Calming the Mind and Discerning the Real

Prepared for
the Columbia College Program
of Translations from the Oriental Classics

Tibetan painting showing a vision of Tsoṅ-kha-pa with hands in teaching gesture, two disciples immediately below, and attendant deities
Courtesy Museum of Fine Arts, Boston

Calming the Mind and Discerning the Real

Buddhist Meditation and the Middle View

From the *Lam rim chen mo* of Tsoṅ-kha-pa

Translated by Alex Wayman

Columbia University Press
New York
1978

Library of Congress Cataloging in Publication Data
Tsoṅ-kha-pa Blo-bzaṅ-grags-pa, 1357–1419.
Calming the mind and discerning the real.

Bibliography: p.
Includes index.
1. Lam-rim. 2. Śamatha (Buddhism)
3. Vipaśyanā (Buddhism) I. Wayman, Alex.
II. Title.
BQ7950.T754L34913 294.3'4'3 78-4535
ISBN 0-231-04404-6

Columbia University Press
New York Guildford, Surrey

Printed in the United States of America

In Memory of
DILOWA GEGEN HUTUKHTU

Was he the last of the
glorious line of Telopas?

Contents

Preface

THE work here presented to the public is probably the most important part of Tsoṅ-kha-pa's *Lam rim chen mo,* an encyclopedic manual of the steps of the path to enlightenment. The portion translated under the title "Calming the Mind and Discerning the Real" is the author's reform in the fields of Buddhist meditation following the teacher Asaṅga and philosophy following the teacher Nāgārjuna. Tsoṅ-kha-pa (1357–1419) is the founder of the Gelugpa sect of Tibetan Buddhism. In his "Discerning the Real" section, he adopts and verifies positions about the Mādhyamika school quite at variance with some of the usual conclusions of modern writers on the topic.

The translator must confess to a generation gap between his initial energetic application to this great work in the year 1951, and the readying of a substantial portion for the press twenty-five years later. During the interim I cited many other works of Tsoṅ-kha-pa for various published books and articles, and changed my translations of certain important Buddhist terms. A wide reading in Buddhist Sanskrit and Tibetan literature during the intervening years undoubtedly turned the delay to the better for a mature presentation of Tsoṅ-kha-pa's text. I had never abandoned my intention to introduce this rich work to the West in an appropriate form, and now fortunately there is a much greater receptivity and evaluating standard for such a work than when I first enterprised it.

Finally, it is a pleasure to acknowledge the generous publishing subvention by Dr. and Mrs. Lex Hixon.

Calming the Mind and Discerning the Real

Prepared for
the Columbia College Program
of Translations from the Oriental Classics

INTRODUCTION

The Lineage, and Atiśa's "Light on the Path to Enlightenment"

THE full Tibetan title of Tsoṅ-kha-pa's work, completed in A.D. 1402, is *Skyes bu gsum gyi ñams su blaṅ ba'i rim pa thams cad tshaṅ bar ston pa'i byaṅ chub lam gyi rim pa.* The title means "Stages of the path to enlightenment, completely showing all the stages to be taken to heart by the three orders of persons." It is generally abbreviated to *Lam rim chen mo* (The great book on stages of the path). The three orders of persons were delineated in Atīśa's "Light on the Path to Enlightenment" (translated below), verses 2–5. Here the theory of "taking to heart" (*ñams su blaṅ ba*) implies "putting into practice."[1] Tsoṅ-kha-pa employs the verbal phrase in the first two lines of his introductory verses to the *Lam rim chen mo:*

/ deṅ dus rnal 'byor brtson rnams thos pa ñuṅ /
/ maṅ thos ñams len gnas la mi mkhas śiṅ /

In our day, enterprisers in yoga have little hearing, while those who hear much are unskilled in the essentials of *putting into practice* (=*taking to heart, ñams len*).

The information on what is "to be taken to heart" or "put into practice" by the three orders of persons is given in the *Lam rim chen mo* by the term *blo sbyoṅ* (exercising, or purifying, the discrimination). This amounts to three kinds of ascetic handbook. This should be clarified by the following general outline of the *Lam rim chen mo,* with folios (f.) from the Tashilunpo edition:

1. Introductory stanzas, general historical background concerning Atīśa, how to study and how to expound the doctrine; ends f. 19b-5.
2. General precepts for the three orders of persons; ends f. 59a-1.
3. The ascetic handbook (*blo sbyoṅ*) for the lesser person; ends f. 123b-3.
4. The ascetic handbook for the middling person; ends f. 169b-1.

5. The ascetic handbook for the superior person, comprising the Bodhisattva path; ends f. 282a-5.
6. "Calming the Mind," expanding the intrinsic nature of the Bodhisattva's fifth perfection, meditation (*dhyāna*); ends f. 337b-5.
7. "Discerning the Real," expanding the intrinsic nature of the Bodhisattva's sixth perfection, insight (*prajñā*); ends f. 486a-6.
8. Brief remarks on the path (just ended) and on the Diamond Vehicle, and colophon; ends f. 491a.[2]

The reader may wonder if my translation in this volume of the part beginning with "Calming the Mind," without the earlier portion of the work, does violence to the author's conception. Tsoṅ-kha-pa expected his disciples to read the entire work, of course; still there is a natural division between the part ending with the three ascetic handbooks and the remainder beginning with "Calming the Mind." The Mongolian translation of the *Lam rim chen mo,* with the abbreviated reference of *Bodhi Mör,* is printed in two parts on this basis. The annotation edition (*Mchan bźi*) is also divided into two volumes on the same basis. In fact, the first part can be roughly characterized as the portion that is the least controversial in terms of the path lineage as it would have been studied in the time of Tsoṅ-kha-pa (1357–1419) in Tibet. The second part, which I have here translated, is the more controversial part, developed extensively because it constitutes Tsoṅ-kha-pa's reform of Tibetan nontantric Buddhist meditation and philosophical position. It is also the part that should be of greater interest to contemporary students of Buddhism.

Before passing to the role of Atīśa, it will be necessary to refer briefly to the two main periods of Buddhism in Tibet, the Early Spread and the Later Spread.

The Early Spread starts with the rather firmly established historical setting of King Sroṅ-btsan-sgam-po. During his reign, beginning in the year A.D. 629,[3] the Tibetan alphabet was created by 'Thon-mi-Sambhoṭa, who had studied the Sanskrit language, perhaps in Central Asia, and then modeled the written form after a late Gupta script. The king was converted to Buddhism, it is said, by his two wives, both princesses, one from Nepal and the other from China. As might be expected, both Nepalese and Chinese forms of Buddhism were immediately represented in Tibet.

Toward the end of the following century (between 792 and 794) there occurred the important debate between the pandit Kamalaśīla, representing the Indian-Nepalese Buddhism, which was a mixture of the Indian Yogācāra and Mādhyamika, and the Chinese teacher (*Hva śaṅ* or *Ho śaṅ*) known by the Sanskrit name Mahāyāna deva, who preached a doctrine of complete quietism and inactivity. According to the Tibetan accounts, Kamalaśīla refuted the Chinese teacher. The teacher and his party acknowledged themselves vanquished and were expelled from Tibet by order of the king. Thenceforth the Mādhyamika (or rather, a mixed form of it) became the dominant school in Tibet.[4] The implications of this dispute are brought up a number of times in Tsoṅ-kha-pa's *Lam rim chen mo* (especially in the parts herein translated), and this matter will be treated later in this introduction.

Presumably in the year 814 the *Mahāvyutpatti* Buddhist dictionary was inaugurated, with exacting standards for the translation of the Sanskrit texts into Tibetan. The translators were forced to adhere to somewhat artificial and even purely arbitrary Sanskrit-Tibetan equivalences. Then in almost all cases, committees, of learned Indian Buddhist pandits and Tibetan *lotsavas* (translators) were formed for the work to be translated. These methods led almost from the beginning of these stipulations to a breach between the spoken language and that of the texts. Oral commentary had to be supplied, for which the translators themselves were the most capable. In this early period of translation, the main bulk of Mahāyāna sūtras was translated into Tibetan from the Sanskrit language, with a few works even now extant from early translations into Tibetan from the Chinese language.

The period A.D. 841–978 represents a gap in the Buddhist doctrine,[5] owing to Glaṅ-dar-ma's persecution. The Later Spread begins with the life of the lotsava Rin-chen-bzaṅ-po (b. 958). While many of the early translations were later recovered from one source or another, the oral lineages had been mostly wiped out. (Later the Tibetan sect called the Rñiṅ-ma-pa disclaimed this discontinuity, insisting that its lineage goes back to the eighth century adept Padmasambhava.) It was necessary to repeat the process of translator committees, and again invite Indian pandits to Tibet, to renew the lineages of oral commentary. The most famous of these teachers is Atīśa (A.D. 982–1054), steward of the Buddhist college of Vikramaśīla, who earlier had studied for twelve years in Śrīvijaya (Sumatra) and who arrived in Tibet in A.D. 1042. When he arrived, Rin-chen-bzaṅ-po was eighty-five but was still able to collaborate with Atīśa in translations. In this second period of translation a huge literature on Buddhist Tantra was translated into Tibetan along with an enormous amount of commentary and exegetical literature. Bu-ston (1290–1364), an encyclopedic writer, compiled all the works that he considered authentic into two great collections called the Kanjur (translated word of the Buddha) and the Tanjur (translation of exegetical works). Since all these works had been translated by the same exacting methods, it became necessary to compose native works that would convert the translated literature into more comprehensible forms, especially into contemporary Tibetan prose style. In the traditions leading to Tsoṅ-kha-pa's *Lam rim chen mo,* the native works were mainly in the broad fields of Buddhist logic and Buddhist path literature.

In the background of the path treatises, we observed that Atīśa's Tibetan pupil 'Brom Rgyal-ba'i-'byuṅ-gnas (A.D. 1005–1064)[6] founded the Bka'-gdams-pa (school of the oral precepts) upon the basis of the master Atīśa's precepts and instructions. In the year A.D. 1056 'Brom founded the monastery of Rva-sgreṅ (Raḍeng). Tsoṅ-kha-pa, coming three centuries later, represented his school as a revival of 'Brom's school and called it the Bka'-gdams-gsar-pa (the new Bka'-gdams-pa), but it became better known under the name Dge-ldan-pa'i-lugs, or Dge-lugs-pa (Gelugpa), and became the dominant school in Tibet in the days of the Fifth Dalai Lama. It was at Rwa-sgreṅ that Tsoṅ-kha-pa completed the formulation of the *Lam rim chen mo,* and then he retired to a solitary monastery nearby to write it down.

The special Tibetan development that led to Tsoṅ-kha-pa's great path treatise may be summarized thus (the material is based on a number of works):[7] As Atīśa's *Bodhi-patha-pradipa* (translated at the end of this introductory section A) had given only the general characteristics, in briefest form, of the three moral orders of persons, it was necessary to supplement this work with the oral instructions. The great translator Blo-ldan-śes-rab (A.D. 1059–1109), a disciple of 'Brom, wrote the *Bstan rim,* while the former's disciple Gro-luṅ-pa Blo-gros-'byuṅ-gnas wrote the *Bstan rim rgyas bsdus,* and thereby the structural foundation was laid for the stages of the path. Blo-ldan-śes-rab translated a possibly related work, the *Abhisamayālaṃkāra,* into Tibetan from Sanskrit and apparently wrote the first independent Tibetan commentary on it. This is a highly compressed metrical summary of the *Prajñāpāramitā* literature from the standpoint of the steps of the path.[8] Nevertheless, while Tsoṅ-kha-pa's first great work was a commentary on this *Abhisamayālaṃkāra* exegesis following the Indian author Haribhadra, Tsoṅ-kha-pa has only a few references to the *Abhisamayālaṃkāra* in his *Lam rim chen mo,* and seems to have conceived the *Lam rim chen mo* along quite different lines, which he makes explicit in his colophon.[9]

The oral explanations were handed down, especially by the second and third hierarchs of Raḍeng (Dgon-pa-pa and Po-to-ba, the first being Ames-chen-po). Dgon-pa-pa (A.D. 1016–1082) gave them to Sne'u-zur-pa (A.D. 1042–1118) and to the great kalyāṇamitra (spiritual guide) Spyan-sṅa-pa (A.D. 1038–1103). These two lines descended unbroken down to the great abbot (*upādhyāya*) of Lho Brag, Nam-mkha'i-rgyal-mtshan, who gave them to Tsoṅ-kha-pa. On the other hand, Po-to-ba (A.D. 1031–1105), who in addition wrote a work on the subject called the *Dpe chos rtsa ba,* gave the explanations to Śa-ra-ba (A.D. 1070–1141) and to the kalyāṇamitra Dol-pa-rin-po-che (born c. A.D. 1048). These two lines descended unbroken down to Mkhan-chen Chos-skyabs-bzaṅ-po,[10] who gave them to Tsoṅ-kha-pa. Those kalyāṇamitras faithfully transmitted the various stages. Thus the structural outline of the Lam rim chen mo descended from the Bka'-gdams-pa.

It is relevant to compare the foregoing with what are called the six texts of the Bka'-gdams-pa—the *Mahāyāna-Sūtrālaṃkāra,* the *Bodhisattvabhūmi,* the *Śikṣāsamuccaya,* the *Bodhisattvacaryāvatāra,* the *Jātakamālā,* and the *Udānavarga.*[11] In fact, Tsoṅ-kha-pa quotes all these works liberally in the first part of the *Lam rim chen mo,* that is, from the beginning through section five, the ascetic handbook for the Bodhisattva. But there are very few references to these texts in the second part of the *Lam rim chen mo,* the part herein translated. This again shows a natural division of the work, consistent with my previous remarks. Of those works, the *Mahāyāna-Sūtrālaṃkāra* and the *Bodhisattvabhūmi* are counted in Asaṅga's tradition. The *Śikṣāsamuccaya* and the *Bodhisattvacaryāvatāra* are of course Śāntideva's tradition, understood to follow the Mādhyamika in the sense of path. The *Jātakamālā* and the *Udānavarga* are important Buddhist works, but are not to be identified with Nāgārjuna's Mādhyamika lineage. The six books do not include any obvious *Prajñāpāramitā* texts, such as the *Abhisamayālaṃkāra.* This suggests that the theory of *blo sbyoṅ,* or different rules of training for the three orders of persons, as they were developed in the three centuries from 'Brom to Tsoṅ-kha-pa, avoids the Prajñāpāramitā exegesis. Of course, there are some quotations from the Prajñāpāramitā scriptures, and a number of verse citations from the *Prajñāpāramitā-sañcaya-gāthā;* but these are cited only for the thought expressed by the particular passage cited, and not to provide the framework for the theory of three orders of persons in the *Abhisamayālaṃkāra* set-up, where each of its three families (Śravaka, Pratyekabuddha, Bodhisattva) has its own description of five stages, since this terminology (although Tsoṅ-kha-pa mentions it) is not used at all for the internal structure of any of the various sections of the *Lam rim chen mo.* Hence, it is not proper to identify the three orders of Atīśa's *Bodhipathapradīpa* with the three families (Śrāvaka, etc.) whose paths are developed in the *Abhisamayālaṃkāra* summary of the *Prajñāpāramitā.*[12]

Furthermore, when we pass to the second part of the *Lam rim chen mo* the authoritative texts change rather drastically. In the "Calming the Mind" section, Asaṅga's *Śrāvakabhūmi* and *Samāhitabhūmi* from the great encyclopedic compilation called the *Yogācārabhūmi,* and Kamalaśīla's three *Bhāvanākrama,* become the main authorities. In the "Discerning the Real" section, the main authorities are the various works that the Tibetan tradition assigns to Nāgārjuna's authorship, Āryadeva's *Catuḥśataka,* Candrakīrti's commentaries on any of the foregoing, Candrakīrti's *Madhyamakāvatāra,* and Buddhapālita's commentary on the *Madhyamaka-kārikā.* Bhāvaviveka is also cited, but mainly to be rejected. Toward the end, some of Asaṅga's materials again appear. But in this "Discerning the Real" section, which is mainly devoted to establishing the Prāsaṅgika-Mādhyamika position—and while the *Madhyamakakārikā* are held in this tradition to represent the Prajñāpāramitā position—there is no use of the type of organization one finds in the *Abhisamayālaṃkāra* of the *Prajñāpāramitā* literature.

As to Atīśa's lineage, carried down to the *Lam rim chen mo,* the Tibetan tradition is given in the commentary preceding the second introductory stanza of the *Lam rim chen mo* (Ṅa: Kha, f. 2a-5 to 2b-1):

Jo-bo-chen-po (the master Atīśa) holds three lineages from the two teachers of the Path which is Profound (*zab pa*) and Far-extended (*rgya che ba*), [and which is the Path] in this śāstra (i.e., the *Lam rim chen mo*), namely: the first one being the lineage from Mañjughoṣa to Nāgārjuna, the later one which was the lineage from Maitreya to Asaṅga and the still later lineage from Mañjughoṣa to Śāntideva.

This represents that Nāgārjuna wrote his profound Mādhyamika treatises, inspired by the Bodhisattva Mañjughoṣa; while Asaṅga wrote his far-extended Yogācāra treatises, inspired by the Bodhisattva Maitreya; and that Śāntideva was inspired about the Bodhisattva path by the Bodhisattva Mañjughoṣa. And moreover that Atīśa's position is a combination of these three lineages.

My translation of Atīśa's *Bodhipathapradīpa* follows, helped by Atīśa's self-commentary—both works being preserved in the Tibetan Tanjur, where Atīśa is catalogued with his alternate name Dīpaṅkaraśrījñāna.[13]

Light on the Path to Enlightenment (*Bodhipathapradīpa*), by Dīpaṅkaraśrījñāna[14]

I bow to Bodhisattva Mañjuśrī the Youth.

1. Having saluted with great reverence all the Victors (the Buddhas) of the three times (past, present, and future), their Doctrine, and the Congregation (of monks), because exhorted by the good disciple Byaṅ-chub-'od I shall light the *Lamp on the Path to Enlightenment.*

2. Three (religious degrees of) persons should be known—as lesser, middling, and superior. Their characteristics will be clarified; their differentiation delineated.

3. Whoever, by whatever means, pursues only his own aim in just the pleasures of this world, he is known as the lesser person.

4. Whoever, turning his back on the pleasures of phenomenal existence, and averting himself from sinful actions, pursues only his own quiescence, he is known as the middling person.

5. Whoever, through the suffering belonging to his own stream of consciousness, completely desires the right cessation of all the suffering of others—that person is superior.

6. To those illustrious sentient beings who desire the highest enlightenment, I shall explain the right means which were taught by (my) gurus.[15]

7.–8a. Facing icons of the Saṃbuddha, *caityas,* and the illustrious Dharma, one should worship them with substances such as flowers and incense as available. Also, seven kinds of offerings are stated in the *Bhadracarī*.

8b.–9. With a mind that cannot be turned back until arriving at the terrace of enlightenment, the one of faith in the three jewels places his kneecap on the ground, joins his hands in respect, and first repeats thrice the refuge formula.

10.–11. Then, preceding with a loving mind toward all the sentient beings, he observes the births in the three evil destinies and the whole world suffering through death and transmigration. Himself a sufferer through suffering, and desiring to liberate the world from the suffering reason for suffering, he should generate the mind of enlightenment pledged not to turn back.

12. The merits of generating the thoughts vowed that way are well explained by Maitreya in the *Gaṇḍavyūha-sūtra:*

13. He reads the sūtras or hears them from a guru.

> Having perceived the infinite merits of the perfected mind of enlightenment,
> For that reason, and in that way
> He should again and again resolve.

14. Its merits are well set forth in such sūtras as the *Vīradattaparipṛcchā*. I shall delineate them here briefly in just three verses (15–17).

15. If the merits of the mind of enlightenment had a form, it would fill the full realm of space and extend beyond.

16.–17. Suppose some man should fill with jewels the Buddha fields numbering the sands of the Ganges and offer those to the Lord of the World. And suppose someone joins his palms and inclines his mind to enlightenment. The latter worship is superior; it has no limit.

18. Having generated the thoughts vowed to enlightenment,
With great endeavor one should enhance those;
So as to remember those even in other lives,
One guards the instruction as it was taught.

19. The mind of entrance (into the Bodhisattva path) does not itself pertain to the vow and does not rightly promote the vow. The one desiring to enhance the vow of perfect enlightenment, therefore assiduously takes hold of it.

20. When one continually holds the other vow belonging to the seven orders of the Prātimokṣa, he has the potentiality of the Bodhisattva vow, not otherwise.

21. Among the seven orders of the Prātimokṣa the Tathāgata ex-

plained the glorious pure life to be the best. (I) maintain (this) to be the vows of the *bhikṣu.*

22. The one with the good behavior stated in the morality chapter of the *Bodhisattvabhūmi* takes the vow from a good guru who possesses the right characteristics.

23. The guru is known as "good" who is skilled in the procedure of the vow, himself is one who adheres to the vow, and who possesses the forbearance and compassion to impart the vow.

24. If by exertions of such kind, one does not find a guru, I shall explain (verses 25–31) another procedure of receiving the vow.

25. In regard to that, how in a former life Mañjuśrī, born as Ambarāja, generated the mind of enlightenment, as explained in the *Mañjuśrī-Buddhakṣetra-guṇavyūha-sūtra,* I accordingly here shall delineate clearly.

26.–31. In the presence of the nāthas one generates the resolve to complete enlightenment, (thinking): "I shall play host to the living beings and rescue them from the cycle of transmigration. Henceforth, until I attain the highest enlightenment, I shall not engage in hostility, wrath, avarice, and envy. I shall practice the pure life and avoid sin and (corrupt) desire. With rapture in the vow of morality, I shall understudy the Buddha. I am not zealous to attain enlightenment by a speedy method; but for the cause of a single sentient being shall remain (in the world) up to the last extremity. I shall purify the measureless, inconceivable fields; hold (to this) from (the time of my present) name (so-and-so), and abide in the ten directions. I shall cleanse all actions of body and speech; also cleanse the actions of mind (= volitions), and refrain from unvirtuous deeds."

32. With the mind of entrance, which is the basis for purification of his body, speech, and mind, while he adheres to his vow—he trains himself in the three instructions of morality, and his devotion to the three instructions of morality waxes.

33. Hence, when one has heeded the two vows constituting the vows of the purified perfected Bodhisattva, he brings to perfection the (two) equipments for the complete enlightenment.

34. All the Buddhas maintain that the cause of perfecting the natural equipments of merit and knowledge is the generation of the supernormal faculties.

35. Just as a bird with unspread wings cannot fly up to the sky, in the same way the one without the power of the supernormal faculties cannot serve the aim of the sentient beings.

36. The merits of a single day that are due to the supernormal facul-

ties would not occur in a hundred births for one lacking the supernormal faculties.

37. The one desiring speedily to perfect the equipments of the complete enlightenment must therefore assiduously accomplish the supernormal faculties. The lazy person does not (accomplish them).

38. As long as calming is not accomplished, the supernormal faculties do not arise. Therefore, one should exert again and again so as to accomplish calming.

39. The one who destroys the members of calming, even should he cultivate the endeavor, would not accomplish *samādhi* even in a thousand years.

40. Therefore, when one is well based in the members stated in the *Samādhisambhāraparivarta* he should settle his mind in virtue on certain ones of meditative objects, as appropriate.[16]

41. When the yogin accomplishes calming, he also accomplishes the supernormal faculties. If he lacks the training of Prajñā-pāramitā, there is no extinction of obscuration.

42. Hence, in order to eliminate all the obscuration of defilement and the knowable, the yogin should continually cultivate Prajñā-pāramitā together with the means.

43. (Various sūtras) say that bondage is consequent upon insight (*prajñā*) divorced from means (*upāya*), or means divorced from insight. So one should avoid both (kinds of one-sidedness).

44. In order to eliminate doubts, whether about insight or about the means, I shall clarify the right distinction of the means and insight.

45. The Victorious Ones have explained as means all the virtuous natures of the perfection of giving, etc., leaving out the perfection of insight.[17]

46. The one with the control of cultivating the means, who (also) cultivates insight, speedily attains enlightenment; but does not if he solely cultivates nonself.

47. The awareness that there is voidness of self-existence, constituting the full comprehension that the personality aggregates, realms, and sense bases do not arise—is explained as "insight."

48. There is no reason for an existing thing to arise; nor for a nonexisting thing like the flower in the sky, because this reduces to absurdity in both cases. Nor for that matter can both (together) arise.[18]

49. An entity does not arise from itself, from another, or from both (itself and another); and does not (arise) without a cause. Hence, it has no self-existence by way of own-nature.[19]

50. Furthermore, when one deliberates all the natures as single and multiple—since one does not perceive their own-nature, their non-self-existence is certain.[20]

51. The *Seventy Principles of Voidness,* the *Mūla-Madhyamaka,* and other works express with proof the voidness of self-existence of all entities.[21]

52. For the reason that (my) text would swell, here I do not amplify (the verses) 48–51. I have expressed (them) only as the proven tenets whose meanings are to be intensely contemplated.

53. Hence, whatever the intense contemplation of selflessness while there is no perception of self-existence of any *dharma*—that is the intense contemplation of insight.

54. According as insight does not see the self-existence of any of the *dharmas* this insight is explained as the "principle." This should be contemplated intensely without discursive thought.

55. This phenomenal world sprung from discursive thought is discursive thought itself. Therefore, the elimination of all discursive thought is the best *nirvāṇa.*

56. Moreover the Lord said: "Discursive thought is the great nescience (*avidyā*) which casts one into the ocean of cyclical flow. The one based in *samādhi* without discursive thought is clear of discursive thought like the sky (clear of light and dark clouds).

57. Also it is stated in the *Avikalpapraveśa-dhāraṇī:* "When the son of the Victor contemplates without discursive thought this illustrious doctrine, he transcends the difficult routes of discursive thought and gradually perfects nondiscursive thought."

58. When he has become certain, by means of scripture (*āgama*) and the principle that all the *dharmas* are unborn and without self-existence, he may intensely contemplate without discursive thought.

59. When in this way he has intensely contemplated this, gradually he achieves "warmth," etc., and achieves Pramuditā [the first Bodhisattva stage], and so on, so that the Buddha's enlightenment is not far off.[22]

60.–61a. By means of (the four rites of) appeasing, prosperity, etc., made successful through the power of Mantras, by the power of the eight great occult powers which are the "good flask," and so on, and others, it is maintained that one perfects joyfully the equipment for enlightenment.

61b.–62. It is stated in the Tantras Kriyā, Caryā, etc., that if one desires to practice the Mantras for the purpose of the preceptor's initiation, he serves, and gives precious objects, etc., to an illustrious guru and delights him by fulfilling austerities, etc.

63. The one who has completed the preceptor's initiation (as con-

ferred) by the delighted guru is thereby purified of all sins, and (so) has the potentiality of accomplishing occult power (*siddhi*).

64.–67. According to the great Tantra of the Ādibuddha, because they would obstruct endeavor, the initiations "Secret" and "Prajñā-(jñāna)" should not be taken by one of pure life (*brahmacarya*). When one takes those initiations, because they exert an obstruction to remaining in the pure life and austerity, the vow of austerity is lost. Transgressions would arise to defeat that vowed person. By reason of evil destiny and transgression, he is never successful. (However,) he may listen to and expound all the Tantras, perform burnt offerings, give offering materials, and the like. He may hold the preceptor's initiation; and there is no demerit in knowing the facts.[23]

68. Having been exhorted by Byaṅ-chub-'od, (I) the sthavira Dīpaṅkara, observing the explanations according to the doctrines of the sūtras and so on, have composed this concise explanation of the Path to Enlightenment.

The Author of the *Lam rim chen mo*

TSOṄ-KHA-PA (1357–1419) has received much attention from biographers.[24] I have constructed the following biography using the Tibetan texts by Mkhas-grub-rje[25] and by Akyā Blo-bzaṅ-bstan-pa'i-rgyal-mtshan Dpal-bzaṅ-po,[26] to achieve a balance between presenting the author's attainments and including the lineages that lead to the *Lam rim chen mo.*[27]

Tsoṅ-kha-pa was the fourth of six children; his father was Da-ra Kha-che Klu-'bum-dge and his mother, Śiṅ-mo A-chos. They lived among the Mal clan in East Onion Valley (*śar-tsoṅ-kha*), a part of lower Amdo that earlier had come under the rule of the Tibetan kings. According to Dge-'dun-grub, he was born at dawn, when the great star (i.e., Venus) had arisen, in the Fire-female-Bird year of the sixth sexegenary cycle. This year is approximately equivalent to A.D. 1357. The biography by Dge-'dun-grub is specific about the time of year: the tenth day of the tenth month. On the assumption that persons living on the frontier with China would be using the Chinese calendar system, this particular day for that year (the seventeenth year of Chih-Chêng) is November 21. Thus, Tsoṅ-kha-pa was born November 21, 1357, and at sunrise if we accept Dge-'dun-grub's information.

Various legends grew up about prodigies connected with his birth. When the child reached the age of three, the Mongol king Togon Temür (1333–1368)[28] sent Karma Rol-pa'i-rdo-rje to visit him. He took the vow of Buddhist layman (*upāsaka*) from this monk, who gave him the name Kun-dga'-sñiṅ-po. As to the "age of three," this is clarified by the biography by Mkhas-grub-rje, stating, much later, that Tsoṅ-kha-pa reached the age of thirty-six in the tenth month of the Ape year. This proves that Tibetans were reckoning age from the beginning of the year of one's life, while in the West it is counted by the number of years completed. Therefore, the Tibetan "age three" is equivalent to the Western "two years old." We shall state the age by the number given in the Tibetan texts.

In his third year, the chos-rje (*dharmasvāmin*) Don-grub Rin-chen brought horses, sheep, and many valuable gifts to the father and commanded, "You must present me this boy of yours!" The father agreed and enthusiastically entrusted the boy to the monk's care. When Tsoṅ-kha-pa's seventh year was close at hand, the chos-rje gave him his first introduction to the Tantras. (Prior to Tsoṅ-kha-pa's reform, maturation in the Buddhist Vinaya was not a stipulated preliminary for tantric practices.) He was initiated in the *maṇḍala* of Lord Cakrasaṃvara according to the method of Ghaṇṭa-pa, the *maṇḍalas* of Hevajra, Vajrapāṇi, and so forth, and given the secret name of Don-yod-rdo-rje. In his seventh year, he "went forth" to the religious life. The lama Don-grub Rin-chen became his "principal" (*upādhyāya*), charged with admitting the candidate to the religious order. Gzon-nu Byaṅ-chub became his "instructor" (*ācārya*). He took the vow of novice (*śramaṇera*), and was given the name Blo-bzaṅ Grags-pa'i-dpal. At the end of both his *Lam rim chen mo* and his *Sṅags rim chen mo* he presents his name as author: Śar tsoṅ-kha-pa (the man from East Onion Valley) Blo-bzaṅ Grags-pa'i-dpal. Since in his later reform one must have the discipline of a monk before practicing the Tantras, his religious name Blo-bzaṅ Grags-pa'i-dpal was employed in preference to the names Kun-dga'-sniṅ-po and Don-yod-rdo-rje. He is also frequently referred to by his followers as the Rje Bla-ma or Rje Rin-po-che. Thereafter, the lama Don-grub Rin-chen prepared him for the continuance of his studies in Central Tibet. When Tsoṅ-kha-pa reached his sixteenth year, the lama gave him final precepts: in short, "You must practice hearing, pondering, and cultivation." He was also advised to study the five treatises of Maitreya and the seven works on logic by Dharmakīrti. The lama counseled him to make offerings to the deities Vajrabhairava, Vajrapāṇi, Mañjuśrī Arapacana, Amitāyus, Vaiśrāvaṇa, the six-handed Mahākāla, and Dam-can-chos-rgyal.

Tsoṅ-kha-pa agreed to do as instructed, was given the blessing of the lama, and never looked back as he went away. Having been previously invited by Rin-chen-dpal, the 'Bul-dpon of 'Bri-khuṅ monastery, he arrived at the grove of 'Bri-khuṅ-dpal in Central Tibet in the autumn of the Ox year (1373), toward the end of his sixteenth year, or going on seventeen.

During the following seven years, he mastered the monastic curriculum of nontantric Buddhism that is called *mtshan-ñid* (the characteristic), i.e., the characteristics of Buddhism. There are five traditional subjects: (*1*) Perfection of Insight (*phar-phyin*), study of the *Prajñāpāramitā* scriptures on the basis of the *Abhisamayālaṃkāra;* (*2*) Metaphysics (*mdzod*), study of the Abhidharma on the basis of Vasubandhu's *Abhidharmakośa;* (*3*) The middle Viewpoint (*dbu ma*), study of the Mādhyamika on the basis of Nāgārjuna's principal works or of Candrakīrti's *Madhyamakāvatāra;* (*4*) Logic (*tshad-ma*), study of "authority" (*pramāṇa*) on the basis of Dharmakīrti's *Pramāṇavarttika;* (*5*) Disciplinary Code (*'dul-ba*), study of the Vinaya scripture on the basis of Guṇaprabha's *Vinayasūtra.* These works are all in superb Tibetan translations from the original Sanskrit. It is customary to commit the basic works, which are all in verse form, to memory by rehearsal and subsequently to review them in a rhythmical process while counting the rosary beads. The examinations are in the form of debates, or questions-and-answers. Learning by heart any of the bulky prose commentaries is considered a feat of memory, especially if done in a record number of days. Tsoṅ-kha-pa's biography shows that his study of the five traditional subjects was not as formalized as it later became. Tsoṅ-kha-pa studied them in the order of his interest, and he constantly moved from monastic college to monastic college, where he sought out the leading teachers of each subject. At 'Bri-khuṅ, his starting point, he took a course of medicine and learned the eight branches of therapy. Then at the Bde-ba-can college, in only eighteen days he completely memorized every word of Haribhadra's basic commentary (*vṛtti*) on the *Abhisamayālaṃkāra.* Previously in Amdo he had memorized the *Mahāyāna-Sūtrālaṃkāra,* and he now listened to new explanations for this and the other Maitreya treatises. In the same period at the hermitage Chos-rdzoṅ, in the presence of the illustrious lama Bsod-nams-rgyal-mtshan, he listened to the permission to invoke Mañjughoṣa Arapacana, the initiation in the body *maṇḍala* of Cakrasaṃvara according to Ghaṇṭa-pa, and the permission to invoke the Mahākāla "Protector of the Tent" (*gur gyi mgon po*). In his nineteenth year he participated in the examinations of the Prajñāpāramitā at both Gsaṅ-phu and Bde-ba-can, becoming—as the biography mentions—celebrated for his intelligence and expository ability.

After listening to the initiation of the "Maitri bcu-gsum-ma" of the *Cakrasaṃvara-tantra* from the translator Rin-chen-rnam-rgyal-ba, abbot of Źa-lu in Tsaṅ, he visited Snar-thaṅ and audited a course at Sa-skya. Subsequently, he took part in the Prajñāpāramitā examinations at Sa-skya, then those at 'Dar-bzaṅ-ldan in Stod-byaṅ and those at Dam-riṅ and at 'Ga'-roṅ. He went to Jo-mo-naṅ and listened to the guidance of the six stages of Yoga from the chos-rje Phyogs-las-rnam-rgyal. Then the abbot at Spyi-bo-lhas offered him the handed-down doctrine of the stages of the path descended from the Bka'-gdams school. He took part in the examinations at the great E school of Bo-doṅ, and at the Gnas rñiṅ of Ñaṅ-stod.

Upon auditing a beautiful course in Prajñāpāramitā from the Na-Dbon Kun-dpal at Rtse-chen, he sought a teacher in Abhidharma and that master recommended his student as more proficient in this topic. This was the Reverend Red-mda'-pa (1349–1412), who had such mastery of Vasubandhu's self-commentary on the *Abhidharmakośa* as to excite utmost admiration in Tsoṅ-kha-pa. Red-mda'-pa became his guru; and the two traveled together for years, starting, it seems, in 1376. Tsoṅ-kha-pa first gained from this teacher the full comprehension of the Mādhyamika and of Buddhist logic that paved the way for his nontantric treatises. But not every master was willing to teach this brilliant student. He followed the yogi-translator Byaṅ-chub Rtse-mo all the way to the Potala, hoping to study Asaṅga's *Abhidharmasamuccaya* under him; but the master frustrated him, saying, "There are many autumns."

At Skyor-mo-luṅ college in Central Tibet, after listening to the instruction, he memorized in seventeen days the great commentary on Guṇaprabha's *Vinayasūtra.* But this effort apparently brought on a serious ailment in the upper part of his body, which continued to bother him for over a year despite prescriptions from specialists. He suffered from the ailment throughout his eleven months of study with Red-mda'-pa at Sa-skya, where he also listened to the Sa-skya interpretation (*salugs*) of the *Hevajra-tantra.* Then he took a prescription from a friend at Sa-skya who was versed in incantations (*mantra*). Proceeding to the reverse side of a ridge, he recited several times a neuter *Ha*—and the ailment left without a trace. That autumn (1378, it seems) his mother wrote him from his birthplace, urging him to visit his native district. The biography represents him as having an intense longing to visit Amdo, but as not seeing the necessity, and so with much sadness deciding not to go there at that time, but to complete his skill in the basic texts. For the rest of the autumn he minutely studied Dharmakīrti's *Pramāṇavarttika* and was provoked to tears by ecstatic faith. His unremitting study takes him up to the next autumn when at E of Bo-Doṅ he studied the manual of poetics, the *Kāvyādarśa,* with the translator Nam-mkha'-bzaṅ-po; along with the usual studies under Red-mda'-pa. Then the master and disciple returned to Sa-skya, where Tsoṅ-kha-pa participated in the examinations on the "great difficulties" (Dka'-chen, i.e., the five traditional subjects). He visited successively Gsaṅ-phu, Sñe-thaṅ, and many other schools, and participated in the examinations of the four "great difficulties," omitting the Prajñāpāramitā because he had previously taken so many examinations in the latter.

His fame was now spreading, and many students were asking him to let them study under him. He felt that he could engage in this activity only by following the example of Śākyamuni, i.e., becoming a monk (*bhikṣu*). After completing the examinations at Rtses-thaṅ, in his twenty-fourth year (which he attained in November 1380) he took the vows of ordination at Rnam-rgyal in the Yar-luṅ district. The Kashipa Tshul-rin, the abbot at the Tshogs-chen (headquarters of the Jo-naṅ sect) and in spiritual descent from Śākyaśrībhadra (A.D. 1127–1225), the great pandit of Kashmir, was his "principal" (*mkhan-po*). The sthavira Vinayadhara Śer-mgon-pa, the abbot of the Tshogs-pa Byi-rdziṅ-pa, was his "counselor" (*las kyi slob dpon*). Bsod-nams Rdo-rje, the head (*dbu-mdzad*) of Byi-rdziṅ, was his "confidant" (*gsaṅ ste ston pa*).

Tsoṅ-kha-pa's ordination marks the beginning of his career as a teacher of nontantric Buddhist treatises. During the subsequent twelve years he not only became an author of such works in his own right, but also himself continued to study under the eminent teachers of the Tantras, both showing to the latter and winning for himself that devotion to the teacher described in his commentary on the tantric writer Aśvaghosa's *Fifty Stanzas in Praise of the Guru.*

Then, having arrived at Gdan-sa, the monastery founded by the lama Phag-mo Gru-pa (1110–1170), Tsoṅ-kha-pa learned from the Spyan-sṅa

Grags-pa Byaṅ-chub-pa (1356–1386; died at age of thirty-one) the complete precepts of the Path and the Fruit, the Six Doctrines of Nāro-pa (*nā-ro-pa'i chos-drug*), the collected sayings (*bka' 'bum*) of Rje Phag-mo Gru-pa and of Chos-rje 'Jig-rten Mgon-po, the precepts in the lineage from Lho-brag Mar-pa to Rje-btsun Mi-la (i.e., Milarepa), and the precepts in the lineage from Lho-brag Mar-pa to Rṅog Chos-sku-rdo-rje.

At the temple Ke-ru of 'On, Tsoṅ-kha-pa explained many nontantric doctrines. Then at Skyid-śod he conducted a minute perusal and consideration of the scriptures and śāstras translated into Tibetan (the Kanjur and Tanjur) while beginning the *Gser-'phreṅ,* his great commentary on both the *Abhisamayālaṃkāra* and its commentary by Haribhadra. This work was interrupted by various teaching assignments, such as going from Tshal to Bde-ba-can for the winter course; and for the spring session, lecturing to seventy students in the Bya district of Dbu-stod. When he finished his *Gser-'phreṅ,* he asked the lama Rtogs-ldan Ye-śes-rgyal-mtshan to teach him the *Kālacakratantra,* which that lama explained in detail to him on the basis of the commentary *Vimalaprabhā*. Tsoṅ-kha-pa studied the astrological calculations and the practical part while at the same place (Skyor-mo-luṅ) himself teaching numerous scripture-memorizers. He continued his study of the *Kālacakra* while teaching the next summer session at Bde-ba-can and the following winter session at Mtsho-smad and Naṅ-dkar. He then taught successively at Smon-mkhar of the Yar-luṅ district at the Rigs-lṅa temple, and at Bkra-śis-gdoṅ of Smon-dkar.

One summer Tsoṅ-kha-pa stayed in the rock cave O-dkar-brag of the Yar-luṅ district and practiced various tantric rites, such as the contemplation-recitation of Cakrasaṃvara; the Yoga at dawn, noon, sunset, and midnight; the visualization cycle of the six Ne-gu Doctrines (*ne-gu chos-drug-gi dmigs-skor*). Every day he trained the wind of the heat (*caṇḍa-vāyu*) eight hundred times. Rejoining Red-mda'-pa at the Potala, they taught jointly. Then Tsoṅ-kha-pa returned to the rock at Skyor-mo-luṅ to teach the *Kālacakra* as well as nontantric doctrines.

In the spring of the year of the Horse (A.D. 1390), Red-mda'-pa and his disciple went to Gtsaṅ and stayed at the Roṅ-gi-snubs Chos-luṅ. It was here that Tsoṅ-kha-pa first met the lama Dbu-ma-pa, at this time receiving from him the evocation permission of Devī Sarasvatī. After studying the basic Tantra *Guhyasamāja* under Red-mda'-pa at 'Ba'-'u

'Ba'-gñer, the guru proceeded to Sa-skya, while Tsoṅ-kha-pa returned to Roṅ Chos-luṅ. There the lama Dbu-ma-pa taught him the doctrinal cycle of Mañjughoṣa, and Tsoṅ-kha-pa in turn explained to that lama the self-commentary on the *Madhyamakāvatāra.* Now Tsoṅ-kha-pa's mind was given over to the Tantras. In the autumn he arrived at Ñan-stod to study under the lama Chos-kyi-dpal, who was the most learned in the *Kālacakra* among the great sons of Bu-ston Rin-po-che (b. A.D. 1290), and remained into the spring, listening to the whole cycle of *Kālacakra.* At Źa-lu, Bu-ston's college, there was a specialist of the Yoga-tantra named Yo-ga-pa Mgon-bzaṅ. Tsoṅ-kha-pa invited him and the two stayed at the 'Khris-rtsa-khaṅ at the edge of lower Ñan-stod, where Mgon-bzaṅ trained him in the great *maṇḍalas* of the Yoga-tantra such as the *Vajradhātu-maṇḍala.* Back at Źa-lu in the fall of 1391 and also for the winter, spring, and summer of the Ape year (1392), in the presence of the aged lama Rin-po-che Khyuṅ-po-lha he heard the great *maṇḍalas* of the Yoga-tantra and the entire mass of promulgations of the lower Tantra divisions (i.e., Kriyā, Caryā, and Yoga) that were accessible in Tibet. He also received much instruction on the Anuttara Tantra *Cakrasaṃvara* according to the schools of Lūi-pa and Nag-po-pa. During this period Tsoṅ-kha-pa invited the lama Chos-kyi-dpal to Mount Pa-rnam-pa Phag-pa and heard the *Rdo-rje-sñiṅ-'grel* and the *Phyag-rdor stod-'grel* as well as Bu-ston's explanations of the two schools (Ārya and Jñānapāda) of the *Guhyasamāja.* After they returned to Sde-che, Tsoṅ-kha-pa invited the Źa-lu specialist Yo-ga-pa Rgyal-mtshan-grags-pa to Mount Pa-rnam-pa Phag-pa, and heard from him Bu-ston's *Rdo-rje-'byuṅ-ba'i rnam-bśad-chen-mo,* and the whole range of commentarial views on the Yoga-tantras. Thus Tsoṅ-kha-pa became a master of the Tantras according to the celebrated Źa-lu school.

In the autumn of 1392, he rejoined the lama Dbu-ma-pa and went with this master to Dga'-ba-dgoṅ of Central Tibet. After worshiping at the Jo-bo statue of Lhasa, they went into solitary seclusion. The biography by Mkhas-grub-rje now digresses to present a biographical sketch of the lama Dbu-ma-pa, who was not intellectually keen like Red-mda'-pa, but had a rich inner life, involved with evoking tutelary deities, especially Mañjughoṣa, and receiving spiritual communications. With this master's guidance, Tsoṅ-kha-pa proceeded with the "service" and soon visualized concretely the face of Mañjughoṣa; and with Dbu-ma-pa as interpreter, received answers to his questions on profound essential points of the sūtras and Tantras. In the case of the middle viewpoint, Tsoṅ-kha-pa sought counsel on deciding between the Prāsaṅgika and Svātantrika systems of Mādhyamika. And he prayed that there be no separation henceforth between the tutelary deity and himself. Having reached the age of thirty-six in the tenth month of the Ape year (1392), he finished up the autumn preaching many doctrines at Skyor-mo-luṅ.

Tsoṅ-kha-pa now had the confidence to start his new school, later known generally as the Gelugpa. At the end of the Ape year, along with eight followers as prophesied by the venerable Mañjughoṣa 'Jam-dkar-ba, he went to Bya-bral. (Of the eight, four were from Dbus: (*1*) Grags-pa dpal-ldan-bzaṅ-pa, (*2*) Rtogs-ldan byaṅ-seṅ-ba, (*3*) Gnas-brtan Rin-chen rgyal-mtshan-pa, (*4*) Gnas-brtan bzaṅ-skyoṅ-ba; and four were from Mdo-smad: (*1*) Bla-ma Rtogs-ldan 'Jam-dpal Rgya-mtsho-ba, (*2*) Dge-bśes Śes-rab-grags, (*3*) Dge-bśes 'Jam-dpal Bkra-śis, (*4*) Dge-bśes Dpal-skyoṅ.) Tsoṅ-kha-pa proceeded to 'Ol-kha and there preached the Buddhist doctrine to the 'Ol-kha family who, filled with faith, became his patrons. At that time he saw the faces of the thirty-five Buddhas of Confession, and often saw Maitreya in the shape of the Sambhoga-kāya, Bhaiṣajya-guru (the healing Buddha) in yellow garb, Maitreya as a seated Nirmāṇa-kāya, and the Buddha Amitāyus. He reviewed in his mind the glorious practice of the Bodhisattva recorded in the *Buddha-Avataṃsaka-sūtra* and modeled his conduct accordingly.

The next several years were replete with visions and growing numbers of disciples. He conferred the initiations of the five *gṛva* (Pañcarakṣā goddesses) on the great siddha Lha-brag-pa Nam-mkha' Rgyal-mtshan, while the latter taught Tsoṅ-kha-pa the stages of the path in the lineage from Spyan-sṅa-pa to Sne'u-zur-pa. After abandoning the idea of going to India, at Lo-ro of Gñal he encountered the book *Bstan-rim* of Gro-luṅ-pa, and conceived the plan of his future work, the *Lam rim chen mo* (Stages of the Path to Enlightenment), taking as point of departure the tiny work by Atīśa, "Light of the Path to Enlightenment" (*Bodhipatha-pradīpa*), and combining the views of Nāgārjuna and Asaṅga. For Tsoṅ-kha-pa, the candidate for entering the Vajrayāna must first train his mind (*blo sbyoṅ*) in the common path, that is, the path shared by the nontantric Mahāyāna and the tantric Mahāyāna, and a preeminent common element in the reliance on the guru. This great work was not completed until A.D. 1402 at the monastery Rva-sgreṅ. In the meantime Tsoṅ-kha-pa had written various related works, such as the commentary on the Morality chapter (*śīla-parivarta*) of Asaṅga's *Bodhisattvabhūmi.* During this time, one summer season while the master was teaching at the Rab-groṅ of Upper Gñal, Rje Dar-ma Rin-chen (A.D. 1364–1432), also called Rgyal-tshab, met him and became a leading faithful disciple, having previously mastered the curriculum of the "ten difficult subjects." This disciple later wrote commentaries on the basic logical works of Diṅnāga and Dharmakīrti. During this period Tsoṅ-kha-pa also had detailed religious discourses with his guru, Red-mda'-pa, and they jointly taught at Rva-sgreṅ.

After the *Lam rim chen mo,* Tsoṅ-kha-pa composed his great compendium of the Tantras, the *Sṅags rim chen mo,* setting forth the four classes of Tantra: Kriyā, Caryā, Yoga, and Anuttarayoga. In the year 1407, Mkhas-grub-rje (A.D. 1385–1438) met Tsoṅ-kha-pa for the first time, and eventually became his leading disciple in the Tantras. This disciple later wrote a great commentary on the *Kālacakratantra,* and presumably met Tsoṅ-kha-pa at Serā-chos-sdiṅs where the latter arrived in the summer of 1406 and stayed for two years. It was during his stay there that, his fame having spread to China, the Chinese emperor Tā-Ming (Yunglo), probably in 1407, sent gold-lettered invitations; but Tsoṅ-kha-pa reflected that the obstacles for traveling to the Chinese capital were numerous, the advantages few, and so declined to go.[29] Instead, he prostrated himself on the "Raga" rock-face and the venerable Mañjughoṣa stated the essential points of the Mādhyamika and Yogācāra philosophical viewpoints. On this basis, at Serā-chos-sdiṅs he now composed his treatise discriminating the "provisional meaning" (*neyārtha*) and "final meaning" (*nītārtha*) of the sūtra called *Legs-bśad-sñiṅ-po,* considered to be among the most beautifully written of all Tsoṅ-kha-pa's works.

In the later part of 1408, at the entreaty of Mi-dbaṅ-grags Rgyal-mtshan, he moved to the Grum-bu-luṅ of Lower Skyid, where the clergy increased to a thousand, so many came to hear Tsoṅ-kha-pa expound the Lam rim, the Cakrasaṃvara-sādhana according to Lūi-pa, and the Stages of Completion (*saṃpanna-krama*) of the Mother Tantra (*Cakrasaṃvara*). Thus Mi-dbaṅ-grags Rgyal-mtshan, as well as Sne'u-pa and Nam-mkha'-bzaṅ-po became patrons for supplying all the equipment and necessities for a great Smon-lam, which Tsoṅ-kha-pa instituted at Lhasa by the Jo-bo Śākyamuni (statue), lasting for the first fifteen lunar days of the first month of the year of the Ox (A.D. 1409), that is, starting from the Tibetan New Year's day. Since Mkhas-grub-rje was already a disciple, the long description in the biography proves that he was a personal witness, held spellbound by this great mass devotional, which turned out to be a capital political stroke in favor of Tsoṅ-kha-pa's new school. It continued as an annual observance down to the 1950s.

After the Smon-lam, Tsoṅ-kha-pa went into a brief meditative retirement and then resumed his teaching at Serā-chos-sdiṅs. Meanwhile, most of his monk followers, headed by Rje Dar-ma-rin-chen and Rje 'Dul-ba-'dzin, began the erection of the monastery Dge-ldan Rnam-par-rgyal-ba'i-gliṅ at 'Brog Ri-bo-che. In those days, the name used for the sect was apparently Dge-ldan-pa rather than the later ubiquitous Dge-lugs-pa (Gelugpa). That monastery is better known later as Dga' ldan (Galdan) and, after the master's passing, Rje Dar-ma-rin-chen became the first abbot; Mkhas-grub-rje, the second. Tsoṅ-kha-pa arrived at the new monastery on the fifth day of the second month of the Tiger year (A.D. 1410) and began clarifying the difficult points of Asaṅga's works, Buddhist logic, and the *Pradīpoddyotana* commentary of the *Guhyasamāja-tantra.* Now he wrote his great commentaries on the *Guhyasamāja* cycle, such as his voluminous commentary on the *Pañcakrama* called *Rab tu gsal ba'i sgron me.*

Then in his fifty-seventh year (A.D. 1413) a serious illness threatened his life. He performed extensive Yantras (occult machinations) of Śri-Vajrabhairava as a means of increasing the length of his life and warding off dangers. In the morning he would perform the "prosperity" recitation-contemplation; and in the evening, the "warding off" recitation-contemplation. After this practice had been repeated many times his body displayed a radiance; the illness cleared up, at least temporarily, and the danger was averted. After that, he put the ācārya Dar-ma-rin-chen in charge of the clergy of the sect. He even resumed his teaching the following summer at 'On-gyi-bkra-śis Do-kha. Then he returned to Dge-ldan Rnam-par-rgyal-ba'i-gliṅ and wrote his great *ṭīkā* on the *Śrīcakrasaṃvara* Lūi-pa system, as well as the *Mchan-'grel* (annotational commentary) on Candrakīrti's *Pradīpoddyotana,* and other commentaries included among his chief tantric works.

Maintaining that the hall for *maṇḍala* preparation and offering had a mistake in construction, in the Bird year (A.D. 1417) he had a wide temple erected on the right side of the Assembly Hall and then performed an extensive consecration. He gave a precious conch shell to 'Jam-dbyaṅs Chos-rje and prophesied that the latter would have an outstanding son by a female recluse. He gave a garment and a vestment for it to Rje Dge-'dun-grub and prophesied that the latter would perform wonderful deeds in the Tsang district and found a Bkra-śis-lun-po'i chos-sde (Tashilunpo). (The latter, who lived 1391–1475, is an important figure for the survival and success of the new sect after the founder's death, and became retroactively called the First Dalai Lama).

In the Dog year (1418) Tsoṅ-kha-pa was still explaining the Tantras to hundreds of new monks who flocked to Dge-ldan-Rnam-par-rgyal-ba'i-glin. He also gave his own views on the *Kālacakra-tantra;* and apparently this is the occasion when he instructed Mkhas-grub-rje on how the latter was to write his great commentary on that system. He also wrote his commentary on Candrakīrti's *Madhyamakāvatara.* In the last year of his life, the Hog year (1419) he wrote one of his greatest works, the *ṭīkā* on the *Cakrasaṃvara* called *Sbas don lta ba'i mig 'byed.*

Then in the autumn of the Dog year Tsoṅ-kha-pa's feet became afflicted. Giving in to entreaties, he was borne from Ri-bo Dge-ldan to Lhasa and to Stod-luṅ, where he was told he must not do any walking at all. When the word spread that he was there, monks flocked to Stod-luṅ to hear his explanations of the doctrine and to get his blessing. Upon being brought to 'Bras-spuṅs (the Drepung monastery) he lectured to as many as two thousand monks. Now he preached both tantric and non-tantric doctrines to laymen and townspeople as well as to monks. When he returned to Ri-bo Dge-ldan his illness became grave. On the evening of the twenty-fourth lunar day of the month he conducted a great devotional to Srī Cakrasaṃvara. In the early morning of the twenty-fifth day he crossed his legs, held his two hands in *samāpatti-mundrā* (level at the chest), and exactly at sunrise ceased to breathe. The biography by Mkhas-grub-rje represents him as passing through various Yoga states, with his body taking on various aspects.

Calming and *Discerning* as Natures and Categories

FROM the beginning of Buddhist literature, we find the terms *calming* and *discerning* paired, as natures to be cultivated. Some of the relevant Pāli passages are these:

Dasuttara Suttanta (D.III,273): Which two natures (*dhamma*) help much? Mindfulness (*sati*) and awareness (*sampajañña*). Which two natures are to be cultivated? Calming (*śamatha*) and discerning (*vipassanā*). Which two natures are to be experienced? Name (*nāma*) and form (*rūpa*).

Mahā-Vacchogottasutta (M,I,494): On that account, you Vaccha, should cultivate two natures further—calming and discerning. You should know, Vaccha, that if these two natures—calming and discerning—are cultivated further, they will conduce to the penetration of the various elements (*dhātu*).

Asaṅkhata-samyutta (S,IV,360): And what, monks, is a path that goes to the unconstructed (*asaṅkhagāmimagga*) (which is the eradication of lust, hatred, and delusion)? Calming and discerning. [Notice that a number of other paths leading to the unconstructed are specified in the same place.]

As a pair, they occur also in the Book of Twos of the *Aṅguttara-nikāya* (A, I, 95). In this case, as in the three citations above, the listing of terms does not sufficiently pin down their usage. However, it is obvious that in early times these two terms stood for natures that were cultivated for various ends, for example, to experience name-and-form (*nāma-rūpa*), to penetrate the elements (*dhātu*), to lead to the unconstructed (*asaṅkhata*).

A significant statement occurs in the *Ākaṅkheyyasutta* (D, I, 33):

Monks, if a monk should wish: "May I be agreeable to my fellows in the pure life, liked by them, revered and respected," he should be one who fulfills the moral rules (*sīla*), who is intent on calming the mind (*cetosamatha*) within, whose meditation (*jhāna*) is uninterrupted, who is endowed with discerning (*vipassanā*), a frequenter of solitary abodes (*suññāgāra*).

This passage relates these terms to the well-known three instructions (which account for the three parts of Buddhaghosa's *Visuddhimagga*). That is, one who fulfills the moral rules is undergoing the "training in morality" (*adhisīla-sikkhā*). One who is intent on calming the mind, whose meditation is uninterrupted, is undergoing the "training of the mind" (*adhicitta-sikkhā*). One who is endowed with discerning is undergoing the "training of insight" (*adhipaññā-sikkhā*). Notice that the expression "calming the mind" is itself equivalent to the second instruction if the remark "whose meditation is uninterrupted" is simply adding more information. Also, the expression "endowed with discerning" can be construed as equivalent to the third instruction because the expression "a frequenter of solitary abodes" is not a qualification of the "discerning" but seems, rather, to go with all three of the instructions. This passage continues the "nature" (*dhamma*) interpretation of the terms, because the passage says, "who is intent on calming the mind within," thus stressing a nature to be cultivated.

However, in the course of time the terms came to be used as inclusive categories (*pakṣa*), as is obvious in the works of Asaṅga. Thus in his *Śrāvakabhumi*[30] he places the seven accessories to enlightenment (*bodhyaṅga*) under these headings: the cathartic (*praśrabdhi*), concentration (*samādhi*), and equanimity (*upekṣa*) in the category of calming (*śamatha*); the analysis of the doctrine (*dharmapravicaya*), striving (*vīrya*), and rapture (*prīti*) in the category of discerning (*vipaśyanā*); and mindfulness (*smṛti*) in both categories. Furthermore, in the same work he says: "A single area of thought is of calming category and of discerning category. Among them, when there is fixation of thought of nine kinds, that is the calming category. Moreover, when there is analysis by insight of four kinds, that is the discerning category."[31] These matters (fixation of thought and analysis by insight) are of course the extended subject of the two sections of Tsoṅ-kha-pa's work herein translated.

The category usage of the terms seems to have been fostered by the identification with the second and third of the three instructions (*supra*). So also in Yüan-ts'ê's great commentary on the *Saṃdhinirmocana-sūtra,* which was translated from Chinese and is found in the Tibetan Tanjur:

Here calming and discerning are samādhi and prajñā. Therefore, in the treatise *Tattvasiddhi,* the chapter "Exposition of Calming and Discerning" teaches that calming is samādhi, and discerning is insight (*prajñā*). Also, the *Commentary on the Buddhabhūmi* explains that calming is samādhi, and discerning is prajñā. Besides, in the *Noble Prajñāpāramitā-sūtra:* calming is a single area of thought; discerning is what sees the dharmas rightly as they are. Moreover, the *ācārya* Asvabhāva, in his commentary on the treatise *Mahāyānasaṃgraha* states that calming is the adversary of the samādhis that stray; discerning is the adversary of wayward insight.[32]

This sets the stage for the dispute which Tsoṅ-kha-pa alludes to at the outset of his treatment of calming and discerning. Here we learn that some of the tantrics of Tibet rejected the authority of the *Saṃdhinirmocana-sūtra* (the chief scripture of the Yogācāra school, headed by Asaṅga) on the grounds that its statements about calming and discerning were refuted by what the tantric literature says about calming and discerning. Tsoṅ-kha-pa resolves the dispute by pointing out that the *Saṃdhinirmocana-sūtra* is using the two terms as categories, so the sūtra can rightly say that all virtuous natures are the fruit of calming and discerning; while the Tantra, using the terms as natures, can rightly claim that calming and discerning are merits achieved by the tantric practices. This shows that the Tantras used the terms about the same way as did the old Pāli scriptures, in the sense that the two terms would occur only occasionally as natures and so not appear with a paramount role as a title. However, when the terms came to be employed as categories, other important terms could be subsumed under them until they could serve as book titles, and thus could be used as the titles for two major sections of Tsoṅ-kha-pa's *Lam rim chen mo.*

This category use is exemplified in the Sanskrit commentary after *Mahāyāna-Sūtrālaṃkāra* (XIV, 6), which sets forth six steps of consciousness:

1. basic consciousness (*mūlacitta*), which is the meditative object in the form of the concise statement of the doctrine—of course, held in mind with calming. There follow five steps of discerning:
2. analytical consciousness (*anucara-citta*);
3. enumerator consciousness (*vicāraṇā-citta*);

4. restriction-to-the-text consciousness (*avadhāraṇā-citta*);
5. classifying consciousness (*saṃkalana-citta*);
6. aspiring consciousness (*āśāsti-citta*).

Sthiramati's subcommentary on the *Sūtrālaṃkāra* may be cited in amplification:[33]

1. "basic consciousness." This is the initial aiming of consciousness at the precise words of the scriptural text after receiving the relevant percept and instruction from the abbot, the Tathāgata, etc.
2. "analytical consciousness." One then well analyzes the words of the particular scriptural text. One defines the words, and relates them to other passages.
3. "enumerator consciousness." This is an enumeration of both the entities and the letters. In the enumeration of entities, there is, for example, the enumeration of *rūpa* as the eleven bases (*āyatana*), to wit, the five sense organs and the five sense objects, making ten, and then counting the *dharma-dhātu* as one, consisting of *avijñapti-rūpa*—thus eleven, no more or less. The enumeration of letters is the judiciousness of using fewer or more words to deal with a given topic.
4. "restriction-to-the-text consciousness." Here the application of insight is to the meaning of the scriptural passage so that one knows it is to be expressed this way and no other way.
5. "classifying consciousness." With whatever the insight one possesses for the meaning of the scriptural passages, using judgment, for example, in terms of the twelve classes of scripture, one knows in which class the passages are to be included.
6. "aspiring consciousness." This is the consciousness applied to a samādhi for the aspired fruit, thus, to enter the stream, or to engage the stages, for such fruits as the powers, the confidences, and so on.

Sthiramati's explanations imply that all sound Buddhist works, such as Vasubandhu's *Abhidharmakośa,* require for their composition these levels of "discerning." Therefore, when Tsoṅ-kha-pa uses the term as an inclusive category for the Mādhyamika position, he is consistent with Sthiramati's subcommentary on the *Sūtrālaṃkāra.* By the same token, Tsoṅ-kha-pa's is not the only solution of Buddhist philosophy that can appropriately be entitled "discerning." Toward the end of the *Lam rim chen mo,* Tsoṅ-kha-pa acknowledges that while he has been mainly expounding the Mādhyamika, the Yogācāra has great treatises that may be followed.

In Tibet a type of religious literature grew up concerning the outer and inner "doctrinal systems" (*siddhānta*). "Outer" means the various non-Buddhist systems; while "inner" refers to the four systems: Vaibhāsika, Sautrāntika, Yogācāra, and Mādhyamika. In the light of Sthiramati's explanations, each of these four systems could represent a kind of "discerning" (*vipaśyanā*).

Asaṅga on the Ancillaries of Calming and the Supernormal Faculties

ATIŚA's "Light on the Path to Enlightenment" (*supra,* verse 39) states: "The one who destroys the members of calming, even should he cultivate the endeavor, would not accomplish *samādhi* even in a thousand years." Besides (verse 38): "As long as calming is not accomplished, the supernormal faculties do not arise. Therefore, one should exert again and again so as to accomplish calming." The word rendered "members," i.e., *aṅga,* is here translated as "ancillaries." Tsoṅ-kha-pa states in the "Calming" section: "Hence, those who desire in the depths of their heart to accomplish the *samādhi* of calming and discerning, must take as supremely important the endeavor in the ancillaries of, or equipment for calming, such as the thirteen set forth in the *Śrāvakabhūmi.*" Asaṅga, in his *Viniścaya-saṃgrahaṇī* on the *Śrutamayī bhūmi*[34] states that the thirteen aspects of the "path of equipment" (*saṃbhāra-mārga*) are set forth in the *Śrāvakabhūmi.* In fact, they amount to one chief, and twelve subordinate, conditions. I here translate Asaṅga's summary statement of these ancillaries from the Tibetan and from the Sanskrit (available starting in the subparagraph "What is lack of defective organs?").[35]

> Among those, if persons have the element of *parinirvāṇa,* and lack defective (organs), but have not approached [the spiritual guides], what are their conditions (*pratyaya*) for *parinirvāṇa?*
>
> He said: There are two conditions. What are the two? [1.] Chief (*pradhāna*) and subordinate (*hīna*). What is the chief condition? He said: As follows—the discourse of others dominated by the Illustrious Doctrine (*saddharma*) and the inner methodical mental orientation (*yoniśo manaskāra*). What is the subordinate condition? He said: There are numerous subordinate conditions, as follows—
>
> 2. personal achievement (*ātmasampat*),
> 3. achievement of others (*parasampat*),

4. virtuous craving for the doctrine (*kuśalo dharmacchandaḥ*),
5. going forth (*pravrajyā*),
6. restraint of morality (*śīla-saṃvara*),
8. moderation in food (*bhojane mātrajñatā*),
9. practice of staying awake (*jāgarikānuyoga*),
10. conduct with awareness (*saṃprajānadvihāritā*),
11. solitude (*prāvivekya*),
12. elimination of hindrances (*nivaraṇa-viśuddhi*),
13. right dwelling in *samādhi* (*samādhi-saṃniśraya*).

2. Personal achievement.

What is "personal achievement"? All of these: (*a*) human birth, (*b*) birth in the middle country, (*c*) lack of defective organs, (*d*) faith at home, (*e*) no bad bodily action.

(*a*) Among those, what is human birth? As follows— Now, some born in this world with human endowment possess the male organ, or are born as women.

(*b*) What is birth in the middle country? Now some born in this world, as above, among the illustrious births mentioned, are born among the men of the middle country, which is the "pure destiny." That is "birth in the middle country."

(*c*) What is lack of defective organs? Now some are neither stupid, nor incoherent in speech, nor mute, nor lack defectiveness of ears, etc., thus lacking defectiveness of major and minor limbs. They have the good fortune (the potentiality) of rightly accomplishing the virtuous side (*kuśala-pakṣa*). That is "lack of defective organs."

(*d*) What is faith at home? This way:—Now some in this world have faith and acquire purity of mind toward the Doctrine (*dharma*) and Discipline (*vinaya*) expressed by the Tathāgatas. That is "faith at home." Here "home" means the Doctrine and Discipline expressed by the Tathāgatas, because it is the home of birth of all the mundane and supramundane "good natures" (*śukla-dharma*). By dint of that [*śukla-dharma*] pulling forward—the faith in that [Doctrine and Discipline] becomes the faith at home, because it frees from all stain and turbulence of defilements.

(*e*) What is no bad bodily action? When one does not commit and is not drawn to commit any one of the five heinous deeds, to wit—matricide, patricide, killing of an *arhat,* causing schism in the Saṅgha, drawing blood with evil intention from a Tathāgata, that is "no bad bodily action." When one is not utterly innocent of committing and accumulating [having done in past lives] these five heinous deeds, he lacks the good fortune (the potentiality) of the Noble Path which proceeds to *parinirvāṇa.* Hence, those are bad bodily action.

Only by oneself does the embodiment (*ātmabhāva*) achieve by means of those five limbs (*aṅga*). Hence, the expression "personal achievement."

3. Achievement of others.

What is the achievement of others? (*a*) Arising of Buddhas, (*b*) teaching of the Illustrious Doctrine, (*c*) preservation of the doctrines taught, (*d*) dissemination of the preserved doctrines, and (*e*) corresponding sympathy from others.

(*a*) Among those, what is arising of Buddhas? As follows—Some individuals in this world generate good will and desire of benefit to all sentient beings. After three immeasurable eons of thousands of difficulties and the equipment with merit (*puṇya*) and knowledge (*jñāna*), they acquire their last ordinary body and take their seat at the terrace of enlightenment (*bodhimaṇḍa*). Eliminating the five hindrances, they well stabilize their mind (*citta*) in the four "stations of mindfulness" (*smṛtyupasthāna*). Then they cultivate the thirty-seven natures (*dharma*) accessory to enlightenment, and fully realize the incomparable, right-completed enlightenment. In that way there is "arising of Buddhas." Moreover, in the past, present, and future, that is the only way any Buddha Bhagavat arises.

(*b*) What is the teaching of the Illustrious Doctrine? When these Buddha Lords—and by their agency, disciples—appear in the world, because of compassion toward the world, they teach the Doctrine, beginning with the four Noble Truths, to wit, suffering, source, cessation, and path, in the groups (= the twelve sets of scripture)—*1*) thread discourses (*sūtra*), *2*) mingled prose and verse, *3*) prophecies, *4*) verses, *5*) joyous impersonal utterances, *6*) instructive personal discourses, *7*) parables, *8*) legends, *9*) Bodhisattva lives of the Buddha, *10*) grand scripture, *11*) marvelous events, and *12*) explanation. That is the "teaching of the Illustrious Doctrine."

(*c*) What is preservation of the doctrines taught? After the Buddha Lords live and tarry and teach the Illustrious Doctrine by setting into motion the Wheel of the Law, up to the time of passage into *parinirvāṇa* of the Buddha Lord, the practice is not destroyed and the Illustrious Doctrine does not decline. That is "preservation of the doctrines taught." Moreover, one should understand that "preservation" to take place by way of direct perception of the supreme doctrine (*paramārtha-dharma*).

(*d*) What is dissemination of the preserved doctrines? The very person who has fully comprehended the Illustrious Doctrine informs people that there is good fortune and power in the direct perception of the Illustrious Doctrine. With precepts only as he has fully comprehended it and that are in conformity with it, he follows it in teaching and follows it in introducing (people). That is "dissemination of the preserved doctrines."

(*e*) What is corresponding sympathy from others? "Others" means donors and patrons. They bring the conditions of things useful for living, as follows: religious garb, alms, bedding, seats, medicaments, and whatever utensils may be in point. One is shown sympathy by them. That is "corresponding sympathy from others."

4. Virtuous craving for the doctrine.

What is virtuous craving for the doctrine? As follows—Now some hear the doctrine from the Tathāgatas or the disciples of the Tathāgatas and acquire faith, but after having heard it stay at home addicted to harmfulness and defilement. However, the "gone forth" (*pravrajita*) has the opportunity. Consequently, one should think, "In this way I shall leave off all the host of women, treasures, foodstuffs, and money; and for the well-expressed Doctrine and Discipline shall leave home, and only when I am indeed 'homeless' shall be 'gone forth,' and having 'gone forth' I shall practice assiduously," and with these words rightly instruct (himself). Whoever has produced the virtuous craving for the doctrine in this way has "virtuous craving for the doctrine."

5. Going forth.

What is going forth? After having come under the influence of just that virtuous craving for the doctrine, by means of petition and the fourfold rite, one becomes ordained; and when he rightly holds the morality of the *śramaṇera,* is called "going forth."

6. Restraint of morality.

What is restraint of morality? The one who is "gone forth" in that way remains in possession of morality, is restrained by the Prātimokṣasaṃvara; has the "perfection of good behavior" (*ācāra-saṃpanna*) and the "perfection of lawful resort" (*gocara-saṃpanna*), views fearfully the major and minor sins; and rightfully takes and learns the "points of instruction" (*śikṣāpāda*). That is "restraint of morality."

7. Restraint of sense organs.

What is restraint of sense organs? When one has taken recourse to just the restraint of morality, he guards mindfulness. His mindfulness is zealous. His mind is guarded by mindfulness. He has the sphere of the even state. When he sees forms with the eye, he does not take hold of sign-sources or details by reason of which sinful, unvirtuous natures would flow according to his mind. He acts in each case to restrain those. He guards his mind sense organ. When he perceives sounds with his ear, odors with his nose, tastes with his tongue, tangibles with his body, natures (*dharma*) with his mind, he does not take hold of sign-sources or details by reason of which sinful unvirtuous natures would flow according to his mind. He acts in each case to restrain those. He guards his mind sense organ. His mind sense organ exerts the restraint. This is called "restraint of sense organs."

8. Moderation in food

What is moderation in food? When he thus has restrained senses, after detailed consideration he eats food, not for sport, not for intoxication, not for smartening, and not for embellishment, but simply to keep his body alive, to maintain it, allay its desire of food, and promote its chastity, with the thought, "I shall eliminate old feeling, and not give rise to new; and I shall have sustenance, strength, delight, no reproach, and an agreeable condition." This is called "moderation in food."

9. Practice of staying awake

What is the practice of staying awake? When one has moderation in food in that way, he purifies his mind from obscuring natures by means of walking and sitting during the day. He purifies his mind from obscuring natures by means of walking and sitting during the first watch of night. When he has (so) purified, then he leaves the monastery and outside the monastery washes his feet. Reentering the monastery, he takes rest on his right side, placing one foot upon the other, with the idea of light (*āloka-saṃjñā*), being mindful, being aware, and orienting his mind just to the idea of rising (*utthāna-saṃjñā*). In the last watch of night he quickly reawakens, and he purifies his mind from obscuring natures by walking and sitting. This is called "practice of staying awake in the former part of night and the latter part of night."

10. Conduct with awareness

What is conduct with awareness? When he has in that way practiced staying awake, he conducts himself with awareness while going forth and returning. He conducts himself with awareness while looking at and looking around; while drawing back and extending his arms; while bearing the upper robe, the religious garb, and the begging bowl; while eating, drinking, chewing, and tasting; while eliminating the fatigue that causes sleep; while walking, standing, sitting, lying down, and staying awake; while speaking and remaining silent. This is "conduct with awareness."

11. Solitude

What is dwelling in solitude? Having engaged in practice according to those (foregoing) rules, he makes his abode in lonely places, forests, bases of trees, deserted houses, mountains, mountain caves, grass huts; wide-open spaces, cemeteries, woods; and remote places. This is "dwelling in solitude."

12. Elimination of hindrances

What is elimination of hindrances? Whether one stays in a hermitage, or at the base of a tree, or in a deserted house, as the case my be, he purifies his mind (*citta*) from the five hindrances: *1*) sensuous lust, *2*) ill-will, *3*) torpor and sleepiness, *4*) mental wandering and regret, and *5*) doubt. When one removes his thoughts from those hindrances, then, free from hindrance, he has vicinity settling in the pleasure of *samādhi*. That is "elimination of hindrances."

13. Right dwelling in *samādhi*

What is right dwelling in *samādhi?* Having abandoned the secondary defilements of mentals and the main defilements as well as the five hindrances, then—

1) Separated from cravings, separated from sinful and unvirtuous natures, with inquiry (*vitarka*) and investigation (*vicāra*), having attained the First Dhyāna, he abides in the rapture and pleasure arising from the separation.

2) Allaying the inquiry and investigation, through inward serenity, through continuity of thought, he accomplishes and dwells in the Second Dhyāna, which is without inquiry and investigation, and has rapture and pleasure arising from samādhi.

3) He dwells with equanimity after losing the feeling of rapture. Mindful and aware, he experiences pleasure by way of body, just as the one of whom the noble ones said, "Equable and mindful, he dwells in pleasure." He accomplishes and dwells in the Third Dhyāna which is without rapture.

4) Through elimination of pleasure, through former elimination of pain and vanishing of satisfaction and dissatisfaction, having attained the Fourth Dhyāna, he abides in the purification of equanimity and mindfulness free from both pleasure and pain.

> This is called "right dwelling in *samādhi.*"
>
> In that sequence, beginning with "personal achievement" and ending with "right dwelling in *samādhi*" one rightly accomplishes in ever higher degrees the superior, very superior, and most superior conditions (*pratyaya*).
>
> When one in that way completely purifies his thoughts, is free from defilement, free from secondary defilement, becomes upright, acquires ease, and is fixed in the immobile state; when he begins with the four Noble Truths, which are (respectively) to be known, eliminated, directly realized, and cultivated, he obtains the precepts from another and from him hears the enunciation of the teaching. Then he pays attention to generating that. The right view, previously laid down, is the good fortune (*bhavya*) and power to be generated. Thereby he fully comprehends the four Noble Truths and accomplishes liberation, reaching *parinirvāṇa* in the realm of *nirvāṇa* without residue of personality aggregates (*skandha*).

As to the supernormal faculties, Tsoṅ-kha-pa says near the end of the "Calming" section: "However, by taking recourse to the Meditations, one also attains the five supernormal faculties. I shall not treat these here, for fear of the many words. As they are found extensively in the *Śrāvakabhūmi,* one should look them up there." By "Meditations" is meant the four Dhyānas described above in "13. Right Dwelling in *Samādhi.*" Since Asaṅga's theory about the supernormal faculties and how they arise is assumed in the reader as preparation for reading Tsoṅ-kha-pa's "Calming" section, besides having an intrinsic interest, it is here presented from the *Śrāvakabhūmi:*

> Among those, by taking recourse to [the four] Dhyānas, one accomplishes the five supernormal faculties (*abhijñā*). Furthermore, how does one accomplish them? As follows: When that meditator has attainment of completely pure meditation (*dhyāna*)—whatever be the doctrine heard, held (in mind) and studied by him with mental orientation of the equipoised stage—he, taking recourse to that completely pure meditation, having oriented his mind (in that way) to just that (doctrine) in order to master the supernormal faculties, namely undertaking *1*) the domain of magical practice, or *2*) the (memory of) former abodes, *3*) the divine hearing, *4*) the (vision of) death and birth, *5*) the (knowledge of another's) mental

make-up—has both special knowledge of meaning and special knowledge of doctrine. As a result of much repetition on the part of the one especially knowing meaning and especially knowing doctrine, who is arousing thoughts in just that way, there comes the time, there comes the occasion when his fruits of the cultivation, the five supernormal faculties, arise.

Furthermore, the person especially knowing meaning, especially knowing doctrine that way, cultivates twelve ideas in order to accomplish all the supernormal faculties, as follows: *1*) idea of lightness, *2*) idea of softness, *3*) idea of the space realm, *4*) idea of great attention to body and mind, *5*) idea of perfect freedom, *6*) idea of remembrance according to their order of previously experienced practices, *7*) idea of assembled utterance of all kinds of sounds, *8*) idea of the sign of manifesting form, *9*) idea of the transformation of form caused by defilement, *10*) idea of liberation, *11*) idea of the base of supremacy, *12*) idea of the base of totality.[36]

The continuation, here presented on the basis of the Sanskrit in the Bihar Manuscript and the Tibetan translation, in part coincides with passages found in the old Buddhist scriptures:

1) Among them, by the idea of lightness, he is convinced that his body is light, like the cotton of the *tūla* shrub or cotton of the *karpāsa* type in a whirlwind. He, being so convinced, at that place dispatches himself by means of a mental orientation derived solely from conviction, as though from the cot to the stool, from the stool to the cot; likewise, from the cot to the grass, from the mat to the cot.

2) Among those, (by) the idea of softness, he is convinced that his body is soft, like silk or hair or fine cloth. By the idea of softness, by the idea of lightness, this idea of lightness which nourishing, fostering, is being fostered, attains great increase.

3) Among those, the idea of the (empty) space realm is the idea by which he is convinced that his body has lightness and softness. If he wishes to go somewhere, whatever intervening corporeal substance creates an obstacle for going there, by means of a mental orientation derived solely from conviction, he is convinced that *it* is space.

4) Among those, the idea of conjoining mind and body is the one by which either he joins mind to body or body to mind, for which reason his body becomes lighter, becomes softer, more serviceable, and more radiant; and following mind, tied to mind, based on mind, it proceeds.

5) Among those, the idea of perfect freedom is the idea by which he transforms (magically) the distant to the near, the near to the distant; the fine to the coarse, the coarse to the fine; earth into water, water into earth; accordingly, with each one of the great elements, what is to be mutually effected at length. And in that way he creates a magical manifestation, either a magical manifestation of form or a magical manifestation of sound.

Thus with those five perfect ideas belonging to the cultivation, he severally experiences the diverse fields of magical power. Having become single, he exhibits himself in multiple form, namely, by means of an idea pertaining to transformation, pertaining to magical manifestation. At that place, furthermore, he exhibits himself in multiple form and becomes single, namely, by means of an idea of perfect freedom pertaining to magical manifestation and disappearance. He goes through the wall, through the hill, through the rampart, with an unhindered body (as though in space). With that he goes and performs submergence and emergence in the earth as though in water. Without sinking, he walks on the streams as though on earth. In the posture of folded legs, he ascends to the sky like a winged bird; or with his hands he strokes and catches these two—the sun and the moon—which are so great of magical power, so great of dignity, so great of splendor. With that body he makes a *tour de force* up to the world of Brahma. He does all that, to be understood according to circumstances, by means of the idea of perfect freedom controlled by the ideas of lightness, softness, space realm, and conjoining of mind and body. Here two kinds of *tour de force* by that body pertain to the world of Brahma: He makes a *tour de force* (*a*) by the fact of going, or (*b*) by a (magical) transformation as desired, from the world of Brahma downwards, of the four great elements and of any (= every) form having those (elements) as condition.

6) Among those, the idea of remembrance according to their order of previously experienced practices is the one by which, starting from the state of childhood, his memory serves and does not fail on any point. Where he went, stood, sat, lay,—the previously experienced practice he remembers and recognizes at length, very roughly, without disturbing the sequence, and without skipping. As a consequence of the cultivation of that (idea), he remembers the diverse kinds of former abodes (of previous lives), up to [as in the sūtra] "together with the aspects and together with location," at length—which is the fruit of the cultivation.

7) Among those, the idea of assembled utterance of all kinds of sounds

(is as follows): In whatever village, town, guild, assembly, audience, long and broad residence, or private chamber, a mixed-up, varied sound, which is called the *kala-kala* sound (confused noise), or the sound of a great flowing river, arises, in that place, taking hold of the sign-source, the idea is the one by which he fastens (his mind) with effort, by means of a mental orientation of the equipoised stage, on the sounds, noble and ignoble, divine and human, far and near. As a consequence of much repetition of that (idea), he acquires the divine ear, which is his fruit of the cultivation, by which he hears the divine and human sounds, whether distant or nearby.

8) Among those, the idea of the sign of manifesting form (of other realms) (is as follows): Having previously taken hold of the sign of light, he orients his mind to just that sign; and having taken hold of the sign that is due to the manifoldness of sentient beings, he orients his mind to just that sign by means of distinguishing their engagement with virtuous and unvirtuous action. This is the idea of the sign of manifesting form. As a consequence of the cultivation of this (idea), he acquires the knowledge of passing away and birth—which is the fruit of the cultivation; by which purified divine eye . . . at length [as in the sūtra, telling what he, the Lord sees] up to, "after the breaking up of the body they are born among the gods in the good destiny, heaven world."

9) Among those, the idea of the transformation of form caused by defilement is the one by which he examines and decides upon the state of form belonging to the sentient beings whose mentality—impassioned, hostile, and stupified—is enveloped by defilements and secondary defilements, (such as) wrath, malice, hypocrisy, anguish, duplicity, craftiness, immodesty and lack of conscience. The state of form, the change of form, belonging to the impassioned person is of such a kind, namely, excitation of sense faculties, prominence of sense faculties, smiling face. The state of form, the change of form, belonging to the hostile person is of such a kind, namely, change in color of face, trembling speech, frowning. The state of form, the change of form, belonging to the stupefied person is of such a kind, namely, muteness, nonassenting even after the meaning is obvious, use of vulgar language. So (also), by means of aspects belonging to such categories, up to the state of form, the change of form, belonging to the person filled with immodesty and lack of conscience. Then, taking hold of the sign, he orients his mind, to wit, as a consequence of much repetition, there arises the knowledge of the make-up of minds—which is

> the fruit of the cultivation—by which he knows with his mind as it really is, the adumbrating (*vitarkita*) and discursively-thinking (*vicarita*) mind of other sentient beings, of other persons.
>
> *10–12*) Among those, the cultivation of the ideas of liberation, of the bases of mastery, and of the bases of totality, is to be understood as previously, namely, as in the *Samāhitabhūmi*—by which cultivation he accomplishes the noble magical power, transformative of substance, magically manifesting, creative through conviction; namely, purifying others (*araṇā*), knowledge of aspirations (*praṇidhi-jñāna*), and the four special knowledges (*pratisaṃvid*), namely, special knowledge of natures (*dharma*), special knowledge of meaning (*artha-*), special knowledge of etymology (*nirukti-*), special knowledge of eloquence (*pratibhāna-*).

Asaṅga's passage continues and concludes as follows:[37]

> Among those, there is a distinction of magical power (*ṛddhi*) as noble (*ārya*) and ignoble (*anārya*). Whatever the entity one transforms, whatever the creation one creates, (in whatever one has conviction), with noble magical power just that thing occurs, not otherwise, and one is completely able to do the required with it (i.e., with noble . . .). Furthermore, with ignoble magical power just that thing does not occur, but is explained as the mere display of a magician.
>
> Thus, by means of those twelve ideas, as a consequence of following (them), as a consequence of (their) cultivation, as a consequence of much repetition, one understands the accomplishment, according to circumstances, of the five supernormal faculties; as well as, according to circumstances, of the merits of the nobles that are not shared by the ordinary person.

Also, while in the above materials only five supernormal faculties were set forth, a sixth one—especially designed as "Buddhist"—is often added, i.e., the "knowledge of flux-destruction" (*āsrava-kṣaya-jñāna*). Asaṅga in his exegesis of the *Śrāvakabhūmi*,[38] explains that knowing the worldly flux and knowing that it won't arise is called "knowledge of flux-destruction." In his discussions in the same place, he treats the supernormal faculties in the order, *1*) domain of magical power, *2*) divine hearing, *3*) knowing others' minds, *4*) remembering prior lives,

5) knowing the passing away of beings to various destinies, and 6) knowledge of flux-destruction. He says that the first three are only supernormal faculties (*abhijñā*) and not clear vision (*vidyā*), while the last three are both supernormal faculties and clear vision, because the latter completely and at all times oppose confusion (*saṃmoha*).[39] (The three "clear visions" are frequently attributed to the Buddha's experiences during the three watches of the night of enlightenment). Asaṅga adds that the last three supernormal faculties avoid the two extremes of eternalism and nihilism, and teach the middle path devoid of pride in the flux-destruction. He seems to intend by this remark that the remembrance of former lives avoids the extreme of nihilism, that knowing the passing away of sentiment beings avoids the extreme of eternalism, while knowledge of flux-destruction establishes the middle path.

Discursive Thought and the bSam-yas Debate

TSOṄ-KHA-PA frequently condemns theories credited to a Chinese teacher called in Tibetan sources usually Hva-śaṅ. Thus, in the "Calming" section: "The positing of no discursive thought whatever to be the contemplation of the profound meaning of discerning is exclusively the school of the Chinese professor Hva-śaṅ. Regard the three *Bhāvanākrama* texts thoroughly and you will understand!" Professor Demiéville has thoroughly examined the late eighth-century (between 792–794) controversy in Tibet between the Chinese party headed by Mahāyāna Hva-śaṅ, representing a form of Ch'an Buddhism, and the Indian party headed by Kamalaśīla, whose position is recorded in his three *Bhāvanākrama,*[40] the first and third of which have been edited in Sanskrit by Tucci. While Demiéville calls the debate the "Council of Lhasa," Tucci points out that it occurred in the bSam-yas monastery outside of Lhasa.[41]

As we shall see, the dispute revolves about the roles of discursive and nondiscursive thought. Tsoṅ-kha-pa's position itself is complicated, but certainly he is following Asaṅga's tradition (*Saṃdhinirmocana-sūtra, Yogācārabhūmi* especially the *Śrāvakabhūmi* portion), as does Kamalaśīla in his three *Bhāvanākrama*. Therefore, the matter will be clearer if Asaṅga's tradition regarding discursive and nondiscursive thought be treated, followed by a discussion of the position attributed to Hva-śaṅ.

Saṃdhinirmocana Tradition on Discursive and Nondiscursive Thought *qua* Calming and Discerning

The *Saṃdhinirmocana-sūtra* states:

"Lord, how many are the meditative objects of calming?" He declared, "One, namely, the reflected image without discursive thought." "How many are the meditative objects of discerning?" He declared, "Only one: the reflected image with discursive thought." "How many are the meditative objects of both?" He declared, "Two, as follows: the limits of the entity and the fulfillment of the requirement."[42]

According to Asaṅga's *Śrāvakabhūmi,*[43] there are two limits of the entity, the phenomenal limit and the noumenal limit; and the fulfillment of the requirement is the meditative object in fruitional stage, so that the meditator is freed from contamination (*dauṣṭhulya*).

Using the same vocabulary, Vimalamitra's commentary on the *Saptaśatikā Prajñāpāramitā* states:

As the Bhāvanā-mārga has been explained, its meditative object (*ālambana*) is the limits of the entity, the reflected image with discursive thought, and the reflected image without discursive thought.

[As to the Aśaikṣa-mārga], the meditative object of those (i.e., Bodhisattvas) on the Tenth Stage and the Tathāgata is the fulfillment of the requirement because they abide at the summit.[44]

This theory of paths (*mārga*) is based on the "five-path" theory of the *Prajñāpāramitā* literature, of which the first three are the *saṃbhāra-mārga* (path of accumulating merit and knowledge), the *prayoga-mārga* (path of praxis), and the *darśana-mārga* (path of vision); and the last two, the *bhāvanā-mārga* (path of cultivation) and the *aśaikṣa-mārga* (path beyond training).[45] Tsoṅ-kha-pa, in his "Guided Tour through the Seven Books of Dharmakīrti,"[46] when defining *yogipratyakṣa* gives as examples the *darśana-mārga* (in the varieties of the śravaka, pratyekabuddha, the bodhisattva). So this must be back of Tsoṅ-kha-pa's hint in the "Discerning" section that the nondiscursive thought of the logician is not the same as that for the meditative object of calming.[47]

The *Saptaśatikā Prajñāpāramitā* gives an example of the meditative object as the limits of the entity:

The Lord asked, "Of what is 'true limit' (*bhūtakoṭi*) a term?" Mañjuśrī replied: "Lord, 'true limit' is a term for the real body (*sat-kāya*)." The Lord asked, "Referring obscurely to what (i.e., having what in back of your mind), do you so speak?" Mañjuśrī replied: "Lord, the unreal body. Since it is not a real body, it neither transmigrates, nor fails to transmigrate. For that reason, this body is an unreal body."[48]

Accordingly, Mañjuśrī mentions the limits of the entity, the noumenal limit being the "true limit," the real body; and the phenomenal limit being the imputed self or five personality aggregates, the unreal body. The *Saṃdhinirmocana-sūtra* states two limits in VIII, sect. 13, as the "mixed *dharmas*" (*miśra-dharma*) massing toward the thusness end, and "unmixed *dharmas*" (*amiśradharma*) for the phenomenal end, or objects taken individually.[49] In agreement, the scripture "Lion's Roar of Queen Śrīmālā" mentions the two ends as "nondiscrete *dharmas*" for the absolute end, and "discrete *dharmas*" for the phenomenal end.[50]

ASANGA'S POSITION ON DISCURSIVE THOUGHT

So far the term "discursive thought" (*vikalpa*) has been used without clarifying what is meant by it.

In the earlier part of his *Yogācārabhūmi* (portion edited by V. Bhattacharya), Asaṅga discusses discursive thought (again, *vikalpa*) in connection with the well-known terms *vitarka-vicāra,* which I have rendered "inquiry" and "investigation" in the First Dhyāna in the previous section (D) under the heading "13. Right dwelling in *samādhi.*" Since a mere translation of this passage would be quite dense, I shall attempt to explain Asaṅga's statements by paragraphs, referring to the portion in Sanskrit as "Asaṅga (Sanskrit)." Asaṅga (Sanskrit) begins:

What is the body (*śarīra*) of inquiry (*vitarka*) and investigation (*vicāra*)? The vitarka(s) and vicāra(s) should be understood to have as body the volition (*cetanā*) which has not inferred the object-support (*ālambana*), and furthermore to have as body the cognition (*jñāna*) which has inferred the object-subject.[51]

Let us turn to Asaṅga's exegesis in a later section of the *Yogācārabhūmi* (his *Viniścaya-saṃgrahaṇī*):

The coarse "insight" (*prajñā*) based on "mental murmur" (*manojalpa*) is "inquiry" (*vitarka,* or "adumbration"); . . . the subtle one is "investigation" (*vicāra,* or "thinking with signs").[52]

Since many commentaries on the words *vitarka-vicāra* takes them as respectively coarse (*sthūla) and subtle* (*sūkṣma*), this shows that in the previous paragraph about volition (*cetanā*) and cognition (*jñāna*) as "bodies," they are each bodies for both "inquiry" and "investigation." Yüan-ts'ê, author of the great commentary on the *Saṃdhinirmocana-sūtra,* makes the same point.[53] Thus, it is the "cognition" (*jñāna*) which is either a coarse or a subtle "insight" (*prajñā*). One may conclude that inquiry-investigation can use only one body at a time—either the volitional, noninferring body, or the cognitional, inferring body. In the case of using the volitional, noninferring body, my alternate translation of the terms as "adumbration" and "thinking with signs" seems more apt.

Asaṅga (Sanskrit) continues:

What is the object-support (*ālambana*) of *vitarka* and *vicāra?* The object-support is the meaning (*artha*) based on the set of terms (*nāma-kāya*), the set of syllables (*pada-kāya*), and the set of phrases (*vyañjana-kāya*).

What is the imagery (*ākāra*) of *vitarka* and *vicāra?* Vitarka has as imagery the consignment (*arpaṇā*) and particular consignment (*vyarpaṇā*)[54] to that very object-support. Furthermore, vicāra has as imagery discrimination (*pratyavekṣaṇā*) of that same one. What do *vitarka* and *vicāra* arouse? They arouse speech (*vāk*).

This shows that what Tsoṅ-kha-pa refers to as "discriminative insight" (*pratyavekṣaṇa-prajñā*) or "discriminative knowledge" (*pratyavekṣaṇa-jñāna*), especially in his "Discerning the Real" section, includes this "imagery" (*ākāra*) of "investigation" (*vicāra*), discriminating that very object-support of terms, syllables, and phrases, or the meaning thereof, to which "inquiry" had consigned and particularly consigned. Furthermore, this shows that this kind of discursive thought arouses speech, e.g., Asaṅga's works and Tsoṅ-kha-pa's works as well. Moreover, one distinguishes the sets of terms, syllables, and phrases from their meaning (*artha*); and this enables one to introduce the well-known levels of "insight": "insight consisting of hearing" (*śrutamayī*), consisting of pondering (*cintāmayī*), and consisting of cultivation (*bhāvanāmayī*). Thus Jñānagarbha's commentary on the Maitreya chapter of the *Saṃdhinirmocana-sūtra,* says that the marks (or signs) of *dharma* are the sets of terms, syllables, and phrases.[55] Asaṅga (*Samāhitabhūmi*) says that the object-support in *dharma* has the mental concomitant of insight consisting of hearing; while the object-support in meaning (*artha*) has the concomitants of insight consisting of pondering and insight consisting of cultivation.[56]

Asaṅga (Sanskrit) continues:

What are the varieties of *vitarka* and *vicāra?* the varieties are of seven kinds, the *naimittika* as previously (*pūrvavat*), and "undefiled" (*akliṣṭa*).

After surveying Asaṅga's text up to that point to ascertain what was meant by "the *naimittika* as previously," I could only conclude that he refers to the *prajñapti* varieties he introduces in the *Yogācārabhūmi* at the outset of his *bhūmis* called *Savitarkā savicārā bhūmi* (the third), *Avitarkā vicāramātrā bhūmi* (the fourth), *Avitarkāvicārā bhūmi* (the fifth), and other *prajñaptis* occurring in the text of the three *bhūmis,* which are combined in Asaṅga's treatment. That is to say, they are the "designation" (*prajñapti*) varieties of *1*) realms (*dhātu*), *2*) birth (*upapatti*), *3*) cause and fruit (*hetuphala*), *4*) characteristic (*lakṣaṇa*), *5*) methodical mental orientation (*yoniśo manaskāra*), *6*) unmethodical mental orientation (*ayoniśo manaskāra*), 7) defilement (*saṃkleśa*), to which one adds the "undefiled" (*akliṣṭa*). Asaṅga thus shows his position that discursive thought or constructive imagination is responsible for the worlds, everything that happens in them, including all the good and bad things.

Asaṅga (Sanskrit) continues:

What is the distribution (*viniścaya*) of *vitarka* and *vicāra?* What is vitarka and vicāra is also discursive thought (*vikalpa*). But while what is vitarka and vicāra is also discursive thought, there could be a discursive thought that is not vitarka or vicāra, namely, in regard to supramundane knowledge (*lokottara-jñāna*). Besides that, when taking into account all the *citta-* and *caitasika-dharmas* that range in the three worlds, there is discursive thought that is not vitarka or vicāra.

According to Asaṅga, "inquiry" (*vitarka*) and "investigation" (*vicāra*) always constitute the development of discursive thought. In fact, "inquiry" covers all discursive thought of question form, e.g., "What is . . .?"; while "investigation" covers all declarative sentences, in furtherance of, or in resolution of, the questions. Thus, Tsoṅ-kha-pa states in the "Calming" section:[57] "The method of non-slipping-away [of the meditative object] is taught by the gurus as the idea, 'The foundation of meditative object is like this,' which can be a question by another person or a personal involvement in discursive thought—and it says nothing about the sheer capacity of mindfulness." This shows that discursive thought, as mentioned previously in the form of coarse or subtle *prajñā,* is necessary for the communication of the guru's precepts. However, "inquiry" and "investigation" do not exhaust all discursive thought, because, outside of those, there is a discursive thought related to supramundane knowledge. In Asaṅga's *Śrāvakabhūmi,* "supramundane" is especially applied to the four Noble Truths and their aspects.[58] Besides, there is discursive thought which takes the yogin through the higher states (the *samāpatti-vihāras*) by the discursive thought, "This state is coarse; the next one is more calm" (the calmness-coarseness sequence).[59] This is the improvement-oriented discursive thought, analogous to when the painter thinks, "This line won't do; another one will be better." Since *vitarka-vicāra* is found in the First Dhyāna but is no longer found in the higher Dhyānas of the "realm of form" (*rūpa-dhātu*), nor in the equipoises of the formless realm (*arūpa-dhātu*), any discursive thought found in the higher states cannot be included in *vitarka-vicāra* which arouses speech.

Accordingly, while "discerning" (*vipaśyanā*) is regularly associated with a kind of discursive thought, the *Saṃdhinirmocana-sūtra* (VIII, sect. 17) mentions that calming and discerning can occur in a *samādhi* attended with "inquiry" and "investigation," in one without "inquiry" and attended with only "investigation," and in one without either "inquiry" or "investigation" (which are the third, fourth, and fifth *bhūmis* in Asaṅga's *Yogācārabhūmi*). Yüan-ts'ê, presumably combining language of the sūtra's chapter VIII, section 24 with section 17,[60] thus attributing the remark to the Bhagavat, says:[61]

> Whatever Calming and Discerning experience and discriminate in a manner coarse and clear with "inquiry" and "investigation" (*a*) those words in the way they are apprehended by both "insight consisting of hearing" and "insight consisting of pondering" and (*b*) the marks (or, signs) (*nimitta*) of the meaning of dharma—is the "samādhi attended with inquiry and attended with investigation."[62]

The sūtra itself (VIII, sect. 17) states that the *samādhi* without "inquiry" and attended with only "investigation" is the one consisting of "discrimination" (*pratyavekṣaṇā*) of those marks (or, signs). It states that the *samādhi* with neither "inquiry" nor "investigation" is the one with support-object of "mixed *dharmas*" (*miśradharma*). The expressions "unmixed *dharma*" and "mixed *dharma*" are explained earlier in the chapter (VIII, sect. 13), and I have already mentioned them in connection with the two limits. When the *dharmas* are taken as objects individually, the object is "unmixed *dharma*." When the dharmas of sūtras, and so on, are taken in a block for object-support of calming and discerning, and thus those *dharmas* are directed toward thusness, toward enlightenment, toward *nirvāṇa*, the object is "mixed *dharma*."[63]

Asaṅga (Sanskrit) continues:

What is the evolution (*pravṛtti*) of *vitarka* and *vicāra?* The vitarka-vicāra of hell-beings have what gesture (*ākāra*), evolve with what contact (*sparśa*) assembling, agitated by what, possessed with what, eager in what, doing what? As is the case of hell-beings, so also in the case of animals, hungry ghosts (*preta*), man, gods ranged in desire, and gods belong to the First Dhyāna, the vitarka-vicāra have gesture, etc. along with the other questions [Asaṅga goes on to describe each of the five destinies of hell-beings, etc. in terms of those questions and according to Buddhist mythology].

It is of course hard to see how the previous translation of *vitarka* as "inquiry" and *vicāra* as "investigation" fits the attributed "discursive thought" (*vikalpa*) of hell-beings, animals, and hungry ghosts (the three bad destinies), as of men, gods ranged in the realm of desire and gods ranged in the First Dhyāna of the "realm of form." Since it arouses speech, the presumed "discursive thought" is whatever mental process arouses animal calls, etc. Perhaps my alternate translation "adumbration" and "thinking with signs" is more apt here.

Asaṅga (Sanskrit) later on states:[64]

What is the occasion (*adhiṣṭhāna*) of the *vitarka-vicāra* that are equipped with "methodical mental orientation"? There are six occasions, follows—*1*) time of certainty (*niścaya*), *2*) time of non-evolution (*nivṛtti*), *3*) time of action (*karma*) *4*) time of worldly dispassion (*laukika-vairāgya*), *5*) time of supramundane dispassion (*lokottara-vairāgya*), *6*) time of assisting sentient beings (*sattvā-nugraha*).

"Methodical mental orientation" was previously mentioned as one of the seven kinds of *vitarka-vicāra*. Various kinds of "methodical mental orientation" are explained in the *Śrāvakabhūmi* and in Tsoṅ-kha-pa's "Calming" section; and they serve as the occasions of the religious life, with "certainty" and so on.

Asaṅga (Sanskrit) also mentions:[65]

What is the search (*eṣaṇā*) of the *vitarka-vicāra* that are equipped with "methodical mental orientation"? In this way: In this world some persons seek possessions (*bhoga*) by a dharma that is considerate, not by a dharma that is inconsiderate. [Asaṅga goes on to explain that the considerate dharma is the one without attachment, that sees possible troubles, etc., and so on extensively, with praxis of the equipment of the Śrāvaka as expounded extensively in the *Śrāvakabhūmi,* praxis of the equipment for the Pratyekabuddha as set forth in the *Pratyekabuddhabhūmi,* and praxis of accomplishing the Perfections as developed extensively in the *Bodhisattvabhūmi.*]

Thus "inquiry" and "investigation," accompanied by a methodical mental orientation, when searching, generate the instructions for the Srāvaka, for the Pratyekabuddha, and for the Bodhisattva.

ASANGA'S POSITION ON NONDISCURSIVE THOUGHT

Asaṅga talks about this topic at the end of his *Viniścayasaṃgrahaṇī* on the Tattva chapter of the *Bodhisattvabhūmi.*[66] Besides, he treats the topic in this *Mahāyāna-saṃgraha,* chapter VIII, devoted to Adhiprajñā-śikṣā.[67] In fact, the five aspects stated in the latter work as the nature of the non-discursive, or nonreflective, *jñāna* (*nirvikalpa-jñāna*) in terms of negatives are given reasons in the former work. Therefore, the matter will be clearer if the two sources are combined, using the signals "Tattva" and "Saṃgraha" to identify the sources of the material.

Tattva: As to the passage, "The insight which grasps the meaning of reality is nondiscursive," how should one understand the "nondiscursive"?

Saṃgraha: There are five aspects to the nature of "nonreflective wisdom."

Saṃgraha: *1*) It does not lack a mental orientation (*manaskāra*).

Tattva: If it were from no mental orientation, it would not be proper to say [as said in the sūtras] "possessed of methodical mental orientation"; and would reduce to the absurdity that dreamless sleep, stupor, and drunken stupor would also be [that insight].

Saṃgraha: *2*) It need not exclude or transcend the stage with inquiry (*vitarka*) and investigation (*vicāra*).

Tattva: If it were from transcendence [over *vitarka-vicāra*], how would this avoid contradicting the saying, "The *citta-* and *caitasika-dharmas* of the three realms are discursive thought"? (And it would contradict!)

Saṃgraha: *3*) It is not inoperative in "cessation of feelings and ideas" (*saṃjñāveditanirodha*).

Tattva: If it were from absence [in some state], then *prajñā* would not occur among the *caitasika-dharmas*. (But it does!)

Saṃgraha: *4*) It has no own-nature of form.

Tattva: If it were from own-nature, then how would insight which is without own-form not be rightly the nondiscursive character? (But sometimes it is discursive!)

Saṃgraha: *5*) It does not make a variety out of objects (the *bhūtārthacitrīkāra*).

Tattva: If it were from instigating the object-support, how would it not scorn the nondiscursive insight which does not instigate? (And it would scorn it!)

Tattva exegesis concludes:

Then how is one to look upon the nondiscursive insight? He said: Since it does not instigate the object-support, its object-support is a nature (*dharma*) inconsistent with presence and absence, i.e., is thusness; and it is nondiscursive. At the time, by virtue of former thrust, there is no instigation, there arises the *prajñā* having the *samādhi* of thusness; at that time it grasps directly the sign of the object-support. That is the nondiscursive (*prajñā*).

A principal conclusion one may draw from Asaṅga's remarks, especially the first four aspects, is that "nondiscursive knowledge" operates wherever there is discursive knowledge, i.e., the yogin applies this "nondiscursive knowledge" to the very object toward which others use discursive thought. Thus it is not the object which is responsible for whether or not there is discursive thought. Furthermore, Asaṅga states in the *Śrāvakabhūmi* (2d Yogasthāna):[68]

When he has exchange of the basis (*āśraya-parivṛtti*), having transcended the reflected image (*pratibimbam atikramya*) he is equipoised in the First Dhyāna and having reached the First Dhyāna has the object-field (*gocara*) of the

First Dhyāna; is equipoised in the Second, Third, and Fourth Dhyānas, and having reached the Fourth Dhyāna has the object-field of the Fourth Dhyāna; is equipoised in the base of infinite space, the base of infinite perception, the base of nothing-at-all, the base of neither ideation nor nonideation; and (in each case) having reached those, has direct perception (*pratyakṣa*), has nondiscursive (*avikalpa*) knowledge and vision (*jñāna-darśana*) of those (eight) object-fields as the knowable entity.

In this passage Asaṅga defines the full range of states involves with discursive thought, but where the yogin applies nondiscursive knowledge and vision. In addition, there is the "cessation of ideas and feelings" in which there is apparently no discursive thought, but where one can have nondiscursive knowledge.

Tsoṅ-kha-pa's Rejection of Hva-śaṅ's Position

If one collects all the references in the "Calming" and "Discerning" sections to the positions advanced by Hva-śaṅ Mahāyāna or his Tibetan followers, one is forced to a striking conclusion: this is not an argument between the "sudden" and the "gradual" schools, as has sometimes been advanced, especially by Tucci in *Minor Buddhist Texts,* part II, where (p. 154) the reader is led to believe that the *Lam rim chen mo* takes up the dispute from this standpoint. This is not to deny Tucci's evidence from various texts that the "sudden-gradual" dispute was present in Tibet. So prevalent is this misapprehension of the nature of the dispute that Demiéville finds it astonishing that the Chinese teacher Mahāyāna would speak of "liberation thought by thought" and so hearken back to the gradual path of *Dhammapada,* 239.[69] But the Chinese text about the debate which Demiéville has translated shows so much reliance on the *Laṅkāvatāra-sūtra* as to make one conclude the Chinese teacher belonged to the *Laṅka* school of Chinese Ch'an. One may easily ascertain that the *Laṅkāvatāra* dwells for a considerable portion of its length on the development of a "body made of mind" (*manomaya-kāya*) in three stages; so this sūtra is not espousing the "sudden" doctrine, except in common with other Mahāyāna scriptures in reference to enlightenment as the culmination of the path.

The view of the dispute as was handed down and later explained in Tsoṅ-kha-pa's *Lam rim chen mo* is, rather, a dispute over what constitutes the proper sequence of *samādhi,* namely, what could be called "right" (*samyak*). And the dispute was over the nature of "discursive thought," which is of course the reason that Asaṅga's treatment of "discursive" and "nondiscursive" thought was expounded above. It seems that this dispute came about partly through terminological inconsistency. Thus Demiéville observes that the *Laṅkāvatāra* continually presses the point that language is tied to *vikalpa.*[70] Now, the use of the term *vikalpa* (discursive thought) differs in various works. According to the foregoing discussions based on Asaṅga's work, one may notice that this *Laṅka* usage of the word *vikalpa* makes it equivalent to the terminology *vitarka-vicāra,* which arouses speech. Besides, for the "realm of desire" it is a use of *vikalpa* tantamount to the Pāli *vitakka* ("conjecture" or "discursive speculation") as a fault for which meditation praxis assigns "mindfulness while breathing in and out" as an adversary.[71] But we have already observed that Asaṅga allows for a kind of "discursive thought" (*vikalpa*) outside of, or transcendent, of, *vitarka-vicāra.* In speaking this way, Asaṅga follows the lead of the *Saṃdhinirmocana-sūtra* which in chapter VIII, section 17, sets forth three *samādhi* situations of "calming" and "discerning," with the third being in a *samādhi* without either "inquiry" or "investigation" (*vitarka-vicāra*). And since, as was cited, the *Saṃdhinirmocana* states the meditative object of discerning (*vipaśyanā*) as being attended with "discursive thought," this shows the sūtra's position of allowing a supramundane type of "discursive thought" as a form of insight (*prajñā*). Hence, the opposition of the Chinese party to the *Saṃdhinirmocana-sūtra,* as Tsoṅ-kha-pa puts it:[72]

It is well known that when the Chinese teacher Hva śaṅ saw this sūtra's exceedingly clear exposition, which cannot be repudiated, in regard to discerning as discriminative insight, he exclaimed "How incomprehensible is this sūtra!" and kicked it with his foot. Conceiving that any discursive thought is all apprehension of sign-source [*nimitta-grāha*], he rejected discriminative insight and paid no attention at all to it. Because he was opposed to the longing to contemplate the profound meaning, he acted that way. There appeared many followers of this school of thought.

Thus to have followed the lead of Hva-śaṅ would mean rejecting the authority of the *Saṃdhinirmocana-sūtra,* and upholding in its place the authority of the *Laṅkāvatāra* and certain other Mahāyāna scriptures. Demiéville mentions that in the list of scriptures to which the Chinese teacher appeals there is included the "Mahā-prajñā" and the *Vajracchedikā,* which also shows some Prajñāpāramitā scripture influence.[73]

From the standpoint of Chinese Buddhism it would be a normal thing to follow one or more scriptures in preference to others, so there arose the Hwa-yen (the Avataṃsaka school), the Lotus school, etc. In contrast, in Tibet the tendency was to follow a philosophical school, prevalently the Yogācāra or the Mādhyamika, rather than a particular sūtra. Tsoṅ-kha-pa is not really a follower of the *Saṃdhinirmocana-sūtra* in the sense of the Hwa-yen for the *Avataṃsaka,* etc. His defense of this sūtra is not a blanket endorsement of everything in it, since it is the basic scripture of the Yogācāra school, containing certain technical philosophical positions that rival the Mādhyamika position that Tsoṅ-kha-pa generally espouses. The reason for Tsoṅ-kha-pa's spirited defense of the scripture has to do with the lineage he is following of combining Asaṅga's school for Buddhist meditational practice with Nāgārjuna's school for the Buddhist philosophical position. In this way he continues the path lineage associated with Atīsa, and this requires also upholding and appealing to the Maitreya chapter of the *Saṃdhinirmocana* (its chapter VIII), Asaṅga's *Śrāvakabhūmi,* as well as Kamalaśīla's three *Bhāvanākrama.*

Then what is the theory of "right" *samādhi* praxis according to the *Saṃdhinirmocana,* the *Śrāvakabhūmi,* and the *Bhāvanākrama* triad? Tsoṅ-kha-pa's "Calming the Mind" section is devoted to clarifying this praxis, and he reverts to the topic at the end of the "Discerning" section. He makes no secret of his view that this correct method of Buddhist meditation had largely fallen into desuetude in Tibet of his day. While there are various qualifications and subtleties involved, simply stated this sequence is necessary:

One trains the mind to stay on an appropriate meditative object without using discursive thought until one has success in calming as indicated by the serviceability of body and mind and at least some rudimentary supernormal faculty. This is equivalent to the ancient Buddhist Instruction of Mind Training (*adhicitta-śikṣā*), the second of the three instructions (the first being of morality).

Then one applies discursive thought according to a laid-down procedure directed toward the meditative object, until one has success as indicated by the cathartic of body and mind, which draws the discerning of objects arising as illusions, or the nonreflective knowledge (*nirvikalpa-jñāna*). This is equivalent to the ancient Buddhist Instruction of Insight (*adhiprajñā-śikṣā*), the third of the three instructions. When by habituation in Calming the Mind and Discerning the Real, one can draw upon both of them without effort to apply to a phenomenal limit or the noumenal limit, there is the pair-wise union of calming and discerning.

Then, what is the "wrong" position which Tsoṅ-kha-pa attributes to Hva śaṅ and his Tibetan followers? They contended that any contemplation without discursive thought is the way to contemplate voidness. This is held to be a complete misunderstanding. The correct procedure requires calming without discursive thought (and which does not contemplate the void), and then discerning with discursive thought, to bring on the discerning of the void.

Besides, the Chinese party held, appealing to the old three levels of *prajñā*—consisting of hearing, pondering, and cultivation—that at the outset one (hears and) ponders the non-self-existence (of the object); and at the time of cultivation, cultivates only nonreflection (*nirvikalpa*). Such a method is rejected on the grounds that one doing it this way, and claiming that his "nonreflection" is cultivation of voidness, would, if he is indeed cultivating voidness, be cultivating a different voidness from the one of his previous pondering, and be unable to avoid realistic imputations (which bind one to *saṃsāra*).

Again, the position of Hva-śaṅ is rejected, since claiming to think of nothing, and claiming to do nothing (or not to pay attention to anything) would, if indeed that is the accurate description of the procedure, amount to nothing more than dreamless sleep (which everybody enters every night of normal sleep).

Another objection that occurs to the present writer—but which Tsoṅ-kha-pa for whatever the reason did not mention—is that the Chinese party did not claim for their procedure any of the fruits which Buddhism sets forth as the signs of success in the meditative procedure, i.e., the serviceability of body and mind, the development of supernormal powers; the cathartic eliminating the contamination of body and mind.

But then, did the Chinese party, according to Demiéville's translation of the Chinese text, actually claim in the manner that Tsoṅ-kha-pa's tradition attributes to them? See Demiéville:

Ancient question: If one is without idea, without reflection, without examination, how would one achieve omniscience?
Answer: If false thoughts are not produced, and one abstains from every false idea, the true nature which is present at the bottom of ourselves and omniscience are revealed by themselves. It is as the *Avataṃsaka,* the *Laṅka* and other sūtras say: just as the sun emerges from the clouds, the troubled water is purified, the mirror is wiped, the gold separated from its veinstone.[74]

And also:

And in the Vajra-sūtra (i.e., *Vajracchedikā*): "Wherein one cannot find even the slightest *dharma,* that is the supreme Bodhi."[75]

Demiéville refers to the *Saptaśatikā Prajñāpāramitā* for an equivalent statement:[76] "Since in Bodhi one does not find, does not apprehend even the slightest *dharma,* for that reason it is termed 'incomparable samyaksambodhi.' "[77] However, if one studies this sūtra starting from the beginning, especially with the help of Vimalamitra's commentary, one can easily notice that the sūtra first goes into the path of vision (*darśana-mārga*), then passes to the path of cultivation (*bhāvanā-mārga*), before treating the path beyond training (*aśaikṣa-mārga*) wherein there is the passage cited. In the sūtra portion devoted to the "path of cultivation," there is the passage: "Moreover, Lord, that is a cultivation (*bhāvanā*) of Prajñāpāramitā which, when one attains the cultivation, one sees all *dharmas* as Buddha *dharmas,* sees all *dharmas* as inconceivable *dharmas,* without reviewing (them)."[78] Notice that in the "path of cultivation" one does indeed see all the *dharmas* in the stated manner, in contrast with the "path beyond training" when "not even the slightest *dharma* is found." But if one were, as in the advice of Mahāyāna Hva-śaṅ, merely to seek a state in which "not even the slightest *dharma* is found," it would amount to claiming one could attain the state "beyond training" before one had ever been in training, because in training one must learn to see all *dharmas* as Buddha *dharmas.*

Consequently, one can conclude that even if the exact words which the Tibetan tradition attributes to Hva-śaṅ are not found in the Chinese text about the debate, the passages above and others that could be mentioned from Demiéville's work are consistent with the Tibetan attribution to Hva-śaṅ, in that those passages by the Chinese teacher amount to taking the final stage mentioned by a scripture and disregarding what that scripture might have said or reported as necessary preliminaries to the final stage. Thus, Tsoṅ-kha-pa's complaint against the Chinese teacher is also what he charges against many of his contemporaries—that they do not study enough, do not read through the scriptures and śāstras from which they cite this or that line.

Tsoṅ-kha-pa's Position on Discerning: Rejection of the Extremes in Favor of the Middle View

To say that Tsoṅ-kha-pa uses his large section on "Discerning" (*vipaśyanā*) to establish his position on the Mādhyamika school would appear anomalous in the light of some ancient and modern studies of the Mādhyamika; so Murti,[79] who repeatedly asserts that the Mādhyamika, while refuting the opponent's views, puts forth none of its own—a "view" (*dṛṣṭi*) is an "extreme" (*anta*). However, in the "Discerning" section, under *A,* the portion entitled "Invalidating the Assailant to Denying the Four Alternatives, Presence, Absence, etc., of an Entity," contains citations which reject "views" in the Mādhyamika, and other citations which accept "views" in the Mādhyamika. Under *B,* there is *b.* "The Establishment of Our Own Position," and *B-2.* "Which One of the Two One Should Follow to Generate the View in the Stream of Consciousness." Then *C* is devoted to "The Method of Generating the View in Consciousness." There is no doubt that Tsoṅ-kha-pa is quite aware of the theory that the Mādhyamika "does not commit himself to a position," and since he replies to this at length and in various subtle ways in his "Discerning" section, I need not dwell here on how he accomplishes precisely what Murti and others disallow for the Mādhyamika. Tsoṅ-kha-pa's method will be barely alluded to by considering his use of Buddhist logic and his treatment of the middle view as well as the *svabhāva* issue.

Besides, Tsoṅ-kha-pa never intended that discerning should be taken in isolation, because he emphasizes the training in both "Calming the Mind" and "Discerning the Real." It is a natural question as to whether the reader must have calmed his mind to understand the matter as Tsoṅ-kha-pa presents it. It should be granted that as the author of the work he had to calm his mind and then come to his conclusions about the

Mādhyamika position. As a translator, I dare say that the reader need not do the same in order to appreciate Tsoṅ-kha-pa's text. That is to say, a reader need not calm his mind in the manner described in the "Calming" section merely to ascertain how Tsoṅ-kha-pa establishes the Mādhyamika position. Readers interested in Mādhyamika Buddhism should find herein valuable suggestions for why the school is called "followers of the middle (*madhyama*)."

Use of Buddhist Logic

There are various reasons for the author's enthusiastic use of Buddhist logic, especially of Dharmakīrti's works. There was an intensive study of this topic in the several centuries before Tsoṅ-kha-pa and it was prevalent in his own day. For the Prāsaṅgika school of Mādhyamika which Tsoṅ-kha-pa accepts, Candrakīrti's own arguments with Bhavaviveka and with the Buddhist logician Dignāga involve a conventional acceptance of the four "authorities" (*pramāṇa*) of the Nyāya school and assume a scholastic study of the "rules of debate" with the rather acute distinctions of the later Indian school of Buddhist logic. Previously, in the introduction to Tsoṅ-kha-pa's life, we noticed how assiduously and devotedly he studied Dharmakīrti's *Pramāṇavārttika*.

This truly remarkable application of Buddhist logic under the category of "Discerning" creates two forms of stark contrast: *a*) the contrast with the usual Western treatment of the Mādhyamika, limited to philology, metaphysical interpretations, and the like; *b*) the contrast with present-day expositions by Theravādins of "insight-meditation" ("insight" rather than "discerning" being the usual rendition from the Pāli *vipassanā*) taking its Buddhist doctrinal base in the Abhidharma.

It is not possible to deal here with all the ways in which Tsoṅ-kha-pa employs Buddhist logic, but since he devotes the first large topic in the "Discerning" section to determining the principle to be refuted by considering the "overpervasion" (*ativyāpti,* Tib. *khyab ches pa*) and "nonpervasion" (*avyāpti,* Tib. *khyab chuṅs pa*), I shall restrict myself here to a consideration of this matter.

According to Ingalls, *ativyāpti* (overpervasion), *avyāpti* (nonpervasion), and *asaṃbhava* (impossibility) are fallacies of the definition in Nyāya.[80]

Indeed, they are about the same as fallacies of the reason (*hetu*) in earlier Indian logic, which includes the Buddhist logic that was transmitted to Tibet and earnestly studied there.

Tsoṅ-kha-pa uses the two terms to cover his various rejections of Buddhist sectarian differences on apprehension of the Mādhyamika refutable (*niṣedhya*). He first treats the overpervasion in lengthy fashion (40 folios), then the nonpervasion rather briefly (4 folios), where the first of these fallacious positions, the overpervasion, affirms *svabhāva* (self-existence); and the second, the nonpervasion, denies *svabhāva*. He follows in many folios thereafter with what he represents as the proper Mādhyamika apprehension of the refutable, which is either the refutable of the path (the hindrance of defilement and the hindrance of the knowable, in Sanskrit the *kleśa-* and *jñeya-avaraṇa*) or the refutable of the principle (the adherence to a delusive thing and to the presence of self-existence).

The opponents thus judged to be guilty of overpervasion are especially the realists, called the *vastu-satpadārtha-vādin*—a name extant in the Sanskrit fragments of Candrakīrti's commentary on Āryadeva's *Catuḥśataka*. Other opponents are the mind-only (*cittamātra*) persons of the Yogācāra school of Buddhism as well as the Mādhyamika-Svātantrika (of which Bhāvaviveka is the most famous exponent). Of the three opponents, Nāgārjuna may have been opposed by only the *vastu-satpadārtha-vādin*—whether or not he knew them by that name—since the Yogācāra and the Mādhyamika-Svātantrika arose after him, although it is possible that arguments similar to those of the latter two schools may also have been advanced in Nāgārjuna's day.

Now the question arises why those opponents should be charged with overpervasion by way of their *svabhāva* affirmation. Or, is their overpervasion a fallacious inference according to the illustration, "It has smoke, as it has fire"? The discussions are complicated, but as I read Tsoṅ-kha-pa's section, the easiest position to pin down under "overpervasion" is that of the Cittamātra. In this case, the *svabhāva* is threefold, the "perfect" (*pariniṣpanna*), the "dependency" (*paratantra*), and the "imaginary" (*parikalpita*). This school takes the dependency character as the reason (*hetu*) for refuting *saṃvṛti* (the conventional world) as *parikalpita;* the reason is overpervasive, since the dependency character is both real (*sat*) and unreal (*asat*), while *parikalpita* is only unreal.

The realist is the opponent assumed in Nāgārjuna's *Madhyamaka-kārikā,* to wit, the opponent who argues (MK, XXIV, 1), "If all this is void, then your position reduces to the absurdity that there is no arising or passing away and there are no four Noble Truths!" And the one who argues (*Vigrahavyāvartanī,* k. 1), "If there is nowhere a self-existence of any presences (*bhāva*) your words, being without self-existence, are unable to refute the self-existence!" Thus the realist says that things either exist or do not exist, and has no middle ground (according to Nāgārjuna, the Buddhist dependent origination). For this realist, a thing exists and works by way of its *svabhāva* (self-existence or own-being). It is held that these realists fall into the faults of eternalism and nihilism, saying (per Nāgārjuna's *Yuktiṣaṣṭikā,* k. 43), "Oh, it is permanent, (or) it is impermanent!" Their fault is more clearly stated in *Madhyamaka-kārikā* (XXIV, 16), "If you look upon the occurrence of entities as being from self-existence, then you regard the entities as without causes or conditions." Otherwise stated: the realist has not distinguished the mean (i.e., the shoot without self-existence, that has arisen from causes and conditions) from an extreme (i.e., absence of the shoot, or presence of the shoot by own-nature). Therefore, the realist overpervades with a reason of "presence" (*bhāva*) or "absence" (*abhāva*). Indeed, when the realist charges the Mādhyamika with nihilism, Nāgārjuna mounts a counterattack, undermining the appeal to authority (*pramāṇa*), as when one says realistically, "The hill has fire, as it has smoke." But Nāgārjuna says (MK, III, 2): "Vision does not see itself as itself. Now, if it does not see what is itself, how will it see what is another?" Thus Nāgārjuna rejects the authority of direct sense perception, anticipating Candrakīrti's argument against the Buddhist logicians.

The argument between Candrakīrti and Bhāvaviveka involves the distinction of supreme truth (*paramārtha-satya*) and conventional truth (*saṃvṛti-satya*). Tsoṅ-kha-pa points out that only Bhāvaviveka's school, the Mādhyamika-Svātantrika, applies *paramārtha* in particular to the refutable principle (the *niṣedhya*), in commentary on Nāgārjuna's *Madhyamaka-kārikā,* I, 1. The fallacy is suggested by Candrakīrti, in *Madhyamakāvatāra,* VI, 32d: "Even according to the world the birth is not from another." So I understand the inclusion of the Mādhyamika-Svātantrika under "overpervasion" to be involved in Bhāvaviveka's appeal to *para-*

mārtha-satya as a reason while he employs the theory of *paramārtha-satya* in overpervasion of *saṃvṛti-satya.*

So in the briefest reply to the question I posed, it appears feasible to interpret the overpervasion of all three opponents in analogy to the way fire overpervades smoke, namely, that the pair *sat* and *asat* overpervade *asat,* that *bhāva* and *abhāva* each overpervade their mean, and that *paramārthasatya,* in a certain theory, overpervades *saṃvṛtisatya.*

Under the nonpervasion, Tsoṅ-kha-pa places the insider of the Mādhyamika, Prāsaṅgika school who has quite properly denied *svabhāva* as a principle and then falsely denies *svabhāva* in the Buddhist path, i.e., takes it as the refutable of the path. Thus this insider misses the meaning of the scriptural passage, "Whether Tathāgatas arise or do not arise this true nature of *dharmas* abides," found both in a Pāli-language scripture and in the Mahāyāna scripture *Daśabhūmika-sūtra.* Nāgārjuna alludes to this *svabhāva* in his *Madhyamaka-kārikā,* chapter XV. Regarding this nonpervasion, Candrakīrti's *Madhyamakāvatāra* has this verse (VI, 141)—extant in Sanskrit as cited in the *Subhāṣitasaṃgraha* (as I translate): "Seeing a snake coiled in a recess of his house, and thinking, 'There is no elephant here' his alarm is dispelled (as to an elephant), and he abandons fear even for the snake. Behold the rectitude of our opponent!" Here the snake can be explained as nescience (*avidyā*). This person does not fear the snake because he thinks, "There is no elephant here" (i.e., there is no *svabhāva,* self-existence). Thereby he loses fear for the snake of nescience and continues to have its threatening presence there in the recess. So "Behold the rectitude of our opponent!" In this case, nonpervasion (*avyāpti*) is construed as "not the *vyāpti,*" meaning that non-self-existence (*niḥsvabhāvatā*) is not the *vyāpti* of the Buddhist path, even though it is a *vyāpti* in Mahāyāna Buddhist philosophy and referred to as the "principle."

Upon reading some of the discussions of these two fallacies of *vyāpti* in a Navya-Nyāya work on *vyāpti,*[81] it appears that Tsoṅ-kha-pa's discussion approximately fits the presumed fallacies of the *kevalānvayī vyāpti* (the universally present pervasion) and the *kevalavyatirekī vyāpti* (the universally absent pervasion). That is to say, the three outer opponents of the Mādhyamika-Prāsaṅgika would universalize their principle that is used for the refutable of *saṃvṛti.* In contrast, the insider opponent of the Mādhyamika-Prāsaṅgika would universalize the absence of *svabhāva.*

Thus, Tsoṅ-kha-pa's usage seems consistent with later Indian logic, where the two terms are nonoverlapping, that is to say, a fallacious inference which is *ativyāpti* cannot be *avyāpti* and vice versa.

The same work sets forth Gangeśa's discussion and rejection of a number of definitions of *vyāpti* as found in previous schools, including the definition by the Buddhist logicians.[82] Of course, to assail the definition of *vyāpti* made by a previous school implies a rejection of the soundness of the arguments in that school. Indeed, Gangeśa thereby takes that definition as the refutable (*niṣedhya*), a kind of *sādhya;* while we know that *vyāpti* is itself a part of the inference involved. This reminds us of Bhāvaviveka's position as cited in Candrakīrti's *Prasannapadā* (chap. I) and explained in Tsoṅ-kha-pa's "Discerning" section:[83]

Now, if one holds such distinctions, there are no agreed-upon conventions for the inference or for the inferable. The reason is as follows: if we hold that sound is derived from the four great elements, that is not proved to the opponent (who is the Vaiśeṣika). On the other hand, when he (the Vaiśeṣika) holds sound to be a quality of space (*ākāśa*), that is not proved to the Buddhist on his side. Likewise, if the Vaiśeṣika sets forth the proposition "Sound is not eternal" and holds that the sound is constructed (*kārya*), that is not proved to those others (i.e., the Mīmāṃsā, who maintain that it is made perceptible, *vyaṅgya,* from its imperishable state). On the other hand, if sound be held as made perceptible (*vyaṅgya*), that is not proved to (the Vaiśeṣika) himself.

In short, one way of disagreeing with another school is to reject its definition of *vyāpti;* another way is to reject the *vyāpti* itself. But, for example, the Buddhists presumably agree that every created thing is impermanent—it is pervaded by impermanence. So when a Buddhist reads that the five personality aggregates are impermanent, he accepts this because he has already accepted the pervasion, oblivious of the definition of "pervasion." While in "inference for others" according to Bhāvaviveka, in the case of the well-known syllogism about the smoke and the fire, when one gives the example "like the stove," it is necessary for the two parties to agree that the example is viable, or it would be futile to go on. Perhaps this is a reason why, when I asked the late Hidenori Kitagawa of Nagoya, Japan, if he had ever noticed in the texts of Buddhist logic the simile of the mirror, he responded negatively. But Nāgārjuna is willing to use more similes than those used by the logicians. Thus, he writes in his *Pratītyasamutpādahṛdaya-vyākaraṇa:*[84]

Just as in the case of a flame from a flame, the reflected image in a mirror from a face . . . a person is not taught . . . that one is different from the other, so also in the case of reconnection of the personality aggregates, the wise person will understand that there is no transfer.

The Middle View

The middle view of course avoids the extremes of existence and nonexistence, or, in the preceding terminology, avoids the alternatives of overpervasion or nonpervasion. But, as was mentioned, it is often held that the Mādhyamika, especially in the Prāsaṅgika form, rejects all views and therefore does not have a position of its own. According to Tsoṅ-kha-pa, there is a great misunderstanding here. Chakraborty mentions: "Khaṇḍanakhaṇḍa Khādya of Śrī Harṣa is a case in point. Śrī Harṣa here with the help of a formidable dialectic disproves the case of the opponents but does not take pains for the positive establishment of any thesis."[85] In fact, Śrī Harṣa in the first chapter takes the Mādhyamika side against the Nyāya opponent and argues that even if he (Śrī Harṣa) does not have a thesis of his own, it is still possible to carry on a debate. Indeed, by disproving the opponents he gradually defines his own position in negative terms, somewhat analogous to when in ancient India the absolute was referred to as "not this, not this" and still the absolute was thereby referred to and was not denied. So Tsoṅ-kha-pa, early in his section "B. Option of Prāsaṅgika and Svātantrika as Refuting Agent" states, ". . . while insisting that the Svātantrika is not valid, he [Candrakīrti] clarified the (Prāsaṅgika) position." Besides, the fact of not putting forth a position of one's own while arguing with opponents is consistent with the middle view not being expressible in the ordinary realistic terms of existence and nonexistence. Hence, the middle view is expressed as nonself; and dependent origination is voidness (*śūnyatā*): the natures (*dharma*) arise like a dream, like a face in a mirror, a flame from a flame, etc. Fire arises by a cause (= the original fire that does not go anywhere) and conditions (combustible materials; exciting agencies, such as friction). And the arising by cause and condition is not equivalent to the Nyāya-Vaiśeṣika *asatkāryavāda,* holding that the clay pot arises from itself (clay) and from the potter, wheel, sticks, etc. This is because the "new" fire is not, according to Nāgārjuna, composed of the "old" fire, since in the case of a flame from a flame, there is no transfer. In short, the "old" fire is the efficient, not the material cause, while in the realist position the clay is the material cause of the clay pot. But the "new" condition (the combustible material, etc.) is the instrumental cause, like the realist's old potter, wheel, sticks, etc.

Pursuant to the middle view, Tsoṅ-kha-pa cites Nāgārjuna's *Yuk-tiṣaṣṭikā* and Candrakīrti's *Yuktiṣaṣṭikā-vṛtti.*
Nāgārjuna:

What arises in dependence is not born;
That is proclaimed by the supreme knower of reality (=Buddha).

Candrakīrti:

(The realist opponent says): If (as you say) whatever thing arises in dependence is not even born, then why does (the Mādhyamika) say it is not born? But if (you Mādhyamika) have a reason for saying (this thing) is not born, then you should not say it "arises in dependence." Therefore, because of mutual inconsistency, (what you have said) is not valid.
(The Mādhyamika replies with compassionate interjection:)
Alas! Because you are without ears or heart you have thrown a challenge that is severe on us! When we say that anything arising in dependence, in the manner of a reflected image, does not arise by reason of self-existence—at that time where is the possibility of disputing (us)!

So when in this Mādhyamika literature one frequently finds such statements as "The natures (*dharma*) arise void of self-existence (*svabhāva*)," the opponents declare this to be a nihilistic position (thus willing to attribute a "position" or "view" to the Mādhyamika), asserting that the Mādhyamika denies self-existence (*svabhāva*) or denies the natures (*dharma*). An example should clarify Candrakīrti's response. If we were to say, "The children came to school without shoes," and another were to make a challenge, "So you deny that there are shoes," we would have to answer, "Alas, you are without ears; we did not deny shoes when we said that the children came to school without shoes." And if another were to make a challenge, "So you deny children," we would have to answer, "Alas, you are without heart; whoever would deny children is heartless, and we did not deny children when we said that the children came to school without shoes." Thus, these Mādhyamikas do not deny *svabhāva* (= shoes) or *dharmas* (= children), when saying, "The natures (*dharma*) arise void of self-existence (*svabhāva*)."

Svabhāva of the Path

Having again and again denied the self-existence (*svabhāva*) of entities, the Mādhyamika followers go on to qualify their denials. It turns out that the *svabhāva* that was denied is the one believed in by ordinary persons called *bāla* (the childish, spiritually immature person), who accept as real what they imagine to perceive, while their eye of knowledge is covered by nescience's caul. So Candrakīrti's *Prasannapadā* commentary on the *Madhyamaka-kārikā* (XV, 2):

> By whatever (deluded) self one approaches the form of entities (form, etc.) perceptively reached by the power of nescience's coat; and by whatever method of nonseeing belonging to the nobles who are rid of nescience's coat one approaches the domain (of *samāpatti*): just that own-form (*svarūpa*) is established as the *svabhāva* of those (entities).

But, as he mentions there, the meditator who can ascend to equipoise (*samāpatti*) may witness the *svabhāva* that is inaccessible to the ordinary person. And as Tsoṅ-kha-pa further cites Candrakīrti (his *Madhyamakāvatāra*): "The reality (i.e., own-form) which no childish person can witness is the principle which (ultimately) is *svabhāva*," and "Consequently, it is for the purpose of witnessing that (ultimate *svabhāva*) that the pure life (and path cultivation) becomes meaningful."

To further explain the witnessing of *svabhāva*, one may refer to the tradition of the Buddha's night of enlightenment when he discovered the formula of dependent origination; and according to Aśvaghoṣa's *Buddhacarita* (chap. XIV) discovered it in the third watch of night by working backward from "old age and death" (no. 12 in the twelve-membered formula) in the formula with ten members, up to "perception" (*vijñāna*) (no. 3 in the twelve-membered formula). Aśvaghoṣa writes:[86]

> 71. When perception arises, name-and-form is produced. When the development of the seed is completed, the sprout assumes a bodily form.

72. Next he considered, "From what does perception come into being?" Then he knew that it is produced by supporting itself on name-and-form.

The significance of this is exposed in Asaṅga's *Yogācārabhūmi* in the *Vastusaṃgrahaṇī* section. Asaṅga explains what is meant by "seeing *dharmas*" as seeing a "place of truth" by seeing either constructed natures or unconstructed natures; and in both cases with either conventional or absolute truth. As to the "place of truth," he says:[87]

Just as there is some place of truth, he rightly knows it as it is, and rightly knows as it is the truth (thereof). What is a place of truth? Name-and-form, called the "own-nature of a man" (*manuṣya-svarūpa* *).

Thus when the terminology "discerning the real" is employed, the "real" may be referred to as "name-and-form."[88]

The foregoing also helps to clarify why Aśvaghoṣa used at that point the ten-membered formula, which omits the usual two first members of "nescience" (*avidyā*) and "motivations" (*saṃskāra*). This suggests the enlightenment situation when both "nescience" (defilement) and "motivations" (the *karma*) have ceased, and so Nāgārjuna writes in his *Yuktiṣaṣṭikā* (k. 10-11AB):[89]

Having seen with right knowledge (= clear vision, *vidyā*) what has arisen with the condition of "nescience," there is no apprehension at all of either arising or passing away. That very thing is Nirvāṇa as this life (= the dharma seen, *dṛṣṭa-dharma*), and the requirement is done (*kṛta-kṛtya*).

This situation is prepared for by the Bodhisattva's contemplation of dependent origination on the sixth stage according to the Mahāyāna scripture *Daśabhūmika-sūtra*. This is said to occur to that Bodhisattva: "Because of the clinging to a creator, activities are known; wherever there is no creator, there also activities are not perceptively reached in the absolute sense," and "These three realms are this mind-only." As I have discussed elsewhere using Tsoṅ-kha-pa's materials,[90] it is "nescience" which clings to a creator, so when "nescience" does not arise, "activities" (= 'motivations') are not perceptively reached, i.e., "percep-

* Theoretical reconstruction of the Sanskrit.

tion" (*vijñāna*) does not perceive them. Then, "perception," in the light of the present discussion, is the conventional mind-only which is tantamount to the three realms. In Aśvaghoṣa's account, it is not the *vijñāna* itself that is to be got rid of. Rather, it is disengaged from dependence on "activities" and instead is promoted by "name-and-form." This may then be the intention of the *Laṅkāvatāra-sūtra* (text 126.11–12): "According to my promulgation, Mahāmati, the warding off of the *manovijñāna* that thinks discursively, is said to be Nirvāṇa." Thus *vijñāna* changes its meaning from "perception" to "understanding," and understands the "name-and-form," also with "insight" (*prajñā*) or with "clear vision" (*vidyā*).

Now it should be pointed out that the *svabhāva* which is here alluded to as "name-and-form," or the reality which is the object of discerning (*vipaśyanā*), is also referred to in this literature as the "true nature" (*dharmatā*). So the *Laṅkāvatāra-sūtra* may be cited (218.8–13):

> Whether the Tathāgatas arise or do not arise, there remains this true nature (*dharmatā*), the rule of *dharma*, the continuance of *dharma*. This abiding of *dharma* is not in the sphere of any of the visualizations of the Śrāvakas, Pratyekabuddhas, or heads of sects; and immature ordinary persons are not awakened to it. It is contemplatively evoked (*prabhāvita*) by the insight-knowledge of the Tathāgatas.

The foregoing should show why the Mādhyamika has over the centuries afforded such difficulties of interpretation, so that it was not only the opponents—who so often do not take pains to ascertain what they are disagreeing with—who were found to be rejecting the Mādhyamika; but also those who counted themselves as the "insiders" were arguing as vociferously with each other on the matter. Small wonder that this Mādhyamika school should be misunderstood, when it vigorously rejects the *svabhāva* that is something to establish by mundane reasoning, and then upholds the *svabhāva* that is something to realize in Yoga attainment. Or when it sometimes denies having a position of its own, and then argues at length and in all sorts of ways to refute the "wrong" views—for why bother to reject views on the grounds that they are wrong, if not wrong in comparison with a "right" view!

The Translation

THE translator is somewhat embarrassed to notice how long ago he promised a significant portion of the *Lam rim chen mo,* starting with a student paper in *Phi Theta Annual* (Berkeley, 1952).[91] It is understandable that some other students of the Tibetan language might in the meantime have undertaken a translation of this important work. However, if anyone has seriously engaged himself on the part here translated while also being aware of my long-promised translation, he did not bother to inquire as to the status of my translation.[92] The delay has doubtless contributed to a better result.

Besides the Tashilunpo edition of the *Lam rim chen mo* I employ the edition of the work to which is added four *Mchan bu* (*ṭippaṇi*), a type of commentary somewhat like our "annotations," but which runs along with the actual text in smaller type.[93] These commentaries have in general been kept separate by identification letters written above the individual annotations. Thus, "Ba" stands for the commentary by Ba-so Chos-kyi-rgyal-mtshan, sixth abbot of Galdan Monastery (A.D. 1402–1473—born the date of the *Lam rim chen mo* composition); "Na" for the compilation by Nag dbaṅ-rab-brtan of the commentaries of Rje 'jam-dbyaṅs Stag-luṅ-grags-pa, thirtieth abbot of Galdan Monastery (1546–1618), and 'Jam-dbyaṅs Dkon-mchog-chos-'phel, the thirty-fifth abbot (1573–1646);[94] while "Ja" stands for the commentary by Rje 'Jam-dbyaṅs-bźad-pa (1648–1721), founder of the Sgo maṅ ("many doors") school, which became predominant in Mongolia and Transbaikalia.[95] In addition, and without special mark, there is the voluminous commentary on the part of the work called "Calming the Mind and Discerning the Real" by the seventeenth-century Amdo scholar, Bra-sti Dge-bśes Rin-chen-don-grub. Presumably because the section "Calming the Mind" is relatively easy reading for the educated Tibetan, it has very little annotation; while presumably because the section "Discerning the Real" is replete with difficulties for the same educated Tibetan, it is profusely annotated in the *Mchan-bu* commentaries described above. I learned how to use the annotation commentaries by my study of Tsoṅ-kha-pa's own annotation commentary on the *Pradīpoddyotana* commentary of the *Guhyasamājatantra.*[96] In the case of the "Discerning the Real" section, the voluminous *Mchan bu* annotations were invaluable in sentence after sentence, providing most of the additions within parentheses. I also make use of the annotations in my notes to the translation, specifying "Ja" for certain comments, and "Mchan" for the remainder.

Whenever possible I exploited the original Sanskrit for Tsoṅ-kha-pa's numerous quotations from canonical texts. In the case of the "Calming the Mind" section, since there is so much reliance on Asaṅga's *Śrāvakabhūmi,* my studies long ago on this text (*Analysis of the Śrāvakabhūmi Manuscript*) went hand in hand with my first-draft translation, begun July 1, 1954, of the "Calming" section. Everyone of Tsoṅ-kha-pa's many quotations from the Tibetan version of the *Śrāvakabhūmi* are, except for one passage missing in Sanskrit, translated with use of the original Sanskrit, either from passages included in my doctoral dissertation (*Analysis*) or from passages I later transcribed from the Sanskrit manuscript.[97] These passages, along with Tucci's Sanskrit editions of the first and third of Kamalaśīla's *Bhāvanākrama,* and the *Mādhyantavibhāga* edited by Nagao and others, solve practically all the terminological problems of the "Calming the Mind" section. Also in the 1950s I made a rough draft translation of the Bodhisattva section of the *Lam rim chen mo;* and here most of the quotations are of passages extant in Sanskrit (in works of Śāntideva, Āryaśūra, and Asaṅga), but I have never had the leisure, beginning with my teaching career and preoccupation with other projects, to revise this large section. For the "Discerning the Real" section I also utilized whenever possible the original Sanskrit of the quotations, and most of the extant Sanskrit for these citations was conveniently available in the notes to Nagao's Japanese version of this "Discerning" section within his book *A Study of Tibetan Buddhism* (1954). I worked on the "Discerning" section sporadically during the early 1970s as time was available, especially during the summers, having had much experience with Tsoṅ-kha-pa's style in his tantric commentaries on which I did much study during the 1960s. Here Tsoṅ-kha-pa relies heavily on Candrakīrti's Mādhyamika works, the *Prasannapadā* commentary and the independent *Madhyamakāvatāra,* so I have naturally consulted the previous Western translations of these works.[98]

It is not necessary here to dilate upon the general theory of translation from Tibetan, since I devoted a full-length article to the topic in the *Indo-Iranian Journal* (vol. XIV, 1972) including, inter alia, a translation of Tsoṅ-kha-pa's "Auspicious Preparation" (*Mdun legs ma*). In some cases my renditions of technical terms are original, although usually I have adopted one of the several renditions in vogue for a given term. Only a few of these renditions need be discussed here.

The article just mentioned went into the matter of the term *śūnyatā,* and I shall resume and develop some of the points. First of all, the possible renditions "emptiness" and "voidness" are used contrastingly in English. The housewife says, "The refrigerator is empty" (referring to the container), and does not use the word "void" here. The legalist says, "The document is null and void" (referring to the content), and does not use the word "empty" here. Consistent with this usage of the term "void" to apply to content, *Webster's New Collegiate Dictionary* defines the word *jejune:* "1. Lacking nourishing quality; 2. Void of interest or satisfaction." Thus, by the authority of this dictionary, when the adjective *jejune* is applied to an object like a book, it should be construed to mean "void of interest"; and this of course does not mean that the book is "empty" (i.e., has nothing in it) or is nonexistent (as though the book is destroyed through being void of something). Since the Mādhyamika treatises say that the natures (*dharma*) are *svabhāvaśūnya,* I therefore translate this as "void of self-existence," and avoid the implication that natures such as hatred are "empty" (have no defiling vitality) or are nonexistent, since the negation is qualified ("void of self-existence").

My translation of *prajñā* by "insight" has to be considered along with my rendition of *vipaśyanā* by "discerning," since frequently we find translators from Pāli translating the equivalent *vipassanā* by "insight." The reason that I do not find "insight" useful to render *vipaśyanā* is that this term occurs in verbal situations, and one cannot say "He insights." After much searching for a good equivalent, I finally settled on "discerning" so one can use such a locution as "Discerning the Real." On the other hand, the term *prajñā* is standardized as a noun and as first member of a compound, especially *prajñā-pāramitā,* so the rendition "insight" nicely fits the usual contexts of the term, such as the three sources of *prajñā* (from "hearing," etc.) and the "eye of *prajñā.*" "Insight" properly indicates the "better-knowledge" intention of the term, while not implying ordinary visual perception. Among the numerous passages that could be cited to demonstrate this visionary sense of *prajñā,* I shall content myself with the one in the *Akṣayamatinirdeśa-sūtra:*[99] "Since it has the Ārya-dharma in direct view (*āvirbhāva* *), Prajñā is the authority (*pramāṇa*)." This passage takes *prajñā* as the authority of "direct perception" (*pratyakṣa*) for the Noble Dharma.

In fact, the renditions of *śūnyatā* by "voidness" and *prajñā* by "insight" are not original with me. On the other hand, the contexts have gradually forced some original renditions on the translator. Such was the case with two terms *dharmin* and *liṅga* of Buddhist logic that are employed in the Mādhyamika texts and utilized in the "Discerning the Real" section. It is usual to translate the term *dharmin* literally as "bearer of the qualities,"[100] where the "qualities" render the word *dharma,* and to translate *liṅga* as "mark" or "logical mark." Instead of *dharmin,* frequently there is used a term to be rendered "substratum" (*āśraya* or *ādhāra*).[101] In illustration, there is the well-known thesis that the mountain is fiery, where the mountain would be the "bearer of the qualities" or the "substratum." One of the qualities is "fiery," which is the quality to be proved; and another one of the qualities is "smoky," which is the *liṅga* that is appealed to as the reason (as when we say, "Because it is smoky"). Now this mountain that is the "bearer of the qualities" or the "substratum" is presupposed by the realist and called into question both by the idealist and by the Mādhyamika. Tsoṅ-kha-pa discusses this matter at length. Ultimately I was forced to more convenient renderings, namely "factual base" for *dharmin,* which has "features" (*dharma*); and "evidence" for *liṅga.* That is, the mountain is the "factual base" because it is the base for the realist to say, "It is a fact that it is a mountain, and not a pot." And the eye is the "factual base" because it is the base for the Mādhyamika to say, "It is not a fact that eyesight is an authority for the mountain."

Besides, it took me some earnest consideration of contexts before arriving at the rendition "elaboration" for *spros pa* (S. *prapañca*). My renditions "idea" and "perception" are justified in a paper "Regarding the Translation of the Buddhist Terms *saññā/saṃjñā, viññāṇa/vijñāna*" (1976).

* Theoretical reconstruction of the Sanskrit.

Tsoṅ-kha-pa's Sectional Titles

IT should be pointed out that Tsoṅ-kha-pa's procedure of sectional titles amounts to stating a set of titles as, e.g., three in number, and then, for example, mentioning that the first one is, say, of two kinds as stated. He will then go on to say "the first (is as follows)." Later, when coming to the place in the text where the second of those two kinds begins he will explicitly give the title, but not always with the exact words as when he originally stated the two kinds. This happens because when he comes to the place in the text, the particular sectional title is in its own context. My presentation of his titles in the actual context of the translation will be to replace his "the first (is as follows)" with a heading that explicitly gives his first title. Thereafter, to preseve the author's style, I will translate his later expression of a title just as he gives it at the particular place. Therefore, the following list of sectional titles agrees with the initial or later statement of the titles in the text, and in every case represents Tsoṅ-kha-pa's words.

CALMING THE MIND AND DISCERNING THE REAL

1. The Benefit of Calming and Discerning
2. The Teaching that These Encompass All Samadhis
3. The Intrinsic Nature of Calming and Discerning
4. The Reason for the Requirement to Cultivate Both Calming and Discerning
5. The Method of Determining the Sequence
6. The Method of Their Individual Instruction

Tsoṅ-kha-pa's Sectional Titles

CALMING THE MIND

The Method of Instruction in Calming

- I. Reliance on the Equipment for Calming
- II. After Recourse to that (Equipment), the Method of Cultivating Calming
  - 1. The Preparation
  - 2. The Main Part
    - a. Exposition of the Cultivation in Terms of the Posture of the Body
    - b. Exposition of the Stages of Cultivation
  - A. The Method of Generating Faultless Samadhi
    - I. How One Performs Prior to Fastening Mind on a Meditative Object
    - II. How One Performs at the Time of Fastening Mind on a Meditative Object
      - A. Determination of the Meditative Object
        - 1. General Fundamentals of the Meditative Object
          - a. Exposition of the Basic Meditative Objects
          - b. Exposition of Which Persons to Have Which Meditative Objects
        - 2. Determination of the Circumstances for Choosing Meditative Objects
      - B. The Method of Fastening the Mind to That Meditative Object
        - 1. Settling the Technique without Fault
        - 2. Clearing Away the Technique with Fault
        - 3. Teaching the Measure of Watches
    - III. How One Performs After Fastening the Mind on a Meditative Object
      - A. How One Performs at the Time Fading or Scattering Occurs
        - 1. Resorting to the Opponent to Nondetermination of Fading and Scattering
          - a. The Fundamental Characteristics of Fading and Scattering
          - b. How to Produce Awareness that Recognizes Fading and Scattering
        - 2. Resorting to the Opponent to the Lack of Effort to Eliminate These
          - a. Determination of the Thinking-Volition and the Method of Opposing Fading and Scattering

b. Determination of the Causes Productive of Fading and Scattering

B. How One Performs at the Time Free From Fading and Scattering

B. The Stages of Generating the Fixations of the Mind

I. The Basic Stages of Generating Mind Fixation

II. The Way of Accomplishing This by Means of Six Forces

III. The Method of Employing Four Mental Orientations

III. By Reason of the Cultivation, the Standard of Accomplishment of Calming

A. Teaching the Demarcation between the Perfected and the Unperfected States of Calming

I. Teaching the Basic Meaning

II. The Marks of Having the Mental Orientation

IIa. The Removal of Doubts

B. The Method of Walking the Path after Taking Recourse to Calming

C. The Method of Walking the Mundane Path

I. Teaching the Necessity of Attaining Calming Prior to Walking the Path Formed of "Calmness-Coarseness"

II. The Method, Relying on Calming, of Becoming Free from Attachment to Craving

DISCERNING THE REAL

The Method of Instruction in Discerning

I. Reliance on the Equipment for Discerning

A. The Texts of Provisional Meaning and of Final Meaning

B. How Commentary on Nāgārjuna's Purport Developed

C. The Method of Establishing the View of Voidness

I. The Sequence of Understanding Reality

II. The Basic Establishment of the Reality

A. Engaging the Principle to Be Refuted

1. The Reason for the Requirement to Determine the Refutable

2. Refuting the Other School Which Denies Without Determining the Refutable

a. Refutation of Overpervasion in Determining the Refutable

(1) Setting Forth the Opponent's Thesis

(2) Showing That the Thesis Is Not Valid

(a) Showing That the Special Refutation of *Dharma*

by That School Is Not Common to the Mādhyamika
- (i) Determining the Special *Dharma* of the Mādhyamika
- (ii) Manner in Which a School Opposes That (Special *Dharma*)
- (iii) How the Mādhyamika Answers This (Challenge)

(b) Teaching How to Avoid Defeat by the Assailant's Discourses
- (i) Avoiding Defeat by Denial Considering Ability and Inability, by Examination of a Principle
- (ii) Avoiding Defeat by Denial, Considering Proof and Nonproof by Authority
- (iii) Avoiding Defeat by Denial, Considering Whether or Not There Is Birth with the Four Alternatives
- (iv) Invalidating the Assailant to Denying the Four Alternatives, Presence, Absence, etc., of an Entity

b. Refutation of Nonpervasion in Determining the Refutable

3. Our Own School's Method of Determining the Refutable
   a. Determining the Refutable with Its Basic Meaning
   b. The Method of Treating or Not Treating the Other Refutables
   c. Explanation of Treating or Not Treating the *Paramārtha* Distinction in Regard to the Refutable

B. Option of Prāsangika and Svātantrika as Refuting Agents
1. Determining the Meaning of Prāsangika and Svātantrika
   a. The Refutation of Other Positions
      (1) Expressing the Position
      (2) Refuting the Position
   b. Establishment of Our Own Position
      (1) Basic Refutation of the Svātantrika
         (a) Teaching the Fault of the Side Which Does Not Prove the Factual Base Substratum
            (i) Stating the (Opponent's) Position
            (ii) Refuting the Opponent's Position

(ii-a) Showing That the Meaning Is Not Cogent
(ii-b) Showing That the Formulation of Example Is Different
(b) Teaching That on Account of That Fault, the Reason Is Also Not Proved
(2) How Our School Differs Therefrom
2. Which One of the Two One Should Follow to Generate the View in the Stream of Consciousness
C. Relying on This Agent, the Method of Generating the View in Consciousness
1. Establishing the Nonself of Personality
a. Basic Establishment That There Is No Self-Existence of Self
(1) Formulating the Example
(a) Showing the Chariot as a Designation Without Self-Existence
(b) Eliminating the Argument About That
(c) Method of Demonstration by Way of Distinction of Names
(d) Based on That, the Speedy Benefit of Attaining the View
(2) Adding the Meaning
(a) Adding the Meaning to the Method of No Self-Existence
(i) Refuting the Position That Self Is Identical with the Aggregates
(ii) Refuting the Position That Self Is Different from the Aggregates
(iii) Hence, the Remaining Positions Become the Problem
(iv) Based thereon, the Method by Which a Personality Rises Like an Illusion
(b) Adding the Meaning to the Method of Demonstrating by Way of the Distinction of Names
b. Thereby Showing That What Belongs to Self Also Rises Without Self-Existence
c. The Method of Adding Other Principles
2. Establishing the Nonself of Feature

CALMING THE MIND AND DISCERNING THE REAL

I bow respectfully at the feet of the
reverend illustrious ones of
great compassion.
Tsoṅ-kha-pa

IN particular, the instruction in the last two perfections is the method of cultivating calming and discerning, because these two in the given order are included in the perfections of meditation (*dhyāna*) and insight (*prajñā*).[1] Here there are six topics: 1. the benefit of cultivating calming and discerning; 2. the teaching that these [two] encompass all *samādhis;* 3. the intrinsic nature of calming and discerning; 4. the reason for the requirement to cultivate both [calming and discerning]; 5. the method of determining the sequence; 6. the method of their individual instruction.

1. THE BENEFIT OF CULTIVATING CALMING AND DISCERNING

All the mundane and supramundane merits of the Great and Small Vehicles are the fruit of calming and discerning, because it is said in the *Saṃdhinirmocana-sūtra:* "Maitreya, one should understand that all the virtuous natures—mundane and supramundane—of either the disciples (*śrāvaka*), Bodhisattvas, or Tathāgatas, are the fruit of calming and discerning."[2]

The questions have been proposed: "Are not calming and discerning merits of the Tantras that arise and are attained through cultivation? How is it valid that all merits are the fruit of those two?" As the concrete nature of calming and discerning will be explained, they are merits of the Tantras that arise and are attained through cultivation. Consequently, while all the merits of the Great and Small Vehicles are not the fruit of those two [limited to their concrete significance], the *samādhis* beginning with a single area of thought in a virtuous meditative object are included in the category of calming, and the virtues of the insight that discriminates the meaning of the noumenon and phenomenon [of that virtuous meditative object] are included in the category of discerning. Therefore, following the deep purport here, there is no contradiction in saying that all the merits of the three vehicles are the fruit of calming and discerning.

Following the deep purport here, it is also said in the *Mahāyānaprasādaprabhāvana-sūtra:* "Son of the (Buddhist) family, you should know in this manner and this way that whether it be the case of faith in the Great Vehicle of the bodhisattvas or of what arises from the Great Vehicle—all those arise from right contemplation of the meaning and *dharma* with nondistracted mind." "Nondistracted mind" is a single area of thought in the category of calming, and "right contemplation of the meaning and *dharma*" is discriminative insight in the category of discerning. Hence, all the merits of the two vehicles require accomplishment by both (a) attending to examination with discriminative insight and (b) a single area of thought on a meditative object, whereas they are not accomplished by a one-sidedness of either cultivation of fixation or cultivation of examination.

Furthermore, the *Saṃdhinirmocana-sūtra* states: "The person who has cultivated discerning and calming is liberated from the bondage of contamination and from the bondage of sign-source."[3] Here "contamination" is the habit-energy abiding in the stream of consciousness that is capable of generating ever higher subjective illusion; and "sign-source" is the reviver of the formerly abated habit-energy of attraction toward objective illusion. The *Prajñāpāramitopadeśa* explains that the former is eliminated by discerning and that the latter is eliminated by calming.

While those benefits are associated with the terms "calming" and "discerning," statements of the benefits of meditation and insight are of like meaning although not associated with the terms "calming" and "discerning." One should understand them as the benefits of these two.

2. THE TEACHING THAT THESE TWO ENCOMPASS ALL SAMĀDHIS

For example, however uncountable be the twigs, leaves, flowers, and fruit on the trunk of a tree, they are all brought together by an essential element, which is the root. Analogously, all the uncountable *samādhis* proclaimed (by the Buddha) of the Great and Small Vehicles are brought together by a sublime essential element, which is calming and discerning, for he said in the *Saṃdhinirmocana-sūtra,* "Whatever the numerous *samādhis* of the disciples, Bodhisattvas, and Tathāgatas that I have taught, one should know that they are encompassed by calming and discerning."

Therefore, those who endeavor to gain *samādhi* need not search for a multitude of distinct species: they should take recourse at all times to well searching for the method that attends to both calming and discerning, which are the general binding thread of all *samādhis.* This is expressed in the *Bhāvanākrama III:*[4] "At that place, when the Bhagavat had finished displaying an uncountable multitude of diverse bodhisattva *samādhis,* he encompassed all *samādhis* with calming and discerning, for which reason we must expound that very path which proceeds as calming and discerning pair-yoked." And it is expressed in the *Bhāvanākrama II:* "Because all *samādhis* are encompassed by those two, all yogins must at all times take recourse to calming and discerning."

3. THE INTRINSIC NATURE OF CALMING AND DISCERNING

The intrinsic nature of calming is just as stated in the *Saṃdhinirmocana-sūtra:*[5]

Having placed himself in solitary detachment, he orients his mind to just that *dharma* (nature, doctrine) so well contemplated through introspection, and he orients his mind, by means of whatever thought, with a mental orientation in continuity within on that mentally oriented thought. The arising of the cathartic of body and the cathartic of mind in that person so engaged, repeatedly dwelling on that (thought)—is called "calming." In that way, the bodhisattva searches for calming.

When one has taken as sensory object a meditative object having that [*dharma* (doctrine, nature)] as aim, whether making definite some aim among the twelve branches of scripture, or some aim among the personality aggregates, etc., as the case may be—by mindfulness and awareness tied to that meditative object, in the sense of nondistraction elsewhere of the mind having that as meditative object, his mind dwells automatically on the meditative object. Upon production of the rapture and pleasure of the cathartic of body and mind, that *samādhi* becomes "calming." This is produced only from holding the mind within, without straying from the meditative object; it is independent of the full comprehension of the entity.

The intrinsic nature of discerning is just as stated in the same sūtra:[6]

When he has obtained the cathartic of body and the cathartic of mind, he remains in just that and eliminates aspects (*ākāra*) of mind.[7] [Then,] he discriminates and has conviction toward the reflected images, which are the range of *samādhi* within, of those so-contemplated *dharmas*. Thus, investigation, supernal investigation, consideration, profound comprehension, forbearance, longing, analysis, views, and discursive thought—of the knowable meaning in those reflected images, which are the range of *samādhi*—is called "discerning." In that way, the Bodhisattva is skilled in discerning.

It is well known that when the Chinese teacher Hva-śaṅ saw this sūtra's exceedingly clear exposition, which cannot be repudiated, in regard to discerning as discriminative insight, he exclaimed, "How incomprehensible is this sūtra!" and kicked it with his foot. Conceiving that any discursive thought is all apprehension of sign-source, he rejected discriminative insight and paid no attention at all to it. Because he was opposed to the longing to contemplate the profound meaning, he acted that way. There appeared many followers of this school of thought. Here (in the sūtra quotation), "investigation" means investigation of a phenomenon; "supernal investigation" means investigation of a noumenon. Āryāsaṅga explains "consideration" as the time of apprehension of sign-sources by means of a mental orientation with discursive thought accompanied by insight; and explains "profound comprehension" as the time of traversing.[8] "Consideration" means crude consideration; "profound comprehension" means subtle comprehension. "Apprehension of sign-source" is not imputation of truth, but consideration in detail of a domain (*viṣaya*). Thus each investigation of a noumenon and a phenomenon has both its consideration and its profound comprehension.

Consistently with the *Saṃdhinirmocana-sūtra,* the *Ārya-Ratnamegha* also explains it clearly in these words: "Calming is a single area of thought; discerning is right discrimination." Furthermore, we find in the *Sūtrālaṃkāra* (XIV, 8) by the Reverend Maitreya:

One should know his path of calming and the concise titles of the doctrines; one should know his path of discerning—the enumeration of the entities going with those (concise titles).[9]

And (XVIII, 66):

When he takes recourse to right fixation, through halting mind in mind, there is calming; and also through supernal investigation of natures, there is discerning.

According to this, when he takes recourse to right *samādhi,* the fixation of the mind is calming, and the insight supernally investigating the *dharmas* is discerning. Because this presentation exactly conforms to the deep purport of the sūtras, it obviates drawing upon other sūtra material.

Also the *Bodhisattvabhūmi* states:[10]

Having fastened the mind on a meditative object that is expressionless (*nirabhilāpya*), a mere given thing (*vastumātra*), a mere entity (*arthamātra*), he absorbs himself in any meditative object with a mental orientation of idea that is free from all (verbal) elaboration, free from all distraction of mind. He settles his mind within on *samadhi* sign-sources, rightly settles it, . . . (up to) makes-it-flow-one-pointedly, naturally concentrates. This is called calming. What is discerning? That mental orientation of sign-source of precisely the *dharmas* thus contemplated by that very mental orientation which had cultivated calming; investigation, supernal investigation, supernal investigation of the *dharmas,* . . . (up to) engagement with learning and insight. This is called discerning.

This is consistent with the previous passages. As it presents the situation just as the earlier deep purport of both the sūtra and the venerable one, it reinforces the previously given foundation of calming and discerning. Moreover, according to the *Bhāvanākrama II:*

When he has calmed the straying to exterior sensory domains, the rapture in proceeding automatically in continuity on the inner meditative object, and the fixation in the nature of mind that is accompanied with the cathartic—are called calming. At the time of dwelling in that calming, the profound comprehension of reality is discerning.

Also, it says in the *Prajñāpāramitopadeśa* (by Śānti-pā):

Among those, the reflected image without discursive thought on the phenomenon and the noumenon is the meditative object of calming. The reflected image with discursive thought on the phenomenon and the noumenon is the meditative object of discerning.

This sets forth that the fixation without discursive thought on the phenomenal and noumenal entity is calming, and that the examination of those two domains is discerning. Furthermore, we find in the *Saṃdhinirmocana:*[11]

"O Lord, how many are the meditative objects of calming?" He declared, "One, namely, the reflected image without discursive thought." "How many are the meditative objects of discerning?" He declared, "Only one: the reflected image with discursive thought." "How many are the meditative objects of both?" He declared, "Two, as follows: the limits of the entity and the fulfillment of the requirement."

That is the deep purport. The *Samuccaya* (of Asaṅga) states that the noumenon and the phenomenon are the limits of the entity. This accords with the previous explanation by Śānti-pā. Because both calming and discerning have a meditative object in both the noumenon and the phenomenon, then by way of the domain of meditative object of calming and discerning there is both a calming that, without discriminating, completely comprehends voidness, and a discerning that does not completely comprehend voidness. Moreover, by reason of the "calm" having validity for domains outside the mind and by reason of "fixation" (of the mind) within on the meditative object, it is called "calming" (*źi gnas*). By reason of seeing better, i.e., in a distinguished manner, it is called "discerning" (*lhag mthoṅ*).

Some claim that calming, having the fixation of mind without discursive thought, is without strength of the vivid part of the clear vision (*vidyā*); and that discerning has the strength of the vivid part; but that is not valid, because it is opposed to the pronouncements of the Buddha, the analytic expositions of the regent (i.e., Maitreya), the texts of Asaṅga, the *Bhāvanākrama* texts (three in number), and so on, which explain, in the course of ample exposition of the characteristics of calming and discerning, that calming is the *samādhi* having a single area of thought in a meditative object, and that discerning is the insight having right examination of the knowable entity. In particular, the formulation "having the fixation of mind without discursive thought, is without strength of the vivid part of the clear vision" constitutes a distinction of whether or not there is a fading of the *samādhi;* but that is not valid for establishing the distinction of calming and discerning, because there is a definite requirement to eliminate fading in the case of all *samādhis* of calming and because there is a definite occurrence of the clear part of mind in the case of all *samādhis* free from fading.

Now, the *samādhi* and insight having a noumenon as their meditative object are to be determined in terms of whether or not there is discrimination of the nonpresence of the sensory domain or of the self, as the case may be; but they are not determined in terms of whether or not there is fixation when there is nondiscursive thought attended with pleasure and vividness of the mind—because there is an infinity of *samādhis* with pleasure and vividness and without discursive thought that do not direct discrimination to the reality of the nonpresence of the sensory domain and of the self. There is no contradiction at all in the production of a *samādhi* without discursive thought even though one does not obtain a view that completely comprehends thusness in that way [of the preceding paragraph]; and even though one does not understand voidness by an accomplishment in immediacy. It suffices to hold the mind with no discursive thought whatever. When one holds the mind for a long time by way of that [nondiscursive thought], by the force of holding the mind the serviceability of wind arises, and when that has arisen there is the true nature of production of rapture and pleasure in body and mind, so there is no contradiction with the production of pleasure. When that has arisen, by the force of the vivid aspect of the feeling of rapture and pleasure, the vivid part occurs in the mind. Consequently, by no means do all *samādhis* with pleasure and vividness and without discursive thought involve the accomplishment with full comprehension of reality.

Now, there are a great many occurrences of pleasure, vividness, and nondiscursive thought in *samādhis* that fully comprehend voidness as well as in *samādhis* that do not direct discrimination to voidness. Therefore, it is necessary to distinguish the two cases.

4. THE REASON FOR THE REQUIREMENT TO CULTIVATE BOTH CALMING AND DISCERNING

Why is it insufficient to cultivate either calming or discerning alone; why the requirement to cultivate both? That will be explained.

For example, if, for the purpose of viewing icons in the darkness of night, one lights a lamp, if the lamp is very bright and not disturbed by the wind, the icons are seen very clearly. However, if the lamp is not bright, or, if bright, flickers in the wind, the forms are not clearly seen. In the same way, for perceiving the profound meaning, if one has both insight, with certainty and freedom from illusion, into the meaning of reality and a motionless state of mind, fixed exactly as desired on a meditative object, he clearly sees reality. However, even if there be the *samādhi* without discursive thought, with the mind fixed so that it does not proceed elsewhere, should there be no insight that fully comprehends thusness, by reason of the lack of the eye that sees reality, no matter how much one cultivates *samādhi* there occurs no full comprehension of thusness. And even if there be the view with perfect understanding of the reality of selflessness, should there be no *samādhi* with a firm fixation in a single area of thought, by reason of the agitation by the wind of shifting discursive thought in an uncontrolled manner there occurs no discerning of the thusness aim. For that reason there is the requirement for both calming and discerning. Thus we read in the *Bhāvanākrama II:*

When he has only discerning without calming, the yogin's mind strays in sensory domains, just as a fire lamp placed in the wind is not steady. So the light of knowledge is not very bright, for which reason he must take recourse to both. For that reason, the Buddha pronounced this in the *Ārya-parinirvāṇa-sūtra:* "The disciples do not see the lineage of the Tathāgata because of their emphasis on *samādhi* with negligible insight. The bodhisattvas see it, although not clearly, because of their emphasis on insight, with negligible *samādhi*. A Tathāgata sees everything, because of his equal calming and discerning. Thus, by the power of calming, like a fire lamp placed where there is no wind, the mind is not shifted by the winds of discursive thought. By means of discerning, one eliminates the whole net of evil views and is not disturbed by others, as said in the *Candrapradīpa-sūtra:*[12] "By the power of calming, it becomes immobile; by means of discerning it becomes like a mountain."

Now, the *imprint of calming* is the adhering stability of the mind at the place where it is deposited when it is not distracted from the meditative object. The *imprint of discerning* is like a mountain that cannot be shaken by an adversary—when through full comprehension of the reality of selflessness, one eliminates the evil views such as "self-view." Hence, those are to be distinguished.

When calming has not been perfected previously, even though one examines the meaning of selflessness with discriminative insight, like a fire lamp in the wind, even the generality of the meaning of selflessness is not clear because the mind is too agitated. And if one examines when calming has been perfected previously, because he has averted the fault of excessive agitation the general meaning of selflessness becomes clear. Consequently, the part of immobility of the mind belonging to discerning is produced from the calming without discursive thought, while the part of full comprehension of thusness is not produced from calming. For example, there is this analogy: the part illuminating form, belonging to the fire lamp, is produced from the previous wick and fire, but not due to the curtain, etc. protecting against the wind; while the part consisting in the nonshifting stability of the fire lamp is due to that curtain, etc. Thus one arrives at right knowledge of the meaning if he examines with the insight that is accompanied by the equipoise of calming that is free from inequality stemming from fading or scattering of the mind. Following the deep purport, the *Dharmasaṃgīti* states: "The equipoised mind has the view of things as they really are," and the *Bhāvanākrama I* says this:[13]

By reason of the commotion of the mind like a stream, there is no fixation amidst the calming base. One cannot know things as they really are with an unequipoised mind, for the Bhagavat has proclaimed, "The man whose mind is equipoised knows things as they really are."

If one accomplishes calming, then by averting the fault consisting in the shifting of the insight that examines selflessness in the correct manner, he has an inexhaustible number of cultivations of examination by discriminative insight [from which to choose]—such as impermanence, *karma* and its maturation, disadvantages of cyclical flow, friendliness, compassion and purification of the aspiration to enlightenment. And in the case of every meditative object, when he has avoided the fault of straying, by proceeding on whatever is his own meditative object without straying to a different one, all his virtuous deeds have exceedingly great strength. However, when he has not previously attained calming, and mainly strays to other meditative objects, all his virtuous practice has meager strength, just as is said in the *Caryāvatāra* (VIII, 1, C-d): "The man whose mind is distracted stands between the fangs of torment"; and (V, 16): "Just in vain does the silly person whose mind is fixed on something else conduct mutterings and privations for a long time, the Omniscient One has declared."

Thus the requirement to accomplish a *samādhi* with fixation in the sense of mind on a single meditative object, no straying elsewhere and nondiscursive thought, is to produce the serviceability that makes the mind serve as desired in a virtuous meditative object. Furthermore, if the mind is tied to a single meditative object and kept in arrest, if one (then) releases it, like the irrigation canal that conducts water to a fertile field, it proceeds exactly as desired to a virtuous meditative object that is boundless. Consequently, after the accomplishment of calming, there is the requirement to attend to the insight having a meditative object in the domain of a phenomenon or noumenon, (to attend to) renunciation, thought of vows, forbearance, striving, faith, aversion, etc.—meditative objects which assemble boundless virtue and ward off boundless fault. However, one should know that there does not arise a great profit for virtuous practice by a settling through tying [mind] to a single meditative object in continuous time, when one does not know the purpose of accomplishing calming. If in that way one rejects the examining-cultivation by discriminative insight of the category of practice and the category of theory, there is very small profit in the cultivation of a *samādhi* with a single area of thought. In particular, if one lacks the discerning with meditative object in the noumenon—consisting in attending through examination by discriminative insight to the means of generating in long continuity the fierce energy of certainty in the meaning of selflessness—then no matter how long one cultivates calming one can only suppress the visible tops of the defilements and there is no possibility of eliminating the seed of those [defilements] from the root. Therefore, one should not merely cultivate calming, but should also cultivate discerning, because the *Bhāvanākrama II* states:

When one has merely cultivated calming, the hindrance of the yogins is not eliminated, but for the time being there is only a suppression of the defilements. As long as the light of insight has not arisen, the traces are not well defeated. Thus it is proclaimed in the *Ārya-Saṃdhinirmocana,*[14] "By means of meditation one suppresses the defilements; by means of insight one well erases their traces." Also, it is said in the *Samādhirāja* (IX, 36–37):[15] "Although he cultivates a *samādhi* in the world, he does not uproot the idea of self. Again his defilements assert their discord like Udraka's cultivation of *samādhi* here.[16] If he discriminates the *dharmas* as selfless; if he, discriminating those, would cultivate, that is the cause of achieving the *nirvāṇa*-fruit. A different cause does not conduce to ceasing." Furthermore, we read in the *Bodhisattvapiṭaka:* "Those who have not heard (or, learned) the noble doctrine and discipline, but who are satisfied with mere *samādhi,* by the power of pride of having attained that position fall into manifest pride; are not liberated from birth, old age, sickness, death, grief, lamentation, misery, dissatisfaction, and perturbation,[17] are not liberated from the cyclical flow of the six destinies; and are not liberated from the aggregate of suffering. Following the profound purport in regard to that, the Tathāgata announced, 'The one who has heard (*śrutam*) from another, comformable to Thus (*evam*), is liberated from old age and death.' "[18] That being the case, the one desiring the origination of completely pure knowledge through elimination of all hindrance should base himself in calming and then cultivate insight. Thus it is also pronounced in the *Ārya-Ratnakūṭa:*[19] "Having based himself in morality, he attains *samādhi.* After attainment of *samādhi* he cultivates insight. By means of insight his pure knowledge occurs. Indeed the perfection of morality belongs to pure knowledge." Furthermore, the *Ārya-Mahāyānaprasādaprabhāvana-sūtra* proclaims: "Son in the family, if one does not stand close to insight, I do not talk about his faith in the Great Vehicle of the Bodhisattvas or how he will develop in the Great Vehicle."

5. THE METHOD OF DETERMINING THE SEQUENCE

The *Caryāvatāra* states (VIII, 4): "The one well yoked to discerning by means of calming makes an end to defilement. Knowing that, calming deserves to be sought for first of all." Accordingly, one first accomplished calming; thereupon, on its basis, one cultivates discerning.

In regard to that, why is there this passage in the *Bhāvanākrama I:*[20] "Its meditative object is not definite"? It sets forth that the meditative object of calming is not definite. As previously set forth, there is both a subject and an object going with the meditative object of calming.

Therefore, the former, when understanding the meaning of selflessness, cultivates with that (latter) as his meditative object. Consequently, although it suffices to generate simultaneously both the calming with the mind not distracted elsewhere and the discerning with voidness as its meditative object, why is it that one first seeks calming and then cultivates discerning? In regard to that, the school of thought which makes discerning precede calming maintains that in generating the understanding of the view with full comprehension of selflessness it is not necessary to precede with calming, because even when there is no calming one sees the production of that view. (And it maintains that) also in the case of producing the experience of an exchange of mind toward that view, it is not necessary to precede with calming because even when there is no calming, that does not contradict the production of the exchange of mind when one again and again cultivates that examination with discriminative insight. This reduces to the sheer absurdity that also one produces the experience of an exchange of mind toward impermanence, disadvantages of cyclical flow, and purification of the aspiration of enlightenment when one depends on calming, for a completely identical reason.

Well then, what is the school of thought that makes calming necessary for discerning? In this regard, the *Saṃdhinirmocana* says that when one cultivates investigation and supernal investigation with discriminative insight, as long as he is unable to generate the cathartic of body and of mind, for that long he has a mental orientation favorable to discerning; and that, thereafter, upon generating the cathartic, there is discerning.[21] Consequently, if one has not attained calming, however much he cultivates examination with discriminative insight, in the end he is unable to generate the rapture and pleasure of the cathartic of body and mind. On the other hand, when he has attained calming he generates the cathartic at the conclusion of cultivating examination with discriminative insight. Hence, for that case calming is necessary as a foundation, as will be explained below.

Now, discerning does occur when there is the ability to generate the cathartic through the power of deliberation, even though one has not settled on a single meditative object with discriminative insight. Therefore, the generation of the cathartic through the power of settling the mind on a single meditative object, even with voidness as the meditative object, agrees with the school of thought that calming is accomplished. Hence, when discerning is attained by merely that [power of examination] one does not settle [the mind on a single meditative object], to wit: when one first seeks the understanding of selflessness and again and again examines its meaning, because he has not previously accomplished calming, then after taking recourse to that [examination], there (still) does not occur an accomplishment of calming. On the other hand, if he cultivates the fixation without examination, taking recourse to that [fixation] he accomplishes calming; and since he lacks the discerning method of attending that does not pertain to the calming method of attending, subsequently he must seek discerning—because he does not violate the sequence when he first seeks calming and then, on the basis of that, cultivates discerning. Accordingly, if the method of generating discerning did not serve to generate the cathartic by examining-cultivation that discriminates, there would be scarcely any reason for first seeking calming, and then, on the basis of that, for cultivating discerning.

Besides, if one does not cultivate according to that sequence, it is highly improper, as is stated in the *Saṃdhinirmocana,* namely, as previously quoted (to the effect that) based on the attainment of calming, one cultivates discerning. And it is said, "Based on the previous one, the subsequent one arises," to wit: the sequence of meditation and insight among the six perfections; producing the instruction of *samādhi* and then, on the basis of that, the instruction of insight. In the case of these sequences, the sequence is previously to cultivate calming and later to cultivate discerning. Also, it is stated in the *Bodhisattvabhūmi,* as previously quoted, and also in the *Śrāvakabhūmi* that based on calming, one cultivates discerning. Furthermore, the *Madhyamaka-hṛdaya,* the *Caryāvatāra,* the three *Bhāvanākrama* works, (the authors) Jñānakīrti and Śānti-pā (all) say that one first seeks calming and then cultivates discerning. Now, some Indian masters maintained that, without seeking calming separately, from the outset one generates discerning through an examination with discriminative insight; as this is in conflict with the texts of the great way-layers, those with good judgment do not find that position acceptable.

Furthermore, that sequence of calming and discerning is at the time when it is newly generated for the first time. After one has done it that way, one may also cultivate discerning previously and then cultivate calming, for which reason the sequence is not definite. But how is it that the *Samuccaya* says this:[22] "Someone has acquired discerning and not calming. Basing (himself) on discerning of that kind he cultivates calming"? That is not a nonattainment of the calming incorporated by the threshold (*sāmantaka*) of the First Meditation (*dhyāna,* of the Realm of Form); rather, it is the nonattainment of the calming belonging to the main part (*maulī*) of the First Meditation and subsequent [stages].[23] This also: having fully comprehended in immediacy the four truths, and basing oneself thereon, one accomplishes the calming belonging to the First Meditation and subsequent [stages], because the *Bhūmivastu* states:[24]

> Moreover, the one who rightly knows them as they really are [i.e., the truths] from suffering to path, does not attain the First Meditation, etc. No sooner does he dwell [on some meditative object] than he settles his mind, and he does not investigate the *dharmas.* He, basing himself on that [preceding] insight, accomplishes meditation.

Generally, for the sake of convenience of terminology, calming is expressed as the nine thoughts and discerning is expressed as the four kinds, inspection, etc. Furthermore, as the substance of calming and discerning will be explained, it is necessary to establish them through the production of the cathartic.

6. THE METHOD OF THEIR INDIVIDUAL INSTRUCTION

This has three divisions: the method of instruction in calming, the method of instruction in discerning, the method of those two pair-yoked.

CALMING THE MIND
(ŚAMATHA)

The Method of Instruction in Calming

THIS has three divisions: I. Reliance on the equipment for calming; II. After recourse to that (equipment), the method of cultivating calming; III. By reason of the cultivation, the standard of accomplishment of calming.

I. RELIANCE ON THE EQUIPMENT FOR CALMING

The yogin should at the outset take recourse to the equipment for calming, which is the foundation for speedily and pleasantly accomplishing calming. There are six parts to this, as follows:

Residence in a favorable place. The place possesses five merits: "good access" because food and clothing are obtained there without difficulty; "good settlement" because savage men and wild beasts, as well as enemies, do not dwell there; "good soil" because it is not pestilential soil; "good companionship" because there are companions of morality and congenial views; "good usage" because by day there are few persons, and by night there are few noises. Also, it is stated in the *Sūtrālaṃkāra* (XIII, 7): "The place where the wise man accomplishes has the merits 'good access,' 'good settlement,' 'good soil,' 'good companionship,' and 'good usage.' "

Meager desire. There is no craving for good, or ample numbers of, religious garb, and so on.

Contentment. This is remaining contented, even though one obtains only mean clothing and so forth.

Elimination of multiple activities. This is the elimination of such deleterious activities as buying and selling, as well as an excessive acquaintanceship with householders and mendicants, and also such activities as preoccupation with herbs or the calculation of the stars.

Purity of morality. One does not violate the points to be learned about the intrinsic nature and the attendant reproachful acts as regards both the Prātimokṣa and the Bodhisattva vows; and if through carelessness one has broken [those vows], with quick repentance he repairs them in accordance with righteousness.

Elimination of discursive thinking of craving, and so on. One contemplates the disadvantages of this life (found) in cravings, such as being killed or imprisoned; and the disadvantages of the next life, such as going to an evil destiny. And one contemplates all the entities of cyclical flow [which]—whether pleasant or unpleasant—possesses a perishable nature and are impermanent; and that if one cannot impede the distant separation of those things from oneself, then why crave them!—and so forth. With such contemplations, one should eliminate all the discursive thinking of craving.

Those have been explained according to the purport of *Bhāvanākrama II:* they may be known extensively from the *Śrāvakabhūmi.* The six natures of that kind comprise the essentials for newly producing a good *samādhi,* holding it without loss after it has been produced, and the cause and condition for promoting it ever higher. In particular, purity of morality, seeing the disadvantages in cravings, and residence in a favorable place are the chief ones.

It was said by Dge-bśes-ston-pa: "We think that only the precept is the answer and seek only the precept; not desiring to generate *samādhi* and not situated in the equipment for that, we are 'men with the answer.' " Here, "equipment" means the six set forth above.

Moreover, the first four perfections go into the equipment for the fifth one, meditation. The *Bhāvanākrama I* states:[25]

Calming is speedily perfected by one who disregards the desire state of acquisition [has the perfection of giving], is stationed in right conduct [has the perfection of morality], has the nature of resignation to suffering [the perfection of forbearance], has inaugurated striving [the perfection of striving]. Consequently, giving, and so on, are described in the *Saṃdhinirmocana* and other sūtras by the state of the subsequent having the preceding as a base.

Also, it is said in the *Pathapradīpa* (k. 46):[26]

> The one who destroys the ancillaries of calming,
> Although he cultivates, earnestly persevering,
> Indeed, even for a thousand years—
> Has no accomplishment of *samādhi.*

Hence, those who desire in the depths of their heart to accomplish the *samādhi* of calming and discerning must take as supremely important the endeavor in the ancillaries of, or equipment for, calming, such as the thirteen set forth in the *Śrāvakabhūmi.*[27]

II. AFTER RECOURSE TO THAT (EQUIPMENT), THE METHOD OF CULTIVATING CALMING

Here there are two sections: 1. the preparation; 2. the main part.

1. THE PREPARATION.

This is the six preparatory natures discussed above. Especially, one cultivates at length the mind of enlightenment; and, as ancillaries of the latter, one also trains himself in the intrinsic elements of the meditative objects shared with the lowest and middling persons.[28]

2. THE MAIN PART.

This has two sections: a. exposition of the cultivation in terms of the posture of the body; b. exposition of the stages of cultivation.

a. Exposition of the Cultivation in Terms of the Posture of the Body

As set forth in the *Bhāvanākrama II* and the *Bhāvanākrama III,* on a very smooth and pleasant seat one should have the eight department natures of the body. Among those, the *legs* should be completely crossed like the crossed legs of the venerable Vairocana; or, again, have the half-cross, as convenient. The *eyes* are neither fully open nor fully closed, and are fixed on the tip of the nose. The *body* should be kept neither bent backward nor stooped forward, but one must stay inwardly mindful to keep it straight. The *shoulders* are kept horizontally even. The *head* is neither raised nor drooping, and not kept turned in one direction; but one maintains the nose and the navel in line. The *teeth and lips* are kept in the ordinary way in their natural disposition. The *tongue* is kept by the upper teeth. The motion in and out of the *breath* should not be withheld, proceed in pants, be excited or constrained; but its movement that way and this way should not be felt; it should proceed without effort, and very gently.

It is stated in the *Śrāvakabhūmi* that the Buddha enjoined one to sit with crossed legs on a seat, stool, or grass mat, for five reasons: 1) If the body is well drawn in, this posture is consistent with generating the cathartic, for which reason the cathartic is speedily produced. 2) By sitting that way, one can be active even after a long period of time; by means of that posture, one's body is less likely to get weary. 3) That posture is not shared by the heretics and the opponents. 4) When others see someone sitting with that posture, they are gladdened. 5) The Buddhas and their disciples employ and authorize that posture. That work states that in consideration of those five reasons, one adopts the posture of crossed legs; and states that the upright straightness of the body is so that torpor and sleepiness will not occur.

Accordingly, one must accomplish at the outset the eight deportment natures of the body and particularly the tranquillization of the breath, exactly as has been set forth.

b. Exposition of the Stages of Cultivation

The stages of the path are expressed in broad outline as the accomplishment of calming by way of the eight motivations that eliminate the five faults, as they are stated in the *Madhyānta-vibhāga*. According to the precepts descended by Dge-bśes Lag-sor-ba, in addition it is necessary to accomplish it with the six forces, the four mental orientations, and the nine thoughts, as they are explained in the *Śrāvakabhūmi*. According to the savant Yon-tan-grags, the nine means of mind fixation are incorporated in the four mental orientations; the eight motivations which are the opponents for the six faults constitute the means of all *samādhis;* and those agree with all the teachings of the means of meditation in numerous sūtras, the *Sūtrālaṃkāra,* the *Madhyānta-vibhāga,* the *bhūmi* compilations of Asaṅga, the three Mādhyamika *Bhāvanākrama* works, and so on. That being the case, the one who is based in the equipment for *samādhi* at the outset, and endeavors with those means, necessarily attains *samādhi.*

In our day, these means are only names, or even do not appear at all, in precepts of meditation hailed as profound. Our stages of the path explain that when a person does not have the equipment for *samādhi* and lacks those means, he may endeavor however long and still not accomplish *samādhi.* This is mentioned in the section on obtaining the pure certainty in the method of accomplishing *samādhi* according to the great texts. In that regard, Asaṅga extensively lays down the general methods of guidance of the stages of the path for the three vehicles in the five *bhumi* compilations.[29] His text, teaching the procedures, is exceedingly detailed. Furthermore, since the explanation is extensive in that single text and the exposition not extensive in other texts; and since he states both calming and discerning in the *Viniścaya-saṃgrahaṇī* as "required to be known from the *Śrāvakabhūmi,*" the Srāvakabhūmi is the most detailed (part). Also, the venerable Maitreya set forth the nine means of mind fixation and the eight climinative motivations in the *Sūtrālaṃkāra* and in the *Madbyānta-vibhāga* (respectively). Following those treatises, Indian servants such as the *ācārya* Haribhadra, Kamalaśīla, and Sānti-pa wrote much on the stages of accomplishing *samādhi.* Apart from dissimilar meditative objects, such as the body of a deity, the drop (*bindu*), and (incantation) syllables—the general contents of *samādhi* are quite consistent in the respective explanations of the above-mentioned great texts and the Tantras. In particular, the defects of *samādhi,* such as the five faults, and the methods of dispelling them are amply treated on the part of the sūtras.

However, the ones who know the procedure on the basis of the great texts appear like the stars of day. In contrast, having burdened those texts with the impurity of one's own faulty discrimination, they are only opened to the extent of external understanding. But when there is alongside a precept that teaches the essential meaning, and one grasps that (precept), then at the time of the procedure in the stages of accomplishing *samādhi* according to those (texts), there is no doubt of how it is. This precept serves to erect the procedure from beginning to end that only has its source in the great texts. Consequently, this work also takes from the great texts the methods of accomplishing *samādhi* that are to be explained. Here there are two sections: *A.* The method of generating faultless *samādhi; B.* After taking recourse to that, the stages of generating the fixations of mind.

A. The Methods of Generating Faultless *Samādhi*

This has three sections I. How one performs prior to fastening mind on a meditative object; II. How one performs at the time of fastening mind on a meditative object; III. How one performs after fastening mind on a meditative object.

I. HOW ONE PERFORMS PRIOR TO FASTENING MIND ON A MEDITATIVE OBJECT

If one is incapable of overcoming the sloth which lacks enthusiasm for cultivating *samādhi* and which delights in the side inconsonant with it, then from the outset one is not granted the entrance to *samādhi;* or, if he once attains it, he is unable to prolong it, and so it is quickly lost. For that reason, the great essential in the beginning is the ending of sloth. For this, if one attains the thorough cathartic with rapture and pleasure of body and mind, since he is unwearied in all the day and night by virtuous practice, he averts sloth.

To generate that (cathartic), the requirement is to be able to carry forward a continuous striving in the *samādhi* that is the basic-cause for generating the cathartic. To generate that (striving), the requirement is the continuity of fierce longing aimed at that *samādhi.* As a basis for that (longing), the requirement is the steadfast faith gratified at seeing the merits of the *samādhi.* Hence, at the outset one should cultivate again and again the faith which thinks volitionally about the merits of the *samādhi.* If one has the viewpoint, through taking their sequence to heart, he has grasped the sublime essential which is perfectly clear and certain; as it is said in the *Madhyāntavibhāga* (IV, 5a-b): "The basis, and what is based thereon; its primary cause and just its fruit." Here, "basis" is longing, the basis of endeavor. "What is based" is endeavor or striving. The "primary cause" of longing is the faith which trusts in the merits. The "fruit" of the endeavor is the cathartic.

The merits of the *samādhi* to be cultivated are as follows: If calming is accomplished, there are both ample rapture in in the mind and pleasure in the body, so that one dwells pleasantly in the nature (*dharma*) that is seen.[30] When one obtains the cathartic of body and mind, he can apply his mind as desired to a virtuous meditative object. By pacifying the uncontrolled straying into the sensory domain of illusion, the numerous demeritorious practices do not take place and there is great power in any virtuous deed he performs. Through recourse to calming, he is able to accomplish the merits of supernormal faculties, magical powers, etc.; and, in particular, through recourse to this, he generates the full comprehension of discerning that fully comprehends the noumenon, so that he is able speedily to cut out the root of the cyclical flow. If one contemplates such merits as those, he recognizes and cultivates whatever promotes enthusiasm in the cultivation of the *samādhi*. When this (enthusiasm) has been produced, it continuously exhorts inwardly the cultivation of the *samādhi*, so that it is easy to achieve *samādhi;* and having attained it, one repeatedly cultivates it, so that it is difficult to lose it.

II. HOW ONE PERFORMS AT THE TIME OF FASTENING MIND ON A MEDITATIVE OBJECT

This has two sections: A. Determination of the meditative object, the ground to which the mind is fastened; B. The method of fastening [*the*] mind to that (meditative object).

A. Determination of the Meditative Object

This has two sections: 1. General fundamentals of the meditative object; 2. Determination of the circumstances for choosing meditative objects. The first one has three sections: a. Exposition of the basic meditative objects; b. Exposition of which persons have which meditative objects; c. Exposition of the synonyms of the meditative objects.

1. GENERAL FUNDAMENTALS OF THE MEDITATIVE OBJECT

a. Exposition of the Basic Meditative Objects

The Lord stated four meditative objects of the yogin, namely, the universal meditative object, the meditative object for purification of addiction, the meditative object for skill, and the meditative object for purification of defilement. Among those, there are four kinds of universal meditative object: reflected image with dicursive thought, reflected image without discursive thought, limits of the entity, and fulfillment of the requirement.

Among those, there are two kinds of reflected image based by way of "agency of the meditative object"; the first is the meditative object of discerning, and the second is the meditative object of calming. The reflected image is the own-character (*svalakṣaṇa*)[31] minus the concreteness of the meditative object—whatever be the meditative object—its imagery (*ākāra*) appearing in discrimination (*buddhi*). Among those (two), there is discursive thought of examination when one is examining the meditative object, so the reflected image is with discursive thought. Also among those, there is no discursive thought of examination when one fixes the mind in a nonexamining manner upon the meditative object, so the reflected image is without discursive thought. Now, of which meditative objects are those reflected images the reflected images? They are the reflected images or imagery of the five meditative objects for purification of addiction, the five meditative objects for skill, and the two meditative objects for purification of defilement.

The limits of the entity are based by way of "scope of the meditative object," viz.,: the phenomenal limit of the entity goes with the statement, "So much is all: there is nothing beyond this"; and the noumenal limit of the entity goes with the statement, "Only like this is it based: it is not based otherwise." Among those, the phenomenon is all the constructed which is comprised in the five personality aggregates, all the natures comprised in the eighteen realms and in the twelve sense bases, and all the knowable entities comprised in the four (noble) truths: there is nothing beyond that. The noumenon is the reality and the thusness of those meditative objects, and is the goal demonstrated by the principle.

The fulfillment of the requirement is based by way of the "fruit," namely, having by means of calming and discerning upon the reflected images of those meditative objects cultivated and frequently repeated the mental orientation toward the meditative object, then by virtue of complete reliance upon it one becomes free from one's own contamination and thereupon has an exchange of the basis (*āśraya-parivṛtti*).[32]

The meditative objects for purification of addiction are those which purify addiction with a preponderance of lust, and so on, namely, the five—the unpleasant thing, friendliness, dependent origination, analysis of the elements, and mindfulness while inhaling and exhaling.

Among those, the meditative object in an unpleasant thing is the thirty-six personal unpleasant things, such as hair, pores; and the external unpleasant things, such as the becoming blue [of the corpse]. The imagery of an impure, unpleasant thing arises in discrimination and one holds the mind on this.[33]

The friendliness object involves taking friends, enemies, and neutrals as the meditative object, and then having a contemplation belonging to the equipoised plane, of accomplishing their benefit and pleasure.[34] The holding of mind on those meditative objects by way of this grasping pattern of friendliness is called "meditative object in friendliness" and it is said that there is friendliness toward both a domain and the possessor of the domain.

The meditative object in dependent origination is as follows: by taking as basis only the nature (*dharma*) arising dependently in the three times, the fruit of the "nature only" arises. So much is all: apart from those there is no doer of the action or enjoyer of the fruit. One holds the mind with a meditative object in that manner in the meaning of that (nature).[35]

The meditative object in analysis of the elements is as follows: one analyzes the subdivisions (or aspects) of the six elements, namely, earth, water, fire, wind, space, and perception. Taking those as meditative objects, one holds the mind thereon.[36]

The meditative object while inhaling and exhaling is the one by way of counting and observing the inward and outward passage of the breath, so that the mind does not stray elsewhere.[37]

There are also five meditative objects for skill, namely, skill in the personality aggregates, realms, sense bases, dependent origination, and possibility and impossibility.[38]

Among those personality aggregates are the five, personality aggregate of form, etc. Skill in these is understanding that there is neither "I" nor "mine" apart from the personality aggregates.

The realms are the eighteen realms of eye, etc. Skill in these is understanding the cause and condition by which those realms arise from their individual seeds.

The sense bases are the twelve sense bases of eye, etc. Skill in these is understanding that the six personal sense bases are the personal conditions for the six perceptions, that the six external sense bases are the objective conditions (for those perceptions), and that the immediately subsequent mind is the immediately succeeding condition.

Dependent origination is the twelve members. Skill in this is understanding the impermanence, suffering, and selflessness in these (twelve).

Possibility and impossibility are (respectively) the possibility of being gratified by the maturation consequent upon virtue and the impossibility of being gratified by the maturation consequent upon nonvirtue. Skill in these is understanding it this way.

That amounts to a diversity of skill regarding dependent origination; and, in particular, it makes known the unlike causes. At the time when one takes those as the meditative object of calming, he holds the mind by way of grasping pattern of certainty in any one of the personality aggregates, and so on.

The purification of defilement means either merely threatening to destroy the seed of defilement, or eliminating the seed from the root. The meditative object of the first kind is the coarseness of the lower planes and the calmness of the higher ones, from the plane of desire to the base of nothing-at-all. The meditative object of the second kind is the sixteen aspects, impermanence, etc. of the four truths.[39]

Also, when one takes those as the meditative object of calming, he holds the mind by way of either the arising of those domains without understanding or the certainty of mind, as the case may be.

Three kinds of meditative objects are mentioned in the *Bhāvanākrama II,* namely, *1*) in each case descending toward, hanging over, and alighting upon the thusness of all the twelve members of scripture, he fixes his mind on that;[40] *2*) the meditative object on how the personality aggregates, etc., incorporate the natures (*dharma*);[41] *3*) settling the mind on the form of the body of the Buddha who is seen and heard.

The method of settling on the personality aggregates, etc., is as follows: When one understands the way of subsuming all the constructed under (one or other of) the five personality aggregates, he thereupon completes the subsumption in sequence under those, and holds the mind with this as the meditative object.[42] If he cultivates the way of individual analysis, he generates discriminative insight; and if he cultivates the way of synthesizing them, he generates the *samādhi* which draws the mind onto the meditative object without dispersal into other domains. This is a precept of the *Abhidharma.* In the same way, having comprehended the method of assembling all the natures into the realms and sense bases, he completes the subsumption under those (categories), and holds the mind (thereon).

Among those (various meditative objects), the meditative objects for purification of addiction, as was explained, easily avert the attachments of those addicted to attachments; taking recourse to those (meditative objects), one easily achieves *samādhi,* so they are distinguished meditative objects. The meditative objects for skill bring about the cessation of the personal self, which does not belong to those natures. These objects are consistent with producing the discerning that fully comprehends selflessness, and so are very fine meditative objects of calming. The meditative objects for purification of defilements, representing as they do the general opponents to defilement, are of great import.[43] The universal meditative object is not a special kind as against those previous meditative objects. For these reasons it is necessary to accomplish *samādhi* on the basis of a meditative object of calming that accompanies a specific requirement. Consequently, it is clear that those who work at *samādhi* by taking a pebble, a twig, etc. as meditative objects, do not know the fundamentals of the meditative objects for *samādhi.*[44]

Some persons—thinking that if one has achieved the resource of a meditative object and then holds the mind on this, that it involves apprehension of signs—go on to maintain that without fixation on a domain of a meditative object of such kind, the very fixation without a basis is the cultivation of voidness. This is a complete misunderstanding of the method of cultivating voidness (as shown) this way: If at that time there is no awareness, neither is there a *samādhi* which cultivates (or, which intensely contemplates) voidness. But if there is (awareness), by reason of awareness of something, it is necessary to posit a knowable that has been fixed while there is awareness (of it). If there is a knowable, this very thing is the meditative object of that discrimination, because "domain," "meditative object," and "a knowable" have the same meaning. This being the case, it is necessary to posit an apprehension of signs for this *samādhi* also, so that school of thought is not valid.

Moreover, whether or not there is passage into the cultivation of voidness depends on whether or not there is the fixation by means of the cultivation through initially establishing the view which fully comprehends thusness, but does not depend in any sense on whether or not there is the fixation by way of discursive thought toward the domain—as will be taught below extensively. Furthermore, the one who maintains that there is settling without a meditative object or domain must first hold his mind in the thought, "I shall hold my mind so that it will not proceed to any domain whatsoever"; hence, he has to make certain to hold it so that it does not proceed to any aspect, while he depends on a meditative object that is "mind only" (*cittamātra*). It follows that the thesis that there is no meditative object is in conflict with personal experience.

Now, many meditative objects are set forth in the great texts about accomplishing *samādhi,* and the requirement of these (objects) has been explained above. Therefore, one should become skilled in the meditative basis for fixing the mind. It is mentioned in the *Bhāvanākrama* (*I,* as previously quoted) that the meditative object of calming is not definite; and the remark in the *Pathapradīpa,*[45] "On certain ones of meditative objects, as appropriate," means that there is a definite stipulation not to adopt the diversity of meditative objects, but it does not indicate the standard for dwelling in some (particular) meditative object.

b. Exposition of Which Persons Have Which Meditative Objects

When persons have a preponderance of lust, and so forth, up to discursive speculation, then, as the *Śrāvakabhūmi* quotes "The Questions of Revata (YS II):[46]

Revata, if a monk-yogin, practitioner of yoga, has only the addition of lust, he fastens his mind upon an unpleasant meditative object; if the addiction of hatred, upon friendliness; if the addiction of delusion, upon the origination in dependence of this condition; if the addiction of pride, upon analysis of the elements; if just the addiction of discursive speculation, he fastens his mind upon mindfulness while inhaling and exhaling. Thus he fastens his mind upon a corresponding meditative object.

The *Śrāvakabhūmi* also states (YS II):[47]

Among those, whoever are among the persons with addiction of lust, hatred, delusion, pride, and discursive speculation—for a while at first their addiction should be purified in a meditative object which purifies addiction. Subsequent to this, they should realize the fixation of the mind; and then their meditative object is adopted with certainty for each single case. Certainly they should practice with this meditative object.

Hence, certainly they should practice in those (respective) meditative objects. If it is a person who has achieved equality (of faults) or one who has weak passion, it suffices that he hold the mind on some one of those previously described meditative objects to arouse rapture (in him); but there is no requirement to have a certain one. This is stated in the *Śrāvakabhūmi* (YS II):[48]

On whichever one the person with addiction of equal parts has upsurge of rapture, there he should apply himself—merely for fixation of the mind and not for purification of addiction. Like the person with addiction of equal parts, so he with weak passion should be understood.

Among those, the five, predominances of lust and the others, are the consequence of following, cultivating, and often repeating the five, lust and the others, in previous lives, so that even in the event of a tiny sensory domain of the five, lust and the others, the five, lust and the others, arise strongly and for long duration. The addiction with equal parts is a consequence of not following, not cultivating, not often repeating lust and the others in previous lives; but also, the individual did not notice the disadvantage of those (five) and was not averse to them, so that in a domain of those (five), lust and the others do not arise with a predominance or for a long duration, but also, it is not the case that the five, lust and the others do not arise (at all). Weak passion is a consequence of not following, and so on, lust and the others in other lives, but of noticing the disadvantages, and so on, so that in great, many, and excessive domains of lust and the others, lust and the others arise feebly, and in medium and tiny domain, do not arise at all.

Moreover, the full comprehension of the mind fixation occurs in case of the five predominances of lust and the others, after a long time; in case of the addiction with equal parts, in not too long a time; in case of weak passion, very speedily.

The persons to endeavor in the meditative objects for skill are as set forth in the *Śrāvakabhūmi* (YS II):[49]

Revata, if a monk-yogin, practitioner of yoga, is confused about the individual characteristic of the motivations, or is confused about the fact of a self, a sentient being, a living thing, a progenitor, a feeder, or a person, he fastens his mind in skill concerning the personality aggregates. If confused about cause, in skill concerning the realms. If confused about condition, in skill concerning sense bases. If confused about impermanence, suffering, or nonself, in skill concerning dependent origination and concerning the possible and the impossible.

These five meditative objects chiefly avert confusion.

Furthermore, as to the persons who should fasten their mind in the meditative objects for purification of defilement, the *Śrāvakabhūmi* states (YS II):[50]

The one wishing to produce equanimity toward the realm of craving, fastens his mind on the coarseness of cravings and the calmness of forms; or, wishing to produce equanimity toward forms, fastens it on the coarseness of forms and the calmness of the formless realm; or, wishing to lose interest in and wishing to become free from the reifying view in every case,[51] fastens his mind on the truth of suffering, the truth of the origin (of suffering), the truth of the cessation (of suffering), and the truth of the path (leading to that cessation).

These meditative objects occur as meditative objects both for cultivating the understanding with discerning and for cultivating the fixation with calming. Hence they are not meditative objects for calming alone. However, some are suitable as meditative objects for newly accomplishing calming, and some occur as meditative objects for a special purpose once calming is accomplished, which is explained in the section devoted to the meditative object of calming.

c. *Exposition of the Synonyms of the Meditative Objects*

The synonyms of the reflected image, or appearance of imagery in discrimination of those previously explained meditative objects which are the foundation in which one holds the mind, the basis for the meditative object of *samādhi,* are as stated in the *Śrāvakabhūmi* (YS II):[52]

And that reflected image is called "reflected image," "sign of *samādhi,*" "domain for the range of *samādhi,*" "means of *samādhi,*" "door of *samādhi,*" "basis of the mental orientation," "body for inner discursive thought," "appearance to the mind." These are the synonyms of the reflected image that matches the knowable entity.

2. DETERMINATION OF THE CIRCUMSTANCES FOR CHOOSING MEDITATIVE OBJECTS

Now, of those numerous meditative objects that have been described, on this occasion which one should be the basis for accomplishing calming? As the sūtra was previously cited, that is not individually definite, but there is the requirement that the diversity of persons perform in the diverse meditative objects; and, in particular, if one who has not gone to the limit of calming that reaches certainty and is among those with a predominance of lust, and so on, he has the requirement to perform with a definite meditative object, because if he does not (so) perform, although he may attain a *samādhi* favorable to calming he will not actually achieve calming; and because—it being taught that it takes a very long time for one practicing in the meditative object for purification of addiction to perfect calming—if he abandons the meditative object for purification of addiction, how much less likely is it (i.e., calming) to be perfected! In particular, the one with predominance of discursive speculation definitely has the requirement to cultivate the breath. If one be a person with addiction in equal parts or a person with weak passion, as previously explained, he is to take a meditative object—his mind filled with enthusiasm—from among the meditative objects previously set forth.

Moreover, the *Bhāvanākrama II* and the *Bhāvanākrama III,* following the *Pratyutpanne Buddhasaṃmukhāvasthitasamādhi* and the *Samādhirāja-sūtra,* state that one may accomplish *samādhi* by taking the body of the Tathāgata as a meditative object. Also, the *ācārya* Bodhibhadra sets forth many in this passage:[53]

Here, calming is of two kinds: (*a*) that attained by looking inwardly, and (*b*) the dwelling on what is seen outside. Among them, (*a*) that attained by looking inwardly, has two kinds: (*a-1*) dwelling on the body, and (*a-2*) dwelling on what is based on the body. Among them, (*a-1*) dwelling on the body, has three kinds: (*a-1.1*) dwelling on the body itself as the aspect of a god; (*a-1.2*) dwelling on the unpleasant thing of skeleton, etc., and (*a-1.3*) dwelling on the outstanding signs of *khaṭvāṃga,* etc. Moreover, (*a-2*) dwelling on what is based on the body, has five kinds: (*a-2.1*) dwelling on the breath; (*a-2.2*) dwelling on the subtle signs; (*a-2.3*) dwelling on the drop (*bindu*); (*a-2.4*) dwelling on the member rays; and (*a-2.5*) dwelling on rapture and pleasure. (*b*) Dwelling on what is seen outside, has two kinds: (*b-1*) outstanding, and (*b-2*) ordinary. Among those, (*b-1*) outstanding, has two kinds: (*b-1.1*) dwelling on the body, and (*b-1.2*) dwelling on speech.[54]

That is quoted in the *Commentary on the Pathapradīpa.*[55] Among those, the holding of mind on the body of the Buddha is mindfulness of the Buddha, which generates an infinity of merits; and when that body is vivid and firm, there is the very special matter of performing in the meditative object of the field which amasses the accumulation (of merit)—bowing, making offerings, fervent aspirations, and so on; and of the field of purification from hindrance by confession (of sins), holding (of vows), and so on. Besides, as was earlier quoted from the *Samādhirāja,*[56] there are the merits of not losing mindfulness of the Buddha at the time of death. Again, if one cultivates the path of the Tantras, there are many requirements regarding Yoga of the deities and other very special matters. The benefit of this and the method of orienting the mind to the Buddha are extensively and lucidly treated in the *Pratyutpanne Buddhasaṃmukhāvasthitasamādhi;* since they are certainly as stated in the *Bhāvanākrama III,* they are to be known in that text, but are not written up here for fear of too many words.

Now, a special requirement in the perfection of *samādhi* follows upon the obtaining of the meditative base: it is the search for skillfulness in the means. How does one operate with a basis of meditative object in such a thing as the body of the Tathāgata? That is stated in the *Bhāvanākrama III,* as follows:[57]

In that regard, first the yogin fastens his mind upon the body form of the Tathāgata as it is seen and as it is heard, and then is to accomplish calming. He orients his mind continuously on the form of the Tathāgata's body, yellow like the color of purified gold, adorned with the (32) characteristics and the (80) minor marks, dwelling within its retinue, and acting for the aim of the sentient beings by diverse means. Generating a desire for the merits of that (body), he subdues fading, scattering, and the other faults, and should practice meditation until such time as he clearly sees that (body) dwelling in front.

And he should make the basis of the meditative object in the way stated by the *Samādhirāja:*[58]

> Whoever engages his mind in that meditative object—
> The Lord of the world, glorious
> With a body like the color of gold—
> That Bodhisattva is declared "equipoised."

Moreover, of the two kinds—generating newly with discrimination, and the vivid recollection (of that body) dwelling naturally—the latter is of great distinction for arousing faith besides being appropriate in the cases of the common vehicle,[59] so one will arouse the aspect of vivid recollection after that has been accomplished naturally. As to the former, when one seeks a basis for the meditative object—the foundation in which the mind is held—he seeks a good replica, such as a painting or metal casting; again and again looks at it and takes hold of its signs, and dwells in the cultivation of its arising in the domain of the mind. Besides, he contemplates the meaning of the good explanations he has heard from the guru, and he should seek the basis of the meditative object in what abides, arising in his mind. Again, the basis of the meditative object is not to be made through the aspects of painting, metal castings, and the like, but one studies (that) in the arising in the form of the substantial Buddha.

Some place an icon in front, and viewing it with the eye, make a quick contemplation; this has been elegantly refuted by the teacher Ye-śes-sde:[60] *samādhi* is not accomplished by what the senses are aware of; rather, it is accomplished by what the mind is aware of. Thus, the substantial meditative object of *samādhi* is the substantial domain of mental awareness—because the requirement is to hold the mind on this, and because, as was previously explained, the requirement is a meditative object in the arising of the reflected image, or entity agreement with the concrete objective meditation object.[61]

Also, there are both detailed and sketched parts of the body. As mentioned in other places, it is necessary to dwell first of all on the sketched parts, and subsequently to dwell on the detailed ones. In that experience it is very easy to have the sketched parts arise (in the mind), so the requirement is to make the basis of the meditative object through the sketched sequence of the body. Of especially great importance for the one who has not yet accomplished such a *samādhi* as explained (above) is the impropriety of all sorts of engagements with *samādhi* through shifting to numerous nonconcordant meditative objects, because the shifting to many different meditative objects constitutes a great obstacle to perfection of calming while cultivating *samādhi*. That being the case, the authoritative texts for accomplishment of *samādhi*. such as the *bhūmi* compilations (of Asaṅga), and the three *Bhāvanākrama* texts, explain that when one accomplishes *samādhi* for the first time, he accomplishes it by subjecting (the mind) to only one meditative object, while they deny that one shifts to numerous meditative objects. This is also clearly stated by Ārya-Śūra in the section on accomplishing meditation:[62]

> And he should fasten his mind firmly to a single meditative object.
> Holding a series of other meditative objects, he just provokes his mind to commotion.

Also the *Pathapradīpa* says:[63] "He should fasten his mind in virtue, on certain ones, as appropriate, of meditative objects." The statement "on certain ones" requires explanation. Thus, first he achieves calming by dwelling on a single meditative object, and subsequently dwells on many. (In this respect), the *Bhāvanākrama I* remarks:[64]

> At whatever time he has conquered a mental orientation, only at that time does he (meditatively) dwell purifying at length by means of the diversity of personality aggregates, realms, and so on. Thus the *Saṃdhinirmocana* and other sūtras set forth various kinds of meditative objects of the yogins by means of the diversity of meditative objects such as the eighteen kinds of voidness.[65]

Accordingly, at the outset one's standard for achieving the foundation of the meditation object on which he holds his mind is as follows: he distinctly recalls several times together the head, the two arms, other major parts of the trunk, and the two feet, in that order. Upon concluding this (exercise), if he has created in his mind the general form of the body, and if only half portions of the rough outlines of the members can arise on the plane of the mind, he should be satisfied with this degree (of visualization) even though an illuminated vividness does not (yet) occur and must hold his mind on this. The reason for that is as follows: if he does not hold his mind, satisfied with this degree (of visualization), but with desire for a greater vividness again and again vividly recalls, his meditative object becomes scarcely more vivid and besides he does not achieve the *samādhi* in the part of mind fixation, and there is no end to the obstacles for achieving it. However, if one holds his mind on just that meditative object of only half parts, and even though the meditative object is quite dim, he speedily achieves *samadhi*. After that, one derives a benefit from the vividness and so he joyfully creates the vivid part. That is drawn from the precepts of the teacher Ye-śes-sde and is of great importance.

In regard to the manner in which the foundation of meditative object arises (in the mind), there is no certainty because of the diversity, although one may take as fundamental that there are four alternatives and two classes, to wit, by reason of the lineages of persons, the arising of an aspect is (*1*) easy or (*2*) difficult, and that arising, in turn, is (*3*) vivid or (*4*) not vivid; and those two, moreoever, are (*a*) steady or (*b*) unsteady.

When one is in the phase of accomplishing the Yoga of deity (*devatā-yoga*) pertaining to the Mantra (vehicle), he must certainly accomplish the vividness of the aspect of the deity. Consequently, as long as that does not arise he must engage himself in a means of generating this (vividness) chosen from among the numerous means. But in the present case, when it is very difficult to get the aspect of the deity to arise (in the mind), it is satisfactory to hold the mind on one suitable meditative object from among those previously mentioned, because the main thing is the requirement simply to accomplish the *samādhi* of calming. In the present case, if one chooses the body of a deity as the meditative object for accomplishing (calming) and tries to hold his mind thereon, if its aspect does not arise then he does not accomplish the desired aim. This is why it is on the aspect (actually) arisen that one must hold the mind.

Moreover, suppose one holds (his mind) on the general features of the body to the extent it arises and some particular part of this body appears especially vivid, whereupon he concentrates on this (particular part).

And suppose when this (particular part) becomes dimmed he again holds (his mind) on the general features. On that occasion there is an uncertainty of color, for example, with red arising when he wishes to contemplate yellow. There is an uncertainty of shape, for example, with the standing shape arising when he wishes to contemplate the seated shape. There is an uncertainty of number, for example, with two things arising when he wishes to contemplate one thing. There is an uncertainty of large and small, for example, with the tiny arising when he wishes to contemplate the large. It is most improper to chase after those (uncertainties) if they arise. Therefore, one must accept the foundation of the meditative object in just precisely the basic meditative object, whatever it is.

B. The Method of Fastening the Mind to That Meditative Object

This has three parts: 1. Settling the technique without fault; 2. Clearing away the technique with fault; 3. Teaching the measure of watches.

1. SETTLING THE TECHNIQUE WITHOUT FAULT

Here, the *samādhi* to be accomplished has two distinguishing features, as follows: it has the strength of the vivid part consisting in exceeding vividness of mind, and it has the nonpredicating fixation part consisting in fixation on the meditative object as a single area. Some persons add "pleasure" as a third (distinguishing feature), and others add also "clarity" as a fourth. However, "clarity" is included in the first distinguished feature, so there is no need to refer to it separately. Again, the rapture and pleasure that are the euphoria of feeling arise in the fruit of the *samādhi* to be accomplished in this occasion; but they do not arise as concomitants of the *samādhi* comprised by the threshold of the First Meditation, and pleasure of body and pleasure of mind do not arise as concomitants of the *samādhi* of the Fourth Meditation stated to be the best foundation for accomplishing the merits of the three vehicles.[66] Consequently, that (ie., pleasure) is not counted here. Moreover, the great strength of the vivid part is not in the *samādhis* comprised by the formless plane(s), according to the *Sūtrālaṃkāra* text, "likewise meditation apart from the formless realm. . . ."[67] That is to say, aside from the Bodhisattvas who have attained power,[68] the Bodhisattvas accomplish their merits by taking recourse to the *samādhi*(s) comprised by the Meditation planes. Consequently, there is no fault in expounding the vivid-part kind of distinguishing feature.

The issuance of that sort of strength of the vivid part is interrupted by fading, and the nondiscursive thought consisting of a single area (of mind) is interrupted by scattering. Hence fading and scattering are the reason that becomes the chief obstacle for accomplishing the aspects of *samādhi*. Therefore, the one who has well determined the subtle and crude forms of fading and scattering, and having determined them does not know any ways to protect the *samādhi* defeated by these two, would have no possibility of calming—we need not speak of discerning! Therefore, the wise who aim at *samādhi* should become skilled in that method. Now, fading and scattering are the condition hostile to the accomplishment of calming. The determination of that hostile condition and the actual method of defeating that (condition) are explained later on. Here I shall set forth the method of generating the *samādhi* which is the favorable condition for the accomplishment of calming.

Samādhi is the fixation of mind in a single area on a meditative object; furthermore, one must dwell continuously on the meditative object.

Again, whatever be the basic meditative object of the mind, there are two requirements: 1) a means so as not to be distracted from that (meditative object); 2) a knowledge of the true state of affairs (viz.:) distraction or nondistraction, the threat of distraction or the nonthreat of distraction. The former is mindfulness and the latter is awareness. The *Commentary on the Sūtrālaṃkāra* states:[69] "Mindfulness and awareness are the fastener, since the former prevents straying from the meditative object of the mind and since the latter recognizes the straying."

When the meditative object slips away through failure of mindfulness, the meditative object is lost immediately after the straying (of mind). Hence mindfulness is the basis for the non-slipping-away of the meditative object. Regarding the method by which mindfulness fastens mind to the meditative object, upon distinct recall of the foundation of the meditative object as previously discussed, in case too low a level (of distinct recall) occurs, the one who recognizes that (state of affairs) generates a force of grasping pattern held in succession and raises the mind aloft, thus again fixing (the mind) without investigation on whatever be (the meditative object). Mindfulness has three distinguishing features, which are alluded to in this passage of the *Samuccaya:*[70] "What is mindfulness? The non-slipping-away of the mind in regard to the familiar entity; the agent of non-distraction."

α The distinguishing feature consisting of the domain of meditative object means "the familiar entity," because mindfulness does not arise in regard to a domain that was previously unfamiliar. In the present context, it is the arising of the foundation of meditative object previously ascertained.

β The distinguishing feature consisting of the aspect of grasping pattern means "the non-slipping-away of mind," i.e., the non-slipping-away of that domain from the mind. In the present context, it is the non-slipping-away of the foundation of meditative object. The method of non-slipping-away is taught by the gurus as the idea, "The foundation of meditative object is like this," which can be a question by another person or a personal involvement in discursive thought—and it says nothing about the sheer capacity of mindfulness. Rather, the mind is tied to the meditative object, has uninterrupted mindfulness of it, and does not stray away in even the slightest measure; for no sooner does it stray, than mindfulness is lost. Hence, one finishes settling the mind, as previously (explained), on the foundation of meditative object, and arouses the idea, "(I am) tied to the meditative object in this manner." Thereupon, again without discursive thought, the force of that discrimination protects without interruption: this is the essential point of the method of taking recourse to mindfulness.

γ The distinguishing feature consisting of the agent and action means the activity of nondistraction of the mind away from the meditative object.

The discipline tying mind in that way to the meditative object is expressed by the simile of training an elephant, for example, a wild elephant is tied with many massive cords to a trunk or post. However the elephant [may] stamp as he has learned to do, he is indeed unable to do anything (about it), and being more and more enmeshed with the sharp hooks, is defeated and subdued ("broken in"). The mind is like the untrained elephant. When it is bound with the cord of mindfulness to the firm post of the previously discussed meditative object, [even] if it is unwilling to remain there, it is gradually brought under control, goaded by the hook of awareness. The *Madhyamakahṛdaya* tells it this way:[71]

Having bound with the cord of mindfulness
To the firm post of meditative object,
The elephant of mind going astray—
It is gradually brought under control by the hook of insight.[72]

Also, the *Bhāvanākrama II* states: "With the cords of mindfulness and awareness, one should bind the elephant of mind to that trunk of meditative object." Although in the former work awareness is compared with a hook, and in the latter work it is compared with a cord, that is not a contradiction. Mindfulness is the thing that continuously binds the mind to the meditative object; however, awareness also in due course fastens the mind to the meditative object. One takes recourse to the recognition through awareness of the actual fact of fading and scattering or of the threat of fading and scattering in order to settle on the basic meditative object without falling into the power of those (faults); and because, as was previously quoted, the teacher Vasubandhu has declared that both mindfulness and awareness are the fastener to the meditative object.[73]

It is said that *samādhi* is accomplished by recourse to mindfulness, and it is said that mindfulness, like a cord, ties the mind continuously to the meditative object in concreteness. Therefore, the chief guardian method for the accomplishment of *samādhi* is the guardian method consisting of mindfulness. Furthermore, mindfulness owns the grasping pattern which has the aspect of certainty. Hence, when one is protecting the *samādhi* and is without the firm grasping pattern of conclusive awareness, even the appearance of the vivid part constituting clarity of mind is a sudden shock to the fixation (of mind); and when there is no issurance of the vivid part issuing with the strength of conclusive awareness, it (i.e., the appearance of the vivid part) does not originate along with the power of mindfulness; and for that reason it only occurs with protection of the *samādhi* when not obstructed by subtle fading.

One should be mindful of this precept: "Without settling on some other foundation of meditative object, such as the body of a deity, one guards only the nondiscursive thought of the mind; thus, one should settle the mind without any discursive thought whatever on any sensory domain." Then he must not allow the mind to issue forth (to another sensory domain), or to stray away (from the meditative object); and that nonstraying means the same as the mindfulness that does not allow the meditative object to slip away. That kind of contemplation without transgressing the method of protecting mindfulness, also must depend on the mindfulness evincing the force of conclusive awareness.

2. CLEARING AWAY THE TECHNIQUE WITH FAULT

One should clear away this certain wayward reflection: "Granted that there is practically no fault of fading when one settles (his mind) with no discursive thought in the manner previously explained, namely, by enhancing the casting of awareness, which restricts; but then there is much scattering (of thought) and one notices that he is unable to prolong the (mind's) fixation part, so the loftiness of the clear vision is again lowered. When one notices that the fixation part is quickly produced by relaxation of the restriction, his great precept is this means (*upāya*)." When they reach the conclusion from this train of thought, they loudly proclaim, "The best relaxation is the best cultivation."

That position makes no distinction between the production of fading and the production of cultivation. Indeed, a faultless *samādhi* requires the possession of two distinguished features as previously explained, but the firmness of the mind's fixation part without discursive thought does not by itself suffice. If it were that way, then (one might as well say) when drowsiness muddies the mind, there is fading; and when that (drowsiness) is absent, there is the vivid part consisting in the clarity of mind, wherefore the *samādhi* is faultless. This position does not distinguish between torpor and fading; consequently, I shall explain these two (states) extensively further on.

It means that either one has the vivid part through engaging in the strong clear vision of intense restriction (of the mind) and finds it difficult, by reason of the preponderance of scattering, to gain the fixation part; or else one has the fixation part through guarding with much relaxation, and, by reason of the preponderance of fading, has no vividness which evinces the strength (of the clear vision). Because it is very difficult to decide on the balance of firmness and relaxation that does not go on to either excessive restriction or excessive relaxation, it is difficult to generate the *samādhi* free from fading or scattering. Following the profound purport, the teacher Candragomin states:[74]

> When one takes recourse to endeavor, scattering ensues;
> When one avoids this, there is shrinking.

> Since it is difficult to achieve equipoise as the balance,
> What should my turbulent mind do?

"Taking recourse to endeavor" is excessive restriction; when one engages in this, scattering ensues. If, in avoiding this restriction, there is excessive relaxation, there arises the retreat of the mind's inward stability. Consequently, the mind's dwelling in equal parts free from fading and scattering is the meaning of the passage "it is difficult to achieve equipoise as their balance." That is the case, moreover, because Buddhaśānti writes in his commentary on that verse:[75] " 'Endeavor' means here proceeding with enclosure with a venture in the virtuous category"; and, "When he avoids this endeavor, i.e., gives up effort after noticing the fault that threatens to be a scattering, he shrinks within the mind."

The *Deśanāstava* also mentions:

> When one engages with zeal, scattering ensues.
> When one relaxes (from) this, there is shrinking.
> Since it is difficult to achieve success as their balance point.
> What should my turbulent mind do?

And its commentary explains it clearly:

> When there is effort, proceeding with enclosure, by reason of the great zeal the mind is assailed by the occurrence of scattering and distraction; so as a result of effort one does not achieve fixation of the mind.

Now, the work pointed out that it is difficult to achieve success as the balance point free from the two extremes of fading and scattering, or to achieve the *samādhi* of equipoise as their balance. Since there would be no occasion for difficulty if relaxation sufficed; and since the work said that fading arises as a consequence of this (relaxation), it is clear that such a method does not manage to accomplish *samādhi*. Āryāsaṅga lays down that it is not enough to have the vivid part with only the mind's clarity when it is overrelaxed, but that one must have the restriction part with the grasping pattern: "Among these, the mental orientation proceeding with enclosure belongs to him who settles and rightly settles (the mind)."[76] He thus refers to the first two thoughts among the nine means of mind fixation. The *Bhāvanākrama I* also says:[77] "He clears away fading and again should grasp more firmly precisely that meditative object." Besides, the *Bhāvanākrama II* says: "Thereupon, having removed fading, with his mind he sees very clearly the meditative object, whatever it be. That is what he should do." When that text speaks of seeing very clearly with the mind, it does not refer to just the vividness of the sensory domain but also refers to the exceedingly vivid and firm grasping pattern of discrimination.

This technique of relying on mindfulness is of highest importance. If one does not know this, then no matter how much he cultivates the tokens of protection he remains with numerous faults such as coursing in great forgetfulness and coursing in dullness of the insight which supernally investigates the natures (*dharma*); and when his *samādhi* is firm, it causes vanity. At the time when the mind is tied to the meditative object by mindfulness in the way previously explained, is it proper to arouse the discursive thought which supervises whether or not the meditative object is well grasped? This should be done, because the *Bhāvanākrama II* states:

> After one has settled his mind in that way on whatever desired meditative object, he should settle his mind continually pursuant to just that (meditative object). When he has settled (his mind) upon that (meditative object) he should investigate his mind this way: he should examine it, thinking, "Is (my) mind well held to the meditative object; or, is there fading; or is there a distraction due to the arising (in the mind) of an external sensory domain?"

Now, there is no such consideration when one abandons *samādhi*. And when one abides in *samādhi,* one may or may not be abiding in the basic meditation object as previously established; in the case when one is not abiding in it, one manages only to notice the passing into either fading or scattering. When one is settled in the *samādhi,* he should supervise at intervals that are neither too short nor too long. When one does it with merely no exhaustion of the strength and force of the previous discrimination, it is necessary to proceed for a long time in possession of that strength by continuous arousal of that discrimination, and necessary quickly to recognize fading and scattering. Accordingly, one protects by being just mindful, at intervals, of the previous meditative object; and because a great power of mindfulness is necessary as a basis for proceeding in continuity, there is the protective method of mindfulness. The *Śrāvakabhūmi* states (YS III):[78]

Among those, what is a single area of mind? He said—The stream of consciousness with mindfulness again and again, with matching meditative object, accompanied with continuity, irreproachable pleasure—is called *samādhi,* as well as a single area of virtuous mind. What is one mindful of again and again? He said—Whatever doctrines are upheld and heard, and whatever precepts and instructions are obtained from the gurus. When one has made that the ruler and faces toward the sign of the equipoised plane, one makes mindfulness conform, fastens it, yoked continuously, to that meditative object.

Furthermore, the *Madhyāntavibhāgaṭīkā* states:[79] " 'Mindfulness' means the non-slipping-away of the meditative object; 'meditative object' means the precept-entity, the mental recitation, to be fixed in the mind." Thus, taking recourse to mindfulness is so as to destroy the forgetfulness involved in straying from the meditative object. The non-slipping-away of the meditative object involving the destruction of that (forgetfulness) is recitation of the meditative object by the mind: again and again one orients the mind to the meditative object. For example, if one fears that he will forget something he knows, it will be hard to forget it if he again and again recalls it in his mind.

Hence mindfulness, at intervals, of the meditative object requires having the power of mindfulness; and supervision through holding the meditative object successively without the mind's straying away is the means of proceeding by having the power of awareness that fully recognize fading and scattering. So one should realize that it is very difficult to generate the possession of the power of mindfulness and of awareness if one is opposed (to those two requirements), thinking, "Such as that is also discursive thought."

3. TEACHING THE MEASURE OF WATCHES

Now, in regard to that tying of mind to the meditative object by mindfulness, is there or is there not a definite measure of watches, that could be termed "settling for so long an interval"? All the preceding gurus of the diverse lineages of Tibet said one must perform many brief watches. The reason given by some is that if one has the cultivation for short watches in good divisions, then he tastes the cultivation even during the in-between times, while if he has a lengthy watch he becomes tired. Others maintained that if one has a lengthy watch, it is easy to fall into the dominion of fading and scattering, as a consequence of which it is difficult to produce the faultless *samādhi*. The measure of watches is not set forth clearly in such great texts as the *Śrāvakabhūmi*. However, the *Bhāvanākrama III* states:[80] "One should engage (in meditation) in that order for as long as one is able, whether for twenty-four minutes, one and one-half hours, or three hours." That remark is made in the phase of watch measure for the time when one cultivates discerning and has already produced calming; however, it is obviously the same from the outset in the phase of producing calming; so one should act accordingly.

Furthermore, if, as previously explained, one practices at intervals with discursive thought the protective method of mindfulness and awareness, consisting in mindfulness of the meditative object and the view which supervises, no fault arises, whether the watch be brief or lengthy. However, generally the beginner observes too long a watch. Then, if he strays through the slipping-away (of the meditative object), his mind may have fading or scattering even for a long time, and unless he is acquainted (with such signs) he has no speedy determination (of what is happening). On the other hand, even if mindfulness does not slip away, it is easy for him to fall under the control of fading or scattering, and he has no speedy determination of the occurrences of fading and scattering. Of these two (possibilities), the former constitutes an interruption in the possession of the power of mindfulness; and the latter represents the interruption in the possession of the power of awareness. So it is very difficult (for that beginner) to break off the fading or scattering.

In particular, the nondetermination of the occurrence of fading or scattering when one strays after the meditative object slips away, is much worse than the nondetermination of the occurrence of fading or scattering when one does not forget the meditative object. Hence, it is of great importance to have the protective method for mindfulness, as previously discussed, that constitutes the opponent which impedes the failure of mindfulness when one is straying. It is necessary to have a brief watch if one has small force of awareness amounting to much forgetfulness in the event of straying and amounting to nondetermination promptly of fading and scattering. There is no fault in having either a brief or a long watch if one is able to recognize promptly the fading or scattering and if it is hard for the slipping-away to occur. Following the deep purport, [that *Bhāvanākrama* passage] expresses no certainty of the watch length, the twenty-four-minute period, and so on. In short, it is necessary to accord with the capacity of one's own discrimination; therefore (that passage) stated, "as long as one is able."

Moreover, if no adventitious impediment to body or mind occurs, one is equipoised. And if it occurs, one gives up the cultivation while performing industriously, and immediately thereupon has a cultivation which dispels the interruption of elements. That is the deep purport of the wise, so one should understand as an ancillary to the cultivation that one should do it that way no matter what the length of the watch.

III. HOW ONE PERFORMS AFTER FASTENING MIND ON A MEDITATIVE OBJECT

This has two sections: A. how one performs at the time fading or scattering occurs; B. How one performs at the time free from fading or scattering.

A. How One Performs at the Time Fading or Scattering Occurs

This has two sections: 1. Resorting to the opponent to nondetermination of fading and scattering; 2. Resorting to the opponent to the lack of effort to eliminate these, although one has determined them. The first has two sections: a. The fundamental characteristics of fading and scattering; b. The means of producing awareness that fully recognizes these at the time of the cultivation.

1. RESORTING TO THE OPPONENT TO NONDETERMINATION OF FADING AND SCATTERING

a. The Fundamental Characteristics of Fading and Scattering

Scattering is just as defined in the *Samuccaya:*[81]

What is "scattering"? The lack of pacification of mind included in the category of craving which follows after pleasant sign-sources; the agent which interrupts calming.

There are three aspects to this definition. The *object* is the sensory domain that is gratifying and pleasant. The *class* is the predominance of craving while the mind is unpacified and proceeds outward, so that one is involved with the class of thirst for sensory domains. The *agent* is the interrupter of fixation of mind on the meditative object.[82]

When the mind is tied to the meditative object, scattering with attachment to forms, sounds, and so on pulls the mind, powerless, to those sensory domains, and makes it stray, just as said in the *Deśanāstava:*

> Of what kind and in what manner calming has a
> meditative object,
> When one fixes the mind again and again thereon,
> The noose of defilement with the cord of craving for
> sensory domains
> Pulls that (mind) powerless from that (meditative object).

Now, is scattering an issuance of mind, causing straying away from the meditative object, by way of other defilements; or, again, is it an issuance to other virtuous meditative objects? Scattering has a preponderance of craving. Therefore, the straying by way of other defilements is not scattering, but is the straying to mental concomitants included among the twenty secondary defilements.[83] The issuance to a virtuous meditative object goes to some sort of virtuous thought or mental concomitant. Hence no (such) issuances are (classified as) scattering.

Regarding "fading," in many translations it was rendered also by "shrinking." That is not the same as the mind's "shrinking" from death.

The general run of meditators of the snowy mountain peaks maintained that the characteristic of fading is the fixation without issuing to other sensory domains and a torpor of mind involving no vividness and clarity (of the meditative object). This is not correct, because torpor is stated to be the cause of fading, and hence the two are distinct. The *Bhāvanākrama II* shows this point: "If, having been oppressed by torpor and sleepiness, the mind has fading or one notices the threat of fading. . . ." The point is also shown by the *Saṃdhinirmocana-sūtra:*[84] "If, by reason of torpor and sleepiness, defilements, with secondary defilements as the case may be, occur along with fading or equipoise, that is the inner straying of the mind." This sets forth that when, by the force of torpor and sleepiness, there is fading of mind, that is the inner straying. Furthermore, although the *Samuccaya* mentions fading in the section of straying consisting in secondary defilements, the straying discussed in that (text) also occurs with virtue, so it is not certain that (fading) is defiled.

Now, torpor is defined this way in the *Samuccaya:*[85]

What is torpor? The unserviceability of mind included in the category of delusion; the agent consorting with all the defilements and secondary defilements.

Therefore, it is the heaviness and unserviceability of body and mind with a predominance of delusion. The *Commentary on the Kośa* states:[86] "What is torpor? The heaviness of body; the heaviness of mind; the unserviceability of body; the unserviceability of mind."

In regard to fading: when the mind relaxes the grasping pattern which holds the meditative object, it fails to hold the meditative object in the sense of its being very vivid and firm. Hence, even if there is the clear portion, when there is no very vivid grasping pattern of the meditative object, one passes into fading, because the *Bhāvanākrama II* says:

At whatever time the mind does not see the meditative object vividly, like one born blind, or like a man entering a dark place, or like the winking of eye—at that time one should recognize that fading is occurring.

Other great texts do not treat clearly the characteristic of fading.

In fading there are both the virtuous and the unassured; while torpor has obscuration with the nonvirtuous and has the unassured, as the case may be, and is only the predominance of delusion.[87] Furthermore, according to the great texts, for dispelling fading, it is necessary to orient the mind to the delightful domain of the form of the Buddha's body, and so on, and to stimulate the mind by the contemplation of light. Hence, when one has opposed the nonvividness of the domain that is like the descent of darkness on the mind and has opposed the casting down and abasement of the grasping pattern of discrimination, it is necessary to have the two parts—vividness of the meditative object and restriction of the grasping pattern; but it does not suffice to have just the vividness of the domain or just the clarity of the domain holder.

It is easy to understand scattering, but fading has not been clearly determined in the great genuine texts. Thus, it is difficult to recognize, and at the same time is of highest importance because it is the great mishap in the faultless *samādhi.* Consequently, with fine discrimination one should well observe and determine (it) as set forth in the *Bhāvanākrama(s)* after relying on experience.

b. The Means of Producing Awareness That Recognizes Fading and Scattering

It does not suffice to have only the understanding of fading and scattering; but at the time of the cultivation, it is necessary to be able to produce the awareness that recognizes the exact situation of whether there is occurrence or nonoccurrence of fading or scattering.

Furthermore, when one develops gradually the possession of the power of awareness, how much more capable is he of arousing the awareness which determines fading or scattering immediately upon its occurrence! It is necessary to arouse the awareness that recognizes the incipient state when the concrete manifestation has not (yet) occurred, because the last two *Bhāvanākrama* (*II* and *III*) assert:[88] "He notices the fading of mind or the threat of fading," and "He notices the scattering of mind or the threat of scattering." As long as one has not aroused such awarenesses, he should not conclude, "From that time to this a faultless cultivation, free from fading or scattering, has been occurring," because he cannot be certain even when fading or scattering occurs, for the reason that he has not aroused the possession of awareness. On the same point, we cite the *Madhyāntavibhāga.*[89] "Full recognition of fading and scattering." Accordingly, when fading or scattering occurs, one does not know it and there is no possibility (of knowing it), when awareness has not been aroused; and even if one cultivates for a long time, say a year, the time may elapse with a subtle fading and scattering without his feeling it as the occurrence of fading and scattering.

Now, if one wonders how to generate that awareness, he should have the protective method of mindfulness that was already set forth: it is the other one of the two outstanding causes. Thus, if one is able to generate the continuous possession of mindfulness, he is able to oppose the slipping-away of the meditative object with consequent straying. Then he averts the lengthy insensitivity to the occurring of fading and scattering, because it is easy fully to recognize fading and scattering. The point becomes very clear when one observes (the situation) by traversing the experience of the long and the short times (respectively) for knowing fading and scattering at the time mindfulness is lost and for knowing fading and scattering at the time when it is not lost. Following the profound purport, the *Caryāvatāra* states:[90] "When mindfulness is seated at the gate of the mind for its protection, then awareness appears." Besides, the *Madhyāntavibhāga-ṭīkā* explains:[91] "Awareness is 'the full recognition of fading and scattering when there is no slipping away of mindfulness'; for mindfulness stationed nearby becomes possessed of awareness. Therefore, he said, 'when there is no slipping away of mindfulness.' "

One cause is the uncommon protective method for awareness. The mind takes as meditative object either holding the form of such things as the body of the deity or holding the form of such things as only the knowledge or only the vividness of the experience. Then, by way of recourse to mindfulness as previously explained, one holds his mind in continuous supervision of the issuance or nonissuance elsewhere than (the meditative object). This epitomizes the protection of awareness. Furthermore, it is just as the *Caryāvatāra* says:[92] "Just this in short is the characteristic of awareness: disciminating again and again the states of body and mind."

Hence, thereby one generates the awareness that recognizes the incipient state of fading and scattering, and the method of recourse to mindfulness opposes the slipping away that proceeds to straying. Therefore, one must well analyze the meditative object. Otherwise, all those discriminations are mixed together. And without the understanding which analyzes the meditative object, one guards according to [i.e., no better than] the guarding of now-a-days. The fruit of accomplishing with a bewildered basis is the fear that such a *samādhi* will collapse. Consequently, the great genuine and competent texts agree that it is of outstanding importance to have a foundation by the procedure of investigating with a very detailed investigation. But one should not place hope in perseverance alone, because the *Pāramitā-samāsa* states:[93] "His striving when exclusive is for utter exhaustion; when protected by insight is for the goal."

2. RESORTING TO THE OPPONENT TO THE LACK OF EFFORT TO ELIMINATE THESE, ALTHOUGH ONE HAS DETERMINED THEM

As previously explained, when one has performed well the protective method of mindfulness and awareness, he arouses the possession of exceeding power of mindfulness and awareness; and when he is able to recognize with awareness even very subtle fading and scattering, he has no fault consisting in the nondetermination of the occurrence of fading and scattering. But when one takes no recourse to the effort of opposing these two as soon as they occur, his submissive lack of effort or nonmotivation constitutes a very great fault of the *samādhi,* because in such a case discrimination goes no further and it is indeed difficult to generate a *samādhi* free from fading and scattering. Hence, one should cultivate the thinking-volition that is called "motivation or effort as the opponent to nonmotivation in the elimination of fading-and-scattering occurrence." This has two sections: a. Determination of the thinking-volition and the method of opposing fading and scattering; b. Whichever (thinking-volition) one takes recourse to, the determination of the causes productive of fading and scattering.

a. Determination of the Thinking-Volition and the Method of Opposing Fading and Scattering

One should understand it according to the definition in the *Samuccaya:*[94]

> What is thinking-volition? The mental action instigating thoughts; the agent which incites the mind to the virtuous, nonvirtuous, and indeterminate.

For example, without power of its own, iron moves by the power of a magnet. In the same way, the three kinds of thoughts, virtuous, nonvirtuous, and indeterminate, as the case may be, are swayed and exhorted by a mental concomitant, thinking-volition. So one takes hold of the thinking-volition that instigates the mind to eliminate fading or scattering, when either of these occurs.

Now, when one has exhorted the mind to eliminate fading and scattering, by what method does one oppose fading or scattering? [Considering that] the fading of mind is the loss of the grasping pattern following upon excessive fierceness in compressing (mind) within, one should orient the mind to a delightful entity constituting the cause for the mind to issue forth; e.g., to the exceedingly beautiful body of the Buddha, but (of course) not to the delight in producing defilements. Or he orients his mind to the sign of light, such as sunlight; and upon clearing up the fading, he immediately takes care to tighten the grasping pattern of the meditative object. The method is just as stated in the *Bhāvanākrama I:*[95]

When, overcome by torpor and sleepiness, and because the apprehension of the meditative object is not vivid, one's mind fades, then he should dispel the fading by the cultivation of the idea of light and by a mental orientation toward a gladdening entity, the merits of the Buddha, and so on. Thereafter, he should apprehend that same meditative object more firmly.

In such a case, he should not cultivate a jaded[96] meditative object, because distaste causes the mind to compress.

One also repulses the fading by being cheered through examination of any desirable sense domain that is examined with discriminative insight. Thus, the *Pāramitāsamāsa* says,[97] "When (the mind) is shrinking, he should stimulate it by a bright vision with the power of striving." Whether it be fading—the casting down and abasement of the grasping pattern of the meditative object, or shrinking—the excessive compression within, he repulses these by being cheered through stimulation of the grasping pattern and enhancement of the meditative object. The *Madhyamakahṛdaya* informs us:[98] "The one who has retreated should extend himself by cultivation of a far-flung meditative object"; and, "The one who has retreated should stimulate by observing the benefit of striving." Further, in agreement with the great scholars, the *Śikṣā-samuccaya* states:[99] "When his mind is shrinking, he should stimulate it with the cultivation of sympathetic joy." This alternate important opponent opposes the fading as follows: one meditates on such merits as the three jewels, the benefit of the resolve of enlightenment, the great purpose of obtaining the favorable states (of rebirth); one must be able to proceed like the man whose sleepy face is doused with cold water, who (then) proceeds with wide-awake cognizance. This (method) is dependent upon the experiences gained through the cultivation of discriminative examination of the categories of benefit.

On whichever cause fading is based for its production—torpor and sleepiness, or the nature attracting these two which has the form of the mind's darkness—when one relies on the opponent consisting of the cultivation of light, the fading based on these (causes) is not produced, or if (already) produced is repulsed.

The dignified deportment is set forth in the *Śrāvakabhūmi:* one walks; having well apprehended the sign of light, again and again cultivates it; stimulates his mind with any one of the six recollections, to wit, Buddha, Dharma, Saṅgha, morality, renunciation, or a deity; or with other pure meditative objects; recites by heart the doctrines which teach the disadvantages of torpor and sleepiness; gazes in different directions and at the moon and stars; douses his face with water.

Moreover, if the fading is very slight, or only occurs once, one should cultivate, restraining the grasping pattern of the mind. But if the fading is very strong, or occurs repeatedly, one should postpone the continuance of the *samādhi*'s cultivation; take recourse to those opponents, as appropriate; and having cleared up the fading, (again) should engage in the cultivation.

When the meditative object held by the mind, whether internally or externally directed, is not vivid, and either a slight or strong form like the descent of darkness on the mind, manifests; and without dispelling that (darkness), one were to cultivate, it is difficult to cut off the fading. As an opponent to that, one should cultivate repeatedly the manifestation of light. Thus, the *Śrāvakabhūmi* states (YS III):[100]

You must cultivate calming and discerning with a mind that is accompanied with light, accompanied with radiance, with a clear light, free from darkness! And when you are thus cultivating the idea of light on the path of calming and discerning, if at the outset there are unclear conviction toward and weak illumination on the meditative object, as a consequence of the cultivation and illumination—by that cause and by that condition—there will occur clarity and abundant illumination. And if at the outset there are clear [conviction and] abundant illumination, there will be even greater clarity and even more abundant illumination.

This sets forth that even if the meditative object is vivid in the beginning, one should cultivate—how much more if it is not vivid! Also, the sort of sign of light one apprehends is just as mentioned in the same work (YS III):[101] "Hold onto the sign of light, whether it be from a lamp, from the glow of a bon-fire, or from the solar disk!" This cultivation of the sign of light is not limited to the time of *samādhi,* but should be done also at other times.

Scattering is the wandering of the mind to sensory domains such as forms and sounds, by way of attachment. Hence, one should orient his mind to a mentally aroused topic that causes a gathering within the mind. As soon as scattering is thereby pacified, one should equipoise his mind on the previous meditative object. Thus the *Bhāvanākrama I* states:[102]

When he notices his mind scattered from time to time through remembrance of former laughter and delight, then he pacifies the scattering through a mental orientation to a sobering (mentally aroused) topic, such as impermanence. Thereupon, he should make an attempt to engage that same meditative object without instigation of the mind.

Also, the *Madhyamaka-hṛdaya* says: "Scattering should be pacified by a mental orientation toward impermanence and the like"; and "Straying should be gathered (back) by observing the disadvantages in the sign(s) of straying." Besides, the *Śikṣāsamuccaya* mentions:[103] "When there is scattering, one should pacify (it) with mental orientations of impermanence." Therefore, when scattering that is vehement or of long duration occurs, for a while one relaxes his cultivation, and the cultivation of aversion is the chief ingredient; but a single issuance of mind does not convey back or settle [the scattered straying]. When the amount of scattering is modest, one gathers in that issuance (of mind) and should tie it to the meditative object. Thus, the *Pāramitāsamāsa* states:[104] "One should restrain the scattering mind by means of calming"; and according to the sūtra, "who well settles the mind," which is mentioned in the *Bhūmivarga* [of Asaṅga] as the opponent to scattering.

Speaking only in generalities, when the mind is scattered, one should settle it on the meditative object; and when the mind has faded, one should activate a delightful sensory domain. Thus, the *Srāvakabhūmi* states (YS II):[105]

And when the mind is compressed within that way, he attains to shrinking, or sees the threat of shrinking. At that time he should promote and gladden (his mind) with one or other promoting sign that is favorable. In that way he promotes the mind. How does he settle (the mind)? At the time of promoting, (his mind) is again scattered or sees the threat of scattering. Then, in turn, he should compress (mind) within; he should settle (it) for calming.

When the mind is scattered, one should not orient the mind to a sensory domain that is cheering and delightful, because this is a cause for straying outward.

b. Determination of the Causes Productive of Fading and Scattering

The *Bhūmi-vastu* [of Asaṅga] states:[106]

What are the sign-sources of fading? *1*) Not guarding the doors of the senses, *2*) not adhering to moderation in food, *3*) not training in the practice of staying awake during the former and latter parts of night, *4*) not dwelling in awareness, *5*) practice in delusion, *6*) sleeping long, *7*) ignorance of the means, *8*) slothful accompaniment to desire, striving, thought, and investigation [*samādhis*], *9*) without performing the cultivation in calming or the pure form of calming, to orient the mind to a single direction of calming *10*) staying in the darkness of mind, *11*) taking no delight in fixation on the meditative object.

One should understand the "sign-sources of fading" in this context to be the causes of fading. Among these, "accompanied by sloth" should be added also to [the other three *samādhis,*] "striving," "thought," and "investigation."

Furthermore, the same work states:[107]

What are the sign-sources of scattering? As previously, the four beginning with "not guarding the doors of the senses," *5*) practice in lust, *6*) lacking the disposition to pacify (the mind), *7*) lacking a repellent object for the mind, *8*) ignorance of the means, *9*) as previously, excessive activation accompaniment to desire, etc. [*samādhis*], *10*) without performing the cultivation in striving or the pure form of promotion, to cultivate a single direction of that (promotion), *11*) discursive thought of relatives, etc. Any one of the natures agreeing with scattering causes the mind to stray.

The "signs of scattering" are the causes of scattering. "Excessive promotion" means an intense holding of mind on a delightful sensory domain. The desire, etc. accompanied by that [promotion] are the four, as previously given.

It follows that the four (practices) beginning with "restraint of the gates of the senses," previously set forth in the section devoted to the procedure of watch intervals, are of great importance for opposing both fading and scattering.[108] Moreover, when one has understood those causes (of fading and scattering) and endeavors to oppose the two (faults), (the four practices) are obviously of surpassing value for cutting off the fading and scattering.

By means of awareness one can recognize even subtle portions of fading and scattering; and no matter of what sort they are, it is necessary to not submit and to resist all (their) forms, because if one does otherwise that is said in the *Madhyāntavibhāga* to be the fault of *samādhi* called "lack of instigation." Hence, if one thinks, "I cut off in the very beginning the subtle forms of scattering and straying; since there is nothing (left) to cut off, I shall not (continue to) cut off," he deprives (himself) of the lessening. When there is no vehement expression of those (faults) and no especially long chain (of them), if one thinks, "Because they are weak and brief, their activity is not cumulative, so I need not cut them off," he lacks the instigation to eliminate those. Both those persons are ignorant of the method of perfecting the *samādhi* but feign to know it and they deceive those who pursue *samādhi,* because (both) are outside the way laid down by the Reverend Maitreya and others as the method of perfecting *samādhi.*

The general case for suppression of fading and scattering is that at the outset scattering and straying form the obstacle, so it is necessary to endeavor in cutting these off. Then, having endeavored that way, when one turns away the coarse part of scattering and straying and arrives at a minor portion of fixation (of mind), at that time he should endeavor to take heed of fading. When he has taken heed of fading by intensifying cognizance, in turn the subtle portion of the former scattering causes an interruption of the fixation. Thereupon, if, while endeavoring to cut that off, he does avert it, he proceeds to a great degree of fixation (of mind); and again at that time fading arises, whereupon he should endeavor to cut off the fading.

In short, one restores the mind from the scattered issuance and seeks the fixation part in an attachment to the meditative object within. When the fixation part occurs, in turn one takes great heed of fading and draws forth a strength of (the meditative object's) vividness. When one has performed these two (stages) in turn, he may perfect a faultless *samādhi*. However, he should not place hope in a fixation part with only clarity and lacking the vivid part accompanied with strength of the grasping pattern.

B. How One Performs at the Time Free from Fading or Scattering

As previously explained, one cultivates that cutting off of even subtle fading and scattering. When neither fading nor scattering occur unequally and one proceeds with equality of mind, at that time motivation or effort is the fault of the *samādhi*. Consequently, equanimity should be cultivated as the opponent to this (fault). The *Bhāvanākrama II* says the same:

> At the time there is no fading or scattering, one notices repose of mind toward that meditative object; then one should relax the effort and be equable; then one should abide (in that state) for as long as he wishes.

Now, what sort of fault is it when one operates with motivation or effort? At the time one becomes confident that fading and scattering do not occur in each suitable watch by reason of the cultivation of summoning the mind within when there is scattering and of stimulating it when there is fading, one guards by taking heed of fading and taking great heed of scattering just as at the outset. When one proceeds this way, it is necessary to know relaxation at that time, because (otherwise) straying occurs, just as the last two *Bhāvanākrama* (*II* and *III*) state:[109] "If one makes an effort when he is equipoised, at that time the mind strays."

Furthermore, although one relaxes the effort, he does not abandon the strength of the grasping pattern. Hence, this cultivation of equanimity is not done in all occasions when fading and scattering do not occur. For although it is done after having broken off the spike of fading and scattering, there is no equanimity (possible) at the time when the spike of fading and scattering is not broken off.

Now, what sort of equanimity is it? In general, three kinds of equanimity (*upekṣā*) are mentioned, namely equanimity of feeling, equanimity among the four boundless states, and the motivation kind of equanimity.[110] Of these, the one meant here is the motivation kind of equanimity. The *Śrāvakabhūmi* (YS III) defines it:[111]

What is equanimity? That sameness of consciousness—driven by repose and its own essence—of unstained mentality, when the meditative object has the category of [both] calming and discerning; and that serviceability of serviceable consciousness which is the effortless activity in the bestowal by consciousness.

When one cultivates a *samādhi* at the time of attaining the equanimity of this kind, he should perform directly this equanimity on the occasion when fading and scattering do not occur and should settle on a mild effort.

Its sign of meditative object is just as the same work states (YS III):[112]

The sign of equanimity is the meditative object by which he renders the mind equable, and just that meditative object toward which there is no engaging in an excess of striving.

Also, the time for cultivation of equanimity is just as the same work states (YS III):[113]

The time of equanimity is the time when the mentality, having the category of [both] calming and discerning, is free from fading or scattering.

These explanations of the method of generating that way the faultless *samādhi* are concordant with what the reverend Maitreya has stated in the *Madhyāntavibhāga:*[114]

The serviceability of the basis there;
Enrichment with all the goals;
The eight elimination motivations for the five faults;—
Arise from the relied upon cause.
Sloth, slipping away (of mindfulness),
Fading, scattering,
Lack of instigation, and instigation,—
The precepts assert to be the five faults.
The basis, and what is based thereon;
Its primary cause and just its fruit,
Not forgetting the meditative object,
Full recognition of fading and scattering,
The instigation to eliminate these (two),
And in the time of calm—repose.

In that passage, "the basis there" is based at the inception of striving so as to dispel the disconcordant side. There the *samādhi* with serviceability of mind is born. Moreover, it is the "foot" or basis of magical power which perfects all the goals, such as the supernormal faculties; hence, it causes enrichment with all the goals. What does one do to generate the *samādhi* of this sort? It arises from the cause of reliance on the eight motivations which motivate for the purpose of eliminating the five faults.

The five faults: At the time of preparation, *sloth* is the fault, because there is no preparation for *samādhi*. At the time of endeavor in *samādhi*, *forgetting the precept* is the fault, because when the meditative object slips away, the mind is not equiposed on the meditative object. When there is equipoise, *fading-scattering* is the fault, because these two produce unserviceability of the mind. At the time fading and scattering occur, *lack of effort* is the fault, because thereby these two are not pacified. When fading and scattering are absent, the *thinking-volition that motivates* is the fault. If fading and scattering are treated as one, there are five; if treated separately, there are six faults [the latter classification] being mentioned in the *Bhāvanākrama*(s).

Among the eight elimination-motivations which are the opponents to those (faults), there are four opponents to sloth: faith, desire, effort, and the cathartic. Then, the opponents to slipping-away, fading-scattering, lack of instigation, and instigation, in the given order, are (respectively) mindfulness, awareness that fully recognizes fading-scattering, thinking-volition that motivates, and equanimity with repose. These were previously discussed extensively.

Those are the chief precepts for perfecting *samādhi.* Accordingly, the great teacher Kamalaśīla in his three *Bhāvanākrama,* moreover the great scholars of India, have explained them in many (textual) sections for perfection of *samādhi:* and they are also explained in the *Commentary on the Pathapradīpa*[115] in the section dealing with calming. For this reason, the former (Tibetan) gurus of the Stages of the Path appear to have explained only the rough sequence and those desiring to cultivate meditation appear not to know how to do it. That is why it is laid down extensively (in this book).

That this *samādhi* with a single area of mind is rid of fading and scattering by means of mindfulness and awareness is the common one of all precepts of protection (of the *samādhi*). Consequently, one should not stick to the idea, "It is a doctrine by way of the vehicle of characteristics [of nontantric Buddhism], but is not necessary in the Tantras," for it is also stated in the *Anuttarayoga-tantra* division, and so is shared. Thus, the *Śrī-Saṃpūṭa* states in the second *rab byed* of the first *brtag pa:*

> The feet of magical power, accompanied with elimination-exertion motivation of desire-*samādhi*—which is based on detachment, based on freedom from craving, based on cessation, transformed into abandonment: by means of that desire one cultivates without further shrinking (within the mind) or overstimulation (of the mind). . . .

The text gives the same formula for striving-, comprehension-, and mind-*samādhi* [in place of "desire-*samādhi*" and "desire"].

That very serviceability of *samādhi* previously explained, having become the basis for accomplishing such merits as magical power, is comparable to feet, and hence (called) the feet of magical power.[116] There are four gates for accomplishing this, as explained in the *Commentary on the Madhyantavibhāga* and other works: 1) attainment through fierce desire, 2) attainment through lengthy striving, 3) attainment of *samādhi* through inspection of the meditative object, are called (respectively) desire-*samādhi,* striving-, and comprehension-*samādhi;* 4) attainment of a single area of mind by relying on the seed of former *samādhi* present in the mind, is called mind-*samādhi.* "Further shrinking" means excessive relaxation, and "overstimulation" means excessive restriction. The point is to guard so as to be free from these two.

B. The Stages of Generating the Fixations of Mind

This has three sections: I. The basic stages of generating mind fixation; II. The way of accomplishing this by means of six forces; III. The method of employing four mental orientations for this.

I. THE BASIC STAGES OF GENERATING MIND FIXATION

The nine thoughts are as follows:

1. *Settling the mind.* Having gathered the mind back from all external supports of consciousness, one fastens it to a meditative object within. Thus, the *Sūtrālaṃkāra* states:[117] "When he has fastened the mind upon the meditative object. . . ."

2. *Right settling.* When there is no distraction elsewhere of the mind which was fastened in the first place, there is right settling on the meditative object. Thus:[118] ". . . he does not distract its course."

3. *Settling in a stable way.* When one has become aware that (the mind) has been distracted by forgetfulness and has strayed outside, he again ties (it) to the same meditative object. Thus:[119] "Quickly perceiving a distraction, he drives (mind) back upon that (meditative object)."

4. *Vicinity settling.* The *Bhāvanākrama I* explains it as the settling by endeavor toward the same meditative object through elimination by awareness of the distraction of the former thought and through elimination of the distraction of the present thought. The *Prajñapāramitopadeśa* explains it as the continually higher settling through again and again condensing it from its naturally spread-out state and through rendering it small. This consistent with the text:[120] "The wise man to an ever higher degree compresses the mind within." The *Śrāvakabhūmi* explains that when at the outset mindfulness is stationed near by, the mind does not stray outside. Thus, when one has generated the power of mindfulness, there is no straying outside due to forgetfulness.

5. *Taming.* Having contemplated the merits of the *samādhi,* one is made delighted with the *samādhi.* Thus:[121] "Then, through seeing the merits [to be gained], he delights his mind in the *samādhi.*" The *Śrāvakabhūmi* explains that if the mind is distracted by any one of the sign-sources of the five sensory domains—form and so on, the three poisons [lust, hatred, and delusion], or the male and female—from the outset he should apprehend the disadvantages in these (sign-sources) and not grant an issuance of mind by reason of these ten sign-sources.

6. *Pacification.* Observing the fault of distraction, he pacifies the lack of delight in *samādhi.* Thus:[122] "Through seeing the fault of distraction, he pacifies the lack of delight in it." The *Śrāvakabhūmi* explains that if the mind is stirred up by such discursive thoughts as the discursive thought of craving and by such secondary defilements as the hindrance of sensuous lust, from the outset he should apprehend the disadvantages in these, and not grant an issuance of mind to these discursive thoughts and secondary defilements.

7. *Extreme pacification.* One pacifies the near occurrences of clinging, melancholy, torpor and sleepiness, etc. Thus:[123] "No sooner has he emerged [from the concentration] than he pacifies clinging, melancholy, and so on." The *Śrāvakabhūmi* explains that when slipping-away[of mindfulness] is produced, one does not accept, (rather) one eliminates these discursive thoughts and secondary defilements, already mentioned, whether arising or arisen.

8. *Making (the mind)-flow-one-pointedly.* One engages in endeavor in order to proceed without endeavor. Thus:[124] "Then the persevering one acquires the automatic driving attended with instigation to the mind. . . ." Furthermore, it is to be understood according to the *Śrāvakabhūmi* (YS III):[125] "He settles the course of *samādhi* without breaks, attended with instigation, and without interruption. Thus he makes it flow one-pointedly." (That text) also refers to the eighth thought with the name "rendering continuous," a name that is easy to understand.

9. *Natural concentration.* According to the *Bhāvanākrama* when the mind becomes even, equanimity is induced. The *Prajñāpāramitopadeśa* sets forth that as a consequence of cultivating [the eighth thought] the making-flow-one-pointedly, one proceeds automatically in a spontaneous manner and attains independence. Likewise:[126] "and [acquires] lack of instigation as a result of meditating on that [eighth thought]." The

Śrāvakabhūmi says "he naturally concentrates," the meaning of which the same work clearly explains, as follows (YS III):[127]

As a consequence of following it, cultivating it, and doing it repeatedly, one attains the path driving without effort, driving automatically. By reason of that lack of instigation and lack of effort, his course and mind-*samādhi* proceeds with no distraction. Thus he naturally concentrates.

Those names of the nine thoughts are derived as mentioned in the *Bhāvanākrama I:* "This path of calming was taught (by the Lord) in the *Āryaprajñāpāramitā* and other scriptures."[128]

II. THE WAY OF ACCOMPLISHING THIS BY MEANS OF SIX FORCES

There are six forces: the force of hearing, the force of pondering, the force of mindfulness, the force of awareness, the force of striving, the force of intimacy. The method of accomplishing which thoughts by which of those is as follows:

1. By the *force of hearing,* one accomplishes the settling thought. Having followed merely the hearing from another of the precepts for settling the mind on the meditative object, there is merely the initial tying to the meditative object, for there is (as yet) no cultivation through meditating (on it) again and again by oneself.

2. By the *force of pondering,* one accomplishes the right settling thought. He again and again ponders and guards the prolongation of the initial tying to the meditative object, because at first he acquired scarce capacity to extend the continuity.

3. By the *force of mindfulness,* one accomplishes both the settling-in-a-stable-way thought and the vicinity-settling thought. When one has strayed or is straying from the meditative object, he should consolidate within through mindfulness of the former meditative object, because if one generates the power of mindfulness at the outset, there is no cause for straying from the meditative object.

4. By the *force of awareness,* one accomplishes both the taming thought and the pacification thought. He recognizes with awareness the disadvantages of issuance to the signs of discursive thoughts and secon-

dary defilements, because he does not grant an issuance to the latter two when he observes their disadvantages.

5. By the *force of striving,* one accomplishes both the extreme-pacification thought and the making-flow-one-pointedly thought. With effort he eliminates and does not accept even subtle occurrences of discursive thoughts and secondary defilements, because when he performs that way, fading, scattering, and the other faults are unable to interrupt the *samādhi;* and he perfects the *samādhi* which arises without breaks.

6. By the *force of intimacy,* one accomplishes the natural-concentration thought, because of the tremendous force of cultivating the previous (thoughts) produces a *samādhi* which proceeds with the character of effortlessness.

These (descriptions) are according to the purport of the *Śrāvakabhūmi.* Hence, one should not place credence in explanations differing from them.

The situation when there is the ninth thought can be illustrated this way: if one highly cultivates the recitation of texts and the like, when he recites subsequently to his initial arousal of recitation, then even though in the interim his mind had strayed to other matters, this recitation by heart is not cut off but comes forth without effort. In the same way, when there is natural concentration for a single time by reason of the mindfulness that fastens mind to the meditative object for the first time, thereafter mindfulness and awareness, (the masters) say, "even if not continually relied upon, are able to proceed for a long time without break when the issuance of that *samādhi* is uninterrupted." The continuity of mindfulness and awareness, they say, "does not require the effort of reliance; hence, there is no instigation or effort of endeavor." For its production by reason of the former effort of mindfulness and awareness, they say, "By relying, it is necessary to produce a *samādhi* that carries on for a long time when the nonconcordant side of fading, scattering, etc. cannot interrupt; and that is the eighth thought. The latter and the ninth one are alike in that the nonconcordant side for the *samādhi* consisting of fading, scattering, etc. cannot interrupt (either one). Besides, in that one (i.e., the eighth) one must take recourse to mindfulness and awareness without gaps; hence it is attended by instigation or the effort of endeavor."

For its production, when even subtle fading, scattering, etc., occur, one must not accept them, (rather) must oppose them; hence, the seventh thought is necessary. For its production, it is necessary to recognize the disadvantages in straying through discursive thoughts and secondary defilements, and to possess the force of awareness that supervises so that there is no issuance to those; hence, the fifth and sixth thoughts are necessary, because these two are accomplished when the force of awareness is already present. Similarly, for its production, it is necessary to have mindfulness quickly of the meditative object when one is distracted from the meditative object, as well as have mindfulness not to create a distraction from the meditative object in the first place; hence, the third and fourth thoughts are necessary, because these two are accomplished by those two mindfulnesses. For its production, furthermore, it is necessary to tie the mind to the meditative object in the beginning, and having tied, not to distract its continuity; hence, one arouses previously the first and second thought.

Accordingly, in short, in the beginning one pursues the precept that was heard and should well perform the method [leading to] the natural concentration of mind. Thereafter, having been settled this way, one again and again meditates on that (precept) and guards the continuity, albeit with scarce capacity to prolong it. Thereafter, if one loses mindfulness and strays, he quickly compresses it and is quickly mindful of the slipping-away of the meditative object. Thereafter, he generates the power of mindfulness and generates the force of mindfulness which does not stray from the outset from the meditative object. Having perfected the possession of the force of mindfulness, he generates intense awareness that supervises by way of observing such faults as fading and scattering which involve straying away from the meditative object. Thereafter, if he is distracted by a subtle slipping-away, he immediately recognizes (the state of affairs) and breaks off its course; and having broken it off, he generates the force of effort which avoids for ever longer duration the course of interruption by the nonconcordant side. When he has generated this (effort), he cultivates through endeavor. As a consequence, he soars into mystic perfection of the cultivation and perfects the ninth thought, which proceeds in the *samādhi* without the effort of the endeavor. Hence, the yogin who is progressing upward but has not yet attained the ninth thought must apply effort to settle the mind in *samādhi*. When he has attained the ninth thought, on that account he does not engage in an effort of concentration, but the mind is enveloped in *samādhi*.

If one does not attain the cathartic although attaining this ninth thought of such a kind, then, as will be explained below, besides not being settled in the attainment of calming, how much less does one attain discerning! Nevertheless, as will be explained below, there are a great many persons who maintain that if one obtains an endowment with the pleasure, vividness, and nondiscursive thought of a *samādhi* like that, he arouses the knowledge which has no discursive thinking and which mingles the natural concentration and the after-attainment; and who in particular maintain that the perfection of the stages of completion (*saṃpannakrama*) of the *Anuttarayoga(tantra)* occurs in this ninth thought that was portrayed in the *Śrāvakabhūmi*.

III. THE METHOD OF EMPLOYING FOUR MENTAL ORIENTATIONS [FOR THIS]

The *Śrāvakabhūmi* states (YS III):[129]

When there is the fixation of mind of nine kinds one should recognize four mental orientations—*1*) proceeding with enclosure, *2*) proceeding with interruptions, *3*) proceeding without interruptions, *4*) proceeding without effort. Among these, the mental orientation proceeding with enclosure belongs to him who settles and rightly settles. The mental orientation proceeding with interruptions belongs to him who settles in a stable way and settles in the vicinity, who tames, pacifies, and extremely pacifies. The mental orientation proceeding without interruptions belongs to him who makes flow one-pointedly. The mental orientation proceeding without effort belongs to him who naturally concentrates.

At the time of the first two thoughts there is (the mental orientation) proceeding with enclosure because of the necessity to enclose (or, restrict) by endeavor. In the phase of the succeeding five thoughts (i.e., nos. 3–7) there is (the mental orientation) proceeding with interruptions because there is no capacity to protect for a long time when fading and scattering interrupt. Afterward, during the eighth thought there is (the mental orientation) proceeding without interruptions because of the ability to protect for a long time when fading and scattering are unable to interrupt. Thereupon, during the ninth thought there is induced the mental orientation proceeding without effort because there are neither interruptions nor the necessity to take continuous recourse to effort.

Now, is it the case that there are also interruptions in the phase of the first two thoughts as well as the requirement of enclosure in the phase of the middle five thoughts? And then why is the mental orientation proceeding with interruptions not set forth for the first two, and the mental orientation proceeding with enclosure not set forth for the middle five? In the case of the first two thoughts, the mind both passes into *samādhi* and does not pass into that, in the latter event for a long time; while in the case of the middle five it is based in *samādhi* for a long time. Consequently, one assigns the designation "interruption of *samādhi*" to the latter group (i.e., the middle five) and does not assign it to the former group (i.e., the first two). For that reason, although the two groups are alike in having the proceeding with restriction, they differ in having and lacking the proceeding with interruptions; consequently, one does not place those five thoughts in the mental orientation proceeding with restriction.

Accordingly, one accomplishes calming if, after becoming based in the equipment that was previously explained, he relies continuously on the striving to perfect *samādhi;* but it is explained that he does not accomplish it if, after having practiced only a few times, he again gives up his training. Thus the *Pāramitāsamāsa* states:[130]

> He should engage in the enterprise of dhyāna with constant yoga.
> For not relaxing and relaxing while applying friction would he get a fire.
> Just that is the praxis in yoga, except for the *viśeṣādhigama.*[131]

III. [BY REASON OF THE CULTIVATION] THE STANDARD OF ACCOMPLISHMENT OF CALMING

Here there are three sections: A. Teaching the demarcation between the perfected and the unperfected states of calming; B. The general teaching of the method of walking the path after taking recourse to calming; C. In particular, teaching the method of walking the mundane path.

A. Teaching the Demarcation between the Perfected and the Unperfected States of Calming

This has two sections: I. Teaching the basic meaning; II. The marks of having the mental orientation, together with removal of doubts.

I. TEACHING THE BASIC MEANING

One protects through well understanding the method of protection of the *samādhi* in the way already explained, and so produces the nine thoughts in sequence, and is able to protect for a long time with the ninth thought free from subtle fading and scattering. Then, has one or has one not attained calming when he has attained the *samādhi* that comes forth by itself without dependence on the effort of endeavor that relies on continuous mindfulness and awareness? That will be explained. Thus, when one has attained this *samādhi* there are two cases: he has or has not attained the cathartic. Then, if he has not attained the cathartic, that (situation) is favorable to calming, but is not an actual calming, and so is called "mental orientation favorable to calming." The *Saṃdhinirmocana-sūtra* clearly states this:[132]

"O Lord! As long as that Bodhisattva orients his mind within, with thought having thought as its meditative object, and has not attained the cathartic of body and the cathartic of mind, what shall this mental orientation be called?" "Maitreya, this is not calming. It should be referred to as 'furnished with a conviction favorable to calming.' "

Also the *Sūtrālaṃkāra* states:[133]

. . . and [acquires] lack of instigations as a result of meditating on that [eighth thought].

Then, when he has attained a subtle cathartic of body and mind,
He is known as "having the mental orientation."

The expression "mental orientation" refers in the present context to calming, as will be clarified below by citation of the *Śrāvakabhūmi.*

Furthermore, the *Bhāvanākrama II,* in the following passage, mentions the requirement both to attain independence when fixed on the meditative object, and to have the cathartic:

When one has cultivated calming that way, at whatever time there is the cathartic of body and mind and there is the mastery of the mind over the meditative object exactly as desired, at that time he has perfected his calming.

For that reason, when the *Bhāvanākrama I* says,[134] "When the mind proceeds as long as desired on the meditative object and is carried without instigation, then calming is perfected," it intends the presence of the cathartic as well, because that was clearly stated in the *Bhāvanākrama II.* Besides, the equanimity mentioned by the *Madhyāntavibhāga* among the eight elimination-motivations is essentially one with the ninth thought of the present context, and this does not suffice because the cathartic is also set forth among those (eight). (Finally), the *Prajñāpāramitopadeśa* also states the case clearly:

This Bodhisattva, solitary, in a lonely place, orients his mind to the so-meditated entity. Abandoning "mind-talk," he orients his mind many times to consciousness itself, so manifesting. As long as the cathartic of body and mind has not arisen, it is a mental orientation favorable to calming. At whatever time (the cathartic) arises, then (the mental orientation) is calming.

All those (citations) also establish the meaning of the sūtra *Saṃdhinirmocana.*

Now, what plane incorporates the highest *samādhi* in which the cathartic has not arisen? That *samādhi* is incorporated by the plane of the realm of craving, because when one incorporates it in any one of the nine planes of the three realms,[135] it is not at or beyond the threshold of the First Meditation, and because if one attains that threshold he assuredly attains calming. While there is a similar *samādhi* in the stage of craving, it is a stage without equipoise. The reason it is not set down as an equipoised stage is that it is not accomplished with lack of regret, the best kind of rapture and pleasure, and the cathartic. That is the position of the *Bhūmi-vastu:*[136]

Why is it that only it is called "stage of equipoise," while any single area (of mind) belonging to the realm of craving is not? As follows:—That *samādhi* is accomplished with lack of regret, the highest rapture, the cathartic, and pleasure. However, the one that ranges in craving is not this way. (Still,) there is no lack of thinking-volition that approaches right doctrine in the realm of craving.

Accordingly, if one has not attained the cathartic, the *samādhi* appearing as though going by means of its own energy when there is no continuous reliance on mindfulness and no inquiry of mind, and able to consort with all the postures of going, walking, lying down, and sitting, is called "single area of craving mind," but one should know it is not proper to posit this as a concrete calming.

Now, of what sort is the way of attaining the cathartic; and having attained it, of what sort is the way of proceeding in calming? Here, one should understand the cathartic as stated in the *Samuccaya:* [137]

What is the cathartic? The serviceability of body and mind for catharsis of the contamination of body and mind; the agent extracting all the obstacles.

The contamination of body and mind is the uselessness for service exactly as desired in accomplishing virtuous deeds of body and mind. Its opponent, the cathartic of body and mind, because freeing from the contamination of body and mind, is the serviceability for service in virtuous deeds of body and mind. Moreover, if one has effort to abandon the defilements constituting the contamination of body—which interrupts the delight in abandoning defilements and which is the category of defilement—and if one has freed (himself) from the unserviceability, such as heaviness, of body, the animation and lightness of his body is the serviceability of body. Similarly, if one has effort to abandon the defilements constituting the contamination of mind—which interrupts the delight in abandoning defilements and which is the category of defilement—and if one has freed (himself) from what is useless for infusing delight and joy in fastening on a virtuous meditative object, his mind's prevailing without hindrance on the meditative object is the serviceability of mind. The *ācārya* Sthiramati speaks along the same lines:

Among those, the serviceability of body arises from the animation and lightness in the body's own actions. The serviceability of mind has its cause in the well-being and lightness of mind causing it to embark upon the right mental orientation and is the exchange (*parivṛtti*) of the mental-concomitant natures. When one possesses the latter (serviceability), he prevails without hindrance on the meditative object, and for that reason it is called "serviceability of mind."

In short, when one attains the cathartic, it is difficult for him to engage, as do those who crave to enterprise the abandonment of defilement and yet engage voluntarily in evil deeds, because he shrinks (from such deeds) and wards off the unserviceability of body and mind, whereupon his body and mind gain superior service and delight.

When one has attained his first *samādhi* that involves the consummation of the serviceability of body and mind of the sort (above described), (only) a subtle fraction occurs. This becomes ever larger, and in the end there is the calming consisting of the cathartic and the single area (of mind). Moreover, in the beginning it is difficult to recognize because of the subtlety; later it is easy to recognize. Thus the *Śrāvakabhūmi* states (YS III):[138] "At first, at the time of inaugurating the right training, a subtle cathartic of body and mind arises that is difficult to discern." And that work states (YS III):[139]

When his subtle single area of mind and his cathartic of mind and body are increasing, he drives toward the single area of mind and the cathartic of mind and body that is obvious and easy to discern, namely, (he drives) in a manner which is a successively higher chain-reaction.

The arising of this cathartic which has its characteristics perfected and which is easy to discern, has a portent as follows: The person who is exerting himself in the cultivation of the *samādhi* imagines a heavy deadweight on his head, and it is not a distressing weight. No sooner does that arise than he becomes free from the contamination of mind which interrupts the delight in abandoning defilements, and the opponent to that (contamination), the cathartic of mind, had arisen prior. Thus the *Śrāvakabhūmi* says (YS III):[140]

A short time before his obvious cathartic of mind and body and the single area of mind become easy to discern, it is said there will occur a portent (*pūrvanimitta*), the appearance of a weight on his head, and this is not a sign of harm. No sooner does this occur, than his mind contamination in the category of defilements that interrupt the joy of elimination, is (itself) eliminated; and, as its opponent {or, supplantor}, the serviceability of mind and the cathartic of mind arise.

Then, on the basis of the power engendered along with that cathartic having the serviceability of mind, a wind that is the cause for the production of the cathartic of body, courses in the body. While that wind is coursing throughout the parts of the body, one becomes free from the contamination of body, and the opponent to the contamination of body, the cathartic of body arises. Moreover, after it has proceeded through the whole body, the power of the serviceable wind gives rise to a radiance which seems to fill up (the body). Thus the *Śrāvakabhūmi* says (YS III):[141]

As a result of its production, the great elements (*mahābhūta*), urged by the wind, and concordant with the production of the cathartic of body, course in the body. By reason of their coursing, there disappears any contamination of body in the category of defilement that creates an obstacle for the joy in elimination. Also, the whole body is filled with its opponent, the cathartic of body, as though it were a radiance.

Among them, the cathartic of body is highly gratifying for the tangibles within the body, but it is not a mental concomitant, because the *ācārya* Sthiramati draws from the sūtras:[142]

One may recognize it as the cathartic of body if one is seized by an extraordinary rapture of the tangibles of the body. While the mind is delighted, the body has the cathartic.

Accordingly, at the time when at first the cathartic of body is produced, the power of wind arouses a great consciousness of pleasure in the body. On the basis of this, there also occurs in the mind a supernal consciousness of rapture and pleasure. Subsequently, the initially generated impetus of the cathartic gradually dwindles; and after the cathartic is exhausted, it (the rapture) does not proceed. However, by reason of that obvious fact, the mind has much perturbation; and when one wards that off, a cathartic slight like a shadow and equal to the immobile *samādhi* occurs. Also, when one wards off (the disquiet over) the disappearance of the rapture of mind, and thereafter fixes his mind firmly on the meditative object, (his mind is) moved by a great rapture, and despite this he attains the calming free from lack of calm. Thus the *Śrāvakabhūmi* says (YS III):[143]

When this takes place for the first time, at that time there appears in the mind a delight of mind, rejoicing in the good mental orientation of the mind, and manifest joy in the accompanying meditative object. Subsequent to this, the impetus of the cathartic taking place for the first time gradually becomes very attenuated, and the following cathartic proceeds in the body like a shadow.[144] And whatever is the delight of mind, that also disappears. The mind—its aspect pacific—proceeds, held fast by calming, upon the meditative object.

When it has transpired in that fashion, it is said that one "has attained calming," or, as (previously) quoted, is "having the mental orientation," which amounts to "has attained the mental orientation," because he has attained the other one (of two)—the small mental orientation belonging to the equipoised stage, by reason of his attaining the calming incorporated by the threshold of the First Meditation. This is also stated in the *Śrāvakabhūmi* (YS III):[145]

Later on, this yogin, a beginner, becomes possessed of the mental orientation, and is counted as "having the mental orientation." For what reason? Because he has attained for the first time the small mental orientation belonging to an equipoised stage and ranging in (the realm of) form. Therefore he is said to be "having the mental orientation."

"Equipoised stage" means the named ones of the two higher realms [i.e., the realm of form and the formless realm].[146]

II. THE MARKS OF HAVING THE MENTAL ORIENTATION

These are the marks and signs to be recognized by oneself and by others with the words "When he possesses these, he has attained the mental orientation." The one who has attained that way has attained in small measure these four (marks): *1*) the mind comprised by the realm of form, *2*) the cathartic of body, *3*) the cathartic of mind, *4*) a single area of mind. Besides, he has these (marks): possession of the capacity to purify defilements by means of the path formed of calmness and coarseness or formed of the (Noble) Truths; the speedy arising of the cathartic of body and mind whenever he equipoises himself within; the nonoccurrence, as a rule, of the five hindrances, sensuous lust, etc.;[147] some cathartic of body and mind even at the time when he has emerged from equipoise. Along these lines, the *Śrāvakabhūmi* states (YS III):[148]

These marks belong to the beginner having the mental orientation: he attains in a small degree the mind ranging in (the realm of) form, (as well as) the small cathartic of body, cathartic of mind, and single area of mind; he has the potentiality, the capability of training in the purification-of-defilement meditative object,[149] and his stream of consciousness proceeds smooth. Since he is enwrapped by calming, he purifies the addiction.

And (YS III):[150]

. The mind and body of that person who is seated in introspection and who is settling the mind, speedily gain the cathartic. The contaminations of body scarcely harm, and the hindrances do not operate inordinately.

And (YS III):[151]

Furthermore, when one has emerged (from that *samādhi*) and is occupied with his (ordinary) mind, some measure of the cathartic continues in his body and mind. The mental orientation's marks and signs consistent therewith should be understood as pure.

Accordingly, when one has attained the mental orientation possessing thses marks, it is very easy for the path of calming to become pure, to wit:—at the conclusion of the equipoise in the calming consisting of a single area of mind, he is able to drive toward the cathartic of body and mind, so that the cathartic increases. Moreover, to the extent that the cathartic increases, the calming of a single area increases, and they mutually increase each other. This is stated in the *Śrāvakabhūmi,* as follows (YS III):[152]

To the extent that the body and the mind gain the cathartic, to this extent they increase the seat of the single area of mind upon the meditative object. To the extent that the single area of mind increases, to this extent the body and mind gain the cathartic. Hence, two natures, namely, the single area of mind and the cathartic, are mutually based and mutually dependent.

In short, when there is the serviceability of mind, the wind and mind proceed together, and so the serviceability of wind arises. At that time, the cathartic of body become superior. When that happens, a special *samādhi* arises in the mind. That, moreover, accomplishes a special serviceability of wind, and so one drives toward the cathartic of body and mind, as previously explained.

IIa. [THE MARKS (cont.):] REMOVAL OF DOUBTS

Accordingly, it was explained in the phase of the ninth thought without predication that it induces *samādhi* of mind although one engages in no effort of endeavor to prolong mindfulness and awareness. Moreover, one possesses the strength of the vivid part which forbids the subtle element of fading. As was explained previously in the phase of the cathartic of body, through the power of the serviceability of wind the *samādhi* confers a surpassing pleasure to the body and mind. As was explained previously in the phase of the marks, there is for the most part no movement of the secondary defilements such as sensuous lust; and besides, at the time of emerging from the equipoise, one has the merit of being not divorced from the cathartic.

[The question is raised:] When this (*samādhi*) is produced, in which phase of the five paths is it posited?[153] There are a great many persons of former and present times who, in connection with the production of a *samādhi* of this sort, generally posit it in the path of the Great Vehicle; and, who in particular, when they observe that by reason of the cathartic and the concordant wind the whole body seems to be filled with pleasure, that based (on the foregoing) a great thought of pleasure in body and mind arises, and that, moreover, (the *samādhi*) possesses the special feature of nondiscursive thought and of exceeding vividness—maintain that it is the *yoga* which perfects the characteristics of the stages of completion of the *Anuttarayoga*(*tantra*). However, when one examines (the matter) after taking recourse to the authoritative texts which clearly teach the stages of *samādhi*—the great texts such as those by the Reverend Maitreya and by Āryāsaṅga, and the *Bhāvanākrama* of the Mādhyamika, etc.—one would be unable to posit it in the path of the Small Vehicle, let alone the Great Vehicle, because the *Śrāvakabhūmi* sets forth that also the mundane paths which are seen to be formed of the calmness and coarseness for accomplishing the main part of the First Meditation take recourse to and accomplish this *samādhi.* For that reason, the outsider seers, who free themselves from attachment to the Base of Nothing-at-all and lower planes by means of the mundane path, must pass to higher paths on the basis of this (*samādhi*). Consequently, the *samādhi* is common to the outsider and the insider.

Furthermore, when one has the view which recognizes selflessness in an errorless manner and well comprehends the fault of the entire phenomenal existence, he is discontented with cyclical flow. When he is seized by the aspiration for the way of emancipation which has liberation as its goal, the path of liberation arises; and when he is seized by the jewel of the mind of enlightenment, the path of the Great Vehicle also arises. For example, it is as when one is seized by those aspirations of giving which feeds a meal of meat and water to an animal and of guarding an instance of morality; in that order they become the equipment for the paths of liberation and omniscience. However, in the present case [of the samādhi under discussion], by way of seizure by a different path, there is no examination of either going or not going along the paths of liberation and omniscience, rather the examination is of the going along a path by way of the essence of that *samādhi.*

Although the Mādhyamika and the Cittamātra schools disagree on how to establish the objective topic for the view of discerning, in general they do not disagree on the determination of calming and discerning or on the general way of arousing in the stream of consciousness the full comprehension of these two. Hence, Āryāsaṅga stated in his *Bodhisattvabhūmi, Viniścayasaṃgrahaṇī,* (*Abhidharma*) *samuccaya,* and *Śrāvakabhūmi* that when one is accomplishing calming among the separate performance of calming and discerning, he accomplishes it by the sequence of the nine thoughts. Furthermore, as it is laid down extensively in the *Śrāvakabhūmi,* (Asaṅga) did not admit those *samādhis* in the course of accomplishing discerning, so in those texts discerning is explained apart from the nine thoughts, and its course of accomplishment is explained separately in the *Śrāvakabhūmi.* Likewise, the Mādhyamika *Bhāvanākra-*

ma texts and the *Prajñāpāramitopadeśa* explain separately the path of calming consisting of the nine thoughts and the path of discerning; and as this does not depart from the statements in the Maitreya doctrine or from their exposition by Asaṅga, all the great way-layers (of the Vehicle) show an identical purport regarding this point.

If pleasure and vividness have proved their occurrence as explained in the *Śrāvakabhūmi,* is it just a calming without the profundity of nondiscursive thought? And if it has nondiscursive thought, is it a *samādhi* of voidness? Whatever be the meaning of "profundity" in "profundity of nondiscursive thought,"[154] one gets the correct view with discriminative insight; and thereupon acts to settle with no discursive thought, or acts only to settle with no discursive thought and no understanding of anything. In the first case, we further maintain that one of this kind is a *samādhi* of voidness. If you grant this, one distinguishes the presence or absence of understanding of the view of the manner of being. It is valid to distinguish and proclaim these as follows: first positing the view of the person with the presence of the view—his guardings of nondiscursive thought are the cultivation of the *samādhi* of profound voidness; the person without the understanding of the view—his cultivation of contemplations with no discursive thought anywhere is not the cultivation of the *samādhi* of profound voidness. But one should not say this: every sort of cultivation of no thinking-volition at all is a meditation on the wishless, the signless, or voidness [gates].

If one maintains that all cultivations which settle the mind with no discursive thought whatever and no examination whatever are a *samādhi* of voidness quite apart from whether there is a presence or absence of the view which fully comprehends voidness, then one would have to acknowledge as *samādhis* of voidness also those *samādhis* which belong to the category of a calming set forth in the *Śrāvakabhūmi,* as previously discussed, and which are not so maintained (in that work). This is because also in their case, at the time of being settled in *samādhi,* there is a weak power of mindfulness and awareness, and aside from a few occasional supervisions when one guards the nondiscursive thought, there is a minimum of ideas of the type "This is this," "This is not this." Hence the *Saṃdhinirmocana-sūtra* sets forth as the meditative object for the *samādhis* which accomplish calming the reflected image without discursive thought.

Besides, of the two, calming and discerning, calming is explained as follows in the *Śrāvakabhūmi* (YS II):[155]

At this time, the meditative object becomes a reflected image without discursive thought, wherein he settles one-pointed mindfulness by a single part, but does not further view, does not investigate, does not supernally investigate, does not consider (that meditative object), and does not fall into profound comprehension.

Also the same work states (YS III):[156]

When the mind has attained calming in that way, if by reason of the slipping-away of mindfulness, or through the fault of lack of repeated practice—sign-sources, discursive speculations, or secondary defilements make an appearance, show an opening, provide a support of consciousness, he should not be mindful of, and should pay no attention to those whether arising or arisen, namely, through his being governed by the former observation of the disadvantages. Thus, by reason of lack of mindfulness and lack of attention, that support of consciousness is destroyed, dispelled and is relegated to nonappearance.

It sets forth this passage in the phase of accomplishing limited to calming, and sets it forth in the phase of accomplishing calming according to authoritative texts as the cultivation of settling without the guarding through understanding. Consequently, the contention that all cultivations with no discursive thought at all are the procedure for cultivating voidness is a jest of scholars. In particular, this *Śrāvakabhūmi* scripture well refutes the contention that any statement about cultivating without mindfulness and without attention (= mental orientation) concerns the cultivation of voidness.

Moreover, the *Bhāvanākrama I* says:[157] "This is the general characteristic of all calmings because only a single area of mind is the intrinsic nature of calming." The *Prajñāpāramitopadeśa* also says, "One should cultivate calming by focusing on that very consciousness which manifests [objective] diversity and by abandoning mind talk (*manojalpa*)." "Mind talk" is the discursive thought "This is this." Besides, we have already explained many times by quotations from scriptures, such as the one previously cited from (*Ārya-*)*Ratnamegha,* "Calming is a single area of mind," and by quotations from the texts of the great waylayers of the Vehicle, that calming has no discursive thought whatsoever.

Hence, there are both a nondiscursive thought of cultivating *samādhi* and a nondiscursive thought which has not even the slightest comprehension of voidness. Therefore, one should not take every sort of occurrence of nondiscursive thought with pleasure and vividness as being cultivation of voidness.

Accordingly, these (remarks) teach only aspects; and when one well endeavors, he should know the way to accomplish calming and discerning as elucidated by Maitreya, Asaṅga, and so on. If he does not proceed in this way, he is mistaken regarding certain *samādhis* which settle with no discursive thoughts but do not arrive at calming, and (is mistaken) regarding the discerning which severs the root of phenomenal existence. Then, having become conceited in the lack of a support of consciousness, as time goes on he will certainly deceive himself and others.

The texts of the authoritative savants declare that when one newly accomplishes calming, he cultivates only the settling without discursive thought, i.e., the fixation cultivation; and that when one accomplishes discerning for the first time, he cultivates the examination through analysis by discriminative insight. But when one holds that all discursive thought is [false] imputation of truth and rejects all of it, he perverts the good understanding of the authoritative texts and fails to reach the errorless view of selflessness. The positing of no discursive thought whatsoever to be the contemplation of the profound meaning of discerning is exclusively the school of the Chinese professor Hva-śaṅ. Regard the three *Bhāvanākrama* texts thoroughly, and you will understand!

B. The Method of Walking the Path after Taking Recourse to Calming

Given a person who has attained the mental orientation involving a *samādhi* with nondiscursive thought as previously explained; should he guard just the nondiscursive thought among the distinguished elements of vividness, nondiscursive thought, and so on? The generation of a *samādhi* like this in the stream of consciousness is for the purpose of generating the discerning which overcomes the defilements. Consequently, when one is based on that (*samādhi*) and does not (go on to) generate discerning, then no matter how much he cultivates that *samādhi*, he is unable to eliminate even the defilements of the realm of desire, let alone all defilements! For that reason, it is necessary to cultivate discerning.

Moreover, there are two kinds of discerning; the one proceeding by the mundane path, which eliminates the manifestation of defilement; and the one proceeding by the supramundane path, which eliminates the seed of defilement from the root; and there is no means of walking along a higher path other than those two. Thus the *Śrāvakabhūmi* states (YS IV):[158]

There, the yogin having obtained the mental orientation, having entered the small joy of the elimination-exertion in that way, has two routes—no others—beyond that. What are the two? As follows—mundane and supramundane.

The person who has attained calming or the mental orientation that way, should cultivate the discerning of the mundane path or the discerning of proceeding by the supramundane path. Again, the person wishing to cultivate that (discerning) should cultivate frequently the previously attained calming; and when he cultivates that way, the cathartic and single area of mind increase exceedingly and that calming becomes very firm. Moreover, he should become skilled in the signs of calming and discerning; and subsequent to that, he should venture upon the particular one of the two paths he desires to go on. Thus the *Śrāvakabhūmi* says (YS IV):[159]

Among those, that beginning practitioner of Yoga, having the mental orientation, thinks, "I shall proceed by either the mundane or the supramundane route." He performs many times just that mental orientation. However many times he performs it, to the same degree after the elapse of these and those nights and days, the cathartic and single area of mind go to great increase. At the time that his mental orientation is firmly steadfast and hard; that his conviction of meditative object becomes purified; and that the signs in the category of (both) calming and discerning are manifestly controlled—at that time he, with desire to proceed by either the mundane or supramundane path, inaugurates in those circumstances the application.

Among those (two paths), the mundane discerning is the cultivation formed of "calmness-coarseness," consisting in observing the coarseness of the lower planes and the calmness of the higher planes. The supramundane discerning is the cultivation of the observation formed of the sixteen aspects,[160] impermanence, and so on, of the four truths. The chief one (of the sixteen) is the view which fully recognizes the selflessness of personality.

At the time of attaining the mental orientation of calming as was previously explained, the sort of person who does not proceed by the supramundane path, but proceeds by the mundane path, is just as the *Śrāvakabhūmi* states (YS IV):[161]

Among those, how many are the persons who proceed by the mundane, not by the supramundane, path in the present life? He said there are four, as follows—all these, 1) he who is outside the fold, 2) he who adheres to this doctrine, but, while having previously practiced calming, has weak faculty. 3) he who likewise (having previously practiced calming) has keen faculty, but whose roots of virtue are unmatured, 4) a Bodhisattva desiring to attain enlightenment in a future life, but not in the present life.

Of those (persons), none of the outsider yogins who have attained the previously explained calming guard through examining the selflessness of personality by means of discriminative insight, because those persons have no conviction in selflessness. For this reason, whether one guards only the nondiscursive thought of calming, or performs only the cultivation of discerning formed of "calmness-coarseness," he consequently proceeds only on the mundane path.

"This doctrine" is Buddhist. But when one has a dull faculty with which previously he relied again and again for the most part on cultivating just the fixation cultivation of calming, then whether he has no delight or has delight in the cultivation through examining the meaning of selflessnes by discriminative insight, he is unable to understand the meaning of selflessness and so proceeds only on the mundane path in this life, because either he protects only the fixation part or he cultivates only the discerning formed of "calmness-coarseness."

The insider Buddhist who has a keen faculty well understands the meaning of selflessness. But if he has not matured the roots of virtue of comprehending the truths directly, he is unable in this life to generate the supramundane, fluxless, noble path, so he "proceeds only on the mundane path." However, he does not lack the ability to cultivate the discerning which has selflessness as its meditative object.

The Bodhisattva who is becoming a Buddha, whether he is "bound to one more birth" or is "in his last existence," in the time of his last (life) takes hold of the path of training and generates in his stream of consciousness the four paths.[162] But he does not generate the noble path at the time when he is "bound to one more birth," so in this life he "proceeds by the mundane path." However, he does not lack the full comprehension of the meaning of selflessness. The *Abhidharmakośa* (VI, 24) explains this:

> The Teacher (i.e., the Buddha) and the rhinoceros (i.e., the Pratyekabuddha), up to (their individual) enlightenment at the upper end of (the Fourth) Meditation, have a single basis (i.e., of the four paths).
> Before that: what is conducive to liberation (i.e., the path of equipment).

The method of becoming a Buddha according to the texts of the Small Vehicle agrees with this (passage), but ācārya Āryāsaṅga's own contention does not (agree).[163]

Accordingly, whether one is the outsider who eliminates the manifestation of defilement through cultivating the path formed of "calmness-coarseness," or is the insider, the Buddhist, who eliminates defilements from the root through contemplating the meaning of selflessness—it is necessary to obtain first of all the *samādhi* of calming previously explained. Hence, both the outsider and insider yogins require the previously explained calming as the basis for the elimination of defilement. And that is not all! Any yogin of the Great Vehicle or the Small Vehicle must also accomplish this *samādhi;* and all yogins in the Great Vehicle, whether belonging to the vehicle of Mantras or to the vehicle of the perfection of insight, must accomplish calming. Hence, this calming is of paramount importance as the basis for all yogins when they walk the path.

The calming explained in the Mantra texts also requires the elimination of the five faults, sloth and so on, of *samādhi,* except that (those texts) have the specific feature of meditative object—through taking as support of consciousness a meditative object of the body of a deity, hand symbols, syllables, and the like—and have the special feature of certain means of generating (calming); and common (to the Tantras and nontantric texts) are all these: the method of reliance on mindfulness and awareness as the opponents for those (five faults), after the attainment of the ninth thought, and the production from the latter of the cathartic, and so on. Therefore, this *samādhi* is most far-reaching. Following the profound purport, the *Saṃdhinirmocana-sūtra* states that all *samādhis* of the Great and Small Vehicles are included in the *samādhis* of calming and discerning. Therefore, the one wishing to be skilled in *samādhi* should be skilled in both calming and discerning.

Although there are a great many requirements in the generation of the mental orientation of calming which is a *samādhi* of that sort, the chief requirement is a discerning common to the outsiders and insiders and common to the Great and Small Vehicles, which is formed of the "calmness-coarseness" for eliminating only the manifestation of defilements; and there is a discerning, a very distinguished feature of only the insider, the Buddhist, which is formed of the reality of selflessness that eliminates the seed of defilement completely. Of these two kinds of discerning, the former is an excellent member, but it is not improper to lack it; while the latter is a member improper to lack; thus, the person with liberation as his goal should generate the discerning which fully comprehends the reality of selflessness.

Moreover, it is this: if one attains a calming of the mind previously explained that is incorporated by the plane of the threshold of the First Meditation, then even if he does not attain the calming belonging to the Meditations beyond this (threshold of the First Meditation) or belonging to the formless realm, by cultivating discerning on the basis of this (threshold) he is able to attain liberation from all the bondage of cyclical flow. On the other hand, if one does not fully comprehend, and does not contemplate, the reality of selflessness, by means of the calming previously explained and by means of the discerning based thereon he may eliminate all the manifestation of defilement in the base of nothing-at-all and below and even attain the mind at the summit of phenomenal existence and yet will not be liberated from the cyclical flow. The *Varṇārhavarṇa* makes a like statement in its "Praise of nonreply" section:[164]

> The person opposed to your doctrine is blinded by delusion.
> Even after proceeding to the pinnacle of phenomenal existence,
> Again his suffering occurs and he undergoes phenomenal existence.

The ones following your teaching
May not attain the main part of the Meditation; and
Still they may dismiss the phenomenal existences
Which are watched by the evil eye of Māra.

Hence, the calming which is the basis of the discerning giving entrance upon the noble path of all the "stream-enterers" and "(non)returners to this world" is the previously explained calming that is incorporated by the threshold of the First Meditation. Accordingly, one should know that all the Arhats lined up only attain Arhatship by cultivating discerning on the basis of that previously explained calming. If one does not attain earlier in his stream of consciousness the *samādhi* of the previously explained calming, it will be shown below that he will have no possibility of arousing an actual full comprehension belonging to the discerning that has a phenomenon or a noumenon as its meditative object. For that reason, although the yogin of the *Anuttarayoga(tantra)* does not generate the discerning which has a phenomenon formed of "calmness-coarseness" as its meditative object and does not generate the calming thereby perfected, still it is necessary for him to generate a certain calming; moreover, the point at which he first produces (that certain calming) is in the phase of the first one of the two stages [of the *Anuttarayogatantra*] (called) stage of generation and stage of completion.

In short, having generated a prior calming, thereafter on the basis of this, he must walk the steps of the path up to the summit of phenomenal existence by means of the discerning formed of "calmness—coarseness," or must walk the five paths to liberation or omniscience by means of the discerning formed of the reality of selflessness. This forms the general seal of the Buddha's teaching; hence, no matter who the yogin, he may not depart from it.

C. The Method of Walking the Mundane Path

This has two sections: I. Teaching the necessity of attaining calming prior to walking the path formed of "calmness-coarseness"; II. The method, relying on calming, of becoming free from attachment to craving.

I. TEACHING THE NECESSITY OF ATTAINING CALMING PRIOR TO WALKING THE PATH FORMED OF "CALMNESS-COARSENESS"

The one who cultivates the path formed of "calmness-coarseness" by way of the realization of the characteristics must first attain that previously explained calming, because when the *Sūtrālaṃkāra* (XIV, 15d, 16a–b) says:

> . . . Then increasing that (cathartic), by means of a far-reaching increase, he attains the main-part fixation,

it sets forth that the person who attains the previously explained ninth thought together with the cathartic and who then takes recourse to increasing the *samādhi,* accomplishes the main part [of the First Meditation].

Furthermore, from the time of taking hold of the ninth thought and as long as he has not attained the mental orientation, he is said to be a beginner in the mental orientation. After he has attained the mental orientation and wishes to purify defilement while he cultivates the mental orientation that realizes the characteristics, he is said to be a beginner in the purification of defilement. Thus the *Śrāvakabhūmi* states (YS II):[165]

> Among these, the beginner in the mental orientation is the first engager until he attains the mental orientation in a single area and appropriates a single area of mind. Among these, the beginner in purification of defilement:—when, the mental orientation having been obtained, there is inauguration of the "mental orientation realizing the characteristics" possessing the desire to free his mind from defilement, and there is receipt [of that mental orientation] repeatedly exercised—this is the beginner in the purification of defilement.

Also, because (that work) states at the head of its Fourth Yogasthāna that having obtained the mental orientation, one then cultivates the path of freedom from passion, whether mundane or supramundane.

This very extensive explanation (i.e., found in the *Śrāvakabhūmi*) of the method of eliminating defilement by first accomplishing calming, as previously explained, and thereafter accomplishing either the mundane or supramundane discerning, does not appear clearly in other Abhidharma treatises. Hence, the former (teachers) who exercised skill in the former upper and lower Abhidharma[166] did not evince clearly this method of first accomplishing the calming of a single area and then eliminating defilement on the basis of that. Therefore, when a person is not well grounded in this *Śrāvakabhūmi* explanation, he may get the mistaken idea, "The lowest part of the path of the (four) Meditations and the formless realm is the threshold of the First Meditation; for this the six mental orientations are explained, and first is the realizing the characteristics; hence, the first-produced thought comprised by the threshold is the realization of the characteristics." It is very invalid to hold this (idea), for these reasons: 1) when one has not attained calming, he has no birth plane of the threshold of the First Meditation; and when one has not attained the threshold, he has not attained calming; 2) the realization of the characteristics is the cultivation of examination, and so the one who cultivates this and has not previously attained calming is unable to accomplish it (i.e., calming) newly.

As was previously quoted from the *Bhūmi-vastu* scripture [above, with note 136, "the one that ranges in craving is not this way"], there is no cathartic in a single area of craving; and because the *Saṃdhinirmocana* and other texts state that when one has not attained the cathartic he does not accomplish calming, then if one has not attained the first threshold he does not attain calming. Hence, the first of the six mental orientations of the first threshold is the inception of the cultivation of discerning incorporated by the threshold. However, (the latter cultivation) is not first of all in the first threshold itself, because it must be preceded by the calming incorporated by the threshold. When a person has not attained the *samādhi* incorporated by the first threshold, all of his previous *samādhis* are only a single area of craving thought; therefore, if one is consistent with the explanations of the great texts, he can hardly insist that [in such a case] there is discerning; there is little of it even when he attains calming!

II. THE METHOD, RELYING ON CALMING, OF BECOMING FREE FROM ATTACHMENT TO CRAVING

When one has cultivated to just the extent of possessing the vividness of the previously explained calming and possessing the numerous special things such as nondiscursive thought, and then either does not cultivate any one of the two (kinds of) discerning, or meanwhile is unable to destroy the manifestation of the defilement of the realm of craving—how much less is he able to eliminate the seed of defilement and the hindrance of the knowable! For this reason, if one wishes to attain the First Meditation that is free from attachment to craving, he should take that calming as his basis and then cultivate discerning.

Now, it was previously explained that when one cultivates just calming, he suppresses the manifested top of defilement. How can (the foregoing remark) avoid contradicting this explanation? The former explanation is without fault, because it is governed by inclusion within calming and mundane discerning, whereas the present remark is governed by the calming comprised by the first threshold which precedes both kinds of discerning.

The (meditative) basis for this is the cultivation both by the outsider who has hardly any view of selflessness and by the one who, adhering to this doctrine, possesses the view of selflessness. The sort of path this person should cultivate for eliminating defilement is just as the *Śrāvakabhūmi* states it (YS IV):[167]

Among these, the yogin engaged toward freedom from attachment to craving obtains freedom from attachment to craving by means of seven mental orientations. Furthermore, what are these seven mental orientations? He said: 1) realizing the characteristics, 2) the kind made of conviction, 3) seclusion, 4) attraction of rapture, 5) orientation with comprehension, 6) final stage of application, 7) fruit of the final stage of application.

Among them, the last one is the mental orientation of the time when one enters the main part [of the First Meditation] after becoming free from attachment to craving; hence, it is the thing to be accomplished. The prior six are the accomplishing agents.[168]

If one has contemplated the meaning of selflessness in this phase and has not caused the elimination of defilement, after what sort of foundation does he contemplate its meaning and eliminate defilement? In that regard, although this path eliminates other manifestations of defilement belonging to the realm of craving, because the text says, "obtains freedom from attachment to craving" it chiefly eliminates by way of the opponent to attachment. Moreover, attachment means in this case the desire for and attachment to the five craved objects of the senses. Hence, as its opponent one observes the many ways of disadvantages of sense objects and cultivates by way of apprehending the opposite of the grasping pattern of that attachment. By so doing he achieves freedom from attachment.

1. This also: even when there is the definite firmness of realization of the characteristics, which is the errorless realization of the demerit of craving and the merit of the First Meditation, if one has not accomplished calming previously, no matter to what extent he cultivates the examination of these two—demerit and merit—he is unable to eliminate defilement; and even when he has accomplished calming, if he does not engage in examination by realization (of the characteristics), no matter to what extent he cultivates that (calming), he is unable to eliminate defilement. Hence, it is necessary for him to eliminate (that) by way of cultivating both calming and discerning. This is basic to all elimination of defilement. Accordingly, the excellent knowledge of the characteristics, consisting in discrimination of the demerit and merit of the higher and lower planes, at one time occurs as hearing and at another occurs as pondering; hence, it is a combination of hearing and pondering.

2. When he has transcended (the forces of) hearing and pondering by cultivating that way, the production of conviction in the meaning of "calmness-coarseness" by a single kind of cultivation is the mental orientation made of conviction. For this phase, the *Śrāvakabhūmi* states (YS IV):[169] "One cultivates the calming and discerning which have precisely that sign as their meditative object." (The same work) also states in the phase of the sixth mental orientation that one cultivates calming and discerning; states in the phase of the first mental orientation that the meditative object is the six elements of meaning, etc.; and states in other phases many times that there is discerning. Hence, even though these (mental orientations) do not cultivate the view of selflessness, they do not oppose discerning. Therefore, one eliminates defilement through cultivating by the method of both calming and discerning during the phases of these mental orientations. The cultivation method for this is the discrimination of "calmness-coarseness." The examination again and again of this very meaning is the cultivation of discerning. At the

conclusion of the examination, the fixation in a single area on the meaning of "calmness-coarseness" is the cultivation of calming. The second and first mental orientations cultivated in this manner are the opponent to denial.

3. When one is based on the cultivation which cultivates calming and discerning alternately that way, the arousal of the opponent to great defilement of craving is called "mental orientation of seclusion."

4. The capacity for eliminating moderate defilements by cultivating calming and discerning in mixture is the mental orientation attracting rapture.

5. Afterward, when the person fixed in *samādhi* has defilements of craving that create an obstacle for his application to virtue, and then on the occasion of his emerging from this (*samādhi*) if he does not notice any coursing (of those defilements), he should examine how to avoid this crude discursive thought, "I have eliminated defilement." He should think, "Do they not course while I am not free from attachment to sensuous lust, or is it that they do not course because I am free from attachment?" So as to test that, he takes as support of consciousness a very pleasant domain of attachment; and upon noticing the arising of attachment, the causing of delight in the cultivation for eliminating that (attachment) is the orientation with comprehension. With that he eliminates the pride which thinks that what has not been eliminated has been eliminated.

6. Then, the production of the opponent to tiny defilement of craving by performing and cultivating, as previously (discussed), both the examining individually of the meaning of "calmness-coarseness" and the fixation in a single area at the conclusion of the examination—is called "mental orientation of final stage of application."

The third, fourth, and sixth mental orientations are the opponents which eliminate defilement. When one has eliminated in that way tiny defilements and has destroyed all the manifestation of the defilement of craving, for a while there is practically no coursing (of defilements), but there is no permanent destruction of the seed. This method frees one from the attachment in the base of nothing-at-all and below, but it is incapable of destroying the manifestation of defilement at the summit of the phenomenal world, and so it cannot rescue one from the cyclical flow.

However, by taking recourse to the Meditations, one also attains the five supernormal faculties. I shall not treat these here, for fear of the many words. As they are found extensively in the *Śrāvakabhūmi,* one should look them up there.

These methods for accomplishing the main part of the Meditations and so on are absent nowadays. As they do not lead one astray, if one arouses the understanding to review frequently just the principal language of these (methods), that will be very beneficial for avoiding the misdirections of other *samādhis.*

Such a *samādhi* of the four Meditations and of the four formless (planes) as well as the five supernormal faculties are in common with the outsider. Therefore, even if one attains a distinguished *samādhi* of this sort, with this alone not only does it not rescue him from the cyclical flow, but also those (kinds of *samādhis*) bind him to the cyclical flow. Hence, one should not be content with just calming, but should seek the discriminative discerning which has the view of selflessness.

If one does not know extensively the ways of accomplishing the main parts of the First Meditation and so on, it is certainly incumbent on him to learn just precisely the teaching while refraining from personal speculations, by well considering the essentials of the way of accomplishing that previously explained calming or "mental orientation," namely [in all the following], the method of fixation of mind as it is stated in the exceedingly profound scripture *Prajñāpāramitā* and others, according as the mention thereof in the Mādhyamika *Bhāvanākrama* was previously cited; its purport expounded in the *Sūtrālamkāra;* Āryāsaṅga's summary statements in the *Bodhisattvabhūmi,* the higher Abhidharma (i.e., the *Abhidharmasamuccaya*), and the *Viniścayasaṃgrahaṇī;* both calming and discerning in the (same author's) (*Mahāyāna*) *Saṃgraha,* expressed like the personal delivery (of a guru) in his *Śrāvakabhūmi,* and extensively expounded in his *Śrāvakabhūmi;* their meanings stated in the Mādhyamika *Bhāvanākrama* texts and in the *Prajñāpāramitopadeśa;* moreover, the statements about the way of accomplishing calming by the eight elimination motivations, together with the method of eliminating the five faults, in the *Madhyāntavibhāga.* These (essentials) do not dwell in some meditators, even by name. And some (meditators), earlier having only the letter at the time of exercising in the great texts, and not well understanding the meaning, later at the time of the procedure see no necessity and then, without building up, (alternately) desert and guard, so that when they do attain a *samādhi* worthy of being included in the category of calming but marked by their not analyzing the meditative object with good understanding, it appears (to them) that they have apprehended a *samādhi* of voidness. And when they attain just the ninth thought which is the common *samādhi* to the outsider and insiders, many of them maintain the occurrence of the complete characteristics of the stage of completion of the *Anuttarayoga(tantra)*; and many of them, having mingled the equipoise and the after-attainment, maintain that it is the uninterrupted knowledge of nondiscursive thought!

When one well attains certainty in those previously explained (essentials), then without being deceived by mere figments through hearing again and again the terms "contemplation of no support of consciousness," "of the signless," "of the final meaning," and so on, he understands the meaning of the *samādhi* in which he has proceeded, and then he understands what is a misdirection and what not a misdirection of the path. Consequently, one should become skilled in the stages of accomplishing *samādhi* as stated in those authoritative texts.

Here I say:

These steps for accomplishing the *samādhi* well stated in the sūtras and in the great treatises which explain their purport, have the constancy of the pronouncement. Hence I, having considered how those of small intelligence have not comprehended; how the demerit of their own discrimination has misdirected them, so that they are without the precepts of guarding nondiscursive thought as in those good texts;—And I, having seen the method by the sort of mind which seeks and finds by many endeavors the stage devoid of search in the many existent texts; [arguing with him,] "If there is no distinction between the *samādhis* of outsiders and insiders, how much less is there a distinction between the *samādhis,* however special, of the Great Vehicle and the Small Vehicle, of the Diamond Vehicle and the Prajñāpāramitā Vehicle!"—have explained in easy language the method of guarding *samādhi* which is the great way of the texts.

Thou friends, who have exercised many years in the great way of the texts, do not take the stone of another, disregarding your own precious jewel! Know that in yourselves is the jewel. You (too), having seen without amiss the meaning of the precepts found in the texts of exercise, are declared by the powerful one of *munis,* "very learned, happy in the forest." It is right for you to deliberate their meaning. May those meditators who are hopeful in mere diligence, although not having received the method of accomplishing for the first time the path of calming which settles with no discursive thought whatsoever, or the standard of accomplishment, or the understanding to analyze well the meditative object—know better the exact method of protection through reliance on skill. If that is lacking, there is small harm in meanwhile taking refreshment in the teaching of the Buddha. In that way, this explanation of the method of accomplishing calming by means of the texts of Maitreya and Asaṅga is so that the teaching of the Buddha may long endure.

From the steps of the path of the great person, for study of the practice of the Bodhisattva—finished is the explanation of the method of how to study calming, which is the intrinsic nature of meditation (*dhyāna*).[170]

DISCERNING THE REAL
(VIPAŚYANĀ)

ACCORDING to the explanation just completed, one establishes himself upon a single meditative object as selected. He stays solidly on whatever he establishes himself upon, and without discursive thought. Moreover, he has the vividness devoid of fading. But he should not be satisfied with merely that calming attended with the rapture and pleasure that are of special benefit. It is necessary to cultivate discerning for generating the conclusive, errorless insight into the meaning of reality. Because, if this is not done, and one merely has that (sort of) *samādhi,* it would mean his being in common with the outsiders, so that although one meditates in that mere (*samādhi*) in the same way as the path of those persons, he does not eliminate the seed of defilement and so does not free himself from phenomenal existence. The *Bhāvanākrama I* says the same thing: [1]

Having fixed the mind on a meditative object in this way, one should examine it with insight. Thereby the light of knowledge arises, so the seed of delusion is thoroughly eliminated. But if this is not done, with only the *samādhi* in the manner of the heretics there would be no elimination of defilement. It is just as pronounced in the Sūtra [*Samādhirāja*]: [2] "Although he cultivates a *samādhi* in the world, he does not uproot the idea of self. Again his defilements assert their discord like Udraka's cultivation of *samādhi* here."

Here the words, "although he cultivates a *samādhi,*" refer to the *samādhi* possessing the outstanding traits of nondiscursive thought, vividness, etc. And although this is cultivated, it cannot eliminate the adherence to self, as in the words, "He does not uproot the idea of self." Because the adherence to self is not eliminated, thereafter defilement will emerge, as in the words, "Again his defilements assert their discord."

Well then, suppose it be asked, "What should one cultivate in order to attain liberation?" As the scripture [the *Samādhirāja*] continues immediately after the foregoing citation, "If he discriminates the *dharmas* as selfless." That is, if one discriminates the natures as nonself, and accordingly generates the insight which comprehends the meaning of nonself. And, "if he, discriminating those, would cultivate." That is, having attained the view of nonself, the cultivation sustaining this view is referred to by the words "that is the cause for achieving the *nirvāṇa*-fruit." Now it may be asked, "Granted that cultivating this [discerning] brings about liberation; but, lacking it, might not some other kind of cultivation bring about liberation?" [The scripture replies,] "A different cause does not conduce to ceasing." Hence, while one cultivates a path different from that [of discerning], as long as he lacks it [i.e., discerning], [that different path] "does not conduce to ceasing" of suffering and defilement.

Moreover, this exceedingly clear teaching that only the insight of nonself can sever the roots of phenomenal life is quoted in the Mādhyamika *Bhāvanākrama* in opposition to Hva-śaṅ.[3] Therefore, one must reach certainty regarding this, because even though *ṛṣi*(s) among the outsiders also have many meritorious qualities of *samādhi* and supernormal faculties, on account of lacking the view of nonself they have virtually no capacity to cross the cyclic flow (*saṃsāra*). Accordingly, as previously cited, the *Bodhisattvapiṭaka* states that when persons do not know Reality as explained in the preaching texts (*pravacana*), "but who are satisfied with mere *samādhi*," "by the power of pride" that they are on the path cultivating the profound meaning, [they] "are not liberated" from the cyclical flow. And it also states that, being mindful thereof, [the Tathāgata announced], "The one who has heard [it] from another, is liberated from old age and death."[4]

In that passage, the Teacher clearly explains by personally drawing from his own memory. The words "The one who has heard [it] from another" means that he heard the exposition of nonself from another. Hence he listened previously to illustrious friendly guides for the meaning of nonself; and having done the hearing and pondering, in order to reject the adherence to the notion "It came from within" he states "heard it from another"—of this there is no doubt.

In general, all the preaching texts of the Victor explicitly teach the reality in some place or other; and those which do not teach it explicitly, only gradually bring one to it.[5] As long as the cognition-light of reality does not arise, one cannot avert the darkness of delusion. If it does arise and one is averting with only the single-area calming, knowledge does not become pure and one cannot avert the darkness of delusion. Therefore, it is necessary to seek certainty of insight by thinking, "I shall seek the insight which gives certainty in the meaning of reality, the nonself," as stated in the Mādhyamika *Bhāvanākrama II:*

Then he should think, "Having accomplished calming, I shall contemplate (by) discerning." All the pronouncements of the Lord are well stated, and either directly or gradually clarify reality to incline one toward the reality. When the light cognizing reality arises, he becomes free from all the net of views in the manner of dispelling darkness. By calming alone, knowledge does not become pure, nor does one dispel the darkness of obscuration. When one well contemplates reality with insight, knowledge become pure and one comprehends reality. One insight rightly eliminates the obscuration. Hence he thinks, "Now that I am stationed in calming, I shall search the reality with insight. I shall not rest content with calming alone." What is that reality? In the absolute sense, all entities, whether personality (*pudgala*) or natures (*dharma*), are the voidness of self.

Among the (six) perfections, it is *prajñā-pāramitā* which comprehends the reality, while *dhyāna* and the others have no capacity to (so) comprehend. Many persons have made the mistake of thinking they have *prajñā-pāramitā* when they have only *dhyāna,* so it is necessary to generate *prajñā* as the *Saṃdhinirmocana-sūtra* states:[6]

"Lord, by which perfection is the lack of self-existence of the *dharmas* seized?" "Avalokiteśvara, it is seized by *prajñā-pāramittā.*"

Following that purport, it is also said in the earlier-cited *Mahāyānaprasādaprabhāvana:*

I have never spoken of any liberation for the Bodhisattvas who have faith in the Great Vehicle but lack *prajñā,* no matter how they practice [with the other perfections] in the Great Vehicle!

The Method of Instruction in Discerning

THIS has four divisions: I. Reliance on the equipment for discerning; II. Varieties of discerning; III. The way to cultivate discerning; IV. Standard for accomplishment of discerning through cultivation.

I. RELIANCE ON THE EQUIPMENT FOR DISCERNING

One should listen to the way of texts by reliance upon the learned person who knows without error the main points of the preaching texts. With insight consisting of hearing and pondering, one generates the view that fully comprehends the reality, that is to say, it is not proper to lack the basic equipment for discerning, because if one lacks the view which goes to the heart of the matter regarding the meaning of the real, there is no possibility of arousing the discerning-comprehension that comprehends as something really is.

The one with a view of such sort, i.e., the nonfinal resort of provisional meaning, must then search the meaning by way of final resort.[7] When one knows the distinction of provisional meaning and final meaning, he should come to understand the meaning of the preaching texts of final meaning. In this regard, a certain great authoritative way-layer has explained the purport. One who does not rely on his treatises is like a blind person, without a guide for his blindness, walking in places of fearful pitfalls. Therefore one must rely on his errorless commentaries. This person whose commentary is to be relied upon is the *ārya* Nāgārjuna of whom the Lord Buddha himself clearly prophesied in many sūtras and Tantras[8] that he would explain the heart of the teaching which is the profound[9] meaning free from the extremes of existence and nonexistence. He is the one celebrated in the three realms,[10] and one should seek the view that comprehends voidness by reliance on his texts.[11] Here there are three parts: A. Deciding upon the preaching texts of provisional meaning and of final meaning; B. How commentary on Nāgārjuna's purport developed; C. The method of establishing the view of voidness.

A. The Texts of Provisional Meaning and of Final Meaning

Those who wish to comprehend that reality must rely on the preaching texts of the Victor. But the preaching texts are diverse by virtue of the diverse mentalities of the candidates. Therefore, one may wonder, which is the one he should rely upon to search for the profound meaning? In fact, in order to comprehend reality it is necessary for one to rely on the preaching texts of final meaning. Then one may wonder which scripture has final meaning and which one provisional meaning. This will be established by way of what it expresses (S. *vācya*), contrasting with the words that express (S. *vācaka*). One takes the preaching text of final meaning to teach the absolute and the one of provisional meaning to teach the conventional. In this connection, the *Akṣayamatinirdeśa* states:

> What are the sūtras with provisional meaning and what are the sūtras with final meaning? Those sūtras which teach and prove the conventional have provisional meaning. Those sūtras which teach and prove the absolute have final meaning. Those sūtras which teach with a diversity of words and letters have provisional meaning. Those sūtras which teach the profound, the difficult to see, and the difficult to understand, have final meaning.

However, one may wonder of what sort is the nature of teaching the conventional that goes with provisional meaning, because this teaches the conventional, and how is taught the nature of teaching the absolute that goes with final meaning, because this teaches the absolute. That is expressed very clearly in the same sūtra [*Akṣayamatinirdeśa*]:[12]

Those sūtras which teach as though there were a proprietor in the case where there is no proprietor, setting this forth with a variety of terms, to wit, self, sentient being, soul, feeder, person, personality, offspring of Manu, man, agent, and feeler—those have provisional meaning. Those sūtras which teach the gates of liberation, to wit, of voidness, signlessness, wishlessness; lack of instigation, no birth, the unarisen, lack of sentient being, lack of soul, lack of personality, and lack of proprietor—those have final meaning.

That passage states as final meaning the teachings by the method of cutting off elaboration (*prapañca*), e.g., no self and no birth, and as provisional meaning the teaching of self and so on; hence, one should know the absolute as no self, no birth, etc., and the conventional as birth, etc. Also the *Samādhirāja-sūtra* (VII, 5) says:[13]

According to how the Sugata taught voidness, one knows how the sūtras of final meaning are distinguished. In whichever one he taught a personality, sentient being, person, one knows all dharmas in the sense of provisional meaning.

One should understand it as the *Madhyamakāloka*[14] states it: "Accordingly, only the one which expresses the absolute has final meaning. The reverse has provisional meaning." Besides, it says in the *Ārya-Sarvabuddhaviṣayāvatāra-Jñānālokālaṃkāra-nāma-mahāyānasūtra:*[15] "Whichever one has final meaning (shows) the absolute." Again, the *Ārya-Akṣayamatinirdeśa* states: "When one is taught the final meaning, he accordingly has been guided to the absolute as only no birth, etc."

Therefore, the set of Madhyamaka principles (i.e., the chief works of Nāgārjuna), along with their basic commentaries, teach the final meaning as it really is, because they lay down extensively the absolute free from all the host of elaboration of arising, ceasing, etc.

One may wonder why there are these two kinds of teaching, with provisional meaning and with final meaning. When there is no capacity to guide to another meaning of this [which is to be expressed], it is called the final meaning (*nīta-artha*), or the meaning that has been (ultimately) guided. That meaning is the meaning of reality, because it is the ultimate to be established. That is not to be guided subsequently, and it is not proper for another personality to guide it to a different (meaning), because it has the (ultimate) proving authority. That is what the *Madhyamakāloka* sets forth:

Furthermore, what sort of one is called "final meaning"? Any explanation with composition possessed of authority and in consideration of the absolute, because that one cannot be guided away from this (meaning) to any other one by another person.

By virtue of this explanation, one can (also) know provisional meaning. Anyone, while not validated for being embraced as teaching the meaning of this [to be expressed], which requires drawing to another meaning after having expressed a purport and which is satisfied merely with holding according to the words (*yathāruta*)[16]—does not have the ultimate reality; and since it is necessary to seek its reality by drawing away from that, it requires the provisional meaning or the guiding meaning (*neya-artha*).

Some persons assert: the sūtras with final meaning are "according to the words"; hence, if there is mention in these sūtras that there is no birth, no personality, and so on, it is necessary to accept that there is no birth or personality at all. For if this were not so, it would be "not according to the words" and would reduce to provisional meaning. This is a wrong argument, for it involves denying the birth, and so on, of the Teacher who speaks that way (i.e., "no birth," etc.). Now, when there appeared numerous sūtras of final meaning composed with the distinction of the absolute (i.e., "no birth," etc.), when there was a single composition with that distinction, and also when none appeared [with explicit distinction of the absolute], they were necessarily composed with a common (affiliated) doctrine (denying birth, etc.). Since there is the reality of the doctrine (*dharma*), why would there not be the final meaning which teaches (explicitly) that way? Because if it is not so, due to the denial of birth in general, there would necessarily be denial of diverse words, and so there would be no capacity to establish even that sūtra of final meaning which teaches that way! Hence, one should know that for a preaching text of final meaning it is not proper to be "according to the words" with only the denotation at face value of each trivial word,[17] not connecting what is said before and after of the general layout of the sūtra or śāstra—and there is no loss (of these final-meaning texts); and know that for (a preaching text of) provisional meaning, it is proper to be "according to the words" with denotation of the words—and there are still (these provisional-meaning texts).

B. How Commentary on Nāgārjuna's Purport Developed

One may wonder how arose the sequence of commentaries of Nāgārjuna which comment errorlessly on the *Prajñāpāramitā* and other sūtras among the preaching texts—which teach in that manner the complete lack of arising or passing away of any *dharma* through self-existence. In this regard, the great Mādhyamikas Āryadeva, *ācārya* Buddhapālita, Bhāvaviveka, Candrakīrti, Śāntarakṣita, and others became authoritative like the *ācārya* (Nāgārjuna); but the Master and his disciples (Nāgārjuna and Āryadeva) are the source for the other Mādhyamikas, so the early teachers of Tibet called the texts of these two the "grandmother Mādhyamika" and applied the term "partisan Mādhyamika" to the others.

Now some friendly guides among the early Tibetan teachers found names for two kinds of Mādhyamika by way of conventional terms. That is, those who in conventional terms held the existence of externals are the Sautrāntika-Mādhyamika, and those who in conventional terms held the nonexistence of externals are the Yogācāri-Mādhyamika. They also found names for two kinds of Mādhyamika by way of the stand on the absolute (*paramārtha*). Those who hold the set appearance-void to be supreme truth (*paramārtha-satya*) are the Sgyu-ma-rigs-grub-pa (who prove illusion with reasons). Those who hold only the cutting off of the elaboration of appearance as *paramārtha-satya* are the Rab-tu-mi-gnas-par-smra-ba (who believe it has no particular location). In the first grouping they included Śāntarakṣita and Kamalaśila among others. They applied the names Sgyu-ma . . . and Rab-tu-mi-gnas-pa to certain Indian *ācāryas.*[18] In general, the Indian *ācāryas* pledged to the Mādhyamika, no matter what their individual theories, have their foundation according to the school of the great Mādhyamikas who followed *ācārya* Nāgārjuna; but who can explain (all) their (diverse) subtleties! Moreover, these two kinds of theories for *paramārtha* were well referred to by the great translator Blo-ldan-śes-rab:[19] "deluded formulations that arouse astonishment." Concerning their theories: [One] held *paramārtha-satya* to be the thing-in-itself (*arthā-mātra*) judged by an inference cognizing reasons (*rigs śes*). [The other] held *paramārtha-satya* to be the appearance, to be judged by reason cognizing. Both appealed to the *Madhyamakā-*

laṃkāra and the *Madhyamakāloka* for the term *"paramārtha-satya."* But this is wrong, because the other great Mādhyamikas do not allow as *paramārtha-satya* that mere entity shorn of elaboration (*prapañca*).

In this connection the *ācārya* Ye-śes-sde[20] relates the following: the Mādhyamika treatises by the *ācārya* the noble father and son (i.e., Nāgārjuna and Āryadeva) did not clarify the existence or nonexistence of an external entity. Later the *ācārya* Bhāvaviveka refuted the Vijñaptimātra school and established a school holding the existence of the external entity in conventional terms. Then the *ācārya* Śāntarakṣita, relying upon texts of the Yogācāra, created a different sort of Mādhyamika which taught that in conventional terms there is no external entity and that in the absolute sense the mind has no self-existence. Thus there arose two kinds of Mādhyamika, the earlier called Sautrāntikacari-Mādhyamika and the later one called Yogācāri-Mādhyamika. The order of arising appears to be that way (i.e., as Ye-śes-sde reports it).

However, Candrakīrti, while maintaining the existence of an external in conventional terms, does not agree with other Siddhānta tenets, and so it is not valid to call him a Sautrāntika, and likewise it is highly invalid to claim that he agrees with the Vaibhāṣika school.[21]

The learned men of the later diffusion of Buddhism in Tibet classified the Mādhyamika into Prāsaṅgika and Svātantrika; they did not make this up themselves, because it is consistent with (Candrakīrti's) *Prasannapadā*. There is certainty as to the Prāsaṅgika (*thal*) and the Svātantrika (*raṅ*) when one applies those names by way of the means of generating in the lineage of views certainty about whether they hold or do not hold an external in conventional terms and certainty about *paramārtha*-voidness.

But should one seek the purport of the *ārya* Master and disciple by following those (later) *ācāryas?* The great Jo-bo (i.e., Atīśa) took as authoritative the school of *ācārya* Candrakīrti; and the great superior gurus (such as Po-to-ba) of this counsel [= the stage of the path to enlightenment], following his indication, also held that school as authoritative. *Ācārya* Candrakīrti, having observed that among the commentaries on the *Mūla-madhyamaka-kārikā* (*Rtsa śe,* by Nāgārjuna) the one by *ācārya* Buddhapālita had fully explained the purport of the *ārya,* accepted this school as a basis; besides he (Candrakīrti) took up various explanations by *ācārya* Bhāvaviveka, refuting certain points that appeared invalid; and thus commented on the purport of the *ārya.* Having observed that the commentaries of these two *ācāryas* (Buddhapālita and Candrakīrti) are the finest explanations of the texts of the ārya Master and disciple, I shall establish the purport of the *ārya* by following the *ācārya* Buddhapālita and *śrimat* Candrakīrti.

C. The Method of Establishing the View of Voidness

There are two ways to establish the view of voidness: I. The sequence in understanding reality; II. The basic establishment of the reality.

The question arises as to what be the *nirvāṇa* which is the reality to be attained in this case; and also regarding understanding the reality of the means of attaining that (*nirvāṇa*), as well as of what sort be the gate through which there is understanding. In this case, the reality to be attained, namely the Dharmakāya, is the ending of all aspects of adhering to an "I" or "mine" through total destruction of this appearance together with habit-energy as reality, which (in fact) is not reality, of the diversity of natures (*dharma*) that are external (form, sound, etc.) and personal (eye, etc.).

I. THE SEQUENCE IN UNDERSTANDING REALITY

First, it is necessary for the mind to get weary of *saṃsā*ra (cyclical flow) through thinking of its troubles, and to arouse a longing to abandon it (the cyclical flow). (Second:) Then, by observing that as long as one has not averted the cause of it (the cyclical flow) one cannot turn away from it, one considers what be the root of *saṃsāra* and extirpates it down to the root. Hence, having summoned, through deep resolve, the certainty in the way of going to the root of *saṃsāra* which is the reifying view (*satkāyadṛṣṭi*) or nescience (*avidyā*), it is necessary to arouse a longing, which is not artificial, to eliminate it. (Third:) Then observing by depending upon the birth of insight which understands the averting of the reifying view and grasps nonself, one observes the necessity to end that self. Relying on the scripture and principles which oppose the existence of that self and which prove its nonexistence, if the obtaining of certainty perseveres toward liberation, there is no lack of means. (Fourth:)

Having in that (foregoing) way obtained certainty that there is no existence whatever of self-existence in "I" and "mine," and by repeatedly contemplating this meaning, one reaches the Dharmakāya. Moreover, the *Prasannapadā* states (in chap. XVIII, sect. 1):[22]

If all these defilements, acts, bodies, agents, and fruits—are not reality (*tattva*), but are only like the unreality of a city of gandharvas, and so on, and it appears to the "children" in the aspect of reality, then what is here the reality and how may one understand this reality? In explanation, the reality in this case is the total destruction of adherence to "I" and "mine" in regard to the external and the personal by the nonperceptive reach of all external and personal things (*vastu*). As to understanding the reality, one may refer to the *Madhyamakāvatāra* including this verse (VI, 120): "Observing with intelligence (*dhī*) that all the defilements and faults arise from the reifying view (*satkāyadṛṣṭi*), and having realized that the self is the sensory domain (*viṣaya*) of that (reifying view), the yogin suppresses the self."

And:

The yogin, desiring to understand the reality and desiring to eliminate all the defilements and faults, examines the root of this cyclical flow.[23] Thus inquiring he observes that cyclical flow has as root the reifying view, that the self alone is the object (conscious support) of that reifying view, and that by not perceptively reaching the self he eliminates the reifying view and thereby averts all the defilements and faults. Hence, at the outset he examines just the self. What is this self which is the object called "I" (*ahaṃkāra*)?

While many principles are stated (in the "Mūla-prajñā" of Nāgārjuna, etc.) denying the self-existence in the innumerable distinct factual bases (*dharmin*), it is the meaning of the *Madhyamaka-kārikā,* chapter XVIII, that at the time the yogin understands (i.e., initially takes to heart) he contemplates, in short, on the foundation of no self-existence of "I" and "mine."*Ācārya* Candrakīrti has written this on the basis of what *ācārya* Buddhapālita said, and has explained extensively in his *Madhyamakāvatāra* that same chapter XVIII with the teachings of nonself of personality (*pudgala-nairātmya*).

The objection is posed: Is it not a fact in this case that there is no teaching of the way of understanding reality proper to the Mahāyāna, otherwise stated that the mere ending of the idea of "I" and "mine" is not a principle regarding the reality which should be attained (i.e., the Mahāyāna *Nirvāṇa*) since it is merely the establishment of no self-existence to "I" and "mine" (i.e., merely *pudgala-nairātmya*) and lacks the establishment of nonself of natures (*dharma-nairātmya*) and thus is not a principle for the path of understanding reality? This is not a fault because, in regard to the total ending of the aspects of grasping the "I" and "mine," whether or not the lower vehicle (i.e., Hīnayāna) among the two vehicles has the permanent elimination so that the defilements do not again arise, it still is a fact that the Dharmakāya is the permanent elimination through no perceptive reach of any elaborated sign-sources of external and personal *dharmas*. And because, if one understands that there is no self-existence in self, one also averts the idea that there is a self-existence in the personality aggregates which are ancillary to that (notion of a self), as (for example), when a chariot burns up, its members, the wheel, etc., also burn up. Also, the *Prasannapadā* (in chap. XVIII) states:[24]

Those who desire liberation should examine the designating that is applied to (the personality aggregates) (designating) which is the seat of attachment to self among those with wayward views due to nescience. Those desiring liberation should think, "For whomever (i.e., an appropriator) this (i.e., the self) appears as the five personality aggregates by reason of appropriating, does it have or lack the characteristic of personality aggregates?" And while examining in every way, when they do not perceptively reach it (i.e., the self) in the sense of the self-existence of a mode of being, then, "Since there is no 'I' (of theirs), how could there occur a 'mine'?" Because they do not perceptively reach the "I," they still less reach the "mine," which is the basis for the designation as "I." Just as when a chariot is burnt one does not perceptively reach its parts which have been burnt, so also when the yogins realize the nonselfness of "I," they also certainly realize the nonselfness of "mine" which is constituted by personality aggregates.

Thus at the time one comprehends that the "I" lacks self-existence, he (by virtue of that comprehension) also comprehends that the "mine," which is the "I" in the personality aggregates, lacks self-existence.

Besides, we read in the *Commentary on the Madhyamakāvatāra:*[25]

Because one goes astray by perceptively reaching the (supposed) self-existence of form and the other personality aggregates, there is no comprehension of *pudgala-nairātmya* for the reason that one perceptively reaches the personality aggregates which are the basis for the designation as "I." It is said (in Nāgārjuna's *Ratnāvalī*): "As long as one adheres to the personality aggregates, for that long one adheres to an 'I.' "

The reason is that if one does not comprehend the non-self-existence of personality aggregates, he does not comprehend the non-self-existence of *pudgala* (personality).

[Now there are two moot points (*dri ba*):][26]

1. If one could comprehend the non-self-existence of personality aggregates by means of that very cognition (*buddhi*) which comprehends the non-self-existence of *pudgala,* there would be the fault that the two cognitions which comprehend the two *nairātmyas* would coincide. Since *dharma* and *pudgala* are diverse, the two cognitions which comprehend these two to be without self-existence are also diverse. For example, like the cognitions which comprehend that the pot and the post are impermanent.

2. The question arises: If one does not comprehend the non-self-existence of personality aggregates with that very cognition that comprehends the non-self-existence of *pudgala,* then how can one posit a comprehending of the non-self-existence of *pudgala* at the time when one is comprehending *pudgala-nairātmya?*

Since we do not accept the first moot point (i.e., the coinciding of the two cognitions), the second moot point must be explained. Although the very cognition that comprehends the non-self-existence of *pudgala* does not give thought to the non-self-existence of personality aggregates, that cognition, without regard to another (object of comprehension) has the capacity to direct a certainty knowledge (constituting another cognition) certain that there is no self-existence of personality aggregates, so it has the capacity to cut off the affirmation which affirms the self-existence of personality aggregates. For this reason it is said that at the time one comprehends the non-self-existence of *pudgala,* one also comprehends the non-self-existence of personality aggregates. One may understand the matter as Buddhapālita expresses it:[27]

> If what in this way is called "I" were to be called "mine," there would be no "I" and for lack of it how could one certify that this ("mine") belongs to that ("I")?

For example, the cognition deciding that a barren woman cannot possibly have a son does not also imagine that he has no ears, etc. But it has the capacity to cut off the affirmation which posits the existence of his ears, because when it merely decides that there is no self it averts the mere positing that there are his eyes, etc.

[The challenge is made:] Well now, do not the Sautrāntika realists (Vastusatpadārthavādin) who believe that a *pudgala* exists by designation and who deny that a *pudgala* is proved in the absolute sense, also comprehend that the eye, etc. are not self-existent? If that were the case, then those who believe that material things like eye, shoot, etc. exist by designation, would comprehend that they lack self-existence. If they think that is the way it is, and claim so, they are certainly in conflict with our thesis. In their position it would not be necessary to prove that the shoot and so forth are not true. Besides, the path of virtuous and unvirtuous acts which is set forth as a stream that comes to fulfillment would in their theory be a stream without self-existence.

The great commentary *Sphuṭārtha* (by Haribhadra) states (the realist's challenge):[28]

> If the ten virtues and (the perfections) giving and so forth do not exist since they are like dreams, then is it not also the case that the phase outside of deep sleep is the same as the phase of deep sleep? (Would not the Mādhyamika fail to distinguish error and nonerror?)[29]

Hence, when Mādhyamikas say that these (natures, such as virtues and giving) are like a dream in the sense of lacking truth, theirs is not the meaning of opponent [whose theory has been presented above, the realist].[30]

For that reason there is a great difference between the *paramārtha* and *saṃvṛti,* whether proved or unproved, of the realist's own school, and the *paramārtha* and *saṃvṛti,* whether proved or unproved, of the Mādhyamika school. The theories they (the realists) use to prove as *paramārtha* are according to the Mādhyamikas the proof for *saṃvṛti.* Their theories (put forth) as *saṃvṛti* are judged by the Mādhyamikas as proving (instead) the (Mādhyamika) *paramārtha.* One should analyze those (differences) because there is no contradiction at all (in the Mādhyamika case).

Furthermore, their (i.e., realists') existence of *pudgala* by designation and this *ācārya's* (i.e., of the Mādhyamika school) existence of *pudgala* by designation are alike (only) in terms, but (decidedly) different in meaning, because this *ācārya* maintains that those (realists) lack the view which comprehends selflessness of *pudgala,* and because (this *ācārya*) maintains that if they do not comprehend selflessness of *pudgala* they do not comprehend selflessness of *dharma.* Hence, this *ācārya* maintains that as long as they do not abandon the school (*siddhānta*) going with the substantial existence of the personality aggregates they will hold that the *pudgala* also has substantial existence, so they will not have the comprehension that the *pudgala* does not exist from the absolute standpoint.

II. THE BASIC ESTABLISHMENT OF THE REALITY

There are three parts: A. Engaging the principle to be refuted; B. Option of Prāsaṅgika and Svātantrika as refuting agent; C. Relying on this agent, the method of generating the view in consciousness (*saṃtāna*).

A. Engaging the Principle to be Refuted

This also has three parts: 1. The reason for the requirement to determine the refutable (principle); 2. Refuting the other school which denies without determining the refutable; 3. Our own school's method of determining the refutable.

1. THE REASON FOR THE REQUIREMENT TO DETERMINE THE REFUTABLE

For example, to be certain about thinking that a (certain) person is not present, it is necessary to know this person with his cause for absence. In the same way, to be certain about the meaning of nonself and non-self-existence, it is also necessary to determine that "self" and "self-existence" with cause for their absence, because as long as the generality of the (principle) to be refuted does not arise (in the mind) there is not certainty that the refutation is without error. This is stated in the *Caryāvatāra* (IX, 140a–b).[31] "As long as one has not contacted an imagined entity, one cannot apprehend its absence."

Now, particular diversified principles to be refuted are innumerable, but when one summarizes the refutable principle and refutes it to the root, one can counter all refutable principles. Besides, if one does not counter all the points to be refuted—even subtle ones—one falls into the extreme of existence and with attachment to things has no capacity for liberation from phenomenal life. On the other hand, when one refutes the refutable principle out of all proportion by not observing the proper measure, he casts aspersion on the series of cause and fruit and of dependent origination, and falls into the extreme of nihilism, and this view leads him to a bad destiny. Therefore it is very important to well apprehend the refutable principle, because if one does not apprehend it, he will certainly generate either the view of eternalism or the view of nihilism.

2. REFUTING THE OTHER SCHOOL WHICH DENIES WITHOUT DETERMINING THE REFUTABLE

There are two parts to this: a. Refutation of overpervasion in determining the refutable; b. Refutation of nonpervasion in determining the refutable.

a. Refutation of Overpervasion in Determining the Refutable

This has two sections: (1) Setting forth the (opponent's) thesis; (2) Showing that (the thesis) is not valid.

(1) SETTING FORTH THE OPPONENT'S THESIS

The generality of modern-day (i.e., Tibetan) adherents of the Mādhyamika, while setting forth its meaning, say: By the principle which examines whether the reality of birth, etc. is proved or not proved one counters all the *dharmas* from form up to omniscience,[32] because when one examines with a principle regarding whatever (*dharma*) be upheld, there is not even an atom that can withstand examination; and because when one refutes all the four alternatives of "it exists," "it does not exist," etc., there is no unconstructed nature (*asaṃskṛta-dharma*) therein (i.e., in the four alternatives). Moreover, when with the noble knowledge that sees reality one sees that there is no (*dharma*) whatever of birth and decease, bondage and liberation, etc., then it must be the case as authorized by that (noble *samāpatti*), so there is no birth, etc. If one claims that there is birth, etc., then either it can withstand or not withstand the examination with a principle that examines the reality in that case. In the event it can withstand (that examination), there would be (proved) explicitly as true that there is an entity which withstands the examination by the principle. In the event it cannot withstand that examination, how could it be valid that there exists an entity countered by the principle?

Accordingly, if one claims an existence of birth, etc., it is either proved or not proved by an authority. In the first case (i.e., proved by an authority), since it is proved by that knowledge (=*ārya-samāpatti*) which sees reality (directly), it is not valid that it sees the nonexistence of birth. If it is claimed to be proved by cognition of the conventional eye, etc. (ear and so on), it is refuted that they constitute an authority, because the *Samādhirāja-sūtra* shows as invalid that they (eye, etc.) serve to prove (form, etc.), as in this passage (IX, 23):

> (The perception based on) eye is not an authority (*pramāṇa*), nor are (the perceptions based on) ear, nose, tongue, body, and mind authorities. If these (perceptions based on) sense organs were authorities, who would need to resort to the Noble Truth!

And also because the *Avatāra* (=*Madhyamakāvatāra,* VI, 31a) states, "The world with its multitudinous aspects is not an authority." The claim that it exists although not proved by an authority is not held by us, and since it is not a principle it is (highly) invalid. If one claims there is birth, while denying it in an absolute sense, it is necessary that he claim it so in a conventional sense, but this is not proper, because this passage of the *Avatāra* (VI, 36) states that the principle by which birth is denied in the absolute sense, also denies it conventionally:

> By whatever principle in the phase of reality there is no reason for birth from oneself or from another, by that principle there is no reason for it conventionally. Therefore, how can there be your birth!

And also because a thing does not arise from itself, from another, and so on—four in all—so if one claims that it arises, he counters by imagining the four alternatives to be a refutation of birth in the absolute sense and so do not disallow (birth); but (the four alternatives means) there is no birth of them at all. Suppose there were birth from a particular one of four alternatives, and denying three of them, suppose it were necessary to be born from another thing—that is not proper, because the *Avatāra* states (VI, 32d): "Even according to the world the birth is not from another." Therefore, when refuting birth, one should not apply the special feature of *paramārtha,* because the *Prasannapadā* refutes the application in particular of *paramārtha.*

In this matter also, some assert that they do not admit birth, etc. even conventionally; and some claim that there is (birth, etc.) conventionally. But all agree with a principle in refuting for the *dharmas* a self-existence produced by own nature, because while this *ācārya*'s school does not affirm and then deny,[33] he simultaneously refutes the production by self-existence in the sense of both truths. If that is the way there is no self-existence, then what (else) is there? Therefore, the special application of *paramārtha* to the refutable principle is now explained with special clarity[34] to be only the school of Mādhyamika-Svātantrika.

(2) SHOWING THAT THE THESIS IS NOT VALID

This has two parts: (a) Showing that the special refutation of *dharma* by that school is not common to the Mādhyamika; (b) Teaching how to avoid defeat by the assailant's discourses.

(a) Showing That the Special Refutation of *Dharma* by That School is Not Common to the Mādhyamika.

Here there are three parts: (i) Determining the special *dharma* of the Mādhyamika; (ii) Manner in which a school opposes that (special *dharma*); (iii) How the Mādhyamika answers this (challenge).

(i) Determining the Special *Dharma* of the Mādhyamika

(Nāgārjuna's) *Yuktiṣaṣṭikā* (verse 60) says:

> By means of this virtue all persons amass
> their collection of merit and knowledge.
> May the two sublimities that arise from
> merit and knowledge, be achieved!

The point of this passage is that the candidates who proceed by the highest vehicle attain the sublimity of the Dharmakāya and the sublimity of the Rūpakāya in the phase of the fruit. In the phase of the path, as was previously explained,[35] they resort to amassing the uncountable collection of merits and knowledge while avoiding a one-sidedness of either means (*upāya*) or insight (*prajñā*).[36] That is to say, they concern themselves with two kinds of certainty: *a*) They associate the causes and fruits of *saṃvṛti* by thinking that from such-and-such a cause comes this benefit (of good destiny) or this trouble (of bad destiny) as fruit, and draw certainty from the bottom of their hearts and with sincerity, thus attaining the certainty of the phenomenon. *b*) And they reach certainty from the bottom of their hearts that there is not even a particle of self-existence (*svabhāva*) produced by own nature in all the *dharmas,* thus attaining the certainty of the noumenon. The reason is that if either one is lacking, the full complement of the path of both means and insight is not being learned from the bottom of their hearts and with sincerity.[37] Accordingly, *a*) the method of establishing the basic view that does not mistake the essential of the causal path for attaining both bodies in the phase of the fruit,[38] and *b*) the method of establishing the view that depends on that (basic view), achieve the (two) certainties in the two truths as just explained.

Except for this kind of Mādhyamika, what manner of other person who observes (only) the gathering of refutation and is ignorant of holding the irrefutable, would be called the Mādhyamika skilled in possession of broad examination and possessed of subtle learning! Thus, the one skilled in the means of comprehending the two truths, who is established without even the question of refutation, and resorts to achieving the ultimate purport of the Victor, engenders wondrous devotion to his teacher and the Teaching and gains understanding guided by the pure voice and words that tell him emphatically again and again the mysterious words: the meaning of the voidness which is void of self-existence is the meaning of dependent origination, but is not the meaning of absence void of efficiency (*arthakriyākāritva*).

The learned realists with their own position may train ever so much in numerous fields of knowledge, but when they deny the Mādhyamika view and dispute the Mādhyamika—it being a fact that all *dharmas* are entirely void of any self-existence at all that is accomplished by self-nature—their theory fails in any establishment of bondage and liberation, *saṃsāra* and *nirvāṇa,* etc. The *Mūla-prajñā* (XXIV, 1) states [presenting the realists' challenge]:

If all this is void, then your position reduces to the absurdity that there is no arising or passing away and there are no four Noble Truths!

That says that if these are void of self-existence, arising and passing away as well as the four Noble Truths are not valid. The *Vigrahavyāvartanī* (k. 1) puts (their challenge) this way:

If there is nowhere a self-existence of any presences, your words, being without self-existence, are unable to refute the self-existence!

This says that if words are without self-existence, they have no capacity to prove the rejection of self-existence or non-self-existence. Thus it disputes, claiming that in the absence of self-existence there is no validity of generator and thing generated, or of refutation and agent and act of proof. Thus they argue, sapient that this principle of opposing self-existence denies all agents and action. Therefore the schools (*siddhānta*) of the realist and the Mādhyamika are not in common; and when these two dispute, the argument merely revolves about whether or not (those holding) the void of self-existence have validity in any establishment of *saṃsara* and *nirvāṇa*. Anyway, while there is not even a speck of self-existence accomplished by own nature, the special *dharma* of the Mādhyamika suffices in its theory for all establishments of generator and thing generated, refutation and proof, etc. and *saṃsāra* and *nirvāṇa*. According to the *Mūla-prajñā* (XXIV, 13, 14):

Furthermore, when you, sir, object to this voidness, the faulty refutation does not apply to the void of our school. For the school which holds voidness as valid, everything becomes valid. For the school which holds voidness as invalid, everything becomes invalid.

This points out that the fault charged by the words, "If all this is void, . . ." does not accrue to the school of non-self-existence; even more, that arising, passing away, are valid in the position (holding) the void of self-existence; and that they are not valid in the position (holding) no void of self-existence. That is also stated in the *Prasannapadā:*[39]

It is not just that the aforementioned faulty refutation does not apply to our school, but also so as to teach that all the establishment of truths, etc. is highly valid, he says: "For the school which holds voidness as valid. . . ."

Thus he (Candrakīrti) explains it in his text.

Chapter XXVI of the *Mūla-Madhyamaka-kārikā* teaches the arising sequence in direct order of dependent origination in twelve members and the cessation sequence in reverse order.[40] Chapter XXV especially teaches the denial of self-existence.[41] Chapter XXIV, by examination of the Noble Truths, extensively lays down that if it is not void of self-existence, all establishments of arising and passing away, and so on of *saṃsāra* and *nirvāṇa,* are invalid; and that if it is void of self-existence, all those (establishments) are valid.[42] Consequently, these chapters are of great importance for understanding all the other chapters.

Hence, those who nowadays claim to speak the meaning of the Mādhyamika and say that such causes and effects as generator and thing generated, when (assumed) without self-existence, are pervaded with invalidity constitute the realist school (*vastusatpadārthavādin*). So one should seek out the Mādhyamika path as it was maintained by nātha Nāgārjuna—that on the basis of this-and-that cause and condition, this-and-that fruit arises and ceases; that the establishment of cause and effect is the void of self-existence in dependence. Chapter XXIV (k. 18, 19) states:[43]

> The origination in dependence we call the "voidness." That is the designation when there is depending. Precisely that is the middle path.
>
> Since no *dharma* originates outside of dependence, it follows that there is no *dharma* whatsoever that is not void.

This states that dependent origination is pervaded by the void of self-existence. So do not deny it and say that birth by reliance on causes and conditions is pervaded by accomplishment of self-existence! Along the same lines, the *Vigrahavyāvartanī* (k. 71–72) proclaims:

> For whatever (school) this voidness is feasible, all things are feasible. For whatever (school) voidness is not feasible, nothing is feasible. I bow to that incomparable Buddha who has expounded voidness, dependent origination, and the middle path with the same meaning.

Furthermore, the *Śūnyatāsaptati* (k. 68) says:

The incomparable Tathāgata has declared that all entities are void of self-existence, giving as the reason that the entities arise in dependence.

Besides, the *Yuktiṣaṣṭikā* (k. 43–45) states:

Those (i.e., outsiders) who insist on a self in a world without dependence, are carried away by views like, "Oh, it is permanent; it is impermanent!"

Those (i.e., the Buddhist realists) who claim that entities in dependence are accomplished in reality, do not recognize the faults of eternalism, etc. as they occur.

Those (i.e., the correct Mādhyamika) who hold that entities in dependence are like the moon in the waters, being not misled by unreality are not carried away by those distorted theories.

Moreover, it is said in the *Lokātītastava* (k. 19–20):[44]

The logicians (*tārkika*) believe that suffering is constructed by oneself, by another, by both, or by chance; but you teach that it arises in dependence.

Whatever is originated in dependence, you regard as void. "There is no independent entity,"—that is your incomparable lion's roar.

This states that it is only void of self-existence because it has origination in dependence. This idea that the meaning of dependent origination is the meaning of voidness of what is non-self-existent is the unshared school of nātha Nāgārjuna. Hence, our school takes the side of Mādhyamika with voidness of what is non-self-existent and thus establishes the cause and effect of dependent origination. If one is loath to so take it, he is guided to other positions and does not have the meaning of dependent origination. Because the (above-cited) passage, "For the school which holds voidness as valid, everything becomes valid," refers to the school of non-self-existence and means that for it everything of dependent origination pertaining to *saṃsāra* and *nirvāṇa* becomes valid.

However, suppose there is the question of how the position accepting voidness is the school validating all of *saṃsāra* and *nirvāṇa*. (In answer:) The one saying that all entities have voidness of self-existence, speaks in that case with the reason that they arise in dependence on causes and conditions; this is to be expounded (below).

That being the case, dependent origination is valid in that (void of self-existence). Since it is valid, suffering is also valid. So it is necessary to posit suffering in anything that arises in dependence on causes and conditions, because suffering is not valid if there is no arising in dependence. If there is the Truth of Suffering, then the Source from which it arises, the Cessation with ceasing of that Suffering, and the Path leading to that (Cessation) are valid, so the four Truths are established. If there are the four Truths, their respective experience, elimination, direct realization, and path cultivation are valid. If there are those, the three Jewels, and so on, are all valid. It is so according to the *Prasannapadā* (on XXIV, k. 14):[45]

For the school in which this voidness of self-existence of all entities is valid, "everything," as was stated, becomes valid. How so? Since we call "voidness" the arising in dependence, it follows that for the school in which this voidness is valid, dependent origination is valid. For the school in which dependent origination is valid, the Noble Truths are valid. How so? For the reason that it is just when there is dependent origination that suffering arises; it does not arise in the absence of dependent origination. And that is void of self-existence. When there is suffering, then the source of suffering, the cessation of suffering, and the path leading to the cessation of suffering are valid. Consequently, the thorough experience of suffering, the elimination of the source, the direct realization of the cessation, and cultivation of the path, are valid. When there are the thorough experience, etc. going respectively with suffering, etc., their fruits are valid. When there are the fruits, those who abide in the fruits are valid. When there are those abiding in the fruits, those who have resorts (to the fruits) are valid. When there are those abiding in the fruits and those who have resorted, the Saṃgha is valid. When there are the Noble Truths, the Illustrious Dharma is also valid. When there are the Illustrious Dharma and the Saṃgha, the Buddha is also valid. Therefore, the three Jewels are valid, and all the distinguished comprehensions (*viśeṣādhigama*)[46] going with mundane and supramundane entities, are valid. And also, virtue, nonvirtue, and their fruits, and all worldly conventions are valid. Hence, "For the school which holds voidness as valid, everything becomes valid." While for the school which holds voidness as invalid, in the absence of dependent origination, "everything becomes invalid."

One may understand from that passage when the valid and the invalid are present or absent.

Regarding the previously cited opponent's challenge in the *Vigraha-vyāvartanī* (k. 1), the *ācārya* (= Nāgārjuna) clarifies his response with a reply that agent and act are valid when they have no self-existence. He states in the *Vigrahavyāvartanī* (k. 22):[47]

> Whatever one of entities occurs in dependence, we declare "voidness." And whatever one arises occurring in dependence, is his (= the Mādhyamika's) lack of self-existence.

And the self-commentary on this states:

> And you sir (= the realist), not understanding the meaning of voidness of entities, try to argue this way: "Since your words lack self-existence, they are impotent to refute the self-existence of entities," But in this case (I reply:) Whatever one of entities occurs in dependence, is a voidness. For what reason? For reason of non-self-existence. Those entities which arise in dependence do not arise with self-existence, because they lack self-existence. For what reason? For reason of depending on cause and conditions. If (according to the realist) entities could exist by virtue of self-existence, they could even exist disallowing causes and conditions. They do not occur that way. Therefore, they are not self-existent. Because they lack self-existence, they are called "void." Thus, my words also have arisen in dependence and so are without self-existence; and since they are without self-existence, it is right to call them "void." Just as the pot, the cloth, etc., by reason of arising in dependence, are void of self-existence, and yet (in the case of the pot) has the capacity to hold honey, water, and milk, and to take (from others);[48] and (in the case of the cloth) has the capacity to protect from cold, wind, and sun—so also, my words, while without self-existence because arisen in dependence, still have the capacity to prove that entities lack self-existence. Therefore, in this case what you say, "Since your words lack self-existence, they are impotent to refute the self-existence of entities," is itself not valid.

Thus he states clearly that if (entities) are produced by their self-existence, they are pervaded by nondependence on causes and conditions; and that if they depend on causes and conditions, they are pervaded by non-self-existence—so present in similar cases and absent in dissimilar cases (*anvaya-vyatireka*);[49] and states clearly that words lacking self-existence have the capacity to do what is needed for refuting and proving.

Need we say there is a common element of the two—*a*) the dependent origination with arising and passing away of defiled and pure *dharmas* in dependence on causes and conditions, and *b*) their lack of self-existence! This incomparable way of reasoning with comprehension that the real nature of such dependent origination is without self-existence, should be known as the special *dharma* of only the learned Mādhyamika. But if one holds that the arising in dependence and the ceasing in dependence is concomitant with accomplishment by own nature, or opposes the dependent origination of arising and passing away, with an opposing principle of self-existence—that is like the descent of a Māra-god[50] and becomes a great obstacle to reaching the meaning of the Mādhyamika as it really is. That being the case, at the time one has drawn certainty that the *dharmas* have not even a particle of self-existence accomplished by own nature, one should give guidance to other sides that have not drawn the certainty of our school in the dependency on causes and fruits. At the time one has well drawn certainty by way of our school regarding causes and fruits, if there is someone who proceeds without having drawn the certainty by way of our school in the lack of self-existence and talks about accepting a (different) purport regarding lack of self-existence, then still more let him know that he has not reached the Mādhyamika view, (and give counsel) that he should settle in the essential of guarding virtue which is the pledge at the basis of attaining that (Mādhyamika) view, should persevere in many ways of amassing the collection (of merit and knowledge) and of purifying the hindrances, should rely on knowledgeable men, and should strive in hearing (the counsel) and pondering (the meaning). The one who proceeded to the summit of the world with the double collection of certainty guidance in that sort of appearance and in the void[51] recalled the extraordinary difficulty of attaining the Mādhyamika view, according to the *Mūla-prajñā* (XXIV, 12):[52]

> Therefore, when the Muni observed that the
> dull-witted were hard-put to fathom this Dharma,
> His mind turned away from teaching it.

Also, the *Ratnāvalī* (II, 16–18) puts it this way:[53]

> At the time the coarse sensory realm, at the
> outset dirtied by body, which is constantly appearing,
> does not stay in mind;—
> at that time how easily does this very subtle, profound,
> Illustrious Dharma beyond the sensory realm, with no
> location, enter the mind!
> The Muni, having been enlightened, turned away
> from teaching the Dharma—having recognised that
> people find this Dharma hard to know because of
> its exceeding profundity.

When it is not that way (i.e., when the Illustrious Dharma has not entered the mind), one can mistake the meaning of some authoritative texts when they state the foundation of non-self-existence by the principle of examining the individual parts of the pot, etc., and oneness and difference; examining what be the individual parts, such as spout, neck, etc. of the pot, etc., and where they are; if one cannot find (the pot), he is led to certainty by thinking, "There is no pot present." Then contemplating that way in regard to the person examining, he becomes certain by thinking, "The examining person is also not present." At the time he does not find an examining person, he wonders, "Who knows the thought, 'There is no pot, etc.'?" He thinks, "Is it present or absent," "Is it simply not here (*prasajya, med pa*) or not here by qualification (*paryudāsa, ma yin*)?" In that way he is drawn to a false certainty by turns with the mere sophism of a principle, and if he posits that he has found the (Mādhyamika) view, it seems an easy thing.

Therefore, those who are wise should draw on certainty, which cannot be led away by another, in the way of having arise (in their minds) the scriptures of final meaning (*nitārtha*) and their authoritative commentaries which are the pure Mādhyamika treatises, wherein in particular the special *dharma* of the learned Mādhyamika is stated, to wit, that the meaning of voidness is the meaning of dependent origination, and wherein the *ācārya* Buddhapālita and *śrīmat* Candrakīrti have explained all the subtle points of the entire purport of the *ārya* Master and disciple (= Nāgārjuna and Āryadeva)—which is the school granting certainty that what arises in dependence is not self-existent—certainty that entities void of self-existence have cause and effect.

(ii) Manner in Which a School Opposes That (Special *Dharma*)

[The older Tibetan school argued:] If the school of nātha Nāgārjuna is that way (= the special *dharma* of the Mādhyamika), i.e., that the *dharmas* have not even a particle of self-existence accomplished by their own nature; and if they were accomplished by self-existence, one could not establish *saṃsāra* and *nirvāṇa;* and there is no validity when they do not effect establishments; then it is necessary to take the position that non-self-existence is certain because it lays down all establishments of bondage, liberation, etc.

And (they say): You sirs: (pray tell) if entities have no self-existence accomplished by own nature—what else is there? Hence, they say, for bondage and liberation, arising and passing away, etc. it is not necessary to add the special thing of *paramārtha,* etc. in connection with the passing away, i.e., they pass away through the principle of cessation of self-existence.[54] But when they talk this way, i.e., that it suffices to posit bondage and liberation, and arising and passing away—observe that they have not in that way refuted the non-self-existence.

Suppose they think, if the theory of the *ācārya* (= Candrakīrti) is the establishments of *saṃsāra* and *nirvāṇa,* including bondage and liberation, etc., as convention—then, because we too claim those conventionally, there is no fault. But that is not right. In fact, the theory of *ācārya* Candrakīrti is that the *dharmas* are not self-existent of accomplishment by own nature, even conventionally. If it were the way those persons believe, then because their principle of cessation of self-existence requires the cessation of that self-existence also conventionally; and because their principle of cessation of self-existence amounts to believing in cessation of bondage, liberation, etc., it is very clear that they have refuted bondage, liberation, etc. even conventionally.

In short, if they wish to refute the non-self-existence, bondage and liberation, arising and passing away, etc. then the two truths which validate all establishments of *saṃsāra* and *nirvāṇa* and the void which is void of self-existence are not proper anywhere, so they have opposed only the special *dharma* of the Mādhyamika.

If they claim that they do not oppose those (establishments of bondage and liberation, etc.) then there is certainly no need to add the special thing (of *paramārtha,* etc.) to the thing opposed (i.e., arising, passing away, etc.) by (their) principle of cessation of self-existence, so there is no genuine reason at all for their belief about arising and passing away, and passing away of bondage and liberation.

Hence, if one opposes the cause and fruit with a principle of cessation of self-existence, this claims it is not proper to attribute arising and passing away to something which has no self-existence. So in this case, it amounts to the argument of the realists formulated in chapter XXIV (*Mūla-P.*, k. 1, previously cited):

If all this is void, then your position reduces to the absurdity that there is no arising or passing away and there are no four Noble Truths!

And in the *Vigrahavyāvartinī* (k. 1):

If there is nowhere a self-existence of any thing, your words, being without self-existence, are unable to refute the self-existence.

So it is very clear that there is no distinction at all (of their theory) from the argumentative position of the realists.

Suppose they think, if arising, passing away, etc. are not valid no matter whether (natures) are void or not void of self-existence, then we have no fault whatever in not accepting that (the natures) are void or not void of self-existence. This is decidedly improper in the meaning of the texts (*Mūla-prajñā,* etc.), because the *Prasannapadā* has proven the point, asserting: our school is free from the fault of invalid arising and passing away, etc.; and not only that, also the four Truths and so on are valid. And because the *Mūla* (*-prajnā*) has well analyzed that these (establishments) are proper in the school believing in the void of self-existence, and not proper in the school believing in the nonvoid of same. Also, because the *Madhyamakāvatāra* states (VI, 37–38B):[55]

Reflections and other entities are void, dependent on an aggregation,[56] and do not go unrecognized.[57] The same way as in that case, from the void reflection, etc. comes a (sensory) cognition born with the form of that (reflection, etc.), so also, all entities being void, from those voidnesses arises [the sensory cognition].[58]

Furthermore, if one opposes with the principle of bondage and liberation, etc., it is not proper to do the refutation in the absolute sense, so one must refute in the conventional sense; and at that time (refuting that way) all establishments of *saṃsāra* and *nirvāṇa* are in conventional terms, and the Mādhyamika refuting that way is new (i.e., belongs to the new school).

(iii) How the Mādhyamika Answers This (Challenge)

Regarding this argument that if (all) entities are void of self-existence, they are not appropriate for positing cause and fruit of *saṃsāra* and *nirvāṇa,* nātha Nāgārjuna wards it off (pointing out) that the fault which (the opponent) flings in this direction is the one which the Mādhyamika has good reason to fling in the opposite (the opponent's) direction. He states it in the *Mūla-prajñā,* chapter XXIV (15–16):

You (the realist) while transferring your own faults to us, are like someone who mounting a horse, forgets it is a horse!

> If you look upon the occurrence of entities
> as being from self-existence, that being the
> case, you regard the entities as without
> causes or conditions.

And he states it with this verse among others (*ibid.,* verse 20):

> If all this is nonvoid, there is neither
> arising nor passing away, and it reduces
> to the absurdity that there is absence in
> your school of the four Noble Truths.

Hence, as to (your argument) saying, "If entities have no self-existence accomplished by own nature, what else is there?"—certainly it is clear that you have not distinguished the shoot without self-existence from the shoot that is absent, although they are distinct. Consequently, you have not distinguished the shoot which exists from the shoot accomplished by its own nature; so it is clear that you claim that if it exists it exists by reason of its own nature and that if it is not accomplished by its own nature it does not exist. (On the other hand), if this is not what (you believe), why do you interpose an objection saying there is only an existent thing and only arising and ceasing, etc. with your principle of cessation of accomplishment by own nature? And if it is what (you believe), you are asserting that for as long as you claim the shoot, etc. to exist, for that long it is accomplished by own nature; and you are asserting that if the accomplishment by own nature is not continuous, it is not continuous. Then certainly you are not distinct from the school of the realist and have fallen into one or other of the two extremes (of eternalism and nihilism), because this is stated clearly in the *Catuḥ-ś-ṭ.*:[59]

According to the realist (*vastusatpadārthavādin*), an entity (*vastu*) exists for as long as its own nature (*svarūpa*), for when according to this school it lacks an own nature, the entity is present nowhere, like the horn of an ass (*khara-viṣāṇa*). So (this school) has not gone beyond the two positions (*dvayavāda,* i.e., the two extremes). Hence, everything this school has claimed becomes difficult to justify.

Anyone who does not comprehend these four—existing or not existing by way of self-existence and existing or not existing (in general)—which is *śrimat* Candrakīrti's analysis—undoubtedly would fall into the two extremes, or would not comprehend the meaning of the Mādhyamika that is free from the extremes. When one takes it in the way that there is utterly nothing (*ye med*) accomplished by self-nature (*svarūpa*) and continues that a *dharma* does not exist at all (*ye med*)—in that way, since there is positively nothing (*gtan med pa*) to posit of cause and fruit in the void which is void of self-existence—one falls into the extreme of nihilism. On the other hand, if one claims that a *dharma* exists and subsequently finds it necessary to maintain that it is accomplished by self-nature, in that way it does not happen that one regards as illusory-like the appearance there, which in fact is the cause and fruit without self-existence, and so one falls into the extreme of eternalism.

Hence, by comprehending that no *dharma* has had from the outset even a particle accomplished by self-nature, one does not fall into the extreme of existence. And this granted, when one does not accept that shoots and other entities are void of efficiency (*arthakriyākāritva*) or that there is no entity (at all), one draws upon the certainty cognition which is certain that each agent and action has its own power, and thus avoids the extreme of nonexistence. Analyzing with clarity both the non-self-existent and the nonexistent, the *Prasannapadā* states as follows:[60]

(The Buddhist realist objects:) If you have established this way the non-self-existence of entities, well then, you have rejected in this manner (= holding to the non-self-existence) all that was said by the Lord when he declared: "The maturation of the act which one committed himself will be experienced by himself." By denying the act and the fruit, you, sir, are the chief nullifier (*nāstika*).

(Reply:) We are not nullifiers. But having rejected both (extreme) positions of existence and nonexistence, we clarify the path without the two (*advaya*) that leads to the city of Nirvāṇa. We do not say that the act, the agent, the fruit, and so on, do not exist. What is it we do? We establish these (act, etc.) as lacking self-existence. You may think, "Due to the nonvalidity of action and agent among entities that have no self-existence, the fault is lasting." But this is not so, because one does not see the action of those (entities) with self-existence and because one sees the action of those that lack self-existence.

Regarding what the realist says in this case, if there is no self-existence, you have rejected *karma* and the arising of *karma*'s fruit by ([our] principle of) cessation of self-existence—this amounts to saying that there is no distinction between the claim to deny (all) cause and fruit through the principle of cessation of self-existence, and the (method of) claim. (As a matter of fact, saying that the denial of cause and fruit is chiefly the nihilistic view is a claim in common of both the Mādhyamika and the realist. However, the Mādhyamika does not claim to deny cause and fruit, while the realist imagines that the Mādhyamika when denying the self-existence certainly must deny as well the cause and fruit, and so he (the realist) ascribes the view of nihilism to the Mādhyamika, who has no such view.

Now, the usual thesis of the Tibetan Mādhyamikas, namely, claiming that if one denies a self-existence, one necessarily, by this principle, also denies the cause and fruit—appears to be the same as that of the realists. However, in the case of the Mādhyamikas, the denial (takes place) by the principle of cause and fruit, which they believe in. In reply to the opponent (i.e., the realist), we (Mādhyamikas) are not *nāstikas* (nullifers, deniers), since denying both the positions of existence and nonexistence we clarify the path of liberation, as was said [in the *Prasannapadā* citation] and since we show by the following way of rejecting the position of existence or nonexistence (=the extremes). (To wit:) In that regard, we deny that there is nonexistence of action and fruit, etc., so we reject the position of nonexistence. Thus, when you claim that action and fruit, etc. are nonexistent, you are the *nāstika* and we reply that we do not claim it. He (the realist) asks, "Well then, what do you assert?" (The Mādhyamika replies.) We claim or posit that these (entities of) action, fruit, etc. are not self-existent, and so we reject the position (i.e., the extreme) of existence. The realist says: "Due to the nonvalidity of action and agent among entities that have no self-existence, the fault continues. Thus, while you, sir, disclaim nonexistence, you assert non-self-existence; and since non-self-existence is the already-stated fault, you are unable henceforth to avoid the nonvalidity of cause and fruit." But arguing that way, they argue as though in our (Mādhyamika) school there is no distinction between non-self-existence and nonexistence. In reply to this, we say (making the distinction explicit) that the presence of self-existence of agent and action which generate cause and fruit, etc. is not proper, and that only the non-self-existence is proper for those. Besides, the *Catuḥ-ś-ṭ* states:[61]

(We reply:) We do not maintain that there is no entity, because we maintain that there is dependent origination (of an entity).

(The realist asks:) Are you asserting that there (really) is an entity?[62]

(Reply:) No. Because we assume that it originates in dependence.

(The realist asks:) What are you asserting?

(Reply:) We assert dependent origination.

(The realist asks:) Then what is the meaning of dependent origination.

(Reply:) It has the meaning of non-self-existence. It has the meaning of effects arising with the nature[63] of a phantom (horse, cow, etc.), a mirage (of water), a reflection (as of a face), a city of *gandharvas* (i.e., a cloud city), a materialization (of a man, etc.), and like a dream. It has the meaning of voidness and nonself.

This passage teaches that by reason of believing in dependent origination, there is the way of rejecting the adherence to two extremes of existence or nonexistence of an entity.

Moreover, one rejects the adherence to existence of the entity by the explanation "not arising by self-existence" as a meaning of dependent origination; and one rejects the adherence to nonexistence of the entity by the teaching of arising of effects like a phantom, etc., as a meaning of dependent origination. Hence, of the two possible meanings of an entity, namely the meaning of self-existence and the meaning of efficiency, the entity held to be existence of entity means only accomplished by self-existence, and the entity held to be the nonexistence of entity means the entity of efficiency; and one rejects both, by teaching the refutation of self-existence (to avoid the extreme of existence) and the existence of cause and fruit which are like an illusion (to avoid the extreme of nonexistence). Furthermore, the *Catuḥ-ś-ṭ* states:[64]

(The Cittamātra people ask:) (According to you, sirs:) Is there no memory of a past subject (*viṣayin*)?

(Reply:) There is not.

(Question:) Who speaks?

(Reply:) We (saying) that there is no rejecting of dependent origination. In what way that (memory) exists, in that way therefore the "memory" occurs only with falsehood toward an object that is false. This the *ācārya* himself established.

[Candrakīrti comments:] Therefore, the object-support (*ālambana*) of memory is the past entity. If it existed by reason of its own nature, the memory of it would exist, because it has (this) object as its object-support. If it (the memory) loses the accomplishment by own nature, then at whatever time the past entity is not self-existent, at that time the memory which has it as object-support would also be not self-existent. Hence, we have proved that it has "falsehood." "False" means non-self-existent and arising in dependence, and it has no other meaning. The meaning of nonexistent entity is not the meaning of "false." It is not the case that the past entity lacks all aspects, because it can be remembered and because its effect can be seen. Besides, it does not exist by way of its own nature, because this would reduce to the absurdity of eternalism, and to the absurdity of its being grasped (i.e., perceived) as a concrete entity.

This passage avers that those entities which are elapsed and so on, are not utterly nonexistent but also not accomplished by own nature, and that the meaning of "false" or lying is the meaning of dependent origination but not the meaning of no entity (at all). Hence, we are neither the realist holding that these natures are accomplished by their own nature, and so falling into the extreme of existence, nor the realist holding that these (natures) simply exist, and so falling into the extreme of existence. In the same way, by holding that among inner and outer entities there are no entities void of efficiency, we do not deny the entity and fall into the extreme of nonexistence. And (simply) by believing that these (entities) have no self-existence we do not fall into the extreme of nonexistence.

Accordingly, when one does not keep separate the distinctions of utterly nonexistent and non-self-existent, and of accomplished by own nature and merely existent, he falls into the extremes of existence or nonexistence. In order to prevent (these falls) we do not profess the simple negation (*prasajya*), but assert the qualified negation (*paryudāsa*) of the existence. When one (i.e., the opponent) has the wishful thinking that we are merely saying that we do not profess the simple presence but assert the qualified negation of absence, he merely expresses the mutual denial and that he has no room at all for the Mādhyamika meaning, because at the time he rejects another (school) he does the rejecting by inspecting the simple presence or absence of self-existence and insists on deciding between these two and then attributes a meaning which in neither case does our school have.

According to that (procedure), whatever be the thing one is inspecting as to whether it has or lacks self-existence, at that time one is supposed to take a position of deciding in terms of the two; but if there is a third possibility[65] in that place, it is not right to inspect it as to whether it has or lacks self-existence. No more (right), for example, than, in the case when given that there is a color, to inquire if it is blue or if it is yellow.

Accordingly, also when deciding between presence or absence of self-existence, one is dependent on deciding between general presence or absence of a knowable (entity). For example, in the case of a real thing when deciding between singleness and multiplicity of the real thing, one is dependent on deciding between general singleness and multiplicity. If one is deciding in that manner, he must avoid a third possibility, so it is rash to believe there is no *dharma* other than among those two, because the *Vigrahavyāvartinī* says (26c–d): "At the time one gets rid of non-self-existence, the thing with self-existence would be proved." Furthermore, the one claiming that way (i.e., that there is no *dharma* other than in those categories) has no instrument to be certain of the count in regard to any *dharma* when not admitting a third possibility, and so would reap only doubt. This is because if one decides about one out of existence and nonexistence, he cannot decide about the other one (of the two). That is to say, if one claims such things as "It exists" or "It does not exist," and that there is no third possibility, then that would apply as well to existence and nonexistence.

Regarding that position, it is possible to mistake the words of the Mādhyamika texts as saying merely, it neither exists nor does not exist. One might grant that it is not proper to say, it either exists or it does not exist; but it is also not right to say (just), it neither exists nor does not exist, because (those Mādhyamika texts) set (the matter) forth as the four alternatives (*catuṣkoṭi*).[66] According to the *Mūla-prajñā* (XV, 10):

Saying, "It exists," one adheres to eternalism.
Saying, "It does not exist," one has the nihilism view.
Therefore the wise person stays neither on existence nor nonexistence.

That clearly states that one should not assert only existence and nonexistence, and that the thesis of entities being accomplished by self-existence is the view of eternalism or nihilism. The *Prasannapadā* explains that when former texts held to existence or nonexistence, this was the view that entities either exist or do not exist; and later it points out (in XV, 11):[67]

Now he has shown that when there is the view of either presence (*bhāva*) or absence (*abhāva*), it reduces to the absurdity of the view of eternalism or nihilism. It is for that very reason that he states (XV, 11):

> Saying that something exists by reason of self-existence and does not fail to exist—reduces to eternalism.
> Saying that something does not exist now but existed formerly—reduces to nihilism.

If one says that something exists by reason of self-existence, then, since there is no ceasing of self-existence, one cannot say that it ever fails to exist. Accordingly, since that person has accepted the existence of self-existence, he falls into the view of eternalism. And when one holds that the own-nature of an entity (*bhāva-svarūpa*) was previously in a present state, but insists that later by reason of its disintegration, now it does not exist, he is reduced to the nihilism view.

This sets forth that the thesis of existence by reason of self-existence is the eternalism view, and that if one claims that the former own-nature later disintegrates, it is nihilistic; but it does not set forth existence-only or disintegration-only. Besides, Buddhapālita clearly explains the teachings of the positions that fall into eternalism and nihilism, when he says:[68]

The explanation (of the *Madhyamakakārikā,* etc.) that the asserting it exists or does not exist, is the view of eternalism or nihilism—takes those (views) as (both amounting to) existence by reason of self-existence.

In short, those who assert that the voidness which lacks self-existence is not the illustrious voidness, by thus opposing (that voidness stated in the *Prajñāpāramitā* and authoritative commentaries) have rejected the *Prajñāpāramitā* and by rejecting the Dharma will go to an evil destiny. And those who, while having faith in non-self-existence and thinking, "If there is no self-existence, what exists?" take the position that all the *dharmas* are completely without existence, they also fall into the abyss of nihilistic view. Because that is alluded to in the passage (*Mūlaprajñā*, XXIV, 11a–b):

> When voidness is ill apprehended,
> it destroys those of weak intelligence.

And because the *Prasannapadā* on that (*kārikā*) states:[69]

First, if one imagines that "everything is void" means that everything is non-existent, at that time his view is a sham. It has been explained (in the *Ratnāvalī,* II, 19):

> This *dharma,* wrongly apprehended, destroys the unwise person, that is to say, he sinks into the unclean view that it does not exist.

But if you do not take the position of denying everything, at that time, however these entities be apperceived and be void, you certainly fall into rejection of voidness when you say that the meaning of non-self-existence is not the meaning of voidness; and having so rejected, you become abandoned by the *dharma,* and as a result of the *karma* thereof, certainly you will go to an evil destiny. As the *Ratnāvalī* (II, 20) says it:

> Besides, as a result of its being understood wrongly, the fool, conceited about his learning, his nature ruined by rejection (of voidness), falls headlong into the Avīci hell.

(You say,) granted that we hold that prior entities did not exist later on, and in that sense do not exist; and we have not claimed that these (entities) exist primordially, so how does that amount to a nihilism view? (In reply) this is the way it has been said to be the nihilism view (*Mūlaprajñā,* XV, 11, c–d):

> Saying that something does not exist now but existed formerly—reduces to nihilism.

Your argument is discussed in the *Prasannapadā* (in XXIV, 11):[70]

> The yogin who is moved only by his deception about conventional truth (*saṃvṛti-satya*) and has understood it to be without self-existence, when he discovers the voidness of it (=*saṃvṛti-satya*) to have the character of *paramārtha,* does not fall into the two extremes. (But:) when you think, "What is that thing which used to be and is not now?" you cannot thus perceptively reach the self-existence of the former entity, and so, also, you cannot discover its later non-existence.

Since that was said, you think it over and say, "That is not right, because if it is necessary to accept a prior entity as a cause of nihilism for the nihilism view, while the Lokāyata sect should have held that earlier there was a previous and a later life, as well as *karma* and its fruit, etc. and later not, in fact they denied (all those) and disclaimed that those exist from the outset," so it reduces to the absurdity of (that sect) not having the nihilism view [when in fact that sect was the classical school of nihilism par excellence].[71] Hence, that passage, "Saying that something does not exist now but existed formerly—reduces to nihilism," means that the realists certainly have the eternalism or nihilism view when they hold that entities have a self-existence accomplished by own-nature, because if they hold that the self-existence never changes in all time, it is the eternalism view; and if they hold that it existed in earlier time and disintegrated in later time, it is the nihilism view. Therefore, when you teach that there is no nihilism view in holding that self-existence was present in a former time and later on disintegrated, this proceeds to a reason for denying that entities have even a particle of self-existence accomplished by own-nature, but (also) this (reason) does not eliminate all nihilistic views (such as the Lokāyata's).

The nihilistic view which holds that there is no *karma* and fruit as well as other different methods, are stated extensively in the *Prasannapadā,* this way: The nihilistic view is the claim that there is no *karma* and fruit and no world beyond; and the Mādhyamika, by claiming that those (*karma,* etc.) are without self-existence are different from i.e., superior to) their thesis. The Mādhyamikas set forth non-self-existence by the reason that those—*karma* and fruit, etc.—arise in dependence. In contrast, you *nāstikas* deny that those—*karma,* fruit, etc.—arise in dependence, and so do not employ that reason. (For you) this is the world of living beings, and reasoning that one does not see the former life coming here and this life going to another one, you say there is nothing. Certainly there is a great difference in reasons. The *Prasannapadā* (chapter XVIII) states:[72]

Now some (realists) accuse us as follows: The Mādhyamikas are not different from the nihilists because they say that the good and bad deed, the agent, the fruit, and the entire world is void of self-existence (*bhāvasvabhāvaśūnya*).[73] The nihilists also say that all those do not exist. Therefore, the Mādhyamikas are not different from the nihilists. (The Mādhyamika replies:) It is not so. Why? Because the Mādhyamikas are among those who profess dependent origination; and they say that all the present world and future world is without self-existence because it (all) arises when reaching (*prāpya*) and in dependence (*pratītya*) on causes and conditions. As to the nihilists, who are among those professing an own-nature (*svarūpa*), it is not by reason of voidness of self-existence through arising in dependence that they understand the absence of another world, etc. On the contrary, they admit the present world to be real (*vastujāta*) by way of its self-existence;[74] but because they do not see the coming here from another world and the passage to another world from this world,[75] they deny other entities that are similar to the entities perceived in this world.

Now, while the reasons for the Mādhyamika and the nihilism view are different, it might be thought that their view of non-self-existence is the same because they have a like comprehension that *karma* and fruit and former and later worlds are without a self-existence accomplished by own-nature. But in this case, they are also different, because their (i.e., the nihilists') non-self-existence is a belief in utter nothingness (*ye med*) so in no wise do they accept the two truths; while the Mādhyamika accepts that *karms,* the fruit, and so on, exist conventionally (*saṃvṛtitas*). This is pointed out by the *Prasannapadā* (chapter XVIII):[76]

But don't they also accept the non-existence of what is not present by way of a thing's own nature, thus agreeing with the given view (i.e., the Mādhyamika)?

Not so! Why? Because the Mādhyamika believes in the existence (of all those things) in the conventional sense, and because (the nihilist) differs from that belief.

In fact, the claim that the Mādhyamika does not believe in the *karma,* the fruit, etc. in the conventional sense is a teaching that they have a view the same as the Lokāyata. Still, the *ācārya* (Candrakīrti), when differing from the nihilist in terms of the reason, does not say, "That's your thesis because it is not ours" [i.e., does not try to pin the Lokāyata doctrine on the opponent the way the latter tries to pin nihilism on the Mādhyamika]. He does not say, "We have nothing like your claim that those things do not exist" [since the *Prajñāpāramitā* scriptures have such teachings in the *paramārtha* sense]. Nor does he say, "We claim that an existent does not exist."[77] But he does speak of non-self-existence and posit dependent origination as its reason; and say that those things (*karma,* fruit, etc.) are established, claiming this in the conventional sense.

You may object, saying, granted that *karma,* the fruit, etc. have no self-existence accomplished by own-nature; then when the nihilistic view also claims that those things do not exist, thus claiming that they have no self-existence, it is the same as the Mādhyamika in the part about non-self-existence. But this is most certainly not the same. In illustration, suppose a man has stolen a treasure, and a certain person, not recognizing that he is the thief, says, by way of lying, "He stole it"; and another person, having observed the treasure being stolen by that thief, says, "He stole it"; then, while both of them say, "He stole it," and the thief and theft are certain, one person told a lie and the other one told the truth. In the same way (the Mādhyamika and the nihilist) are not the same So we read in the *Prasannapadā* (chapter XVIII):[78]

Suppose (the opponent) says: "They are the same basically (*vastutas*)." (Reply:) Even if we take them basically, it is not proved that they are the same. Indeed, they are not the same by difference of persons who assess the situation. For example, suppose a man has committed a theft; and a certain person, not having actually recognized him as such, but urged on by an enemy of that (thief), falsely reports him, saying, "He stole it"; and another person, having witnessed (the theft) directly, denounces him. Then even if there is no difference basically, there is, by difference of the subject [who reports]. One is called the liar; the other, the truth-teller. One is rightly considered with ill-repute and with demerit, but not the other. Here it is a like case. To the extent the own-natures of entities are recognized by the Mādhyamikas, they have been fully understood and spoken of; and to the extent the own-natures of entities are not recognized by the nihilists, those two (the Mādhyamika and the nihilist) are not the same in terms of knowing and expressing.

Now, some persons, having understood the non-self-existence, oppose *karma,* the fruit, etc. by principles (of pondering *paramārtha*); but that is not how *karma* and the fruit, having been understood, are posited in our school. (Those persons) have falsely approached *saṃvṛti* which is the appearance-side (*snaṅ phyogs*), and assert that they have attained without error the view of the void-side (*stoṅ phyogs*).[79] This we must oppose. Thus, (what we mean by) the void is the efficiency (*arthakriyākāritva*) void. But, when one does not take the void (in that meaning), then even though (he accepts) non-self-existence, he still needs to posit dependent origination of cause and fruit. The *Catuḥ-ś-ṭ* (Commentary on chapter XV, 10a–c) clearly answers the question, "If it has no self-existence, what is it?"

Accordingly, whatever be the entity, it neither come to birth, nor, likewise, goes to decease.[80]

[Candrakīrti's commentary:] It certainly has no self-existence, then what is it? That will be told. Whatever thing has a nature created by defilement and purity and arises in dependence, that is it.

Besides, *ācārya* Buddhapālita, having clearly analyzed the difference between presence and accomplished by own nature, makes reply in his commentary on chapter XX (of *Madhyamaka-kārikā*):[81]

(The realist challenges the Mādhyamika): If (as you hold) time does not exist, and cause and fruit and their aggregate do not exist, then what else is there? That being so, you speak as a nihilist.

(The Mādhyamika) will explain this. It is not (as you say). The way you have conceived that time and so on are present through their (individual) natures, winds up as not valid, for those are "accomplished" as designations when there is dependence.

Thus he opposes, saying that accomplished by own-nature, as in the theory of the realist, is not valid, because (they are) "accomplished" as designations when there is dependence, to wit, (only) are present in dependent origination.

Accordingly, if one analyzes the four—presence and absence by self-existence, and presence and absence (generally speaking)—one can turn away innumberable faulty conceptions (that lead to the two extremes); and the principles which oppose presence by self-existence do not engender mistakes when opposing presence-only (in general). Hence, the Mādhyamikas' chief answer to the learned men among the realists is by way of those four, so I have explained it somewhat (in the present section).

(b) Teaching How To Avoid Defeat by the Assailant's Discourses

There are four parts: (i) Avoiding defeat by denial, considering ability and inability of examination by a principle; (ii) Avoiding defeat by denial, considering proof and nonproof by authority; (iii) Avoiding defeat by denial, considering whether or not there is birth with the four alternatives; (iv) Invalidating the assailant to denying the four alternatives, presence, absence, etc. of an entity.

(i) Avoiding Defeat by Denial, Considering Ability and Inability of Examination by a Principle

The methodical examination (or search)[82] by way of such considerations as presence or absence, and arising or nonarising in regard to the manner of being of the entities with these features (*dharma*) such as form, is called the principle of examining reality and the principle of examining the ultimate. And unless by this principle there is examination-ability as to the arising of form, etc.,[83] we make no claims, so we have no fault that is basically fallacious of truth. If there is inability to examine those (the arising, etc.) with a principle, then how could it be valid that there is the meaning of denial by a principle [and it is not valid]. Concerning this [last statement], it is a mistake to identify the inability (*akṣamā*) of examining by a principle with opposition (*bādhā*) by a principle, but many persons talk as though these two were identical. When they say that there are the arising, etc., even though there be negation by a principle which examines reality,[84] this is reckless talk, and we (Mādhyamikas) do not accept it.

The meaning of ability and inability of examining by a principle is whether one finds or does not find reality by that principle of examining. Furthermore, the *Catuḥ-ś-ṭ* (in chapter XIII) states:

> Because our examination has taken pains to search for the self-existence.[85]

This passage refers to the search for the presence or absence of self-existence of the arising, stoppage, etc. of form and so on. Accordingly, it is the search for presence or absence of arising and stoppage that are accomplished by own nature, of form, etc., but it is not the search by that principle for merely the arising and stoppage.

Now, that principle is called "examination of reality" because it is the examination of whether arising, stopping, and so on are accomplished or not accomplished in reality. When examining or searching with that kind of principle, the nonfinding of even a scarce amount of arising, etc. is "inability of examination"; and one cannot deny (the arising) simply through not finding it by that principle; but if there is (the basis of the search) it is necessary to prove it by that principle, and then if it is not proved by that (principle) it can be denied. It is proved by cognizing the arising and stoppage of form, etc. as conventions (*vyavahāra*), but it is not proved by cognizing their presence by the principle. So how can they be denied (simply) by not finding them by that (cognition of the principle)? For example, just as when eye cognition does not find sound (the sound) is not to be denied by that (eye cognition)!

For this reason, it is necessary to find out by that principle whether the arising, stoppage, etc. are accomplished by own-nature or accomplished in reality (*de kho nar*), because by that principle there is methodical examination of whether form, etc. is present or absent, whether arising and stopping, accomplished by own-nature. When that sort of (principle of search) does not manage to find out the arising, and so on, that negates the arising, stoppage, etc. accomplished by own-nature or accomplished in reality, because it is necessary to find by that (principle) if (those things) are accomplished by own-nature, and then were not (so) found. For example, suppose a pot is situated in the eastern quarter and a guide searches with determination to find it; if he does not find it at the time he searches for the pot in the east, it can be denied that there is a pot in the east. But the pot has mere presence;[86] how can it be denied (just) by that (not finding of it)! In the same way, if one searches the pot by the principle with determination to find out if there is arising accomplished by own-nature, the not finding of the arising serves to deny an arising by self-existence or by own-nature; but how is the arising per se (*utpatti-mātra*) to be denied? This is also clearly stated in the *Catuḥ-ś-ṭ* (from chapter XIII, on k. 321c—d):[87]

Therefore, when the sense organs, sense objects, and (their respective) perceptions are examined by a principle (*rigs, yukti*) of such sort (which examines *paramārtha*), there is no accomplishment by an own-nature since no (own)-nature is found. If they had accomplishment by their own-nature, then when they are examined by a principle (= by a valid method) they would be perceived by their own nature as it stays (*yathāsthita*). But they are not (so) perceived. For that reason, it is proved (*siddha*) that they are void of self-existence.

This *ācārya* (Candrakīrti) says again and again that these *saṃvṛti* things, form, sound, etc. are mere presence, since the principle of examining their reality or examining the presence or absence of their self-existence does not give positive proof [of anything more than that mere presence]; so a consideration of the principle does not infuse into them (the sense organs, etc.). He frequently states that unwise persons, having done the examination of the principle, and not finding (those things) by that principle, (erroneously) posit *saṃvṛti* as the destruction (*'jig pa*) of those *saṃvṛti* things. If it were possible to deny those things by the principle of examining the presence or absence of self-existence, it would be most obligatory to subject those *saṃvṛti* things, form, feelings, etc. to a consideration of the principle (of examining the presence or absence of self-existence); but it is precisely this which is refuted in every way in this *ācārya*'s writing. This being the case, (you sirs), taking your stand in the aim of opposition by your principle whose meaning is not finding by the principle (otherwise valid) of examining the presence or absence of self-existence, have strayed far afield from the method of the Mādhyamika.

On the same grounds, since with noble equipoise (*ārya-samāpatti*)[88] one does not see the arising and stopping of form, etc., how can one see with it that there is no arising and stopping! Even though one does not find arising, etc. at the time he uses the principle of examining the presence or absence of self-existence, he should not judge that there is no arising, stoppage, etc. Therefore, while inability of examination by a principle and opposition by a principle are different; not seeing arising and stoppage by noble equipoise, and seeing that there are no (arising and stoppage) are different; not finding the arising and stoppage by cognition through the principle which examines the presence or absence of a self-existent, and finding that there is no arising and stoppage are different—then when present-day teachers (who profess to be Mādhyamika), not to speak of some former learned men,[89] who, not distinguishing those two (in each set), take them as one, are led to be mistaken, intelligent persons must (henceforth) distinguish those with keen examination!

According to the above, the great power of conventional cognitions derives from the authority of the one having *paramārtha* as his object; and we do not believe in opposing, with conventional cognitions, the authority of the one having *paramārtha* as his object. However, suppose someone does not find (the arising, etc.) by that (principle) after examining the conventional form, feelings, etc. by the principle of examining reality, and then claims to deny (the conventional form, feelings, etc.) by means of that principle. (We reply:) not only has this person been unable to deny them away by that (principle), but also, using that method, we can oppose that negating expert by an authority acknowledged by the world. The *Madhyamakāvatāra* (VI, 83) states (the reason):

If the world does not oppose you[90] (with its acknowledged authority), deny this (*saṃvṛti*) while regarding the (conventions of this) world itself! Then let you and the world argue in this case (about the presence or absence of *saṃvṛti*)! After (your quarrel), we will rally with the power (of the Buddha).

Also because the commentary on this verse explains:

As for us (Mādhyamikas), we are very sorely placed to assail (these erroneous appearances of) worldly *saṃvṛti:* may you (the believer in mind-only) refute the *saṃvṛti* of the world! If the world does not give you opposition, we will join your cause. But it does give opposition.

In this passage, "we are very sorely placed to assail worldly *saṃvṛti*" refers to (our) endeavor on the path for the sake of purifying [which is a difficult thing to do] these appearances of error belonging to the subject (*viṣayin*) who has eye cognition, etc. and of error belonging to the object constituted by form, etc.; and to the fact that we do not care to have them (the appearances) refuted by a principle, but would make them be refuted by cultivating the path. The words "may you refute the *saṃvṛti* of the world" and so on, mean that when (the Cittamātra's theory of) *paratantra* as substantial is refuted by the Mādhyamika, you (the Cittamātra followers) say, "We also shall refute your *saṃvṛti* by a principle," thus are put in the same boat;[91] and if you have the capacity to refute by a principle the *saṃvṛti* as we have the capacity to refute the self-existence of *paratantra,* "we will join your cause." Now, if you can deny (*saṃvṛti*) by a principle, we explain that in such a case it is not necessary to engage in austerities of cultivating the path in order to ward off these (erroneous appearances of *saṃvṛti*), but we hold (that it is necessary), so we teach that one cannot deny by a principle the *saṃvṛti* things. Not only can you not deny (*saṃvṛti* by a principle), but if you refute (by that principle), the celebrated persons of the world "give you opposition"; i.e., give opposition by conventional cognition to such a principle which is a fallacy (*ābhāsa*); and still we maintain that there is a great power from those (principles).

Hence, when the realists also engage in the examination of a principle, and refute such *saṃvṛti* things as external entities, (at that time) they do not find (those *saṃvṛti* things), so they cannot deny (them).

Besides, some persons assert that the meaning of not denying in conventional terms the form, etc. is to not deny independent wordly individuals such as cowherders; but by the principle of examining reality they are to be denied, so this (particular) assertion is highly invalid. A wise person with the principle of examining reality needs to deny or not to deny (form, etc.), and to have the independence of a discrimination not affected by a theory-system (*siddhānta*), because there is no stipulation that he not deny; and because if he denies by a principle which examines reality, it is necessary that he take this denial conventionally.

That there is no denial of all arising by the principle of examining reality, is also clearly stated by *ācārya* Candrakīrti, as he states in the *Catuḥ-ś-ṭ* (on chapter XV, k. 360):

If one claims to teach that this examination refutes all forms of arising, so that there is no arising of constructed (natures), then there could not occur such a thing as a phantom (*māyā*), for example, such things as the son of a barren woman—and it would reduce to the absurdity that there would be no dependent origination. When one is fearful he does not accept concord with those (similes of illusion). But one should accept those, the phantom, etc., which do not conflict with that (dependent origination).

"This examination" means the principle of examining reality. "Refutes all forms of arising" means refutes all measure of arising without adding a qualification to the refutable things. The meaning of "barren woman" and so on is that if one refutes all arising (by that principle)—so also the son of a barren woman, the horn of a hare, and so on—there would be no void entities, with all their efficiency; and in the same way there would occur the fault of no dependent origination, and "fearful," i.e., that there is no efficiency at all. But unlike that nonarising of the son of a barren woman, and so on, we assert the denial of arising by self-existence or in reality, since it is like a phantom, etc. Also, the *Catuḥ-ś-ṭ* (on chapter XIII, k. 311a–b) says:

If the sense organs such as the eyes were not possible, then how could one posit the nature of maturation of (i.e., cast by) fluxional) *karma* of those sense organs such as the eyes? Why should we (Mādhyamikas) refute the nature of maturation of those (sense organs)? [And we don't] Or, if you prove your denial of sense organs such as the eyes, why may we not refute that (own-nature of maturation)? [And we do]. Because our examination has taken pains to search for the self-existence. When we here deny the accomplishment by own-nature of the entities, we do not deny that what was done by the eyes, etc. has a maturation of *karma* in dependent origination. For that reason, since there is that (maturation), whatever is reported as maturation is the existence of eyes, and so on.[92]

Thus, with principles, this passage explains clearly that so much is to be denied and so much is not to be denied, and the analysis in this manner is stated on the same occasion. How necessary it is to add such (information) in all cases (where it is not actually mentioned)!

Hence, what was searched on our side has been based on the object (*viṣaya*), and we have denied the existence through own nature by principles, but have not denied existence itself. The principles are stated as taking pains to search for the self-existence; thus the principle is the search for the presence or absence of self-existence, so that is the meaning of saying "refutation by that (principle)" or "refutation of self-existence." Hence one must distinguish the two (Commentary: i.e., not denying the object which is searched, and denying the self-existence which is searched).

It is said that the Mādhyamika not only must not deny the fruits (pleasant and painful) of *karma* (good and bad) but also must believe in them, according to the continuation of that scriptural passage (the *Catuḥ-ś-ṭ*):[93]

Therefore, a wise man, regarding the worldly entities, should see the reality by examining (them) as already explained, and should not be drawn into their same direction. He should believe in the inconceivability of the maturation of actions, and should believe in all the world in the manner of a materialization (*nirmita*) arisen from a materialization.

Accordingly, on our part, we have established both truths. But if a person opposes the establishment of *saṃvṛti* by the principle of establishing *paramārtha,* this creates an inner conflict in establishment of what has been established as the two truths. Since it is impressive wisdom to establish both truths, how to do it right (must be discussed). You claim to have practically no inner conflict in those two establishments, and yet by the principle of establishing *paramārtha* you have a conflict which wrongs the establishment of *saṃvṛti*. We read in the *Prasannapadā* (on chapter I):[94]

You sirs, engage upon some principle with muddle-headed intelligence concerning the distinction of *paramārtha-satya* and *saṃvṛti-satya* and then destroy it by a bad principle (*a-nyaya*). We (Mādhyamikas) take a stand in the worldly side through wisdom in establishing conventional truth; and then combat with one principle your other alluded-to principle which denies the single side of *saṃvṛti.* We, like an elder of the world, combat just you who falls away from good behavior of the world, but do not combat *saṃvṛti*.

This passage states that a person is muddle-headed about establishing the two truths when, having engaged in examination by the principle of examining reality, he destroys *saṃvṛti*. Therefore, it is certainly not the purport of this *ācārya* (Candrakīrti) to deny by a principle the form, etc. of *saṃvṛti.*

In short, not only should the Mādhyamika concern himself with the inside schools described in the *siddhāntas* of India for establishing of the two truths, but also (with *siddhāntas*) by other persons expressing hostility to the way we establish the two truths. To the person who wishes to wrong the entities of *saṃvṛti* by a principle partial to *paramārtha* among the two truths which we have established, we say: you do not have even one.[95]

(ii) Avoiding Defeat by Denial, considering Proof and Nonproof by Authority

The belief in form, etc. is claimed to be not proved by an authority but it is proved by an authority. However, how is it proper to say (*Madhyamakāvatāra,* VI, 31a, as cited in Candrakīrti's own commentary):

By all means, the world is not an authority.

This argues against the reality of worldly cognitions of eye, etc. as being authorities, but does not argue against all sense objects as having authorities. Accordingly, we read in the *Madhyamakāvatāra* commentary (on VI, 30) as follows:

Consequently, in the contemplation of reality, it is only the *āryas* who are authorities, not the non-*āryas.*[96] But if (the authorities of) the world have the desire to express opposition, and believe in the authority of what is seen by the world (with eye cognition, etc.) as examination of reality, it is the case (as the verse 30 now tells):

If the world is the authority,
then the world sees reality, and

what is the use of the others, the *āryas;*
and what is the use of the Noble Path?
(But) the stupid do not have the principle
to be authority.

And because the commentary thereon (leading to 31a–b expands:

When there are only the eyes, and so on, to serve for determination of reality, to serve for understanding the Noble Path, then there is no endeavor in morality, learning, pondering, intense contemplation, and so on, nor fruit; and it is not the case; hence:—

By all means, the world is not an authority;
When it is a matter of reality, the world
cannot oppose.

And the *Yuktiṣaṣṭikā-vṛtti* (on verse 3) explains:

The view (by eye cognition, etc.) that those (form, etc.) have existence is proved to be the not seeing of reality. For this reason the Lord said,

The eye, ear, nose are not authoritative.[97]

By such citations he renders it exceedingly clear that the specialized sensory organs (eye cognition, etc.) are refuted as authorities for reality, and that the others, sensory objects (form, etc.), are not (authorities, either). If one does not take it this way, there would be no connection (between prior and later purpose), that is, if those cognitions such as the eye and conventional entities such as form and sound were authorities for viewing of reality, we say there is the absurdity of no need to seek the Noble Path, and we (further) say there is the absurdity of no (individual) purpose for eye cognition to cognize form and the ear to hear sound;[98] and similarly, we say there is the absurdity of no purpose to seeking the Noble Path (for no other reason than) because one observes form, sound, etc. We put much stress on this, and if one does not so accept (that those are absurdities), how could he accomplish anything! [And he can't.] This is what the *Catuḥ-ś-ṭ* says (on k. 301 in chapter XIII):

When a person[99] exaggerates (the function of) sensory perception as being direct realization, and understands the others (sense objects that are self-existent) as being the authority (devoid of error), he is highly disconnected (from purpose). While the world regards undeceived cognition as authoritative, the Lord declared (sense) perception (*vijñāna*), because it is constructed, to be false, a deceptive factual base (*dharmin*), and illusory.[100] As to a thing that is false, a deceptive factual base, and illusory—it lacks nondeception, because it is a thing which is present in one way (namely, not existent by way of own-character) but appears in another way (namely, existent by way of own-character). Since it appears in this (deceptive) way, it is not a principle to be considered as authority: indeed, all (vulgar) perceptions are absurd as authority!

But one may properly wonder how (simply) saying this, constitutes the general refutation of the cognitions, such as eye, as authority. It is set forth in such passages as, "The eye, ear, nose are not authoritative," and as there are weighty points of seeming contradiction, I must explain them in detail.

Accordingly, the refutation of eye and other sensory cognitions as constituting direct perception and authority, is the refutation of the logicians' thesis, so first of all, we speak of the school which is their thesis. It is as stated in the *Catuḥ-ś-ṭ* (on chapter XIII):[101]

Let us suppose a (novice) like a child (who does not know the words for things), because he has not gained experience in this logician's system for worldly entities, would involve himself for the very first time, and so as to be instructed, would ask him:

Novice: What is your direct perception (*pratyakṣa*)?

Logician: That is something to be argued and considered. Anyway, direct perception is (sense) awareness.

Novice: Then, what is (sense) awareness?

Logician: That which is free from discursive thought (*vikalpa*).

Novice: Then, what is discursive thought?

Logician: A swinging bell[102] of ideas which engage in attributing a name[103] and a genus[104] to an entity. Because they are free of that (swinging bell), the five perceptions (*pañcavijñāna*) clarify only the inexpressible particular of the object, so one should call them "direct perception" (*pratyakṣa*).[105]

The awareness free from discursive thought and unmistaken is claimed to be direct perception itself. Here "unmistaken" means that the five direct perceptions (*pratyakṣa*), which are sensory perceptions grasping the object-particular exactly according to its presence, appraise the particular; and the particulars of form, sound, etc. are the things to be appraised by those five direct perceptions. Consequently, it is claimed that those (direct perceptions) go as authoritative, and the particular consists of the five objects (*viṣaya*).

According to the way this *ācārya* (Candrakīrti) explains, he does not maintain "accomplished by own-nature" or "accomplished by own-characteristic [or by a particular]" in conventional terms. So how could he maintain that those sensory perceptions are authoritative for (proving the) particular! [And he does not maintain it.] Hence, here we refute those as authorities, and oppose the claim that those particulars in the five sense objects are authorities. Our manner of opposition is how the Lord opposed (them), saying that the perceptions are false and deceptive. Furthermore, since it (the scripture) declared them deceptive, on that account it refutes them as being nondeceptive and opposes them as authorities; because being nondeceptive is the characteristic of authority.

However, if one wonders what is the manner of deception, it was said (previously): "it is a thing which is present in one way, but appears in another way." That is to say, those five sense objects, form, sound, etc., while not accomplished by particular, appear to the sensory perceptions as though (accomplished by) particular. And so we say that those particulars are not authorities. In short, those sensory perceptions and those five object-particulars are not authorities; and because the act of observing the five object-particulars is deceptive, and because the appearance as a particular is in fact void of the five object-particulars, one should remember to think of them, for example, like perceiving the appearance of a double moon.

Regarding this (method of opposition), the realists claim that if form, sound, etc. have no self-existence accomplished by particular, then those (form, sound, etc.) would be void of all efficiency, and entities would be absent. So they (the realists) claim that if the five object-particulars do not pass as authoritative of direct perception, then the five sense objects do not go as authorities; but also that if the five sense objects pass as authorities, then their particulars may go as authorities.

According to this *ācārya* (Candrakīrti), if something were accomplished by particular or its own-nature, it would occur in reality, so a sensory object would be accomplished in reality with its authority established, and it would be incumbent for a particular to pass as an authority. But he adds that the sense object is false, and so it is not incumbent for it to have its authority established and for a particular to pass as an authority. That is shown in the *Catuḥ-ś-ṭ* (chapter XIII, on k. 312):

The principle is not for dispelling the world's viewing that views reality (with eye, etc. perception) (just) because this (viewing of the world) is an authority only to the world, and (just) because the entity apperceived by (viewing the world) is proved to be false, a deceptive factual base (*dharmin*).

Now, having refuted the particular as an authority, it is not incumbent to deny an authority per se. Thus we do not oppose in general the conventional cognitions as authority. Otherwise, it would be without principle to say that a nondeceptive cognition is viewed as an authority in the world, and also this would deny authority to any of all the conventional cognitions. Besides, the *Prasannapadā* (chapter I) gives a further reason:[106]

That being the case, by these four authorities (or "sources of knowledge"), the world's understanding of entities is established.

That is, otherwise there would be a contradiction to establishing the authorities of direct perception, inference, testimony, and analogy.[107]

Besides, we refute the accomplishment through their natures, of the authority and the cognizable object, but we do not oppose the dependent origination which posits the (subjective) authority and the cognizable object in mutuality. Thus, the *Prasannapadā* states:[108]

And they are accomplished through mutual dependence. There being the (subjective) authorities, there are the cognizable objects; and there being the cognizable objects, there are the (subjective) authorities. But there is no accomplishment by way of self-existence of either the (subjective) authority or the cognizable object.[109]

Now, if there is no trouble of darkening due to the personal or external causes of error consisting of cataract (*timira*), etc., then when sensory perceptions in the power of nescience's darkening apprehend the object as present with self-existence although it is without self-existence, the errors which appear (in this situation) do not (actively) trouble the correctness of convention. The *Avatāra* (VI, 24–25) informs us;[110]

And those who see falsely are of two kinds, those whose sense organs are clear, and those whose sense organs are impaired. The cognition of those persons having impaired organs is held to be false relative to the cognition of those persons having sensory organs in excellent condition. That which the world considers as perceived by the six sense organs when unimpaired, that is true just to the world itself; the rest[111] is imagined by the world as false.

This passage lays down that the conventional cognition and the object which is relative to the conventional cognition, have each their two kinds of error and nonerror.[112]

Regarding the personal causes of trouble to the sense organs, the *Avatāra*- commentary gives this explanation:[113]

Among those, the cataract, jaundice of the eye, (colored vision) from eating the poisonous *dhattūrika,*[114] and so on, are personal conditions for trouble to the sense organs.

As to those (causes) which are external, we read in the same work (the *Avatāra*-commentary):[115]

Oil, water, and mirror;[116] sound echoing in caves,[117] and so on; special encounter of sunrays, place, and season, etc.;[118] are external conditions causing trouble to the sense organs. In the absence of personal causes of trouble to the sense organs, these cause an apperception of reflected images, echoes, and water in mirages.[119] One may similarly understand the incantations and herbs employed by an expert in creating hallucinations. The causes of trouble to the *manas* (the sixth sense) are those (above mentioned) and moreover the heretical theory-systems and the fallacies of inference (*anumānābhāsa*).

So bad theory-systems (*siddhānta*) and fallacies of inference are causes for darkening the mind-based perception (*mano-vijñāna*). Besides, during sleep and other states of consciousness the mind is darkened by dream, and so on.

Although the objective realm, which is the grasping pattern for nescience, as will be explained below, is not a matter of convention—the trouble of darkening by nescience (the beginningless cause of error) is not taken as the cause of the trouble (of error) here. If these five sensory cognitions with no other (immediate) cause of error were without error conventionally, it would be necessary (to posit) that these (five) have the particular of their appearance, conventionally; and this is not what the *ācārya* (i.e., Candrakīrti) maintains. So the question arises: If it is necessary to maintain that there is error, is it improper for those cognitions to be the authority for positing conventionally the form, sound, etc., because of the error of form, etc. conventionally? That will be told. In this regard, *ācārya* Bhāvaviveka maintains that form, etc. have a nature conventionally accomplished by particulars (or, own-character, *svalakṣaṇa*). He refutes the claim by the Cittamātra followers that the imaginary (*parikalpita*) lacks a nature accomplished as "own-character," i.e., that it lacks the nature of a character (*lakṣaṇa*). He (Bhāvaviveka) having considered the two, affirmation of the imaginary and thing affirmed, (in the phase of considering the first one, affirmation) says, "If you (Cittamātra followers) claim that (*a*) the expression of a nature and of the affirmation of a distinction, and (*b*) the mental factor, do not have conventionally a nature of 'own-character,' you perforce deny the dependency (*paratantra*) entity."[120] Thus refuting, he makes clear his belief that dependency has conventionally a nature accomplished by own-character. That is (the purport of) what he says in his *Prajñāpradīpa* on chapter XXV (of *Madhyamaka-kārikā*):

Well, if (for you Cittamātra followers) there is a mental murmuring of "form" and expression of it by the word, is there no nature at all of the "imaginary" (of them)? Because then you would deny the entity and deny the mental murmur and the expression of it by the word!

And because the commentary on that by Avalokitavrata (the *Prajñāpradīpa-ṭīkā*) explains:

According to this (passage), the Yogācārin (= Sems tsam pa) asserts, The imaginary nature (*parikalpita-svabhāva*) has no real nature, since it has no nature of character (*lakṣaṇa*). And if he says, "Any mental factor of mental murmur of a nature (of form) and of a distinction (of the form), and any expression of it as a word, to wit, a conventional nature of affirmation, is without the nature of character," then he (the Yogācārin = Cittamātra follower) would deny the dependency (*paratantra*) entity in a *saṃvṛti* (conventional) sense, and so would teach without validity.

Thus he says that (the Yogācārin), holding that there is no nature of character (*lakṣaṇa*) in conventional terms, denies the dependency (*paratantra*) consisting of word and mental factor.

Concerning the character in the expression "without nature of character" of this discussion, the Cittamātra person claims that in the imaginary there is no own-character (*svalakṣaṇa*) or nature, and also claims that the dependency has that character and so the nature; and that since it involves birth from another (cause and condition) and no nature born from itself, there is no self-existence (when there is an arising through dependency). In the same manner, the *Saṃdhinirmocana-sūtra* expounds obscurely (*dgoṅs pa can*) that all natures (*dharma*) are devoid of self-existence. The *ācarya* Kamalaśīla teaches (clearly) on the basis of this scripture the purport (*dgoṅs pa*) of three kinds of non-self-existence (*niḥsvabhāvatā*);[121] and he (the *ācarya*) in order to teach the middle path free from the two extremes, states that he starts out with the text of only final meaning (i.e., the *Saṃdhinirmocana*).[122] Thus he claims to teach the middle (*madhyamaka*) meaning by affirming a nature of the dependency in the absolute sense and that it (the nature) is absent by way of the imaginary; that the dependency is present in conventional terms with own-character, and thus he removes the denial; and this *ācarya* maintains that there is own-character in conventional terms.

According to the *Avatāra-Comm.* when one ascribes a snake to a rope, the snake entity which is imagined (*parikalpita*) is a dependency (*paratantra*), created in dependent origination and with a nature as though moving in reality (*pariniṣpanna*). Thus, the *Saṃdhinirmocanasūtra,* in the manner of the Buddaha's domain, establishes the three natures (*svabhāva*), positing them in reality (*pariniṣpanna*). It is explained, namely (*Avatāra,* VI, 95b–c):

Which sūtra explains nonreality as the meaning? The one which expresses the guiding meaning (*neyārtha*), which is to be guided (*neya*) further through understanding.

The commentary on this makes clear the position that the establishment of the three natures in the *Saṃdhinirmocana-sūtra* is *neyārtha.*[123] The imaginary of (Candrakīrti's) own school is dependency. And as to the "dependency" present and made of *svabhāva,* he denies (even) conventionally the *svabhāva* accomplished by own-character.

The Cittamātrins do not maintain non-self-existence of character in the case of the dependency and the perfect (natures), as they do in the case of the imaginary (nature);[124] so they maintain that the other two are self-existent or have the character of accomplishment by own-nature.[125] This position appears to be mainly based on the *Saṃdhinirmocana-sūtra;* consequently, they claim that those two (dependency and perfect) are accomplished in the absolute sense. Now, the *ācāryas* Buddhapālita and Candrakīrti maintain that if these (two) have a nature accomplished by self-character, they are accomplished in reality; while the *ācārya* Bhāvaviveka and others maintain that with only this (i.e., accomplishment pursuant to the theory that they have a nature accomplished by self-character) they would not be accomplished in the absolute sense. Moreover, the Cittamātrins take the position that atoms in isolation are not the objective substratum for sense perception because they do not manifest; and also take the position that when many atoms are massed together, they again are not the objective substratum for this (perception) because they are not material but are like the appearance of a double moon.[126] In answer to this (i.e., the first case), the *Tarkajvālā* says:[127]

When the atoms are not amassed, if you could prove that they are not the substratum of sense perception, you would prove (to us) that they are accomplished (i.e., are really there).[128]

And in answer to the second case (when the atoms are amassed):—

If you (Cittamātrin) use the reason of denying that a mass of atoms of one genus assembled in a space (*dik*) is a cause (for sense perception to have their arising as an object), on the grounds that they are not material; then the same reason would disprove the other (reverse) case (as well).[129]

In the case of any part of the whole substratum:—

When there is a certain nature of atom (aggregation) belonging to one genus, and assistance is applied to it by another (aggregation), it follows that the (objective) substratum is made up of parts and may give rise in cognition to an aspect (of the substratum) which is the manifestation of a set of atoms (i.e., the rough manifestation, *rags snaṅ,* of a part of the whole substratum). For example, there are such things as pots from the aggregation of atoms of one genus, and those are atom (aggregates) we have maintained to be material.

The reason for claiming that the aggregation is material:—

Just as the atoms are aggregated into eight substances[130] and (you)[131] maintain those to be substance, also (we maintain) that such things as pots, made up of aggregations, are substance. But that much per se (*'ba' źig*) is not a proof.

By saying this, he maintains that through the individual aggregation of the atoms, there is the basis (constituting a support substratum) for sensory perception, and that it (the aggregation) is material (*dravya*); (also) maintains that ultimately it is resolved into atoms (*paramāṇu*); and maintains that in appearance the atoms are impartite (*cha med*) as the perceptual support (for sensory perception).

Therefore, (*ācārya* Bhāvaviveka) maintains that there is no error (only) when one is not corrupted by those previously explained personal and external causes of error, such as the (nearby) sensory perception, and maintains the perceptual support (for sensory perception) in consistency with the Sautrāntikas in conventional terms.

The *Avatāra-Comm.* states:[132]

Some (Mādhyamikas) explain certain matters of the Sautrāntika school in the *paramārtha* sense, which matters the Mādhyamika school (in fact) asserts in the *saṃvṛti* sense. One should recognize that what those persons say stems from their confusion about the genuine teaching of the Mādhyamika texts.

Besides, some (Mādhyamikas) explain certain matters of the Vaibhāṣika school in the *paramārtha* sense, which matters the Mādhyamika school (in fact) deems to be in the *saṃvṛti* sense. Such persons also fail to understand these texts.

(In reply to both:) In that way they equate the supramundane natures (*lokottaradharma*) (which are the domain of the *āryas*) with the mundane natures (*laukikadharma*) (which are the domain of ordinary persons, *pṛthagjanas*). Since this is not proper, wise persons should become certain about this school, which is not in common (*asādhāraṇa*).

It is not in common with the theories (*siddhānta*) of those schools (Sautrāntika and Vaibhāṣika); and (this *ācārya,* Candrakīrti,) does not maintain even in conventional terms the apprehended thing which is designated (i.e., the impartite atoms of the object) or the impartite apprehender (i.e., the momentary consciousness of the subject). In his *Catuḥ-ś-t* he also opposes a belief in the impartite atoms (i.e., on chapter XIV, k. 343a):

It is not proper for the insider schools (*svayūthyā*)[133] to believe as do the (outsider) Vaiśeṣikas in atoms as material (*dravya*).

What those two schools (Sautrāntika and Vaibhāṣika) accept as *paramārtha* the Mādhyamika does not claim to be *saṃvṛti.*[134] Their *paramārtha* means an entity that is impartite. We do not accept as *saṃvṛti* everything those two schools hold to be true; but when they claim as true such entities as form and sound, the Mādhyamika does accept them as *saṃvṛti.* The *Catuḥ-ś-t* says:[135]

Having refuted the position (of others) that there is the basis (furnishing the dominant condition, *adhipati-pratyaya*) for sense perception through each single section of the atom-aggregation of the sense organs, (in our school) there is the basis for perception tied in dependence on those atoms of sense organs when there are those (atoms of sense organs) and they are not accomplished elsewhere, and in the same way, there is the substratum for sense perception, with tied existence, tied in dependence on those sense objects (form, etc.).[136]

This maintains that perceptions are the things with direct-perception kind of tie, and that the dense domains have the character (*lakṣaṇa*) of the direct perception. So this *ācārya* (Candrakīrti) and *ācārya* Bhāvaviveka both agree about the external object, but disagree on the way of positing the sense organs and their sense objects.

Previously, in the phase of denying the own-character of sense perception as an authority, it was said, "Because it is a thing which is present in one way, but appears in another way."[137] In accordance with that saying, to the sense perceptions the form, sound, etc. appear as accomplished by own-character, but the own-character that so appears is in fact not present even conventionally. That being the case, this *ācārya* (Candrakīrti) maintains that these (sense perceptions) are mistaken (about those objects) even in conventional terms.

Now, while the sense perceptions are not valid as authorities for positing the aspects of such sense objects as form and sound, this is not the whole story. The reason for positing those (sense perceptions) as mistaken is the meaninglessness of the accomplishment by own-character as it appears (to those sense perceptions), and this (reason) is proved by knowing the principle of examining the presence or absence of self-existence, and is certainly not proved by authority of conventional terms. But it is not an error to use that (sense) perception in conventional matters.

Regarding the sense perceptions to which appear the double moon, reflected images, and so on, in situations where there are no double moons, faces, and similar entities as they appear (to sense perceptions), these are proved to be nonexistent when the cognition of the principle regards (them) with conventional authority. Therefore, it is valid to distinguish these and the former by genuine (*tathya*) and misleading (*mithyā*) *saṃvṛti*.

Let us assume mere presence[138] of the distinction between (two kinds of) mistaken understanding, namely, when one depends on cognition of a principle (using sense perception to judge form, etc.), or when one depends on conventional authority (using sense perception to apprehend reflected images, etc.). Then, just as there is no entity (*artha*) at the time (the reflected image of) a face appears, and so on, also there is no entity at the time the own-character (of form, etc.) appears. And just as there is form, etc. that is void of own-character, also there is the reflected image, etc. that is void of face, etc. In this case when the conventional cognition observes those (objects) at its own pleasure, is there no distinction of whether it is misleading or not misleading? Well, (just as) the two things, the nature accomplished by own-character and the seeming entity appearing as a face, are alike in not being present conventionally; (so) the two things, form, etc. and reflected images, etc. are alike in being present conventionally. The *Avatāra-Comm.* (on VI, 28) says:

There are some things, arising in dependence, such as reflected images and echoes, which appear as false even to those persons affected by nescience; while some other things, colors such as blue, and personal elements such as body, thought, feeling, appear (to those persons) as true. But in no way does self-existence (*raṅ bźin*)[139] appear to those persons who are affected by nescience. Therefore, that (self-existence) as well as anything that is false conventionally (*saṃvṛtitas*), is not conventional truth (*saṃvṛti-satya*).

This passage can be expanded upon as follows:[140] What is the answer if someone asserts:—It is not proper to differentiate a positing of blue, etc. as *saṃvṛti-satya,* and a nonpositing of reflected images, etc. as *saṃvṛti-satya.* (Reply:) Those two are alike in the fact of appearing to conventional cognition; but reflected images and so on are acknowledged by worldly cognition to be false, so the world does not posit them as conventional truth (*saṃvṛti-satya*); while at the same time blue and so on are false, and yet worldly cognition is incapable of comprehending them to be false, so the world posits them as conventional truth. And thinking this over, (someone asserts:) If that's the way it is, when conventional cognition observes both those (objective) domains (the blue, etc., and the reflected images, etc.), it has the right (to discriminate between) truth and falsehood; accordingly, when conventional cognition observes both subjects, it has the right (to discriminate between) the one that misleads and the one that does not mislead. (Reply:) If one posits the conventional cognition as nonmisleading when it observes, this is in conflict with positing it as mistaken conventionally (i.e., when sense perception apprehends blue, etc.). Thinking this over, (someone asserts:) Now, about the conventional cognition which is mistaken in conventional matters, and the conventional cognition in the case when any observing cognition is unmistaken—if one takes these two are one, there is a contradiction; but if the two conventions[141] are distinct, where is the contradiction! (Reply:) It is this way: The denial by a principle that form, etc. have a self-existence accomplished by own-nature is not valid in the absolute (*paramārtha*) sense, but must be taken in the conventional sense. Accordingly, there is no contradiction that on the side of conventional cognition of that sort, the sensory perceptions are mistaken, while on the side of conventional cognition differing from the foregoing kind and autonomous, those (sensory perceptions) are not mistaken. For example, in worldly convention, it is said that some men are present, and some men are absent; in that remark the expression "some" (T. *la la*) is one term, and while there are two "somes"—one with "present" and one with "absent"—they have one meaning. Likewise, we do not posit them (the cognitions) (as separate). Moreover, it has been posited that the one which is unmistaken is the mundane cognition that depends on autonomy;[142] but the Mādhyamika denies that it is without error. Besides those various assertions, it has been said that truth is from the world itself.[143]

Hence, there is no contradiction when the Mādhyamika posits those sense perceptions as mistaken, and accordingly posits (their) sense objects as mistaken; but there would be a contradiction if one were to posit the sense objects as true and then take the position of charging the subject with error. Besides, we take the position that conventionally all natures (*dharma*) are illusory, and so they (form, etc.) are false conventionally, and so also there is no contradiction in positing them (form, etc.) as conventional truth. Thus it was said,[144] "Because nescience obscures real nature (*svabhāva*), it is (called) 'all-obscuring' (*saṃvṛti;* T. *kun rdzob*)." According to this, the convention (*saṃvṛti*) consisting of nescience is the truth (*satya*) (of form, etc.) on its side, and the side on which it is posited denies the natures (*dharma*) accomplishment by own-nature, so there is no contradiction between the two falsities on the side of that convention. The statement (of the *Avatāra-Comm.,* above-cited),[145] "(and anything) false conventionally, is not conventional truth," refers to what conventional authority understands to be false (namely, reflected images, and so on), so it is not proper to take (this passage) to refer to conventional falseness generally.[146]

Now, the Mādhyamikas, in our school, are able to posit conventionally many establishments of *saṃsāra* and *nirvāṇa;* and because they do not share the theories espoused by the realists, oppose the existence conventionally of the designated entities. Still, these methods are exceedingly difficult, and the errorless understanding that establishes the two truths appears at the summit of the world.

In consideration of that, the many persons who are proud that they have reached the Mādhyamaka reality, who claim they have contemplated the right meaning of the (Madhyamaka) view, have posited without grasping anything in common with that kind of understanding when opposing existence conventionally (against) the theories of the realists, when they think, "It is necessary to oppose by examining with a principle; and as to our thesis that there is birth, cessation, etc. conventionally, whether there is a thesis or not by way of examination is a matter of whether or not there is a syllogism, and I have taken recourse pursuant to the principle." When opposing with a principle, and when opposing with a principle both the conventional things of our claim and the things imagined by the realists, they deny them equally; and when they do not deny them, they fail to deny them equally. When they deny a lord (*īśvara*) and primary matter (*pradhāna*) conventionally, they need to deny also form, etc. (conventionally). When they affirm these (form, etc.) conventionally, they need to affirm also a lord, etc. (conventionally). Thus they see both equally. Thus, in the case of any nature (*dharma*), our own school becomes unable to determine or claim that this is present and that is absent.

Such (explanations) as those do not appear in accounts that please persons skilled (in the examination). As was previously explained, the principle that denies self-existence (*svabhāva*) without determining the principle's refutable destroys all conventional establishments, because it is a great wayward view that takes the genuine view and the misleading view to be equally mistaken when there is a mistake, or equally unmistaken when there is no mistake. Hence, for as long as one contemplates in this manner, for that long he scarcely manages to get close to the genuine view, because (his view) is totally incompatible with the path of dependent origination which serves in our school for all establishments of dependent origination going with *saṃsāra* and *nirvāṇa*. Consequently, the *Madhyamakāvatāra* (VI, 26) states:

> The things imagined according to (misled) personal theories by the heretics corrupted through the sleep of ignorance; the imaginary conceptions of phantoms, mirages, and so on; as well as those things (horses, water, etc.) which exist according to the world, are (all) nonexistent.

That passage refers to the things imagined in the theories of the heretics not in common (with our position); and, as mentioned before, the things imagined in the theories of the Svātantrika realists not in common (with our position) that are not the convention (*saṃvṛti*) of our school.

The meaning of this must be further elucidated. In this regard, one may wonder through what avenue one may posit the theory that things exist conventionally and the theory that things do not exist (conventionally). (In reply:) (α) (An entity) reported in conventional cognition, (β) an entity as so reported with lack of opposition by other conventional authority,[147] and (γ) (an entity) not subject to opposition by a principle which methodically examines the presence or absence of reality or self-existence[148] (thus an entity with three features)—(such is the entity) claimed to exist conventionally; and (the entity) the opposite (of the three features) is claimed not to exist (conventionally).

α) Among those, the conventional cognition just follows after any entity (*dharma*) according to how it appears. This cognition does not engage in consideration, does not examine with the question. "Does that appearing entity just appear that way in cognition, or does the entity have an existent manner that is accomplished that way?" This is precisely what is called the "nonexamining cognition," but it is not the case that it utterly refrains from consideration. In whatever manner something appears to, or enters as reported in that mundane or conventional cognition, because it does not enter with examination concerning of what manner is its manner of being (*yin lugs*), it is called 'worldly report." The cognition of that type occurs in all intellects (*blo*) whether altered or unaltered by theory-systems (*siddhānta*); and in whatever kind of stream of consciousness (*saṃtāna*)[149] it has a place, it is called "the nonexamining cognition or reported of worldling"; but one should not hold that it is only in the stream of consciousness of a worldling whose intellect is not altered by systematic theories. Even though there are many intellects altered by systematic theories and examining with the thought, "Is it as reported conventionally, or is it present in reality?" how is it necessary that it be an examining cognition of what be the true manner of all cognitions! (And it is not necessary.) Thus, to satisfy the condition to be a worldly report, it is not a question of whether it keeps free from the systematic theories of the worldly elders; but it suffices to observe the way of entering and how it stays in the nonexamining intellects of the streams of consciousness of (both) the debater (*vādin*) and opposing debater (*prativādin*). (The entities) reported in this cognition are the substratums for conventional attribution (=affirmation) of appearance or experience. *Karma* and fruit, the path of stages (*bhūmi*), and so on, are not acknowledged among the populace;[150] that is, even when (religious) learning, experience, etc. are made the object, they appear as the autonomy[151] of a cognition which does not examine what be the manner of being, so there is no fault (in saying) they are not acknowledged among the worldlings.

β) [In this case], the opposition by another conventional authority is as follows: for example, if there is the cognition that imagines a snake in a rope or the apperception thinking there is water in a mirage, one holds that with an intellect that does not examine what be the manner of being (*yin lugs*). Furthermore, the entities (snake, water) held by this (intellect) are opposed by conventional authority, so even conventionally those do not exist.

γ) [In this case], being not subject to opposition by a principle which methodically examines the presence or absence of self-existence, is as follows: while it is necessary to prove by conventional authority the entities posited conventionally, it is certainly necessary that there be no opposition of any sort by a cognition with a principle that methodically examines the presence or absence of self-existence; for if one proves presence by that principle, this proves that it is present by its own-nature, so it is in contradiction to its being a conventional entity. Therefore, there is no holding as the same thing, what are in fact two—not denying with a principled cognition, and proving with that (cognition)—the occasion for the wayward reflection about happiness and sorrow arising from virtue and vice, or happiness and sorrow arising from a lord (*īśvara*) and primary matter (*pradhāna*) conventionally,[152], that if they are present they are present equally, or if they are absent they are absent equally. That is, the generating of happiness and sorrow by a lord and primary matter, or the generating of happiness and sorrow by virtue and vice, are equally unproven by the principle which methodically examines presence or absence of self-existence; still, denying and not denying by a principle are not at all the same.

In that connection, at the time when our school and the other school of the realists, who have views not in common, posit the imagined apprehended thing and apprehender, to wit, the partless (atom) and the self, primordial matter and a lord, and examine by principle whether such things (the partless atoms, etc.) exist or do not exist accomplished by own-nature, then, by means of this principle so examining, (our school) thinks to have found those entities and to posit (those entities); so in regard to this (positing) it is necessary (for us) to believe that the examining with principle as done by others (i.e., other sects) does examine the presence or absence of self-existence—because the ability to examine those entities by a principle is claimed (by both our sect and the realists).

At the time of examining this way (methodically), should there not be an ability to sustain (*khur bzod*) consideration with a pure principle, and one could not find those (partless atoms, etc.) with a principle, they (the partless atoms, etc.) would be debarred, because if they do exist they certainly would be found by those principles.

Form, sound, and so on, are only posited as they are reported to conventional cognitions that are not assailed by external and personal causes of error. But when one examines them, thinking, "Are these merely conventional (appearances), or are the entities' manner of existence accomplished that way?"—so examining, one cannot accept the formulation in the school that finds them with self-existence accomplished by own-nature; because when those (form, etc.) are not examined with the principle of examining the presence or absence of self-existence, we deny that there is the ability to examine those entities with a principle. For example, if somebody says, "This is a sheep," it would not be proper for us to examine it, thinking "Is this a horse or a cow?"

Even when an entity has been acknowledged in the world from time immemorial, when one denies it by the principle it does not exist even conventionally. That is, the entities designated by nescience to have own-nature, the adherence by reifying view (*satkāyadṛṣṭi*) to "I" and "mine" accomplished by own-nature, the insistence that yesterday's mountain is today's mountain (i.e., belief in permanence)—while all these objects are acknowledged in the world, the Mādhyamika does not accept them conventionally.

Some (former Tibetan teachers) said that form, sound, etc. and the things imagined by the heretics differed conventionally by existing and not existing, because the former (form, sound, etc.) are acknowledged throughout the world, and the latter (things imagined by the heretics) are acknowledged only in their theory-systems (*siddhānta*). What they failed to note is that, in addition, the conventional forms, etc. that are illusory would be necessarily nonexistent (because not acknowledged throughout the world), and a thing accomplished by own-nature would be necessarily existent (presumably because acknowledged throughout the world, i.e., naïve realism). And there are many like arguments.

Also, the *Yuktiṣaṣṭikā-Comm.* (on 7b) says:

Moreover, the wayward object (*viparyāsa*) is the clinging to happiness, and so on (i.e., also to the pure, permanent, and self),[153] because conventionally its nature (i.e., of happiness, etc.) is not found in those entities (suffering, etc.). One should adhere to the nonwayward entities (suffering, etc.) because these entities have a nature conventionally.

This explains that the four, permanence, etc. are commonly acknowledged in the world, and that the adherence therein is conventional and wayward; also that the four, impermanence, etc., are not acknowledged throughout the world, and that the adherence therein is not [conventionally] wayward. Accordingly, the conception that adheres to the impermanence of personality aggregates, etc. is the grasping pattern of certainty regarding the error in the appearing-realm (*snaṅ yul*) and is not opposed by authority; therefore, it is called "nonwayward" or "not mistaken." On the other hand, the sense perceptions (of eye, etc.) are mistaken about their (respective) appearing-realms and have no unmistaken part elsewhere; therefore they are not called "not mistaken."

The sensory perceptions have likeness to the error in appearance, and the (objective) entities are consistent with the (respective) appearance on the (cognitive) side of the world. By way of the (distinct) avenues of the existent (form, etc.) and the nonexistent (face in mirror, etc.), the sensory perceptions with appearance of reflected image (of face), etc. constitute misleading convention (*saṃvṛti*); and the sensory perceptions that differ from that (namely, with appearance of form, etc.) which are not denied, constitute genuine convention.[154]

The objective domain of the grasping-pattern of the conception adhering to permanence of personality aggregates, etc., because it is conventionally nonexistent, can be refuted (by a different authority); while the objective domain (of the grasping pattern) adhering to impermanence, etc., because it is conventionally existent, cannot be refuted by a principle.

Just as the four, permanence, etc. are not possibly accomplished either in an absolute sense or by own-nature, also the four, impermanence, etc. are not possibly accomplished in either way (absolute sense or own-nature). Hence, obscurely referring to reality, with no division into wayward and nonwayward in the grasping as present of those eight,[155] it was said (in the *Prajñāpāramitā* scripture) that any ranging in form as permanent or impermanent, in happiness or sorrow, in existence or nonexistence of a self—is ranging in sign-sources.[156]

If one refutes with a principle the grasping-pattern of nescience that attributes self-existence to entities, and does not refute conventional entities, the contradiction is to have two. Thus, the *Avatāra* (VI, 28, first 3 lines) states:

> Delusion, because it obscures *svabhāva,* is (called) all-obscuring (*saṃvṛti*). And whatever construction appears true by reason of that (delusion) the Muni has declared "conventionally true" (*saṃvṛti-satya*).

Well, it posits form, sound, etc. as "conventionally true" by virtue of nescience. How is that? There is no fault in positing form, sound, etc. as conventional truth (*saṃvṛti-satya*), in which case *satya* is a truth by virtue of intention (not a truth by virtue of entities), and this intention must mean the imputation of truth, so it is a truth on the side of nescience which attributes self-existence (to entities). Hence those persons who eliminate the defiling nescience,[157] namely the two *arhats*[158] and the Bodhisattvas on the eighth and higher stages (of the Ten Stages) view (all) these appearances as (only) the nature of construction (*bcos ma*) and not existing in truth, because (those persons) have no clinging (to *dharmas*) as true. That is the reason for saying that to persons without imputation of truth, (appearances) are *saṃvṛti*-only.

For that reason, while form, sound, etc. have truth on the side of nescience, (in fact) form, sound, etc. are not posited by that nescience; just as in the case when one apprehends a snake in a rope, that rope is a snake on the side of the wayward perception, but (in fact) the wayward perception does not posit the rope aspect. The intelligence (*blo;* S. *buddhi*) that posits form, sound, etc. is the set of the six perceptions based on eye, etc.,[159] which are not denied, so the objects proved by these (sense perceptions) exist conventionally and we do not oppose them by a principle. On the other hand, the objects as they are apprehended by nescience do not exist even conventionally, because this (nescience) attributes to entities a self-existence accomplished by own-nature, and such self-existence is not present, even conventionally. For that reason, the principle must refute even conventionally; and if this (entity) were not debarred by the principle, one could not prove conventionally that entities are like an illusion.

Regarding the self-existence attributed by this delusion (= nescience) when there are (appearances like) the pleasant, the unpleasant, etc., after attributing differences to them, it generates passion (for the pleasant), repulsion (for the unpleasant), and so forth. Also one can refute, by the principle, the grasping-pattern of these (the passion, repulsion). That is also the point of this passage in the *Catuḥ-ś-ṭ* (on chapter VI, 10 = k. 135):

> Moreover, passion, and so on, follow the differentiating attribution of the pleasant, the unpleasant, etc., because delusion has assigned these to the nature of entities. They (passion, etc.) follow the same from delusion, occur again in dependence on delusion, because delusion is the leader.

Accordingly, those defilements (passions, etc.), cohabiting (i.e., adventitious to the intellect) from time immemorial, are a grasping pattern that can be refuted by a principle, so their attachment-realm does not exist even conventionally. Consequently, while the intellect that is cohabited is a fact, there is both capability and incapability to refuse its objective realm by a principle; and these (conventional entities) such as form and sound, which are the objective realm of the conventional cohabiting authorities that posit them, cannot be refuted by the principle, since they exist conventionally. Therefore, in the school of the *ācāryas* Buddhapālita and Candrakīrti one refutes the self-existence accomplished by own-nature even conventionally. That being the case, while it appears very difficult (to make the demarcation line) about positing the entities conventionally, if one does not know well how to posit (those entities) without refutation (by a principle) he certainly does not gain certainty in the matter of (religious) practice (of the six perfections, etc.). Prevalently, it seems that people fall into the condemnatory view. Those who are wise should learn (with whatever assiduous application be required) the manner of positing *saṃvṛti* in this school. But as this could lead to many more words, I shall leave it after saying this much.

(iii) Avoiding Defeat by Denial, considering Whether or Not There Is Birth with the Four Alternatives

[It is asked:] "Since you have refuted birth from oneself, another, both, or by chance, have you not debarred birth (in general)? In this school (i.e., Mādhyamika) arising according to the four alternatives does not occur even conventionally, so there is no need to add a (further) particular to the refutation of arising. And if there is no debarring (of birth in general), then the rejection of birth according to the four alternatives would not also debar birth in the absolute (*paramārtha*) sense."

[We] do not accept the former remark (i.e., about the conventional side); and I will expound the reply to the latter one (i.e., about the absolute side). If one is to accept the *paramārtha* (sense of) arising, one should claim it through ability to examine by the principle which examines reality; and at that time it is necessary to examine by principle the arising from any one of the four alternatives—itself, another, etc. So the one claiming the *paramārtha* arising must certainly accept as appropriate the examination in terms of the four alternatives.

We claim that there is only birth as this occurrence in dependence on some cause and condition, so do not accept the reality (i.e., *paramārtha*) kind of birth. We do not accept it (i.e., birth in that sense), because no matter how one examines, using the principle of examining reality, thinking, "From what does it arise"—from self, another, etc.—when there is ability to examine by principle (such a birth), there is no need to believe (in the birth).

Furthermore, it is precisely because it arises in dependence that we oppose its arising through the four alternatives, since the *Avatāra* (VI, 115) states:

These conceptions (of eternalism and nihilism, of birth from oneself, etc.) are unable to examine the entities arising in dependence. Accordingly, with this principle of dependent origination, one may destroy the entire net of false views (such as eternalism and nihilism).

Hence, Candrakīrti maintains that birth in dependence opposes birth through the four alternatives; and he rejects your theory that if there is no birth from any of the four alternatives, then there is no birth in general. Furthermore, the same work (*Avatāra,* VI, 114) states in opposition to your theory:

Since entities do not arise by chance, from a lord, and so on (primal matter, time, atoms, self-existence, Puruṣa, Nārāyaṇa, etc.), or from themselves, others, or both (themselves and others), then they arise in dependence (on causes and conditions).

Hence, whatever arises in dependence, for example, with dependent origination, rules out the four alternatives; and so it is an improper question to ask which of the four alternatives is that ruling out of alternatives.

Besides, it is a mistake to not distinguish these two things: nonarising by self-existence, and nonarising. However, what is the meaning of this passage (*Avatāra,* VI, 36a-c, previously cited)?

By whatever principle in the phase of reality there is no reason for birth from oneself or from another, by that principle there is no reason for it (substantial birth) conventionally.

This (passage) teaches opposition by those principles to belief in the kind of arising accomplished substantially or by own-characteristic (*svalakṣaṇa*), or even conventionally; but positively does not oppose arising per se (**utpattimātra*). That text (*Avatāra-Comm.*) associates these remarks:[160]

Suppose someone says that only a material thing, the basis for defilement and purification, can be generated. (In reply:) If that were the case, what that person says (being faulty), i.e., word-only, would be all remaining. What is the reason? It is said, "In the phase of reality. . . ."

The commentary to that citation gives the reason:[161]

Therefore, the arising by reason of own-character does not happen even in the categories of either Truth. While (this person) apparently denies it, it should (undoubtedly) be accepted.

Hence if one believes that the arising accomplished by own-nature is the *paramārtha*-arising, it would also be proper to believe in it conventionally (but who would believe that!). In fact, it is the ultimate position of this teacher (Candrakīrti) that one must definitely oppose birth and cessation in the paramārtha (sense). Hence one should not accept that there is arising accomplished by own-nature even conventionally, because the *Avatāra* (VI, 111) says:

The son of a barren women is not born by himself either from the standpoint of reality or from the standpoint of the world. Likewise, none of these entities is born by reason of own-being (*svarūpa*) from the standpoints of the world or of reality.

Thus, when someone (i.e., the realist) holds that the nonarising by reason of self-existence, or the non-self-existence of arising, is pervaded by no arising (in general), he contends to refute both the arising in dependence and the not arising by self-experience; and he is the one (Candrakīrti) calls "without ear or heart." That is to say, when the phrase, "nonarising by reason of self-existence" was said, the expression "by reason of self-existence" is what he did not hear when he settled on the "nonarising." So, following the purport of his situation, he is "without ear." And since he does not have the basis for understanding the meaning of the expression "self-existence" (*svabhāva*), following the purport, he is "without heart." This is the position of the *Yuktiṣaṣṭikā* (48c–d):

> What arises in dependence is not born;
> That is proclaimed by the supreme knower of reality (= Buddha).

The commentary on this (the *Yuktiṣaṣṭikā-vṛtti*) states:

When one observes dependent origination, he does not give heed to entities as (accomplished by) self-existence—because whatever the entity that arises in dependence (on causes and conditions) it, like a reflected image, does not arise by reason of self-existence.

(The realist opponent says): If (as you say) whatever thing arises in dependence is not even born, then why does (the Mādhyamika) say it is not born? But if (you Mādhyamika) have a reason for saying (this thing) is not born, then you should not say it "arises in dependence." Therefore, because of mutual inconsistency, (what you have said) is not valid.

(The Mādhyamika replies with compassionate interjection:) Alas! Because you are without ears or heart[162] you have thrown a challenge that is severe on us! When we say that anything arising in dependence, in the manner of a reflected image, does not arise by reason of self-existence—at that time where is the possibility of disputing (us)!

Therefore it is a precious thing to distinguish those qualifications![163] Also, we read (a consistent statement) in the *Anavatapta* (*nāgarāja*) *paripṛcchā:*[164]

Any (thing) that is born (in dependence) on conditions, is not born (to wit): The birth of this (thing) does not occur by self-existence. Any (thing) that is dependent on conditions, is declared void. Any person who understands voidness, is heedful.[165]

This passage shows the way in which it is "not born," namely, the second *pāda,* "The birth of this thing does not occur by self-existence," adds the qualification to the disputed point (*dgag bya*), i.e., (the entity) does not arise by self-existence. Some persons, who have heard those words but do not understand them in that way, assert, "There is no arising with just arising, and there is no dependence with just dependence." Those persons, so speaking, express hostility and their grandiloquence seems to constitute an arrogant view. Besides, the *Prasannapadā* explains it very clearly, citing the *Laṅkāvatāra-sūtra:*

O Mahāmati, it was in connection with nonbirth by reason of self-existence, that I said, "All *dharmas* are void."

While the reply (given above) about adding or not adding the *paramārtha* qualification to the refutation of birth, etc., treats the meaning, a (concrete) reply will be expounded below, that analyzes by way of the support-object (*ālambana*).

The foregoing discussions show that all those rejections have been incapable of rejecting the (Mādhyamika's) method of establishing the cause and fruit, etc. and by way of no self-existence (*svabhāva*). In general the rejection ends up as a fallacy. We consider how you the opponent has constructed the attack; and we destroy without remainder the (principle of) refutation, so your formulation ends up as a fallacious refutation. That is, we consider what is denied or not denied by your principle; and in the same way that (your) other side opposes, we "turn the tables" on you, and your own principle of refutation becomes the disputed point.

Now, suppose you were to think, "We claim that there are such things as form, and considerations thereof do involve (some fault). But we have no thesis of our own, so those considerations do not involve (a fault for us)." Not by so stating is there a capacity to avoid faults: this will be taught (below) in the phase of individually establishing the Prāsaṅgika and the Svātantrika schools.

(IV) Invalidating the Assailant to Denying the Four Alternatives, Presence, Absence, etc., of an Entity

You suppose that according to the Mādhyamika texts the four alternatives, namely the existence of an entity or of a self-nature, its nonexistence, both (existence and nonexistence), and neither, refute everything; and while *dharmas* are not included therein, all (*dharmas*) are refuted by a principle. [In reply, we shall explain the way it is according to the Mādhyamika texts.] Now, as was previously explained, there are two possibilities for an entity (i.e., accomplished by own-nature, and efficient); and of these, the theory that an entity accomplished by own-nature exists must be rejected in the case of both truths (*saṃvṛti* and *paramārtha*), while the efficient entity is not rejected conventionally (although it is opposed in the *paramārtha* sense).

Likewise for the nonexistence of an entity, if you claim the nonexistence of an entity accomplished by own-nature among the unconstructed (*asaṃskṛta*) natures (*dharma*), we must also reject that sort of nonexistence of entity.[166]

Likewise, we reject that the existence of that sort of entity (the efficient one) is simultaneous with the nonexistence of the other sort of entity (the one accomplished by own-nature); and reject that there are neither, even when accomplished by own-nature.

In that way (the wise) one should understand all methods of rejecting the four alternatives. (However,) if one opposes the four alternatives without the basis of adding the (*paramārtha*) qualification, then at the time he rejects the existence of an entity and the nonexistence of an entity, and rejects (the previous two) thinking, "Both together do not exist," and (finally) thinking, "It is not the case that there are neither," his thesis is essentially inconsistent; and if he insists falsely that there is no fault in rejecting (the four alternatives) in that manner, we do not contend with his false assertion (because it would be beneath our dignity).

Moreover, at the time one rejects that the personality aggregates are self-existent accomplished by own nature, or (rejects) the self, the insight (*prajñā*) arises which understands that there is no self-existence or self. But when you also reject the non-self-existence of *prajñā*'s objective domain, you damage the Mādhyamika view, because *prajñā* comprehends the non-self existence of *dharmas,* and you are rejecting (the voidness of) *prajñā*'s objective domain.

Now, concerning your position rejecting both existence and nonexistence by way of *svabhāva,* this deserves a question: Since *prajñā* is certain that the personality aggregates have no self-existence, pray tell how you can object to the non-self-existence of its objective domain!

The *Mūla-prajñā* (XIII, 7) states:

> If something could be nonvoid, something that is void could exist (by reason of self-existence). If there is not something nonvoid, how can a void thing exist?

Now, what does one make of this position that if there is not anything nonvoid, also there is no void thing without self-existence? Here (i.e., in the *Madhyamaka-kārikā*), the terminology "void" and "nonvoid" is used from the beginning to the end of the text in the sense of void or nonvoid of self-existence (*svabhāva*). For this reason, a thing nonvoid of self-existence is perforce accomplished by self-existence; and when (you) say that since there is not anything accomplished by self-existence there is also no void thing not accomplished by self-existence, what could be more laughable! Moreover, the one with certainty, holding to the idea that such things as shoots (*myu gu*) have no self-existence accomplished by own-nature, holds to the idea that the shoot is not present with self-existence; and does not hold in any way to the pair of ideas, "Is this thing with no self-existence present, or is it absent?" So, closing your eyes, direct yourself within, and understand! Then it will be very easy to learn (the proper method of holding).

Accordingly, since it is improper to hold the nonexistent by *svabhāva* to be existent (by it), so as to avert the imputation of existence (by it) to what is nonexistent by *svabhāva* there is voidness by the principle. [As to what you assert:] if that refutation is a valid thing, then when a different cognition (by principle) holds that what is nonexistent by *svabhāva* is existent (by it), it is necessary to believe in refuting the objective domain of that cognition; so when *prajñā* comprehends the shoot to be nonexistent by *svabhāva*, one may refute the objective domain of *prajñā*. That is extremely invalid. We reject that the shoot has a self-existence accomplished by own-nature, and are certain in our conception that it has no self-existence, and then with a different cognition we hold to the conception that the very thing exists which is nonexistent by *svabhāva,* and there is no need to refute by a principle the objective domain of that cognition; but if one claims that voidness is accomplished by own-nature, we (certainly) refute that.

However, if one wonders how arises the conception that what is nonexistent by *svabhāva* is existent by *svbhāva,* (it happens in the following manner:) when one puts his mind on a shoot that does not exist by reason of *svabhāva,* there occurs to him (the conception), "There is no proof (i.e., no apprehending in this place) that the shoot has *svabhāva* (self-existence)"; still he does get the conception, "The shoot's nonexistence by *svabhāva* is its existence in *svabhāva.*" For example, having put his mind on the absence of a pot, it does not occur to one, "It is true that a pot is present," yet it does occur to him, "It is true that this pot is absent."

Taking it that way, then there are not any (*dharmas*) that are nonvoid of self-existence, so when we say that the shoot is void of self-existence and is not accomplished by own-nature—that amounts to a genuine reason. Also the *Catuḥ-ś-ṭ* (chapter XVI, on k. 382) denies that a voidness thing is accomplished by own nature, with these words:

If there were something accomplished by own-nature called "voidness," entities would exist upon becoming possessed of self-existence; to show this is not so, he explains (Āryadeva's k. 382):

When there is no nonvoid thing, from what does a void thing arise and become that thing? How is it that the other one is not, and its opposite arises?

Were it otherwise, and one would refute the existence with voidness of self-existence, there would be no case of nonexistence by self-existence, and so (all *dharmas*) would exist by self-existence accomplished by own-nature. Therefore, it is improper to reject in all possible ways the self-existence (*svabhāva*). Along the same lines, the *Vigrahavyāvartinī* (k. 26) states:[167]

If with non-self-existent (words) one could prevent non-self-existent entities, now that there is prevention of non-self-existent entities, it would be proved than an entity has self-existence.

And the commentary on this makes it very clear:

Could this be a valid example? Like somebody preventing a sound by the sound, "Don't say it!" (*mā śabdam iti*). Likewise with non-self-existent words one can prevent non-self-existent entities. (It is not valid!)[168] In such an event, with those very non-self-existent words one would be able to refute the self-existence of entities. Accordingly, if non-self-existent words could refute the non-self-existence of entities, as a result of the non-self-existence being refuted the entities would have self-existence; and as a result of having self-existence they would be nonvoid.

Hence, it is as in the previous citation of the *Mūla-prajñā* (XIII, 7d): "How can a void thing exist?" and in the immediately following verse (XIII, 8):

The Victors have proclaimed voidness
as the escape from all views,
and have pronounced as incurable those
for whom voidness is a view.

When this passage refers to (the phase in which) "voidness is a view" it does not intend the view which thinks, "void of self-existence," but speaks about (the situation of) imputing reality (*bden par bzuṅ ba*) to the void which is void of self-existence, or viewing substantially (*dṅos por lta ba*) that (void). This point is expressed clearly along with example by Buddhapālita:[169]

> Those persons who mention voidness in regard to (i.e., so as to dispel) those attachments to entities as existing by reason of their own-nature and who designate an entity by way of causes and conditions in the sense of dependent origination, teach that entities do not exist by reason of own-nature but (exist) in the voidness of own-nature, and so are able to ward off attachments.
>
> Those persons who use a different method in regard to those attachments to voidness as substantial (or; as a mode of being) are unable to ward off attachments. For example, it is as if someone says, "There is nothing-at-all," and then says, "Give (me) that nothing-at all!" Thus engaging in imputation to nothingness (*med pa ñid*) how could he be able (to ward off those attachments)!

Were it otherwise, the example would also not be right. If somebody (the interlocutor, *sloṅ pa po*) says regarding a certain (point of discussion), "That begs a mistake!" then at the time of (your) replying, "There is no mistake," there is no fault to impute with the thought, "In this case a mistake is not present." But if he (the interlocutor) takes what is not a mistake to be a mistake, then there would be no source for certainty that there was no mistake. In the same way, when one asks whether the entities exist or do not exist by self-existence and if one says they do not exist by reason of self-existence, when the speaker takes the thought that they do not exist by reason of self-existence, where is the fault in desiring to generate this (cognition, *blo*)! However (at the same time, we should mention), it is a (great) fault to regard the entity that is without self-existence as though it were (accomplished) by self-existence. According to the way you take it (i.e., that asserting non-self-existence is also a kind of imputation), at the time of saying there is no mistake, since you are imputing when you think there is no mistake, it would turn out necessary to refute that (cognition of yours, as well), so what we have stated above is a lovely thing[170] to rely on (even for yourself)!

The *Prasannapadā* (on XIII, 8) also explains, "for those who cling to a mode of being in regard to voidness,"[171] and so there is for them not only no refutation of voidness (of self-existence), but also there is no fault in just viewing voidness. Hence, the *Saṃcaya(-gāthā)* (I, 9 c–d) says:[172]

The Bodhisattva who courses in sign-sources while he imagines that these personality aggregates are void, is not devoted to the abode of nonbirth.

Also, the *Ratnāvalī* (II, 3c–d) puts it this way:[173]

For that reason the great Muni warded off the views related to self and nonself.[174]

Besides, other scriptures and *śāstras* have statements about the impropriety of views on the void and nonself, and it is necessary to understand them as already explained.

But that is not the way (the *Heart-sūtra*) puts it:[175] Sāriputra, desiring to practice the profound Prajñāpāramitā, asked Avalokiteśvara how he should train himself. In reply, he was told rightly to observe that those five personality aggregates are void of self-existence. Also, the *Saṃcaya (-gātha)* (I, 28c–d) says:[176]

(The Bodhisattva) recognizes that *dharmas* are not present by reason of an underlying nature. This is his coursing in the perfection of best insight.

Besides, the *Avatāra* (VI, 165c–d) states:

Consequently, the yogin who views self and what belongs to self as void (of self-existence) becomes liberated (from *saṃsāra*).

There are many such passages which (by alluding to "views") oppose the other ones.

Hence, the root of all adversities is nescience which attributes self-existence (*svabhāva*); and by way of the basic conflict between that and the grasping pattern (*'dzin staṅs*) (the way of grasping the objective domain), only the *prajñā* (insight) which comprehends non-self-existence or nonself extirpates that (nescience) from the root; so when you refute the grasping pattern of (*prajñā*) (the non-self-existence of the objective domain), you reject the view of reality. In short, it is necessary (for you) also to accept it, disavowing (your rejection), to wit: "The door to quiescence which has no second one . . ." (*Catuḥ-s,* k. 288a):[177] The *Catuḥ-ś-ṭ* states:

The destruction of attachment is the cause of attaining *nirvāṇa*; and there is no cause for that kind of destruction of attachment other than the view that there is no self-existence. For that very reason, the non-self-ness which has the character of no self-existence is the door to quiescence which has no second one, namely this is the sole incomparable gate for entering the city of *nirvāṇa.* Though voidness, signless, and wishless are called the three gates to liberation, even so the view (*darśana*) of nonself is the substratum (for the other three). For the one who has realized the non-self-ness in all *dharmas,* having destroyed the attachment to all entities, nowhere is there any assiduous pursuit, and how could he apprehend (by way of) sign-sources! For that reason, non-self-ness is the door to quiescence which has no second one.

For the same reason the *Byaṅ chub kyi tshogs* says this:[178]

When the void is by reason of no self-existence, there is the void. Also what is there to do with sign-sources! Since all sign-sources lead astray, how would a wise man form a resolution!

These texts explain that there are three doors to liberation and explain that the view which observes the void of self-existence is the sole gate to liberation.[179] And having, by scripture and principle, eliminated the conflict, only this (view) accomplishes the gate of liberation.

Also, why should merely deciding about self-existence require a rejecting of the objective domain! That is, the view understanding in this manner (i.e., nonexistence by self-existence) is the adversary to the adherence to sign-sources (the reifying imputation) in terms of the two selves (self of *dharma* and self of *pudgala*), so it is not just a question of adhering to sign-sources therein. But clearly the position which permeates the texts of the Chinese teacher Hva-śaṅ is to regard even such a (distinguished) reflection as this (which is the basis of the path to *nirvāna*) to be a fault, thus rejecting good reflections and bad reflections (indiscriminatively).[180]

b. Refutation of Nonpervasion in Determining the Refutable

Some persons say that the refutable thing (in this case), namely, the self-existence, has three distinctions, namely, (the distinction of) own-nature, i.e., not generated by causes and conditions; (the distinction of) level, i.e., not changing into something else; and (the distinction of) establishment, i.e., not dependent on another. They say, moreover, (it is) because the *Mūla-madhyamaka(-kārikā)* states (XV, 1–2):

It is not right that a self-existent arise from causes and conditions. If it arose from causes and conditions, a self-existent would be create (*kṛtaka*).

Besides, how could a self-existent come to be called "create"? For a self-existent is uncreate and not dependent on another.

In general, if one claims that such external and personal entities as shoots are accomplished as self-existent in that fashion (with the three distinctions), the Mādhyamika must refute this. However, in this case the determination of the refutable thing (should be as follows): when one refutes something, he should generate in the stream of consciousness the Mādhyamika view which comprehends the non-self-existence of *dharmas,* and thus determine the basis of the refutable thing. Accordingly, when insiders (i.e., the Vaibhāṣikas, Sautrāntikas, etc.) hold that constructed natures (*saṃskṛta*) are generated by causes and conditions, if it is not required for them (i.e., those insiders) to hold the non-self-existence, and if it is a fault for them (those insiders) to comprehend that entities lack self-existence, with that (i.e., your determination) where is the unshared refutable (pertaining to the view that comprehends voidness)!

If (an entity) were produced by self-nature and produced in self-existence (as the realist believes), it follows that (the entity) would be independent of causes and conditions and would not change into something else. Now this evaluation is frequently found in the Mādhyamika texts (such as the *Madhyamika-kārikā* and the *Prasannapadā*). Still, such (evaluations) express the fault by way of the pervader (*vyāpaka*), but do not determine the refutable by way of self-nature.

Moreover, if (an entity) were (produced) in the absolute sense, were genuinely produced and really produced, it would follow that it is not generated by causes and conditions, (does not change into something else) and so on. Still, those (criteria) do not explain "production in the absolute sense" and so on. For example, let us grant that a pot is pervaded by impermanence; still, the impermanence is unable to explain the pot, while a large bulbous pot is able to establish the meaning of that (i.e., a pot).[181] Likewise, if (an entity) were produced in the absolute sense, and so on, it would follow that it is an impartite entity. Now in this (context) an impartite entity is not held to be the basic refutable, although this (impartite entity) is just imagined by adherents of theory-systems in an unshared manner—because this (impartite entity) is not the root that binds the subject (*dehin*) to the cyclical flow; and because even when one contemplates those (partless entities), establishing them as devoid of self-existence, this in no way injures the adherence to immemorial nescience, so that even at the climax of understanding directly the meaning of those (partless entities as non-self-existent) there is no averting of the concomitant defilements.

Hence, at the time one establishes with a view, to the extent that he grasps it with concomitant nescience he mainly grasps the establishment without the meaning, and ancillary to that, he does not know how to oppose the objective domains that are the grasping of imagination. Since he fails to oppose the grasping pattern of concomitant nescience, at the time he rejects the *pudgala*-self, i.e., a self that is permanent, unique, and independent; and at the time he rejects the *dharma*-self, i.e., the apprehender partless atom, the apprehender partless moment, the self-existence possessed of the three distinctions—imagined only by the adherents of theory-systems—he is completely incapable of the rejections. If he were not (incapable), at the time of establishment with a view, even when he contemplates without having established it through those rudiments (permanence, etc.) he would necessarily contemplate those rudiments, because establishment with a view is the meaning of the contemplation.

For that reason, even when one realizes directly after contemplating, and reaches the climax of the contemplation, it amounts to those rudiments; accordingly, viewing the two *nairātmyas* (i.e., nonself of *pudgala* and of *dharma*) is just a figmental tenet of the imagination; and if one claims to have warded off the concomitant defilements by just that (viewing) he has certainly missed the mark. In this connection, the *Avatāra* (VI, 140) states:

At the time one understands nairātmya (of *pudgala*) and rejects (by such vision) the permanent self, he also denies the basis [182] for this ego (the permanent self). For that reason, when one says that by knowing *nairātmya* he also has finally expunged the view of self, this is astonishing!

And the commentary states:

In order to clarify by way of example that the meaning (of that person) is incoherent, (the *kārikā* VI, 141) states: [183]

> Seeing a snake coiled in a recess of his house and thinking, "There is no elephant here" his alarm is dispelled (as to an elephant), and he abandons fear for the snake. Behold the rectitude of our opponent!

This is stated in regard to nonself of *pudgala,* but it applies likewise to nonself of *dharma,* as added (in the verse): [184]

At the time one comprehends the nonself (of *dharma*) and rejects the imaginary self (of *dharma*), he also denies the nescience basis. Therefore, when one says that by knowing nonself he also has finally expunged nescience, this is astonishing!

However, the *ācārya* (Nāgārjuna), as previously explained, said that the uncreate and the not-dependent-on-another have the characteristic of self-existence. The question arises: Is that stated by way of positing alternatives of consideration (e.g., is it self-existent or is it create) or does it refer to some entity that is self-existent? (In answer,) it is said: "This is the true nature of *dharmas.*" [185] And he posits *svabhāva* that is uncreate and not dependent on another. That (*svabhāva*) exists. (Informing us of this) the *Avatāra*-commentary says: [186]

Regarding this sort of *svabhāva* as written in particular (*Madhyamaka-kārikā,* XV, 1–2), received from the mouth of the *ācārya* (= Nāgārjuna), does it exist? (In answer:) As to its authorization, the Bhagavat proclaimed that whether Tathāgatas arise or do not arise, this true nature of *dharmas* abides,[187] and so on, extensively. The "true nature" (of that text, = *svabhāva*) (necessarily) exists. Which (elements) have this "true nature"? These, the eye, etc. have this *svabhāva.* And what is their *svabhāva?* Their uncreate nature and their nondependence on another; the self-nature which is to be understood by knowledge (in *āryasamāpatti*) free from the caul of nescience (and its associated habit-energy). When it is asked, "Does that sort of thing exist?" who would answer, "No"? If it does not exist, for which goal do the Bodhisattvas cultivate the path of the perfections? For what reason do the Bodhisattvas, in order to comprehend the true-nature, assume myriads of difficulties that way?

Thus he proves it along with sūtra information. (The adversary says:) However, is it not the case that previously you refuted the accomplishment by self-existence (*svabhāva*) of all the dharmas? (In reply:) Did we not answer many times that there is not even an atom that is self-existent, accomplished by own-nature, among the *dharmas* which (however) are not present by dint of inner notion's conception? Hence, we need not speak of other (*saṃskṛta*) *dharmas* as self-existent that way! True nature, the absolute truth, is not at all accomplished (as self-existent that way)! (Informing us of this,) the *Prasannapadā* (in chap. XV) states:[188]

By *svabhāva* one understands this innate nature, uncreate, which has not deviated in the fire in the past, present, and future; which did not arise earlier and will not arise later; which is not dependent on causes and conditions as are the heat of water, (one or another) of this side and the other side, long and short. Well, then, does this own-nature of fire that is of such manner (i.e., uncreate, not dependent) exist? (In reply:) This (*svabhāva* of such sort) neither exists nor does not exist by reason of own-nature.[189] While that is the case, still in order to avoid frightening the hearers, we conventionally make affirmations (such as "*svabhāva*" and "*dharmatā*") and say it exists.

Thus that *svabhāva* is also said conventionally to exist, after its accomplishment by own-nature was denied. Now, while that represents to teach with designations so as to avoid frightening the hearers, does that not contradict the *ācārya* himself? (In reply:) That is not right, because it is necessary (to avoid frightening the hearers); in fact, all other *dharmas* as well are expressed by designations, because they are (all) nonexistent! As was cited above (*Avatāra*-commentary), if there were not that meaning (i.e., that sort of *svabhāva*), the pure life (*brahmacarya*) would be purposeless; and so he (the *ācārya*) proves it by showing the absurdity of denial, because the *Avatāra*-commentary says:[190]

Not only was this "*svabhāva*" received from the mouth of the *ācārya* (=Nāgārjuna), but also so other persons could be brought to accept this meaning (this sort of *svabhāva*), this *svabhāva* was established so as to prove it to both (the disputants and his adversary).

If it were otherwise (i.e., if one were to deny that sort of *svabhāva*), it would be necessary to believe that the Mādhyamika school has no possibility of achieving liberation, because attaining *nirvāṇa* means realizing *nirvāṇa;* and *nirvāṇa* is explained (in this context) as the Truth of Cessation (*nirodha-satya*), and the latter is also said to be *paramārtha-satya;* and because there would not be *paramārtha-satya* (if it were otherwise). That it is necessary, at the time of attaining *nirvāṇa,* to realize directly the Truth of Cessation which is *paramārtha,* the *Yuktiṣaṣṭikā-vṛtti* attempts to prove at length.

Accordingly, not only are these *saṃskṛtas* of eye, etc. not accomplished as self-existent, accomplished by own-nature; but also the true nature (*dharmatā*) posited as self-existent, is not proved in that (self-existence), so (neither) is proved in any self-existence. Also, *Paramārtha-satya* is the true nature posited in *svabhāva* and accomplished in it. But the uncreate and the nondependent on another, which are posited in that *svabhāva,* are only accomplished in conventional terms because there is no (accomplishing) at all in that *svabhāva* which is "accomplished by own-nature." Here, "create" means caused to newly arise because not previously existing; and "dependent on another" means dependent on causes and conditions.

The (elements) such as form are not accomplished in either of the two *svabhāvas* (the *svabhāva* in the meaning of true nature and the *svabhāva* accomplished by own nature). Since one cultivates the path so as to view the *svabhāva* that is the *svabhāva* in the meaning of true nature, it is also said that the pure life is not purposeless. (And that is not all:) it is explained that there is no conflict between our positively not accepting the *svabhāva* of *dharmas* accomplished by own nature, and our accepting the *svabhāva* in the adventitious sense (with individual designations). Such is the position of the *Avatāra*-commentary:[191]

Some persons, exclaiming, "Fooey," go on to say: You not only do not believe in any entities, but you also believe in a self-existence (*svabhāva*) that is uncreate, yet adventitiously (designated), and not dependent on another. Your meaning is mutually inconsistent and incoherent. (In reply:) We shall explain (that there is no inconsistency). As to your own *śāstra,* its purport is nescience;

its purport is as follows: If even the childish, ordinary person may apprehend the own-form of eye, etc. that arises dependently, this (own form) is (ultimately) the self-existence of those (the eye, etc.). But such a self-existence is wayward, because it can be comprehended directly; and then there is no purpose for the pure life (*brahmacarya*), because there is no (ultimate) *svabhāva* of those (own-forms of eye, etc.). Consequently, it is for the purpose of witnessing that (ultimate *svabhāva*) that the pure life (and path cultivation) becomes meaningful. Moreover, it is in dependence on *saṃvṛti-satya* (with adventitious designations) that I (*ācārya* Candrakīrti) speak of the uncreate and the nondependent on another. The reality (i.e., own-form) which no childish person can witness is the principle which (ultimately) is *svabhāva;* and with just that (which cannot be witnessed), there is no *paramārtha*-entity, but also it is not the case that there is no entity, because that (*paramārtha*) is intrinsically quiescent.

In this context, the existence and nonexistence of the entity was explained previously when speaking of the two possibilities, to wit, it exists with its own-form or it doesn't exist at all.

Nowadays, they establish the *dharmas* that are without even an atom accomplished as self-existent, accomplished by own-nature, as the voidness of what is void of self-existence. Now these *dharmas* of form, etc. amount to the "special basis" (*khyad gźi*) (i.e., void of self-existence); and thereupon there is a presence in the sense of the "special *dharma*" (*khyad chos*)[192] (i.e., voidness), thus in the scope of a single discrimination (*eka-buddhi*). (They say that) there is no contradiction in there being both of these (i.e., the special basis—form, etc.; and the special *dharma*—voidness), and that the second appearance is not wayward. But this voidness is the factitious (*kālpanika*) *paramārtha-satya*.

At whatever time, by habituation in that view which comprehends the absence of self-existence, one comprehends this entity in immediacy—on this face (of comprehension) one wards off all delusive appearance that takes what is without self-existence to be self-existent. The awareness which realizes directly that true nature (*dharmatā*) does not have in view the factual bases (*dharmin*) form, etc. Thus the two, the true nature of that sort (= voidness) and factual bases (form, etc.), are the absence on the face of *buddhi*. So the positing of those two, the true nature and the factual base, requires a positing by the face of a different *buddhi* that is conventional.[193] That being the case, *paramārtha-satya* is the quiescence of all elaboration (*prapañca*) accomplished by own-form, and on it is the absence of self-existence; but whatever appears there, namely all the elaboration of delusive appearance, is what one posits just in waywardness. So, while accepting that (*paramārtha*), where is the necessity to accept a self-existence accomplished by own-form! Also, the *Prasannapadā* (on chapter XV, 2) states:

By whatever (deluded) self one approaches the form of entities (form, etc.) perceptively reached by the power of nescience's coat; and by whatever method of nonseeing belonging to the nobles who are rid of nescience's coat one approaches the domain (of *samāpatti*)—just that own-form (*svarūpa*) is established as the *svabhāva* of those (entities).

And that is the (ultimate) *svabhāva* with unoriginated nature of the entities. Moreover, by reason of nothing-at-all, by reason of absence-only, and because it lacks self-existence, one should understand that there is no self-existence of entities.

Those persons[194] who do not posit the *paramārtha-satya* refutable, which is only the cutting-off of elaboration of the two selves (*dharma* and *pudgala*), and understand the manner-of-being (*yin lugs*) as green, yellow, etc., (at that time) claim that the objective domain arises in discrimination (*buddhi*) by independent accomplishment and without mistake, and claim that the certainty (of the arising of the objective domain) that way is the (ultimate) view which understands the profound meaning. And they claim that those persons (i.e., Nāgārjuna, Haribhadra, etc.) who understand as without self-existence these external and personal *dharmas* that are the occasion of attachment to the two selves, have been misled[195] from the right view. But those claims are outside (i.e., heretical) of all the Buddhist scriptures whether Hīnayāna or Mahāyāna. The reason is that it is necessary to avert the positing of self, which for all sentient beings is the root of bondage in the cyclical flow (*saṃsāra*); and those claims have an understanding of non-self-existence that is an occasion of adhering to self (*ātma-grāha*), and do not avert it because their other incoherent *dharma* claims to avert the adherence to self by understanding that there is a presence in truth.

This (meaning, indeed astonishing) is like the case of a man who perceiving that there is no snake in the eastern corner, becomes frightened (of a snake) and suffers; then to ward off his suffering, (someone else) says to him, "You perceived that no snake at all was actually in the eastern corner, and cannot ward off your adherence to a snake (*āhi-grāha*); well then, imagine that there is a tree in the western corner and adhere to that; by such (adherence) you will (certainly) ward off your snake-adherence and suffering," and that by no means appears a superior (solution).

Hence, those who wish to prove our good side should eliminate at length those kinds (of wayward views) and apply the means which opposes the grasping pattern of nescience that is the root of all the troubles of bondage in *saṃsāra*. For that means you must rely on the scripture of final meaning (*nītārtha*); and since it is not proper to be led away from that meaning (i.e., final meaning), (rely) on the texts of *ārya* Nāgārjuna and disciples which clearly state the extensive set of principles (*rigs tshogs*) which penetrate the depth of certainty; and may you (thereby) cross the ocean of phenomenal life!

Those rejections of wayward conception regarding the refutable thing constitute the most important essential for getting rid of the misleading point for reaching the Mādhyamika view. Consequently, I have explained the matter extensively.

3. OUR OWN SCHOOL'S METHOD OF DETERMINING THE REFUTABLE

There are three parts to this: a. Determining the refutable with its basic meaning; b. The method of treating or not treating the other refutables; c. Explanation of treating or not treating the *paramārtha* distinction in regard to the refutable.

a. Determining the Refutable with Its Basic Meaning

In general for the refutable there are two kinds—the refutable of the path and the refutable of the principle. Regarding the first of these (the refutable of the path), the *Madhyāntavibhāga* states (II, 17):

> The hindrance of defilement (= consciousness, *citta*) and the hindrance of the knowable (= of consciousness, *cittasya*)[196] are taught. In these (two) are all hindrances, by the destruction of which, liberation (= *nirvāṇa*) is claimed.

According to this there are two hindrances—defilement and the knowable. As long as there is this knowable there is the refutable, because when this is absent, the subjects (*dehin*) have no more endeavor and become liberated.

(The second of these,) the refutable of the principle, is stated in the *Vigrahavyāvartinī* (k. 27):

Suppose a man, in regard to a female body that was magically manifested, would think, "That is a woman," and a magical manifestation would destroy the (sensual) adherence to the delusive thing. In the same way (as that example), would be this (my words).

The self-commentary states:

Suppose a man, in regard to a female body magically created, that is void of self-existence, would think with adherence to the delusive thing. "That is positively a woman." In that way the adherence to a delusive thing would arouse sensual desire toward her. Accordingly the Tathāgata and his *śrāvakas* magically manifest magical creations, and these (magical creations) ward off that man's adherence to a delusive thing. In the same way (as that example) my words, like a magical creation that is void, would, in regard to all the entities that are without self-existence like the magically created woman, ward off the adherence to them as having self-existence.

As this states, the refutable is the adherence (by the subject with *ātmagrāha*) to a delusive thing; and one takes as another refutable the presence of self-existence as it is apprehended by that (subject's adherence). However, (of these) the chief refutable is the latter one, because, for warding off the waywardness of the subject, it is necessary first to oppose the objective domain that is apprehended by that (subject). And this (opposition to such a domain) is tantamount to the various opposing arguments[197] to the presence of self-existence accomplished by own-nature superimposed on the *pudgala* and *dharma* that (in fact) arise dependently. This refutable is necessarily the nonexistent knowable, because if it were existent one would not be able to deny it. If it be this way (i.e., nonexistent) then it is necessary to refute the attribution (*sgro 'dogs*) which apprehends it (this refutable) as existent.

As to the (method of) refutation—when a pot is shattered by a hammer and ceases to exist, one generates the cognition with certainty that recognizes what is not as not; in the same way, if one arouses the certainty that (the refutable) is not existent, one averts the erroneous cognition that apprehends it as existent. In the same way, for proving with a principle, one generates the cognition with certainty, recognizing the *dharma* as it exists in the manner in which it exists, for example, in the manner that a seed generates a shoot—thus there is not a new accomplishment of something that was not before.

Also the *Vigrahavyāvartinī* (k. 65) states:

Besides you say: in the absence of words, there is proof that words can refute *asat*. It this connection, (we reply:) the word informs of *asat* but does not dispel it.

And the commentary on this states the matter clearly:

Besides, you (the logician) say: "Even in the absence of words, refutation of *asat* is proved. So why do you (Mādhyamika) resort to words, to wit: 'All entities lack self-existence'?" In this connection, we (Mādhyamika) say: "You should know (*khalu*) that when we say, 'All entities are without self-existence,' the words do not cause all entities to be without self-existence. However, since there is not the self-existence, the fact is reported (to others) with the words, 'Entities are without self-existence.' "
Here is an example: While Devadatta is not at home, someone says, "Devadatta is at home." Then, since he is not there, someone (else) retorts, "He is not there." But the latter's words do not cause Devadatta's absence; rather they only report Devadatta's absence from the house. Likewise, the words "Entities have no self-existence" do not cause the non-self-existence of the entities, but (they report) the absence of self-existence in all entities. [For example, when persons lack genuine nature like a phantom person and so are deceptive, and a childish fellow, deceived by his nescience, attributes possession of self-existence (to them), again (those words) report the absence of self-existence.][198] Therefore, what you say, to wit: "Since there is no self-existence, why use your words that there is no self-existence, a fact proven even without words?" has no validity.

One should understand it in that way. For this reason, (when some Tibetans) claim that if it exists one cannot oppose it (with a principle) and if it does not exist there is no necessity to oppose it (with a principle), so (all *dharmas*) are free from refutation and proof, and (our) numerous examinations with the principle of refutation and proof are just aimless wandering[199] in conventional words, (their claim or any like argument) is a specious expression of mutual contradiction, in which apparently there has not occurred the general meaning (*don spyi*) as regards any refutation and proof of the principle and of the path. Because, when you yourself show as reason, "If it exists one cannot oppose it, and if it does not exist there is no necessity to oppose it," as though to refute the other person's examination of refutation and proof, you desire not to hear what is to be the refutation and proof; and because even with that form of reason you claim a necessity that there be a refutation and proof aimed at the other person, who cannot properly be opposed, by your very words, "If it exists one cannot oppose it, and if it does not exist there is no necessity to oppose it."

The refutation by means of an illustrious principle is for the sake of warding off the mistaken conceptions of waywardness, and proving by the principle is the means of generating the certainty without waywardness;[200] so the one desiring to avert the wayward kind of discrimination, and desiring to generate the nonwayward kind of discrimination, should generate the discrimination (*buddhi*) of errorless certainty of refutation and proof following the collection of principles (i.e., the six books) of Nāgārjuna, and so on.

Now, since the refutation by a principle is for the sake of generating the errorless certainty by way of refuting the erroneous grasping-pattern, of what sort is the discrimination that has the domain of grasping-pattern which the principle refutes? (In reply:) In general, the refutable grasping conceptions are numberless; however, one should well apprehend that wayward conception which is the root of all faults, and should refute the attachment-domain (*źen yul*) of that (conception), because if one averts this (root of all faults), one averts all faults (*ñes skyon*). Furthermore, (in the scriptures of the Buddha) the opposites of other (defilements) such as lust, etc. are stated to be the opposites of each particular (defilement), and the opposite of nescience is stated to be the opposite of all (defilements). Therefore, nescience is the basis (or root) of all faults. The *Prasannapadā* puts it this way:[201]

The nine kinds of teaching of the Buddhas, sūtras, etc.,[202] are based on the two truths (*saṃvṛti-satya* and *paramārtha-satya*). On the side of the worldlings' conduct (with 84,000 defilements),[203] there is something far-spread, celebrated as genuine in this world (i.e., the *Dharma-skandha*). In that (*Dharma-skandha*), in order to dispel love, it was said that hatred is not brought to an end. And in order to dispel hatred, it was said that love is not brought to an end. It was said that in order for someone to end pride, and so on, he could not conquer defilements other than those. For that reason, those (individual defilements acting as counteracting agents of other defilements, love, ect.) are said to not be great pervaders of those (others), and (just) those are not of great purpose.[204] (However,) it was said that in order to end delusion (= nescience, which is the root of all faults), whatever (is the counteracting agent) destroys all defilements. The Buddhas have declared that all defilements are based on (only) delusion.

However, of what sort is delusion? The cognition (*buddhi*) which attributes to the external and personal *dharmas* a self-existence apprehended as accomplished by own-characteristic, is in this context, nescience (*avidyā*). The *Catuḥ-ś-ṭ* (on chapter XIV, 25 = k. 350) states:

(Any) *vijñāna,* attached to entities, under the power of defiled nescience, that attributes (accomplishment) by own-nature, is the seed which enters *saṃsāra;* by its complete cessation, it establishes the warding off of *saṃsāra.* In order to show that, he explains:

> *Vijñāna* is the seed of phenomenal life.[205] The (inner and outer) objects are its field (of apperception). When it sees the object as selfless, the seed of phenomenal life ceases.

By the method as just explained, when *vijñāna,* which by the cause of attachment is the seed of phenomenal life, sees the object as without self-existence, as a result of averting that in every fashion, it establishes that the *śrāvaka* (*arhats*), *pratyekabuddha* (*arhats*), and the Bodhisattvas (of the eighth stage) who have attained the forbearance of the unoriginated natures, avert *saṃsāra.*[206]

That same (nescience) is also called "apprehender as true"; (informing us of that) (*Catuḥ-ś,* k. 135; chapter VI, 10):

> In the same way as (all) bodies are (pervaded) by sense organs of the body, so delusion (= nescience) is situated in all (other defilements). For that reason, by the destruction of delusion, all defilements are also destroyed.

The *ṭīkā* on that explains:

In the manner that delusion conceives (or, apprehends) as true those (entities of the objective domain), as a result of the consequent deception, one engages in attributing to entities an own-nature as true.

If, in that way, nescience is the root of *saṃsāra,* then when the *Madhyamakāvatāra* and the *Prasannapadā* explain the reifying view (*satkāyadṛṣṭi*) to be the root of *saṃsāra,* would this not be invalid on the grounds that it (*saṃsāra*) could not have two (different) chief causes? (In reply:) The theories of other *ācāryas* about the method of maintaining it to be nescience or the reifying view, have already been explained in the section on the middling person.[207]

Hence (not needing to go into those matters), in this section there is *ācārya* Candrakīrti's theory—as well as the theory of other Mādhyamikas (i.e., Svātantrika) that it is the hindrance of the knowable—and of those (two theories) the apprehension of entities as true is maintained to be nescience; and besides it is maintained to be the defiled nescience, since the *Catuḥ-śataka-ṭīkā* explained in the previous quotation this (apprehension as true) to be defiled. Moreover, the *Avatāra-Comm.* (on VI, 28) states:

By means of this (nescience which is apprehension as true) the sentient beings are deluded about how the entities are present. Delusion, i.e., nescience, which causes the attribution of own-nature to entities although they do not have it, and has the nature of hindrance so that they see a self-existence—is called *"saṃvṛti."*

Also (on VI, 28):

Accordingly, *saṃvṛti-satya* is established by the power of defiled nescience incorporated in the members of phenomenal life.

Thus it is explained as the first of the twelve-membered dependent origination, and so it is (the hindrance of) defilement (*kleśa*), and not the hindrance of the knowable. But then, where does one put the hindrance of the knowable? This will be explained below.[208]

Hence the explanation that this nescience, which is the first one of the twelve members, is the root of *saṃsāra;* and that the reifying view is also the root of *saṃsāra,* is not a contradiction, because nescience is general (*spyi*) and the reifying view is particular (*bye brag*).[209] Among those (two), nescience is the reverse of clear vision (*vidyā*); and this does not mean as relevant any particular clear vision, but the insight kind of clear vision (*vidyā-prajña*) of the reality of nonself. The reverse of that (kind of clear vision) is not properly only the absence of insight or only something different from it, because it is the enemy of that (insight).[210] That (nescience) is the attribution as self, and since it is both the attribution as self of *dharma* and the attribution as self of *pudgala,* both the *dharma-ātmagrāha* and the *pudgala-ātmagrāha* are the (defiled) nescience. Therefore, when the reifying view is taught to be the root of all the other defilements, it is not the case that nescience is denied to be the root (of all other defilements); and it is said (*Ratnāvalī,* I, 35): "As long as there is adherence to personality aggregates (as accomplished by own-nature), for so long there will be adherence to a self." Thus, the nescience of deception that there is a self of a nature (*dharma-ātma*) is taught to be the cause of the deception that there is a self of a personality (*pudgala-ātma*). This shows how to include both (nescience and reifying view) in the category of nescience in the sense of cause and effect. Hence, there is no contradiction in teaching that the reifying view is the root of all defilements other than this nescience. If one does not know the explanation according to the purport of the *ācārya* (Candrakīrti), it is very difficult to reject the contradiction involved in teaching that there are the two (above mentioned) roots of *saṃsāra.*

This way of apprehending that kind of nescience is nātha Nāgārjuna's position, as he writes in the *Śūnyatāsaptati* (k. 64–65):

> Any conception that the entities arisen from causes and conditions, are genuine—the Teacher has declared to be nescience. Starting with that (nescience), the twelve members (of dependent origination) arise.
>
> When so as to observe the genuine, one well knows the entities as void, nescience does not arise. That is how nescience ceases. As a consequence, the twelve members cease.

Besides, he tells us in *Mūla-prajñā,* chapter XXVI (v. 11–12):

When nescience ceases, there is no origination of the motivations (*saṃskāra*). The cessation of nescience results from the contemplation by knowledge of just that (*paramārtha*-reality).

By the cessation of this and that (preceding member of dependent origination), this and that (subsequent member) does not manifest. The (entire) mass of suffering (leaving out happiness) only truly ceases in this way.

This indeed agrees (with the above quotation from *Śūnyatāsaptati*), and is very concordant with the (*Ratnāvalī*) text, "As long as there is adherence to the personality aggregates," which states adherence to the personality aggregates to be the root of *saṃsāra*. In Āryadeva's position, it is clearly shown by such passages as "In the same way as bodies are (pervaded) by sense organs of the body, . . ." and "*Vijnāna* is the seed of phenomenal life, . . ." which were cited above (from his *Catuḥśataka*).

Now, as many as are the principles stated by the *ācarya* (*ārya* Nāgārjuna) in the Mādhyamika treatises about the refutable and the refutation, they all teach the lack of self-nature of the *dharmas* by refuting the self-existence which delusion attributes to the *dharmas* as their accomplishment by own-nature. Thus were stated innumerable different principles for the sake only of opposing the grasping-pattern of nescience (the root of *saṃsāra*). So Buddhapālita writes (Comm. on chapter I):

Why was it necessary to instruct about dependent origination? I shall explain. The *ācarya* (*Nāgārjuna*) having observed with compassionate heart the sentient beings miserable through a wide assortment of sufferings, so as to liberate them, deemed to teach the genuine thusness of entities. So he set about instructing them in dependent origination, because he said:

> Observing the false, is bondage;
> observing the genuine, is liberation.

What is the genuine thusness of entities? He explains: It is the lack of self-nature. Those who are ignorant of that (lack of own-nature) because their perspicacity (which analyzes the *dharmas*) is obscured by the darkness of delusion, imagine that entities have their own-nature; and at that time those persons develop attraction (for entities to which they attribute pleasantness) and aversion (for entities to which they attribute unpleasantness). At the time the darkness of delusion is dispelled by the light of knowledge of dependent origination, and one observes with the eye of insight that the entities have no own-nature—then there is no opportunity (for the rise of attraction and aversion), and in that person attraction and aversion do not arise.

In the transitional comment (*pratisaṃdhi*) of chapter XXVI, he (Buddhapālita) writes:

At this point it was said (by others): You have finished explaining how to understand *paramārtha* by the school of Mahāyāna texts. Now, please teach how to understand *paramārtha* by the school of *śrāvaka* texts! (In reply:) Here it is explained: "Obscured by nescience, for rebirth, . . ."[211]

And in the transitional comment of chapter XXVII, he writes:

At this point it was said (by others): Now that you have resorted to the alternative of the sūtra class consistent with the *śrāvaka* vehicle, please teach the forms of (wayward) views that are not feasible! (In reply:) Here it is explained: " 'In past time, I arose,', . . ."[212]

Thus Buddhapālita clearly maintains that nescience, as the first of the twelve members, attributes to entities the self-existence; and besides maintains that also in the case of *śrāvakas* and *pratyekabuddhas,* one must understand (directly) the nonself of natures (*dharma-nairātmya*). Hence, the *śrāvaka* and *pratyekabuddha* (*āryas*) have the great work of having to comprehend (directly) that *dharmas* are without self-existence. May they realize that what adheres to a self of *dharma* is this nescience among the twelve members!

The *Catuḥ-ś* (k. 399c-d) says:

Observing (entities) with discursive thought (*vikalpa*) is bondage. That (discursive thought) is the refutable in this case.

The "discursive thought" of this verse is not the agent for everything, but is the discursive thought which attributes to *dharmas* accomplishment by own-nature. The commentary (the *ṭīkā*) explains: "Discursive thought attributes (to entities) the meaning of self-existence which is false." Moreover, that (discursive thought) is maintained to be the defiled nescience. So when (other Tibetans), reflecting on what this is, took the position of opposing by principle the objective domain of all discursive thought, they surely did not examine the matter in fine detail![213] If it were otherwise, then when ordinary persons (*pṛthagjana*), for whom the meaning of reality is remote (*lkog tu gyur pa*), grasp the meaning of voidness, they would have the means for it without discursive thought; thus, whatever the discursive thought, all of it would be toward the nonexistent; and denying by principle the objective domain, it follows that the objective domain of certainty knowledge would be like the one attributed self-existence by mistaken wayward cognition. If it were that way (i.e., with mistaken knowledge treated the same as certainty knowledge), there surely would be no right view for guidance to the stage of *nirvāṇa,* and so there would be no purpose in engaging in all those practices laid down in the Mādhyamika texts, of learning, pondering, etc. For the *Catuḥ-ś* says (k. 182):

When the person who has viewed nonvoid as though it were void, thinks, "Let it be my *nirvāṇa,*" he has no *nirvāṇa* because his view is wayward—the Tathāgatas have declared!

When one has posited as a basis that very attachment domain (*źen yul*) with the grasping-pattern of nescience, as previously explained, there are many distinctions by the realists among the insider sects (Buddhist) and other sects (non-Buddhist); and all (the bad views) posited by way of the theory-systems that attribute (those distinctions) have (as a basis) the domain with the grasping-pattern of nescience. If one refutes that (attachment domain), cutting out its root as though it were a tree, one averts all (those faulty distinctions, now without a basis). So the wise should understand the attachment domain of co-natal (or, native) nescience to be the refutable root, and should not persevere in opposing the sheer figments imagined by only the adherents of a theory-system. It is this way: one should not engage in refuting the refutable while destitute of occasion (i.e., not having obtained a cause by someone else's instigation). Rather, the refutable (as an objective domain) goes with the wayward discursive thought of the subject. Having observed the sentient beings in *saṃsāra*'s bondage by reason of that (nescience), one refutes the objective domain of that (wayward discursive thought), because the bondage of all sentient beings in *saṃsāra* is the co-natal nescience; and because it is not valid that the nescience of imaginations, existing as it does only for the sectarians, could be the root of *saṃsāra.* It is of extreme importance to gain the perspicacity[214] of certainty in this matter.

Accordingly, in the final analysis the wayward discursive thought which clings to the refutable is the co-natal nescience which is the first of the twelve members and forms the prior basis also for the refutables of imagination which are only attributions. So all the grasping-patterns of nondiscursive knowledge (*avikalpa-jñāna*) (the undeniable nearby cause of error) of (eye-) sense consciousness and so on, are never to be refuted by principle. For that reason, the intellect (*buddhi*) that would use a principle to refute the grasping-pattern is only the discursive thought of mind-based perception (*mano-vijñāna*) and moreover is the two graspings as self (*dharma-* and *pudgala-ātmagrāha*) or the discursive thoughts which attribute distinctions to the objective domain as imagined by those (two). But this by no means takes in every kind of discursive thought!

However, of what sort is the method by which that nescience attributes self-existence? In general, in the texts of this *ācārya* (Candrakīrti) there appear many designations, such as "self-existence" or "own-nature," that are applied to the natures accomplished only in the conventional sense. In this (section about the refutable) the objective domains of *pudgala* or *dharma,* as the case may be, are not posited by the power of intellect (*buddhi*), but are the situation (*gnas tshul*) or layout (*sdod tshul*) of those natures on their respective side, which are grasped (or given attribution). That (intellect, which attributes), insofar as it posits as attachment-realm the layout of the natures on their respective side, calls it (i.e., the layout) "self" or "self-existence." One may determine this by positing alternative considerations, i.e., (*Catuḥ-śataka,* k. 348c-d, in chapter XIV): "This (entity) is entirely lacking in independence. Hence it is not a self." And the *Catuḥ-ś* on this sets forth alternate references:

In this (world) any entity that has own-nature is self-existent, independent, and not dependent on another. . . .

Among them, "not dependent on another" does not mean it is not dependent on causes and conditions, since the subject (*viṣayin*) or conventional cognition is called "other" and does not posit it, so it is "not dependent on another." Hence, "independent" means that those domains (entities) have their individual situation or layout, their unshared nature. That same (layout) is called "own-nature" and "individual self-existence."

Moreover, to take an example, at the time (cognition) imagines a rope to be a snake, and on the side of the cognition which apprehends that (rope) as snake, one posits (wondering) how it is imagined; and one examines that snake by way of its layout, (wondering) how it is—then because the snake itself is not realized in superimposition upon the objective domain (= rope), the examination does not find the distinction of such a snake. In the same way, examining the way of appearing, (wondering) how these *dharmas* appear on the side of conventional cognition; having posited (the agent), one wonders how be the individual situations of those *dharmas*—then if one has examined the (individual) superimposition on the objective domain—they are not at all realized (as parts, as a collection, etc.). When one does not apprehend it that way, and does not posit it by dint of conventional knowledge, those *dharmas* have a situation that remains to be judged on their respective (or individual) side, a situation that is independent of conventional cognition.[215] This is what is referred to in the *Catuḥ-ś-ṭ* as the manner of nonaccomplishment by own-nature (i.e., on k. 178 in chapter VIII):[216]

Just when they are imagined, they have existence. And certainly when they are not imagined, they have no existence. Like a snake imagined in a coiled mass of rope, their nonaccomplishment by own nature is certain.

Hence, when there is no positing (i.e., imagining) by power of cognition within, one may speak of a "self" or a "self-existence" (the refutable) by way of own-nature accomplished in superimposition on that objective domain; and when that is not superimposed on the personality (*pudgala*) as the specialized basis (*khyad par gyi gźi*), it is said to be "nonself of personality" (*pudgala-nairātmya*); and when that is not superimposed on such natures as the eye (as the specialized basis), it is said to be "nonself of natures" (*dharma-nairātmya*). So one can understand of his own accord that when the self-existence (the refutable) is apprehended as superimposed on *pudgala* and *dharma*, there is apprehension of the two selves. That is the position of the *Catuḥ-ś-ṭ*:[217]

That which is called "self" (*ātman*) is the self-existence, own-nature, not dependent on another, belonging to the entities. And by dividing that into *dharma* and *pudgala,* one understands two kinds—*dharma-nairātmya* and *pudgala-nairātmya*.

Now, some persons say, it is not right that the apprehension of personality realized by individual character (*svalakṣaṇa*) is *pudgala-ātmagrāha* and, if (it were right), then (just by) looking at another person and apprehending him as realized by individual character, would amount to *pudgala-ātmagrāha.* (You) accept that it is necessarily the reifying view, but because one does not judge the other person as "I," it is not right that it is like reification. Is this not so? (In reply:) When one apprehends the personality as self-existent, then as previously explained (on the basis of the *Catuḥ-ś-ṭ*) it is said that the personality's self-existence is *pudgala-ātmagrāha.* Therefore, it is necessary to accept that as the *pudgala-ātmagrāha.* However, (you were not wrong in your point that) the *pudgala-ātmagrāha* is not pervaded by the reifying view. (We add:) But what is the necessity for a "positing of self" (*ātma-grāha*) to belong to the reifying view? (In reply:) As to "positing of self" belonging to the imagination of the reifying view, some followers of the Sammatīya sect[218] (held) that there is no certainty that observing the personality aggregates (*skandha*) is like "positing a self" (*ātma-grāha*). As to the concomitance of the reifying view, the *Avatāra* refutes the observation of those personality aggregates;[219] and the *Avatāra-Comm.* states that the observing of the self is a designation in dependence[220] on (the personality aggregates). So (because of the concomitance) one does not observe the personality aggregates, but observes personality-only (*pudgala-mātra*). Moreover, a personality is necessarily the basis for the occurrence of apprehending the "I," so one does not observe (that concomitant reifying view) in the personality going with a different stream of consciousness (from oneself). The aspect (of grasping-pattern) by which observation apprehends this ("I" of one's own stream of consciousness, *saṃtāna*) is stated in the *Avatāra-Comm.*:[221] "The reifying view issues forth (with a grasping-pattern) as thoughts 'I' and 'mine.' " So this is not determined by just presence of self-existence realized by own-character, but is necessarily determined as the thought of "I." Also, the *Avatāra-Comm.* states:[222]

. . . one should abandon (first) just the reifying view, and this is abandoned by comprehending the nonselfhood of the self (which is observed).

This states that it is abandoned by way of refuting the grasping-pattern, by comprehending the nonselfhood or non-self-existence of that self which is observed, so that (concomitant reifying view) must be an apprehension on the opposing side to insight.

Furthermore, since (empirical observation) apprehends the personality to be realized by own-character, it apprehends the thought of "I" realized by own character. Also the reifying view which apprehends "mine" is to be understood as brought forward by that (reifying view which has the grasping-pattern of "I").

When one does not apprehend with thought "I" and "mine" but still apprehends the personality as existing materially (with self-capability[223]), this is nescience with deception of personality-self; so it is not the way defilements disappear.

That being the case (i.e., as explained above), the cognition which, in regard to just self-existence realized by own-nature, posits it as self and has only the thought of "I"—has as its objective domain two forms as self. Of these, the first one is the refutable by principle, and the second one is not refutable, since one must believe in it conventionally. Hence, we teach not to refute the observation of concomitant reifying view; but one should not fail to refute the grasping-pattern of its aspect, since it is the realization by own-nature. For example, we do not oppose the sound experienced empirically—even when sound is apprehended as permanent—but there is no refuting our opposition to the attachment-domain of that (empirical experience), namely, that sound is permanent.

Accordingly, the texts of the noble father and son (Nāgārjuna and Āryadeva) and of the two *ācāryas* (Buddhapālita and Candrakīrti) have stated their opposition to "presence by self-existence," "presence by own-nature," "presence by own-character," and "presence materially." Those terms, "self-existence," and so on, should be understood in the manner already explained; and since there is no purpose in the way of attachment by ignoring the meaning of those words which teach the nonpresence of those things ("self-existence," etc.), one should understand the matter according to that teaching.

b. The Method of Treating or Not Treating the Other Refutables

For example, at the time one says (to the opponent) that the positively nonexistent things like the horn of hare and son of a barren woman are nonexistent, it is not necessary to treat those distinctions. Likewise, when knowables exist, and some objects and times are present and some objects and times are absent (as when spring is absent when winter is present), at the time one tells (the opponent) that this thing and this time is not present, it is not necessary to treat those distinctions.

Furthermore, we Mādhyamikas do not believe in conventional accomplishment (*tha sñad du grub pa*), and do not share the theory of the realists, whether insider (Buddhist) or other (non-Buddhist). Hence, we oppose their attributions (birth from another, the partless atom, etc.). However, except for occasional places where it is necessary to treat their theories, it is not necessary again to treat their entity, i.e., "self-existence accomplished by own-nature," etc.) which the sectarians espouse.

Over and beyond those (realist theories, such as birth from another, etc.), when Mādhyamikas would establish entities conventionally and would reject those entities, in that event if we did not treat the distinctions ("in the conventional sense," "in the absolute sense," etc.), the fault which adheres to the (opponent) refuter's principle would apply equally (to our side), so it is necessary to treat certain fallacies of refutation.

Moreover, as was previously explained, the Mādhyamikas must examine the entities posited conventionally as to whether or not they have self-existence; and it is necessary that there be no detriment by way of the principle (which examines in the *paramārtha* sense) and conventional authority. If there were not such (a stipulation), it would hardly be valid to differentiate between denying conventionally an Īśvara (creator of the world) and accepting conventionally form, sound, etc. There would be no means for mundane and supramundane establishments of the sort, "Such as this is the path"; "Such as this is not the path"; "It is right according to this treatise"; "It is wrong according to this treatise"; and so forth. Because the special *dharmas* (*khyad chos*) which validify all establishments of *saṃsāra* as void of self-existence, and *nirvāṇa,* would not be feasible.

Accordingly, if one claims to refute those (entities established by the

Mādhyamika), while not assailing them with authority, wise persons have an occasion for mirth. Hence, in the event someone says he has refuted those (*dharmas,* such as form, which must be established conventionally), most certainly one should treat the distinctions (of "in the supreme sense," etc.).

This same (method) appears a great many times in the commentaries (by Candrakīrti) on the *Catuḥ-śataka* and the *Yuktiṣaṣṭikā,* where, in the event of opposing the refutable, they treat those distinctions (of self-existence, etc.). And also in the *Mūla-prajñā* (of Nāgārjuna), and its commentaries, the *Buddhapālita,* the *Prasannapadā,* as well as in the basic commentary on the *Madhyamakāvatāra,* there are numerous instances of treating (those). So, observing that words would multiply inordinately, they do not treat (all the distinctions): it is easy to comprehend with the essential of those treatments. Bearing this in mind, then even in the place where there is no treatment (i.e., where the text does not use the qualification), it is necessary to treat it (i.e., to understand the distinction or qualification), because it does not matter whether or not there is the treatment (in the texts of Nāgārjuna, Āryadeva, Buddhapālita, and Candrakīrti). (If not explicit, it is implicit.)

Moreover, when one examines (in the manner of those texts), and examines, thinking, "Is it present, or is it not present," there are many instances of treating the distinction. Furthermore, as previously explained (above), if there is accomplishment by own-nature, it is necessary to find it by the principle of examining the mode in which it is, after which when one does not find it, one thinks, "There is no entity accomplished by own-nature." So he should understand that there is no self-existence accomplished by own-nature, and take it as the main essential. That meaning is also presented in the *Catuḥ-ś-ṭ* (on k. 327 = chapter XIV, 2):[224]

If those entities (*padārtha*) like the whirling firebrand, the magical manifestation (of an army),[225] and so on, could not, by reason of [successful] deception, be nonmaterial (*avastuka*)—then certainly when they are examined by a valid principle (*upapatti*) their own-natures should be perceived clearly like gold and so on. And if they are not burned by the fire of examination, due to their [inveterate] basis of waywardness, they are not brought close to absence of self-nature.

c. Explanation of Treating or not Treating the Paramārtha *Distinction in Regard to the Refutable*[226]

In this case, what some Tibetans have said, that treating the *paramārtha* distinction regarding the refutable is done only in the Mādhyamika-Svātantrika school, is positively not right, as can be seen in the *Avatāra-Comm.'s* citation (on VI, 173) of the *Prajñāpāramitā* scripture:

(Śāriputra spoke to Subhūti;) Āyuṣmat Subhūti, why is there no attaining and no comprehending? Subhūti replied: Āyuṣmat Śāriputra, there is attaining and there is comprehending, but not both together. Āyuṣmat Śāriputra, attaining and comprehending are worldly conventions. Also, the one who has entered the stream,[227] the one with one more life,[228] the nonreturner, the arhat,[229] the pratyekabuddha,[230] and the Bodhisattva[231] are worldly conventions. But in the absolute sense (*paramārtha-tas*) it is said that there is no attaining and no comprehending.

Thus one must accept it as stated in the *Avatāra-Comm.,* to wit, their so-called "Svātantrika" sūtra as well as the sūtras of final meaning (*nītārtha*) show many examples of treating the *paramārtha* distinction.

Besides, (Nāgārjuna) reports in the *Śūnyatāsaptati* (k. 1):

That (entities) stay, (initially) arise, and (finally) pass away; that (persons) are lower, middling, and distinguished;—the Buddha has stated by virtue of worldly convention, but not by virtue of the genuine.

He tells us in the *Ratnāvalī* (I, 28a–b):

In the absolute sense it is wrong to say there is a self or what belongs to self.

And (I, 29c–d):

For whatever (fruit) the seed is untrue, how could there be in truth a germination for it!

As well as (II, 11):

Likewise there appears to be birth and death in the illusory world, but in the absolute sense there is no birth or death.

Thus he frequently uses such expressions as "in the absolute sense," "in truth," and "by virtue of the genuine" while treating the refutable; and even at the time when he does not treat those (distinctions), he has numerous treatments of the distinction that there is no accomplishment by own-nature, by self-existence, or by self-character (*svalakṣaṇa*).

Also Buddhapālita explains:[232]

> "The dharma teaching by the Buddhas is rightly based on two truths—the *saṃvṛtisatya* of the world, and the *satya* from the standpoint of *paramārtha*" (XXIV, 8).

According to that verse, by way of conventional truth (*saṃvṛtisatya*) of the world one says, "There is a pot," "There is a grass mat." And by way of that same (conventional truth) one says, "The pot is broken," "The grass is burnt," expressing the fact that they are impermanent. At the time one occupies himself with reflecting on (examining) the reality (the true nature of *dharmas*), he decides that the pot and the grass mat are designations in dependence, and (in the way they were previously spoken about) not valid, so how could the view of them as broken and burnt be valid!

Furthermore, in regard to the Tathāgata, by virtue of *saṃvṛti* of the world, it was said, "The Tathāgata has grown old," "The Tathāgata has entered *nirvāṇa,*" expressing the fact of his impermanence. At the time one reflects on the supreme (*paramārtha* = the true nature of dharmas), then he decides that the Tathāgata (thus-come or thus-gone) is himself not valid, so how could the view that he grew old and entered *nirvāṇa* be valid!

The *ācārya* Candrakīrti also rejected origination as true (or truly produced), but did not reject origination per se, when he said in the *Yuktiṣaṣṭikā-vṛtti* (on k. 48):

Whatever the aspect (of form), the observation of its reflection is generated in dependence (on the mirror, the form, and the appearance); and that (appearance of independent arising) is purely false, because there was no arising in the way observed; but we do not assert that there was no arising. However, in whatever personal nature (*bdag ñid*) (or self-existence) one posits the nonoccurrence of that (reflected image), in that very (personal nature or self-existence) we assert that it (the reflected image) does not arise. (But, then), what is that personal nature (or self-existence) in which one posits the nonarising? It is the self-existence believed to occur truly (or be accomplished in reality), but it is not a false nature, because that (reflected image) is what we hold to arise dependently in that nature.

He means not to reject the false, illusory arising, but to reject the arising in truth, so there is no conflict between arising in dependence and not arising by means of self-existence. He says that (in part) in the same work:[233]

For that reason, in that way, since there are these two different domains—the one that arises and the one that does not arise; where is the mutual contradiction!

and:

At the time we (Mādhyamikas) use the illustration of a reflected image for something arising in dependence and say that it does not arise by reason of (its) self-existence, it is then that the opponent has an opportunity to improve his understanding.

In that way he replies to the (opponent's) argument against both "origination in dependence" and "not arising by reason of self-existence." He also states in the *Avatāra* (VI, 93c–d):

Consequently, one should realize by that sequence, that immemorially the entities have not arisen in reality, but have (only) arisen according to (convention of) the world.

There he treats the distinction of reality in respect to not arising. And (VI, 113):

Just as the pots and so on which do not exist in reality, are acknowledged (as existing) in the world, so also it should be in the case of all entities: there is no absurdity in likening them to the son of a barren woman.

Thus he states that all the external and personal entities are nonexistent in reality and are existent conventionally. Hence, he does not fail to treat the *paramārtha* distinction in respect to the refutable.

In short, if one is positively against treating the *paramārtha* distinction in regard to the refutable, then he does not make any differentiation between the two truths by the (inspections), "this and that in the absolute sense" and "this and that in the conventional sense." So this kind of Mādhyamika has only a wayward reflection of what was never explained his way (in any of the Buddha's scriptures or in their authoritative commentaries). According to the *Prasannapadā* the denial of treating the *paramārtha* distinction occurs in (the phase of) rejecting the arising from itself,[234] but there is not (such a denial) in (rejecting) arising alone.[235] This is made very clear in that commentary. And besides, he gives this meaning in his *Avatāra-Comm.* (on VI, 12):

> The *ācārya* (Nāgārjuna) did not make the (*paramārtha*) distinction when he rejected the arising in general with the words "not from itself." One should reflect that whoever (i.e., *ācārya* Bhāvaviveka's school) makes the distinction, to wit:[236]
>
> (Thesis:) From the absolute standpoint, entities do not arise from themselves;
>
> (Reason:) Because they exist;
>
> (Example:) Just as the (unchanging) conscious principle (of the Sāmkhya),
>
> the distinction from the absolute standpoint is useless.

Hence, in regard to the refutable of the two Mādhyamika schools, the Svātantrika and the Prāsaṅgika do not differentiate by way of treating or not treating the *paramātha* distinction. However, (those two) are qualified by opposing or not opposing conventionally the self-existence accomplished by own-nature. Thus, at the time of denying to the external and personal *dharmas* the self-existence accomplished by own-nature, according to the Prāsaṅgika it is not necessary to involve the distinctions "in the absolute sense," "in the genuine sense," or "in truth," because if there were self-existence accomplished by own-nature, it would be necessary to prove the *paramārtha* and so on (i.e., the genuine, the true). According to the Svātantrika, for (denying) it (self-existence accomplished by own-nature), one could not refute it if one did not treat (the distinctions of) "in the absolute sense" and so on, so they say that (there is no self-existence accomplished by own-nature) in the absolute, the genuine, or the true sense.

Generally speaking, in regard to (the conventional presence of) arising and passing away, bondage and liberation—those two do not treat other distinctions such as *paramārtha,* accomplishment by own-nature, etc., so neither (the Prāsaṅgika nor the Svātantrika) find it necessary to oppose (the conventional presence).

However, what is the meaning of nonpresence in the absolute sense (*paramārtha-tas*)? Here, *artha* is what is to be known, *parama* means "supreme." The two are a compound ("consistent basis") (i.e., there being the *artha,* and there being the *parama,* there is *paramārtha*). Furthermore, *parama* is the knowledge of impermanence (in *ārya-samāpatti*); and the goal (*artha*) of that (knowledge) or the objective domain (of the knowledge) being present, there is *paramārtha.* Besides, when there is the knowledge of impermanence which comprehends directly the *paramārtha,* and the insight (*prajñā*) consistent with that (knowledge), there is *paramārtha.* (Informing of that), (Bhāvaviveka writes):[237]

> Here, earth and the other elements,
> do not arise in the absolute sense.

And in its (self-) commentary, the *Tarkajvālā:*

> Concerning *"paramārtha,"* the *artha* means what is to be known; hence the *artha* is referred to as the thing to be considered, the thing to be understood. *Parama* is a term for the supreme. The compound *paramārtha* means that when there is (both) the *artha* and the *parama,* there is *paramārtha.* Furthermore, concerning the *"artha* of *parama,"* when there is the goal (*artha*) of the supreme (*parama*) nondiscursive knowledge (*avikalpa-jñāna*) there is *paramārtha.* Besides, concerning *paramārtha* consistency, when there is comprehension of *paramārtha* and insight consistent therewith, there is *paramārtha,* so that (insight itself) is *paramārtha*-consistency.

Now is *paramārtha* expressed as "qualified negation (*paryudāsa*) there" or as "simple negation (*prasajya*) there"?[238] The *paramārtha* (of the occasion) is the latter one (i.e., that insight itself which is consistent with the comprehension directly of *paramārtha*). The same work (i.e., *Tarkajvālā*) states:

> (The question is raised:) Well, now, is it not the case that *paramārtha* transcends all cognitions of any (*dharmas*), and that the refutation of the entities

having an own-nature is in the realm of words, so there is no refutation (possible of the own-nature of entities according to your words "do not exist in the *paramārtha* sense")? (In reply:) There are two kinds of *paramārtha*. Among them, one involves no instigations (*anabhisaṃskāra*) (to reflections), and is supramundane without flux, without verbal elaboration (*prapañca*). The other one involves instigations (to reflections) and is the pure "mundane knowledge (*laukika-jñāna*) with verbal elaboration that is consistent with the collection of merit and knowledge. So there is no fault (as you alleged) in our accepting the distinction of that (sort of) thesis in this case (namely, saying, "do not exist in the *paramārtha* sense").

That is accepted for the insights (*prajñā*) consisting of hearing (*śrutamayī*) and pondering (*cintāmayī*), and beyond, which examine methodically reality, and does not mean only the "knowledge afterwards obtained by the nobles" (*ārya-pṛṣṭhalabdha-jñāna*).

Also the *Madhyamaka-āloka* (of Kamalaśīla)[239] is consistent (with the *Tarkajvālā*) in this passage:

Whatever (the words) which express "do not arise in the *paramārtha* sense," the meaning (of those words) is claimed to be this way: all the knowledge consisting of right learning, pondering, and cultivation, is the errorless subject (*viṣayin*) and for that reason is called "*paramārtha*"—because this (right knowledge) has the supreme object (*paramārtha*). The direct vision (*mṅon sum*) (of the *paramārtha* where there is no arising in the *paramārtha* sense) and the distinctions formed in lineage (from that vision) are real (*yod de*); and by virtue of those (the distinctions of subject knowledge and object *paramārtha*), one knows only (i.e., without error) that all these entities do not arise. Hence, with the words "do not arise in the *paramārtha* sense," one rightly knows these (entities) and explains (as the meaning), "(there = in that state) their arising is not accomplished."

Besides, (Kamalaśīla) writes in the *Madhyamaka-alaṃkāra-pañjikā:*[240]

To the question, "How is it without self-existence?" he replies: "When it is genuine (*samyak*)." By the expression "genuine" one understands the nature of reality to be comprehended by inference aroused on the strength of a present fact.[241] One calls it "void" when it is examined by way of reality. By this (explanation), one explains "in reality," "in the *paramārtha* sense," (and "in the genuine sense"). Moreover, when there is only right knowledge (*samyagjñāna*), one applies the terms *samyak,* and so on (including *paramārtha, tattva*) for the reason that (the *samyak,* etc.) is observed by that (right knowledge). By virtue of being meditated with right knowledge, it is called "present not by reason of self-existence"; but by virtue of conventional knowledge (*saṃvṛti-jñāna*) it is not called that.

The use of the distinction *samyak,* etc. for the non-self-existent occurs frequently in both the *Prajñāpradīpa* and the *Tarkajvālā* (Bhāvaviveka's commentaries on the *Madhyamakakārikā* and on his own work, the *Hṛdayakārikā*); and in particular the *Prajñāpradīpa* commentary on chapter XV states:[242]

In this case, moreover, (some realists speak as follows:) "If (entities) lack an own-nature, how do entities happen? But if entities exist, they are not without own-nature." Thus, using the very same (words) of the thesis, they cast aspersions on the meaning, labeling it a fault.

Thus, regarding the (Mādhyamika) thesis, "The entities lack an own-nature," they argue that it has the fault of inconsistency of its own words. In reply, the same work (*Prajñāpradīpa*) states:

We accept that entities have an own-nature in the *paramārtha* sense, since we deny that they lack an own-nature (in that sense). Hence, your aspersions are not being cast on the meaning of our thesis. And since the meaning of our reason has not failed of proof, we have no fault.

Thus, since he maintains that the aspersion was not cast on the claim that entities have no own-nature in the *paramārtha* sense, it is clear that (this *ācārya* Bhāvaviveka) maintains that the aspersion was cast on (the theory that) there is no nature accomplished by own-nature in the conventional sense. Furthermore, the same work (*Prajñāpradīpa,* on XV, k. 2c–d) states:

In the *paramārtha* sense, the personal entities (such as eye, etc.) are without self-nature because they are created and are specialized as said ("created") because they have dependence on a basis (formed from causes and conditions), for example, like a phantom man, and so on, by a magician, and cease by their own-nature,[243] because they have been constructed as a *paramārtha* distinction. In this regard, what is the manner of being of the thing (*artha*) said to be nonexistent in the *paramārtha* sense? At the time one examines (it) by a principle of methodical examination, that (principle) proves that it does not exist, which is completely consistent with this *ācārya* (i.e., Nāgārjuna). Hence, according to the texts of this *ācārya,* at the time one posits *saṃvṛti,* to wit, not engaging in an examination consistent with seeing reality—at that time, as stated previously, they cease by their own nature, while at the time they are examined by the principle, they are nonexistent.

Since such statements are frequent, they are like the previous citations (of Candrakīrti's *Avatāra*).

However, while there is ability to examine with the principle that examines the manner of being in regard to accomplishment by own-nature, there is disagreement about whether or not a thesis is required. These two *ācāryas*[244] share the ability to examine by the principle which examines reality in regard to accomplishment by own-nature, and moreover agree about accomplishment in the absolute sense, as was often previously explained.

B. Option of Prāsaṅgika and Svātantrika as Refuting Agents

In regard to whether the opposing of the refutable is to be done by the Prāsaṅgika or the Svātantrika schools, there are two parts: 1. Determining the meaning of Prāsaṅgika and Svātantrika; 2. Which one of the two one should follow to generate the view in the stream of consciousness.

1. DETERMINING THE MEANING OF PRĀSAṄGIKA AND SVĀTANTRIKA

The ācārya Buddhapālita in his commentary made the division into Prāsaṅgika and Svātantrika, but did not clarify the school of Prāsaṅgika. However, when he commented upon (*Madhyamaka-kārikā,* I, 1)—

There is no entity anywhere that arises from itself, from another, from both (itself and another), or by chance—

he opposed the four alternatives of arising by way of refuting other schools (such as the Sāṃkhya).

Then *ācārya* Bhāvaviveka set about proving his own side and refuting the other side (especially Buddhapālita's position), but his refutation used faulty formulations (i.e., fallacies) that were ineffectual (for the purpose).[245]

Accordingly, *ācārya* Candrakīrti extensively commented (in the *Prasannapadā*) on the reasons that the sort of fault (as formulated by Bhāvaviveka) did not engage Buddhapālita's position. He highlighted the absurdity of the method employed by the opposing Mādhyamika (i.e., Bhāvaviveka) to generate the Mādhyamika view in the stream of consciousness (*saṃtāna*); and in the course of opposing and showing the absurdity, while insisting that the Svātantrika is not valid, he clarified the (Prāsaṅgika) position.[246]

There are two parts to the method of setting forth the Prāsaṅgika and Svātantrika (positions) in that manner: a. The refutation of other positions; b. Establishment of our own position.

a. *The Refutation of Other Positions*

Here there are two subdivisions: (1) expressing the position, and (2) refuting it. (In general,) although there appear to be numerous ways of setting forth the Prāsaṅgika and Svātantrika (positions), it is necessary to expound by means of selection out of the totality (of ways). For this reason, only some of those will be expounded.

(1) EXPRESSING THE POSITION

αFirst Position. Among them, (Pandita) Jayānanda said in his *Madhyamakāvatāra-ṭīkā:*[247]

In that connection, some (others) assert, if the Prāsaṅgika believes in a reason, it would prove by authority or disprove by authority. In the first case, then at the time (of proof), for both (the adversary and the defendant) there would be proof, and so how could one say that the thesis was (only) by the adversary! In the second case, the adversary's thesis would be unworthy, and so how could one say that the adversary has a thesis! In reply: We do not know what you say, to wit, "For both (the adversary and the defendant) there would be proof." In explanation:—At the time the defendant has formulated a syllogism, then even though there is proof by authority to whoever is the formulator of the reason, how does he know if there is proof by authority to the adversary, because the (subtle) distinctions of the adversary's mind are not the object-domain (*viṣaya*) of his direct perception (*pratyakṣa*) and inference (*anumāna*)! How does (the other) know whether there is proof by authority to the defendant, because he (the adversary) has been dominated for a long time by the causes of error, with the possibility of deception. Consequently, both the defendant and the adversary, by virtue of espousing that reason itself, espouse the self-existence of entities! Accordingly, while the defendant may claim he has refuted the adversary's position by way of the adversary's thesis, the defendant does not know whether or not there was proof by authority of the evidence to the opponent, since what the latter thinks is not proved by either of the authorities (direct perception and inference) at the defendant's disposal. Besides, (the other) does not know if he has proved by authority the evidence to the defendant; while the latter also decides that he has proved by authority, with the possibility of deception. For that reason, there is no evidence that for both (the adversary and the defendant) there would be proof by authority. Consequently, since they arrive at the thesis that there is authority, and yet there is no proof by the authority (to either side), it is right to refute (the opponent's position) by way of the thesis (that there is authority).

So he (Jayānanda) expounds. Moreover, that same work (Jayānanda's *Madhyamakāvatāra-ṭīkā*) states:

Furthermore, in regard to the Svātantrika's kind of reason, if one demonstrates the pervasion (*vyāpti*) by authority (*pramāṇa*) when there are both a reason (*hetu*) and a thesis (*sādhya*), at that time is the Svātantrika syllogism. However, the pervasion is not demonstrated (to both sides). In explanation —The authority of the syllogism with pervasion, is direct perception or inference. Among these, firstly, the pervasion is not demonstrated by direct perception, as is now shown. Accordingly, to (the sequence of) direct perception (with presence of cause, *anvaya*) of the kitchen, and non-perception (with absence of cause, *vyatireka*) there, when there is (smoke), there is (fire); and when there is not (fire), there is not (smoke). When there is not the thought of that (sequence), there does not occur the comprehension (which connects the presence and absence of cause with the fire of direct perception); so when there is (smoke, directly perceived) in all the sensory domain (*viṣaya*), there is no (demonstration of pervasion of smoke by fire). Also, there is no (demonstration of that pervasion connection) by inference, because it (the authority of inference) firmly decides the object (*viṣaya*), as is now shown.[248] The object of inference (as an authority) is the qualified negation of all (*thams cad ma yin*).[249] Consequently, in whatever (object) there is something to prove (such as the impermanence of natures) and an evidence (*liṅga*) with connection (of presence and absence of cause), the inferential) cognition of impermanence, etc, arises (from the object) alone, and does not arise (in this qualified sense) in all (dissimilar) times and places. (Accordingly, the two disputants fail to demonstrate such a pervasion when employing the two authorities, direct perception and inference.) Hence, the demonstration of the pervasion (*vyāpti*) is (posited here) only by way of worldly assumption, but it is not (posited) by way of authority. So why is it not proper for the Prāsaṅgika to refute with a reason (*hetu*) the position of the opponent? (And it is proper.)

Thus, the pervasion of smoke by fire, and the pervasion of a created thing by impermanence, is valid according to the Svātantrika school, insofar as being proved by authority, but (the pervasion) is not proved. For, if it could be proved by authority, it would be necessary to prove (by authority) that in all places and times smoke and a created thing are pervaded (respectively) by fire and impermanence; and the direct perception and inference for proving the pervasion can prove only upon the kitchen fire and the pot, because (the method of proving by authority) is restricted in scope (*prādeśika*).[250]

Thus, when someone asserts that one may prove even the pervasion by the thesis alone, he (Pandita Jayānanda) does it (i.e., proves) by using the three marks[251] as evidence of proof by authority—while one does it with the Svātantrika by the three marks as just the conclusion of the thesis—and he appears to believe in the Prāsaṅgika.

β Second Position. Besides, the translator disciples of that paṇḍita[252] said this: the Mādhyamika should just refute the claim of the opponent, and not be the one with a thesis of his own; and since there is no proof of a shared field of acceptance between the two (disputants) as concerns the factual basis (*dharmin*), etc., the Svātantrika is not valid. Moreover, the fruit (or, aim) of the examination by the principle is just to abandon the (bad) theory-systems of others (the adversaries); and we have no position of our own other than that (i.e., the casting aside of another's theory-system); thus, the kind of reason of the Svātantrika school is not at all worthy of being expressed. Hence, it is only the Prāsaṅgika school (that effectively opposes the wayward conceptions of the opponents); and in that regard, (from among the two activities, proving and refuting) the Prāsaṅgika of proof, as the finality of the Svātantrika, is only the reductio ad absurdum. And this, moreover, is the reduction (to absurdity) of the thesis, along with the evidence (*liṅga*) and pervasion (*vyāpti*), or of the aim envisaged by the thesis, so there is no genuine authority. When one takes recourse to this (reduction to absurdity, *prasaṅga*), one does it to cut off the opponent's thesis or verbal elaboration (*prapañca*), (amounting to three reductio ad absurdum and one reason).

Among these, the *reductio at absurdum with mention of the contradiction* is as follows: the opponent claims that arising is meaningful and established by arguments, and claims the arising from self (i.e., the position of the Sāṃkhya). But if there is arising from itself, arising is an existence; so the arising is not meaningful or established by arguments, and it is not right to believe that it is meaningful and established by arguments. In that case, one says, "What you claim, namely, the arising from itself, is not valid." Thereby mentioning the mutual contradiction, one acquaints (or, confronts) the opponent (with the contradiction), with the effect of his abandoning the theory (of arising from self).

The inference reported by the opponent is as follows:[253] (according to the Sāṃkhya) the shoot is claimed to arise from itself, because if it did not arise from itself, it would exist as oneself (would have to claim it would). Having mentioned the factual base (*dharmin*) and the evidence (*liṅga*), etc. as reported in the opponent (school = Sāṃkhya), we reject the (thesis of the) opponent. Although we say, "does not arise from itself," we only reject (or refute) the arising from self as in the other school (the Sāṃkhya), but do not prove our own statement, "does not arise from itself," so there is no thesis (of our own to prove).

Equivalence of syllogism and thesis is as follows: whatever formulation with example and evidence that the opponent makes to prove his own side, all that is unproven, as previously.

Common denominator, equating reason is the common denominator[254] by way of no distinction of reason, as when (the opponent) says, "If there is this thesis, then this (other) thesis (is necessary)." (In this case, some others say:) "However, you either do or do not wish to deny the opponent's position. If you do wish to, that very (desire to deny) is a thesis, so it amounts to the Svātantrika's evidence for proving it. And if you do not (wish to deny the opponent's position), it would not be right to mention the principle of denying the opponent's position. Is that not so?" (In reply:) If one claims that there is a thesis of lack of self-existence and lack of arising in the phase of examining *paramārtha,* it is necessary to believe in the thesis and evidence of the Svātantrika. But we do not claim that, so have no fault. If it were (perforce) a thesis simply by our wishing (namely, to reject the opponent's thesis), that amounts to explaining everything (e.g., believing in water) as a thesis.

According to this (translator[255]), there is no basis for proving our own side and we simply deny the other side; also we make no claims, have no thesis, have no position of our own; and in the phase of examining *paramārtha* do not posit as a thesis, the non-self-existence, and so on. But it is not claimed (by this translator[256]) that there are no theses whatever; so he assumes that the thing to prove in the phase of examining *paramārtha* is the non-self-existence, and that proof in our school, not accepting the Svātantrika and its theories, performs only the denial of what is claimed by the opponent; and that appears to be done as the Prāsaṅgika.

γ *Third Position.* Nowadays, what some others (Tibetans) claim to be Prāsaṅgika is as follows: The thesis of *paramārtha,* and of the convention from which one begins, is not in our school even conventionally. Thus, if there were such a thesis, it would be necessary (in our school) also to believe in the example proving that (thesis) and in the evidence (*liṅga*), in which case, (rather than being the Prāsaṅgika) it would be the Svātantrika. Hence, our school, the Prāsaṅgika, has none at all. (Informing of this), the *Vigrahavyāvartinī* (k. 29–30) states:

If I were to have any thesis (*pratijñā*), it would be my fault. But since I do not have a thesis, I do not have a fault (in my school).

If (according to your thinking) by means of (an authority, such as direct perception), something (to be judged as to self-existence) could be witnessed, it would be proven (according to your own school) or disproven (otherwise). But by virtue of its absence (even conventionally), I am not confuted.

Also, the *Yuktiṣaṣṭikā* (k. 50) has this:

Those lofty individuals (= learned Mādhyamikas), having no side (or, thesis), are without contention. For those with no side (of their own), how could there be the other (opponent's) side!

Besides, the *Catuḥ-śataka* (k. 400 = XVI, 25) states:[257]

For the one with no side (*pakṣa*), whether that a thing is present (by self-existence), or absent (even conventionally), or both present and absent (in that way) (or neither present nor absent)—then to confute him would not be possible, even in a long time.

Those passages give the reason that the Mādhyamika has no side or thesis. The *Prasannapadā* (p. 16.2) has this:

And it is not right for the Mādhyamika to make an independent inference of his own, since he has no assumption (of accomplishment by own-character) of the opponent's side.

And (p. 23.3):

Besides, the theory which is the opposite of the absurd one is associated with just the opponent (the Sāṃkhya) since we have no thesis of our own.

And also because the *Avatāra* (VI, 173) says there is no involvement of fault since we have no side of our own:

(Suppose) someone who refutes does not encounter a refutable and says, "(I) engage in refuting, but will do it upon encountering (the refutable)." What person would here have the fault (of such a remark)! Certainly it (the fault) occurs when one has the side (of a thesis); but for us, this side does not exist and so there is no possibility of this absurdity (to be charged to us).

Hence, all those establishments are, according to the Mādhyamika, only establishments constructed on the part of the opponent, as is stated in the *Avatāra* (VI, 81):

In the way you (Cittamātra follower) believe in dependency (*paratantra*) concretely (i.e., accomplished by own-character) we (Mādhyamika) do not accept even conventionally (*saṃvṛti-tas*). While these (entities) are not present, it is for the sake of the fruit that we say on the part of the world that they exist (as designations only).

Also, because the *Vigrahavyāvartinī* (k. 63) states that there is no refuting of the other's side:

Since there is nothing to refute, I do not refute anything. Even so, you object, alleging, "You are refuting."

So they say.[258]

δ *Fourth Position.*[259] Certain former Mādhyamikas, learned Tibetan followers of the *ācārya* Candrakīrti well refuted the positions which claim in that manner (i.e., as in the Third Position) that the Mādhyamika does not have its own side or the authority of those syllogisms. The own school (of those learned men) is as follows: Having examined (*paramārtha*) with the principle, we reject both authorities—direct perception, and inference of authority aroused by strength of a present fact,[260] to wit, with thing to prove by the own-character of examining with the principle, and with thesis establishing the authority. We accept only the authority and the authorized as acknowledged by the world, without examining conventionally. Our business as Mādhyamikas is to use the opponent's formulations of proof, and with a genuine reason to demonstrate that his meaning is false.

They explain that in that manner they do not pass into the Svātantrika position, because they posit (only) by way of the authority acknowledged in the world, without examining it.

(2) REFUTING THE POSITION

Second, there are four parts to the rejection of those (positions).

α *Rejection of the First Position.*[261] According to this school of *Madhyamakāvatāra* commentary, there is no proof by authority of the evidence (*liṅga*) or pervasion (*vyāpti*), but the reason advanced for no proof by authority of the evidence is not right. In that way of explaining, it is necessary that the evidence had already been proven by authority for both the defendant and the adversary. According to the position which claims thus, if the defendant does not know what is proved (by authority) to the adversary but does not deny the evidence, it would follow that necessarily there is proof by authority to the adversary, because it is not refuted. And if you posit that you do not know what is proved by authority to the opponent on the grounds that you do not know the mind of another, i.e., belonging to the adversary, then you would also not know the entity (*artha*) postulated by the opponent, and so it would not be right for you to oppose by way of the opponent's theory. For that reason, when one directly hears the words, "We believe this way because of the opponent," how can he be certain that it was said this way (by us), because there is no certainty of (our) theory, and because one does not know the mind of another!

Also, the reason advanced that the pervasion is not proven by authority is not valid. When on the basis of the kitchen one proves that the present smoke is pervaded by the present fire, the substratum to be comprehended is the kitchen (itself); and the meaning to be comprehended on that basis is that the present smoke is entirely pervaded by the present fire. But there is positively no apprehension that there is smoke present in the kitchen pervaded by fire present in the kitchen, so how could one apprehend the pervasion of the restricted scope[262] of a spacial domain or of a time! If it were not so, that sort of pervasion would not be valid at the kitchen, which is the substratum of certainy, so it is necessary to teach that a substratum (a different one) is required for the certainty on the basis of this substratum. For example, the impermanence of natures as a thing to prove has a certifying reason on the basis of sound. It is necessary to have *anvaya* (presence in similar cases) in the case of both sound and pot, but it is not valid to posit impermanence of what is the *avayava* (part of a whole) of sound. By that principle, one should understand that it is not right to believe that there is no authority, even in the inference of proving the pervasion.

Accordingly, since (in your position), there is no proof (of the evidence and pervasion) by authority (*pramāna*) it is not proper to say that the defendant and the adversary prove (the evidence and pervasion) by the mere thesis. If one takes as the reason the mere thesis; there is no defeat of the opponent, because one's mere thesis would not prove the entity (*artha*), and the authority is lacking in both our side and the opponent. However, if one analyzes the qualification of the thesis, to wit, (the thesis) is proved by this, or (the thesis) is disproved by this; thus discriminating, if one discriminates by way of a reason for the thesis, it is equivalent to a thing to prove; and if one discriminates by way of presence or absence of authority, (your) claim that there is no authority, is destroyed.

β Rejection of the Second Position.[263] (According to you, i.e., translator followers of Jayānanda,) one does not hold a thesis of no self-existence in the phase of examining reality, and you claim that this (nonholding of a thesis) enables you to avoid the Svātantrika's thesis. (Given your stance), is it your claim that you do not hold the thesis (in that phase) because you have not proven the thesis through knowing the principle of examining presence and absence of self-existence, or is it your claim that you do not hold the thesis (in that phase) through having formulated in your understanding, "because it is the phase of examining reality"?

In the first case, since you have not proven, by knowing the principle, that meaning of the thesis that there is no self-existence, you are also unable to refute, through knowing the principle, that meaning of the thesis that there is self-existence, because the reason is the same. Besides, if one supposes he need not deny the meaning of the theory that there is self-existence in the phase of examining reality, this is exceedingly improper, because you said previously that you oppose the other school in its examination by principle; and because, lacking the knowledge derived through pondering, you are unable to reject other schools. Even more: what purpose is there in disclosing with the observation, "We claim no position of our own," because you also do not claim to reject and reduce to absurdity the opponent's school. To refute and reduce to absurdity the theory-system (*siddhānta*) of the opponent, one perforce rejects the presence of self-existence and proves the absence of self-existence—as was previously mentioned from the *Vigrahavyāvartanī*. So in this case there is no third alternative (*phuṅ sum med*). Otherwise (we say to you), it would amount to proving the non-self-existence, but not refuting the self-existence. And what, indeed, can you say in reply to that! If you suppose that deciding that there is no self-existence unquestionably entails a deciding of self-existence; on the same grounds, deciding that there is self-existence entails a deciding of non-self-existence.

If you suppose that since it is the phase of examining reality, it is inappropriate (at that time) for any position such as non-self-existence—then please resume your reason for that (inappropriateness)! But if you suppose that when realizing in the phase of examining reality, one must realize that there is *paramārtha* and consequently he can have no thesis, that is (surely) not right, to wit: you (in effect) deny even the phase of examining reality, i.e., you must claim that there is no possibility of a time for examining with the Madhyamaka principle. And if you posit that phase (of examining according to your school as you have formulated it), you would certainly have to claim, as the opponents do, that the examination is associated with an examiner (by which it is examined), a principle of examining (to which he resorts), and a substratum of examining (on which he is based); so everything proves to be in the phase of that (examination of reality) and what is the necessity of realizing that there is *paramārtha!* Your reductio ad absurdum itself amounts to the theory or theory-consummation (of the evidence and pervasion) (held) by the opponent, so when you say that you perform reductio ad absurdum even in the absence of authority (of evidence and pervasion), this talk does not satisfy the mind of the wise, so it should be rejected as the previous school (that of Jayānanda) was rejected.

Furthermore (in the second case),[264] since you do not hold a thesis in the phase of examining reality, (generally) you hold the thesis conventionally. But this position is also not valid, for these reasons: There is a contradiction that the phase of examining reality is not appropriate for (establishing) in the *paramārtha* sense, but is, for extablishing in the conventional sense. And if there were an entity absent in the *paramārtha* sense outside of the phase of examining reality, there would not be in the Mādhyamika the claim to have a position in the *paramārtha* sense, which would invalidate the special *dharma* (*khyad chos*) of the Prāsaṅgika.

γ Rejection of the Third Position.[265] You say that there is no thesis, even conventionally, among the Mādhyamikas. According to the previous explanation you have not well determined the refutable by the principle. On that account, when you refute the opponent by principles which reject the self-existence, at that time (the opponent, probing) defeats this side, and one can notice that our own school has been rendered equal (to the opponent's) in precisely the same (enunciation of refutation). When one does not know at all (*ye ma śes pa*) how to obviate the faults when posing our position, all of dependent origination going with *saṃsāra* and *nirvāṇa* becomes the same in presence and absence as the lord (espoused by the heretics). For that reason, it is a most despicable insult to the Mādhyamika, and we have already discussed at length in opposition to that (position).

An examiner of presence or absence of a thesis in the Mādhyamika, if he has any meaning to be called "Madhyamaka," must have a thesis to posit in that "Madhyamaka," namely, not even an atom proven in the *paramārtha* sense (i.e., avoiding the two extremes of eternalism and nihilism); and he must also claim a comprehension of the meaning of dependent origination (free from the two extremes); and that all (*dharmas*) are illusory in the conventional (*saṃvṛti*) sense, so there must be a thesis. Moreover, for those two (i.e., not realized in the absolute sense, and illusory in the conventional sense) there is the contrariety, the vile statement claiming presence in the absolute sense and absence in the conventional sense (i.e., the two extremes of eternalism and nihilism); one must refute (all those vile statements) and posit (the Madhyamaka which is free from the extremes), because there is an authority which comprehends the meaning of (the two:) refuting (the wayward side) and proving (the genuine side), and there are the telling and witness of the Mādhyamika who teach errorlessly to others (the candidates) just as they comprehended (by way of that authority) and when those (the authority and the thing to judge) are established (made clear), the opponents can scarcely confute the consistency with *dharma,* so this school (of Mādhyamika) has the pure *dharma* (which is superior to all).

That being the case, a wise person, even if he does not know how to posit by himself the school of Mādhyamika free from fault, does not criticize, saying (such a superior school) does not exist; and by that very assumption of the principle of dependent origination, he destroys the entire net of bad views. Intelligent persons, cherishing this in mind, will become free from all mutual inconsistencies by establishing the (Prāsaṅgika) school of Mādhyamika, and will not pin their hopes on just avowing and then disavowing.[266]

That is clarified in the *Prasannapadā* (on chapter XXIV):

> In that way, our side is perfectly pure and is founded devoid of conflict with any establishment (of *paramārtha* or of *saṃvṛti*). Your side (the realist) has the fault of excessive grossness (simplification), of excessive nearness (obviousness), and of conflict with those (establishments of *paramārtha* or of *saṃvṛti*). You are too stupid to see how the faults and merits are evaluated, to wit: "You while transferring your own faults to us, . . ." (XXIV, 15a)

Thus, as was previously cited, the Mādhyamika school proceeds on the path with the authority that establishes *paramārtha* and the authority (which establishes the meaning) of convention and with these establishments is perfectly pure since it is not to be designated as faulty, and suffices since it posits all establishments of *saṃsāra* and *nirvāṇa.* One should gain certainty about this.

But you, not having that way (of establishment), say that the Mādhyamika does not have a position of his own; and if (what you say) is not to be designated a fault, then whatever words are expressed (by the Mādhyamika), all of them would be false words. No one (of you) would be able to refute this, because all reasons reduce to equivalence.

Besides, there is no use for you to say, "When we said there was no thesis, there was no thesis present to be examined, so there is no fault to by charged (to us), because we have no thesis at all." If it were (as you say), then when we said, "All words would be false," and when we say, "All expressions would be false," those expressions are true, there being no expressions present to be examined, because there is no use to show a contradiction of our words. And the *Avatāra* (VI, 147, c-d) states:

If (as you the realist believes) some self could be proved to be a substance, it would be a substance accomplished like the mind, and would not be inexpressible.

This refers to the theory by the (Buddhist school) Vātsīputrīya[267] that the substantial self (*bdag rdzas*) is inexpressible as the same or different from the personality aggregates (*skandha*). But (according to the Mādhyamika) if it existed substantially, (for that reason) it would be necessary to say whether it is the same or different from the personality aggregates, so it is not possible (for the Vātsīputrīya) to refute the argument that it is not valid that those (the substantial self's sameness or difference from the *skandhas*) are inexpressible.[268] Thus (when you, the Vātsīputrīya,) say, "According to us, the substantial self is inexpressible as to being the same or other," (we, the Mādhyamika,) say that it is necessary to express whether it is the same or other, because it suffices to answer what you say, "It is because an examination cannot be performed."

If you say that the personality (*pudgala*) is material, it contradicts that there is no (expression of whether the *pudgala* is the) same as or other than the *skandhas*. So it is not valid that those (the sameness or otherness) are inexpressible. Thus if (you, the Vātsīputrīya,) say, "I engage in that examination," (we reply) (However, when you) say, "Since we assume nothing at all, we have no assumption," because of (your) expression of hostility (*źe ba*[269]) it is not proper, (for the reason) being completely the same (i.e., the hostility itself is an assumption). (Thus), if you say, "We are unmistaken," others may say, "Give (us) that mistake which is unmistaken!" and if (you) say, "We have no assumption," (we) say, "That lack of assumption is itself the assumption," and "Both are the same." Thus the former side (your side) speaks without understanding. Still, we do not say (in general) that the lack of a thesis is itself a thesis. However, (you) ask, "What is the point of the discussion?" (In reply:) When with expression of hostility you say, "We have no assumption," it is necessary to assume that there is no assumption. And so explaining, (you) are unable to set aside the refuting force of our words.

(Now) you ask, "Is not such a saying (i.e., 'We have no thesis of our own,') (in fact) the Mādhyamika position?" (Concerning your attribution of the negative position:) That is in conflict with what has been proven by the ārya (Nāgārjuna) master and disciples by citation from the scriptures;[270] and besides that is not posited in the school of Candrakīrti; and it is not valid in other Buddhist schools as well, so it is outsider with respect to this (insider) *Dharma*.

If (you) say it is the school of Mādhyamika and therein the school of Candrakīrti, this conflicts with (what you asserted:) "they have no position of their own."

Accordingly, if (you, sirs,) wish to be liberated from a thesis, it is improper to say that the establishments are posited only on the other side. While you say that the existence of form, etc. must be a thesis only of the other side, in fact (those words) "existence of form, etc." attributed to the other side as not (your) thesis, are not liberation from a thesis, because they require a thesis.

Should you say that at that time (of thesis requirement) it is the other person positing (form) on any side and himself the positer (on that side) who needs to have a thesis, so the thesis is just on the other side—you derive no benefit from having no position of your own, but also reap inexhaustible harm.

If you say, "You have no position of your own, and assume only the other side," we reply: "That is not what we say; it comes as what you prefer." And if you deny direct perception (*pratyakṣa*), which is not denied even by the Lokāyatas, since you do not sense our words while we hear (what you say), your wit (vidyā) is astonishing!

If it is the way you say, it must be enough for you to possess certainty about your words of having no thesis, etc.; and whatever be the words you express, in the end you are satisfied with (only) denial because no fault will be charged (to you).

If you assert that the Prāsangika posits only the opponent's side and does not believe in a position of its own—then, what is the use of believing in Candrakīrti's school which is installed in the Prāsaṅgika texts through refuting the Svātantrika school! The Svātantrika would be invalid as one's own school; and the Prāsaṅgika also would be invalid (as one's own school); the Prāsaṅgika would be valid as the other side; the Svātantrika likewise; because by virtue of (your) insistence, they operate on the other side.

Anyone who believes in the "Mind-only" (Cittamātra) school as the other side and does not believe in a school of his own, (asserting) that this is how the Prāsaṅgika invalidates the Cittamātra and establishes the Madhyamaka meaning; that the Prāsaṅgika, not valid as an "own position," poses only the other side—(that person so asserting) has no validity for establishing either the Prāsaṅgika or the Svātantrika (the two Mādhyamika schools), so we teach that it is obvious he is not our Mādhyamika.

Besides, it was cited (*Avatāra,* VI, 81c-d):

While these (entities) are not present, it is for the sake of the fruit that we say on the part of the world that they exist (as designations only).

This (passage) shows that it is especially invalid to require the other side for all establishments. Because the lack of self-existence to accomplish natures by their own essence is established on the side of knowing the principle of examining methodically the presence or absence of self-existence, and is not established on the side of autonomy (*raṅ dga' ba*) in knowing conventions (without comprehending voidness). Because it would reduce to absurdity that there is no purpose to knowing the principle (of examining reality) if one could realize non-self-existence by that (autonomy in knowing conventions). And because when that text says "they exist" and "on the part of the world" it states the positing on the part of the world when it posits the existence of form, etc.

And the cited words, "(we) do not accept (even) conventionally" (*Avatāra,* 81b, cited above) mean "we do not accept" (even conventionally) the dependency as accepted (i.e., accomplished by own-character) by the Cittamātra people; but do not mean that our school rejects *saṃvṛti* itself, because it was stated (in the same verse), "In the way you believe in dependency concretely." Furthermore, as to the introductory words of that text (i.e., "in the way")—they argue (i.e., the Cittamātra followers say to the Mādhyamika:) "If you are using reason or principles to reject your (Mādhyamika) *saṃvṛti.*" In reply: "in the way you believe concretely" that sustains examination of dependency by a principle—we do not believe the conventions that way, because the meaning is that capability and incapability of denying with a principle are not the same. When the text says, "on the part of the world," it is not the (Mādhyamika's) own school, but does not assert (merely) the side of the other (person); rather, it amounts to no denial of conventional cognition, because all positing that there are *saṃvṛti* entities requires positing on the side of that (conventional cognition) and because the Svātantrika-Mādhyamika also accepts those authorities that posit conventionally.

Hence, the words of that text (*Avatāra,* VI, 81), "not present," mean "not present" through own-character (*svalakṣaṇa*). They are there, but not present through own-character; it is not valid to take the words "are not present" universally, because this (text) has our (school's) way of positing conventional entities and holds there is no accomplishment by way of own-character even conventionally; and because the commentary on this text, while informing about it (the text "are not present"), regarding the belief in the world "It exists" and "It does not exist," quotes the scripture "I (the tathāgata) also believe that way," so it is not right that it does not exist (at all).[271]

Hence, we find in many places a remark like "It does not exist in the absolute sense, but it exists conventionally." So when that text says "are not present," there is no fault at all in the fact that there are different meanings for it.

Now, it has been explained in the *Vigrahavyāvartanī* that we have no position or thesis of our own; and whatever be the meaning of that will perforce be explained (by you). One has to claim that if there is a thesis "the shoot lacks self-existence for being accomplished by own essence," it has the reason "because it arises dependently" and, for example, the illustration "like a reflected image." So the reason has (the three marks, to wit:) (1) *pakṣa-dharma* (*pakṣa,* the factual base;[272] and thereon a *dharma,* the feature); and (2-3) the two marks of pervasion (*vyāpti*) (which are *anvaya* and *vyatireka*); and has the thesis (*sādhya*) to be proved thereby. By taking recourse to the verbalization associated with the inference which comprehends that (thesis), if one desires to generate it in the opponent (*prativādin*), at that time, it just amounts to ill-will toward the name "Svātantrika" when one thinks, with whatever the fatigue I shall refute the Svātantrika.

(In reply) to that, there are also found (general) explanations of no thesis or position, similar to what you cited [in your case, with added "of our own"], and there are numerous statements (in the *Vigrahavyāvartinī,* etc.) of the requirement to posit a thesis (of one's own school). Hence, how is one able to prove a nonposition by citing just that (i.e., saying, "no thesis" and "no position")! However, that one gets a fear of becoming a Svātantrika if one has a thesis of non-self-existence is something very true, and the meaning here appears to be a point that is most subtle and difficult. The resolution of this problem will be explained in the section on establishing our own school. In regard to this, while the *Vigrahavyāvartanī* states (in k. 29) that there is no thesis, the Mādhyamika says, "An entity has no self-existence." The realists argue, "In that case, if there is self-existence in the words of (your) thesis, then (your insistence that) all entities are without self-existence is invalid; while if there is no self-existence (in the words), you are incapable of denying self-existence." The continuation (or, amplification) of this argument as well as of the "non-self-existence" is as found in the previous citation of the *Vigrahavyāvartinī* basic commentary regarding validating the agent and action (*bya byed*) of the refutation and proof (*dgag sgrub*). Hence, the argument of whether there is or is not a thesis is not in general an argument of (i.e., restricted to) existence or nonexistence (of the thesis), but is an argument about presence or absence of self-existence (*svabhāva*) in the (Mādhyamika's) words of thesis, "All entities are without self-existence." Consequently, if we were to accept that there is self-existence in that sort of wording of thesis, we would have the fault of conflicting with the thesis of non-self-existence. But since we do not claim that way, the meaning is that the fault (alleged by the realists) is not ours. So it is not valid to maintain (universally) that there is no thesis, because there is a great distinction between *a*) non-self-existence, and *b*) absence (generally).

Such passages as "If . . . such as direct perception,"[273] assert that there is no witness at all by way of direct perception and the other (authorities). As previously cited from the *Prasannapadā*[274] the (subjective) authority and cognizable object are taught to be not a witnessing agent (produced by own essence) and not a witnessable object (produced by own essence); but it is not taught that there is no authority (of direct perception and inference) or (no) cognizable object that arises in dependence (on causes and conditions).

Moreover, (the realists assert:) "In our opinion the own-character of entities is proven by direct perception." Since it is valid to reject this (own-character of entities), the Mādhyamikas aver: "All entities are void of self-existence." At the time of saying that, it is necessary that there be direct perception and with it a judgment of the objective domain included within entities, so that one finds it necessarily the case that they are void of self-existence. If that (direct perception and judgment) be lacking, he (the Mādhyamika) may deem himself unable to deny (the own-character of entities). The *Vigrahavyāvartinī* (k. 5) states the textual passage:

(The realist says:) Now, if you have witnessed entities by direct perception, you may deny them. Then, by whatever (direct perception) the entities are witnessed (that way), that direct perception is nonexistent (to wit: it is void of self-existence).

While replying thereto, the commentary on that (textual passage) states:

(The realist argues:) If he (the Mādhyamika) witnesses with direct perception all the entities, he may deny the entities, saying all entities are void of self-existence; but that is not valid. Why? Because the authority of direct perception is also included within "all entities" (or states of being) and would be void (of self-existence). And anyone that witnesses entities is also void (of self-existence). For that reason, there is no witness by an authority (i.e., direct perception). Since it is not witnessed, also the denial is not valid. Therefore, what you (Mādhyamikas) say, to wit: "All entities are void"—is not valid.

Also, the *Catuḥ-śataka* (k. 400) says: "is present, or absent, or both present and absent" and so on. And the commentary on this states (the meaning as follows):[275]

This shows that even in a long time one cannot confute the speaker of voidness. Since you say that you do not accept voidness, how is it proper for you to be a guide on any position!

The *Avatāra-Comm.* (on the same point) explains, citing the four lines (of Aryadeva's verse, k. 400):[276]

For the reason that in either case (asserting that the entity is present, or asserting that the entity is absent) there is no validity for you to talk to those who express the conceptuality (of entities), it follows that, whether you try to confute by resorting to the two (extremes of "present" or "absent") or whether there is a reply (by the Mādhyamikas to your attempted confutation), in no case do you obtain argumentative advantage over the Mādhyamikas. As Āryadeva says: "is present, or absent. . . ."

The citation (of that text, "is present, or absent" and so on,) informs us that there can be no confutation by means of the two (extremes, i.e., of nihilism or eternalism) of those (i.e., Mādhyamikas) who claim that the presence of a substance produced by own essence is the presence of a hindering figment of imagination, i.e., not (a confutation) by means of *1*) saying that a substance is present, claiming that it is accomplished by own essence, or by means of *2*) saying that a substance is absent, denying all activities of entities, form, etc. Consequently, it is not valid to take it (i.e., the *Avatāra*) as a source for denying (to the Mādhyamika) an own school. It is exceedingly clear (by the citation of the *Catuḥśataka* in the guidance of the *Avatāra-Comm.*) that the sides (*pakṣa*) of, it is present, it is absent, (and it is both present and absent, or neither present nor absent,) are like the sides of speaking in either way (the extremes of eternalism and nihilism) and therefore the previous explanation of denying the four alternatives in the phase of refuting the adherence to "it exists" and "it does not exist" also applies (in present case).

Now, in the commentary on that passage cited from the *Yuktiṣaṣṭikā* (i.e., k. 50, above) we read about "absence" (*abhāva*) as the reason for no side:

At the time when there is no possibility (on the part of intelligence, *buddhi*) of one's own or another's side since there is no presence (*bhāva*) (or no "own-presence," *svabhāva*, at that time, there is certainly a cessation of defilements in those (i.e., yogins) who see that way.

And when one posits a presence in terms of an own-character or self-existence, or when in the case of activity one sees absence, that opposes the situation said to be the cessation of defilements.

Hence, it is the absence of the side which accepts presence by way of self-existence that is said to be the absence of side (or absence of thesis) (of the Prāsaṅgika school). Because prior to that scriptural citation, the *Yuktiṣaṣṭika-vṛtti* (on k. 46) states:

The ones who do not plumb this (deep) true nature of dependent origination, imagine that entities have an own-character. "Those persons (with this thesis), accepting presence (accomplished by self-existence)" are only certain to "have a quarrel arisen from adherence to intolerable and delinquent views aroused by passion and hatred (among other defilements)."

Thus it mentions the attribution of own-character to entities and the acceptance of presence.

Hence, those scriptural passages do not teach that the Mādhyamika lacks a position of his own. Thus, the *Prasannapadā,* after citing the *Vigrahavyāvartinī* and the *Catuḥ-śataka,* said, "since he has no assumption of the opponent's side"; and the meaning of this should be understood accordingly (as was explained above).

Now to the citation (which you, sirs, made from the *Vigrahavyāvartinī,* the k. 64), namely, "Since there is nothing to refute, I do not refute anything." Generally speaking) there are two kinds of refutable (the object and the subject). Of these, having referred to the refutable of object (*viṣaya*) (as the grasping pattern belonging to nescience) which attributes presence to self-existence, then, by reason of the absence (of the object) he says, "I do not refute anything"; and refers to the attribution constituting the refutable of the subject (*viṣayin*) because it is wrong. The commentary on this states that the one who refutes is also not present. Thus, the absence of the two (refutable and one who refutes), to wit, absence of the refutable realized by own-character, and absence of the one who refutes. These you (the realist) take as present, and you deride (us), asserting that (the Mādhyamika) does refute this (refutable). But those two (refutable and refuter) are like an illusion; and it is not the case that we deny them (in dependent origination).

For it is said in the Vigrahavyāvartanī (k. 23):

Just as a magician, himself a magical manifestation, would suppress the magical manifestation (of army, etc.) that had been emitted by his magical craft (*māyā*), so also is this suppression (of refutable and refuter).

And (*Vigrahavyāvartanī,* k. 67–68):

If this (wayward) apperception (of a mirage) is present by way of self-existence, then it does not arise in dependence (on causes and conditions). But if any apperception does arise in dependence, would it not be voidness!

If the (wayward) apperception is present by way of self-existence, what apperception could ward it off! This is also the method (i.e., perceiving as illusory) in the remaining cases. Hence, there is no fault (in accepting the entity which arises dependently).

Thus it says that if a mirage holding water exists (accomplished by self-existence), then it is not valid that it arose in dependence on its own causes and conditions, and it is not valid that any apperception whatever could ward it off.

Furthermore, as to the passage of *Prasannapadā* which you (Svātantrika) cited above, to wit, "since we have no thesis of our own," that is not a textual source disregarded in our school, because (according to the Prāsaṅgika) it means "no thesis of the Svātantrika."

As to the passage of the *Avatāra* about this side not existing, our school (of Mādhyamika) holds that neither the refutable nor the refuting agent are produced by self-existence. So, as to your (realist's) claim that the cause and fruit are accomplished by self-existence, since we have examined with the principle that the fruit is produced by the cause whether one encounters or does not encounter (refutables), we (Mādhyamikas) do not engage in refuting rejections, because (whatever the entity) there is no necessity (for us) to claim a capability of examining with a principle. That is the meaning, but (we grant that the meaning of) no school of one's own is not constant. The *Avatāra-Comm.* states (on VI, 173):

Our side (Mādhyamika) is not reduced to equality (i.e., we do not refute as you do). For this reason, in our school the one who refutes, upon not encountering a refutable, also does not refute. The reason is that neither the refutable nor the refuter is accomplished by self-existence. For this reason, we do not give thought to encountering and not encountering.

Thus, it formulates nonaccomplishment by self-existence as the reason for not engaging in the examination of principle as formulated by the realist. The reason is that it does not formulate an absence of a theory (i.e., of the sort, "We have no theory at all"). Informing of this, it (the *Avatāra-Comm.)* cites the Prajñāpāramitā scripture:[277]

Sāriputra, having pondered, asked Subhūti whether one attains the attainment of the unarisen *dharma* by a *dharma* arisen or by one not arisen. When he denied an attainment by means of either one, Sāriputra then asked why there is no attaining and no comprehending.

And as previously cited,[278] while there are both of them, "there is no (attaining or comprehending) by the method of both." Besides, it states that they (these two) are present (only) conventionally but are absent in the absolute sense. That points out by way of an example, and one should accept the same way (in general, i.e., that all establishments are present conventionally and absent in the absolute sense). Because the *Avatāra-Comm.* says with clarity:

This (Prajñāpāramitā-sūtra passage) denies that one attains the attainment by either a *dharma* arisen or by one not arisen, for the reason that it would reduce (to absurdity) in either case (i.e., to the extreme of either eternalism or nihilism). Since it is not right that there is no presence for the two (attaining and comprehending), one accepts that there is attainment in the sense of worldly convention without examination. Accordingly, while there is neither encounter nor nonencounter of refuter with refutable, still one should understand that in a conventional sense the refuter refutes the refutable.

Thus, when one examines the principle of encountering or nonencountering, there is no refutation in either case (of encountering or not encountering), still (by that examination), since there is no obstruction to refutation (in general), one must accept that there is refutation of the opponent's side in a conventional sense.

That is not all. He (*ācārya* Candrakīrti) also maintains that there is proof of the thesis (*sādhya*) by means of a reason (*hetu*). Right after the foregoing citation, he says (including VI, 174–175):

Moreover,

Just as when you see the distinctions that are present regarding the solar disk, such as reflected images (in water), planetary seizure (i.e., eclipse),

> and so on, (so also at that time) it is not right that you encounter and then do not encounter (both) the sun and its reflected image. However, by taking recourse (to the sun while not examining that way), one has the happening of mere convention, because one may beautifully prove that it (the reflected image) is like a lie in the manner of (taking recourse to) one's own face (a looker upon the mirror while one washes one's face). Just as that (reflected image) exists, so also in this situation, there is a seeing capable of purifying the face of insight (*prajñā*) (from nescience), and the reason (whether dependent origination, freedom from singleness and multiplicity, and so on) should be known as the cognition comprehending the thesis (=non-self-existence) after becoming free (by that seeing) from the acceptance (that there is self-existence).
>
> That "reflected image" has no existence at all (accomplished by self-existence); consequently there is no possibility of any kind of inquiry (*vitarka*) that thinks, "Does it happen through encountering the solar disk or happen through not encountering it?" And notwithstanding that, when one witnesses a reflected image by approaching a form serving as the condition one engages with certainty in the desired purpose (such as washing the face, etc.) while imagining (the viewer on the mirror). In the same way, one can prove the thesis by a reason (dependent origination, and so on) that refutes the refutable with a refutation void of self-existence; and, besides that is void of self-existence while free from the acceptance (of accomplishment of self-existence); in which case it does not reduce to (the fault of) the two (extremes). Therefore one should know that it is not correct that our words (which refute you) equally reduce (to absurdity).

In that way the passage replies by disallowing that the principle of refuting the other side applies equally to (or, is compatible with) our own side, but it does not assert that there is no position of our own (as some Tibetans insist).

Furthermore, when one has examined that claim (of the opponent) that the cause and fruit is accomplished by self-existence, and that the fruit is (personally) engendered whether or not it is encountered by the cause, one disallows to one's own side the fault refuted (of the opponent), rejecting (that fault) by taking the claim of non-self-existence to be the reason (for the causal state of affairs); but one does not reject (that fault) by saying, "We have no position of our own." The *Avatāra-Comm.* (on VI, 170c-d) has this to say:

> How is it (the acceptance) according to you?

"For the reason that these two parts (cause and fruit) are like an illusion (i.e., appear as present with self-existence although not present with self-existence), no fault accrues to me, and worldly entities also exist."

According to which (school, of opponent) there is the generated thing and generating agent by own-character (of cause and fruit), in that (positing) there is the examination (fault) (of encountering and not encountering). According to which (school, the other's opponent—the Mādhyamika) the entities are generated by virtue of the wayward imaginary, have an unborn nature like an illusion, although being without self-existence are witnessed by cauled eyes and become an objective domain imagined like hairnets and the like—in that (case) they do not sustain imagination. Therefore, on our side there is no scope for the aforementioned fault (of engaging in the pondering of encountering and not encountering); and all (establishments) are proved (by convention), since (we accept that) worldly entities are accomplished without examination.

That states the formulation of accepting own-character (accomplishment) as the reason for charging a fault to the other (school), and our claim that (entities) are like an illusion as the reason that we are free from the fault. So having understood it that way, you should know the Mādhyamika school that posits free from the fault!

In general, this (meaning) is talked about in innumerable ways in the (Buddha's) scriptures of final meaning (*nītārtha*) and Madhyamaka śāstras, to wit: "it is like this," "it is not like this," "it is not the same as this," "it is the same as this"—which are claims (*bźed pa*) of their authors. Why is it necessary to prove it by citation from other exceptional texts! Since it is not so (i.e., not necessary to so prove), we maintain this way: in the case of those texts which do not mention a "thesis" (*khas len*), at the time of explaining the meaning of those (texts), this amounts to the position (*lugs*) of that author, or his claim (*bźed pa*). It is this, because there is no capacity to differentiate (into various schools), saying, "It is not like this." If you ask whether it is necessary to have distinct terms, "*'dod,*" "*khas blaṅs,*" and "*dam bca' ba*"—many such are used. The *Vigrahavyāvartanī* (k. 28c-d) says:

We do not explain without accepting (or taking for granted) (*abhyupagamya, khas blaṅs*) a convention.

Also the *Yuktiṣaṣṭikā* (k. 7) says:

Just as in regard to an entity which (formerly) had arisen and (subsequently) passed away, one designates it as "ceased" (*'gog pa*), so also the illustrious ones (Buddhas, etc.) claim (*bźed*) it is ceased as though it had been created by magic.

And (its k. 45) says:

Those persons who hold (*'dod pa*) that entities, having depended upon (causes and conditions), are like the moon in the waters, are not genuine, are erroneous, and not (constant)—they are not taken in by false views.

Besides, the *Lokātīta-stava* states (k. 4):[279]

The entities which arise by reason of a cause, and do not (arise) in the absence of that (cause)—why would one not admit (*'dod*) that they are clearly equivalent to a reflected image (e.g., like that in a mirror)?

And (its k. 6):

Feeling (*vedanā*) does not exist by virtue of itself, since it is absent in the absence of the sensible.[280] So you (the incomparable Buddha) maintain (*bźed*) that feeling, also, is devoid of existence by virtue of self-existence.

And (its k. 8):

You (the incomparable Teacher) teach that the doer (of the act) and the act (done by the doer) are (both) present (only) conventionally. Because you maintain (*bźed*) that they are accomplished by mutual dependence.

And (its k. 15):

At first consideration (*tāvat, re śig*), it is not right that an effect could arise from a cause that had been cut off, nor from a cause that it not cut off.[281] But you (thinking more deeply) hold (*bźed*) that birth is like a dream.

And (k. 20a–b):[282]

The very entity that arises in dependence (on the set of causes and conditions), you (Buddha, Teacher) regard (*bźed*) as void.

Furthermore, the *Avatāra-Comm.* includes (on VI, 160) this:

The ones skilled (in pondering the meaning), having considered this side (of Mādhyamika) to be free from fault (of contradiction, etc.) and also attended with advantage (of delivering from *saṃsāra,* etc.) would doubtless admit it (*khas blaṅ*).

And (on VI, 158):

Hence, (we, Mādhyamikas,) accept (*khas blaṅs*) "the designation when there is depending"[283] (on causes and conditions) while (those) like (the realists and other opponents) accept only "this condition" (*idaṃpratyayatā*) of dependent origination; so our side does not shatter any conventional expressions. Our opponent (realist, etc.) ought to admit (*khas blaṅ*) this very (position).

They certainly express the requirement of an "acceptance," and there are many other passages like them.

Moreover, the *Avatāra-Comm.* (with VI, 8a–b) states:

Referring to the four propositions,[284] so as to demonstrate them with a principle, the author explains:,

> That (shoot) does not arise from itself; how would it arise from others? That does not arise from both (itself and others); how would it arise without a cause?

Thus he explains the four propositions (*dam bca'*), and he speaks in the *Prasannapadā* the same way as that found (in the *Avatāra-Comm.*). So a claim, an accepting, and thesis of their own is present in the school of *nātha* Nāgārjuna and Candrakīrti.

δ *Rejection of the Fourth Position.*[285] This school appears to accept (accomplishment by) own-character conventionally, while denying the examining-ability (*dpyad-bzod*) by a principle of (such an) own-character (*svalakṣaṇa*) conventionally. This is faulty, as has already been explained (at length, in the phase of denying accomplishment by own-character).

Furthermore (according to this school), it is held in the school of Candrakīrti that in both the positions of Mādhyamika and the adversary realist there is demonstration by way of "inference for the sake of others" with the evidence of "three marks" of proof. That is not right, because the *Prasannapadā* is like that only in the exceptional case of engaging in refutation; and because if one holds it like that, it would obviate in convention the evidence "aroused on the strength of a current fact" (= first kind of inference) which is the evidence of the Svātantrika school and would not serve to ward off (such an opponent). These matters will be explained now (i.e., below, at length), so I will not extend them here.

b. Establishment of Our Own Position

The aim is for the Prāsaṅgika to refute the Svātantrika, and for this he must (first) set forth the Svātantrika school, and then analyze both (the Prāsaṅgika and the Svātantrika). In this regard the *Prasannapadā* has a great deal of material; but lest we be too wordy, here only the chief points will be dealt with, namely, under two headings (1) Basic refutation of the Svātantrika; (2) How our school differs therefrom.

(1) BASIC REFUTATION OF THE SVĀTANTRIKA

This has two parts: (a) Teaching the fault of the side which does not prove the factual base substratum; (b) Teaching that on account of that fault, the reason is also not proved.

(a) Teaching the Fault of the Side Which Does Not Prove the Factual Base Substratum

This has two parts: (i) Stating the (opponent's) position; (ii) Refuting it.

(i) Stating the (Opponent's) Position

This case, although among those set forth in the "clear worded" (*Prasannapadā*), yet appears extremely difficult to analyze. As expressed in the language of the *Prasannapadā* (chapter I):

[Statement of Bhāvaviveka:] However that may be, in regard to (the proposition) "Sound is not eternal" (maintained by the Buddhist on the side of the Vaiśeṣika), both the factual base (*dharmin*) and the feature (*dharma*) (in this case) are held in their generality (*sāmānya*) (by both the Buddhist and the Vaiśeṣika), while (the factual base and feature) in their distinctions (*viśeṣa*) (such as held by the Vaiśeṣika) are not (held by the Buddhist). Now (*hi*),[286] if one holds such distinctions (of the factual base and feature), there are no agreed upon conventions (*vyavahāra*) for the inference (the syllogism) or for the inferable (to be proved by that reason). This is why: If we hold that sound (*śabda*) (the factual base) is derived from the four great elements, that (factual base) is not proved to the opponent (who is the Vaiśeṣika). On the other hand, when he (the Vaiśeṣika) holds sound to be a quality (*guṇa*) of space (*ākāśa*), that (factual base) is not proved to the Buddhist on his side.[287] Likewise, if the Vaiśeṣika sets forth the proposition "Sound is not eternal" and holds that the sound (the factual base) is an effect (*kārya*), that (factual base) is not proved to those others (i.e., the Mīmāṃsā, who maintain that it is made perceptible, *vyaṅgya,* from its imperishable state). On the other hand, if sound (the factual base) be held as made perceptible (*vyaṅgya*), that is not proved to (the Vaiśeṣika) himself. So it is (not proved) in all like discussions (*yathā-sambhavam*), e.g., (when the *sādhya* is the feature) "destruction." If, furthermore, it be held that it ("destruction") is accompanied by a cause (*sahetuka*, that (feature) is not proved to the Buddhist on his side,[288] but when the latter holds to uncaused destruction, that is not proved to his opponent (the Vaiśeṣika). For that reason, just as (in the case above discussed), the factual base and feature are held only in their generality, in the same way, here also (in connection with the Mādhyamika considerations), there should be holding of the factual base in its generality only, with rejection of the distinctions.[289] (Such is the formulation held by the opponent, the Svātantrika, as expressed by Bhāvaviveka).

The meaning of that (formulation by the opponent) is as follows: At the time the Buddhist makes a proposition to the Vaiśeṣika, to wit, "Sound is not eternal," if he holds to the factual base (*dharmin*) (while introducing the distinction.) "sound that would arise," he does not prove that (factual base) to the Vaiśeṣika. But when (the latter) goes into the factual base (along with the distinction) "Sound is a quality of the *ākāśa,*" neither does he prove that (factual base) to the Buddhist. Likewise, when the Vaiśeṣika puts the proposition that sound is not eternal to (his opponent, who argues for) the *vyaṅgya* theory, and take the factual base (along with the distinction) "Sound is constructed," that (factual base) is also not proved to the believer in the *vyaṅgya.* And when (the latter) apprehends the factual base (along with the distinction) "Sound is made perceptible (*vyaṅgya*) by the condition of a preexistent reality," he does not prove his own side (to the Vaiśeṣika). Accordingly, it is not valid to hold to the factual base (*dharmin*) with no generality (i.e., by making distinctions) of the various beliefs, because the factual base is the substratum (*gźi*) for the two adversaries to examine the feature (*dharma*) which has the distinction (*viśeṣa*), and the proof must take place in a show of agreement by the two (adversaries). Just as it is necessary for them to prove in a show of agreement on the factual base (*dharmin*), so also it is necessary for the two (adversaries) to prove (in a show of agreement) the feature (*dharma*) (which is the *sādhya*), i.e., "impermanence," in mere generality without interjecting distinctions; and, besides, it is necessary for the proof of the *sādhya* (i.e., "Sound is not eternal") to be preceded by a proof in a show of agreement (of the two adversaries) when formulating any example (such as "pot," etc.).

In the same manner as that example (i.e., the method of proof in the case of the proposition "Sound is not eternal"), when the Mādhyamika takes the personal sense bases of eye, etc. and the external sense bases of form, etc. (as the substratum, *gźi*) and at that time non-Buddhists (such as Sāṃkhya, etc.) make proof that they do not arise from themselves, and among Buddhists the realists make proof that they (the sense bases) do not arise from another, (both) taking as the factual base (along with the distinction of given reality) that the eye, etc. is real (*bden pa*), then they do not prove that (factual base) to (the Mādhyamika) himself. Furthermore, when he takes as the factual base (along with the distinction of given falsity) the eye, etc. as false (*brdzun pa*), he does not prove that (factual base) to the opponent (the realist). Hence, it is necessary to posit as the factual base just the eye and form, while leaving out such distinctions (of truth and of falsity), in which case both the Mādhyamika and the realist have a (common) substratum of examining the feature (*dharma*) with the distinctions of "do" arise from themselves, or "do not," etc., because it is necessary to prove in a show of agreement of the two (Mādhyamika and realist). So he thinks.

Well, then, what is the meaning of proving in a show of agreement (*mthun snaṅ*)? Whatever sort of authority (proves the factual base, etc.) to the opponent, that sort of authority proves (the factual base, etc.) also to our partisan.

(ii) Refuting the Opponent's Position

There are two parts to the refutation: (ii–a) (Showing) that the meaning is not cogent; (Showing) that the formulation of example is different.

(ii-a). Showing that the Meaning Is Not Cogent

The *Prasannapadā* (chapter I) states:

It is not so (i.e., referring to the claim of proof by show of agreement without distinctions, etc., and the requirement to hold as the fact with generality only)! The reason it is not cogent follows:—At the very time that he denies in this phase (of proof) an arising (in the absolute sense) and believes in a feature to be proved (the *sādhya-dharma*), precisely at that time he (the *ācārya* Bhāvaviveka) himself admits the failure (of proof) of the factual base (*dharmin*) which is the substratum of that (*sādhya-dharma*) and which (with eye, etc.) has reached embodiment along with sheer wayward awareness. Now wayward awareness (imbued with nescience) and correct awareness (which sees the reality of noble *samāpatti*) are indeed dissociated. Therefore, at whatever time the cauled eye with its waywardly apprehending of presences that are not really there, apprehends hairnets and so on, at that time it could not possibly witness even a minute particle of anything that is real. And at whatever time the uncauled eye, without wayward awareness, does not affirm unreality such as hairnets, at that time it could not conventionally witness even a minute particle of any unreal thing. Hence, the *ācārya* Nāgārjuna said (*Vigrahavyāvartanī,* k. 30):

> If (as you realists think) there are entities to be witnessed by direct perception (and the other authorities), they could be affirmed (by us), or (otherwise) denied. But since they do not exist, there is no point to your argument with me.

Now for the reason that wayward awareness and correct awareness are dissociated, then, since there is no possibility of waywardness in a nonwayward state belonging to masters (of *samāpatti*), certainly there is no conventional eye to serve as the fact for anyone (i.e., to serve for proof in a show of agreement in the Mādhyamika and the realist). Hence, there is no way for you to escape the fault of side in the sense that the substratum (the factual base) is not established (i.e., the fault that there is nothing to prove) or to escape the fault of reason with no proof of the substratum (i.e., the fault that the evidential "marks," *tshul,* cannot be established). You have no answer to this.[290]

The meaning of that is as follows: Take "the sense base of form" (as the factual base), (and add) "does not arise from self" (and to demonstrate this last remark, formulate) "because it is present" (as the reason); (and to clarify with a consistent example, add) "like a bright pot in front." Since it is easy to understand by that illustration, it should be explained on that (syllogistic frame).[291]

Those replying passages (of the *Prasannapadā*) teach the position of disproving the show of agreement (of the two adversaries) regarding the factual base (*dharmin*). And how do they teach it? In this (context) there is disproof of that factual base which proves a show of agreement with any opponent. That opponent who is (the object of) teaching the way of disproving is stated in the *Prasannapadā;* and in this context the opponent belongs to (the context of) denying the arising from itself. However, (in terms of Buddhist schools) generally it is the realist who holds that entities have self-existence in the absolute sense; while it is the Mādhyamika-Svātantrika who holds that those (entities) in conventional terms have self-existence and are accomplished by own-character. Granted that the Mādhyamika-Svātantrika dubs itself "school of non-self-existence" (*niḥsvabhāva-vāda*); but here (in the context of the *Prasannapadā* and such works), for the sake of simplifying the discussion,[292] one should understand the school of non-self-existence to be the Prāsaṅgika, and should understand the school of self-existence to be the realist and the Svātantrika.

The school (Svātantrika, and so on) which would prove that positing of the sense base of form as a factual base has to prove it by means of the authority of direct perception, which is the eye awareness that perceives this (sense base of form). Since it is not valid in the case of direct perception that it would prove the entity if there is disproof by those (direct perceptions) of nonerror, the nonerror (as to form, etc.) is stipulated. In the case of those schools (Svātantrika and the realist) which prove while (the various direct perceptions of eye, etc. are) without discursive thought and free from error, there is necessarily a dependence on the presence of the place (the object, *viṣaya*) to which there is passage without error, as it (the object) appears, appearing (to nondiscursive thought) as realized by own-character (or, "unique particular"). That being the case, the opponent's authority which proves the fact (the nonerroneous form, etc.) by an authority of that sort is not valid to our partisan (the Prāsaṅgika), because there is no authority to prove any feature (*dharma*)—the nature accomplished by own-character not being present even conventionally. So considering, one rejects the Svātantrika by the purport of this *ācārya* (Candrakīrti).

Moreover, he explains (in this context) the method of refuting the Svātantrika's requirement of assent (*aṅga*) to generating anew in the opponent (i.e., in his stream of consciousness) a view that comprehends the non-self-existence of entities. But we will meanwhile rest the matter[293] of examining the necessity or non-necessity of Svātantrika (authority) of assent to generating an inference for understanding certain phenomenal (*saṃvṛti*) (knowable) entities in mutuality within the Prāsaṅgika.[294]

(Now) to explain in association with (the words of) that text (the *Prasannapadā* citation):— the part from "At the very time (that he denies) *down to* admits . . . (wayward awareness)," has the following meaning: Bhāvaviveka himself admits that there is only failure, i.e., no proof, of the eye or (its object) form, and so on, which are the factual base (*dharmin*) or substratum of the feature to be proved (*sādhya-dharma*). (However,) it will be questioned as to how the factual base (is admitted to be unproved) (and this must be answered). (That factual base) has reached embodiment only with wayward awareness imbued with nescience; and the objects (form, sound, etc.) are proved by mere conventional awareness belonging to eye-awareness, etc. (which is imbued with nescience). (But why is) that position (to be regarded as) admitted (by Bhāvaviveka)? Because he denies an arising in the absolute sense, and at that time bases his *sādhya-dharma* on those factual bases (to wit, form, etc. imbued with nescience); and because it would indeed be a contradiction (with his own position) to base that (*sādhya-dharma*) on a (factual base) proved as reality (i.e., as absolute, *paramārtha*).

One may wonder that while one may not accept that way (i.e., may concede that there is no proof of the reality of form, etc. constituting the factual base that in the absolute sense is the unarisen basis for the feature to be proved), how there is (a fault) thereby (if one were to accept that way). (In reply, the fault arises as follows:) Those (factual bases) form, etc. which are not proved to be real and which are not entities of reality—do not serve for the purpose of attainment (by way of appearance on the side of noble *samāpatti*) with unmistaken awareness, and are themselves attained (merely) with conventional awareness which bears falsehood, wherefore those are (just) mistaken things imbued with nescience. Hence, the entity attained without error (i.e., in noble *samāpatti*) does not appear to mistaken awareness; and the entity which appears to mistaken awareness is not reached by unmistaken awareness, because there is a difference (of subject) in engaging in an object by way of mutually exclusive individual objects belonging to the mistaken awareness and the nonwayward unmistaken awareness. Thus (in that passage) the meaning is stated as the dissociation of the wayward and the nonwayward.

That same (meaning) is explained in the portion from "And at whatever time" down to "any unreal thing."[295] The expression "wayward" means the eyes, etc. with their conventions of cognition, imbued with nescience. Their "apprehending presences that are not really there" means that sense awareness apprehends form, sound, etc. as present with particulars (*svalakṣaṇa*) accomplished by their own-nature—which are not so. Apprehending with awareness devoid of discursive thought (*vikalpa*) (i.e., with direct perception *pratyakṣa*) means an appearance (to sense awareness) of form, etc. as a "particular" (*svalakṣaṇa*) because of the stipulation to be appearance-only. The line "at that time it could not possibly witness even a minute particle of anything that is real," means accordingly (as explained above) that when there is appearance of the particular (in form, etc.)—which is not so—it is said for that reason that those (sense-organ) awarenesses (mistaken as they are) could not possibly prove (i.e., witness) even a minute particle of anything present by reason of a particular (*svalakṣaṇa*). The passage says "such as hairnets" as an example of appearance to mistaken sense awareness of entities accomplished by own-character (*svalakṣaṇa*)—which are not so. Those (lines of the text) set forth that the sense awarenesses of appearing form, sound, etc. are mistaken and so do not serve to prove the particularity (of form, etc.).[296]

What is taught by saying that unmistaken awareness does not apprehend any form, sound, etc. is shown by the line "And at whatever time the uncauled eye. . . ." Here the "nonwayward" is the unmistaken awareness. That is present in the one who experiences reality in direct perception, and is not present in any other person. The nonattribution of fictitious sound when one has that (knowledge in noble *samāpatti*) is the nonattribution of sound in the sense of form, sound, etc. that do not serve for the goal of reality, and one does not apprehend it as present (when one has that *samāpatti* knowledge). For example, it is like the eye awareness free from caul that does not witness the appearance of the hairnet droppings.

The expression "conventionally" means the falseness of form, sound, etc. "Unreal" means not accomplished (i.e., not present) by particularity (*svalakṣaṇa*). The awareness that is not mistaken about that sort (of false form, etc.), i.e., the reality subject (*viṣayin*) (immersed in noble *samāpatti*) does not accomplish even a minute particle; and that is the meaning of saying: "because that (noble *samāpatti*) does not see those (i.e., form, sound, etc.)."

Those senses are a formulation reported in *nātha* Nāgārjuna's text (i.e., the *Vigrahavyāvartinī,* k. 30), "If. . . ." This verse states that the four authorities of direct perception, etc. are unable at all to prove that an entity is accomplished by own-character (*svalakṣaṇa*). His (Nāgārjuna's) composition serves as the guide in this case.

The part "now for the reason" and so on, is a condensation of the meanings previously explained. Besides, the phrase, "certainly there is no conventional eye to serve as the factual base for anyone" does not mean to deny a fact of conventional eye, etc., but rather means, as explained above, that there is no (possibility of) proving, even conventionally, form as a fact accomplished by own-character or proven by unmistaken direct perception.

The meaning of the words from "Hence" onward, is as follows: At the time that both the (Mādhyamika-Prāsaṅgika) school (which holds) that there is no self-existence accomplished by own-nature, and the realist (school), posit the sense base of form as the factual base, there is no proof in a show of agreement that direct perception (belonging to eye awareness, etc.) is unmistaken (regarding form, etc.) and there is no authority proving that factual base (form, etc.) with proof in a show of agreement between the two schools. Hence (in the absence of demonstrating that substratum, the factual base), the opponent, with the evidence of the Svātantrika, fails to establish that his *sādhya* side is faultless. Such is the meaning.[297]

Suppose you would assert: even though your side (admits) no self-existence accomplished by own-nature that way even conventionally, our school does not believe it is that way conventionally, and because there is present the factual base, etc. (the *sādhya* and evidence) of the Svātantrika, our side has no fault. (In reply:) I have explained above that such presence of self-existence is not valid, even conventionally, and I shall explain it still more (below). So your retort is not right.

(ii-b) Showing That the Formulation of Example is Different

This is set forth in the *Prasannapadā* (chapter I):[298]

The case (about the impermanence of sound, which you have advanced) is not comparable. For in that instance (of example) there is no intention to state a difference between the sound universal and the impermanence universal. Thus, there is no agreement, either conventionally or in the absolute sense, between the voidness school and the nonvoidness school regarding the eye universal.

As to the meaning of this passage:— You say that whether the sound (universal) is derived from the (four great) elements, which is not so (to the Vaiśeṣika) or is quality of the *ākāśa,* which is not so (to the Buddhist); whether it is constructed, which is not so (to the Mīmāṃsā), or is made perceptible from its imperishable state, which is not so (to the Vaiśeṣika); and whether there is dependence of (the feature to be proved) on a (later) cause, which is not so (to the Buddhist), or not dependence on a (later) cause, which is not so (to the Vaiśeṣika)—still there is precisely an impermanence universal (suitable for positing a feature to be proved).[299] And do you teach that there is no eye, etc. which fails to be either true or false? You do not, because either those disputants do not claim it (that factual bases are in no case with those features); or if they (claim it), who cannot demonstrate that those two cases are not the same!

However, if one wonders what (that citation really means), (it is this way): (At the time that the Buddhist demonstrates to the Vaiśeṣika that sound is impermanent), whether "sound is derived from the (four) elements" or whether "sound is a quality of the *ākāśa,*" it is certain that the sound (universal) is present without being constructed of features, i.e., by whatever relevant features[300]—a certainty to be conceded in the schools of both disputants (the Buddhists and the Vaiśeṣika). In the schools of both the "void of *svabhāva*" adherents and the "not void of *svabhāva*" adherents, neither is it proven by unmistaken awareness (by way of noble *samāpatti,* and so on), nor is it proven by mistaken awareness. No universal of eye or form is proven by authorities (alone). What (i.e., factual base) is proven by mistaken (sensory) awareness is not proven to the opponent (the realist, etc.); and what (factual base) is attained by unmistaken awareness is not proven by the authority of our partisan. That is the meaning of the line "The case is not comparable."

The "unmistaken"[301] is generally the *samāpatti* which assesses absolute truth in direct perception. However, in this (context) it is necessary to define it as both the authority of direct perception (of eye awareness, etc.) which is unmistaken regarding the particulars (*svalakṣaṇa*) of the objective domain (*viṣaya*) that is manifested (*snaṅ yul*);[302] and the authority of inference which is unmistaken regarding the particulars of the objective domain of clinging (*źen yul*). Such an authority (direct perception and inference) for proving the factual base and for proving the triple mark of evidence is fundamentally lacking (in our school), for it does not serve the aim of attaining with unmistaken awareness to (posit) the fact.

In this (context) the "particular" (*svalakṣaṇa*) does not mean only efficiency (*arthakriyākāritva*), as the logicians claim. But it (also) means self-existence, as previously explained, with the claim (by others) of self-existence in each respective presence or absence; so the adherents of presence by reason of self-existence claim that even the inference which assesses an absent thing (*abhāva*) is unmistaken regarding the "domain of clinging" (*źen yul*) of such a self-existence.

When there is the unmistaken awareness toward such self-existence, there is also no mistake regarding any "manifesting domain" (*snaṅ yul*) or "clinging domain" (*źen yul*), and it amounts to no mistake regarding the meaning of reality (supreme truth); so there is the claim of our school that such authority does not prove the factual base, and so forth; but not the claim that in the stream of consciousness of both disputants (the Mādhyamika and the realist) there is no conventional authority to assess eye and form, etc.

Also, the sense awareness of the opponent only has certainty of the presence of form, etc. when called up without absurdity (*gnod*) (of mistake causes) as previously explained; and there is never absurdity of principle in the domain of certainty awareness (of awareness by the mind). Besides, if that is explained in detail, like the apprehending of a shoot, there are three ways of apprehending (as follows):—*i*) apprehending the shoot as present with self-existence accomplished by own nature, i.e., apprehending it as present in truth; *ii*) apprehending the shoot as present like an illusion, not accomplished by own nature, i.e., apprehending it as present in falsehood; *iii*) apprehending (the shoot) as merely present generally, without making any distinction whatever as to truth or falsehood.

While there is also apprehension of the shoot as present in the manner of permanent, impermanent, etc., still there is no apprehension without the manner of apprehending of self-existence in one of those three ways, so it is not necessary to explain here those manners (apprehension of permanent, impermanent, etc.) (as an additional category).

Among those (three ways), in the sentient beings who have not given birth in their stream of consciousness to a view that comprehends that entities have no self-existence, there are the two apperceptions, to wit, that (the shoot) is merely present or that it is present truly, while there is no occurrence of the apperception (of the shoot) that it is present like an illusion without own-nature.

The aforementioned sentient beings who have not attained the view that the *dharmas* are like an illusion, take as apprehended in truth everything which their discursive thought grasps as being present. That their belief is totally invalid I have previously explained at length in the earlier phase of explaining conventional authority as well as in the phase of analyzing the presence and absence of self-existence and the four distinctions of presence and absence (in general).

(You, sirs, for whom) it is not that way, with the aforementioned discursive thought that misunderstands the view that there is no self-existence, should apprehend in truth (i.e., realistically) everything which is given conventionally. However, those who are not imbued with the cause of mistakes—the autonomy of worldly conventions—as was previously explained, all those must believe with the Mādhyamika in the convention of the entity established, and for these the absurdity of the principle falls away—because the wayward views that are occupied with a lord, or that fail to distinguish presence and absence, become a great obstacle to comprehending the meaning of the Mādhyamika.

Formerly there were many who held in those ways in the marks of wayward understanding of voidness that the side of virtuous practice is a requirement set by discursive thought. Later the view was made into a school, with the opinion that all previous (virtuous) practice amounts to holding to signs (*nimittagrāha*) that bind one to *saṃsāra,* and which asserted that these applications to virtue are meant for persons who have not as yet achieved this sort of (voidness) view which is the final meaning (*nitārtha*). There are many who, like the former Chinese teacher,[303] have come up with this misunderstanding; and with the wayward reflection that views all discursive thought (*vikalpa*) as a fault, have rejected many (illustrious) doctrines (*dharma*).

Among those (three ways), those aforementioned persons who have not achieved the view of no self-existence cannot possibly distinguish between the two—merely present (generally) and present accomplished by own-character, because, as the *Catuḥ-ś-ṭ* was previously cited,[304] whatever is present, those persons apprehend it as pervaded by presence accomplished by own-nature. By reason of that point (i.e., apprehending pervasively that way), they also grasp non-self-existence as pervaded by utter nothingness and make many arguments that (natures, *dharma*) void of self-existence cannot serve to establish cause and effect.

In the stream of consciousness (of persons) arousing continuity of view that comprehends non-self-existence, there occur the three ways of apprehending presence; however, after that view has arisen, as long as the motivation (*saṃskāra*) (of that view) has not passed away, at the time of nonaccomplishment by own-nature, there does not occur for the time being a realistic imputation (*bden 'dzin*) (an imagination, *parikalpa*) which accepts accomplishment by own-nature, but it is not the case that in that (stream of consciousness) there is no occurrence of natural ("co-natal") realistic imputation (involved in from time immemorial).

Hence, there is not an apperception of everything as present like an illusion when apperceiving the presence of shoot (etc.) in a (person's) stream of consciousness in which the view has arisen and not passed away, of comprehending that there is no self-existence accomplished by own-nature, because if it were otherwise (i.e., if persons only apperceived everything as like an illusion) it would reduce to the absurdity that there would be no possibility of directly grasping the presence when there is truth in (the streams of consciousness of) those (persons).

(Thus,) the Mādhyamikas like *ācārya* Bhāvaviveka presume that features (*dharma*) have conventionally an own-character accomplished by own-nature—and this is the reason for their subscribing to the marks of Svātantrika as their own school. This (subscribing) itself is the presence of own-character conventionally accomplished by own-nature, so whether it posits or does not posit the marks of Svātantrika of Bhāvaviveka, etc.), the sense awareness with appearing self-existence accomplished by own-nature (which, as explained above, is a cause of mistake) is without absurdities and there is no mistake conventionally regarding the (individual) appearing domain (*snaṅ yul*); and likewise (according to their school) such a discursive thought of apprehending the presence of shoots, etc. with self-existence is without mistake regarding the (individual) clinging domain (*źen yul*). (Some persons assert): If it were not that way (i.e., that claim that it is without mistake) those (sense awarenesses and discursive thought) would be held to be erroneous (in the individual appearance domain and clinging domain),[305] and so would be any authority which proves a show of agreement between the two schools, the realist and (the Mādhyamika).[306]

According to Candrakīrti's position, while there is no self-existence with its semblance of own-character, when it is proved to the realist by way of sense awarenesses of the appearances there, or the factual base is proved (to the realist), of what use is the Svātantrika's evidence for proving non-self-existence?

Notwithstanding that, one may wonder, since the opponent (the realist) is satisfied with his own proof (of factual bases, etc.), whether it is not necessary for the Mādhyamika and (his opponent) to prove in a show of agreement. But not only do you reject that yourself, but it is not a valid principle, because if it were that way (i.e., necessary to prove in a show of agreement), all applications of syllogisms would be only what is acknowledged by others (*para-pratīta*),[307] so they (Bhāvaviveka, etc.) would be followers of the Prāsaṅgika.

Those (Mādhyamikas) such as ācārya Śāntarakṣita among others, who maintain that external entities do not exist conventionally, claim that blue and other (objects, *viṣaya*) are the material of cognition conventionally, like the belief in truth of aspect (i.e., that the objects are mind-only), so taking a stand on those sense awarenesses with appearance of those (sense objects) they hold that the entity (as it appears) is accomplished by own-character (or, "particular," *svalakṣaṇa*), that is, taking their stand on the blue alone, they do not misconstrue (those sense awarenesses).

In that (context, the writings of Śāntarakṣita, etc.,) the eye, and so forth, is posited as a factual base or entity that is remote (*parokṣa*). That (remote factual base) is not demonstrated concretely by direct perception. Still, if there is an ultimate base for demonstrating it, the Siddhānta-vādins (sectarians) believe it is necessarily up to a (or, some kind of) direct perception (*pratyakṣa*), because inference (*anumāna*) is like a series of blind men, and because (the adherents of theory-systems) believe that it is up to direct perception to give a demonstration of the base of that (inference). At that time (when it is up to direct perception), they believe that direct perception of the base is either in unmistaken extroversion (*gźan rig*) or an unmistaken introspection (*raṅ rig*).[308] and as explained above, it appears to that direct perception that the entity (respective object) is accomplished by its particular (*svalakṣaṇa*), and the semblance (*snaṅ ba ltar*) must be accomplished on the basis of that object (*viṣaya*). Since they (i.e., the Svātantrikas Śāntarakṣita, etc.) believe it (i.e., that those direct perceptions are unmistaken), in the two schools—they (Śāntarakṣita's kind of Svātantrika) and the Mādhyamikas who say there is no self-origination accomplished by own-nature—there is certainly no unmistaken direct perception to prove a show of agreement.

One can answer (the opponent) regarding direct perception in that way (i.e., to demonstrate the base of inference) although it does not reach (the remote factual base), as follows: those who say there is self-existence (i.e., the Svātantrika and the realists) must prove that whatever the constructed (*saṃskṛta*) or unconstructed (*asaṃskṛta*) natures (*dharma*) that are proved by authority, those natures are (individually) present upon the respective objective domain (*viṣaya*) with its form of layout (*sdod lugs*). Because one can refute that with a principle, it does not validify the authority of proof.

(b) Teaching That on Account of That Fault, the Reason Is Also Not Proved

It is taught by this passage of the *Prasannapadā* (chapter I):

> What constitutes the method to refer to the fault of the side (or thesis) whose substratum (=*dharmin*) is unproved is also applicable to refer to the futility of that reason (used by Bhāvaviveka) which says "because of presence."

In regard to this (passage), as previously (in the phase of showing the fault of the thesis whose substratum is not proved) there is no authority to prove the factual base, proving in a show of agreement of the two schools of disputants—the one for whom there is the void of self-existence accomplished by own-nature (the position of our Mādhyamika partisans) or the not-void (the position of the Svātantrika and the realist). That explains that the Svātantrika evidence does not have a side or thesis which ties together the (substratum) factual base, which is the sense base of form, and the feature, which is the nonarising from self. Also, the reason which says "because of presence, by reason of that principle" is not an authority that can prove (the substratum factual base), proving a show of agreement in the schools of the two (disputants); so the methods by which that evidence is undemonstrable should be understood in the same way as explained above.

Moreover, the *Prasannapadā* (on chapter 1) states:[309]

In the same manner (as we have shown the fault), so also (we can add the following):—Hence even this logician (i.e., Bhāvaviveka) himself has admitted the meaning exposed above. How so? (He gives a syllogism, as follows):

(Thesis). The causes and so on, that generate the personal sense bases are actually present.

(Reason). Because the Buddha has so declared.

(Major premise). Whatever has been declared by the Buddha, that is exactly so (i.e., he says it without mistake).

(Example). (As he said:) "*Nirvāṇa* is quiescent."

This syllogism has been formulated by another (opponent, i.e., realist). He (Bhāvaviveka) rejects the formulation: "What do you sirs presume to be the meaning of the reason (to wit, 'Because the Buddha has so declared')? Was it because the Buddha declared it from the conventional standpoint, or because he declared it from the absolute standpoint? If it was from the conventional standpoint, the reason is futile even for yourselves (the realists)."

And further on:[310]

"Because in the absolute sense there is no proof either of the thing to be effected or of the effecting agent, there is the futility and inconsistency of the reason (you have advanced)." With these words (Bhāvaviveka) refers to the fault (to the opponent).[311] Consequently, this one himself (Bhāvaviveka) in that way (of his own words) by this method (of showing the fault) admits that there is no proof of that reason. Since according to his own school (of the Mādhyamika) there is no proof of the reason (as well as the factual base), etc., it follows that in the case of all inferences with a reason alluding to a material feature, all syllogisms (formulated by Bhāvaviveka) are crushed (by himself).

As to the meaning of the above passage:—Some (Tibetans) who claim to be followers of Candrakīrti refer to (Bhāvaviveka's) formulation in the *Tarkajvālā:*[312] (Thesis) Earth (*sa,* S. *mahī*) does not have the nature of solidity in the absolute sense. (Reason) Because it is a factor of becoming (*bhūta*). (Example) Like wind. They say (that this is the meaning:) that if one formulates (the reason), "Because it arises in the absolute sense," it is disproved by (the *ācārya* Candrakīrti) himself; while if one formulates (the reason), "Because it arises in the conventional sense," it is disproved by the opponent, the realist. (And they continue:) If thereby one does not posit the evidence, it being disproved, the disproof by way of the two (truths, conventional and absolute) is pervaded by disproof of the evidence, so (you, *ācārya* Bhāvaviveka) are inconsistent with your own acceptance.

Some persons assert:[313] if one formulates (as the reason) a factor of becoming (*bhūta*) alone, it is refuted, since it is disproved with knowledge of the principle (at the time of examination).

Criticism by such means (as employed by those Tibetans) is decidedly not the purport of the *Prasannapadā*. In fact, the *ācārya* (Bhāvaviveka) does not maintain it that way (i.e., either formulating his syllogism with a distinction of the two truths, or formulating it by disallowing the distinction of two truths); so it is wayward assertion toward both schools (those of the two *ācāryas*).

Well, how then are we to regard (the meaning of that passage)? It said: "Hence even this logician has himself admitted the meaning exposed above." The meaning of the phrase "exposed above" is the previously explained method that there is no proof of the factual base (*dharmin*), and stated to be applicable as well to the reason; and because that passage ("Hence even that logician . . .") comes immediately after that (passage about no proof of the factual base or of the reason). That being the case, the meaning here is as follows:—(An authority) like direct perception for proving the factual base, and the reason does not transcend error or nonerror. When the entity is arrived at with error (of direct perception) and one posits the reason, (also, the factual base), etc., it is not proven to the realist. When the entity is arrived at without error (of direct perception) and one posits those (the reason, the factual base, etc.), it is not proved by the authority of our (school, the Mādhyamika). So the Svātantrika's evidence (*liṅga*), factual base (*dharmin*), etc. are not proved, as previously explained, to wit, "exposed above."

As to how Bhāvaviveka himself posits it as unproven through such an avenue—it has been asserted that when he considered the reason, "Because the Buddha has so declared," this involves a consideration by way of the two truths (conventional and absolute). There is emphatically no (*ye ma yin*) meaning to that (consideration), to wit, whether one formulates the reasoning "Because the Buddha has so declared from the conventional standpoint" or formulates the reasoning "Because the Buddha has so declared from the absolute standpoint." That is, as previously discussed in terms of that partisan, it requires a positing (of a show of agreement) without making a distinction by way of either truth or falsehood of the factual base. Otherwise (i.e., positing a factual base distinguished as true or false while positing a show of agreement), when there is no proof to a particular one among the two adversaries, and one claims that the reason, example, etc. (in this case) is according to the position (of *ācārya* Bhāvaviveka), this amounts to such a coarse fallacy that this error is simply impossible for the accomplished pandit Bhāvaviveka!

Hence (since that *ācārya* is learned) he inquires whether the two truths are meant in that formulation (by the realist), "Because the Buddha has so declared"—and if it is conventional, since that side (realist) does not believe so (that the reason is conventional), it is not proved to himself (that opponent); while if it is absolute, our own position (Mādhyamika) denies that in the absolute sense the effects (the personal sense bases, etc.) that arise from a cause are present, absent, or both; so it is not proved to us (the Mādhyamika). This means that neither of the two truths is involved, and he does not believe they are. Therefore, it is not necessary (for *ācārya* Bhāvaviveka) to clarify this point.

In that regard, in the case of the reason "Because it is a factor of becoming" (for the thesis, earth lacks solidity in the absolute sense), if one asks whether the "factor of becoming" formulated in evidence is which one of the two (truths, conventional and absolute), it is like the foregoing; but if one asserts that the "factor of becoming" formulated in evidence goes with the two (truths), this person definitely misunderstands that partisan (the *pūrvapakṣa* of the *Prasannapadā,* i.e., the viewpoint of Bhāvaviveka). Accordingly, how can it be proper to say that, if one inquires about which one of the two truths, if it (the factor of becoming) is (termed) absolute (*paramārtha*) it is not proved to us (Mādhyamika), while if it is (termed) convention (*saṃvṛti*) it is not proved to the opponent (the realist)? It is not so (i.e., not proper to talk that way), because the personal sense bases that are posited as a fact (by the opponent) exist conventionally; and because they are not proved by those opponents (the realists).

However, as was exposed above (the reason not proved, etc.), how are we to consider the school accepted by Bhāvaviveka when he examines the two truths in the evidence (of the opponent)? I shall explain. Here, the *ācārya* (Candrakīrti), having intended the absolute (*paramārtha*) when (the entity) is arrived at with unmistaken awareness, and convention (*saṃvṛti*) when (the entity) is arrived at by mistaken awareness, (asks,) "Which of the two truths?" (He asks), "By which one of the two (mistaken awareness or unmistaken awareness) is it arrived at?" and thinks it is necessary to settle on a single essential. In this way, if the entity formulated in evidence is neither *saṃvṛti* nor *paramārtha,* it is necessary that the evidence (itself) be disproved. And if the entity formulated in evidence is not an entity arrived at by either unmistaken or mistaken awareness, it is necessary that the entity formulated in evidence be disproved. The reason is the same, and (the *Prasannapadā*) said that this one (Bhāvaviveka) himself admitted (that the reason "because of presence" is not proved), but he (Bhāvaviveka) does not so admit expressly (*dṅos su*). Therefore, in the passage (of the *Prasannapadā*) stating "with a reason alluding to a material feature" (i.e., alluding to a material accomplished by own-character) he (*ācārya* Candrakīrti) points to the isolation (*bkar nas*)[314] through witness of the material feature. Some of those evidences (such as the sense base of form and the factor of becoming) formulated by Bhāvaviveka himself are (demonstrated) definitely by unmistaken direct perception; and some (such as what cannot be demonstrated definitely by direct perception due to inaccessibility) are claimed in a syllogism about the ultimate to involve unmistaken direct perception. However, the *ācārya* (Candrakīrti) rejects it (i.e., such a syllogism's unmistaken direct perception). Moreover, as was previously cited (from the *Prasannapadā*), "It is not right for the Mādhyamika to make an independent inference of his own since he has no assumption of the opponent's side," i.e., it is not right to accept that the entity is accomplished by own-character. But the followers of *ācārya* Bhāvaviveka's position prove in syllogisms, citing such passages as "If he witnesses with direct perception . . . ," and saying that there is no authority to judge the own-character.

(2) HOW OUR SCHOOL DIFFERS THEREFROM

(Others may retort:) "Do not the faults you have expressed about the factual base (*dharmin*) and reason (*hetu*) being unproved in the inferences of the opponent, apply as well to your own inferences? (They indeed are the same!). Hence, you should not quarrel with others!"

(In reply:) The occurrence of those faults in others (Svātantrika and realists) happens through their acceptance of the Svātantrika inference. We (Prāsaṅgika-Mādhyamika) do not accept the Svātantrika inference, and so we do not have the faults mentioned (in the *Prasannapadā*). Here "inference" is to be understood as syllogism.[315]

In the case of the Svātantrika acceptance, one presumes a show of agreement of the two disputants with an authority of taking an own-character (*svalakṣaṇa*) as authoritative; and one must prove the thesis with a proof to both (disputants) that has the three marks (*pakṣadharma, anvaya,* and *vyatireka*). Accordingly, if that authority (with its syllogism) is absent, there is no proof of the factual base (*dharmin*), and so forth.

In the case of rejecting the Svātantrika, the opponent, the realist, is content to prove (the factual base, etc.) to himself with that sort of authority (having a show of agreement); but it is not necessary that he prove to himself with that (kind of) authority (*pramāṇa*).

Hence, the inferences occurring in the texts (such as the *Prasannapadā*) have the requirement only to refut the theses of the opponent and are the inferences acknowledged by others (the factual base, etc. demonstrated to others) but are not (the inferences of the) Svātantrika. An example of this (inference acknowledged by others) is in the *Mūla-Madhyamaka-kārikā,* chapter III (i.e., III, 2):

> The eyesight does not view its own self as that. Because it does not see itself, how can it see those others (the forms)?

Thus, it (the inference) is like taking as evidence that the eyesight does not view itself for proof that it does not view other things (forms). Not only is this (proposition) the evidence claimed by ourselves (Mādhyamikas), but also the thesis which others observe. Thus, the Mādhyamikas claim there is nonaccomplishment by own-nature, and such propositions (*prayoga*) are called "inference acknowledged by others."

Furthermore, the *Prasannapadā* (on chapter 1) states:[316]

> We (Prāsaṅgikas) do not apply independent inferences, because our inferences have the effect of merely refuting the (wayward) theses of the opponent.

This (passage by Candrakīrti) maintains that the formulations of proposition (belonging to the Prāsaṅgikas) are not independent (*svatantra*), but require the effect of merely refuting the opponent's thesis. Besides, the method of dispelling the thesis of that (opponent) after formulating a (Prāsaṅgika) proposition, is stated immediately after the foregoing passage (i.e., on chapter 1):[317]

It is this way: The opponent constructs (the thesis) "The eye sees," and is contradicted by an inference acknowledged by him (the realist). "You believe in the feature (*dharma*) of the eye that it does not witness itself, and you agree that ('The eye sees') does not occur in the absence of features of witness in the other (features such as blue and other colors of form). Therefore (to refute you, I make the following inference in syllogistic form):

"(Major premise:) In whatever (factual base) constituting the substratum) there is no witness of itself, in that (factual base) there is also no witness of another (the special features of blue, etc.).
"(Example:) Like a pot.
"(Minor premise:) There is in the eye (the factual base of the occasion) no witness of itself (as having features, *dharma*).
"(Conclusion:) Therefore the witness of (features of) the other, i.e., form, is lacking in this (the factual base, eye)."

Consequently, the witness of another, with blue, etc. is contradicted by the nonwitness of itself. And he (the realist) is contradicted by an inference acknowledged by himself.

(Here) there is the one essential of both the opponent's acknowledgment by himself, and what depends on the proponent Mādhyamika, the acknowledgment by the other.

This way of averting the wayward discursive thought (of the realist), through our school (the Prāsaṅgika) formulating a syllogism acknowledged by the other, is of great importance. So saying that it is "proven to him" when one explains it in detail, to wit, the factual bases (*dharmin*) of eye and of pot as example, the evidence (*liṅga*) that it does not see itself, and the thesis that it does not see the features (*dharma*) of blue, etc.—does not mean that the evidence, the pervasion (*vyāpti*), and so on, are proven only to the opponent (the realist), with our own school (the Prāsaṅgika) not accepting it, and only the opponent (realist) accepting it.

However, if one wonders how (it is "proven to him"), (it is this way:)

While those (the above two bases, etc.) are also accepted in our school (the Prāsaṅgika), the authority (*pramāṇa*) for proving them, with the thesis (*prameya*) of accomplishment by own-nature, and the resultant judgment (*pramiti*) are not in our school (the Prāsaṅgika) even conventionally. And the proof of those to one who believes they are present with self-existence certainly depends on that (sort of) authority proving them, so there is no authority with judgment of accomplishment by own-nature, proving in a show of agreement between the two (the Prāsaṅgika and the espouser of presence by self-existence); so it is not proven to both (schools), and it is said to be "acknowledged by the other" or "proven to the other."

(In regard to this, some others say:)—However, such an authority (which proves in a show of agreement) does not exist even conventionally. The claim to prove (the factual base, etc.) by means of that (authority) is an absurdity (*bādha*) by way of principle comparable to the (nescient) attribution of self-existence (*svabhāva*). That being so, how is the Mādhyamika view to be reached by recourse to those syllogisms, because if one could attain the errorless view by recourse to a reason that is absurd by way of authority, could one not also attain (the errorless view) with any of the wayward theory-systems (*siddhānta*)! (In response to that argument:)—This opponent (who espouses the presence of *svabhāva*) apprehends as present the "eye," the factual base (*dharmin*); that it "does not view itself," the reason; the example "pot" (a factual base);[318] that it "does not view (other things) such as blue, etc.," the feature (to be proved). But the objects (the eye, form, pot, etc.) are held in our school as well to be present conventionally, so there is no absurdity by way of principle toward those (objects). However, since that opponent does not distinguish between presence (of those objects) by own-nature and presence (of them, generally), he has an absurdity by way of principle toward the object along with conceit that he has proof by authority of assessing the thesis that those (objects) are accomplished by their own-nature. Indeed, how can the conventional awareness (which is the cause of error without a why and a wherefore[319]) of his (the opponent's) stream of consciousness prove without absurdities and oppose with a principle (the object, form, etc.)? (And it cannot). Hence, in both his school (which espouses the *svabhāva*) and our own school (the Prāsaṅgika) there is no acceptance in a show of agreement of authority to judge the thesis that there is accomplishment by own-nature. Since it is not proved by (the evidence of) our stream of consciousness, it serves only to show the contradition in an acceptance by the adversary and ourselves.

The way that (contradiction is exposed) is by exhibiting the syllogism that is acceptable to the other, as was previously formulated. Therein the factual base of eye (the substratum), for which there is a reason (a feature) that it does not view itself, is present conventionally. The (features of) viewing blue, accomplished by own-nature, are not present in that (substratum eye-factual base) even conventionally. That being the case, the former (feature based on the substratum eye-factual base, "does not view itself") serves to refute the latter (feature "views from its own side the other, form"). But that reason ("does not view itself") in that eye and the feature to be refuted ("views from its own side the other, form") if both present, are present equally; and if absent, turn into equal absence; so how is it feasible (to posit) those two—the refuting agent (i.e., the evidence) and the refutee (the feature to be refuted)!

Thus, while it is necessary that there be present conventionally the syllogism's factual base (*dharmin*) respected by the other, the feature (*dharma*) (to be proved), and the evidence (*liṅga*) (which proves), it does not suffice for only the adversary to accept them as present.

But since he himself (i.e., the adversary) accepts as present those (objects), the eye-factual base, etc., why is it necessary for the Mādhyamika to prove them (the eye-factual base, etc.) (to him)! (And it is not necessary). And if he, falsely disclaiming that (acceptance), were to demand of us, "Prove them (the eye-factual base, etc.) because they are not proved!" since it is fruitless to argue with those theologians who unfailingly falsely disclaim, what is the use for anyone to have them as associates (in a debate)?

In this (context) some persons say:—If you would show that it is a contradiction for the opponent (the espouser of *svabhāva*) to believe in both *a*) that (the eye-factual base) does not view itself, and *b*) that the view of blue, etc. is toward a presence of self-existence (*svabhāva*) accomplished by own-nature—then on what (grounds) (pray tell) does one know there is a contradiction? A proof with the (opponent's) authority that there is a contradiction requires proving (that contradiction) to both (schools, the Prāsaṅgika and the opponent's), but you are unable to engage in (the inference of) what is called "acknowledged by others." If the opponent indicates the contradiction by his acceptance, and claims that the two—not viewing itself, and viewing something else (that has an own-nature)—do not constitute a contradiction, it is not valid to point to a contradiction by his (the opponent's) acceptance. (Moreover,) our school (the Prāsaṅgika) accepts that there is a contradiction (of those two), so it is ridiculous to indicate (to the opponent that there is a contradiction). (That being the case), how is it proper to say to the opponent, "You are not right in claiming that there is no contradiction between these two, because we accept that these two are in contradiction"?

(We reply:) The fault (you mention is yours), not (ours). The contradiction between (the eye's) not viewing itself and the presence of self-existence accomplished by own-nature, is proven by authority (*pramāṇa*) and is not established merely by the opponent's acceptance. However, while it suffices for us to render certain the contradiction by pointing out to the opponent that authority (which proves that sort of contradiction), it is questioned why it is necessary to take recourse to his acceptance. (In reply to that):—The proof with authority of syllogism that the realist has a contradiction on his side depends on proving the judgment of the thesis that there is accomplishment by own-nature; and if that (proof of the judgment) is not present (on the opponent's side), how is our side (the Prāsaṅgika) going to prove that contradiction (to the opponent) by accepting that (judgment)! (And it is not possible to prove it). And if the thing to be proved (with that authority) be that there is not self-existence accomplished by own-nature, and one has finished proving to him (the realist) that it is not the authority itself which is contradictory, and then proves with that sort of authority (the contradiction to him), whereupon he receives the view which understands that the *dharmas* are without self-existence, why is it necessary to prove the contradiction by saying, "Since it does not view itself, it is a contradiction that it views something accomplished by own-nature"! Hence, if one would hold the understanding of Candrakīrti's school, he must examine those (essential points) in detail and must come to comprehend (those essentials)!

Suppose it be asked: Well, given that the opponent (the realist) takes recourse to his personal acknowledgment, then how is one to teach him that when something does not view itself and views another it is the manner pervaded by no accomplishment by own-nature? I shall explain that according to the *Buddhapālita-vṛtti*.[320] The witness that earth is moistened by having water, that water is heated by having fire, that clothing is perfumed by having the jāti flower (the Jasmicum grandiflora), requires a dependence on the witness that the three things, water, etc. (i.e., water, fire, and the jāti flower) have the three things, moisture, etc. (i.e., moisture, heat, and perfume). Observing that, if there were any entities with self-existence accomplished by own-nature according to the claim of your own school, it would be necessary for that self-existence to (first) have witness of itself and then for (the entity) possessed of that (witness) to witness another (feature). If at first that (self-existence accomplished by own-nature) does not have witness of itself, how is (the entity) possessed of that (nonwitness) to see something else? (And it does not see it.) For example, an unpleasant smell is not noticed at the jāti-flower, and so a stench is not noticed in clothing possessed of that (jāti flower). It is like that. The opponent (the realist), having by these illustrations of presence in similar cases (*anvaya*) and absence in dissimilar cases (*vyatireka*) become convinced, with the validity acknowledged to himself, then the attaching to the meaning of the context is as follows: thus, if there is a self-existence in what the eye sees, at first (the eye) would view and notice itself, and then view (objects), forms, etc. and forms in aggregates; and there would be a validity in the noticing. (But) because the eye does not view itself, it also does not view forms (by way of own-nature). Such is the teaching. That is also stated in the *Catuḥ-ś* (k. 316 = XIII, 16):[321]

Were the self-existence (*svabhāva*) of any entity (*bhāva*) to be first noticed in itself, then why would not the thing perceived by the eye arise in the eye!

If he argues, "In the same way as the fire does not burn itself but burns something else, so also the eye which does not see itself views something else, and there is no contradiction," we reply:—(In this context) we are not denying in general the mere burning of fuel by fire and the mere viewing of form by the eye; but we deny that when the eye views something else, that it is present by virtue of own-nature. When that is the case, it is necessary to take as example the burning of fuel by the fire, with accomplishment by own-nature; and at that time (of taking the example) the thesis (the accomplishment by own-nature of what is viewed by the eye) is also accordingly not valid. It is this way:—If both the fire and fuel have a self-existence accomplished by own-nature they have not transcended a single self-existence or two distinct self-existences, and hence are one or other of those two. If a single (self-existence), fire would burn itself, and besides (if fire and fuel have a single self-existence) how would fire be the burner and fuel the thing burnt! And if they be (that way), we announce, "Fire would be burnt, and fuel would do the burning!" And what answer do you have (if those two are by way of *svabhāva*)? But if (the fire and fuel) have a diverse *svabhāva,* then even in the absence of a fuel, a fire would be noticed, just as (by reason of diversity of *svabhāva*) a cow is noticed in the absence of a horse. That is also stated in the *Catuḥ-ś* (k. 341 = XIV, 16):[322]

Heat is precisely fire. How could it (i.e., fire) burn without heat? Hence,[323] there is no "fuel" (without fire), and in the absence of that (fuel), there is no fire.

Accordingly, given the acceptance of a self-existence accomplished by own-nature in that burning, if (that fire) does not burn itself, it also does not burn something else (fuel, etc.). Along the same lines, given the acceptance of a self-existence in that eye, if (that eye) does not view itself, it also does not view something else (i.e., form). It is necessary to maintain that, so that he is not swung by the former fault.

Thus, when he sees the acceptance of self-existence as ridiculous teachings, he repudiates the (realist) theory-system that maintains the presence of self-existence accomplished by own-nature. Thereupon, he is also able to comprehend the validity of functioning (of arising, decease, etc.) when there is no self-existence. So he distinguishes between absence of self-existence and absence (generally), and therefore also distinguishes between presence by reason of self-existence and presence (generally). Hence, that (opponent) also comes to comprehend the thesis of no self-existence, the judgment by authority of no self-existence, and so forth.

The question may be raised, though if it is necessary for this (opponent) who has comprehended the non-self-existence of fire and the fuel, to believe in the authority in the sense of an inference without validation of direct perception, of what sort is the reason having that (authority) as a basis? (In reply:)—When that (opponent) has observed that were there self-existence it has not gone beyond a single one or distinct ones, when the self-existence as single or distinct baffles him, he comes to observe the pervasion by no self-existence. That is, it is proved (to him) by the two marks (i.e., presence in similar cases, absence in dissimilar cases), and his certainty that there is no single or multiple self-existence is the method of "premise feature" (*pakṣa-dharma*), to wit, when he comprehends the three marks. And when he takes recourse to that (reason), his certainty of thinking that there is no self-existence in that (substratum fact), fire and fuel is the inference. By this (way of generating certainty), one may understand the syllogism acknowledged by another, as was formulated above (i.e., the eye does not see form with own-nature, because it does not see itself, for example, like a pot), and also the method of generating the inference with the three marks.

The Prāsangika formulates the opponent's acceptance into evidence, to wit, "If there is a self-existence in the fire and the fuel, it is proper that they are single by way of self-existence or multiple by way of self-existence," and "If single, the fire would burn itself," and so on. And illustrates to the opponent with these sorts of considerations what is the wrong belief, so that he will understand still other confutations.

Accordingly, as long as the opponent does not repudiate the realist theory-system, for that long he proves in an authority which proves the entity by depending on the proof of the judgment of thesis that there is accomplishment by own-nature. But at whatever time he comprehends with an authority that any entity is not accomplished by own-nature, he repudiates the realist theory-system. (In this connection), the *Prasannapadā* (on chapter I) also remarks:[324]

(Others say:) Well then, is there an absurdity (to the opponent) of inference in the case of an inference demonstrated to just one of the two (disputants)? Yes, there is (an absurdity), by way of a reason proved (acknowledged) by himself (the opponent who espouses the presence of self-existence), but not (an absurdity to the opponent) when proved by the other (partisan of the Mādhyamika school)—as can be observed in everyday life. (For example,) in common life sometimes a referee is appointed by both a disputant and his opponent, and by the (referee's) decision someone (among the two parties) wins or loses. But never does one win or lose by the disputant's say-so (alone) or by his opponent's say-so (alone). As it is in common life, so it is in the life of reason, because worldly conventions are the point of view in the treatises concerned with (examination by) reasons (for acceptance).

That sets forth both *a*) an example suitable as evidence (in the Prāsaṇgika school) and acknowledged by the other (i.e., the opponent), and b) a precept.[325] And it states that whatever the authority among the opponent logicians, it is necessary for both the disputant and his opponent to prove with that authority that proves the three marks, etc., and that for refuting a belief it is necessary to prove to both the disputant and his opponent. The same work states (on chapter I):[326]

Whoever thinks that whatever (i.e., mark, etc. of the reason) be expressed with certainty (i.e., proved) to both disputants, it is a proof or a refutation, but that whatever one be proved to only one of the two disputants or be expressed with doubt, it cannot be (a proof or a refutation)—he (forsaking that Svātantrika way and adopting our Prāsaṅgika manner) should accept the reasoning as expressed (previously in the *Prasannapadā,* chapter I) in an inference adhering to worldy establishment (as cited above). It is this way: The absurdity through scripture is not only by way of a scripture proved to both (disputants). Well, then, by what (other)? Also (an absurdity) by way of (the opponent's) proof by himself. In the case of inference for one's own sake, in every situation the proof by oneself is more weighty (or more dear); but the proof (in a show of agreement) to both disputants is not (more weighty). For that very reason, there is no necessity to bespeak the characteristics (a reason, etc.) of logic (in the manner of the Svātantrika). The Buddhas, so as to assist persons to be trained who did not know these characteristics, used principles according to what would be individually convincing (to each trainee).[327]

Accordingly (i.e., the above explanation), the proof of the thesis by an evidence demonstrated to both disputants, with an authority of the kind explained above, is (called) "the Svātantrika's evidence"; and because it is not proved by that (i.e., by that sort of evidence), this proof of the thesis by the three marks acknowledged by the other, the opponent—which is posited as the Prāsaṅgika, is the exceedingly clear (i.e., the "clear worded," *Prasannapadā*) in the purport of the *ācārya* (Candrakīrti).

2. WHICH ONE OF THE TWO ONE SHOULD FOLLOW TO GENERATE THE VIEW IN THE STREAM OF CONSCIOUSNESS

Thus, in those (explanations above) of the great Mādhyamika following the *ārya* father and sons (Nāgārjuna and Āryadeva, etc.), there are two different schools, the Prāsaṅgika and the Svātantrika. One may wonder which of those two one should follow. Here we embrace the school of Prāsaṅgika.

Moreover (as to this embrace of Prāsaṅgika), as previously explained, one rejects a self-existence accomplished by own-nature, even conventionally. It is necessary to reject that so as to validate all establishment of *saṃsāra-nirvāṇa*. So one should gain certainty about those two methods.

(Moreover, as to those methods), if one accepts that entities have a self-existence accomplished by own-nature, one must engage in an examination by a principle of pondering how (those entities) exist (that way). There is much said on this matter in the texts of the two ācaryas (Buddhapālita and Candrakīrti), which are observed to be quite consistent with the texts of the noble father and sons (i.e., *Mūla-Madhyamaka-k, Catuḥ-ś.*, etc.) so one should accept that school (i.e., of the two *ācāryas*). And (the acceptance of that school) being the case, then according to the above explanations, there is certainly the requirement to accept this Prāsaṅgika side.

C. Relying on This Agent, the Method of Generating the View in Consciousness

There are three parts to this: 1. Establishing the nonself of personality (*pudgala*); 2. Establishing the nonself of feature (*dharma*); 3. Method of eliminating obscuration by cultivating those views.

1. ESTABLISHING THE NONSELF OF PERSONALITY

This has a triple division: a. Basic establishment that there is no self-existence of self; b. thereby showing that what belongs to self also arises without self-existence; c. the method of adding other principles.

a. Basic Establishment That There Is No Self-existence of Self

This has two parts: (1) Formulating the example; (2) Adding the meaning.

(1) FORMULATING THE EXAMPLE

As a *sūtra* is cited in *Madhyamakāvatara* (under VI, 135):[328]

'I' is a thought of Māra. You have become a view (that clings). This (fivefold) heap of constructions (*saṃskāra*) is void. In this there is no sentient being. Just as, based on a set of members one speaks of a "chariot," so also, based on the heaps (*skandha*) one conventionally speaks of a "sentient being."

That passage takes as example the designation of chariot, based on its members, wheel, etc. and then mentions the designation of sentient being or self, also based on aggregates (*skandha*). Therefore, first I shall explain the example of chariot. There are four parts to this: (a) Showing the chariot as a designation without self-existence; (b) Eliminating the argument about that; (c) Method of demonstration by way of distinction of names; (d) Based on that, the speedy benefit of attaining the view.

(a) Showing the Chariot as a Designation without Self-existence

The *Avatāra* (VI, 151) states:

One cannot believe that a chariot is different from its members. Nor that it is nondifferent. It is not possessed of those (members). It is not in those members; those members are not in it. It is not just an assemblage (of members), nor their shape.

This sets forth (that when one searches for) the identity or difference of the chariot from its members, there is negation in seven ways, so (the chariot) is only a designation; and in the same way, in the case of self and aggregate (searched in seven ways by identity or difference), it (the self) is like that (chariot, i.e., also only a designation).

In this (context of example), if the chariot had a self-existence accomplished by own-nature, doubtless it would be identical or different, etc. (from its members in regard to self-existence), in those seven ways as appropriate; it is necessary to demonstrate (i.e., find) this by a principle which ponders the presence or absence of self-existence. But because it is not demonstrated by that (principle) in any of those seven (ways), it follows that (the chariot) has no self-existence (accomplished by own nature). In that (pondering), the members of the chariot are the axle, the wheels, pegs, and so on. The chariot does not have an identical self-existence with those members. If it were identical, then since those members are multiple the chariot would also be multiple; and (on top of that), since the chariot is single, those members would have to be one, and there would be other faults (if the possessor of members and the members were one), such as the agent and the *karma* of activity also becoming one.

Furthermore, the chariot does not have a dissociated accomplishment by own-nature, from its members. If it had (dissociation), then like the flask and the fine cloth (which are mutually dissociated), they would be noticed separately in individual relief;[329] but they are not noticed (in dissociation), and the designation "chariot" has no (substratum) basis.

(Examining) as two sides the support and thing supported, the chariot is not a support for its members like a dish in which curds are placed; and the chariot is not supported by its members, like Devadatta in his warrior's gear; because in both cases they would be diversified by own-nature, and demonstrably the chariot is not that way. Moreover, in this (case of examining the support and thing supported) we do not reject their mere mutual presence, but we do reject the accomplishment by own-character (*svalakṣaṇa*) of the support and thing supported. The opponent (who espouses the presence of self-existence) demonstrates those (the chariot and its members) as support and thing supported by way of own-character (thereby falling into the extreme of eternalism), but those two examples that have been mentioned are formulated as an acknowledgment by the other. One should know that in all similar situations, (those examples have been applied) the same way.

Also, the possession possibility is not valid, as follows:—If one claims that the chariot possesses its members, like Devadatta possesses cows who serve a different purpose (from himself), then just as how the cows and Devadatta are apprehended separately, so also it is necessary that the chariot and its members be apprehended separately; and because they are not thus apprehended (separately), there is accordingly no possession (by the chariot of its members). (But you retort)—"How about Devadatta's possessing an ear?" In the sense (of this example) the chariot's possession of members is also not cogent, because we have already refuted a difference of self-existence, and because we have previously refuted that method of possessing something accomplished by own-nature which is the position of an identical self-existence.[330] As to this (method of rejection), just as we do not reject presence conventionally of Devadatta's mere possession of an ear, so the chariot also is present, wherefor the rejection is of its possessing (members) accomplished by own-character.

There are two remaining possibilities (i.e., that the chariot is an assemblage of parts, or their shape). (From the *Avatāra,* VI, 152):

If the chariot were only an assemblage, in this case the chariot would be in fragments, for which reason the members would lack a member possessor. Since that is not so, it is also not right (to posit) a mere shape as the chariot.

This passage considers the chariot both as a mere collection of members and as the distinction of the shape of the members. Among them, that the chariot is just an assemblage of its members is also not valid, as is shown in two ways (γ and ω).

γ. The contradiction with evidence is as follows: Having dissected the members into wheel, etc., it is when the assemblage lacks incompleteness of the fragments that the chariot is present (as previously seen), because only the assemblage of members is the chariot (i.e., just a heap of the members, provided they are all there, is enough to constitute a chariot).

ω. The contradiction with acceptance is as follows:

ω-1. In this (context of example), the realists among the Buddhists claim there is no possessor of the members, but only an assemblage of members; and that it is that way because, when the members are absent, there is no possessor of members. Well, in that case, not only is there no chariot when the assemblage is absent, but also there is no chariot when the collection is present.

ω-2. In regard to that rejection of the chariot being only a collection of its members, in the opinion of this *ācārya* (Candrakīrti) it is not necessary to add distinctions (such as "by reason of self-existence," "on its own side," and "by reason of own nature"), because that collection (of members of the chariot) is the substratum (*gźi*) for the designation of chariot; and because he says that the collection of *skandhas* is the substratum for the designation of self, and that this collection is not valid for (establishing) a self.

If (one says) he does not claim that the chariot is just a collection of members, but thinks that the distinction of shape (*saṃsthāna*) at the time when the members are arranged posits the chariot—then as explained above, because it is a belief (held by the realist) that there is no possessor of the members, it follows that there are no members either, so it is not right to posit as the chariot just the shape of the members. And such a fault is in contradiction with his own (realistic) acceptance. The word "also" (in the phrase "it is also not right," *Avatāra,* VI, 152) means that a mere assemblage does not exhaust the improper positions regarding the chariot.

Moreover, if you (the realist) claim that kind of shape as the chariot, then is your claim for the chariot that the shape is of separated members (ω), or that the shape is of a collection of members (ω)?

In the first case, either (γ-1) the shape has no distinction from the shape of the time previous to arrangement, or (γ-2) it is another shape differing from the former shape.

γ-1. In the first subcase, (the *Avatāra,* VI, 153) teaches the fault in these words:

> (As to the claim which) you (the realist) have of the shape, if when (after arrangement) each member belongs to the chariot in the same manner (as part of the same shape) as it did previously (before arrangement), then the chariot is not present (after arrangement) in the same manner as (it was not present) in those isolated parts (before the members were arranged).

Now, since there is no distinction of difference between the shape of the wheels and other members in the prior time when they are not arranged and (the shape) in the later time when they are arranged, then just as there is no chariot at the time when it is dissected (into its parts), so also there is no chariot at the time of arranging (those parts).

γ-2 (second subcase). If the shape of those members, wheel, etc. at the prior time when they are not arranged, is different from the shape at the later time when those members are arranged, is a chariot posited? (The *Avatāra,* VI, 154) states the fault:

> If the shape of the wheels, etc. were (formerly) different from the state of chariot at the present time, that (difference of shape) would be perceived (by way of eye awareness), but that (perception) does not happen. Therefore, a mere shape (of separate chariot members) does not exist as a chariot.

If there were another distinction of different shape of the wheels, axle, etc. at a prior and a later time (such as unarranged at both times or arranged at both times), it would necessarily be witnessed, and however looked at, there is no witness of such, so it is not right that a chariot has a later shape different from the prior shape (of the members).

γ. If he does not claim that diverse shapes of members constitute diverse chariots, but thinks to establish as the chariot that generality (*spyi*) of shape of the (material) collection of members, (the *Avatāra,* VI, 155) also states this to be a fault:

Since the collection according to you (the realist) is (held to be) nothing,[331] this shape is not of a collection of members. In this (situation), how could anything like a shape be based on nothing?

It is not proper for a shape based on a collection in this way (i.e., with this fault) be (established as) a chariot, because the designation as shape is (surely) not valid as based on a collection where the collection (of members) is not accomplished materially, and because you have accepted the substantiality of the designating substratum of all imaginary presences.[332] The collection of members is free from material or of a self-existence accomplished by own-nature; because, if there were a self-existence (of that sort) the members of the collection-possessor would not go beyond a single self-existence or a multiple one, as the case may be, and if those (the single or multiple possibilities) are claimed, it can be refuted in the same manner as previously explained (in the section) regarding the chariot.

In our school (the Prāsaṅgika), which does not believe in the substantiality of the designating substratum of imaginary presence, there is (only) a designating substratum of the chariot, to wit, the shape of the collection of members, but we do not maintain this (i.e., such a shape) to be the chariot since it (the chariot) is an imaginary feature (*btags chos*) attributed to this (shape of the collection). Therefore, it is not necessary to add a distinction ("by reason of self-existence," etc.) to the refutable, to wit, rejecting that this shape of the collection is the chariot.

If you (the realist) claim there is no invalidity in designating the truthless (imaginary) collection as the truthless (imaginary) shape (of the chariot) which is based on that (collection as the designating substratum), in that event it would be necessary to claim there is no invalidity in a truthless cause of nescience, seed, etc. and in all the truthless fruit of motivations, shoot, etc. arising in dependence on (that cause),[333] according to what is said (*Avatāra,* VI, 156):

In the manner in which you (the realist) claim this (designation), you should know that all truthless *svabhāvin(s)* with the (respective) aspects of fruit would arise in dependence on truthless causes.

This example of the chariot also refutes the establishing of pots and other entities when there is just the collection of eight "atoms" of form, etc. i.e., form, odor, taste, tangible; earth, water, fire, wind); and, moreover (this example of the chariot) refutes the theory of designating pots, etc. based on the eight "atoms" materially accomplished, as well as (designating) the distinction of shape of materially accomplished form, etc. (constituting the designating substratum) and pot, etc. (constituting the imaginary feature)—because those things, form, etc. have no self-existence, since they do not (i.e., get accomplished) by means of self-existence; and because there is no validity in material accomplishment. Along the same lines the *Avatāra* (VI, 157) states:

By this (example of chariot), neither is there a reason to have the notion of "pot" in regard to form (and other "atoms") thus cohering. Because they do not arise (by reason of self-existence), form and the others are not present. And for that reason, it is not right (to posit) the shape (constituted by form and other "atoms") of those (entities such as pots).

(In that regard, the opponent) considers: If, like the chariot, the pot had no shape of the collection of its own members, then such things as "pot belly" would have no characteristic of that (pot), because those (things) like a (pot belly) do have a shape. (But there is no fault in the *Avatāra*'s position):—We believe that any "pot-belly," long-neck, etc. is a pot (as far as measurement is concerned), but we do not maintain that the shape of a "pot-belly" and so on, is a pot; otherwise it would be necessary to believe also that a belly and a neck (are a pot).

(b) Eliminating the Argument about That

In this (context), some realists say: If one searches the chariot by seven ways in the manner above decribed with a principle of examining the presence or absence of self-existence, there must be no chariot if it cannot be found thereby. That being so, it should be that in the world, designations of a chariot are not made conventionally. But that is not valid. One notices such (conventional expressions) as, "Fetch me a chariot!" "Buy (the chariot)!" "Build (a chariot)!" For that reason, do not such entities as chariots have existence? In reply to this, the *Avatāra-Comm.* states two ways (γ and ω)—that the fault is only among the realists,[334] and that it is not among us (the Prāsaṅgika).

γ. First (the way that the fault lies with the realists): When you (the realist) resort to mundane conventions of the type "Fetch me a chariot!" it must not be there. The entities which you have posited are not there with self-existence when sought by a principle, because when one demonstrates with an examination and searches with the principle even in the seven ways one cannot find a chariot; and because you do not accept any other means for demonstrating that entity, since there is no chariot there.

Nowadays (in Tibet) some persons who claim to espouse the Mādhyamika meaning and claim to be in the Mādhyamika school (of the Prāsaṅgika), adopt the realist argument, saying, "At the time one searches with a principle of searching for the presence or absence by self-existence, and thereby does not find a chariot, then a chariot is not present." Undoubtedly, the theories of this sort fall into the fault that they are unable to make any conventional establishments.

ω. (Second): The way there is not the (aforementioned) fault among us (the Prāsaṅgika) is held (by ācārya Candrakīrti himself) as taught by this passage (the *Avatāra,* VI, 158):

> While this (chariot) is not demonstrated in the sense of reality or in (conventions of) the world by any of those seven manners, still according to the world which does not do that pondering, (the chariot) is designated on the basis of its own members.

This is the meaning of the passage: If one searches with a principle of search for the presence or absence of self-existence, and by any of those seven manners does not find the chariot, this is (so) in the two truths equally. Consequently, how is the chariot a problem when not found by a principle in terms of those seven? That being the case, the acceptance of the chariot is not from the demonstration by a principle of examining the presence or absence of self-existence, but it is only the mundane, conventional awareness, autonomous, not engaging in the principle's examination, that demonstrates (the chariot) as free from absurdity. Hence, the way of demonstrating it (i.e., the chariot) proves it to be (only) a figment, imagined by reliance on its members.

Suppose a yogin, examining (the chariot) that way (in seven manners) by a principle, does not find a chariot, should think that although that (chariot) has no self-existence accomplished by own nature, still its members (the wheels, etc.) have a self-existence. (In reply:)—You, searching for the threads in the ashes of a burnt-up cloth, merit scornful laughter—as the *Avatāra* (VI, 161a–b) says:

If there is no existence of the chariot,
then in the absence of the one having members,
the members are also absent.

Because if there is no member possessor, there are also no members.

If (you say): That's not valid, because one witnesses the set of members, the wheels, etc., even when a chariot is broken up, (we reply):—It's not that way (as you claim). You only saw the chariot previously (when the members were arranged). (Later) you apprehend those things, wheels, etc. and think they are (parts of) a chariot, but other persons (who did not previously see the chariot) do not apprehend (the pieces) that way (as members of a chariot). At the time the chariot is broken up, the wheels and so on are dissociated from the chariot, and so they are not members of the chariot. Therefore, there is no possibility of chariot members being present, as there is no chariot which possesses the members. At the time (of chariot breakup) there are neither members nor member possessor (to be established) by way of a chariot. But also the wheels, and so on, are themselves member possessors by dependence on their parts (i.e., a wheel possesses spokes, rim, and nave); and since those parts are members of a nonexistence member possessor. Moreover, the meaning of no members in the event of no member-possessor may be understood according to the example stated (in the *Avatāra,* VI, 161c–d):

Just like the example of members not existing when the chariot is burnt up, so also the members when the member possessor is consumed by the fire of intelligence (analyzing those members).

(c) Method of Demonstration by way of Distinction of Names

It is as said in the *Avatāra-Comm.:*

In our position (that of the Prāsaṅgika) we do not rest with just demonstrating clearly the conventional designation of the chariot by way of acknowledgment in the world, but we must also accept the distinction of its names, whatever they be, by way of acknowledgment in the world which does not engage (in the principle of examining the chariot). These are the names (*Avatāra,* 159a–c): "The same chariot is a member possessor (*aṅgin*), a composite (*avayavin,* 'which has parts'); the same one is called 'agent' in the world; men designate it a grasper (*upādātar*)."

Thus, the chariot is designated in conventional meaning as a "member possessor" and a "composite" with respect to its members of wheel, etc. It is also designated in terms of the grasper, using "agent" and "grasper" in consideration of the grasping of wheel, etc.

Also, some (realist) persons within Buddhism, for whom there is only the collection of members and of parts, because they do not observe any different thing beyond those, say that there is no member possessor or composite; and, along the same lines, say there is only action (*karma*) and no agent; and because they do not observe any different thing beyond the grasping (part), say there is only grasping and no grasper. Those remarks are wayward in worldly convention (*saṃvṛti*), because if it were that way (as you, the realist, claim), also there would be no members, etc. With that purport, the *Avatāra* (VI, 159d) states: "Do not smash the convention acknowledged in the world!"

Hence, in the absolute sense, there are no members and so on, just as there are no member possessors, and so on; while in the conventional sense, there are member possessors, and so on, just as there are members, and so on. Saying this involves no falling away from the method of the two truths.

(d) Based on That, the Speedy Benefit of Attaining the View

The *Avatāra-Comm.* says:

Since when one examines that way (with a principle) the convention (*saṃvṛti*) of the world, it is not present; and since by acknowledgment (in the world) which does not examine (with a principle), that same thing is present—it follows that the yogin, when examining this (convention) in the same sequence (i.e., as to when it is present and when not present), will speedily plumb the depth of reality. How (can he plumb the depth)? (The *Avatāra,* VI, 160) states: "That which is not present in any of seven manners, how could it be termed 'present'? The yogin does not find the presence of this (chariot), and by that (above sequence) he also easily enters into reality, so one should believe, in this (phase of Prāsaṅgika), according to the demonstration concerning that (chariot)."

This sets forth that by means of the kind of examination of the chariot (i.e., in seven manners), one speedily plumbs the depth of the meaning of reality or of non-self-existence, so this is indeed a crucial point.

Accordingly, the yogin who is examining the manner of presence (of the features, *chos*) (thinks:)—If the "chariot" were something accomplished by self-existence, doubtless when investigating (this chariot) by the principle of search of the presence or absence of self-existence by way of the seven manners, to wit, identical, different, etc. one should find it in one or other of these seven manners, but it is never found in any of those (seven).

Even though he does not find the chariot by that (method), (the yogin) has no need to disavow the convention of a chariot. When he has the certainty to think:—"The 'chariot' is a figment produced only when the eye of discrimination[335] is impaired by the caul of nescience, and it is not accomplished by self-existence," then that yogin easily enters reality. The word "also" in that phrase "by that also into reality" (*Avatāra,* VI, 160) teaches that convention is also not impaired (when he "also" enters into reality).[336] The method of deciding the alternatives when denying the presence of self-existence in the chariot is the examination in the seven manners. This (method) is quite clear, and the principle of denying (the alternatives) is also very clear, so by recourse to this (principle) it is easy to comprehend the no self-existence of the chariot.

In short, there are three virtues in doing this establishment in the manner explained above for engaging with the chariot: α) the virtue of ease in refuting the eternalist view that attributes self-existence to the features (*dharma*); β) the virtue of ease in refuting the nihilist view that thinks there is no validity in dependent origination when there is no self-existence; γ) The sequence of the yogin's consideration which thus is fulfilled by how he performs the examination of those two virtues.

α. First: With denial of only identity and difference as the method of denying the presence of self-existence, it is difficult to comprehend when curtailed and troublesome when protracted. But the examination by way of the seven manners is exemplary.[337]

β. Second: At the time of initial refutation (of the substratum's form, arising, etc.) one adds a qualification to the refutable things and refutes. So by that gateway, even though denying the presence of self-existence, there is no negating the presence of conventional performance.

γ. Third: When the thing pervaded is the accomplishment by self-existence, and the pervader is the seven kinds (or, alternatives), namely, identity, difference, etc. and one draws certainty that is not exterior to (one or other of those seven), he shows the absurdity in each of those (seven). At that time he sees the objection descend into whatever one of those seven (is being considered). With the knot of the pervader he first ties the thing pervaded in a knot, and again and again draws certainty that cuts the cord in (the meaning of) non-self-existence. After that, when he notices that even though there is no self-existence he has no need to disavow a conventionality of the chariot, he thinks, "Oh, how marvelous is this illusion of the chariot and the other things that are created by the magician who is *karma* and defilement! It is this way that there is nothing at all wrong in each thing arising (in sequence) from causes and conditions; and also because there is no self-existence at all accomplished by its individual nature." Thus, he (the yogin who has rejected the two extremes) will (easily) obtain the certainty that the meaning of dependent origination is that things do not arise by reason of self-existence. It is just as stated in the *Catuḥ-ś:*[338]

Pots and other things do not occur from their own cause when investigated by that very (substratum) and by a different (substratum). Despite its being that way, honey-water and other things do occur by designation in dependence (on a substratum) which is suitable for effecting the activity of holding (the honey-water) or of scooping it up. Is this not wonderful!.

And:[339]

Of whatever (entity) there is no self-existence, it is perceptively reached and is void of self-existence like a whirling firebrand (which gives the illusion of a solid ring).[340]

(2) ADDING THE MEANING

There are two parts to it: (a) Adding the meaning to the method of no self-existence; (b) Adding the meaning to the method of demonstrating by way of the distinction of names.

(a) Adding the Meaning to the Method of No Self-existence

This has four sections: (i) Refuting the position that self is identical with the aggregates; (ii) Refuting the position that self is different from the aggregates; (iii) Hence, the remaining positions become the problem; (iv) Based thereon, the method by which a personality rises like an illusion.

(i) Refuting the Position That Self Is Identical with the Aggregates

In general, one observes in the world (i.e., acknowledged conventionally) that when there is a decision by the intellect (*buddhi*) along with a partner,[341] it is a decision involving the one lacking a partner; and when there is a decision (by it) lacking a partner, it is a decision involving the one along with a partner. Hence, in general one denies a third possibility for identity and difference, or singleness and multiplicity, because "along with a partner" and "lacking a partner" are (respectively) multiple or single.

In general, when there is a unanimity concerning whether there is singleness or nonsingleness, there is also a unanimity concerning whether there is identity or difference accomplished by own-nature in diversity. Accordingly, if there were a self-existence accomplished by own-nature in the sense of the self or personality it would not be outside of identity and difference. So one should examine, thinking whether this self is identical with its personality aggregates while accomplished by its own-nature, or is different from it while accomplished by own-nature. In the course of that (examination of two alternatives) the yogin, thinking, "Is there any absurdity at the outset in demonstrating an identity by way of self-existence of the pair, self and personality aggregates?" should search out whatever be the incongruity in this position of identity. In this regard, *ācārya* Buddhapālita has stated three incongruities, to wit, α the meaninglessness of holding that there is a self, β there would be multiple selves, and γ it would have birth and decease.

α Among those, the first one: if one believes in a single self-existence for both self and aggregates, there is no sense in accepting a self, because it would only be a synonym of the aggregates, for example, like the moon and the "rabbit-possessor." This is mentioned in the *Mūla-Prajñā,* for we read in chapter XXVII (verse 5):

At the time you formulate, "There is no self apart from the grasping (aggregate)," (do you mean) that very grasping (aggregate) is the self? Well, then, your so-called "self" does not exist (for it is just a name for the aggregates)!

β Second: if it could be demonstrated that the self and the aggregates have an identical self-existence, then there would be the fault that there is a multiplicity of selves; and if there is no more than a single self, so also there would be only a single aggregate (but Buddhism recognizes five of them). The *Avatāra* (VI, 127a–b)[342] also states it: "If the aggregates were the self, then on account of their multiplicity, there would be multiple selves."

γ Third: chapter XVIII (of *Mūla-Prajñā,* verse 1a-b) states: "If the self were the aggregates, it would be subject to birth and decease." And chapter XXVII (verse 6a-b) states: "The grasping (aggregate) is not the self, (otherwise) it (the self) would arise (one moment) and pass away (the next moment), (as do the aggregates).[343] In this (context), "grasping" should be understood as the personality aggregates (*skandha*).

Now, if one should wonder how in that way there is a fault if one believes that the self is subject to momentary arising and decease, in that regard the *Avatāra-Comm.* sets forth three faults, to wit, *γ*-1 the invalidity of remembering a life, *γ*-2 the wasting of *karma* performed, *γ*-3 the encounter with *karma* not performed.

γ-1. First: Now, if the self were momentarily to arise and pass away, the self would arise and pass away by accomplishment through own-nature, so the self would be diversified by the own-character (*svalakṣaṇa*) of former and later (moments). In that case, he (the Teacher, the Buddha) would not have said, "In that life, at that time I was the King Māndhātṛ,"[344] because there would be diversity, accomplished by own-character, the two, the self of (King) Māndhātṛ and the self of the Teacher. For example, it is like the nonmemory of Devadatta when, recalling (his own) life, he thought, "I became Yajñadatta."[345] If it were otherwise (than above), there would be no contradiction for the later (self) to remember the thing experienced earlier, even though accomplished elsewhere by own-character. It would not be possible for

Yajñadatta to remember Devadatta's experience. And if it is necessary to show the reason for the difference (of remembering and not remembering), that (reason) would also not be found. This is not only a claim that both the earth and sprout are in a self-existence accomplished by own-nature, but also a claim that they differ in the sense of cause and fruit. And if it is valid to posit cause and fruit in that way, then darkness would even arise from a (bright) tongue of flame. Although it resembles the principle which denies birth from another, it is a claim only in terms of difference; and one does not do (the denying of birth from another) by impartiality of that type.

(Others say): Do you think that this scripture teaches an identity of the Teacher and Māndhātṛ? (In reply): This pronouncement denies a difference in their stream of consciousness (*saṃtāna*), but it does not teach a (mere) identity. Hence, the *ācārya* Candrakīrti maintains that (the denial of such earlier and later *saṃtāna*) is referred to in that scripture: "If you think the one called so and so was someone else, you should not look at it that way!"[346]

Some persons, mistaken regarding the purport of that scripture, say that (the Teacher,) the Buddha is identical with the sentient beings born earlier who are those (persons mentioned by the Buddha in Jātaka stories). Now, if that scripture were speaking of an identity of those two (the former and later persons) when it says, "It was I in this case of former time," then, if that (basic) person is constructed (*saṃskṛta*) he would pass away in each second, and so it would be improper to identify (those former and later persons). For that reason, the statement "Those two (such a former and later person) are permanent" is the first[347] among the four wrong views based on the prior limit that were promulated (by the Teacher).[348] To refute that (identification of persons), *nātha* Nāgārjuna stated in chapter XXVII (of *Mūla-Prajñā,* and verse 3):

The statement, "I was born in a former time," is not valid. For whatever (self) was in previous lives, precisely that (self) is not this (self).

If it were that way (i.e., that the self is permanent as you claim), a single destiny (*gati*) would be the six destinies,[349] because those persons (of former and later lives) would take bodies in each of the six realms, and, moreover, those former and later persons would be permanently identical!

Likewise, (the *Mūla-Prajñā*) has expressed its denial regarding the claim that those earlier and later (births) have diversity of accomplishment by own-nature. Moreover, if the self is present with self-existence and is also in those prior and later (births), those (selves of former and later birth) would be identical by reason of own-nature, and at that time (because free from birth and decease) would be permanent. Besides, if it were diverse by reason of own-nature, that would be the nihilism view, so a wise person (who ponders the meaning) will not accept that the self has self-existence.

γ-2. The fault that there is waste of *karma* performed:[350] If it is claimed that the self at each moment is subject to birth and decease accomplished by own-character, and that the fruit of the *karma* performed by the prior (momentary) self is experienced by the later (momentary) self, (that claim) is rejected below. At this (place) (a different fault will be explained, namely,) it is that there would be no experience of the fruit of the former *karma* amassed (by oneself), because the self which is the agent of the *karma,* having previously been annihilated, would not experience the fruit (of that *karma*); and because there is no other self (that can possibly experience that fruit). And furthermore, it would be necessary, since a prior and later entity (a thing of single series) is not accomplished elsewhere by own-nature, that there be no later self different in nature from the former one (a self of single series); and necessary, since the former (self, the agent of the *karma*) does not experience the fruit (of that *karma*), that there be no experience (at all) of the fruit (of that sort of *karma*). Since the reply in terms of there being a single stream of consciousness (i.e., reply to the question of whether there is no fault in such a case), is a rejection below, you cannot escape (this fault) that the *karma* is wasted (i.e., does not come to fruition).

γ-3. The fault of encounter with *karma* not performed: Now, if he thinks that a prior self is destroyed and a later self enjoys the fruit, so there is no fault in a waste of (*karma*) performed—in that case, some other person who has not (himself) amassed the slightest bit of the *karma* which serves as the cause for the experience of a fruit of that *karma* (amassed by the prior self), experiences a fruit of *karma* amassed by another person—because the fruit is of (*karma*) amassed by one person accomplished by own-nature and the experience is by another person different by way of own-nature from that (collector of the *karma*). That point is also alluded to in the *Avatāra* (VI, 128b–d):

There would be birth and decease in the moments prior to *nirvāṇa*. By destruction of the agent (of the *karma*) there would be no fruit of that (*karma*). And the *karma* earned (*arjita*) by one person would be experienced (*bhuñjita*) by another person.

The *Avatāra* mentions three further faults; but, as they are directed to refute the exclusive theory of the Svātantrika, they need not concern us here where the theory to be rejected is the one in common (or general). Also, the two (above) principle are stated in chapter XXVII (of *Mūla-Prajñā*) (verses 10–11):

If this (self of the present life) were different (from the self of the previous life), it (the present self) would come into existence, repudiating (the prior self). Accordingly, it (the prior self) would remain there (not having passed away); or (the prior self) not having died there, would (as a later self) be reborn. (k. 10.)[351]

It would reduce to various absurdities,[352] to wit, (the stream of consciousness of the former self) would be cut off and his acts wasted; the (volitional) acts committed by one (stream of consciousness) would (have their fruits) be experienced by another (stream of consciousness). (k. 11.)[353]

Those two, the waste of *karma,* etc. (i.e., and experiencing fruits of acts committed by someone else) are formulated by Candrakīrti (in the *Avatāra*).

The phrase "If this (present self) were different" means: "if there were a difference by own-nature of the two, the self of the time belonging to a former life and the self of this life." If that is the case (i.e., the difference by own-nature), since there is no dependence whatever on a former (self), there can be arising (of the present-life self) without reliance on that former one; and for example, as a fine cloth is not destroyed at the time of creating a pot, so a prior (self) remains without dying when the later self is born; and without dying in the previous (life) it can be born in this life—such is the meaning.

(Suppose it be asked:) Is it that the selves of the previous and the later lives are distinct, accomplished by own-nature, and there is no fault in the *karma* (committed) being wasted or encounter with the noncommitted, for the reason that there is a single stream of consciousness (*saṃ-*

tāna) (of the two selves, prior and later)? (In answer): This is like demanding a demonstration of distinctness through own-character because there has been no demonstration of such distinctness. If the (self in a former and later life) is different by own-nature, it is not valid that those two constitute a single *saṃtāna*. For example, like love and hostility (which are dissociated *saṃtāna*). The *Avatāra* (VI, 129a–b) also sets this forth:

Is there no fault if (one accepts that) there is a (single) *saṃtāna* in reality? (Yes, there is, and) we have explained the fault of (such) a *saṃtāna* at the time of our previous consideration.

As to how was that previous consideration, the same work (*Avatāra,* VI, 61) states:

(For example), the *dharmas* (aggregates, etc.) based on love and hostility, because of their contrast, do not belong to a single *saṃtāna*. It is not right that those (former and later series proceeding at variance) which are distinct by own-character belong to a single *saṃtāna*.

Thus, if they are demonstrated to be distinct through own-character, then like two different streams of consciousness (of one or another persons), they are not to be posited as a single stream of consciousness. Also the chapter XXVII (*Mūla-Prajñā,* verse 16c–d) states:

If a man and a god (of a previous and later life) are different, a (single) stream of consciousness (*saṃtati*) (of those two) is not valid.

In short, if they are different, accomplished by own nature, it is necessary to believe in an examination-ability by way of a principle of examining the manner of being. Now, when one considers it in detail by such a principle, the entity subjected to the examination-ability is absent even of atoms. Accordingly, when the later experiences the deeds amassed by the former, who are different by nature, although they have different streams of consciousness (*saṃtāna*) (the examination-ability) cannot distinguish them on account of the sameness (of the *saṃtāna*-parts). Understand it in every case as in the present context (of evaluating the faults)!

Suppose it be asked: However, since the person who experiences in the previous time and the person who remembers in the later time are two, not one, in our school according to the difference of stream of consciousness is there no validity in the (later) memory of previous experience and in the later (self)'s experience of the fruit of *karma* amassed earlier? There is no fault, because in this (school) there is no contradiction of there being a single *saṃtāna,* while in the other school (that of the realist) a single *saṃtāna* is not feasible. For example, the foot of a bluish pigeon was perched on the grass lid of a vessel full of milk, and did not go into the vessel of milk, but one can observe its (the pigeon's) footprint there (on the grass lid). In the same way, the person of this life does not (personally) get into the time of the previous life, but still there is no contradiction in his remembering in this life the experiences of yore (the time of the previous life).[354] The way in which there is no contradiction is shown in the *Catuḥ-ś-ṭ:*[355]

Abandoning the discursive speculation that, given the reality of cause and fruit, imagines them otherwise (than they are), the series of constructions (*saṃkāra*) (the stream in consciousness of entities one after another) is transfigured by virtue of the distinction of cause. If that (stream) is only impermanent, it is proper to say that the self which remembers a life is (only) imagined to possess the grasping (*upādāna*) of that (kind of stream). The entities are not accomplished by own-character; and it is positively right that those (entities, present in imagination) approach with that sort of aspect (the distinction of cause) as the condition, and that they become something else (i.e., the aspect of fruit). Therefore, the (fruitional) entity has a cause that is not accomplished by own-character, to wit, a distinction that serves (as the cause) and which should be considered to be inconceivable. For example, a vessel that is filled with milk is covered on top with layers of grass; and on top of that can be (clearly) noticed the footprint left by a bluish pigeon, as though on wet clay.[356] However, there is no possibility that its (the pigeon's) foot ever entered (into the vessel of milk).

For the extensive exposition of that (meaning), one should consult the (*Madhyamaka-*) *Avatāra.*

Now, to explain the everyday meaning—regarding the belief that the self is identical with the personality aggregates (*skandha*), chapter XXVII (*Mūla-Prajñā,* verse 6c–d) says: "For how will grasping (the aggregates) become a grasper (the self)?" This (belief that the two are identical) is the great incongruity. As to the meaning, it is common parlance to say that this person has taken this body, in which case, the aggregates (or body) is to be grasped, and the self is the grasper (of the aggregates). If one claims that those two are identical, then the *karma* which is done and the agent are identical, for which reason the cutter and the thing cut, the pot and the potter, the fire and the fuel, and so on, are identical (in each set of two). Also, Chapter X (of *Mūla-Prajñā,* verses 1a–b and 15) states:

If fire is the fuel, then the doer and the deed are identical. (k. 1a–b).

By means of the fire and the fuel, along with the flask and the cloth, and other (examples), the manner of self and grasping is all explained completely. (k. 15).

Besides, the *Avatāra* (VI, 137a–b) states:

It is not right that the grasper (the self) and the grasping (the aggregates) are identical. For in such a case, the deed and the doer would be identical.

Accordingly, if the self is identical with the aggregates, there is no sense in accepting a self, there would be multiple selves, the doer and thing done would be identical, the *karma* committed would be wasted, one could encounter the not-committed, and one would remember lives! Those just mentioned are not valid, and constitute six (faults). So one should not accept as identical (the self and the aggregates).

(ii) Refuting the Position That Self Is Different from the Aggregates

But if the two, self and aggregates, are not identical with respect to self-existence, one may wonder what is the fault in claiming that they are different with respect to self-existence. In regard to this (claim), chapter XVIII (*Mūla-Prajñā,* k. 1c–d) states the fault:

If it (the self) were other than the aggregates, it would lack the characteristics of the aggregates (birth, staying a while, and perishing).

In that regard, if the self were different, accomplished by own-nature, from the aggregates, it would not have the characteristics of the aggregates, to wit, birth, perishing, and staying. For example, this horse is granted to be different from the cow, and so it does not have the characteristics of the cow. But if one wonders about that being so—well, there is the substratum for conventional designation as a self, and there is not in the objective domain an apprehending as a self, because unconstructed (*asaṃskṛta*). One should add the acknowledgments of others, for example, "like a flower in the sky," or "like *nirvāṇa,*" mentioned in the *Prasannapadā.*[357]

(Furthermore), if the self lacks the characteristic of birth and decease, it would be permanent; and at that time there would be no way to divorce it from permanence, so there would be no sense in designating it as a self, because there would be no feasibility for it to engage (by way of accepting) and to disengage (by way of rejecting),[358] as *ācārya* Buddhapālita points out.[359]

And another reason: If this (self) were different by self-existence from the characteristics of the aggregates, forming (*rūpaṇā*), etc.,[360] it would be necessary to notice it that way, for example, as one notices the difference between mind and body. But since there is no apprehension that way (i.e., the mind does not entertain such a difference between self and the characteristics of the aggregates), the self has no meaning when abstracted (from those characteristics of the aggregates). That is said in chapter XXVII (k. 7):

> Besides, it is not reasonable that the self is other than the grasping (the aggregates). If it were other (than them) it would be apprehended (by the intelligence) even in the absence of the graspings, but it is not so apprehended.

Also, the *Avatāra* (VI, 124a–b) says:

> Hence there is no self different from the aggregates, for it has not been demonstrated (to intelligence) that a self is perceived outside of the personality aggregates (*skandha*).

Thus, the heretics who attribute to the self that it is something different from the personality aggregates fail to comprehend that it is only a name (conferred upon the aggregates); and the attribution stems from their theory-systems (*siddhānta*) through noticing the invalidity of identifying it with the aggregates. But since their streams of consciousness have an autonomy of conventional awareness, they do not actually see it that way.

One should apply oneself again and again to gain the firm certainty by observing, with such principles (as have been explained above), [certainty's] assailant that the self is different by own nature from the aggregates; because if one does not draw upon the purity of certainty about the assailant in these two sides, the identity and the difference, he does not gain the purity of view which goes ahead with just acceptance until it cuts the thong of the personality in the sense of non-self-existence.

That way one believes in the examination of whether or not the personality is demonstrated in reality. Then, if the personality is present in reality, one examines whether it is identical with or different from the aggregates. If one believes it is identical, this is a radical assailant, to wit, like the identity of such things as fire and fuel, and of the doer and act. If one believes in the identity of those (fire and fuel, etc.), it is necessary to reject it with this authority which is the viewpoint of the world; this (authority) does not become the assailant since it does not share the theory-systems of the adversary and his opponent.

Likewise with the difference. If it is that way, one would have to observe mind and body, for instance, as separate things. Still they are not observed that way, and this shows that the assailant is not grasped (that way) by autonomous awareness; this (authority) does not become the assailant since it does not share the theory-systems.

Therefore, the most radical of assailants in the phase of examining reality is not an absurdity in the conventional awareness in the streams of consciousness of the adversary and his opponent, so it is said (*Avatāra*, VI, 32b), "The absurdity in the phase of reality is not the world's." As previously explained, this maintains that (the worldly cognitions) are not authorities for reality. Still, this does not deny that the nonabsurdities for conventional awareness may be assailants [of certainty] in the phase of examining reality. Otherwise, those who do not share the sundry beliefs would have no place to teach [what are] the assailants. Also, there is a multitude of acceptances and nonacceptances by resorting to scripture; and since such acceptances do not agree in the matter of provisional meaning (*neyārtha*) and final meaning (*nītārtha*), it is also necessary to demonstrate this with a principle.[361] Teach whatever other kinds of principles there be![362] In regard to the opponent's acceptance, if you are accepting it, you should teach, "One ought to accept it!" And if you are not accepting it, you should teach, "One ought not accept it!" If there were no principle of reason in that way, how would one become certain?

Hence, the most radical of all assailants (*bādhaka*) and champions (*sādhaka*) do not touch the absurd conventional cognition of the adversary and his opponent. To see that if they were to accept a position contradictory with that (way in which the most radical . . .), it would be their absurd self-enjoyment; and not to transgress (the way of conventional appearance)—this is at the head of all principles!

In that way, there is no fault in that conventional cognition itself demonstrating non-self-existence, and so on. For example, although one demonstrates with direct perception that a sound has been made, it is not necessary to use direct perception to demonstrate that it is impermanent. In short, the most radical of assailants and champions also arrives at direct perception (*pratyakṣa*); still, why is it necessary to use direct perception to prove the root thesis (*sādhya*)? (And it is not necessary).

(iii) Hence the Remaining Positions Become the Problem

If there were a difference by self-existence (of self and aggregates) as there is of milk in a metal basin, then there would be two sides, to wit, the basis (*ādhāra*) and thing based (*ādheya*), i.e., as the self based on the aggregates, and the aggregates based on the self. But since they are not different in self-existence, there is no basis and thing based, as was explained in the case of the chariot. Also, the *Avatāra* (VI, 142) states:[363]

> The self is not in the aggregates, nor the aggregates in the self, because this conception would be possible if there were a difference here (*iha*). But there is no difference, and so this is a (wayward) conception.

Also, the position that the self is possessed of the aggregates is similar to what was explained in the case of the chariot; and one should understand it accordingly. The same work (*Avatāra,* VI, 143) states:[364]

> The self is not admitted as possessing form (*rūpa*), because the self does not exist. Consequently there is no cogency in "possession." When there is difference (and cogency in possession) one possesses cattle. When there is no difference (and cogency in possession) one possesses form. But self is not the same thing as form, nor different from it.

"One possesses cattle" is like Devadatta possessing cattle; and "one possesses form" is like Devadatta possessing a form.

Well, then, is the self just a conglomeration of aggregates? That is also not right, since it is said (in the scripture) that one designates as a self by dependence on the five personality aggregates, and because there is no validity in the designation substratum and the designated feature. That is also stated in the *Avatāra* (VI, 135c–d):

Since the sūtra states that there is a self by dependence on the aggregates, it is not just a conglomeration of the aggregates.

Furthermore, if the self were just the conglomeration of the aggregates, there would be the fault that the deed and the doer would be identical, as mentioned in the *Avatāra-Comm.* Besides, the belief that there should be acceptance of a self by reason of the individual aggregates requires the belief that one should accept the five aggregates, because in such a case it is necessary to accept also the conglomeration of the aggregates.

When it is said that the conglomeration is not the self while it is the designation substratum of the self, this also clarifies the necessity to believe in the *saṃtāna* (conscious stream) of the aggregates to be (the self) that way.

Well, then, are those (aggregates) also not the self—for example, when arranging the wheels, axle, etc. of the chariot, one arrives at the distinction of its shape which in turn is posited as the chariot; so also, when there is the distinction of shape of the conglomeration of form and the other aggregates, may one posit that (shape) as the self? However, since the shape is only formal (*rūpin*), it cannot serve to posit the self as mind and so on. The *Avatāra* (VI, 136) states:

Is it a shape? Since that is formal, your school is calling the "self" just those formal features, but not (positing) a self in the conglomeration of mind and so on,[365] because those (the formless aggregates) have no shape (*saṃsthāna*).[366]

Therefore, (when one searches for) the self-existence of the chariot as an example, it is not present (according to the above expositions) in any of those seven ways; and that being the case it is a designation based on its own members. Like that (example), (when one searches for) the self-existence of identity, difference, etc., between the self and the aggregates, it is not present in any of those seven ways, and, nevertheless, is a designation in dependence on the aggregates—because those two (chariot and self) are similar. Taking those two in the meaning of the example, we have demonstrated what was briefly stated (by the Teacher, the Buddha).

(iv) Based Thereon, the Method by Which a Personality Rises Like an Illusion.

(Generally) two meanings of illusion (*māyā*) are stated:—what is stated as the illusory supreme truth (*paramārtha-satya*) amounts to just what it is, while its truth is made the problem; and what is stated as the illusory form, etc. (*saṃvṛti*-features) is the illusory appearance which, while void of own self-existence, appears as the form, and so on. Of those two, in this (context) it is the latter. Moreover, it is not certain whether the former meaning of illusion is in the latter, and whether the latter meaning of illusion is in the former.

The way of demonstrating the latter one (i.e., the *saṃvṛti* kind of illusion) is the demonstration by recourse to two kinds of discrimination (*buddhi*), the apprehension of appearances and the certainty that they were void.[367] For example, with eye perception one sees illusory appearances of horses and cows (projected by a magician), and with mind perception relies on the certainty that there are no horses and cows as they appear and thus arouses the certainty that this appearance as horses and cows is an illusory or false appearance. Likewise, when one relies (simultaneously) both on the conventional awareness of personality, etc. that appears without disavowal, and on the certainty by knowing the principle that it (the appearance) is void of self-existence accomplished by own-nature, then one arouses the certainty that this personality (*pudgala*) is an illusory or false appearance. As to this (personality like an illusion), knowing the principle does not demonstrate that there is that appearance (as a personality), and conventional authority does not demonstrate that it is void of self-existence. So that is the reason for requiring both the knowledge of the principle that searches the presence or absence of self-existence, and the conventional discrimination that perceives the presence of form, and so on.

Hence, if one does not believe that form, etc. may rise like an illusion, he need not exert himself in the means of generating the conventional discrimination that apprehends those (form, and so on), since this (conventional discrimination) is automatically present. Rather, he should frequently examine with the principle that examines the presence or absence of self-existence in those (form, and so on); and having generated a strong certainty in the problem of self-existence, then when he observes the rising (in that conventional discrimination) of the appearance (of form, etc.) those (form, etc.) may arise like an illusion. Apart from that, there is no method of establishing the illusory void.

The former learned men[368] had the terminology (of two kinds of voidness). They called "voidness like the sky" the void of just cutting off, by means of knowing the principle, (the attribution of) the self-existence of arising, passing away, etc. in the appearance of a factual base (*dharmin*). They called "illusory voidness" the subsequent voidness of self-existence while there arises the appearance of form, etc. that appears to be self-existent. Accordingly, at the time one engages in the side of practice with praising, circumambulating, reciting, and so forth, one then examines those very preceding practices with the principle of examining the presence or absence of self-existence and thus should reject the self-existence (in those practices). Having completed the certainty evaluation, then while engaging in those (practices), he should learn the rising (of those practices) like an illusion, and should purify those (religious practices) through the spontaneous (illusory rising). If one understands this essential, he contemplates the "voidness like the sky" during equipoise. Then, by dint of that (attainment), in after-attainment, he comes to well understand the methods by which the voidness like an illusion arises.

In regard to this (method of rising like an illusion) as has been explained above, if one examines with the principle the identity, difference, etc., while not having well grasped the dimensions of the refutable thing, at the time he sees the absurdity in those (identity, etc. by reason of self-existence), he has the great nihilistic view if he thinks, "There are no personalities, and so on, at all," or thinks, "The entities such as personalities are like the horn of a rabbit, are entities void of all efficiency," so one should understand this as the wrong road to (get to) the right view. Because immediately after the verse lines (*Catuḥ-ś.*, k. 360c–d) "If it were that way, how would the phenomenal world not be illusory!" the *Catuḥ-ś-ṭ* states:[369]

When one sees as it really is this dependent origination, it becomes as though made of illusion, but not like the son of a barren woman. If (you, espouser of self-existence), using this consideration (which ponders the absolute) should reject all arising (in dependent origination), it would follow that you maintain a teaching that constructed entities (*saṃskṛta-s*) do not arise, and at the time (when you are thus maintaining) these (constructions) do not occur like an illusion. However, we use the "son of a barren woman" and other examples (such as the "horn of a rabbit") (only) for their (legitimate) illustrative purposes; and fearing that they would reduce to the fallacy that there is no dependent origination, we do not practice in agreement with those (examples such as "son of a barren woman"), but we do practice (in agreement with) illusion and other (experiences) that do not conflict with that (way of dependent origination).

Hence, there may even be a fault by the knowledge of the principle which searches the presence or absence by way of self-existence when apperceiving that the entity is just an illusion. But there is no fault, when pondering with that principle, to apprehend that the very entity that is just an illusion is among entities along the road of the self-existence problem and must certainly arise. Because the *Catuḥ-ś-ṭ* (on k. 375) states:[370]

So when entities are examined that way, their self-existence is disproved. The illusory nature of entities in their discreteness (*so so nas*) is left over.

This refers to the requirement that the illusory entity be left over.

Furthermore, given that a shoot has the problem of self-existence accomplished by own-nature, as long as the motivation of that principle is not lost, for that long one should ponder the validity and the nonvalidity by the principle, and there will not occur an apprehension that there is self-existence in the shoot. Also, if one thinks that the shoot devoid of self-existence is a real thing there, and if one thinks that the shoot void of self-existence has an appearance real like an illusion—such an apprehension has a fault requiring rejection by the principle. When those apprehensions are lacking while one apprehends that there is an illusory entity, but one thinks, "I should give it up, because it is a clinging (*abhiniveśa*) of illusion-apprehension," such a (diverted) apprehension never listens! If it were otherwise (i.e., valid to have such apprehensions), there would be the great fault of no certainty whatever of dependent origination, and I have previously explained much on this point.

As to that (kind of belief), furthermore, that is no doubt that it fails to distinguish between the presence of an illusory entity and presence in reality.

Moreover, the first time the examining person (*dpyod mkhan*), using the principle of that examining, cuts to pieces that objective domain, he then thinks that it (the objective domain) is not there. Thereupon he, observing it like that, becomes certain that it is not present; and since it is not present, he arrives at no place where he can be certain regarding any (feature, *dharma*) that this is and this is not; and the arising of the appearance has gone into a fragmentation of appearance. He has refuted everything with the principle, failing to distinguish between presence and absence of self-existence and mere presence and absence; and such a void, since it arises in dependence (on his universal refutation) is a void that destroys dependent origination. Hence, the rising in fragmentation of an appearance guided by that understanding is definitely not the illusory entity.

Hence, when one examines with the principle and thinks in regard to personality and so on that there is scarcely no way to fix it in an objective domain that is accomplished by own-nature, and it is not there, then, having taken such recourse, there is no difficulty that these appearances only arise in fragmentation. But that kind (of rising) occurs to all (persons) who have faith in the Mādhyamika theory-system and who have heard a little bit of the *dharma* that teaches the method of no self-existence. What is difficult to draw in depth is the certainty establishing that the problem is without remainder of the self-existence accomplished by own-nature, and that those very personalities (*pudgala*) and so forth that are without self-existence are amassers of *karma* and enjoyers of the fruit, etc. And since the two collections capable of establishing those (the void of self-existence, the amasser of *karma,* etc.) go only with the summit of phenomenal life, the Mādhyamika view is extremely difficult to gain.[371]

As long as one has not gained that sort of (view), there is no doubt that either he proceeds in only a great certainty of view and in small certainty on the side of practice, or he proceeds in only a great certainty on the side of practice and in small certainty of view. Thus he lacks the means of generating the great certainty in equal strength in both (the sides of view and of practice). Therefore, even when there is a certainty, one may fall into the extreme of over-affirmation that holds to accomplishment by own-nature, (the extreme of) the eternalist view and the view that entities exist; and besides (even with a certainty) one may fall into the extreme of over-repudiation, which holds that entities are void of all efficiency, (the extreme of) the nihilist view and the view that entities do not exist. Showing this, the *Samādhirāja-sūtra* (XIX, 13–16) says: [372]

At that time the victorious one, sinless and endowed with the ten powers, pronounced this best of *samādhis:* All the destinies of phenomenal life are like a dream. No one is born or dies.

One does not find a sentient being, a man, or a soul; These features (*dharma*) are like foam and plantain trunks, like a magical display, like lightning in the sky, like the moon in the waters, and like a mirage.

No man who has died in this world either shifts or goes to another world. The deed committed is never lost, but yields a fruit, good or bad, by way of the round of births.

There is neither eternity nor annihilation, neither accumulation of deeds nor their remaining. What was committed does not fail to be contacted; but what another committed, one will not experience.

One should gain certainty as stated (in that passage) that while one does not find with a principle that a person is born, dies, and shifts; and that while features (*dharma*) are like illusions, still good and bad fruits arise—so having committed a deed, one does not fail to experience it, and the fruits of deeds committed by one person are not subject to experience and enjoyment, or encounter, by another.

The manner of gaining that certainty is as follows: One should be installed by well reviewing (in discrimination, i.e., *buddhi*) the general (meaning) of the refutable with the principle (of examining) as previously explained; and should determine by well considering how one over-affirms the self-existence through the nescience of one's stream of consciousness. Then, considering the method which stays within identity and difference in case such a self-existence were present, and (considering) with analysis of the meditative object (*ālambana*) the way in which there is [certainty's] assailant is an acceptance of those two (identity and difference) simultaneously—one should fortify the certainty which, drawing certainty from observing the assailant, thinks, "In conclusion there is not even a speck of self-existence in the personality (*pudgala*)," and in that way should frequently purify the side of the void. Then, he should be installed by reviewing in the domain of discrimination (*buddhi*) the appearances while one cannot disavow the convention of personality, and should orient his mind to the sides of dependent origination which posit the amasser of *karma* and the experiencer of the fruit, and should gain the certainty in the way of validating the validity of dependent origination without self-existence.

At the time there appears to be a contradiction between those two (the appearance of a personality, and the void), one should contemplate the method whereby there is no contradiction by taking the example of reflected image, etc. It is this way: Wherever the reflected image of the face (appears) to the eye, and so on for ear, etc., there is the void of the appearances; and one associates them on the common ground (*samānādhikaraṇa*) since one cannot deny both the arising in dependence on the face and mirror and the passing away at the time when any of these conditions are removed. In the same way, while the personality has not even a speck of self-existence, one should purify (consideration) by thinking that there is no contradiction between it, the amasser of *karma,* the enjoyer of the fruit, and its arising in dependence on former *karma* and defilement. All situations should be understood along analogous lines in the manner of this example.

However, when the certainty that these reflected images and so on are void of the appearance, wherever they are, is the understanding of their non-self-existence, then it is the understanding of non-self-existence by direct perception of ordinary persons (*pṛthagjana*) whereby they become noble. Suppose this point (of criticism) is raised: "If there is not (this understanding), how would it be valid that these (reflected images, etc.) are examples of non-self-existence? If it is necessary to understand those examples themselves as dependent on the evidence that they are non-self-existent, when one reflects by such methods as positing anything (else) as an example for this (understanding), it entails a succession without meeting (= the "infinite regression")." In reply to this, some former (learned Tibetans) said: "Although one comprehends with direct perception that reflected images, and so forth, lack self-existence, one does not become noble (or superior), because the understanding (with direct perception) is just of the voidness of a limited (*prādeśika*) factual base. For becoming noble (or superior) it is necessary to understand with direct perception the non-self-existence of all *dharmas*." However, this is not right, because the *Catuḥ-ś* (k. 191; VIII, 16) says:[373]

> Whoever is a seer of one entity,
> he is said to be a seer of all,
> Precisely the voidness of one,
> is the voidness of all.

That is, by understanding the voidness without self-existence of a single feature (*dharma*), one can understand the voidness of all features.

Hence, how is there any contradiction for the one who understands the reflected-image face to be void of self-existence, although not holding the face (as a reflection) to be true, to hold the reflected image (purely as such) to be true? (And there is no contradiction). Now, small children who are not trained in signs, having seen the reflected image of a face make sport with it and impute truth to the face (which is only a reflection); while adults who are trained in sign-sources are certain that those (reflected images) are appearances that are not faces, to wit, are void of faces. To impute existence accomplished by own-nature to that reflected image which appears to be a face is the realistic imputation (or, "imputation as truth"); and that, moreover, is demonstrated by experience to be present in one's own stream of consciousness.

That being the case, the way to validate examples of non-self-existence is as follows: The appearance somewhere is void of its nature. That is, it is demonstrated by direct perception that the appearance somewhere is without its self-existence, so that very (reflected image) is taken as the example. When one demonstrates with authority upon a shoot, etc., that it is an appearance somewhere void of its self-existence, then to understand that the shoot has no self-existence is not similar to reflected images, etc. By this (way of validating examples), it is said (*Avatāra,* VI, 113a-b), "These pots do not exist in reality in the manner that they exist as acknowledged by the world." Thus as an example that pots, etc. are without self-existence, there is the formulation to the realist that they are void in limited scope like reflected images, etc., but it is not their lack of self-existence, because as previously explained it is often stated to demonstrate that there is no self-existence in those chariots, etc.

Accordingly, one imputes reality to an illusion, to wit, a spectacle, dismembered cow, chariot, etc.; that is, a magician's chariot one knows to be false and void in the limited scope. Also, when one has witnessed in a dream the entity of elixir flask, then in the situation of waking up he apprehends those things that appeared that way as false, to wit, void of it. Then anything he holds that way at the time of deep sleep again appears as the man and woman in a dream; and he holds it as void of another man and woman, but he does not understand the dream as without self-existence. For example, it is the certainty that there is no face in the reflected images, etc. (and yet there is no denial that there are reflected images). It is as previously cited (*Avatāra,* VI, 26c-d), "Whatever those things imagined as illusions, mirages, etc. they also do not exist according to the world." Thus, when one apprehends water in mirages, horses and cows in illusions, men and women in dreams, etc., conventional authority recognizes that they are spontaneous absurdities, according to their desires but without the entities (of water, etc.). But this is not the view which understands that features (*dharma*) are without self-existence.

The meanings of illusion previously explained that way should also be contemplated according to what is said in the profound words of verses of the sūtra. That should be according to what is said in the *Samādhirāja* (Chapter IX):

Like the city of gandharvas and mirages, like illusions and like dreams, so also know all *dharmas,* by contemplation of signs, as void of self-existence. (11)

Like one sees the reflected image in a serene lake of the moon in the clear sky, but there is no transit of the moon into the lake, so know all *dharmas* to have that character. (12)

Like men dwelling in mountain forests hear singing, speaking, laughter, and weeping, by echoes, yet do not see (the agents), in that way know all *dharmas.* (13)

Although the echo issues in dependence on the singing, musical performance, and weeping; yet never is the sounding in the resounding. Know all *dharmas* to be like that. (14)

Just as the desires which a man resorts to while dreaming he does not see after he awakes. And the fool, clinging to desires, is impassioned. Know all *dharmas* like that. (15)

Just as a magician has created various forms, horse-chariots and elephant-chariots; and there is nothing there as seen there, in that way know all *dharmas*. (16)

Just as one sees in a dream a girl as one's daughter being born and dying, and at the birth one rejoices and at the death grieves, in that way know all *dharmas*. (17)

Just as one sees the moon at night in a water pot, in water that is clear and unruffled; and the ungraspable flimsiness[374] is void of the moon in the water. Know all *dharmas* accordingly. (19)

Just as when at noontime in summer a man wanders tormented by thirst, he sees a mass of water in a mirage. Know all *dharmas* like that. (20)

While there is no water in the mirage he, confused, expecting to drink craves it; but is unable to drink the unreal water. Know all *dharmas* like that. (21)

Just as a man approaches a trunk of Plantain tree, seeking its pith, but neither without nor within is a pith. Know all *dharmas* by that example. (22)

(b) Adding the Meaning to the Method of Demonstrating by way of the Distinction of Names

Just as when one designates a chariot in dependence on the wheels, etc., one grasps those members and grasps a chariot; in the same way, when one designates a self in dependence on the five aggregates, the six realms, and the six sense bases, one must grasp those. And just as the self is the grasper and the creator and the artisan of the chariot and those members, in the same way, the self performing the grasping of aggregates is called the agent, and the aggregates, etc. are called the *karma* to be taken by that (self). Thus, the *Avatāra* (VI, 162) says:

In the way (as the chariot), we claim that the self and the grasper acknowledged by the world is in dependence on the sixfold of aggregates, realms, and sense bases. The grasping (aggregates) is the *karma;* and this is also the agent.

This is like the chariot. When one ponders the reality, the self is not found even in any of the seven ways; but also, when one does not ponder that there is not a bit of self-existence (in that self), it is present conventionally.

b. Thereby Showing that What Belongs to Self Also Arises without Self-Existence

Accordingly, when one has searched with the principle of searching for the presence or absence of self-existence of that self, one does not find it in any of those seven. Hence, by the principle at the time when self-existence in the self is the problem, how could one find what are called "eye," etc. of this self? (And one does not find them). That being the case, neither is there self-existence in what belongs to self. When the yogin does not witness any self-existence at all of self or of what belongs to self, he is liberated from the cyclical flow (*saṃsāra*); and this will be explained. Chapter XVIII (M.K., 2a-6) says: "Since there is no self, how will there be what belongs to self?" And the *Avatāra* (VI, 165):

For the reason that there is no creator, and not his creation, for that reason, where there is no self, there is not what belongs to self. For that reason, by the view that self and what belongs to self are void, the yogin is liberated.

One may know from what was previously explained that by dint of comprehending the non-self-existence in self one also comprehends the non-self-existence of what belongs to self along with elimination of misgivings.

c. The Method of Adding Other Principles

In the way that examining self and aggregates is the same as examining the chariot likewise one should know the pot, the cloth, etc. When by examining the identity and difference, etc. of pots and so on, with their own form, and so on, having searched in seven ways by the principle which searches the presence or absence of self-existence; and having not found it in those (seven ways) by either of the two truths (conventional and absolute), still it is posited on the side of conventional awareness which does not examine. Because we find this in the *Trisaṃvaranirdeśaparivarta:*[375]

(The Lord said): "The world quarrels with me. I (the Tathāgata) do not quarrel with the world. What the world assents to as being present and absent, I also assent to."

Hence, it was received by audience (of the Tathāgata) that he does not deny with a principle what is acknowledged by the world. The *Avatāra* (VI, 166, 167) also states this:

Whatever the entities, be they pots, cloth, shields, armies, forests, garlands, beautiful trees, dwellings, chariots, parts of the body, foreign places, and so on; and likewise through whatever (conventional) gate this worldling has related them, they are to be understood, because it is for this reason that the Munendra does not quarrel with the world.

Whether the entities be the members, the qualities (*guṇa*), the cravings, the characters, the fuel, etc., and whether they be (respectively to the foregoing) the possessor of members, possessor of qualities, the craver, the character-base, fire, etc., these are not present in the seven ways, as when one ponders the chariot. Being otherwise (i.e., not pondering that way) they are present by way of acknowledgment of the world.

In that regard, by whatever (conventional) gateway this worldling person relates them without examining, one should understand them only as present. Besides what are they? When the members and possessor of members, etc., illustrate the pot, the pot is the possessor of members, the possessor of qualities, and the character-base. Gravel, and so on, are the members; blue, and so on, are the qualities; pot-belly, hanging lip, long neck, and so on, are the characters. One may accordingly attach (to the pot) cloth, and so on. Craving is the attachment, and the craver is the support of it. That (craver) is also explained in the commentary[376] as the craving person. Fire is the kiln, and fuel what is fired. Here, one designates a member-possessor in dependence on members. Also, one designates members in dependence on a member-possessor; and one adds the same for the remainder up to, one designates fuel in reliance upon fire, and fire in reliance upon fuel. Also, chapter VIII (MK, 12) states:

> The doer proceeds in dependence on the deed,
> and this karma in dependence on the doer.

Not otherwise (than origination in dependence)
is seen a cause for accomplishment.

And MK, 13c-d):

In the manner of the doer and the deed, one should contemplate the remaining (pairs of) entities.

Accordingly, the thing generated and the generator, the going and the goer, thing viewed and viewer, authority and the object of authority, and so on—none of these is accomplished by own-nature. One should know that they are accomplished only in mutual reliance. That being the case, if one knows how to ponder one thing like the self, and knows the method of positing the two truths to validate the void of self-existence as well as the deed and doer while there is no self-existence, then when undertaking all *dharmas* he is easily capable of understanding the non-self-existence of all of them. Hence, one may obtain certainty in the two example-entities, as previously explained. That is also in accordance with the *Samādhirāja* (Chapter XII, 7; XI, 16);[377]

In the manner in which you have known the idea of self, discrimination (*buddhi*) should be urged on in every case. All *dharmas* have the nature of that (self), are pure like the sky. By means of one (*dharma*) he knows all (of them). By means of one he sees all (of them). However many he has explained he gets no pride.

2. ESTABLISHING THE NONSELF OF FEATURE

The five aggregates which are the basis for the designation as a personality (*pudgala*), the six realms of earth-element and so on, and the six senses of eye and so on, are the "features" (*dharma*). And the void of self-existence accomplished by own-nature is the nonself of those features (*dharma*). While there are many methods of establishing this, the *Avatāra,* when setting forth in its commentary the nonself of *dharma,* establishes the non-self-existence in entities by way of denying birth through the four alternatives. Here it will be expounded in brief.

Chapter I (MK, verse 1) states:

There is no entity anywhere that arises from itself, from another, from both (itself and another), or by chance.

This states that there is no inner or outer entity anywhere that arises from itself, and along the same lines one adds the other three theses (*pratijñā*).

α. Accordingly, the denial by a reductio ad absurdum (*prasaṅga*), of arising from itself, teaches that when there is a thesis without expressing for it an example and evidence (*liṅga*) of syllogism, one controverts such theses; and (teaches) the absurdity (*bādhā*).

Here, if there were arising by self-existence, there should be a unanimous decision concerning both reliance and nonreliance on a cause, hence a unanimous decision concerning both an effect and cause in reliance on a case, and concerning both identity and difference of self-existence. Among them, the arising with an identical self-existence of cause and effect is the arising from itself; and the arising with a different self-existence is the arising from another. Hence, there is a certainty concerning both arising from those as itself and another taken separately, and from those as itself and another grouped together. In the case of being taken separately, there is both arising from self and arising from another, so the way of rejecting other alternatives with denying only an arising with the four alternatives is in that way.

As to the shoot (a factual base, *dharmin*): If it arises from its own self of shoot there would be no purpose of arising, because the arising (of something) is to be the arising somewhere and the attaining of its self; and because the shoot would have already attained its self. For example, like a shoot which was already manifest (**abhivyakta*). Furthermore, it could not reach birth, because if a seed which had already sprouted were again to arise, it would require that seed to sprout repeatedly. Accordingly, there would be the fault that shoots and so on, since they arise in the continuity of just a seed, would not reach the phase of arising. Also, chapter XX (MK, verse 20a-b) states: "If cause and fruit were identical, producer and product would be identical." Also, the *Avatāra* (VI, 8c-d, 9a-b) says:[378]

There is no virtue (*guṇa*) in its arising from itself, and there is no reason (*yukti*) for something already born to be again born. If you imagine that something already born is born anew, it would follow that you would not find in this world the birth of shoots.

And (*Avatāra,* VI, 12c-d) says:[379] "Therefore, what you have imagined, namely that an entity arises from itself, is not reasonable, either according to reality or according to the world."

β. Or if you suppose that it arises from another, because it was said (by the Tathāgata) that a fruit arises from four conditions which have the state of being otherwise (*anyathātva*),[380] (we reply as follows:). "If the effect arises from a cause with different self-existence, then a thick darkness would arise from a bright flame, because it is different. Furthermore, all entities, whether they are or are not cause, because they are the same in being otherwise." The meaning of this is as follows: If one accepts that the shoot of rice has a self-existence accomplished by own-nature, it is not right to take it as its own generator; but when it passes with a different self-existence by way of own-nature from fire and so forth, that is a way of passing (*soṅ lugs*); the passing with a different self-existence from its own cause, the seed of rice, is a way of passing; and those two appear to be simultaneous and the same in every way. Accordingly, at the time it appears to occur with a different self-existence from what is not feasible to so generate it (i.e., fire, etc.); and at the time it appears to occur in dependence on an independent different thing, i.e., different from its rice-seed—the parts of difference appear that way. When that method of appearing different is the self-existence accomplished by way of their own-nature, in no way at all can one separate the distinction of nonbirth from fire, etc. and birth from a rice-seed. To separate the distinction of birth and nonbirth would involve a contradiction between the method of being different as the difference of self-existence and what is called a separation of distinction. This is clearly stated in the *Avatāra-Comm.* (on VI, 14):

In the same way as the rice-seed which generates (the rice-shoot) is different from its fruit, which is the rice-shoot, in that way are its nongenerators whether fire, charcoal, barley-seed, etc., also different. Moreover, in the same way as is the arising of the rice-shoot from the rice-seed which is different, so also would it be from fire, charcoal, barley-seed, etc. Also, in the same way as a rice-shoot which is different arises from a rice-seed, so also might pots, cloth, etc. occur, but one never sees this. Hence, this does not happen.

Hence, what is claimed (by some Tibetans) as proof—that the army with a single turnabout is pervaded by victory—is not the opinion of the *ācārya* (Candrakīrti). The absurdity of it I have already explained in the section of denying as nonproof—that only the presence of smoke in the kitchen is pervaded by only the presence of fire. Also, chapter XX (MK, verse 30c-d) says: "If cause and effect were different, the cause would be equal to what is not a cause." And also the *Avatāra* (VI, 14) states:[381]

If in dependence on another, some other would arise, then thick darkness might arise from a flame. For the reason that from everything would occur the birth of everything, the state of being other would be the same among all nongenerators.

(The realist) gives no reply to that sort of reductio ad absurdum about belonging or not belonging to a single series, etc., because if (cause and effect) were other by virtue of difference of self-existence there is no proof of belongingness to a single series, as (was explained) previously. Also, when one sees with certainty the arising or not arising, it is not feasible to reply, because when one does not posit with the attitude of difference convention, it is the phase of examining (reality) to think, "How is that seeing with certainty valid when it is demonstrated upon an objective domain by way of own nature?"

γ. Those who say that there is arising from both (itself and another) say that the clay pot which arises from clay has arisen from itself, and arising from the potter, etc. (wheel, sticks), has arisen from the other; and they say, in regard to the inner (=stream of consciousness) that Devadatta in another life takes birth from only what he is, a living being (*jīvita*), because Devadatta and a living being are one, thus is born from self; and being born from a father and mother, and from good and bad *karma,* is born from another. That is, arising is not from just itself, and not from just another, but arising is from the set of two. This claim is a problem by way of the very principle previously expounded. That is, the part of arising from itself is refuted by the principle which rejects arising from itself; and the part of arising from the other is refuted by the one which rejects the arising from another. Also, the *Avatāra* (VI, 98) states:

Why is the arising from the two also not the nature of the principle? Because it reduces to the faults already explained above. It is not so according to the world (i.e., worldly convention), nor is it so according to reality, for the reason that an arising is not demonstrated from either (itself or other) (in isolation).

Those who say that there is arising from self-nature say that one does not see any (agent) endeavoring and making the lotus roots rough and the lotus leaves smooth; and likewise one does not see any (agent) taking hold and arranging colors and shapes in the peacock, etc. (i.e., its tail, and so forth); hence the arising of entities only occurs from their own-nature. This is not right. If there is arising from no cause, it would entail the arising in a place and a time to be in all places and times; moreover, it would entail this arising nowhere (in no place or time), because there is no teaching of presence or absence of a cause for those reasons of it to occur or not to occur in this place and time. The peacock tail would happen in the raven, and so on. In short, if one thing arose, it would arise in all (times), or, again, it would never arise and still attain a fruit; on which account, all the many endeavors of worldlings in the motive of that (attainment of fruit) would be fruitless (*anarthaka*). Also, the *Avatāra* (VI, 99) says:

If (as you, the Lokāyata, believe) something surely arises without a cause, then any (entity) always would arise from anything. And these men would not dispose the seeds, etc., by countless (efforts), envisaging the occurrence of a fruit (= harvest).

Accordingly, one resorts to viewing the absurdity in the arising of the four "limits" (*mu bźi*) and demonstrates that there is no arising from any of the four alternatives (*mtha' bźi*). This is pervaded by nonbirth through self-existence, as was demonstrated in the previous explanation in the phase of denying other alternatives. Consequently, the entities certainly occur in dependence while there is lack of self-existence. At the time this (principle) makes the reductio ad absurdum, there is an inference based on making that (reductio ad absurdum), but there is no syllogism which proves those theses concretely. The *Avatāra* (VI, 104a-b) states:[382]

The entities (*bhāva*) are devoid of self-existence (*svabhāva*) because there is no birth, whether from self, from another, from both, or without reliance on a cause (*hetu*).

This expresses briefly the meaning of [certainty's] assailants expounded for the four alternatives of arising. It shows how the inference arises in dependence on the fruit of formulating the refutation; but from the outset there is no such formulation acknowledged by others, i.e., among the opponents. If in that way one gains the certainty, by recourse to refuting the arising through self-existence, that the entities are devoid of self-existence, it is easy to gain the certainty that the non-entities (i.e. the features, *dharma*) are devoid of self-existence, and so easily to gain the Madhyamaka view which understands that all *dharmas* are void of self-existence. Moreover, chapter VII (MK, verse 16a-b) says: "Whatever arises in dependence, that is bereft of self-existence." And it is just as the *Avatāra* (VI, 115) states:

> Because it is impossible to imagine these discursive thoughts (of the four alternatives) when entities arise in dependence, this principle (*yukti*) of dependent origination destroy the whole net of false views.

When, relying on the evidence of dependent origination, one gains the certainty that the shoot, etc., is void of self-existence, the exceeding clarity in the discrimination (*buddhi*) which avoids the wrong road (of views) (is the principle) to be told (only) briefly.

Here, the shoot (= the factual base, *dharmin*) has no self-existence accomplished by own-nature (= the thesis, *pratijñā*), because it arises in dependence on its cause and condition (= the evidence, *liṅga;* or reason, *hetu*), for example, like a reflected image (= similar instance, *sādharmyadṛṣṭānta*). That amounts to inference acknowledged by others (*parapratīta-anumāna*). In illustration, when there appears (in a mirror) the reflected image of a face, for a small child who has notions of such sort (i.e., does not know conventions) that appearance of eyes, ears, etc., as that way the object appears is not its own situation." While that is so, sentient beings with experience apprehend that object (the reflected image) by its situation or layout (*gnas lugs* or *sdod lugs*) as it is and do not posit the appearing features (*dharma*) by dint of fallacious notions. The apprehension of those objects as the layout upon the objective domain through own-nature as the way they appear is the method of over-affirmation that they have self-existence; and such a self-existence of its objective domain is the own-nature, the self-existence, the independent entity, so if it is that way it contradicts the reliance on other causes and conditions. If it were not in contradiction, a finished pot could duplicate itself with no need of arising through a cause and a condition, and it would not be valid to accept this. Along the same lines, the *Catuḥ-ś*. (k. 348; or chapter XIV, 23) says:

> When any (entity) arises in dependence,
> it does not occur with independence.
> Since this is entirely without independence,
> a self (or self-existence) is not present.

And its commentary states:

> Were there in this (world) anything with own-nature, self-existent, independent, and reliant on others,[383] that very thing would be self-accomplished and not arise in dependence. (But, rather,) all constructed entities arise dependently. Accordingly, when any entity arises in dependence, it does not occur with independence, because it arises in reliance on a cause and a condition. Since this is entirely without independence, it follows that for any entity there is no self or self-existence.

"Independent" means that at the time it appears to be accomplished by own-nature, it appears "reliant on others," i.e., on those awarenesses, and also accomplished according to appearance. However, when one denies the production by reliance on other causes and conditions, there is no need for the *raṅ-sde* (Vaibhāṣika, Sautrāntika, etc.) to demonstrate (what has already been demonstrated); and with this crux it is impossible to posit the gaining of the Madhyamaka view. Thus, it amounts to an independence in a layout self-reproductive by way of own-nature upon the objective domain. Hence, the meaning of being void of self-existence amounts to lack of independent nature, but does not amount to lack of an efficient entity. So it is possible to refute the self-existence by reason of the dependent origination. The continuation of the previous citation (*Catuḥ-ś-ṭ* on Chapter XIV, 23) states:

> For that reason, in this case anything arising dependently lacks an independent nature. Consequently, the meaning of lacking an independent nature is the

meaning of voidness. But there is no meaning of no (constructed, efficient) entities at all.

Hence, the view that there is no efficient entity scorns the illusory dependent origination which washes out all (sins), and is wayward. The view that there are entities accomplished by self-existence is also wayward, because there is nowhere such a self-existence. That is mentioned in the immediate continuation of the previous citation (commentary on chapter XIV, 23):

For that reason, the view which scorns the arising dependently which is illusory and the cause of washing away the *saṃkleśa,* i.e., (the view) which denies it, is wayward; and since there is no self-existence, the view that there is an entity (with self-existence) is wayward. Consequently, those who say in that way that entities are attended with self-existence deny dependent origination, and have the fault of eternalistic or nihilistic views.

Therefore, the one wishing to be free of the eternalistic and nihilistic views should accept the view of no self-existence and of the illusory dependent origination which washes out all (sins).

You (the Buddhist realist) may retort: "If after refuting by means of the efficient dependent origination that independent nature, the meaning of dependent origination is the meaning of lacking independence, how are you (the Mādhyamika) going to refute us? Because we too accept the efficient dependent origination. Hence, there is no difference (in belief in dependent origination) between you and us." (In reply:) While you accept dependent origination, that dependent origination is like the realistic imputation in the small child that there is a face when there is a reflected image of face. You have over-affirmed it as being accomplished by self-existence and refer to it as having own-nature of entity. Hence you have not understood it as it is, but refer to it (waywardly) as it is not. We (Mādhyamikas) believe it lacks self-existence, and so speak. Hence, the distinction (of our two schools) is in that. This is also mentioned in the immediate continuation of the previous citation (commentary on chapter XIV, 23):

And suppose you (the Buddhist realist) retort: "If the meaning of nonindependence is the meaning of dependent origination, even so why do you point an absurdity toward us? What is the distinction between you (Mādhyamika) and us?" I shall explain that. Whatever is the meaning of dependent origination, as to the way in which you have understood it and do not know to expound it, that is the distinction. In the way that a young child is not trained in conventions and so over-affirms that there is reality in a reflected image, and thus avoids (*bsal nas*) the voidness of self-existence as it is located, imagines that the reflected image is attended with self-existence and does not know that it is imaginary, in that same way, you also, while having accepted dependent origination, do not know that dependent origination is like a reflected image, void of self-existence, and have understood it as it is located to have an own-nature; because while it lacks self-existence, you do not apprehend the lack of self-existence; and because you apprehend what is present without own-nature by over-affirming it to be present with own-nature. Also, you do not know the expounding, because you do not expound the non-self-existence, and you expound the self-nature of entities.

Although they are similar in accepting the dependent origination of cause and effect, by way of (the Mādhyamikas') saying that it is without self-existence and (the realists') saying that it is with self-existence, there is taught the distinction of understanding or not understanding dependent origination as it is and the distinction of knowing or not knowing the expounding. In this regard, while accepting efficient entities, the realists called them "really accomplished" (*bden par grub pa*), so (former Tibetans, and so on) thought that the dispute over whether they were really present or absent was a dispute over the name (i.e., what they were called). Likewise, while believing in efficient entities conventionally, (they thought) the dispute with the Svātantrika over whether or not there is a self-existence accomplished by own-character conventionally was a dispute over just the name (i.e., the terminology "self-existence accomplished by own-character"); and they clearly refuted what the Svātantrikas purport to apprehend when they say those (entities) are accomplished by own-character.

(Those former Tibetans also said:) Along the same lines, for example, the Sāṃkhya says that this entity acknowledged in the realm of hearing cognition is permanent. So while believing that this entity is acknowledged in the realm of hearing cognition, (those Tibetans) said the rejection of permanence of sound appears as just the name (i.e., "permanence"). (This argument of yours) appears like that.

Other (unskilled) sentient beings, when taking birth in dependence on causes and conditions, on this basis apprehend that there is a self-existence accomplished by own-nature, and so they are in bondage. The skilled ones, taking recourse to this reason, reject the self-existence and draw certainty that there is no self-existence and sever the bondage of views that adhere to the extremes, wherefore this demonstration of no self-existence by the evidence of dependent origination is the great skill in the means (*upāya-kauśalya*). Having seen this powerful one among meanings, the Lord spoke (in the *Anavatapta-nāgarāja-paripṛcchā*):[384]

α Any (thing) that is born (in dependence) on conditions, is not born (to wit): β The birth of this (thing) does not occur by self-existence. γ Any (thing) that is dependent on conditions, is declared void. δ Any person who understands voidness is heedful.

The first two lines (α, β) state the ubiquity by which anything born through a condition is born not by reason of self-existence. The third line (γ) states that the meaning of dependent origination with reliance on conditions (*pratyaya*) is the meaning of "void of self-existence." The fourth line (δ) teaches the benefit of understanding voidness that way. Likewise,[385]

> The wise man understands the *dharmas* in dependence
> and does not take recourse to views of the extremes.

This tells that by understanding dependent origination one cuts off the adherence to extremes (of eternalism and nihilism).

Furthermore, if there were a self-existence accomplished by own-nature, the Victor (= Buddha) and his disciples would by necessity have seen it that way. But didn't see it. And the self-existence has nothing to do with conditions, and nothing for cutting the net of elaboration that adheres to sign-sources. As the *Hastikakṣya-sūtra* states:[386]

> If there were a self-existence for the *dharmas*,
> the Victor and his disciples would know it in them.
> There would be no liberation for the unchangeable *dharmas*,
> and wise men would never be without elaboration (*prapañca*).

While the nonself (*nairātmya*) of *dharmas* is very well established by principles in chapters III, IV, and V (of the *Madhyamaka-kārikā*) that refute a self-existence in the sense bases, aggregates, and elements, through fear of verbosity I shall not elaborate.[387]

3. METHOD OF ELIMINATING OBSCURATION BY CULTIVATING THOSE VIEWS

Having in that way seen that self and what belongs to self have not even a speck of accomplishment by self-existence, having repeatedly contemplated the meaning of that (seeing), one wards off the reifying view that adheres to a self and what belongs to self. Having warded that off, one wards off the four indulgences (*upādāna*) that were previously explained, i.e., indulgence in desires, etc. Having warded that off, gestation (member no. 10) does not occur by condition of indulgence (member no. 9), so there ceases the birth (member no. 11) with reconnection of the aggregates by condition of gestation. Chapter XVIII (M.K., verse 2c–d) says: "By the extinction of self and what belongs to self, one loses the 'I' and 'mine.' " And (XVIII, 4):

> By extinction of the idea of self and what belongs to self regarding personal and external entities, indulgence ceases and by eradication of that, birth is destroyed.

When that happens, since indulgence (*upādāna*) is defilement and gestation (*bhava*) is *karma,* there is liberation by extinction of the *karma* and defilement which are the cause of birth. The same work (XVIII, 5a) says: "There is liberation through eradication of *karma* and defilement" and continues (5b–d): "*Karma* and defilements are from (deviant) discursive thoughts (*vikalpa*); these are from elaboration; and elaboration ceases by voidness." According to that passage, the succession of cyclical flow of birth and death arises from *karma.* Only the motivation (member no. 2) of the three gates[388] imbued with defiled consciousness is the *karma* that accomplishes the cyclical flow. Thus *karma* arises from defilement. When one does not engage in the wrong discursive thought that over-affirms the objective domains with signs of "pleasant," "unpleasant," etc., then there does not arise the defilements which have as root the reifying view; so those defilements of passion, aversion, etc., having as root the reifying view, grow through the wrong discursive thoughts. Only the clingings (*abhiniveśa*) by discursive thought with wrong mental orientation have the ideas that these eight worldly *dharmas,*[389] as well as men and women, pots and cloth, form, feelings, and the other aggregates are real (*bden*); and create the discursive thoughts toward the objective domain (of eight worldly *dharmas,* etc.). Consequently, that discursive thought arises from the elaboration which imputes reality.[390] Thus, the *Prasannapadā* (on XVIII, 5):[391]

This worldly elaboration is destroyed without remainder by voidness, when all entities are viewed as void (of self-existence). How so? Because when an entity is perceptively reached, there is the (net of) elaboration as was described. But in the absence of perceptually reaching the daughter of a sterile woman, passionate persons do not introduce elaboration to that sensory object (as a maiden of lovely appearance). When not introducing elaboration, they do not introduce wrong discursive thought to that sensory object. When not introducing discursive thought, they do not generate, through clinging to the ideas of "I" and "mine," the host of defilements (of lust, etc.) which have as their root the reifying view (*satkāyadṛṣṭi*). When not generating the host of defilements which have as their root the reifying view, they do not commit the acts (*karma*) (which are the cause of cyclical flow). (The persons) who do not commit acts, do not experience the cyclical flow called "birth and old age and death."

The method of warding off those (elaborations and discursive thoughts) by understanding voidness is clearly stated in the same work (*Prasannapadā,* subsequently in commentary on XVIII, 5):[392]

For the reason that, in this way, by recourse to the voidness with the character of extinguishing every last elaboration, every last elaboration is lost; and by loss of elaboration, discursive thought is warded off; and by warding off of discursive thought, every last *karma* and defilement is warded off; and by warding off of *karma* and defilement, birth is warded off—for that reason, only voidness is called "*nirvāṇa*" by reason of its character of warding off all elaboration.

This (passage) teaches with right demonstration that the view of voidness cuts off the root of phenomenal life (*bhava*) and is like the life of the path to liberation; so it is necessary to gain steadfast certainty in this (method).

Accordingly, those texts of the *ārya ācārya* (i.e., Nāgārjuna) (namely, the *Madhyamaka-kārikā,* and so on) clarify that the *śrāvaka* and the *pratyekabuddha* also understand the non-self-existence of all *dharmas,* because those texts express that the liberation from the cyclical flow (*saṃsāra*) is the accomplishment by the view of voidness with non-self-existence. Also, the *śrāvakas* and *pratyekabuddhas* contemplate this view as long as they have not exhausted their defilements; and when the defilements are exhausted, if they are satisfied with that much, and do not engage in cultivating (this view) for a long time, it will not be possible for them to eliminate the obscuration of the knowable. The Bodhisattvas are not content with just personal liberation from the cyclical flow by way of only the exhaustion of defilements; with enterprising aspiration to become Buddhas for the sake of all sentient beings they cultivate to exhaust completely the obscuration of the knowable; they cultivate for colossal length of time, becoming adorned with immeasurable collections (of merit and knowledge).

Thus, the adversary which ejects down to the seed of both obscurations (of defilement and of the knowable) is the previously mentioned view of voidness. However, by dint of not continuing the cultivation for a long time, there is only the possibility to eliminate the obscuration of defilement but not to eliminate the obscuration of the knowable. For example, a single understanding of nonself is the adversary of both what is to be eliminated by view (*dṛṣṭi-heya*) and what is to be eliminated by cultivation (*bhāvanā-heya*).[393] However, by merely viewing directly non-self there is the possibility of eliminating the *dṛṣṭi-heya,* but not the possibility of eliminating the *bhāvanā-heya;* and for eliminating the *bhāvanā-heya* one must cultivate for a long time—it is like that. Along the same lines, in regard to eliminating the obscuration of the knowable, also there is no possibility of eliminating it by a cultivation of just it for a long time; but one must also resort to a training in many other lofty degrees of practice (such as the six perfections, and the four means of conversion).

It is said that by cultivating only the means for eliminating the obscuration of defilement, and without cultivating the adversary of the obscuration of the knowable, the *śrāvakas* and *pratyekabuddhas* do not cultivate to consummation the understanding of *dharma* nonself. The *Avatāra* (on VI, 179) says:

The *śrāvakas* and *pratyekabuddhas* also view just this conditional state of dependent origination. But also by such as this they do not cultivate to consummation the nonself of *dharmas*. They have a means of eliminating the defilements that range in the three realms.

Now, other Mādhyamikas (Bhāvaviveka, Śantarakṣita and his followers—Svātantrikas) claim that it (the obscuration of the knowable) is the adherence to the self of *dharmas*, while this *ācārya* (Candrakīrti) claims that it (adherence to the self of *dharmas*) is the defiled nescience and states (in the *Avatāra-Comm.*) that cultivation of *dharma* nonself eliminates it (the defiled nescience) to exhaustion, but that it is not the cultivation to consummation of *dharma* nonself. One may know this according to those previous expositions and as explained in this context.

Suppose it be asked, "Well, then, of what sort is the obscuration of the knowable according to this school (the Prāsaṅgika)?" (In reply:) The obscuration of the knowable is the errors of two appearances—α There being the immemorial clinging to the presence of self-existences, through the channel of clinging to given things habit-energy is firmly planted in the stream of consciousness; β by dint of the habit-energy, there is the appearance of self-existence where there is no self-existence. It is as stated in the *Avatāra* on VI, 28):

And these (conventional form, etc.) are for the *śrāvakas, pratyekabuddhas,* and Bodhisattvas who having abandoned the defiled nescience see constructions (*saṃskāra*) as though they were reflected images, and the like—an artificial constructed nature and not real, because (for those persons) there is no pretense that (these forms, etc.) are real. These (objects) which deceive the "children" (ordinary persons) are for others (*śrāvakas,* etc.) only convention (*saṃvṛti*) by reason of arising in dependence like illusions, etc. And these (appearances as only *saṃvṛti*) have the characteristic of obscuration of the knowable, because they behave with only nescience. They appear to the *āryas* who range in the sphere attended with appearances (obtained later, *pṛṣṭhalabdha*), and do not (appear) to those (in *samāpatti*) who range in the sphere (only void) not attended with appearance.

The Bodhisattvas (of the present context), by having abandoned the defiled nescience, have attained the Eighth Stage, because as was previously cited from the commentary on the *Catuḥ-ś,* they are Bodhisattvas who have attained the forbearance of the unoriginated natures. For that reason, the two arhats of the Hīnayāna as well as the Bodhisattvas who have attained the Eighth Stage[394] no longer promote again the habit-energy (*vāsanā*) for the mistakes of the two appearances. Still, even if they have often had the motive of purifying the habit-energy of the two appearances promoted from time immemorial (of cyclical flow, *saṃsāra*) by this (repetition of defiled nescience), they must for a long time to come purify (the habit-energy); and when they have removed without any remaining bit the habit-energy for the mistakes (of the two appearances), they will be Buddhas.

The *ārya* (i.e., Nāgārjuna) and his sons claim that both the Hīnayāna and the Mahāyāna teach a similar view of final meaning (*nitārtha*). This is the cause of drawing two wondrous certainties. It is this way: Having drawn the certainty that the only liberation from the forlorn[395] *saṃsāra* is to be a Buddha and that there is no means for it except for the view which understands that there is no self-existence in any of the *dharmas*—is how one acts to gain the immaculate view by great endeavor through numerous means. And having drawn from deep in the heart the certainty of the special *dharma* distinguishing what is unshared between the Hīnayāna and the Mahāyāna to be the jewel of the bodhi-mind and the glorious practices of the Bodhisattva—is how one acts to gain the immaculate view by great endeavor through numerous means. And having drawn from deep in the heart the certainty that the special *dharma* that distinguishes what is unshared between the Hīnayāna and the Mahāyāna is the jewel of the bodhi-mind and the glorious practices of the Bodhisattva—is how one embraces the chief of precepts in a superior way regarding the categories of practice, and having embraced the vow of the Jina and his sons (the aspiration mind), trains in the practice (the entrance mind).

Here I say:

Having appeared at that most marvelous of mountains,
The famed Vulture-peak of Magadha,—
And made the Great Earth move in six ways,
And with magical transformations, filled with light the myriad fields,
The Muni pronounced from his resplendent throat
The Great Mother giving birth to all the Noble Sons,

Like the life of the Path of both *sūtras* and *mantras* (= Tantras),—
Elegantly expressed, incomparable *Prajñā-pāramitā*.
The heroic Nāgārjuna, who had obtained a prophecy,
Explained (her), as (she) really is—in that best of texts,
His magnificent *Mūla-prajñā,*
Incomparable exposition honored like the sun.
That superb explanation was superbly explained
In the text of Buddhapālita, offspring of the Jinas;
And, having been well analyzed, was then explained extensively
In the splendid text of Candra (kīrti)—the *Prasannapadā,*
Their unblemished school—the method of validating
Saṃsāra and *nirvāṇa,* dependent origination, the act and the agent,
While entities are without self-existence and are illusory—
I shall express in easy words in a merely summary way:
"Thou friends who train in the profound Mādhyamika texts,
Although it be difficult to establish in your mind the
Dependent origination with cause and fruit and no self-existence,
There is such a Mādhyamika school.
It is a fine thing to take recourse to the method here spoken of:
Lacking it, you were unable, by your own school, to abandon
The faults, as they are, of formulation in the other (system).
So study hopefully at length in (our) 'non-school.' "
That being the case, the method of search according
To the texts of the noble Father and Sons
Has been here well explained, so that
The teachings of the Jina may long endure.

II. VARIETIES OF DISCERNING

Accordingly, one relies on illustrious persons, searches for much hearing, and thinks methodically. Having taken recourse to that triple equipment of discerning, with reliance as stated in *Bhāvanākrama II,* when one gains the view which understands the two *nairātmya,* one should cultivate the discerning.

It is asked: Well, then, how many are the discernings to be cultivated? (In reply:) Here is not taught chiefly for the while the discernings of the exalted realm, but is taught chiefly the discerning to be cultivated at the time of the ordinary person.[396] The fulfillment of his discerning is the cultivation of discerning of four kinds, of three kinds, and its six kinds.

The four kinds are the "investigation" and so on, stated in the *Saṃdhinirmocana-sūtra*.[397]. "Investigation" is witness of a phenomenon. "Supernal investigation" is witness of a noumenon. The first one has both a consideration and a profound consideration; the second one also has both a consideration and a profound consideration—with their meaning differentiated by crude and subtle. Along these lines, the *Śrāvakabhūmi* states (YS III):[398]

Here what are the four kinds of discerning? A monk, having based himself within on a calming of the mind, investigates the *dharmas* (natures, features, doctrines), supernally investigates them, fully considers them, is immersed in profoundly comprehending them. How does he investigate? He investigates according to phenomenon either the meditative object for purification of addiction, or that for skill, or that for purification of defilement. He fully considers, just making images, by the mental orientation along with insight and with discursive thought. Traversing,[399] he is immersed in profoundly comprehending them.

The fourfold path of discerning is mentioned in the (*Abhidharma-*) *Samuccaya,*[400] and the *Prajñāpāramitopadeśa* sets forth the fundamentals in accordance with the *Śrāvakabhūmi.*

There are also the three kinds which the *Saṃdhinirmocana* tells (chapter VIII, sect. 10):

Lord, how many kinds are there of discerning? Maitreya, there are three kinds: discerning consisting of images, that consisting of thorough search, that consisting of discrimination. α What is the one consisting of images? It is the discerning with mental orientation only to the reflected image in the range of *samādhi* and attained with discursive thought. β What is the one consisting of thorough search? It is the discerning with a mental orientation to that (image) and there (on the equipoised plane according to the *Śrāvakabhūmi*) where the *dharmas* have so far not been understood by insight, in order to rightly understand them. γ What is the one consisting of discrimination? It is the discerning with a mental orientation to that, and there, liberating the *dharmas* that were rightly understood by insight, in order to touch bliss (*sukhasparśārtham*).

In the *Śrāvakabhūmi,*[401] those three are referred to as the three doors of discerning,[402] to wit, orienting his mind with a mental orientation of the equipoised plane on the *dharma* heard or precept embraced, α he does not pay attention (to something else), does not reflect, or judge, or understand, but engages himself just with the image. β At the time he ponders (i.e., using the second kind of insight) and inspects (that image with discursive thought), he is engaging himself with search. γ When he discriminates (i.e., using the third kind of insight) that (image) as it was established (previously), he is engaging himself with discrimination on what was searched. Those meanings are in brief:—α Having taken a meditative object for instance, in the meaning of nonself, one orients the mind to the image of that, and does not engage in multiple establishments (i.e., avoids distractions). β In order to become certain about what one was previously not certain, he establishes it (with intellectual processes). γ The entity on which he had become certain in the previous manner, he (now) examines.

The six kinds are the meditative objects in six given things, and, moreover, are the way of search of the (β) discerning with thorough search. Besides, thoroughly searching, one searches meaning (*artha*), entity (*vastu*), characteristic (*lakṣaṇa*), category (*pakṣa*), time (*kāla*), and reason (*yukti*); and then (γ) discriminates those.[403] Among those, the search of meaning is the search, thinking, "That expression has this meaning." The search of entity is the search, thinking, "This is a personal entity." "This is an external one." The search of characteristic involves two kinds—the search, "This is an individual characteristic (*svalakṣaṇa*)," "This is a general characteristic (*sāmānyalakṣaṇa*)," or unshared and shared. The search of category is the search by way of the "black category" including faults (*doṣa*) and troubles (*ādīnava*) and the search by way of the "white category" including merits (*guṇa*) and benefits (*anuśaṃsa*). The search of time is the search, thinking, "Thus it occurred in past time. Thus it will be in future time. Thus it is now in present time." The search of principle involved four principles (*yukti*). Among them, the dependency principle is the dependence on causes and conditions for the arising of the fruits. Besides, it is the search by the diverse standpoints of convention (*saṃvṛti*), absolute (*paramārtha*), and their underlying cause (*nidāna*).[404] The principle of act and agent is the individual act and agent by means of *dharmas,* for example, the act of being burned by the agent fire. Besides, one searches, thinking, "This is a *dharma.* This is an agent. This is a deed by this *dharma,* the agent." The principle of proof by demonstration is the proof of the meaning when there is no contradiction with authority (*pramāṇa*). Besides, what is it? It is the search, thinking, "Is this or is this not of the three, direct perception (*pratyakṣa*), inference (*anumāna*), a hand-down from authoritative persons (*āptāgama*)?" The principle of true nature (*dharmatā*) produces conviction in the true nature acknowledged (*prasiddha-dharmatā*) by the world as the true nature of fire to heat, water to moisten, etc., as well as the inconceivable true nature (*acintyadharmatā*) (the inconceivable cause of the fruitional entity,[405] magical feats of the Buddhas, and so on), and the abiding true nature (*avasthita-dharmatā*),[406] and does not produce a thinking that there is a different reason for being that way. In that way one searches.

The positing that way in terms of six is so the yogin may know the certainty in terms of three: the meaning of what is said, the phenomenon and the noumenon of a knowable, [and the true condition (*yathābhūta*)].[407] Among those, on behalf of the first one, the first search (i.e., of meaning) is prescribed. On behalf of the second one, both the search of entity and search of individual characteristic is prescribed. On behalf of the third one there is prescribed the search of the other three (category, time, and principle) and of the general characteristic. The *Śrāvakabhūmi* (YS III) states:[408] "That in brief is three-doored discerning and its meditative objects in the varieties of six given things. Thereby, all of discerning has been summarized." This states, as explained therein (i.e., in the *Śrāvakabhūmi*), that all of discerning is summarized by those (varieties of discerning). Moreover, it states that the three are doors to the four kinds of discerning first explained, and that the six ways of search are involved in the thorough search of those three; so the three doors and the six searches appear to be included in the previous four.

The previously explained (in the "Calming the Mind" section) four mental orientations, "proceeding with enclosure" and so on, are in common between "Calming" and "Discerning," as stated in the *Śrāvakabhūmi,*[409] so those four mental orientations also pertain to "Discerning." Hence, it is as stated in the *Prajñāpāramitopadeśa:*[410]

Accordingly, by fulfilling the cultivation of the four kinds of discerning, one is liberated from the bondage of contamination; and by fulfilling the cultivation of the nine aspects of calming, one is liberated from the bondage of sign-source.

That is stated in many great texts, so the cultivation of discerning is by way of the four, investigation, etc., as stated in the *Saṃdhinirmocana;* and the cultivation of calming is by way of the nine thoughts established with no discursive thought at all.

III. THE WAY TO CULTIVATE DISCERNING

Here there are two parts: A. Refutation of other schools; B. Establishment of our school.

A. Refutation of Other Schools

1. THE FIRST REFUTATION

Some (former Tibetans) said: Even when one does not gain any view which understands nonself (of personality and of *dharma*), (one's) mind may hold with no discursive thought at all (of space, time, etc.) and thereby contemplate the meaning of the manner of being. That manner of being, i.e., voidness, determines whether this is or this is not and is devoid of everything, because this way of establishing is installed in agreement with the situation, and because not only is there no demonstration at all of an objective domain, but also there is nothing at all apprehended by the intellect.

This is said (in reply:) α Is it, accordingly, that the contemplater, having failed to demonstrate objective things, and knowing that he has not demonstrated them, thereupon, consistently with that (nondemonstration) needs a positing that there is no apprehension at all by the intellect; β or is it, accordingly, though knowing[411] that he has not demonstrated anywhere the situation of the objective domain, thereupon he posits the "shocker"[412] that when the intellect does not embrace anything at all, it is contemplating the situation of that (objective domain).

α In the first case, it contradicts his (the contemplater's) not having gained the view, because he (himself) claims this to be the final meaning of that (nondemonstration). According to us, such as this (your view) disregards the principle's refutable. Thus, while accepting something, you (purport) to envisage the absurdity by means of the principle; and then if you take whatever you determine as not arising, it is an insulting view (or, the nihilistic view); and certainly there is no errorless contemplation of voidness to be founded upon *this* (view), as was extensively explained above.

β. And if you have evaluated with a principle that evaluates the way of being of these *dharmas,* and have not demonstrated with that principle any presence or absence at all among these (*dharmas*), whereupon you imagine that these (*dharmas*) are devoid of any elaboration in the absolute sense, a person (like you) posits the method this way by not having thus understood (the method of no elaboration). And when you take this position (i.e., that they are devoid of any elaboration), if you claim to contemplate (their) voidness, it reduces to a monstrous absurdity. It never occurs to you that with every sense cognition there is the thinking, "This (object, form, etc.) pertains to this, or does not pertain to this," for which reason, in agreement with the situation of the object, all these (positings by sense cognition) also happen to contemplate with contemplation of the manner of being. And as was explained, in past time there have been many heresies which take calming's no discursive thought at all to be in every case a contemplation of voidness (i.e., faint, deep sleep, etc. would then be a contemplation of voidness). Moreover, if you are satisfied with what another person knows (while you do not know), to wit, the agreement between the two—the situation of the object and the intellect's way of positing, you cannot avert the various heresies which occur there (i.e., in the contemplation of voidness). But suppose you think, "Ours is not like that (of the various heresies). Here (i.e., our school), that person (who is the contemplater) knows that these two are in agreement, and then posits this way (i.e., the intellect's way)." Then (in reply), if he knows the way of agreement of this sort, that conflicts with what you claimed, namely, that one contemplates voidness by the mere positing, and without understanding a view and without apprehending anything at all. If you think that all discursive thought, no matter in what (good or bad) there is discursive thought, creates bondage to *saṃsāra,* so positing the "shocker," and that the liberating consists in positing no discursive thought, this was in previous times much refuted. You would have practically no cause to attribute fault to the school of Hva-śaṅ which is like this (position of yours). So, the *Bhāvanākrama III* states:[413]

Some claim: "By dint of the good and bad *karma* generated by discursive thought of the mind, sentient beings circle in the cyclical flow, experiencing the fruits of heaven and the other destinies. Those, however, who do not think of anything at all, and do not do anything, are liberated from the cyclical flow. Therefore, one must not imagine anything. One should not engage in such virtuous practices as giving (*dāna*). The practice of giving, and so forth, was taught only on behalf of stupid persons (*mūrkha-jana*)." Now those who talk this way will reject all of the Mahāyāna. As the Mahāyāna is the root of all vehicles, if one rejects it, he will reject all vehicles. When one says, "Therefore, one should not imagine anything," he will reject the insight (*prajñā*) with the character of right discrimination (*bhūta-pratyavekṣaṇā-lakṣaṇa*). The root of right knowledge is right discrimination; so if one rejects this, one destroys the root, wherefore one rejects the supramundane insight. When one says, "One should not engage in such virtuous practices as giving," he rejects the giving, etc., which constitute the means (*upāya*), the major portion of the perfections (*pāramitā*). In short, it is this way: insight and means are the Mahāyāna. This is also stated in the *Ārya-Gayāśīrṣa-sūtra:* "The path of the Bodhisattvas in short amounts to two. What are the two? It is this way: The part of means, and the part of insight."[414] It is also proclaimed in the *Ārya-Tathāgataguhya-sūtra:* "The whole path of the Bodhisattvas is comprised by these two—means and insight." For that reason, the rejection of the Mahāyāna produces a great karmic obscuration. That being the case, the one who rejects the Mahāyāna has heard little, overweeningly values his own views,[415] has not given due deference to wise men, has not understood the way of the Tathāgata's good teachings (*pravacana*), himself ruined brings others to ruin; whose words, being infected with the poison of contradiction with reason and scripture, are like poisonous food to be cast away far off by a wise man who wishes well for himself.

This clearly sets forth the positions, i.e., the formulation held by Hva-śaṅ; and that if one claims like this he rejects all of the Mahāyāna. May you be acquainted with those positions of yore!

Suppose you think, "We are not like him (i.e. Hva-śaṅ) because we practice giving (*dāna*), etc." We (in reply) teach that if you have to distinguish yourself from him by way of mere giving, etc., both you and Hva-śaṅ are alike in contemplating the view of final meaning. Otherwise, you would have found it proper to distinguish yourself in the matter of the *samādhi* with no discursive thought at all. Moreover, you hold that whatever the discursive thought, all of it binds to *saṃsāra,* so you are not pursuing the aim of liberation from *saṃsāra,* for one has to give discursive thought to renouncing with giving (*dāna*), guarding with morality (*śīla*), etc. (as the cause of liberation). So what need is there to perform these (the giving, etc.—they in fact binding to *saṃsāra* by their attendant discursive thought)! This was previously explained *in extenso.* Hence, if you claim that whatever the discursive thought it all binds to *saṃsāra,* it is assuredly that (position) of Hva-śaṅ, so in your position, one droops with the burden of contradiction.

Moreover, some (former Tibetans), inclining toward that (position), thought, (at first) one frequently ponders the sensory domain (*viṣaya*) held to as sign-sources in the manner of the two selves. Next, to ward off the subject's (*viṣayin*) adherence, one then cuts off the elaboration (*prapañca*) which is like when a stone (is thrown) a dog runs after it. So from the outset one holds thought within, not letting it go out to any (sense object), just as when a hand throws a stone (to a dog), one holds it near the head; and by virtue of doing it (one's thought) does not go forth to those sense objects which are held as sign-sources, and one cuts off (within) all elaboration. Hence, they say, the exertion in scripture and principles when establishing a view is a wandering aimlessly in merely conventional words. This (person who so talks, rejecting the sūtras and śastras) has the most vile of wayward discursive thought that rejects all of the Buddha's preaching (*pravacana*) and the learned text of the six ornaments[416]—because only those (ornaments) have established the meaning of the scripture and principles.

Moreover, given the intellect (*buddhi*) that adheres to sign-sources as the two selves (*pudgala* and *dharma*) and how they are apprehended by it, when one well ponders them as they are (i.e., as existent or nonexistent), and with pure scripture and principles—it is necessary, by way of drawing certainty that they do not exist in the way they are apprehended by us (i.e., by the intellect that adheres to sign-sources); and it is then that the falseness of illusion undergoes an interior collapse. That being the case, as long as one does not gain such a certainty, just holding thought within, and being satisfied with it (i.e., thought) not going out to the object consisting of the two selves (*dharma* and *pudgala*), with just that much, one does not comprehend the meaning of nonself. Otherwise, it would reduce to the great absurdity that at the time of dreamless sleep, fainting, and the like, since the mind does not go forth to those (objects, to wit, the two kinds of self), one would understand selflessness. For example, at nighttime, if one is frightened, wondering if there is or is not a demon motionless in a cavern, as long as one does not dispel the fear (of a demon) by lifting a lamp and well settling whether there is or is not (a demon) there—one has the discursive thought that there is a demon. It is like saying, hold the mind so the discursive thought does not engage in going forth!

The *Bhāvanākrama III* points out that at a time of battle, one keeps the eyes open to see where the enemy may be, and like a sword-wielding hero does not move there when one notices that the enemy is powerful, but his eyes are wide-open—just like the previous (discussion of) fixation (of mind in *samādhi*):[417]

> It is as stated in the *Ārya-Mañjuśrī-vikrīḍita-sūtra:* He asked, "Girl. How does the Bodhisattva win the battle?" She suggested, "Whoever, Mañjuśrī, when examining (by principle), does not apprehend any *dharmas.*" Accordingly, the yogī having opened the eye of knowledge, with the sword of insight (*prajñā*)[418] cuts out the enemy defilements, and abides fearlessly. He does not, as does a timid man, close his eyes.

Hence, if one is frightened by mistaking a rope for a snake, he should reach certainty by thinking, "That coil is a rope, not a snake." It is necessary to ward off the mistake and the anxiety of fear. Likewise, when one is deluded by accepting the two selves as existent and has the suffering of *saṃsāra* generated by that delusion—he should draw upon the certainty of cord-cutting scripture and principles that there is no object consisting of the imputed selves, and should understand the imputation of selves as an illusion. Then repeatedly dwelling upon that meaning, he averts (the self-imputation), and having warded it off, he averts all the suffering of *saṃsāra* generated thereby. Accordingly, in the Set of Mādhyamika Principles, etc., the pondering of sense objects is given as the reason for cessation (*nirodha*). Thus Āryadeva (*Catuḥ,* k. 350c–d):

> When he sees the objective domain as selfless,
> the seed of the phenomenal world ceases.

Also the *Avatāra* (VI, 116a–b):

When there are the discursive thoughts (positing the extremes of nihilism or eternalism), there are the given things (supposedly accomplished by own-nature). The way in which those given things are not existent is settled by examination (with the principle).

This states that when, with the discursive thought that adheres to extremes, one accepts entities as existent, they (i.e., those discursive thoughts) arise, so one examines in many ways that their (clinging-) object is nonexistent. ". . . and having realized that the self is the sensory domain (*viṣaya*) of that (reifying view), the yogin suppresses the self"[419] Also, the Lord of Principles (*rigs pa'i dbaṅ phyug*) (i.e., Śrī-Dharmakīrti) states (*Pramāṇavārttika,* I, 222–223a–b):[420]

Unless one reviles his objective realm (of clinging), one is incapable of eliminating it. The attraction and aversion that (respectively) follow upon merits and faults, is not an observation in the objective domains of those two, nor is it a way in external things.

There are many similar passages.

Others say: Since whatever the discursive thought, it all binds to *saṃsāra,* one should contemplate voidness, and at that time one suppresses all discursive thought. This (method) should be examined as follows: If an ordinary person (*pṛthagjana*) [Ja: "one who looks hither" (*tshur mthoṅ*)] contemplates voidness, is the voidness the meaning of nonself with direct perception (*pratyakṣa*), or is it out of sight (parokṣa) [=inferential]? In the first case, this person would be an *ārya* [which is absurd], because he realized directly the meaning of nonself. But if you assert that even though he realizes directly the meaning of nonself it is not in contradiction with his being an ordinary person, we reply, then even if the meaning of reality is remote for a person, it is not in contradiction with his being an *ārya,* because it comes out exactly the same.

Besides, this sort of person (i.e., the ordinary one) who (according to you) has directly realized reality, does not know that his own sense objects have the meaning of reality, and it is necessary for some other person to explain to him the accomplishment of reality by comprehension of the scriptures—so (what you say) is a case of mirth for the wise, because it claims that the student directly realizes (the meaning), while the teacher has to prove it (to the student) by inference. Consequently, the sort of account (as you have put forward) should not be told in the presence of those who know the principles!

Also, there is no point to saying (as you do) that the proof of the meaning of reality by direct sight is a proof by conventional understanding. The Lord of Principles (i.e., Dharmakīrti, in *Pramāṇavārttika,* II, 99c–d) said:[421] "That is a highly deluded thing, because acknowledged as an *āgopāla*[422] ('cowherd') (= 'a boner')." This states that if one proves the meaning (so easily), the meaning is acknowledged as a "cowherd," which is a conventional illustration, and one sets that down as evidence of a delusion. Hence, if one claims to have realized directly reality, though with that sort of delusion, speak of it as a sort of stupidity that does not realize reality! Although (you) are satisfied it is reality—it is not valid, just as for example in the case of a white heifer to posit this as the characteristic of a cow; so also with just seeing directly it is not valid to posit this as the character of reality. (To posit such a characteristic) is in contradiction to your own thesis, so to say it is proven conventionally is clearly a poverty-stricken communication; and I shall not expand upon it (further).

(But) if [i.e., in the second case] the nonselfness to be contemplated as the meaning of voidness is out of sight to the contemplator of voidness, the claim to hold with knowledge free from discursive thought that the entity is out of sight is an occasion for mirth.

In short, if the intellect (*buddhi*) of the ordinary person who contemplates voidness is not directed on the side of intellect[423] that is toward the selflessness of the objective domain, it is a contradiction that it contemplates voidness. And if it is directed on the side of intellect toward that (nonself), it would be certain in one way whether the objective domain was directly realized or out of sight. And among these (cases), it is necessary to hold that if one directly realizes the nonself he is an *ārya* (noble), while if the meaning of nonself is out of sight he is an ordinary person. (Still,) if at that time, the meaning of nonself is an understanding by a method of general meaning, this contradicts that it is free from discursive thought.

Moreover, insofar as one claims that the person who is great in the best *dharmas*[424] of the "path of praxis" (*prayoga-mārga*) understands the meaning of nonself by the method of general meaning, it amounts to the gross contradictory claim that the present-time beginner (who is an ordinary person, *pṛthagjana*) has an intellect that contemplates voidness and is free from discursive thought. If the meaning of nonself amounts to being free from discursive thought, that (ordinary intellect) would be unmistaken, could prove easily, and would have *yogi-pratyakṣa,* because it would know free from discursive thought and unmistakenly the meaning of nonself.

Hence, if one does not obtain the right view which reviles with principle the objective domain posited as a self, the claim to contemplate the meaning of selflessness with merely holding the mind that goes toward the two selves, etc. to not go toward (them) and the claim that the ordinary person contemplates nonself with a knowledge free from discursive thought—wander far away from the path of scripture and principle.

2. THE SECOND REFUTATION OF OTHER SCHOOLS

Some (other Tibetans) assert: We also hold it to be not a valid contemplation of voidness when one has not achieved the view of voidness with nonself and merely lays down no discursive thought at all, so the former school is not valid. However, when one has achieved the view of final meaning (*nitārtha*) of nonself, subsequently, in all cases when this person lays down the nondiscursive thought, he contemplates voidness.

This is not valid: Since this person has achieved the view of final meaning, any and all of his contemplations with no discursive thought are contemplations of the meaning established by the view of final meaning. But, when this particular person contemplates the mind of enlightenment [and this requires discursive thought], let those (Tibetans) tell for what reason he is not contemplating the view of final meaning!

If you admit that this contemplation of the mind of enlightenment is the contemplation by a person who has achieved the view of final meaning, (and yet assert) that this view (of final meaning) is remembered at that time, because there is no contemplation through being based upon that (view), (we reply:)—However, at the time of contemplation by the person who has achieved the view of final meaning, and that view is remembered—when the contemplation is founded pursuant to the view, he is satisfied that it (the view) is a contemplation of voidness. Now, how is that person going to protect the view that all establishments are without discursive thought? (And he can't.) Hence, even when one has achieved the view (of final meaning), at the time he guards (that view) it would be necessary to contemplate voidness by remembering the meaning established by way of the former view, so he does not manage to contemplate voidness by just engaging in the fantastical positing that there is no discursive thought at all!

Here, what our own school calls "no discursive thought" has occurred numerous times in the previous "Calming (the Mind") and in the present section ("Discerning the Real"), namely, adopting and staying on a meditative object without the multiple examinations of the type, "It is this; it is not this," but this is not a claim of being free from discursive thought.[425]

3. THE THIRD REFUTATION OF OTHER SCHOOLS

Some (other Tibetans, differing from the two previously mentioned) assert: We do not accept the first position, i.e., that being based without discursive thought and not having achieved the view, is a contemplation of voidness; and we do not accept that when one has achieved the view any positing without discursive thought is a contemplation of voidness. However, (in our school) when previously there was a single session of pondering with discriminative insight by an instance of guarding that there be no discursive thought at all, then when that is given up, subsequently all establishments with no discursive thought are contemplations of the meaning of voidness.

That is not valid. In that case it reduces to the absurdity that having had a single session of examining the view in sleep, subsequently the nondiscursive thought in dreamless sleep is a contemplation of voidness, because both[426] are equally preceded by examination of the view, and because in their own (individual) time it appears (clearly) that there is no necessity to contemplate with an establishing upon the view (by virtue of no discursive thought). Hence, when one has examined with the view and has posited the meaning establishing that there is no self-nature; and then scarcely anything happens;—then losing the positing pursuant to the view, in general, when one's mind stays without imagining anything, this is not a contemplation of voidness, but an exercise of imagination, and it is necessary to protect with uninterrupted attention to whether one stays or does not stay pursuant to the view.

4. THE FOURTH REFUTATION OF OTHER SCHOOLS

Some (other Tibetans) assert: We do not accept those previous three positions. At the time of contemplating voidness, we draw certainty in voidness; then we give thought to the meaning of this; and other than this, the positing without examining is a wayward contemplation of voidness—because in the manner of the first school there is no facing of the mind to voidness; in the manner of the second school, at the time of guarding that there be no discursive thought there is no lack of remembering the view of voidness; and in the manner of the third school, having previously given up examining the view, then there is no nondiscursive thought in abandonment pursuant to the view.

This claim of yours, to wit, having a meaning (*artha*) said to be the examining of view, and only remembering the view, and then only contemplating with a positing pursuant to the view—that this is contemplation of voidness is not valid. Because if it were that way, there would be only calming (the mind) that engages in stoppage-cultivation of the voidness, while there would be no method of guarding the discerning with examining-cultivation. So there would be a one-sidedness that does not guard to combine both calming and discerning.

B. Establishment of Our School

As long as one has not achieved the view of final meaning of nonself, none of the person's contemplations in his stream of consciousness are with the face of *buddhi* directed to nonself, so it is necessary that he acquire the view of nonself. Moreover, it does not suffice to just understand, i.e., it is necessary at the time of guarding that he examine while remembering the view and that the contemplation be on the very meaning he examines. For this, it is necessary that there be both the stoppage without examining the meaning of nonself, and the cultivation through examining with discriminative insight, while a one-sidedness does not suffice. Here there are three points: 1. The reason for requiring both stoppage-cultivation and examining-cultivation; 2. Rejecting the argument against it; 3. Summarizing the essentials of the method of protection.

1. THE REASON FOR REQUIRING BOTH STOPPAGE-CULTIVATION AND EXAMINING-CULTIVATION

As long as there is no certainty of the view by errorless exhaustive reflection on the meaning of nonself, the comprehension of discerning does not arise, because that (certainty) is stated to be the cause of that (discerning), and because not to learn the accounts that explain that view is stated to be a hindrance to discerning. Because the *Saṃdhinirmocana* (chapter VIII sect. 32) says:

"Bhagavan, through which causes do calming and discerning arise?" "Maitreya, they arise through the cause of pure morality, and through the cause of pure views consisting of hearing and of pondering."

And (in VIII, sect. 33): "Not learning the noble accounts according to their position is a hindrance to discerning." And because the *Nārāyaṇaparipṛcchā,*[427] just as the many previous citations (i.e., in the Bodhisattva section), says: "Insight arises from hearing; the one with insight eliminates defilement."

The way discerning arises from the view (of nonself) is as follows: At the time of initially deciding (on the view) one decides by examining through many avenues of scripture and principle. Then, when one has decided, he examines again and again with discriminative insight. By a mere stoppage-cultivation without guarding, there is no arising (of discerning), so it is necessary at the time of contemplating (discerning) after having accomplished calming, to guard through the examining (by principle).

In regard to this (manner of guarding), some (Tibetans) assert: We deny that there is no examining (with principle) at the outset. Indeed, after having decided (the view) by hearing and pondering, if at the time of cultivating[428] one performed the examining-cultivation (with principle) it would be the discursive thoughts that adhere to sign-sources (*nimitta-grāha*) (which keep men enchained). If one does not guard accordingly, any reflection is adherence to sign-sources; and there are many refutations of the thesis that the nondiscursive-thought awareness of the ordinary person is a contemplation of nonself, so that is not valid. Moreover, all those reflections are realistic imputations, so if at the time of contemplating (the view) there is cessation, then at the time of deciding (with hearing and pondering) there is reflection (or discursive thought); hence, the requirement to do those must be refuted. The explanations to the disciple, the disputes (with opponents), the enterprises (to write up the explanations and the disputes), the views (going with the foregoing) that arouse discursive thoughts, and so forth—all these activities which you find necessary to do with discursive thought must at that time (i.e., when stopping discursive thought) also be suppressed, because at the time of contemplation it is necessary to suppress the realistic imputation, and because at other times (than contemplation) there is no particular qualification that it is not necessary (to suppress it). And because if you do not accept it this way, even so your examining by many avenues of scripture and principle does not comprehend the meaning of nonself to be understood. Having already acquired the view (of nonself) it is not necessary at the time of contemplation.

If it were that way, one would understand nonself in direct perception on the path of vision (*darśana-mārga*). Then, having already seen nonself, there would be no purpose to cultivating it (i.e., on the *bhāvanā-mārga*).[429] If it were necessary to cultivate it, it would amount to believing that (the defilements) to be eliminated by *bhāvanā* will be eliminated by *bhāvanā* and were not eliminated by just *darśana*. And here it is because having previously established the matter and decided by hearing and pondering, it would be necessary to cultivate the establishment. And because to the extent one has cultivated the establishment, to that extent the certainty (that understands nonself) would see in the manner of strong surge, for a long time, very clearly, and steadfastly. Hence, it is as said in the *Pramāṇavarttika,* I, 50a–b:[430]

Since there is the presence of the defender (*bādhya*)—certainty (that sees the nonself), and of the assailant (*bādhaka*)—the mind superimposing (self upon the object).

Thus those two are (respectively) the defender and the assailant; so to the extent the certainty continues steadfastly, with strong surge, and so on, to that extent the superimposition is the assailant. So also in this case, it is necessary to be steadfast in increasing ever more the certainty of no self-existence; moreover, because it is necessary to examine by many avenues the assailant (*bādhaka*) and the upholder (*sādhaka*). Otherwise, having achieved an understanding of impermanence, *karma* and fruit, disadvantages of *saṃsāra,* the mind of enlightenment, friendliness, compassion, and so on, then without pondering them, it would be necessary (i.e., would suffice) to guard by adopting the single grasping-pattern of just thinking, "I shall die," because it would amount to the same reason.

Hence, for drawing upon the purity of certainty, it does not suffice to resort to a single pledge from among the separate thoughts, to wit, "I shall die," or "I shall attain Buddhahood for the sake of sentient beings," or the thought of wishing happiness for sentient beings, and so forth. It does not suffice to adopt a single pledge on account of the requirement to examine the reason by many avenues for the certainty of no self-existence with steadfastness, strong surge, etc. And it is necessary to examine by many avenues the assailant and the upholder, as was already explained extensively in the section of the lesser person.[431]

Along the same lines, the three *Bhāvanākrama* state that when one has accomplished calming (*śamatha*), at the time of cultivating (the discerning, *vipaśyanā*) one cultivates by performing the pondering in many ways. Also the *Avatāra* (VI, 120d) states: ". . . the yogin suppresses the self," and so forth, mentioning the examinations to be made at the time of the cultivation. This is because the yogin performs in the gaining of calming or discerning, as the case may be; and because if calming is not previously accomplished it is not that there is no search for understanding of the view (of voidness). And (those works) state the examining of the view in the phase of insight (*prajñā*) after meditation (*dhyāna,* as the fifth *pāramitā*), so after accomplishing *dhyāna* by the essential of that sequence, there is the purport of examining both kinds of nonself (*pudgala* and *dharma*). Also the *Madhyamaka-hṛdaya* (III, 21) says:

> With his good mind (*mati*) he should get equipoised and afterwards should grasp by way of convention the *dharmas* or given things; and these he should examine this way with insight.

And the commentary on it (the *Tarkajvālā*) says that one engenders the *samādhi* (of calming) and thereafter should engage in the examinations of the view (in the phase of cultivating the discerning). And because also the *Bodhicaryāvatāra* (VIII, 4) shows that one accomplishes calming according to the *dhyāna* chapter, and after that at the time of cultivating insight (*prajñā*) one cultivates with examining of the principle.

Hence the sequence of the two last perfections (*dhyāna* and *prajñā*), and the sequence of the two last instructions (*adhicitta* and *adhiprajñā*), all are the sequence of first accomplishing *samādhi* and then cultivating *prajñā;* and for the method of cultivating that *prajñā,* all the stages of cultivation [perhaps meaning the *Bhāvanākrama* texts] have stated it by way of examining the noumenon and the phenomenon, so one should not examine in a way deviating from that (the foregoing). And not only that, but many great texts have stated it this way, so doubtless at the time of cultivating (the discerning) one should examine (with the principle).

Accordingly, after accomplishing calming, if at the time of cultivating with discerning one engages with solely the examining-cultivation, the previous calming would be lost. Since it is not generated anew, there would not be calming; and on that account discerning also would not occur—as was previously explained [cf. beginning of the "Calming the Mind" section]. Hence, it is not only necessary to guard the calming accomplished in the prior fixation (of consciousness) but also necessary to perform the examining-cultivation, so both are necessary. Moreover, at the conclusion of performing the examining-cultivation of discerning one should perform the stoppage-cultivation on that entity (treated with examining-cultivation), and so will accomplish the pair-wise calming and discerning with the meditative object of nonself. One may also consult the *Bhāvanākrama II:*

Besides, the *Ārya-Ratnamegha* promulgates: "Accordingly, in order that the person skilled in (eliminating) faults may get free from all elaboration (*prapañca*) (of sign-sources, *nimitta*), he should practice Yoga in the contemplation of voidness (of self-existence). He having frequently contemplated voidness, in the event of mental straying to whatever object which gladdens the mind, would search the nature of whatever is this object, and at that time would comprehend that it is void. Whatever was the thought, searching it, he would comprehend that it is void. Whatever was the thought by which he comprehended, upon searching the nature of this, he comprehends it also to be void. By comprehending in this manner, he enters the Yoga without sign-sources (*ānimittayoga*)." This passage teaches that the inquiry into (and investigation of) (*dharmas*) and the prior renunciation is the entry into (the discerning way of) that non-sign-source. And it very clearly teaches that with only renouncing a mental orientation, or not examining with insight the nature of a given thing, there is no possibility of entering the state of no discursive thought.

This text (i.e., the *Bhāvanākrama II*) explains that when there is the object to which the mind issues and there is the issuing person's examination of his thoughts, he comprehends that they are void (of self-existence); searching or pondering his comprehension as void, comprehends that it is void; and at that time these (i.e., method of examining with principle) are his contemplation of voidness. And (the text) explains that by examining (in this manner) and comprehending as void, one enters the non-sign-source Yoga. Thus, it clearly teaches that there is no possibility of entering the non-sign-source or nondiscursive (voidness) if one follows the theory of Hva-śaṅ wherein one does not give up at the outset the examination with principle of search by examining, or by a mere mental orientation that draws back the mind that was straying and eliminates (everything).

Hence, as previously explained, one shatters by the sword of principle, to wit, that there be not a single atom accomplished of the two selves for the *dharmas,* and draws certainty in nonself. Accordingly, upon finding no given thing of the two selves (*pudgala* and *dharma*), the nongiven thing of the refuted (two selves) is something rightly produced. The grasping as existent the nongiven thing of the absent son of the barren woman, depends upon a support, to wit, the son of a barren woman. At the time those two (the barren woman and her son) are not witnessed, that there is true existence of the absent son of the barren woman bursts apart like (a *pudgala*) not given a name. When one does not witness a single given thing that is real or a single substratum, there does not arise a reflection grasping the nongiven thing upon that (given thing) as a present real thing.

Hence, one should ward off all reflections that grasp sign-sources. Where there is a reflection with realistic imputation, there is the reflection with realistic imputation whether of a given thing or a nongiven thing, since it is said in the *Bhāvanākrama* that if the pervader (the realistic imputation) goes astray, the thing pervaded (the truly existent) also goes astray.

Accordingly, one should generate the certainty that pulls from the depths of certainty that there is not as much as an atom of real existence in a given thing, whether present or absent; and should fix (without examining) upon the entity whose cord has been cut by this (certainty)—and doing each of those with conviction generates the nonreflective wisdom (*nirvikalpa-jñāna*). But it is not possible to generate it merely by drawing attention within, while not examining objects at all, because (then) it is not possible to eliminate the realistic imputation; and this (denial of attention) is merely a nonreflection on whether a self is present, because, there being no comprehension of nonself, such a contemplation does not oppose in the slightest the imputation of self.

Hence, it is necessary to distinguish between not reflecting on whether there is real presence or on whether two selves are present (on the one hand), and comprehending the nonreality (of the object) or both nonselves (on the other). Hold this as the meaning of essentials (than which there is no greater one)!

2. REJECTING THE ARGUMENT AGAINST IT

Suppose one thinks: The pondering on the meaning of nonself is reflection (or discursive thought), so it is a contradiction that from it could arise the nonreflecting wisdom (*nirvikalpa-jñāna*), because it is necessary that cause and effect agree. In regard to this, the Lord spoke together with an illustration in the *Kāśyapa-parivarta:* [432]

"Kāśyapa, it is this way: for example, when two trees are rubbed together by the wind, and fire arises (from the friction), (that fire) having arisen, burns the two trees. In the same way, Kāśyapa, (when given things are analyzed) by the most pure discrimination (*pratyavekṣaṇā*), the faculty of noble insight is born; and (that Fire) having been born, (it) burns up that most pure discrimination itself."

Thus he declared that noble insight (like a fire burning up defilement) is born from discrimination. The *Bhāvanākrama II* makes the same point:

Thus, accordingly, at whatever time the yogin, pondering with insight (*prajñā*), does not hold as certain in the absolute sense the nature of any given thing (that was pondered), at that time he enters the nonreflecting (or nondiscursive thought) *samādhi.* Also he comprehends the non-self-existence of all *dharmas.* Whoever (the foolish person) that does not contemplate with insight while examining the nature of given entities, but merely eliminates the mental orientation as he contemplates something, he never averts his discursive thought and he never comprehends the non-self-existence (in the absolute sense of the given entities), because there is no light of insight. It is this way: from the right discrimination there arises the fire of right knowledge (of given things) as they really are; and like the fire from the friction wood, it burns up the tree of discrimination, as the Lord proclaimed.

If it were not that way, it would not be possible for the nonfluxional path to arise from the fluxional path, so an ordinary person could never attain the noble state, because the cause and fruit are not alike. Likewise, there are an uncountable number of unlike causes and effects, such as a green shoot arising from a yellow seed, smoke arising from fire, a male child born from a woman, etc.

The nonreflecting wisdom of the nobles (in *samāpatti*) is the comprehension in direct vision of nonself that is void of the domain (which the wayward mind clings to) that imputes the two selves (*dharma* and *pudgala*); and when this (wisdom) arises, it perforce contemplates from that time on by way of comprehending, by discrimination, that the domain with adhering to self does not exist; and so it is a reflection with nonreflecting knowledge as the highly consistent cause, just as the *Samādhirāja* teaches in the previous citation:[433] "If he discriminates the *dharmas* as selfless," etc. Besides, the *Bhāvanākrama III* has this:[434]

If there is its (*pratyavekṣā*'s) nature of reflection (or discursive thought = discrimination), namely, because it is the nature of right mental orientation, then it brings the arising of (true) nondiscursive knowledge. The person who seeks that knowledge should take recourse to this (discrimination, *pratyavekṣā*).

Suppose one claims: It says in the *Prajñāpāramitā* scripture that if a person ponders, thinking, "Form, etc. are void and nonself," he is coursing in sign-sources; so it is not valid that one should discriminate toward voidness. (In reply:) Such (scriptural) statements as that one refer to the realistic way of taking voidness, but not just taking the thought, "It is void (of self-existence)," as has been explained in many previous places. It is not the way (that person claims), because those scriptures (i.e., the *Aṣṭasāhasrika-Prajñāpāramitā*) teach:[435]

The Bodhisattva great being who is coursing in Prajñāpāramitā, who is cultivating Prajñāpāramitā, should examine it this way, should put his mind to it this way. What is this Prajñāpāramitā? Whose is this Prajñāpāramitā? What it is when any *dharma* is not found, not apprehended, that is Prajñāpāramitā.

This passage intends that if he "should examine it this way, should put his mind to it this way," it is the examining at the time of contemplating with Prajñāpāramitā. And the *Prajñāpāramitā-hṛdaya,* in answer to the question of how to practice profound Prajñāpāramitā, states: "observed that the five personality aggregates are void of self-existence." Also, the *Sañcaya-gāthā* (VII, 3a–c) puts it this way:

At the time he is dissecting[436] with insight a nature (*dharma*), constructed or unconstructed, good or evil, he does not find even its atoms. At that time, he goes measuring with Prajñāpāramitā in the world.

This says that when the person who examines the *dharmas* with insight does not see as an object even their atoms, he goes in the manner of Prajñāpāramitā. How could (your claim) be in contradiction with the many statements (cited from the scriptures) that require the examination with this kind of principle? (And it is in contradiction).

If you do not accept it this way, (we put to you the question:) What is the reason for saying (as it does in the scriptures, etc.) that one should not have discursive thought toward the *dharmas?* If one believes, as does Hva-śaṅ, that whatever the reflection one engages in, it all binds to *saṃsāra,* it would be necessary to believe in bondage (to *saṃsāra*) by all such thoughts, "I request the precept of that nonreflection," and "I contemplate (with nonreflection)." And this (belief) has been refuted many times already. Of course, not to impute reality to those (*dharmas*) is the meaning of the scripture.

There is no other means (e.g., to remove distress) as when one stops the reflection that imputes reality, for example, as when one is distressed having mistaken a rope for a snake, and one removes that mistake by certainty that there is no snake as apprehended by that notion. (So also:) when an object is apprehended as real, it is necessary to be certain with a proper reason that there is not that real thing, and to be accustomed to the meaning of this (certainty); but it is not possible, by a mere beckoning of mind toward the subject, stop the mind from imputing reality.

Besides, it is necessary to believe that the (imagination) which imputes reality (to the object) is mistaken, for if it were not mistaken, there would be no purpose to cessation. If one accepts that the notion (imputing reality) is mistaken, how is one to recognise it as mistaken if one does not know that there is not the object as our minds apprehend it? This is because whether the intellect (*buddhi*) is mistaken or not mistaken involves only the presence or absence of the object which is the purview of apprehension. For demonstrating that there is no object in the way it is apprehended by imputation of reality, and that it is not proven by mere thesis, one should look to the scriptures and the Set of Principles which are unsullied. Doing it what way, foundation is the nonreality, and then the fixation with nonreflection on reality—this is our position, so it is necessary to have nonreflection as the preliminary to right discrimination, but it does not suffice to have just nonreflection. That is also the position of *Bhāvanākrama III:*[437]

Therefore, in the Illustrious Dharma are mentioned the nonmindfulness (*asmṛti*) and the non-mental-orientation (*amanasikāra*) and they are to be viewed as preliminary to right discrimination (*bhūta-pratyavekṣā*). Consequently, nonmindfulness and non-mental-orientation are possible with right discrimination, not otherwise.

And,[438]

Discerning has the nature of right discrimination according to the *Āryaratnamegha* and the *Saṃdhinirmocana.* And in the *Ārya-Ratnamegha,* it is said that there is entrance into non-sign-source through the comprehension of non-self-existence by the inspection with discerning. And in the *Laṅkāvatāra* it is said: "For what reason, Mahāmati, one does not understand the individual and general characteristic of things that are being inspected by *buddhi,* for that reason all *dharmas* are declared to have non-self-existence." If (as others assert) one should not do the right discrimination, that would be in contradiction with the many kinds of promulgations by the Lord of right discrimination in these and those sūtra passages. Accordingly, one should know the principles that were declared, to wit, who is himself of small insight, small striving, he cannot learn much, cannot search, and that the Lord praised the one of much learning (or hearing), so at all times, (your) abandonment is not right.

Likewise, that (the *dharmas*) from form up to omniscience are nowhere located by *buddhi* is stated (in the Prajñāpāramitā scripture), and it is not valid to apprehend as real the domain (*viṣaya*) where those (*dharmas*) will be located. That it is not this way (i.e., real) is also stated along the same lines in regard to the six perfections, etc., and it is also necessary to take them as without location.

It is not valid to locate (those *dharmas*) by apprehending them as real, as was previously explained. That those (*dharmas*) are not real depends on comprehension, so it is stated (in the sūtras) that there is no place and no reflection of that sort (of *dharmas*); and it is stated (in the sūtras) that all those domains (*viṣaya*) (where there is no place, and which are not subject to reflection = discursive thought) only precede the right discrimination that refutes the accomplishment by own-nature or the real existence. May you (the intelligent and persevering ones) be informed of that!

Of course, the statements in the scriptures (*pravacana*) of the inconceivable and of transcending the *buddhi* are there so as to defeat the (beginner's) pride of understanding the profound meaning by mere hearing and thinking. Those (profound meanings) may be introspected (in the *samāpatti*) of the nobles, so (those scriptures) teach the inconceivability, etc. on the part of others (the ordinary persons). Moreover, the profound meaning was stated (as inconceivable, etc.) so as to oppose the improper (muddle-headed) thinking that apprehends it (the profound meaning) in realistic manner, but one should know that it does not oppose the methodical examining with discriminative insight, as the *Bhāvanākrama III* mentions:[439]

Accordingly, in whichever places (of sūtras) is heard the verbal elaboration[440] of the "inconceivable," etc., in those places, it was so that those who deem to comprehend reality by a mere hearing and thinking would have their pride defeated, and was to show the introspective realization of the *dharmas*. One should understand that the defeat is of the improper thinking, and not a defeat of right discriminations. Otherwise, it would be in contradiction with numerous principles and scriptures.

The way in which it would contradict many scriptures is, for instance, as the *Kāśyapaparivarta* puts it:[441]

> Kāśyapa, what is the middle path that is the right discrimination of the *dharmas?* Kāśyapa, in whatever place there is discrimination of no self, and discrimination of no sentient being, no living being, no feeder, no man, no person, no one born from Manu, no descendent of Manu, Kāśyapa, this is the middle path that is the right discrimination of *dharmas.*

It would be in contradiction with such passages as that one. Moreover, the *Bhāvanākrama I* states:[442]

> As to what the *Avikalpapraveśadhāraṇī* says, namely, "By non-mental-orientation (*amanasikāra*) one avoids the sign-sources of form, etc."—in that place also the purport is that the one without apperception as a result of inspecting with insight, has no mental orientation there. But it is not merely no mental orientation, because, just as in the case of the nonideational equipoise (*asaṃjñi-samāpatti*), the immemorial clinging to form, etc. is not destroyed by a mere avoiding of the mental orientation.

This *ācārya* (Kamalaśīla) has written a commentary on this *dhāraṇī* (the *Avikalpapraveśa-dhāraṇī-ṭīkā*) that clarifies the matter.

In short, the Mahāyāna has two methods of views of the extensive commentaries in the texts of Ārya-Nāgārjuna and Ārya-Asaṅga, and no views other than those. Also, the illustrious savants of India and Tibet appear to have relied on a certainty in one or other of the two views as commented by those two (Nāgārjuna and Asaṅga), so doubtless one should search in accordance with what occurs in the individual texts of the respective views of those two (Nāgārjuna and Asaṅga).

Moreover, the way of search by recourse to the texts of the *ārya* father and son (i.e., Nāgārjuna and Āryadeva) was previously explained (at length); and if one follows Ārya-Asaṅga (whose way of search was not explained)—(it is this way): in reality, the subject and object (apprehender and thing apprehended) are void in every way of diverse material, but to immature beings (i.e., ordinary persons) these appear as though of diverse material. As in the manner in which this appears, the imaginary domains are imputed reality; and upon the dependency (character) is the perfect (character) whose nondual entity has refuted, according to the scripture and principles, all (the imaginary). Having gained steadfast certainty in that (perfect character), one disposes upon that view the stoppage-cultivation as well as the examining with discrimination and it is necessary to perform both cultivations. But given the understanding of such as that (view), at the time of cultivation, there does not go with contemplation of that voidness a mere (disposing of) nonreflection which is not disposed upon that view. The method of establishing the view of this school is very clear; and the aim of the establishment, the method of separate protection of calming and discerning, and the method of their pair-wise union is very clear in the *Prajñāpāramitopadeśa* (of Ratnākaraśānti), so one should look there. When one well understands this school, the engagement in contemplation as found in its texts is very much a marvel.

The scriptures of the Mahāyāna contain the profound meaning (i.e., the *paramārtha*) in compressed form, and therein many points are explained. However, there are also many points that are not explained, so it is necessary to draw upon the texts which explain what is not explained there (i.e., in the scripture). It is necessary to draw upon (those texts) which expand upon what is not expanded there (in the scripture). Likewise, it is necessary that the side (the steps of the path) that is far extended (i.e., the *saṃvṛti*) be known; but it is not valid thus to embrace a single side, leaving out one or other of the profound and the far-extended. In reference to this (meaning), the complete character of the guru who teaches the path, and the skill in all the vehicles are set forth in many (authoritative commentaries).

3. SUMMARIZING THE ESSENTIALS OF THE METHOD OF PROTECTION

As previously explained, the person who has gained the view of final meaning, having for the first time established the non-self-existence of self and self's, which are the substratum giving rise to any adherence to the thought of "I" and "mine," should examine many times with discriminative insight and finally would generate the impetus of certainty in the meaning of this, and would mix the stoppage-cultivation which holds (the mind) not to stray and the examining with discriminative insight.

At that time, (if) the examining-cultivation becomes predominant, and the fixation part gets less, one should increase the stoppage-cultivation and engage the fixation part anew. (If) the fixation part gets predominant by virtue of stressing the stoppage-cultivation and there be no enthusiasm for examining, then upon not examining there is no strong impetus for steadfast certainty in reality. When this (kind of certainty) does not occur, there is no opposition with that much on the side of certainty-reversal to the over-affirmation (or superimposition) that posits the presence of the two kinds of self. Therefore, by way of stressing the examining-cultivation, one cultivates calming and discerning with equal portions. Thus, in the *Bhāvanākrama III:*[443]

At what time he would cultivate discerning, and insight become excessive, then on account of diminution of calming, like a fire lamp in the wind, one would not see reality clearly due to the stirred-up nature of consciousness. Hence at that time one should cultivate calming. When calming predominates, like of a person in deep sleep, one would not see reality clearly. Hence, at that time one should cultivate insight.

One may learn according to the explanation in the section on the lesser person how to perform in the (initial) praxis, in the final (phase), and during the in-between states (or watch).[444]

Likewise, one may learn according to the explanation in the previous section on "Calming the Mind" how at the time one contemplates the meaning of nonself, one determines the occurrence of fading and scattering, has the way of recourse to mindfulness and awareness, and attains the equanimity (*upekṣā*) proceeding automatically with no inequality of fading and scattering—the way of relaxation of effort, etc.

It is said in the *Prajñāpāramitopadeśa* that whatever be the object to be contemplated, toward it one practices the method for protecting calming, and generates the cathartic. Besides, toward it one performs the examining-cultivation of discerning, and perfects the cathartic. Accomplishing those separately one unites them pair-wise. According to this (summary of the *Prajñāpāramitopadeśa* exposition) it is held that there is no assurance in doing both the examining and the stoppage in a single current (of watch), while it is satisfactory to do them in separate watches.

In this (phase) the important thing is by way of refuting the grasping-pattern, which is how one's own nescience over-affirms (the object); and for the side reversing that (grasping-pattern) it is necessary to contemplate voidness through generating the impetus of certainty toward that voidness which is void of self-existence. But should one, not refuting the imputation of self and the grasping-pattern of nescience, engage in a private (idiosyncratic) voidness which he contemplates, he does not oppose at all the two imputations of self. So very true was the oft-repeated remark of the former gurus, "For the alarming demon at the East gate, he sacrifices a scapegoat at the West gate."[445]

The previous explanations along those lines are only rough. But for the subtle faults and merits going with the phase of contemplation, one should resort to the skilled kalyānamitras. Since a personal contemplation (by the meditator is necessary for what is to be known, it is not expatiated upon here.[446]

For those methods of cultivation one should abandon the (modern) inflated forms, and make essential the ancient precepts of the Stages of Path, as given in the *Be'u Bum* of Potoba:

Some claim that at the time of (initial) hearing and pondering, one establishes with principle (of *paramārtha*-pondering) the non-self-existence (of the object), and at the time of cultivation (*bhāvanā*) cultivates only nonreflection (*nirvikalpa*).

If one cultivates that way, he cultivates at another time a voidness not associated (with that voidness established by hearing and pondering), and there is no adversary (to the realistic imputation).

That being so, at that very time of cultivation, the one cultivating the freedom from one or many, dependent origination, or another (topic of reasoning), thereon examining separately, would hardly dwell in the state of nonreflection.

Contemplating that way, there is an adversary for (defeating) the defilements (of nescience, etc.). For whoever wants to follow the One Deva (= Atīśa), and wants to ponder the pāramitā—it is the way of cultivating insight.

Besides, he (first) contemplates the nonself of personality, and then is to follow it in that way (i.e., the method of realising the nonself of *dharmas*).

Jo-bo (i.e., Atīśa) also mentioned this (in the *Satyadvayāvatāra*):

> If one asks, by whom was voidness comprehended,
> It is whoever was given a prophecy by the Tathāgata.

He sees the truth of true nature, does
Nāgārjuna and his disciple Candrakīrti.
By the precepts descended from them,
One will comprehend the truth of true nature.

As to the method of the guidance for that, it is according to what Jo-bo (Atīśa) said in his *Madhyamakopadeśa-nāma,*[447] namely, he said it is the mixture of pondering-cultivation and the stoppage-cultivation on the entity which was so pondered.

This (method of guidance) is not distinguished from the school of *ācārya* Kamalaśīla; and, as was previously explained, the purport of the *Madhyamakāvatāra* (of Candrakīrti), the *Madhyamaka-hṛdaya* (of Bhavaviveka), and *ācārya* Śāntarakṣita is similar. Also, it is explained at length in the texts of Maitreya-dharma[448] and Ārya-Asaṅga. The savant Śāntipa, who has mastered that school in errorless manner, has written upon it clearly in his *Prajñāpāramitopadeśa.* That being the case, the method of protection for discerning appears consistent in the texts and precepts descended from Nāgārjuna and Asaṅga.

IV. STANDARD FOR ACCOMPLISHMENT OF DISCERNING THROUGH CULTIVATION

When one cultivates through pondering in that manner with discriminative insight, and while the previously explained cathartic has not yet arisen, it is consistent with discerning; and upon the arising of the cathartic, there is the characteristic of discerning. The nature of the cathartic and the way it arises are as it was explained earlier (i.e., the "Calming the Mind" section).

Furthermore, when the previously accomplished calming is not lost, and the cathartic is attracted by its presence, also there is (the discerning), but in general when there is only the presence of the cathartic, there is not (the discerning). However, if one wonders which one it is (i.e., which is the cathartic that establishes the attainment of discerning), it is, namely, when one performs the pondering cultivation: by its own power it is capable of attracting the cathartic, whereupon discerning occurs. This is the same for both kinds of discerning, the one with a phenomenon as meditative object, and the one with a noumenon as meditative object. The *Saṃdhinirmocana* (VIII, 5) speaks along those lines:

"Lord, as long as he has not attained the corporeal and mental cathartic, and his mental orientation is on the inner reflected image as the domain of *samādhi* of those *dharmas* as they were well pondered, what is the mental orientation?" "Maitreya, it is not discerning. One should call it 'equivalent to a conviction consistent with discerning.'"

And besides, the *Prajñāpāramitopadeśa* states:

He abides in that very attainment of corporeal and mental cathartic; and should examine (or review) with conviction the inner *samādhi* domain of reflected image of the very entity as it had been pondered. As long as the corporeal and mental cathartic has not arisen, for that long it is a mental orientation consistent with discerning. At whatever time it arises, at that time there is (the characteristic of) discerning.

The foregoing amounts to saying that the methods for calming, discerning, and their union pair-wise with the meditative object of a phenomenon is equivalent (to the methods for calming, and so on) with the meditative object of a noumenon.

(Generally,) when the cathartic is able to draw by its own power, there is a single area of thought; and since there is ability to guide by that (own power), the discriminating examining-cultivation by its own power draws the single area (of thought). This is the quality (i.e., the signature) of accomplishing the calming.

A person who has in that way well accomplished calming, and by performing the examining-cultivation proceeds in the associates of calming, should not accept the thought that by performing the discriminative examining-cultivation he would be proceeding in a tiny fixation (of calming).

The standard of whether there is proceeding or not proceeding in the contemplation of discerning when one performs the (mixture of) stoppage-cultivation and examining-cultivation with a meditative object on a noumenon, is whether one obtains the pure faultless understanding in either one of the two views of nonself; and taking that (entity as it was understood) as a meditative object, it is necessary to distinguish by way of presence or absence of the contemplation, and one cannot distinguish by way of anything else.

If one wonders about the inability to distinguish by some (other) sort (i.e., by post-attainment), it is, namely: by the contemplation one stops the coarse appearances among the twofold appearance of object and subject; then his mind is stainless like a (cloudless) sky, attended with a special awareness (*rig ciṅ*), brightness (*gsal*), and clarity (*dvaṅs pa*), and abides for a long time like a fire-lamp not buffeted by the wind. And should appearances of inner and outer objects, such as a rainbow or fine smoke, arise upon the face of the mind and stay there a long time; and should the mind fix itself on any arisings in the domain of apprehension on the side of mind-awareness, than no matter how slight is the fixing, he proceeding with pure calming does not tolerate it. Furthermore, when external entities, form, sound, and so on, initially arise that way, one contemplates them, and at the conclusion (of the contemplation) the forms of prior principles of subjective introspection and (objective) experience depart like an exodus; and at the time of fixing on them with the mind one tolerates scarcely any fixing (and fixation of the mind dwindles). Hence, when one is involved in gaining the view which comprehends the reality without the two (eternalism and nihilism), and (illusory) appearances arise little by little, one has no capacity to establish even slight comprehension of the illusory entity as it was explained in the Mādhyamika (section), because when a person does not direct his intellect (*buddhi*) to the view (of reality), at the time he guards for a long time the fixation part (the *cittasthiti*) there are many arisings little by little of such sort (of illusory appearances).

Accordingly, the illusory entity, as it was explained (previously in the Mādhyamika section), requires an occurring (to the meditator) through resort to both (α) the certainty with knowing the principle which decides that there is no accomplishment by own-nature, and (β) a proof by conventional logic that does not disavow the appearance. For the arising of form, etc. on the face of mind as the attenuated and very clear aspect like a rainbow is only the commingling of both (α) freedom from the tangible, with removal of impediment, and (β) the glittering-light appearances, but not with removal of impediment. Because according to that (method), while there is the certainty of no self-existence, the certainty would not last. And because one applies the name of non-self-existence through apprehending together the self-existence to be refuted and the tangible with impediment.

If you say it is not that way, then accepting that sort (of arising) as a false entity and accepting illusion as explained by the Mādhyamika, there would not arise the reflection that attributes presence of self-existence in those, the rainbow and the fine smoke, upon apprehending that there is the basis of their distinction, because that very certainty that there is the basis of the distinction (the rainbow, etc.) is the certainty of non-self-existence in the appearance.

There is nothing to draw certainty of non-self-existence in that tangible with impediment through apprehending it as the basis of a distinction, because that very certainty of a basis of distinction is an imputation that there is self-existence.

Hence, at the time when form, etc. arise that way (as discussed above), precisely that arising in the aspect attenuated and clear (*srab ciṅ dvaṅs pa*) is the adherence to the manner in which those objects are laid out as being the situation, but that arising is without a bit of refutation of the object (with the grasping-pattern of nescience), and so it is not an illusory entity; but when a person previously gains the pure view (of reality) and does not forget it, those (appearances) arise as illusory (thus as composites of appearance and void). This was previously explained.

From among the stages of the path descended from the kalyāṇamitra Dgon-pa-ba, the method of arising of that comprehension of voidness is held to be as follows: First one contemplates the nonself of personality. Then one contemplates the meaning of nonself of *dharma* with the control by mindfulness and awareness. Furthermore, in the case of a long watch, failing in the control by mindfulness and awareness, sometimes there occurs a fading, sometimes a scattering (of the meditative object), so there is meager benefit. Hence, one must halt in the four watches of morning, evening, dusk, and dawn, dividing each watch by four, making sixteen watches in a single day—thus with a clarity of contemplation, or (derivative) experiential thinking. By contemplating in this way, then not having given thought to contemplation for a long time, when one observes for the space of a day and night, speedily there occurs a control of mind in case of an appearance. If one thinks a superior contemplation is a long one, having observed however long, there is no control of mind (toward the meditative object). At the time of controlling the mind, one's stream of consciousness has few defilements, there is no reason to get sleepy or to have idle thinking. Then observing in each watch, the morning one, etc. (that *samādhi*) is endowed with four characteristics:

α. Nonreflection (*nirvikalpa*). At the time of equipoise (*samāpatti*), without feeling the motion of breath in and out, the breath and reflection flow in a subtle manner.

β. Bright (*vyakta*). (Like) noontime in autumn when the circle of sky is bright and undifferentiated.

γ. Clear (*accha*). As when one pours (clean) water into a shiny oblation cup (*tiṅ*), puts it in the sun (to be struck by sunrays), and it is clear to the view.

δ. Subtle (*sūkṣma*). At the time one observes (an object) after being in the realm of those three (foregoing) characteristics, one comes to see the given thing, although arisen in one piece, as though a tip of hair had been fragmented.

This sort of (*samādhi*) is a nonreflection (*nirvikalpa*) consistent with the arising of knowledge (of *ārya-samāpatti*); and nonreflection is compared to (*ārya-*) wisdom (*jñāna*); so to take the own-nature (of that *samādhi*) to be reflection (*vikalpa*) is said to be "contrary." This is set forth in the *Madhyāntavibhāga* (IV, 11A): "It is consistent and contrary" (*anukūlā viparyastā*). According to what is said in the *Madhyāntavibhāga,* one must posit the "consistent" and the "contrary" (*samādhi*) by the voidness of the ordinary person (= contrary) and the other one, the good contemplation (= nonreflection in *ārya-samāpatti*).

If, as previously explained, other characteristics do not arise, one contemplates the view (of reality) with errorless meaning, it is the contemplation of the meaning of nonself. If there is no contemplation of the meaning establishing the view in errorless fashion, even if those four characteristics arise, there is no capacity to posit a contemplation of final meaning (*nitārtha*). Therefore, it is as previously explained, to wit, whether or not there is a contemplation of the meaning of the noumenon (=*paramārtha*); and one should understand as previously explained, to wit, after contemplating that (meaning of noumenon) there follows the method of arising as an illusion.

The Method of Pair-Yoking Calming and Discerning

As it was explained in the sections on the standard for accomplishing those two, if one has not attained both calming and discerning, there is no cause for uniting them in a pair, so for the pair-yoking it is certainly necessary to attain both of them.

And this achievement of pair-yoking is at the time after first attaining discerning. As to its method, one has earlier taken recourse to calming, then upon performing the examining-cultivation, it (the pair-yoking) arises by the sequence of the four mental orientations, "proceeding with enclosure," etc. which are mentioned in this (phase) also. As the four mental orientations were previously explained (in the "Calming the Mind" section), if their time of birth is (here also) they proceed in the pair-yoking. Furthermore, at the conclusion of performing the examining-cultivation, since one has performed and protected the stoppage-cultivation, of what sort was the attainment of calming, of that sort is the stoppage-cultivation present (in the pair-yoking). The *Śrāvakabhūmi* (YS III) speaks along the same lines:[449]

Among those, how does calming as well as discerning occur in equal union when the pair is mixed, whereby it is called "path with pair-yoked driving"? He said: in thought fixation of the nine kinds, to wit, whoever attains the equipoised state of nine kinds. And he, having taken recourse to that perfect samādhi, engages the (instruction of) insight, namely, of discerning the *dharmas*. At that time, for him discerning the *dharmas* there is the path which proceeds by its own essence (*svarasavāhana*), and the one which proceeds without effort by reason of no instigation. Just as is the path of Calming, (at that time) a pure and purified Discerning proceeds, controlled by being yoked to calming and by elation. Therefore, it is said, his calming as well as his discerning occur in equal union when the pair is mixed. And one says there is the path with calming and discerning proceeding pair-yoked.

Besides, the *Bhāvanākrama III* explains:[450]

> So (having taken recourse to calming), at whatever time, by freedom from fading and excitement, the mind engages equally, proceeding by its own essence, it occurs there on the reality with exceeding clarity. At that time, by reason of relaxation of effort, it becomes equable. And at that time, it is to be known as the perfect path, with calming and discerning proceeding pair-yoked.

However, why is that sort (of engagement with calming and discerning) called "pair-yoking"? When one has not previously attained the fixation part with no reflection, that discriminative examining-cultivation is not able by its own power to attract it (the single-pointedness). Hence, one must contemplate individually and separately the endeavor of both the examining-cultivation and the stoppage-cultivation. And when one has attained those two, the very performance of the discriminative examining-cultivation is able to attract calming, so it is "pair-yoking."

Furthermore, the examining (of this context) is discerning. The fixation at the conclusion of the examining has calming in a distinguished way: it has voidness as the meditative object.

The *Prajñāpāramitopadeśa* further explains:

> After that (stationing in calming), one takes that same reflected image of form as the meditative object along with reflection (or, discursive thought). (Otherwise stated:) At whatever time that very thought (the meditative support) is uninterrupted, and (on that basis) the mental orientation (with the thrust of examining-cultivation) is without gap, and one experiences the two by that current, at that time it is called "path which is pair-yoking calming and discerning." Here, calming and discerning are the "pair," and "yoking" means "possessing (both)"; thus they proceed mutually bound.

The meaning of "without gap" is that, having established the continuance of precisely that examining-cultivation, it is not necessary to establish the nonreflection, for the nonreflection is attracted by virtue of that examining-cultivation. "Experiences the two" means that one experiences both the calming with meditative object in a reflected image with no reflection, and the discerning of that meditative object in the reflected image together with discerning. Moreover, it is not the identical time, but one experiences that very mental orientation of the cultivation by a current without gap.

However, it may be wondered whether it is a contradiction to explain that after having accomplished calming, the fixation part is accomplished by the discriminative examining-cultivation. (In reply:) That (explanation) amounts to this: when calming is not accomplished previously, then when one examines again and again and if at its conclusion one mixes it with fixation, it is not possible to accomplish calming. But when one has achieved calming and one does it that way (i.e., mixing examining with fixation), it is taught that by the contemplation there is accomplished a special calming—so there is no contradiction. Moreover, when there is the previous accomplishment of discerning by means of an examining-cultivation, immediately thereafter there is a phase[451] with capacity to attract one-pointedness. So, on the other hand, one may examine in that (situation when one has first accomplished calming). Therefore, if prior to accomplishing discerning, one examines again and again, and at its conclusion mixes with fixation, it is impossible to accomplish calming. And as to having acquired calming, with the examining-cultivation being unable to attract the nonreflection, this previous explanation has to do with the situation when previously one had not accomplished (discerning) and sets aside the meditative object, or abandons it.

In short, when one has not previously accomplished calming, at the conclusion of an examining's (examining-cultivation) along with a single fixation (on a meditative object), then performing a stoppage's stoppage-cultivation—there is no possibility to accomplish calming. And having accomplished calming, but not having previously accomplished discerning, the examining-cultivation does not draw by its own power a firm fixation part with a single area (of thought). But that very examining which frequently examines with discriminative insight achieves a firm fixation part (of calming); thus, it having come after attaining discerning, the pair-yoking thereupon is established.

Therefore, just as a tiny fish darts out over a place of still water, from the realm of the nondeteriorating honey of nonreflection which is the firm fixation part, it suffices to discriminate the meaning of nonself. Make no mistake that there is pair-yoking of calming and discerning in those two sets!

According to that, the method of pair-yoking of calming and discerning may be known according to those cited texts (*Śrāvakabhūmi, Prajñāpāramitopadeśa,* etc.), and one should put no trust in explanations that diverge from those with idle speculations. By way of these (sources) while it appears also necessary to differentiate many special points in the method of protecting calming and discerning, through fear of the many words I shall not write upon the matter.

[Brief Statement of the Meaning of the Path]

Now I shall speak a little on the general summary meaning of the path. At first one reaches the method of resort to a spiritual guide (*kalyāṇamitra*) who is the root of the path; so one must analyze minutely that (method of resort). Then when one generates a genuine desire to take heart in the favorable states (*dal ba*), he exhorts from within himself the continuous accomplishment of that (attitude which so desires). So in order to generate that (attitude) he should contemplate the elements of the favorable states (*dal 'byor*). Then he endeavors not to veer from the kind of attitude that pursues the goal in the present life, while contemplating that it was because he did not strongly pursue the goal in former worlds that his present acquirement of a body will not last long with its impermanence, and that he will die and wander in evil destinies. At that time with the arising of his authentic mind remembering the fears (of evil destinies), he cherishes the virtues of the three refuges, and for generating certainty takes the shared vow of going to refuge, and studies the points of instructions for that (taking of refuge). Then he generates and makes firm by many avenues the faith with trust in *karma* and fruit—the great essential for all the good *dharmas;* of the ten (paths of *karma*) he should endeavor to induce the good (side) and to avert the evil (side), and he should continually engage the path with four powers.[452] Having proceeded that way, he stores for future use the elements of the *Dharma* for the lesser person (*skyes bu chuṅ ṅu*); and giving much thought to the general and special disadvantages of cyclical flow (*saṃsāra*), he should put his mind on how to avert the generality of cyclical flow. Then having determined the cause from which arises *saṃsāra* to be the nature of *karma* and defilement, he should generate a genuine desire to eliminate that (*karma* and defilement), and having drawn certainty in the generality of the three instructions for the path that liberates from *saṃsāra,* as a particular case one should endeavor in the *prātimokṣa* (vow) which is taken by oneself. Having proceeded that way, he stores for future use the elements of the *Dharma* for the middling person; and having oriented his mind to the thought that just as oneself has fallen into the ocean of phenomenal life, so many have gone likewise; and he must endeavor in how to arouse the exercise of the mind of enlightenment, which constitutes the root of love and compassion. If that (generation of the mind) is absent, then such practices as the six perfections (of the Bodhisattva) and the two stages (of generation and completion in the Tantra) are like constructing the superstructure minus the foundation. When a little aspect of tasting that (aspiration mind) has arisen in the stream of consciousness, one should embrace it ritually, and how one should fortify the aspiration is through endeavoring in what should be learned of it. After that, he should hearken to the glorious practice of the mind of enlightenment and know the demarcations of what to ward off (i.e., reject) and what to engage (i.e., accept), and should generate a strong desire to learn those (demarcations). Having engendered those attitudes (of accepting and rejecting), he should take ritually the vow of entrance (into the Bodhisattva practice) and should learn the six perfections (*pāramitā*) which mature one's own stream of consciousness; and especially should risk his life with fierce endeavor for (i.e., against) the basic transgressions (which destroy the vow of the enlightenment mind).[453] He should endeavor to be not stained by the minor and middling sins (the lower basic transgressions); and if stained, should endeavor to make amends. Then, he must study especially the two last perfections (*dhyāna* and *prajñā*); thus having become skilled in the way of protecting meditation (*dhyāna*) he should accomplish *samādhi;* and wherefore arises in the stream of consciousness a pure view, free from eternalism and nihilism, of the two kinds of nonself (i.e., of *pudgala* and *dharma*), so he should have done. Knowing the pure method of protection which protects the attainment after positing just there the view, he should have done and protected. Calming and discerning are designations for the *dhyāna* and *prajñā* of that sort, and are not an official function withdrawn from *dhyāna* and *prajñā*. That being so, having taken the vow of enlightenment mind, one comes forth from between the study of that study-topic (calming and discerning).

Furthermore, when in the process of cultivating the lower from the lowest (steps of the path, from recourse to the spiritual guide) he goes ever greater in his desire to attain the higher to the highest (up to discerning the real), and when hearkening from the higher to the highest, he goes ever and ever greater in his desire to accomplish the lower from the lowest—he passes to the essential point. And when he omits some of the earlier ones (recourse to the spiritual guide, etc.) and tries with only the single part of mind fixation, or only the single part of understanding the view, even beating the dust for a year, it is exceedingly difficult for him to attain the essential point. So it is necessary that he draw certainty in fulfilling the body of the path.

At the time one cultivates those (parts of the path), having practiced reflection (of certainty), it is necessary to have equal parts (in terms of upper, lower, and middling) of attitudes (about the path cultivation), as follows: If (at first) there appears meager devotion to the spiritual guides who provide guidance on the path, one should endeavor in the method of recourse (to the spiritual guide) by way of the accounts that show them to be the root of all the collections of good (fruit) (in the future). Likewise, if the enthusiasm for the accomplishment be weak, it is necessary to emphasize a contemplation on the elements of favorable birth, and should there be a gross attachment in the present life, (contemplation) on the disadvantages of impermanence and evil destiny. If laziness should show up in one who has taken vows, and scant certainty in *karma* and fruit should take over his mind, he should emphasize the contemplation of *karma* and fruit. If one is impenitent for all of *saṃsāra*, his attitude of pursuing the aim of liberation amounts to just words, so he should give thought to (the full list of) the disadvantages of *saṃsāra*. If there is no strong urging of mind on how to perform the benefit of sentient beings, one cuts off the root of the Mahāyāna, so one should much exert himself (sincerely) in the mind of aspiration together with its motive (i.e., compassion). If one having taken the vow of the sons of the Victor is studying the practice (of the Bodhisattva) and has a strong inclination to the bondage of adherence to sign-sources, then by knowing the principle he should destroy all the directing (by grasping patterns) to objective supports as held by the mind that adheres to sign-sources, and should train his mind in the voidness that is like the sky (i.e., the initial arising as void), and like illusion (i.e., the subsequent combination of appearance and void). If (one's) mind does not stay on a virtuous meditative object and appears to be a slave to distraction, one should especially guard the fixation part, which is the single area (of thought). So spoke the former (gurus of the path-stages).

One should know as well the points not made explicit by what is shown by that (foregoing method of equal emphasis); and in short, it is necessary, without passing into a one-sidedness, to employ as is appropriate all virtuous sides of the stream of consciousness.

From the stages of the path of the great person, finished is the explanation of the method, when one is training in the practice of the Bodhisattva, of how to learn discerning (*vipaśyanā*) which is the nature of insight (*prajñā*).

[Brief Introduction to Vajrayāna]

(*Tantra*). Second,[454] there is the particular method of studying the Diamond Vehicle (*vajrayāna*). By the previous method one has trained in the path which is common to both Sūtra and Mantra (= Tantra). And afterward doubtless one should enter the Tantra, because this path is a more rare *dharma* than other *dharmas,* and speedily fulfills the two collections.

If one enters that (path of the mantras), as stated in the *Pathapradīpa* (of Atīśa) one pays respect to the guru and pleases him by acting according to his preaching, and he (the guru) must do more than what was explained previously (the nontantric steps of the path). Moreover, as explained therein (the *Pathapradīpa*) he (the guru) should have the complete characteristics, without upper limit, and one should act accordingly (to rely upon him, etc.).

Then, since the initiation (*abhiṣeka*) is what matures (the candidate), at the outset one should get the stream of consciousness matured by someone (i.e., the guru) who explains according to the (authoritative) tantric sources. Then, at that time he makes (the candidate) listen to the pledges and vows to be taken, fully informs, and makes (the candidate) guard (them as stipulated), and should basic transgressions strike, have him renew (his vows). When there is an undue delay in the arising in the stream of consciousness of the virtues of the path, (the candidate) should exert himself strenuously not to be stained by those (basic transgressions) and should exert himself not to be stained by coarse transgressions. And if unintentionally (*brgyal*) stained, should resort to the means for making amends. These (instructions in the pledges and vows) are the main thing for cultivating the (diamond) path, because in their absence, it is comparable to a foundation giving way and the house caving in. The *Mañjuśrī-mūla-tantra* proclaims:[455]

The munindra (lord of silent sages) denied that a person of impure morality has success of Mantras.

This passage amounts to denying superior, middling, and inferior success (for such a person). Also, it is said in the *Anuttarayoga-tantra* that when a person tries to accomplish with the three, to wit, not guarding the pledges, poor initiation, and not knowing the reality, in no case does he accomplish; so the one who announces his cultivation of the (tantric) path while not guarding pledges and vows, has (merely) strayed away from the method of the Vajrayāna.

Accordingly, that person who (properly) guards his pledges and vows may cultivate the Mantra path; and (among the two stages) he first of all should contemplate the full deity-circle of the Stage of Generation (*utpatti-krama*), as set forth in many (authoritative) tantric sources. The unshared thing to eliminate in the Mantra path is this ordinary (or vulgar) discursive thought which clings to the autonomy of the (impure) aggregates, elements, and sense bases, because, besides eliminating that (sort of discursive thought), the Stage of Generation transforms into a distinguished appearance the place (where one is), the body (on which perception is based), and the food (which nourishes).

Having in that way purified the ordinary discursive thought, one is at all times blessed by the Buddha and his sons (the Bodhisattvas), and one easily fulfills an immeasurable collection of merit. That being the case, one is a proper vessel for the Stage of Completion, and then one must contemplate (the methods) occuring in the tantric sources of the Stage of Completion. But that one should contain himself within the later stage (i.e., the Stage of Completion), casting aside the first stage (i.e., the Stage of Generation), thus exerting himself in a single portion of the path, is not the position of the Tantras or of the learned men who have written the authoritative commentaries on them. Therefore, one should retain in memory the essential of the two stages that complete the body of the Anuttarayoga path.

These (methods) are here taught only roughly as the entrance in the Tantra, and only by some terminology. For the extensive treatment, one must know them from the works on the stages of the Mantra path.

If one trains by the foregoing method, one is training in the completion of the body of the path which comprises all the essentials of the Sūtras and the Tantras. So it serves for having the aim of attaining the favorable conditions, and is the jewel of the Buddha's teaching that is able to enhance (with certainty) one's own and another's (the candidate's) stream of consciousness.

[Final Verses and Colophon]

When his one eye sees the far-spread promulgations of the Muni, (the other's) one well knows as they are all the texts and schools. When this (text) arouses joy in those with knowledge, this sort of method was trained in (by another, Tsoṅ-kha-pa) relying on the spiritual guides. Who being the primordial Buddha, Mañjughoṣa (the presiding deity), by whom (Tsoṅ-kha-pa) well took refuge; by whose power one becomes skilled in analyzing the manner of being, may those best of skilled men always guard!

(Śastra sources)

1. Who are head ornaments of all the learned men of India,
   the famed emblems of victory, shining for living beings
   —Nāgārjuna and Asaṅga—the steps of the path to enlightenment
   have well descended in accordance with the steps from those two.
2. Completely fulfilling all the desired aims of the countless
   beings, it is the powerful king of jewels;
   And by gathering in the thousand rivers of texts and schools,
   it is the ocean of glorious well-expressed teachings.
3. The one who is the great Pandit, Dīpaṅkara (i.e., Atīśa),
   illumined the snowy range; and in this country (of Tibet)

the eye which views the good path of the Victor,
did not close for a long time.

4. Then, in time, all the essentials of the teaching, as the learned men had understood them, were dissipated;
And this good path for a long time was lost.
Having seen that method (of decline) and so as to enhance the Teaching,—
5. Given that the Jina had stated all the method of *Dharma,* however much it be, and was the driver of the best vehicle, whereby a single fortunate being may travel (to the city of omniscience), namely, the method to take to heart that is well comprised in the steps of the path.
6. I tried to draw all the essentials of the meaning, without verbosity, though not incomplete, so that even a person of slight intelligence could understand it easily, and do this by way of the path of methodical pondering with scripture and principle.
7. (However,) the entrance passageway for the sons of the Victor (i.e., the Bodhisattvas) is very difficult to comprehend; and even among fools I am very foolish—so I confess whatever faults have arisen here (in this work) in the presence of the witnesses as to how (the scripture is).

(Aspirations)

8. May I there through long endeavor amass the two collections (of merit and knowledge) as wide as the sky, and as a powerful Jina act as guide for all the living beings whose *buddhi*-eye (which sees *dharma*) is blinded by nescience.
9. Even if in all my lives I do not attain there (i.e., the Buddhahood-goal aspired to), may Mañjughoṣa, in his compassion, assist me, so that I may attain the best of paths with full complement of stages as taught; and by accomplishing it, please the Buddhas.
10. In the way I have personally understood the essentials of the path, using skill in the means drawn by spirited compassion, may I, by dispelling the mental darkness of living beings, cause them to embrace for a long time the teaching of the Victor.
11. In a place which is not pervaded by the excellent jewel of the Teaching; or if (once) pervaded, (now) it had declined, may I with great compassion sway the mind (of the people there) and reveal the treasure of benefit and happiness.
12. The steps of the path to enlightenment have been well framed from the (combining of the) marvelous acts of the Buddhas and Bodhisattvas; so may they confer glory on the mind pursuing liberation, and protect for a long time the deeds of the Jina.

13. May the concordant conditions for arranging the good path be effectuated, the discordant conditions be dispelled, so that in all lives (henceforth) no human or nonhuman will be deprived of the pure path extolled by the Buddha.
14. At whatever time persons enterprise the methodical accomplishment by the ten practices of *dharma*[456] in the highest vehicle, may at that time they always associate with the powerful (guardians), and may all directions be pervaded by the ocean of good auspice.

(Perfection of *Dharma*)

Thus the waylaying by the two chariots, Nāgārjuna and Asaṅga, who comprise the essentials of all the scriptures of the Victor (the Buddha)—the manner of *dharma* of the best person (belonging to the Mahāyāna) who travels to the stage of omniscience: "The stages of the path to enlightenment, showing completely the steps to be taken to heart by the three orders of persons".

(Perfection of Influential Persons)

The great son of the Jina, Rṅog (the translator) Blo-ldan-śes-rab, the great rgyal-tshab,[457] gained skill in the *piṭaka* of inner science and practiced its meaning, i.e., properly took it to heart.

Dkon-mchog-tshul-khrims, the illustrious friend of the jewel of the Teaching by way of guiding numerous beings; and the ones faithful to their vows of yore, on the one hand—the Rgyal-tshabs, who were the honored, illustrious Vinayadharas—adorned with many jewels of merits of understanding, to wit, learning, compassion, etc., and merits of scripture;

And among the ones faithful to their vows, of the snowy range, the great Vinayadhara on high like a topmost banner, the Mkhan chen Zul-phu-ba[458] Dkon-mchog-dpal-bzaṅ-po. Moreover, many seekers of the goal, who were influential in past time. In later times, there were those who gained skill in the extensive Sūtras and Tantras, and thereby became preeminent among those (skilled in) the texts and schools, and were highly esteemed among those with the three jewels of the instruction (morality, mind training, and insight).

And on the other hand, the unrivaled bilingual speaker (i.e., translator) who carried the burden of the jewel of the Teaching, the perfect spiritual guide, the mahāsattva called Skyabs mchog dpal bzaṅ po; and those who accepted that illustrious person's influential pronouncements.

(Perfection of Spiritual Guides)

I heard from the venerable illustrious one with the name SPACE (Nam-mkha', i.e., Lho brag mkhan chen Nam-mkha'-rgyal-mtshan) the lineage from Dgon-pa-ba to Sne'u-zur-pa, and the steps of the path descended from Spyan-sna-pa. Also, I heard from the venerable illustrious one whose name ends in GOOD (bzaṅ-po, i.e., Chos-skyabs-bzaṅ-po) the steps of the path in lineage of Po-to-ba to Śa-ra-ba; and of Po-to-ba to Dol-pa. And heard (those lineages) together with the meaning. The text going with these precepts, the *Bodhipathapradīpa* (of Atīśa) teaches only the general characteristics of the three orders of persons; it is conceptually easy without needing more words, so is not cited (here). Having taken as essential the organization of the steps of the path according to the great translator (i.e., Rṅog, his *Bstan rim*), and the master's disciple Gro-luṅ-pa (his *Bstan rim rgyas bsdus*), (I) compiled the essential points from many (works on) steps of the path (by other spiritual guides), and gladly took on the task of completing the parts of the path, so that this arrangement, without disturbing the sequence (would be) a great vehicle for the snowy range, and would methodically accomplish the aims of the great virtuous texts and schools with confident eloquence toward the far-extended scriptures. So with my head I take the dust at the feet of the great being who has wondrously given delight to the Buddha and his sons—the venerable illustrious Red-mda'-pa; and of other illustrious gurus.

(Perfection of the Author)

The bhikṣu who hears much, who eliminates (by meditation), Śar-Tsoṅ-kha-pa Blo-bzaṅ-grags-pa'i-dpal, has well composed this; the scribe is Bsod-nams-dpal-bzaṅ-po.

(Perfection of the Place)

In the yaṅ-dgon of Byaṅ Rva-sgreṅ-rgyal-ba'i dben-gnas;[459] at the Brag-seṅ-ge'i źel gyi ri-khrod.

May this enable the spread of the jewel of the Teaching in all directions by all agencies.

OM SVASTI.

NOTES, GLOSSARIES, AND BIBLIOGRAPHY

Abbreviations Used in the Notes and Bibliography

Avatāra-comm. Candrakīrti's self-commentary on the *Madhyamakāvatāra.*

BHS Dictionary. Franklin Edgerton's *Buddhist Hybrid Sanskrit Dictionary.*

Catuḥ-ś. Āryadeva's *Catuḥ-śataka.*

Catuḥ-ś-ṭ. Candrakīrti's commentary on the *Catuḥ-śataka.*

fol. folio.

MK. *Madhyamaka-kārikā.*

Mūla-prajñā (=Tibetan *rtsa śe*). Tsoṅ-kha-pa's reference to *Madhyamaka-kārikā.*

PTT. The Tibetan Tripitaka, Peking edition. . . ., reprinted under the supervision of the Otani University, Kyoto, ed. by Daisetz T. Suzuki, vols. 1–168 (Tokyo-Kyoto, Tibetan Tripitaka Research Institute, 1955–1961).

YS. *Yogasthāna* (one of the four of the *Śrāvakabhūmi*).

Notes

INTRODUCTION

1. As to the translation of *ñams su blaṅ ba'i* by "to be taken to heart," I got the idea from "The Story of the Jar," which is Jātaka no. XVII in Āryaśūra's *Jātakamālā,* and argued this matter in my "Introduction to Tsoṅ kha pa's Lam rim chen mo," *Phi Theta Annual,* vol. 3 (Berkeley, 1952), pp. 61–65, but now have reservations about part of my arguing there long ago.

2. The *Lam rim chen mo* was translated into Mongolian, with its abbreviated reference of *Bodhi Mör* corresponding to *byaṅ chub lam* (path to enlightenment). G. Z. Zubikov edited a Mongolian translation up through no. 3 of the above outline (ending fol. 123b-3) in Vladivostok, Vostochnye Institut, *Isviestiia,* 1914, and translated this portion into Russian on the basis of the Mongolian (*ibid.,* 1913). The entire work was translated from Tibetan into Chinese by Fa-tsun, published Peking, 1936. Gadjin Masato Nagao, with the help of Fa-tsun's translation rendered the "Discerning the Real" section (no. 7 in the above outline) into Japanese in his book *A Study of Tibetan Buddhism* (Tokyo, 1954). Prof. Dr. Johannes Rahder, emeritus of Yale University, once informed me that a short summary of the *Lam rim chen mo* was printed in an Italian book, *Il Nuovo Ramusio,* vol. 2 = *I Cappuccini Marchigiani,* part 4, p. 157–59 (Libreria dello Stato, Rome, 1953), reproducing the record written in 1738 of an Italian missionary in Tibet-Nepal at the beginning of the eighteenth century.

3. According to *The Blue Annals,* part I, by George N. Roerich (Calcutta, 1949).

4. E. Obermiller, "A Sanskrit Ms. from Tibet—Kamalaśīla's Bhāvanā-krama," *The Journal of the Greater India Society,* January 1935.

5. These important dates are from Roerich, *Blue Annals,* part I.

6. This and other Bka'-gdams-pa dates are from Roerich, *Blue Annals,* part I.

7. *a*) The colophon to the *Lam rim chen mo* and *Mchan* annotation; *b*) section Ra of the complete works of the Kloṅ-rdol Bla-ma; *c*) *The Blue Annals,* by G. Roerich; *d*) *Tibetan Painted Scrolls,* by G. Tucci; and *e*) Introduction by Stcherbatsky and Obermiller to the Sanskrit and Tibetan texts of the *Abhisamayālaṃkāra* (Bibliotheca Buddhica, vol. XXIII).

8. For a translation, there is Edward Conze, *Abhisamayālaṃkāra,* Serie Orientale Roma VI (Rome, 1954).

9. Giuseppe Tucci, *Minor Buddhist Texts,* part II (Rome, 1958), p. 102, speaking of the *Abhisamayālaṃkāra,* says "sGam po pa, the disciple of Milaraspa, writes a Lam rim which unlike that of Tsoṅ k'a pa, ignores the book." As we shall see below, the Lam rim literature generally ignores the *Abhisamayālaṃkāra,* and so the avoidance of this type of Prajñāpāramitā exegesis is not a matter of rejecting the gradual or progressive path, as Tucci suggests at this point. One may survey the con-

tents of sGam-po-pa's book in Herbert V. Guenther, *Jewel Ornament of Liberation* (London, 1959). In fact, Tsoṅ-kha-pa takes up the same subjects in his *Lam rim chen mo* but goes much deeper into each topic.

10. The meeting of Tsoṅ-kha-pa with this lama is discussed by Tucci, *Tibetan Painted Scrolls,* p. 418.

11. Cf. Alex Wayman, *The Buddhist Tantras: Light on Indo-Tibetan Esotericism* (New York, 1973), p. 228.

12. The terminology of three orders of persons may very well have been derived from a rather lengthy section in Asaṅga's *Viniścayasaṃgrahaṇī* on his third, fourth, and fifth *bhūmis,* Japanese photographic edition of the Peking Tibetan canon (PTT), vol. 111, p. 7-5-5 to p. 9-3-5, which is devoted to stating many ways of classifying persons as lesser, middling, and superior; and starts by saying, "These three persons, the lesser person, middling person, and superior person, have their inception in praxis (*prayoga*)." That the three orders of persons are distinguished by respective practices rather than by "family" (*gotra*) is clear enough from Atīśa's "Light on the Path to Enlightenment," translated below.

13. There are two previous translations: *a*) the one by Sarat Chandra Das, in *Journal of the Buddhist Text Society of India,* I (1893); *b*) the second one by Alaka Chattopadhyaya, in *Atīśa and Tibet* (Calcutta, 1967).

14. Translated from the edition in the Peking Tanjur (PTT, vol. 103), p. 20-4-1 f., and taking a few notes from Atīśa's own commentary, the *Pañjikā-nāma,* p. 21-5-6, f. (cited hereafter as Comm.).

15. Comm.: the gurus are the Reverend Śrībodhibhadra, the Reverend Suvarṇadvīpa, etc.

16. These members are cited by Tsoṅ-kha-pa in the "Calming" section.

17. Atīśa, of course, means the first five Perfections: giving (*dāna*), morality (*śīla*), forbearance (*kṣānti*), striving (*vīrya*), and meditation (*dhyāna*). The first four are elaborately set forth in Tsoṅ-kha-pa's ascetic handbook for the superior person. Then "meditation" along with "insight" are developed at length in the "Calming" and "Discerning" sections.

18. Comm.: the principle that denies existence by four alternatives.

19. Comm.: the principle called "diamond grain" (*vajrakaṇa*).

20. Comm. appeals to Śāntideva, especially his *Bodhicaryāvatāra,* chap. IX.

21. Comm.: the principle of dependent origination.

22. For various theories about the four successive states, "warmth," "summits," "forbearance," and "supreme mundane natures," cf. A. Wayman, "Buddhism," in *Historia Religionum,* pp. 437–38. The theory that these usher in the first Bodhisattva stage is found in the *Sūtrālaṃkāra* (XIV, 29): "That—which is the revolution (*parāvṛtti*) of his basis—we claim to be the First Stage. And that becomes purified through immeasurable eons." But this seems inconsistent with Atīśa's "not far off."

23. The terminology "great Tantra of the Ādibuddha" refers to the *Kālacakra-tantra.* For initiations "Secret" and "Prajñā-jñāna," cf. Lessing and Wayman, trans., *Mkhas grub rje's Fundamentals of the Buddhist Tantras* (The Hague, 1968), pp. 317–25. For the "transgressions," cf. *Mkhas grub rje's,* pp. 328–29. For the "preceptor's initiation," cf. *Mkhas grub rje's,* pp. 315–17 (there called "Hierophant's Initiation").

24. More recently there is Rudolf Kaschewsky, *Das Leben des Lamaistischen Heiligen Tsongkhapa Blo Bzan-Grags-Pa (1357–1419), dargestellt und erläutert anhand seiner Biographie "Quellenort allen Glücks"* (Wiesbaden, 1971). However, my present biographical materials were prepared during the 1960s, mainly in the summer of 1964, using Tibetan texts of the East Asiatic Library, University of California, when I was in Berkeley with the aid of summer research grant from the University of Wisconsin, of which I was then a faculty member.

25. The *Rje-btsun bla-ma Tsoṅ-kha-pa chen-po'i rnam-par-thar-pa yoṅs-su-brjod-pa'i-gtam-du bya-ba dad-pa'i-'jog-ṅogs źes-bya-ba* (Lhasa edition).

26. The *Rje thams-cad-mkhyen-pa Tsoṅ-kha-pa chen-po'i rnam-thar-gyi bsdus-don cuṅ-zad brjod-pa* (Peking edition).

27. Inaccessibility of Dge-'dun-grub's biography made it necessary to rely for some remarks on Alexandra David-Neel, *Textes tibétains inédit, traduit et présentés* (Paris, 1951), pp. 39–72.

28. Cf. René Grousset, *Histoire de L'Extrême-Orient* (Paris, 1929), pp. 495–96.

29. Instead, he sent his disciple Byams-chen chos-rje to China, where the latter preached the *Kālacakra-tantra.* This disciple, upon his return, founded the monastery of Sera, near Lhasa, in 1419 (the year of Tsoṅ-kha-pa's death), hence not to be confused with the Serā-chos-sdiṅs (below).

30. Cf. Alex Wayman, *Analysis of the Śrāvakabhūmi Manuscript* (Berkeley, 1961), p. 101.

31. Wayman, *Analysis,* p. 108.

32. PTT, vol. 106, p. 178-1.

33. The *Sūtrālaṃkāra-vṛtti-bhāṣya,* PTT, vol. 108, p. 317-5.

34. PTT, vol. 111, p. 19-5.

35. Some excerpts from the Sanskrit MS. along with English translation are found in Wayman, *Analysis,* pp. 60–63.

36. Wayman, *Analysis,* pp. 128–29.

37. Wayman, *Analysis,* p. 129. For this distinction of *abhijñā*-only and clear vision (*vidyā*), cf. Lamotte, *Le Traité,* vol. IV, 1824–1826.

38. PTT, vol. 111, p. 47-4-1.

39. PTT, vol. 111, p. 47-4-3.

40. Paul Demiéville, *Le Concile de Lhasa* (Paris, 1952).

41. Giuseppe Tucci, *Minor Buddhist Texts,* part II, chap. 1, "The Debate of bSam yas According to Tibetan Sources," pp. 3–154.

42. The Maitreya chapter of the sūtra, as cited in Tsoṅ-kha-pa's "Calming" section.

43. Wayman, *Analysis,* p. 86.

44. PTT, vol. 94, p. 179-3.

45. The theory is elaborately set forth in E. Obermiller, "The Doctrine of Prajñā-pāramitā as Exposed in the Abhisamayālaṃkāra of Maitreya," *Acta Orientalia,* vol. XI, reprint, 1932.

46. The *Sde bdun la 'jug pa'i sgo don gñer yid kyi mun sel źes bya ba* (Sarnath edition).

47. See Notes, "Discerning the Real," note 425.

48. Cr. *Mahāyāna-sūtra-saṃgraha,* Dr. P. L. Vaidya, ed. (Darbhanga, 1961), p. 345.10-13.

49. Cf. Étienne Lamotte, *Saṃdhinirmocana Sūtra* (Louvain, Paris, 1935), pp. 94, 215.

50. Cf. Alex and Hideko Wayman, trans., *The Lion's Roar of Queen Śrīmālā* (New York, 1974), index, p. 140, under "*Dharma* (natures)" the entry "constructed or non-discrete (melting of)."

51. Cf. Vidhushekhara Bhattacharya, ed., *The Yogācārabhūmi of Ācārya Asaṅga,* part I (Calcutta, 1957), text 112.12 ff.; equivalent Tibetan in PTT, vol. 109, p. 239-2 ff.

52. PTT, vol. 110, p. 281-3.

53. PTT, vol. 106, p. 202-1-6.

54. Bhattacharya, ed., *The Yogācārabhūmi,* p. 112.16, has incorrectly edited, or else the MS. was faulty, *anarpaṇā.* Cf. Edgerton, *BHS Dictionary,* for *arpaṇā* and *vyarpaṇā,* the readings verified by the Tibetan translation of Asaṅga's text: *gtod ciṅ bye brag tu gtod pa.*

55. PTT, vol. 109, p. 204-3.

56. PTT, vol. 109, p. 272-1.

57. See p. 119, above.

58. Wayman, *Analysis,* pp. 125, 130.

59. Cf. Wayman, *Analysis,* pp. 127–28, for the coarse and calm characteristics.

60. Lamotte, *Saṃdhinirmocana,* pp. 96–97, 105.

61. PTT, vol. 106, p. 202-2-5.

62. This information can be taken together with the previous mention of the word *naimittika* in connection with the varieties of *vitarka* and *vicāra*—and observing that V. Bhattacharya, ed., p. 112, notes that the word *naimittika* was rendered into Tibetan equivalent to *vitarka* and *vicāra*—to explain an important sentence of Vasubandhu's own commentary on the *Abhidharmakośa,* namely, on IV, a-b: *ato nimitte naimittikopacāraṃ kṛtvā aṣṭau mārgāṅgāni vyavsthāpyanta iti.* Here, take *nimitta* as "sign (of the dharma)"; and *naimittika* as "inquiry" (*vitarka*) and "investigation" (or, the previously mentioned "coarse" and "subtle" insight). The sentence can now be translated: "Thus, when there is the 'sign' (of the *dharma*) and one makes the approach of 'inquiry' (directed to the teacher) and 'investigation,' this amounts to saying: the eight path members are established."

63. Cf. Lamotte, *Saṃdhinirmocana,* p. 215.

64. V. Bhattacharya, ed., text 114.16; equivalent Tibetan, PTT, vol. 109, p. 239-5-8 f.

65. V. Bhattacharya, ed., text 115.1; equivalent Tibetan, p. 240-1-4 f.

66. PTT, vol. 111, p. 75-5-4 to p. 76-1-5.

67. Cf. Etienne Lamotte, *La Somme du Grand Véhicule d'Asaṅga,* vol. II (Louvain, 1939), pp. 233–34.

68. For this passage, cf. Karunesha Shukla, *Śrāvakabhūmi of Ācārya Asaṅga* (Patna, 1973), 196.18 to 197.5.

69. Demiéville, *Le Concile,* p. 125.

70. Demiéville, *Le Concile,* p. 147, note.

71. Cf. Alex Wayman, "Aspects of Meditation in the Theravāda and Mahīśāsaka Buddhist Sects," *Studia Missionalia,* vol. 25, 1976.

72. See p. 85, above.

73. Demiéville, *Le Concile,* p. 160.

74. *Ibid.,* pp. 94–95.

75. *Ibid.,* pp. 61–62.

76. *Ibid.,* p. 62, note.

77. Cf. *Mahāyāna-sūtra-saṃgraha,* p. 349.4-5, for the Sanskrit passage.

78. Cf. *Mahāyāna-sutra-saṃgraha,* p. 344.25-26, for the Sanskrit passage.

79. T. R. V. Murti, *The Central Philosophy of Buddhism* (London, 1955), pp. 131, 136, 145, etc.; and for the identification of *dṛṣi* with *anta,* pp. 123, 125, 217. Since Buddhism from ancient times rejected the "extremes" (*anta*)—indulgence and mortification, or existence and nonexistence—it is notable that Murti's interpretation would have the Mādhyamika identify every dṛṣṭi with an *anta,* and disallow any *dṛṣṭi* for the middle (*madhyama*).

80. Daniel Henry Holmes Ingalls, *Materials for the Study of Navya-Nyāya Logic* (Cambridge, Mass., 1951), p. 81.

81. Tarasankar Bhattacharya, *The Nature of Vyāpti according to the Navya-Nyāya* (Calcutta, 1970).

82. *Ibid.,* chap. IV.

83. In "Basic Refutation of the Svātantrika," Teaching the Fault of the Side.

84. Cited in A. Wayman, "The Mirror as a Pan-Buddhist Metaphor-Simile," *History of Religions,* vol. 13, no. 4 (May 1974), pp. 258–59.

85. Nirod Baran Chakraborty, *The Advaita Concept of Falsity—A Critical Study* (Calcutta, 1967), p. 40.

86. Cf. E. H. Johnston, *The Buddhacarita,* part II (Calcutta, 1936), p. 211. These verses are in the portion not extant in Sanskrit, and I have adopted Johnston's rendering from the Tibetan except for changing his "consciousness" (for *vijñāna*) to "perception."

87. PTT, vol. 111, p. 175-3-8. I have cited Asaṅga's passage at length and discussed it in an article, "Dependent Origination—the Indo-Tibetan Tradition," *Journal of Chinese Philosophy,* 1978 volume.

88. This appears to be compatible with the *Chāndogya Upaniṣad,* VI.3.2, vision of *nāma-rūpa* as a divine reality which a creative divinity (replaced in Buddhism by *vijñāna*) enters. See Sengaku Mayeda, "On the Cosmological View of Śaṃkara," *The Adyar Library Bulletin,* Centenary issue, vol. XXXIX (1975), pp. 191–93, for the continuance of this position in Śaṃkara's Vedānta system.

89. As cited in the article of note 87, above.

90. Cf. the article of note 87, above.

91. A. Wayman, "Introduction to Tsoṅ kha pa's *Lam rim chen mo.*"

92. An announcement of my translation labor on the *Lam rim chen mo* was included in *Philosophy East and West* (October 1970), p. 443, in the list "Research in Progress" among members of the Society for Asian and Comparative Philosophy. On February 22, 1977, at Dharmsala, H.P., India, I informed H.H. the Dalai Lama of my translation of this major portion of the *Lam rim chen mo;* and he in turn informed me that as far as he knew no one else had translated into English this portion of Tsoṅ-kha-pa's great work. He explained that the work on "Path to Enlightenment" mentioned in

issues of *The Tibet Journal* (published in Dharmsala) was of the oral tradition going with the path literature.

93. This edition, along with the Tashilunpo printing of the *Lam rim chen mo,* was brought back from Peking by a Berkeley student (now professor at Vancouver), Arthur Link, from whom I obtained them early in the 1950s. I am pleased to report that the annotation edition has been reprinted by the Tibetans in North India: *Lam Rim Mchan Bźi Sbrags ma, Tsoṅ-kha-pa,* vols. I and II (New Delhi, 1972).

94. For dates of the abbots of Galdan, cf. Giuseppe Tucci, *Tibetan Painted Scrolls* (Rome, 1949).

95. Cf. E. Obermiller, *Analysis of the Abhisamayālaṃkāra* (London, 1933), p. v.

96. These researches are embodied in my *Yoga of the Guhyasamājatantra; the Arcane Lore of Forty Verses* (1977).

97. A reader familiar with the fact that in recent years a Sanskrit edition of the *Śrāvakabhūmi,* prepared by K. Shukla, has appeared in India might question my citation of the Sanskrit text from the Bihar M.S. rather than from his edition. But one will understand the justification for my practice by referring to the review of the Shukla edition by De Jong in the *Indo-Iranian Journal,* 1976.

98. There is a good bibliography of Western translations of the Mādhyamika works and associated literature in Jacques May, *Candrakīrti: Prasannapadā Madhyamakavṛtti* (Paris, 1959). Since May's work there has been an increasing study of the works of Bhāvaviveka (Candrakīrti's rival) by scholars in Japan, notably Y. Kajiyama, H. Nakamura, and Y. Ejima; and the works were the topic of a doctoral dissertation at Madison, Wisconsin, by S. Iida. See also Hajime Nakamura, "A Brief Survey of Japanese Studies on the Philosophical Schools of the Mahāyāna."

99. Narthang Kanjur, Mdo, vol. Pha, fol. 202a-3: / 'phags pa'i chos mṅon par gyur pas na śes rab ni tshad mar gyur pa'o /.

100. So Ernst Steinkellner, *Dharmakīrti's Hetubindu,* part II, p. 33, where he translated *dharmin* as "Beschaffenheitsträger," equivalent to the English "bearer of the qualities." The German language capability of nominal compounding renders Steinkellner's translation convenient in his language, while an equivalent operation in English would be clumsy. Mookerjee and Nagasaki, *The Pramāṇavārttikam of Dharmakīrti,* first chap., kārikās I-LI, pp. 8–11, distinguish between the *sādhyadharmin* (the logical subject) and the *dṛṣṭāntadharmin* (the example). The expression "logical subject" is unsuitable for translation purposes of the "Discerning" section. Notice how the renditions "logical subject" and "example" fail to convey the common element of *dharmin,* for which the Tibetan equivalent *chos can* occurs numerous times in Tsoṅ-kha-pa's "Discerning" section.

101. Ingalls, *Materials,* p. 43, distinguishes the two terms by English equivalents: substratum (*ādhāra*), or abode (*āśraya*). Since Tsoṅ-kha-pa's text uses only the one term *gźi,* I employ in translation only "substratum."

CALMING THE MIND

1. Cf. Introduction, section on "*Calming* and *Discerning* as Natures and Categories."

2. Cf. Lamotte, *Saṃdhinirmocana,* chap. VIII, in sect. 32. Yüan-ts'ê, PTT, vol. 106, p. 230-3,4, discusses the passage as controversial in China. Since there is no mention (as would be expected) of

pratyekabuddhas, one theory was that the "śrāvakas" of the passage included the pratyekabuddhas; and another theory was that the "Bodhisattvas" implied the pratyekabuddhas. Again, it was a problem as to how mundane virtuous natures would apply to the Tathāgatas. It is explained that there are two kinds of "mundane"; the first kind naturally accompanied with flux (*āsrava*), and the second kind naturally devoid of flux, because having the world as meditative object. Thus, this second kind is meant in the present context as thoughts equivalent to the "knowledge afterward obtained" (*pṛṣṭhalabdha-jñāna*).

3. Also chap. VIII, in sect. 32. Asaṅga, *Viniścayasaṃgrahaṇī of Cintāmayī bhūmi,* PTT, vol. 111, p. 21-2, states that the characteristic of "contamination" (*dauṣṭhulya*) is in short the characteristic of nonserviceability (*akarmaṇyatā*), and this is of five kinds: *1*) the characteristic of heaviness, *2*) the characteristic of rigidity, *3*) the characteristic of hindrance, *4*) the characteristic of sloth, *5*) the characteristic of inability through lack of exerting control. For the "sign-sources," see Introduction, section on "Asaṅga on the Ancillaries," the paragraph "Restraint of Sense Organs."

4. Giuseppe Tucci, *Minor Buddhist Texts,* part III, *Third Bhāvanākrama* (Rome, 1971), hereafter *Third Bhāvanākrama;* and here p. 1.2-5.

5. Cf. Lamotte, *Saṃdhinirmocana,* chap. VIII, in sec. 3.

6. Cf. Lamotte, *Saṃdhinirmocana,* chap. VIII, in sect. 4. Yüan-ts'ê, p. 183-4, explains the sequence "forbearance . . . discursive thought" as references to the four kinds of "discerning," which are "investigation," "supernal investigation," "consideration," and "profound comprehension": "Among them, 'forbearance' is the forbearance of understanding (*adhigama*); 'longing' is for having conviction (*adhimukti*); 'analysis' is insight (*prajñā*); 'views' is the search (*paryeṣaṇa,* or *eṣaṇā*); 'discursive thought is discrimination (*pratyavekṣaṇa*)." According to Jñānagarbha, the *Kevala* commentary, p. 197-5, "forbearance" is toward the *dharmas* with inexpressible and nondual meaning.

7. Jñānagarbha's *Kevala* commentary, p. 197-4-2, explains: the aspects of mind are the wayward appearance (*log par snaṅ ba*).

8. The Sanskrit original for "traversing" is *saṃtīrayan;* cf. A. Wayman, *Analysis of the Śrāvakabhūmi Manuscript,* p. 110, there improperly (following Edgerton, *BHS Dictionary*) rendered as "judging." For the meaning of "traversing," Jñānagarbha's *Kevala* commentary, p. 197-4-1, explains: "In the phase of (profound) comprehension, one has unified the *dharmas* without aspect (*nirākāra*) and the mind with aspect (*sākāra*)."

9. The expression "concise titles" refers to the list, Sūtra, Geya, etc. For "enumeration," cf. Introduction section on "*Calming* and *Discerning* as Natures and Categories," the "enumerator consciousness" as explained by Sthiramati.

10. Unrai Wogihara, ed., *Bodhisattvabhūmi,* I, p. 109.

11. Cf. Lamotte, *Saṃdhinirmocana,* chap. VIII, in sect. 2.

12. *Candrapradīpa-sūtra* is an alternate name for the *Samādhirāja-sūtra.* The passage is in chap. VII, verse 10a-b (Vaidya, ed.): / akampiyaḥ samathabalena bhoti / śelopamo bhoti vipaśyanāya /.

13. The Sanskrit is in *First Bhāvanākrama,* G. Tucci, ed., in his *Minor Buddhist Texts, Part II* (Rome, 1958), p. 205. A similar citation is in *Śikṣāsamuccaya* (text p. 119.11) from the *Dharmasaṅgīti: samāhitamanaso yathābhūtadarśanaṃ bhavati,* "The vision of things as they really are occurs to the man whose mind is equipoised."

14. Cf. Lamotte, *Saṃdhinirmocana,* chap. IX, in sect. 9.

15. This passage from the *Samādhirāja-sūtra* also partially occurs in *Bhāvanākrama I,* as cited in Tsoṅ-kha-pa's Discerning the Real section where he comments on the words of the sūtra passage.

16. Cf. E. H. Johnston, ed., *The Buddhacarita,* XII, 84–88 (my translation): "Then, desirous of hearing something superior, he (the future Buddha) proceeded to the hermitage of Udraka. But on account of the *ātmagrāha* (adherence to self) neither did he accept his system. For the *muni* Udraka, knowing the fault of both ideation and non-ideation, found beyond nothingness a state consisting of neither ideation nor non-ideation. For the reason that the pair ideation and non-ideation have each a subtle object, he thought that beyond them was a state 'neither ideation nor non-ideation' and thereon went his enthusiasm. And since the intelligence (*buddhi*) remains just there, without wandering elsewhere, subtle and incompetent; therefore, in that state there is neither the conceived nor the nonconception. And since after reaching this, one returns to the world, the Bodhisattva, desiring the highest, thereupon left Udraka."

17. The list from birth down to perturbation constitutes the last two members of dependent origination, namely "birth" (no. 11) and "old age and death" (no. 12), followed by the usual appendage to dependent origination of the suffering aroused in others, "grief" down to "perturbation." Here the set is called the "aggregate of suffering."

18. The citation interprets the opening of the Buddhist scriptures "Thus by me it was heard" (*evaṃ mayā śrutam*) as a hearing from another—according to the suggestion of Tsoṅ-kha-pa's "Discerning" section, that "nonself" cannot be learned from "self."

19. The Sanskrit is available in *First Bhāvanākrama,* Tucci, ed., p. 213, by a citation without name of source.

20. *First Bhāvanākrama,* p. 207: *ālambanaṃ tu tasyāniyatam eva.*

21. Cf. Lamotte, *Saṃdhinirmocana,* chap. VIII, in sect. 5.

22. Asaṅga's *Abhidharmasamuccaya,* Pralhad Pradhan, ed., p. 75.21: ekatyaḥ vipaśyanāyālābhī na śamathasya / tatprakārāṃ vipaśyanāṃ niśritya śamathabhāvanā /.

23. Cf. Introduction section on "Asaṅga on the Ancillaries," Right Dwelling in *Samādhi,* where the four Dhyānas are here referred to as "First Meditation and subsequent stages." Each of these four is said to have a threshold and a main part.

24. Cf. Wayman, *Analysis,* pp. 42–43, for the information that the title *Bhūmivastu* stands for the seventeen *bhūmis* of Asaṅga's *Yogācārabhūmi.* Asaṅga follows the seventeen basic *bhūmis* with four kinds of exegetical treatises called *saṃgrahaṇī.*

25. Sanskrit in the *First Bhāvanākrama,* Tucci, ed., p. 205.

26. Cf. Introduction, section on "The Lineage, and Atīśa's 'Light on the Path to Enlightenment.' "

27. Cf. Introduction, section on "Asaṅga on the Ancillaries."

28. For a brief indication of these meditative objects and elements shared with the lowest and the middling persons, cf. Tsoṅ-kha-pa's "Brief statement of the meaning of the path" near the end of the *Lam rim chen no.*

29. For the five, cf. note 24 above. They are the *Bhūmivastu* and the four *saṃgrahaṇī.*

30. The *dharma* that is seen, i.e., the *dṛṣṭadharma,* is frequently to be understood as "present life" (so Edgerton, BHS *Dictionary,* s.v.). So also, La Vallée Poussin, trans., *Abhidharmakośa,* VIII, 27c–28 (p. 193) for *dṛṣṭadharmasukhavihāra,* "béatitude de ce monde." Therefore, the "present life" and dwelling pleasantly in it, may well be what Tsoṅ-kha-pa intends in the present context. Asaṅga, *Paryāya-saṃgrahaṇī,* p. 236-4-3, the meditative object (*ālambana*) of the *dṛṣṭadharmasukhavihāra* is the "auspicious given thing" (**bhadravastu,* Tib. *dṅos po bzaṅ po*). The early Tibetan

translator Dpal-brtsegs writes in his *Chos kyi rnam grans kyi brjed byan* (PTT, vol. 147, pp. 117–18) that when *dṛṣṭadharmasukhavihāra* is a variety (the first kind) of Dhyāna-pāramitā, it is the nondiscursive *samādhi* (*nirvikalpa-semādhi*) and cessation-equipoise (*nirodha-samāpatti*). Dpal-brtsegs mentions two other kinds as follows: "As to the Dhyāna that accomplishes merits, by means of the samādhis Śūraṅgama, etc. one obtains all the glorious merits of the Buddha." "As to the Dhyāna that performs the aim of sentient beings,—having obtained the six supernormal faculties (*abhijñā*) through accomplishing Dhyāna, having gladdened their minds by magical performances of body, and knowing the make-up of others' minds, he teaches the dharma consistent with their mentality, turns them away from unvirtue and installs them in virtue."

31. Here the use of the term *svalakṣaṇa* seems compatible with Buddhist logic, in which the *svalakṣaṇa* is the object-field of direct perception (*pratyakṣa*). The subjective *svalakṣaṇa* is here called the "imagery" (*ākāra*), which is also an important term of Buddhist philosophy including logic, and said to occur in the discriminating, or mirroring, function of the mind, *buddhi*. Now there are four kinds of *pratyakṣa* allowed by the Buddhist logician—of the five senses, of the mind-sense, of introspection, and of the yogin; and so the question arises of which one would be meant here. It seems it would have to be the *yogi-pratyakṣa*. Also the "imagery" appears equivalent to what Asaṅga (Wayman, *Analysis*, pp. 110–11) calls the first door or gateway for discerning, namely lhe image-only (*nimittamātra*), which is also the *samādhi*-sign.

32. The meaning of the term *āśraya-parivṛtti* is exposed by Asaṅga's passage in the *Śrāvakabhūmi* of this very context which I have translated in the Introduction, at the conclusion of the section on "Asaṅga's Position on Nondiscursive Thought."

33. The thirty-six personal elements are given in the *Śrāvakabhūmi*, Second Yogasthāna. In the old Buddhist canon, an equivalent context is in the *Aṅguttara-nikāya*, Book of Sixes (text iii, 323; or E. M. Hare translation, pp. 227–29), although the list is less than thirty-six.

34. The two steps appear to involve the distinction made by Ratnākaraśānti (cf. A. Wayman, *The Buddhist Tantras*, p. 84): "Because they take the sentient beings as object, the four boundless states (*apramāṇa*) of friendliness, etc. are called 'boundless.' When they take as object the sentient beings involved with the realm of desire, they are called 'pure abodes' (*brahma-vihāra*)." This indicates that "boundless states" are meant to apply to the meditation when the meditator is in the realm of desire; and then when he ascends to the equipoised planes and in those planes takes beings in the realm of desire as meditative object, the mental acts of friendliness, etc. are called "pure abodes."

35. As is indicated in the "Discerning" section, this meditative object is a favorite with the Mādhyamikas, who identify dependent origination with voidness (*śūnyatā*) and then contemplate the *dharma* that arises dependently.

36. The *Śikṣāsamuccaya*, in its chap. XIV on "self-purification," is especially devoted to the topic of the six elements.

37. This was a favorite topic of the early Buddhists, and Asaṅga gives it a generous treatment in his *Śrāvakabhūmi*. Cf. Buddhadāsa Bhikkhu, *Ānāpānasati* (*Mindfulness of Breathing*), translated from the Thai version by Bhikkhu Nāgasena (Bangkok, 1971).

38. The meditative objects for skill, defined in the subsequent paragraphs, are of course the topics of the Abhidharmists, which Tsoṅ-kha-pa specifically mentions a few pages later.

39. For these sixteen aspects according to Asaṅga, I cite from Wayman (*Analysis*, p. 130): "Among them, the practitioner of *yoga* having held, through hearing, the four Noble Truths attended with concise presentation and detailed explanation, possessing either the well-cultivated mental orienta-

tion or the attainment of the basic *dhyāna* [of the realm of form (*rūpadhātu*)] or of the formless realm, realizes the characteristic of the Truth of Suffering by four aspects, as follows: by the aspect of impermanence, by the aspect of pain, by the aspect of voidness, and by the aspect of non-self; realizes the characteristic of the Truth of Source by four aspects, as follows: by that of cause, by that of source, by that of production, by that of condition; realizes the characteristic of the Truth of Cessation by four aspects, as follows: by that of cessation, by that of calm, by that of excellence, by that of exit; realizes the characteristic of the Truth of Path by four aspects, as follows: by that of path, by that of method, by that of process of accomplishment, and by that of way of deliverance. That is his mental orientation realizing the characteristics."

40. The three steps of "descending toward" and so on, in Sanskrit with the terms *nimna, pravaṇa,* and *prāgbhāra,* are used in this context in *Saṃdhinirmocana,* chap. VIII, sect. 13. This section was already alluded to in the Introduction, "Discursive Thought and the bSam-yas Debate," in terms of the "mixed *dharmas*" massing toward the thusness end. Jñānagarbha's *Kevala* commentary explains, p. 200-1-7: " 'Descending toward thusness' is the gathering together toward thusness; 'hanging over thusness' is having thusness as main object; 'alighting upon thusness' is the entrance into thusness."

41. This refers to the subsumption of the multiple *dharmas* according to the *Abhidharma* precepts; cf. La Vallée Poussin, *L'Abhidharmakośa de Vasubandhu,* chap. I, 18a-b: "All the *dharmas* are included in a personality aggregate (*skandha*), also in a sense base (*āyatana*), also in a realm (*dhātu*)." Hence the *Pañcaskandha* books in the Tibetan Tanjur, which explain the five personality aggregates, the twelve sense bases, and the eighteen realms. As to how the *dharmas* are subsumed under the five personality aggregates, three of the five, namely "feelings" (*vedanā*), "ideas" (*saṃjñā*), and "perceptions" (*vijñāna*) are counted as one *dharma* each, although each of the three have varieties. The aggregate "motivations" (*saṃskāra*) includes all the remaining mental and nonmental natures (*dharma*) amounting to fifty-eight in the Sarvāstivadin system, which exclude the aggregate of "form" (or matter, *rūpa*) amounting to eleven *dharmas*. So there is a total of seventy-two here.

42. Sthiramati explains this as "enumerator consciousness," as shown in the Introduction, above.

43. As an illustration from the *Prajñāpāramitā* literature, Jñānakīrti's *Pāramitāyāna-bhāvanākramopadeśa* (PTT, vol. 103, p. 263–2) states: "Then the Lord taught in the Great Mother Prajñāpāramitā that nine cravings are of great import, to wit, 1. craving for shape, 2. craving for touch, 3. craving for sweet-smelling body through anointments of sandlewood, etc., 4. craving for a body beautified by adornments of jewels, 5. craving for complexion of body, 6. craving for firmness of flesh, 7. craving for public amusement, 8. craving for beautiful teeth, 9. craving for color and shape. Nine uncleanlinesses serve (respectively) as their opponents (or, adversaries), as follows:
For 1: 'idea of a corpse swollen by putrefaction' (*vyādhmātaka-saṃjñā*)
For 2: 'idea of a corpse infested with worms' (*vipaḍumaka-*°)
For 3: 'idea of a corpse reduced to putrefaction' (*vipūyaka-*°)
For 4: 'idea of a bloody corpse' (*vilohitaka-*°)
For 5: 'idea of a corpse turned blue-black' (*vinīlaka-*°)
For 6: 'idea of a corpse being devoured (by scavengers)' (*vikhāditaka-*°)
For 7: 'idea of a dismembered corpse' (*vikṣiptaka-*°)
For 8: 'idea of a skeleton' (*asthi-*°)
For 9: 'idea of a corpse burnt by fire' (*vidagdhaka-*°)."
This shows how specific defilements, here in terms of cravings, are assigned specific meditative objects.

44. Tsoṅ-kha-pa's remark not only means that those taking any object such as a pebble as meditative object do not recognize that persons differ in what would be proper or preferable meditative object for them, but also that such an attitude leaves no room for the spiritual guide (*kalyānamitra*) to advise a disciple on what would be the most appropriate meditative object in his case.

45. See the translation of Atīśa's work "Light on the Path to Enlightenment," verse 40, in the Introduction, above.

46. See Wayman, *Analysis,* pp. 86–87, for the summary.

47. Bihar MS., 10B.8-7a: / tatra ye rāgadveṣamohamānavitarkacariteṣu pudgaleṣu pūrvaṃ tāvac caritaviśodhane ālambane caritaṃ viśodhayitavyaṃ / tataḥ paścāc cittasthitam adhigacchanti / teṣāṃ pratiniyatam eva tadālambanam avaśyaṃ tais tenālambanena prayoktavyaṃ /.

48. Bihar MS., 10B.8-7c: / samabhāgacaritasya tu yatra priyārohitā / tatra tena prayoktavyaṃ / kevalaṃ cittasthitaye na tu caritaviśuddhaye / yathā samabhāgacarita evaṃ mandarajasko veditavyaḥ /.

49. Cf. Wayman, *Analysis,* pp. 86–87, for the summary.

50. Bihar MS., 8A.1-3c: / kāmadhātor vā vairāgyaṃ kartukāmaḥ / kāmānām audārikatve rūpāṇāṃ śāntatve rūpebho vā vairāgyaṃ kartukāmaḥ / rūpānām audārikatve ārūpyaśāntatāyāṃ ca cittam upanibadhnāti / sarvatra vā satkāyān nirvektukāmo vimoktukāmaḥ / duḥkhasatye samudayasatye nirodhasatye mārgasatye cittam upanibadhnāti /.

51. The expression "in every case" (*sarvatra*) would mean according to the *Abhidharmakośa,* La Vallée Poussin, trans., ch. V, pp. 15–17, the five personality aggregates, because the *satkāyadṛṣṭi* is the view that the five aggregates are self.

52. The full passage is available in the Tibetan translation of Asaṅga's text as cited by Tsoṅ-kha-pa. The Bihar Sanskrit manuscript omits the Sanskrit words for 'sign of *samādhi*' down to "appearance to the mind"; but Karunesha Shukla, *Śrāvakabhūmi of Ācārya Asaṅga* (cf. p. 195.10–12) does not notice the omission. Asaṅga gives a further alternate term in his *Viniścayasaṃgrahaṇī,* PTT, vol. 111, p. 25-2: "The form of the reflected image belonging to the range of samādhi (*samādhi-gocara*) is called *manas-gocara-rūpa.*"

53. This is in his work *Samādhisambhāraparivarta,* in the Derge Tanjur, *Dbu ma,* Ki, fol. 90a-3 ff.

54. These data are tabulated in Alex Wayman, *The Buddhist Tantras; Light on Indo-Tibetan Esotericism,* p. 112.

55. This is Atīśa's self-commentary.

56. This is a citation of the sūtra in the ascetic handbook (*blo sbyoṅ*) for the lesser person, fol. 83a-b in the Tashilunpo edition. There Tsoṅ-kha-pa cites the two verses, *Samādhirāja-sūtra,* IV, 20–21.

57. *Third Bhāvanākrama,* Tucci, ed., p. 4.12-18.

58. *Samādhirāja-sūtra,* Vaidya, ed., chap. IV, 13: / suvarṇavarṇena samucchrayeṇa samantaprāsādiku lokanāthaḥ / yasyātra ālambani cittu vartate samāhitaḥ socyate bodhisatvaḥ /.

59. By "common vehicle" Tsoṅ-kha-pa means both nontantric and tantric Buddhism, and so the recollection of the Buddha's body will serve for frequent reinforcement of faith.

60. Ye-śes-sde was a celebrated translator of the early period of Buddhism in Tibet. He apparently himself translated or was in charge of rendering the entire huge *Yogācārabhūmi* of Asaṅga. Some works by the early translators (late eighth to early ninth centuries) are preserved in the Tibetan

canon, *Tanjur, Ṅo-tshar* section, where several brief works by Ye-śes-sde are found (PTT, vol. 145) and presumably contain the passage to which Tsoṅ-kha-pa refers.

61. That is, the reflected image matches the knowable entity, as mentioned in the previous citation of the *Śrāvakabhūmi* for synonyms of the reflected image.

62. *Pāramitāsamāsa* by Āryaśūra, ed. A. Ferrari, in *Annali Lateranensi,* vol. X (1946), V, verse 12.

63. Atiśa's "Light on the Path to Enlightenment" (in the Introduction, above), verse 40.

64. *First Bhāvanākrama,* Tucci, ed., p. 206.

65. The eighteen kinds of voidness are set forth in *Saṃdhinirmocana,* VIII, 29.

66. For the First and Fourth Meditations (*dhyāna*), see the Introduction, above, "Asaṅga on the Ancillaries," Right Dwelling in *Samādhi.* Tsoṅ-kha-pa points out that while there is pleasure in the *samādhi* of the First Dhyāna, this pleasure has not yet arisen in the threshold of the First Dhyāna.

67. The Sanskrit is *vinārūpyaṃ tathā dhyānaṃ*. The line is within two verses, *Mahāyāna-Sūtrālaṃkāra,* XIX, 28, 29: "For the right praxis of the wise in the six perfections is the giving of the one without wish, the morality of the one without enthusiasm for re-existence, forbearance everywhere, the striving to bring forth all-good; likewise meditation (*dhyāna*) apart from the formless plane, and insight (*prajñā*) tied to the means (i.e., the other five perfections)." Tsoṅ-kha-pa suggests the meaning here of *dhyāna* as requiring "vividness" as the reason it is apart from the formless realm, since "formless" means without shape or color and this situation does not lend itself to vividness.

68. By thus alluding to the Bodhisattvas who have attained power, namely, those of the eighth and higher states (in the ten-Bodhisattva-stage theory), Tsoṅ-kha-pa may well be referring to a teaching, found for example in Asaṅga's *Samāhitābhūmi,* that Tathāgatas and Bodhisattvas of the last three stages can enter any of the four Dhyānas and any of the formless realms from any other one. There is a good treatment of this matter in J. May's article CHŌJŌ in *Hobogirin,* IV, 1967.

69. *Sūtrālaṃkāra* (Lévi's edition), under XVIII, 53: / smṛtiḥ saṃprajanyaṃ copanibandhakaḥ / ekena cittasyālambanāvisārāt / dvitīyena visāraprajñānāt /.

70. *Abhidharmasamuccaya,* Pradhan, ed., p. 6.6: smṛtiḥ katamā / saṃsmṛte vastuni cetasaḥ asaṃpramoṣo 'vikṣepakarmakā /.

71. The work is by Bhāvaviveka.

72. As the Mongolian lama Dilowa Hutukhtu once explained to me, *śes bźin* (awareness) is a form of *śes rab* (insight), while the latter is a larger category. Hence, it is not inconsistent to replace "awareness" by "insight" in the present context.

73. The attribution to Vasubandhu is due to the Tibetan literary tradition that the initial commentary (still preserved in Sanskrit) on the *Sūtrālaṃkāra* verses was by Vasubandhu.

74. *Mchan* (here: Ba) identifies the work as the *Deśanāstava.*

75. The *Deśanāstava-vṛtti.*

76. Part of a citation from the *Śrāvakabhūmi* in "Calming the Mind," B-3. The Method of Employing Four Mental Orientations.

77. *First Bhāvanākrama,* Tucci, ed., p. 206: . . . layam upaśāmya punas tad evālambanaṃ dṛḍhataraṃ gṛhṇīyāt /.

78. Part of the Sanskrit was in Wayman, *Analysis,* p. 108. The entire passage reads (11B.4-5c): / tatraikāgratā katamā / āha / punaḥpunaḥsmṛti(ḥ) sabhāgālambanā pravāhānavadyaratiyuktā cittasaṃtatir yā / sā samādhir ity ucyate / kuśalacittaikāgratāpi / kiṃ punaḥ punar anusmarati / āha / ye dharmā udgṛhītā śrutā yā cānuvāda-anuśāsanī pratilabdhā bhava (n) ti gurubhyas tām adhipatiṃ kṛtvā samāhitabhūmikanimittaṃ saṃmukhīkṛtya tadālambanāṃ pravāhayuktāṃ smṛtim anuvartayati / upanibadhnāti /.

79. Sthiramati commentator; cf. Susumu Yamaguchi, *Madhyāantavibhāgaṭīkā,* text, p. 175, 7–8; and R. C. Pandeya, *Madhyānta-Vibhāga-Śāstra,* p. 131, last line, to p. 132.1.

80. *Third Bhāvanākrama,* Tucci, ed., p. 11: evam anena krameṇa ghaṭikām ekapraharaṃ vā yāvantaṃ kālaśaknoti tāvantaṃ kālaṃ tiṣṭhet /. *Mchan* (here: Ba) explains "for as long as one is able": to stay free of fading or scattering. In India the twenty-four minutes was the water-clock unit, which is one-half of a *muhurta* of which there are thirty in a full day and night. The period "one and one-half hours" is one-half watch (= three hours).

81. *Abhidharmasambuccaya,* Pradhan, ed., p. 9.9–10.

82. Asaṅga's meaning is further observed in his *Paramārtha-gāthā* and self-commentary (cf. Wayman, *Analysis,* p. 185), since he distinguishes between desire for given things (*vastu*) and desire for defilements (*kleśa*), establishing two kinds of release (*mokṣa*)—release from defilements and release from given things. "Scattering" is a fault involved with given things, or sign-sources (*nimitta*), although presuming defilements.

83. The number may have been rounded to "twenty" to be free of the controversy over the exact number of *upakleśa*(s), usually stated in the twenties. See La Vallée Poussin, *L'Abhidharmakosa de Vasubandhu,* ch. V, p. 89, for the agreement of Vasubandhu and Sanghabhadra on the number "twenty-one." But see *Dharmasaṃgraha,* reprinted in P. L. Vaidya, ed., *Mahāyāna-sūtra-saṃgraha,* p. 333, item no. 39, for a list of twenty-four *upakleśa*s. The longer list seems to agree more with the Yogācāra system, while the list closer to twenty would be of the *Abhidharmakośa* lineage. Cf. P. Cordier and L. de La Vallée Poussin, "Les soixante-quinze et les cent dharmas, d'apres l'*Abhidharmakośa,* la *Vijñānamātrasiddhi* et la *Mahāvyutpatti,*" *Le Muséon,* Nouvelle Série, vol. VI (Louvain, 1905). Without going into the details, which would take much space, it seems that the difference between "defilements" (*kleśa*) and "secondary defilements" (*upakleśa*), is that "defilements"—principally "lust," "hatred," and "delusion"—are the "root of unvirtue" (*akuśala-mūla*) and forge the bondage to *saṃsāra;* while the "secondary defilements" are the transient ones that may be of limited occurrence, or consort with every unvirtuous idea, or may be unassured, e.g., "lack of shame."

84. Cf. Lamotte, *Saṃdhinirmocana,* chap. VIII, in sect. 34, para. 3.

85. *Abhidharmasamuccaya,* Pradhan, ed., p. 9.8.

86. This is the Vasubandhu's own commentary on II, 26, and its quotation drawn from the Vaibhāṣika book *Jñānaprasthāna.*

87. Tsoṅ-kha-pa here alludes to the theory of multiple *dharmas* which include such *dharma* sets as "virtuous" (*kuśala*) and "unassured" (*aniyata*); see, for example, Th. Stcherbatsky, *The Central Conception of Buddhism,* pp. 85–89. Concerning the "virtue" which Tsoṅ-kha-pa mentions, the Dilowa Hutukhtu explained to me that the "virtue" in the "fading" is a very small one, like a small amount of milk in black coffee. N. H. Santani, *The Arthaviniścaya-sūtra and Its Commentary* (*Nibandhana*) (Patna, 1971), text, p. 237, may be giving a different tradition of the meaning of the term *laya* (in its alternate form *līna*) in the commentarial remark, "for the 'fading' occurs through association

with torpor and sleepiness (*tathā hi styānamiddhayogāl līnaṃ bhavati*)." Regarding the "torpor and sleepiness," see note 147, below. Note that Tsoṅ-kha-pa differentiates between "fading" and "torpor." The "fading" in his tradition is the sinking or shrinking of the meditative object into the darkness of consciousness, just as when one falls asleep while having something in mind. However, it does not require any sleepiness to have this "fading," since one can be wide awake and have a meditative object on which one is concentrating fade away either through sinking or shrinking.

88. Cf. *Third Bhāvanākrama,* Tucci, ed., p. 9: *līnaṃ cittaṃ paśyet, layābhiśaṅkitaṃ vā . . . cittam antarā samuddhataṃ paśyed auddhatyābhiśaṅkitaṃ vā.*

89. *Madhyāntavibhāga-bhāṣya,* Gadjin M. Nagao, ed., p. 52 (IV, 5b): *layāuddhatyānubuddhyanā.*

90. Śāntideva's *Bodhisattvacaryāvatāra,* V, 33a-c.

91. Sthiramati commentator; cf. Yamaguchi, *Madhyāntavibhāga-ṭīkā*, text, p. 175.9–11.

92. *Bodhisattvacaryāvatāra,* V, 108. Prajñākaramati's *Bodhicaryāvatārapañjikā,* ed. by Louis de La Vallée Poussin, pp. 165–66, commenting upon this verse, explains the "states" (*avasthā*) as "all dignified deportment" (*īryāpatha*), which for the body are while walking, standing, sitting, and lying down. For the mind, cf. Tsoṅ-kha-pa's reference below to the *Śrāvakabhūmi.*

93. Āryaśūra's *Pāramitāsamāsa,* VI, 15ab: niṣkevalaṃ vīryam api śramāya prajñāsanāthasya tu tasya kārye /.

94. *Abhidharmasamuccaya,* Pradhan, ed., p. 5 (last line) to p. 6.2. According to Vasubandhu this eliminates Asaṅga from the ranks of the Sautrāntika because *Abhidharmakośa,* IV, La Vallée Poussin trans., p. 169, "Les Sautrāntikas ne reconnaissent pas la volition (*cetanā*) comme acte mental (*manaskarman*)."

95. *First Bhāvanākrama,* Tucci, ed., p. 206: / atha yadā . . . tad evālambanaṃ dṛḍhataraṃ gṛhṇīyāt /.

96. The Mongolian lama Dilowa Hutukhtu explained to me this term *skyo ba* as the state of being "tired of," as when one eats only one food for a long time.

97. Āryaśūra's *Pāramitāsamāsa,* V, 13a-b: vidarśanād vīryabalāl līyamānaṃ samuddharet /.

98. The author is Bhāvaviveka.

99. *Śikṣāsamuccaya,* Bendall edition, p. 203.6: tatra līne manasi muditābhāvanayottejanaṃ kuryāt /.

100. Bihar MS., 12A.7-6b: / ālokasahagatena cittena saprabhāsa-sahagatena prabhāsvareṇānandhakāreṇa śamatha-vipaśyanāṃ bhāvaya / evaṃ ca te śamatha-vipaśyanā-mārge ālokasaṃjñāṃ bhāvayataḥ / saced ādita eva avispaṣṭo 'dhimokṣo bhaviṣyaty ālambane mṛdv-ābhāsaḥ / sa tena hetunā tena pratyayena bhāvanābhāsād vispaṣṭatā bhaviṣyati / pracurābhāsagatā(s) ca / sacet punar ādita eva vispaṣṭo ['dhimikṣo] bhaviṣyati / pracurābhāsaḥ / sa bhūyasyā mātrayā vispaṣṭataratā(s) pracurābhāsataratās ca gamiṣyati /. Compare K. Shukla, *Śrāvakabhūmi of Ācārya Asaṅga,* p. 421 (last line) to p. 422.9, on *mṛdv-ābhāsaḥ* and some other words.

101. Bihar MS., 12A.6–2a,b: / ālokanimittam udgṛhāṇa yad uta pradīpād vā agniskandhaprabhāsād vā sūryamaṇḍalād vā /.

102. *First Bhāvanākrama,* Tucci, ed., pp. 206–7: / atha yadā . . . yatnaṃ kurvīta /.

103. *Śikṣāsamuccaya,* Bendall edition, chap. XII, p. 203.5–6: / uddhate tv anityatā-manasikāraiḥ praśamaḥ /. (Continues with passage of note 99, above).

104. Ātyaśūra's *Pāramitāsamāsa,* V. 13c–d: uddhatyamānaṃ ca manaḥ praśamena nivārayet /. (Second half of verse, whose first half is above, note 97).

105. K. Shukla, ed., *Śrāvakabhūmi,* p. 312.3–10, is satisfactory for this passage, except for where the Sanskrit goes with "or sees the threat of shrinking," and he has *līnatvābhiśaṃki caivaṃ paśyati* (which is indeed in the Bihar MS.), it should probably be amended to *līnatvābhiśaṃkitaṃ,* as in *Bhāvanākrama III* (see note 88, above).

106. The passage is in Asaṅga's *Samāhitabhūmi,* PTT, vol. 109, p. 273-2-4. Notice that the first four sign-sources (*nimitta*) are failure to observe nos. 7–10 of the ancillaries of calming set forth in a summary way in the Introduction, section on "Asaṅga on the Ancillaries."

107. The passage is in *Samāhitabhūmi,* PTT, vol. 109, p. 273-2-7. Again, the first four sign-sources here are failure to observe the same nos. 7–10 of the ancillaries of calming.

108. Tsoṅ-kha-pa here refers to the early part of his *Lam rim chen mo,* beginning fol. 37a–2 of the Tashilunpo edition, where he heads a section saying, "Moreover, one should learn the four 'sets' that are the cause of easily giving rise to the path of calming and discerning, namely, guarding the doors of the senses, practice with awareness, knowing the measure of food, and how to perform at the time of sleep, enterprising the Yoga of staying awake." He then devotes individual sections to the four and relates these matters to the "watches."

109. Cf. *Third Bhāvanākrama,* Tucci, ed., p. 11: / yadi, samapravṛtte citte, ābhogaḥ kriyate, tadā cittaṃ vikṣipyate /.

110. The *Artha-viniścaya-ṭīkā* (author unknown), in the Tibetan Tanjur, PTT, vol. 145, p. 208–2, defines the three kinds of equanimity (*upekṣā*): "Among them, the equanimity of feeling (*vedanā*) is the feeling which is neither pleasure nor pain. The equanimity of the boundless states (*apramāṇa*) is the character (*lakṣaṇa*) of neither the arising of passion toward, nor the arising of hostility toward, sentient beings. The equanimity of motivation (*saṃskāra*) is the character of acting automatically without work or effort toward the object that is to be the consciousness-support (*ālambana*). We claim that here (i.e., in the Third Dhyāna) the equanimity of motivation is meant." Besides, cf. *Abhidharmakośa,* under II, 25, La Vallée Poussin, trans., p. 159. Of course, the equanimity of the boundless states is the fourth of the set "friendliness," "compassion," "sympathetic joy," and "equanimity"; cf. note 34, above.

111. Cf. Wayman, *Analysis,* pp. 117–18.

112. Cf. Wayman, *Analysis,* p. 118.

113. Cf. Wayman, *Analysis,* p. 118.

114. *Madhyāntavibhāga-bhāṣya,* Gadjin M. Nagao, ed., chap. IV, verses 3–5.

115. Atīśa's self-comment on his "Light on the Path to Enlightenment."

116. Cf. Wayman, *Analysis,* p. 100 (translation modified for this note): "For what reason is it called 'feet of magical power'? He said as follows: That person who has feet is able to approach, return, and march forward. In just the same way, for that person who has those natures (*dharma*), this *samādhi* exists; and when his mind has been thus thoroughly purified, thoroughly cleansed, is without blemish, free from secondary defilements, straight, serviceable, immobile (*āniñjya-prāpta*)—he is able to approach, return, and march forward, so as to reach and touch the supramundane natures. That is the supreme magical power, the supreme prosperity; i.e., the supramundane natures, hence called 'feet of magical power.' "

117. *Mahāyāna-Sūtrālaṃkāra,* S. Lévi, ed., XIV, 11b.

118. *Sūtrālaṃkāra,* XIV, 11a.

119. *Sūtrālaṃkāra,* XIV, 11c–d.

120. *Sūtrālaṃkāra,* XIV, 12a–b.

121. *Sūtrālaṃkāra,* XIV, 12c–d.

122. *Sūtrālaṃkāra,* XIV, 13a–b.

123. *Sūtrālaṃkāra,* XIV, 13c–d.

124. *Sūtrālaṃkāra,* XIV, (14a–c of the Tibetan version).

125. Bihar MS.,11A.5-6a: / sābhisaṃskāraṃ nicchidraṃ nirantarasamādhipravāham avasthāpayaty evam ekotīkaroti /.

126. *Sūtrālaṃkāra,* XIV, (14d of the Tibetan version).

127. Bihar MS., 11A.5–6b; / āsevanānvayad bhāvanāvayād bahulīkārānvayād anābhogavāhanaṃ svarasavāhanaṃ / mārgaṃ labhate / yenānabhisaṃskāreṅaivā 'nābhogenāsya cittasamādhipravāhaḥ / avikṣepe pravartate evaṃ samādhatte /.

128. I have noticed in various places this same remark, attributing the precepts of nine thought fixations to the "Great Prajñāpāramitā." The closest so far that I have come to a definite location was through Jñānakīrti's statement, because soon after presenting the material (see note 43, above) from the "Great Mother Prajñāpāramitā" about nine cravings and their nine adversary ideas—namely, the nine corpse ideas—this author attributes the usual statement of the nine thought fixations to the same "Mother Lordess (scripture)." This suggests that the teaching of the thought fixations was in close proximity to the previous passage that Jñānakīrti cited. However, making use of the Japanese index volumes to the Taishō Tripitaka (with the help of my wife, Hideko) for the "nine ideas" various places were found, with the nine ideas in association with the thirty-seven *bodhipakṣya-dharmas* and the eight Liberations, but so far not Jñānakīrti's passage nor the passage about the nine thought fixations.

129. Cf. Wayman, *Analysis,* p. 109.

130. Āryaśūra's *Pāramitāsamāsa,* V, 10c–d and 11.

131. Here this term must mean "attainment of distinction"—what has been referred to as the "ninth thought" or the mental orientation proceeding without effort, in which case the very efforts that were necessary to arrive at this level become the fault here.

132. Cf. Lamotte, *Saṃdhinirmocana,* chap. VIII, in sect. 5.

133. *Sūtrālaṃkāra,* XIV, (14d of the Tibetan version), 15a–c.

134. *First Bhāvanākrama,* Tucci, ed., p. 207: / yadā tu tatrālambane 'nabhisaṃskāravāhi yāvadicchaṃ cittaṃ pravṛttaṃ bhavati / tadā śamatho nispanno veditavyaḥ /.

135. The number nine is apparently arrived at by taking the "realm of desire" as plane no. 1, taking four more as the four Dhyānas of the "realm of form," and taking a final four as the four levels of the "formless realm."

136. The passage is probably in Asaṅga's *Samāhitabhūmi.*

137. *Abhidharmasamuccaya,* Pradhan, ed., p. 6.19 f.

138. Bihar MS., 13B.2–6a: / pūrvam eva samyakprayogam ārambhakāle / sūkṣmā [kāya-] cittapraśrabdhir durupalakṣyā pravartate /.

139. Bihar MS., 13B.2–6c: / tasya saiva sūkṣmā cittaikāgratā / cittakāyapraśrabdhiś cābhivardhamānā audārikāṃ sūpalakṣyāṃ cittaikāgratāṃ [citta] kāyapraśrabdhimāvahati / yad uta hetupāraṃparyādānayogena /.

140. Bihar MS., 13B.2–7b: / tasya na cirasyedānīm audārikācittakāyapraśrabdhiś cittaikāgratā ca / sūpalakṣyotpatsyatīti yāvad asya pūrvanimittaṃmūrdhani gauravapratibhāsam utpadyate / na ca tad bādhalakṣaṇaṃ / tasyānantarotpādād yat prahānarativibaddhakāriṇāṃ kleśānāṃ pakṣyaṃ cittaṃ dauṣṭhulyaṃ ca prahīyate / tatpratipakṣeṇa ca cittakarmaṇyatā cittapraśrabdhir utpadyate /.

141. Bihar MS., 13B.2–8c: tasyotpādāt kāyapraśrabdhy-utpādānukūlāni vāyūdṛktāni mahābhūtāni kāye 'vakramanti / teṣām avakrāmaṇahetor yat kāyadauṣṭhulyaṃ tad vigacchati / prahāṇarativibaddhakārakleśapak ṣyaṃ kāyapraśrabdhyā ca tatpratipakṣikayā sarvakāyaḥ pūryate / syād iva dyoti /.

142. I failed to locate the Sthiramati quotation in this author's commentary on the *Madhyāntavibhāga* by using the works of S. Yamaguchi and R. C. Pandeya. Sthiramati's great sub-commentary on the *Mahāyāna-Sūtrālaṃkāra* is a good bet.

143. Bihar MS., 13A.3–1b: / tataḥ [tat] prathamopanipāte cittaudbilyaṃ ca cittasumanaskāre pramodya sahagatālambane sābhirāmatā ca / cittasya tasmin samayekhyāti / tasyordhvaṃ yo 'sau tatprathamopanipātī praśrabdhivegaḥ / sa śanaiḥ śanaiḥ pariślathataro bhavati / cchāyevānugatā praśrabdhiḥ / kāye ca pravartate / yac ca tadaudbilyaṃ cetasas tad apy avahīyate / praśāntākāracittam ālambane śamathaupastabdhaṃ pravartate /.

144. The Dilowa Hutukhtu explained to me the "attenuated . . . like a shadow" as being comparable to the sensitive consciousness of a person in light sleep, who hears the voices and noises around him, and can wake up accordingly.

145. Bihar MS., 13A.3–2c: / tata ūrdhvam ayaṃ yogī ādikarmikaḥ samanaskāro bhavati / samanaskāra iti ca saṃkhyāṃ gacchati / tat kasya hetoḥ / rūpāvacara(s) tena samāhitabhūmiko manaskāraḥ parīttas tatprathamataḥ pratilabdho bhavati / tenocyate samanaskāra iti /.

146. The various Western books on Buddhist meditation, and even those that simply survey Buddhist doctrine, list the various divisions of the "realm of form" (*rūpa-dhātu*) and "formless realm." Those of the "realm of form" are describable both by deity residents and by the mental and physical concomitants in the case of a yogin. The "formless realm" has the four levels "base of infinite space," "base of infinite perception," "base of nothing-at-all," and "base of neither idea nor no-idea."

147. The five hindrances in the standard listing are sensuous lust, ill-will, torpor and sleepiness, mental wandering and regret, and doubt. Ratnākaraśānti states in his *Prajñāpāramitābhāvanopadeśa,* following the *Saṃdhinirmocana-sūtra,* chap, VIII, namely, at PTT, vol. 114, p. 235–3: "Here of the five hindrances, 'mental wandering and regret' is a hindrance to calming; 'torpor and sleepiness' and 'doubt' are hindrances to discerning; 'sensuous lust' and 'ill-will' are hindrances to both."

148. Bihar MS., 13A.3–3b: / tasayāsya samanaskārasyādikarmikasyemāni liṃgāni parīttam anena rūpāvacaraṃ cittaṃ pratilabdham bhavati / parīttā kāyapraśrabdhiś cittapraśrabdhiś cittaikāgratā bhavyo bhavati pratibalaḥ / kleśaviśodhanālambanaprayogasya snigdhā cāsya cittasantatiḥ pravartate / śamathopagūḍhāc caritaṃ tadānena viśodhitaṃ bhavati /. As to the word *snigdha* (smooth), cf. Asvabhāva, commentary on *Mahāyāna-Sūtrālaṃkāra,* chap. XIV, in PTT, vol. 108, p. 171–2: "Calming (*śamatha*) is like water."

149. This statement agrees with the *Mahāprajñāpāramitāśāstra* (cf. Étienne Lamotte, *Le Traité de la Grande Vertu de Sagesse de Nāgārjuna,* vol. III, p. 1289) that such contemplations as those of revolting objects, i.e., the cadaver in decomposition (cf. note 43, above) were actually practiced in the

First and Second Dhyāna by those ranging in the realm of form and employing what were called the first two Liberations and the first four Masteries. Thus the "purification-of-defilement" meditative object was best adopted by those who had attained the realm of form and from that vantage point were contemplating an object in the realm of desire. I have discussed this matter in "Aspects of Meditation in the Theravāda and Mahīśāsaka Buddhist sects," *Studia Missionalia,* vol. 25, 1976.

150. Bihar MS., 13A.3–5b: / niṣaṇṇasya cāsya pratisaṃlayane cittaṃ praṇidadhatas tvaritatvaritaṃ cittaṃ praśrabhyate / kāyaś ca kāyadauṣṭhulyāni ca nātyarthaṃ bādhante / na cātyarthaṃ nivaraṇasamudācāro bhavati /.

151. Bihar MS., 13A.3–6a: / vyutthitasyāpi manasa-carataḥ / praśrabdhamātrā kācit kāye citte [MS.: kācic citte kāye citte] cānugatā bhavatīty-evaṃbhāgīyāni manaskārasya liṃgāni nimittany avadātāni veditavyāni /.

152. Bihar MS., 12A.3–1a: / tasya yathā yathā kāyaḥ praśrabhyate cittaṃ ca tathā tathālamban(e) cittaikāgratāyāś ca yad utāśraya(ṃ) vivardhayati /yathā [yathā] cittaikāgratā vivardhate / tathā tathā kāyaḥ prasrabhyate cittaṃ ca ity etau dvau dharmāv anyonyaṃ niśṛtāv anyonyaṃ pratibaddho yad uta cittaikāgratā [praśrabdhiś ca] /.

153. The context indicates that the question is asked by adherents of the *Abhisamaālaṃkāra* exegesis of the Prajñāpāramitā scriptures, which describes five paths in different terms for each of the three families, śrāvakas, pratyekabuddhas, and Bodhisattvas (cf. E. Obermiller, "The Doctrine of Prajñāpāramitā as exposed in the Abhisamayālaṃkāra of Maitreya," *Acta Orientalia,* vol. XI, 1932). The five paths are *1*) path of accumulating merit (*saṃbhāra-mārga*); *2*) path of training (*prayoga-mārga*); *3*) path of vision (*darśana-mārga*); *4*) path of cultivation (*bhāvanā-mārga*); *5*) path beyond training (*aśaikṣa-mārga*). The sequel is not a specific answer to this question, because Tsoṅ-kha-pa then presents the suggestions of other partisans, to wit, those who would put the *samādhi* in the Mahāyāna and even in the Tantra. Tsoṅ-kha-pa concludes that the *samādhi* has nothing to do with particular paths of the Prajñāpāramitā, with vehicles, such as Hīnayāna and Mahāyāna, in short with "families." In taking this position he is consistent with the findings in the Introduction, section on "The Lineage," showing (see note 12 to Introduction) that Artīśa's "Light on the Path to Enlightenment" does not establish the "lesser," "middling," and "great person" in terms of families, but in terms of practice.

154. It is because "nondiscursive thought" is such an important matter to these discussions, that I included Asaṅga's position on discursive and nondiscursive thought in the Introduction, "Discursive Thought and the bSam-yas Debate." As Tsoṅ-kha-pa denies that a *samādhi* with nondiscursive thought is by virtue of that fact alone a *samādhi* of voidness, he now clarifies his position to the effect that when one understands the view of the manner of being—and understanding requires discriminative insight—when one then stays on the same object, called "manner of being" (*yin lugs*), with nondiscursive thought, this is the *samādhi* of voidness. But if one simply calms the mind without employing discursive thought, this does not amount to a *samā*dhi of voidness.

155. Bihar MS., 8A.4–5b: / tasya tasmin samaye nirvikalpitaṃ pratibimbaṃ ālambanam bhavati / yatrāsāv ekāṃśenaikāgrāṃ smṛtim avasthāpayati / tad ālambanaṃ no tu vicinoti / parivitarkayati / parimīmāṃsām āpadyate /. Some of the words of the Tibetan version are lacking in the Bihar MS., namely, "does not further view," and "does not supernally investigate."

156. Bihar Ms., 12A.6–5c: / sacet punaḥ smṛtisaṃpramoṣāt tathā śamathaprāpte cetasi nimittavitarkopakleśā 'nabhyāsadoṣād ābhāsam āgacchanti / mukham ādarśayanti / ālambanīkurvanti / teṣūtpannotpanneṣv asmṛty-amanasikāraḥ kartavyaḥ / yad uta [ādinavaṃ] pūrvadṛṣṭam evam adhipa-

tiṃ kṛtvā evaṃ tad ālambanam asmṛty-amanasikāreṇa vibhāvitaṃ viśvastam anābhāsagatāyām avasthāpitaṃ bhaviṣyati /.

157. *First Bhāvanākrama,* Tucci, ed., p. 207: /. etac ca sarvaśamathānāṃ sāmānyalakṣaṇam / cittaikāgratāmātrasvabhāvatvāt śamathasya /.

158. Cf. Wayman, *Analysis,* p. 125.

159. Cf. Wayman, *Analysis,* p. 125.

160. Cf. note 39, above.

161. Cf. Wayman, *Analysis,* pp. 125–26.

162. The terminology "four paths" here seems to be those implied by the *Abhidharmakośa* verse, namely, the four Dhyānas of the "realm of form."

163. It would have been helpful if Tsoṅ-kha-pa had enlarged upon this remark. It depends on which works the Tibetan tradition ascribes to Assaṅga.

164. Cf. D. R. S. Bailey, "The Varṇārhavarṇa Stotra of Mātṛceṭa (II)," Bulletin of the School of Oriental and African Studies, XIII (1951), pp. 947 ff. The "Praise of Nonreply" renders the title Apratikarastava. The main difference here with Bailey's translation is my "watched by the evil eye of Māra" where he has "as if (wiping away) the eye-grease of Māra." My rendition agrees with the Tibetan *bdud kyi mig ras btsa' bźin du* ("as though being watched by Māra's eye"), verified by the entry *btsa'* in the Tibetan dictionary by Dge bśes Chos kyi Grags pa. Bailey's interpretation is based on the Sanskrit reading *vasāvata(ḥ).* It is only necessary to alter his reading to *vaś-* (the *s* and *ś* are frequently confused in old Buddhist texts) and note the expression *vaśaṃvada,* "submissive" (Monier-Williams *Dictionary*) to promptly improve on Bailey's rendition with "submissive to the evil eye of Māra," which may have been the original intention of the verse. In any case, the passage suggests that Māra is the creature depicted as holding the "Wheel of Life" in both the Chinese and Tibetan forms, but that creature is popularly referred to as Yama (King of the Dead).

165. Cf. Wayman, *Analysis,* p. 95.

166. The lower Abhidharma is the *Abhidharmakośa* of Vasubandhu, and the higher Abhidharma is the *Abhidharmasamuccaya* of Asaṅga. The terminology seems related to Hīnayāna and Mahāyāna.

167. Cf. Wayman, *Analysis,* p. 126.

168. Cf. Wayman, *Analysis,* p. 127: "Just as there is equipoise of the First Dhyāna by means of the seven mental orientations, so also there is equipoise of the Second, Third, and Fourth Dhyānas and equipoise of the base of (boundless) space, of (boundless) perception, of nothing-at-all, and of the base of neither the idea nor no-idea, by means of precisely the seven mental orientations."

169. Bihar MS., 13B.4–3b: / tannimittālambanām eva śamatha-vipaśyanāṃ bhāvayati /.

170. "Intrinsic nature of meditation" is a terminology which stems from Asaṅga's *Bodhisattvabhūmi.* Each of the perfections (*pāramitā*) has an intrinsic nature (*svabhava*) and other explanations such as varieties (referred to as the totality, *sarva,* of the perfection). Accordingly, "Calming the Mind" is the intrinsic nature of *dhyāna-pāramitā,* just as "Discerning the Real" is the intrinsic nature of *prajñā-pāramitā.*

DISCERNING THE REAL

1. *First Bhāvanākrama,* Tucci, ed., pp. 209–10: / tad evam ālambane cittam sthirīkṛtya prajñayā vivecayet / yato jñānālokotpādāt saṃmohabījasyātyanta-prahāṇaṃ bhavati / anyathā hi tīrthikānām iva samādhimātreṇa kleśaprahāṇaṃ na syāt / yathoktaṃ *sūtre,* "kiṃ cāpi bhāvayet samādhim etam / na vāpi bhāvayet sā ātmasaṃjñā / punaḥ prakupyati kilesu tasyā / yathodrakasyeha samādhibhāvanā" / iti /.

2. Although the verse cited here is only *Samādhirāja,* IX, 36, after commenting thereon Tsoṅ-kha-pa goes on, as he indicates, to comment on the next verse, IX, 37, both of which verses are cited in *Bhāvanākrama II,* as in the passage of the "Calming" section above, with note 15. And see "Calming," note 16, for Udraka.

3. See Giuseppe Tucci, *Minor Buddhist Texts, Part II,* pp. 38–39, for the Tibetan account that Hva-śaṅ was defeated and that Kamalaśīla's victory meant that Nāgārjuna's doctrine, i.e., the Mādhyamika, was, by the king's decree, to be followed thereafter. While Kamalaśīla's three *Bhāvanākrama* treatises are not obviously in the orthodox Mādhyamika tradition, it could be argued that while Kamalaśīla certainly draws much material from Asaṅga's tradition (*Sūtrālaṃkāra, Yogācārabhūmi*) and justifies by sūtra citations, he also avoids the well-known distinctly Yogācāra terminology (such as the three *svabhāvas*) and so his *Bhāvanā-kramas* could be said to be Mādhyamika by virtue of not being Yogācārin.

4. The cited lines are all in the *Bhāvanākrama II* passage of the "Calming" section (see there, going with note 15), but in fact in the Introduction to both "Calming" and "Discerning," so now commented upon in the "Discerning" section.

5. *Mchan* (Ja) here refers to the passage, Āryadeva's *Catuḥśataka,* XII, 23 (=verse 298, which is available in Sanskrit): "The Tathāgatas have stated in short that the *dharma* is non-harming (of others), and that voidness is *nirvāṇa.* Here there are only these two." As Candrakīrti explains in part this passage, "Nonharming and voidness—these two *dharmas* attain heaven (*svarga*) and liberation (*apavarga*)."

6. Cf. Lamotte, *Saṃdhinirmocana,* chap. IX, sect. 26.

7. By "final resort" the terminology of *pratisaraṇa* is meant. There are four of these (*Mahāvyutpatti,* nos. 1545–49), and the one here intended is: "One should cultivate by resort to a scripture of final meaning (*nītārtha*), not by resort to a scripture of provisional meaning (*neyārtha*)." In Tsoṅ-kha-pa's context, the nonfinal resort precedes the final resort.

8. The sūtra that is especially appealed to is the *Laṅkāvatāra-sūtra;* and the Tantra, the *Mañjuśrī-mūla-tantra.*

9. For "profound," Ja says: "difficult to plumb" (*dpag dka' ba*).

10. *Mchan:* the beneath-realm, the upon-realm, the above-realm (*sa 'og, sa steṅ, sa bla*).

11. In the Gelugpa tradition, for which see Lessing and Wayman, *Mkhas grub rje's Fundamentals of the Buddhist Tantras,* p. 87, there are six Mādhyamika treatises by Nāgārjuna, of which five are undisputed: 1) *Madhyamaka-kārikā,* 2) *Yuktiṣaṣṭikā,* 3) *Vaidalya,* 4) *Śūnyatāsaptati,* 5) *Vigrahavyāvartanī.* Tsoṅ-kha-pa accepts as 6) *Ratnāvalī;* while his teacher Red mda' pa accepted only the first five as the essential Mādhyamika treatises. Candrakīrti frequently quotes the *Ratnāvalī.*

12. See Louis de La Vallée Poussin, *Mūlamadhyamakakārikās de Nāgārjuna avec la Prasannapadā Commentaire de Candrakīrti,* p. 43, note.

13. This verse is cited in *Prasannapadā,* chaps. 1 and 15, and in *Madhyamakāvatāra* commentary on VI, 97.

14. This is a work by Kamalaśīla preserved in the Mādhyamika (*Dbu-ma*) section of the Tibetan Tanjur.

15. Some further citations from the *Jñānālokālaṃkāra* are in Alex and Hideko Wayman, *The Lion's Roar of Queen Śrīmālā,* per Index. Still more in Jikido Takasaki, *A Study on the Ratnagotravibhāga* (Rome, 1966), per Index.

16. *Mchan:* For example, such precepts taken on trust as "Through giving, possessions; through morality, good destiny." There is a fuller statement of this kind of precept in Ratnakīrti, *Dharmaviniścaya-nāma-prakaraṇa,* PTT, vol. 114, p. 279: "Through giving he obtains enjoyment (*bhoga*); through morality, good destiny (*sugati*); through forbearance, beautiful body; through striving, glorious countenance; through meditation, [supernormal faculty]; [through] insight, liberation."

17. Ja: "a slave being summoned" (*'khol 'don byas nas*).

18. Ja: The Kashmirian Lakṣmī, etc. Presumably this is the Lakṣmī who has written the tantric commentary *Pañcakrama-ṭīkā-kramārtha-prakāśikā-nāma;* cf. PTT, vol. 63, p. 11–5. Here the author quotes a verse: "If one would see the oneness in the *parama-artha,* he would see the single self-nature (*svabhāva*) of all living beings. For example, if one drinks water at the shore of the ocean, he knows all of its water." And goes on to quote: "A single entity is the self-nature of all entities; all entities are the self-nature of a single entity. When one sees a single entity as *paramārtha,* he sees all entities [that way]." But then this author classifies these passages as "provisional meaning" (*draṅ ba'i don*), and goes on to classify as "final meaning" (*ṅes pa'i don*) the direct viewing of the "lights" or "voids"—what is called in this literature the *saṃvṛti-māyā* (conventional illusion)—followed by an instant of comprehending the "clear light" along with great ecstasy (*mahāsukha*). There is much material on this subject in A. Wayman, *Yoga of the Guhyasamājatantra; the Arcane Lore of Forty Verses* (1977).

19. This translator has been referred to in my Introduction, above, "The Lineage" section.

20. For this personage, cf. "Calming the Mind," note 60.

21. *Mchan* here, f. 86a–6, goes into why some thought Candrakīrti was a Vaibhāṣika.

22. *Prasannapadā,* La Vallée Poussin, ed., p. 340.

23. This sentence is missing in the Sanskrit text, *Prasannapadā,* p. 340.

24. Equals *Madhyamaka-kārikā* (hereafter, M.K.), XVIII, 2a–b, according to *Prasannapadā,* p. 345, n. 3.

25. See the translation of L. de La Vallée Poussin, *Muséon* XIII (1911), p. 269. This is part of the long commentary under I, 8d, with citation of *Ratnāvalī,* I, 35a–b f.

26. According to Ja, saying *1)* is *dri ba daṅ, 2)* is *dri ba gñis pa.*

27. The *Buddhapālita* commentary, on XVIII, 2a–b, per Nagao.

28. This is the *Abhisamayālaṃkāra-vṛtti,* and on *Abhisamayālaṃkāra,* IV, 60, per Nagao. Cf. Edward Conze, *Abhisamayālaṃkāra* (Rome, 1954), pp. 74–75. Nagao points out the equivalent

sūtra treatment in Haribhadra's *Abhisamayālaṃkārāloka,* U. Wogihara, ed., pp. 728–30. Also now Edward Conze, *The Large Sutra on Perfect Wisdom,* pp. 415–16.

29. According to *Mchan*'s suggestion.

30. According to the realist, as his position is here presented, the waking state is true and the dream or deep-sleep state false. Thus, for the Mādhyamika to say that the various natures that are considered virtues in the waking state are like dreams is to have undercut virtues by equating them with nonexistence. But the Mādhyamika, in agreement with the Prajñāpāramitā sūtra passages alluded to in note 28, above, retorts that the realist completely misses the point. The Mādhyamika, rather states that whatever can be said of a nature in the waking state can be said of that nature in dream. Therefore, as in the sūtra in that place, the Bodhisattva's virtues increase in the waking state, so do they also in dream. This position is also the basis for the theory of auspicious dreams, since dream is comparable to the waking state. So the Mādhyamika says that the natures in the waking state are not true, like a dream. *Mchan* adds that Haribhadra is here cited in the sense that his position is tantamount to the Svātantrika, so the intention is to show that the Mādhyamika as a whole agrees in this matter. The disagreement between the Svātantrika and the Prāsaṅgika would be on other grounds, namely, as refuting agent, to be discussed in Tsoṅ-kha-pa's next subsection.

31. *Bodhicaryāvatārapañjikā,* La Vallée Poussin, ed., p. 571: kalpitaṃ bhāvam aspṛṣṭvā tadabhāvo na gṛhyate /.

32. "Omniscience" for *rnam mkhyen,* on the authority of the Dge-bśes-chos-grags dictionary.

33. The phrase *bsñon can* means "affirmation followed by denial" according to Dge-bśes-chos-grags dictionary.

34. Here the reading in the Tashilunpo edition, *mgrin pa bsal nas,* had to be rejected in favor of the reading in the *Mchan 'grel* edition, *mgrin pa gsal nas.*

35. Explained in the Bodhisattva section of the *Lam rim chen mo.*

36. The matter of avoiding a one-sidedness is well presented in the Introduction, the section "The Lineage, and Atīśa's 'Light on the Path to Enlightenment'." In the present context, according to *Mchan,* the means goes with comprehending *saṃvṛti* as the phenomenon (*ji sñed pa*), and insight goes with comprehending *paramārtha* as the noumenon.

37. The phrase "from the bottom of their hearts and with sincerity" is for *gtiṅ thag* which, according to *Mchan,* is an abbreviation for *sñiṅ gi gtiṅ daṅ źe thag pa.*

38. That is, attains the Dharmakāya from the knowledge collection, and the Rūpakāya from the merit collection—according to the Bodhisattva section of the *Lam rim chen mo,* and as indicated by the *Yuktiṣaṣṭikā* verse above.

39. *Prasannapadā,* La Vallée Poussin, ed., p. 500.1-2.

40. The "direct" and "reverse" order does not mean, as would be expected, the order from one end of the series and the order from the other end. Rather, by consultation of that chap. XXVI, we see that "direct" order means the origination order, starting with no. 1, "nescience" (*avidyā*), and continuing down to the last member of dependent origination, no. 12, "old age and death" (*jarā-maraṇa*); and "reverse" order means the cessation order, starting with that same no. 1, "nescience," and continuing down to that same no. 12, "old age and death."

41. But also by teaching the denial of self-existence, it presumes the self-existence, as becomes clear from Candrakīrti's commentary, to be cited later by Tsoṅ-kha-pa.

42. This is the teaching of voidness as efficiency, which serves to establish the Noble Truths, and all the rest.

43. When Tsoṅ-kha-pa refers simply to "Chapter" it is because the work is the most famous of all, the *Madhyamaka-kārikā* of Nāgārjuna. Sometimes he refers to this work as *rtsa śe* (*mūla-prajñā*).

44. As L. de La Vallée Poussin points out in "Les quatre odes de Nāgārjuna," both verses are extant in Sanskrit, no. 19 cited in the *Prasannapadā,* pp. 55 and 234, and no. 20 cited in the *Bodhicaryāvatārapañjikā,* p. 427, under IX, 34.

45. La Vallée Poussin, ed., p. 500.5 to p. 510.8 omitting p. 500.7-12, the words *rocate kṣamate* in 500.13, the words *sugatir durgatir* in 501.5 and 501.7.

46. For this term *viśeṣādhigama,* cf. Jacques May, *Candrakīrti, Prasannapadā Madhyamakavṛtti,* p. 235, on the textual references. *Mchan* here annotates the *adhigama* (T. *rtogs pa*) as "comprehension" (*khoṅ du chud pa*), and the *viśeṣa* (T. *khyad par du*) as "higher and higher" (*goṅ nas goṅ du*). But see "Calming the Mind," note 131, above, for another interpretation.

47. *Vigrahavyāvartinī,* Kunst, ed., pp. 23–24.

48. The expression "to take," apparently missing from the Sanskrit text, suggests here the function of the pot as a begging bowl.

49. According to *Mchan,* the first statement represents the *vyatireka,* absence in dissimilar cases, by nondependence on causes and conditions; and the second statement represents the *anvaya,* presence in similar cases, by dependence on causes and conditions.

50. In the theory of multiple Māras, this is the variety called "son-of-the-gods Māra"; cf. now, using some of my own researches, James W. Boyd, *Satan and Māra; Christian and Buddhist Symbols of Evil* (Leiden, 1975).

51. The "appearance" and the "void" are explained in the verses cited below from the *Ratnāvalī,* namely, II, 16–17. Verse 16 speaks of the coarse sensory realm which is constantly appearing; and verse 17 speaks of the Illustrious Dharma beyond the sensory realm, with no location—hence the "void."

52. Cf. Discerning the Real, note 43, above.

53. Giuseppe Tucci, "The Ratnavali of Nagarjuna," *Journal of the Royal Asiatic Society* (1936), p. 238.

54. Compare Asaṅga, *Paramārtha-gāthā,* verse 9 (in Wayman, *Analysis,* p. 168): "Another does not destroy this; nor is it destroyed of itself. When there is the condition, things arise; and having arisen, are perishable by their own essence." But later the position is shown to be Bhāvaviveka's.

55. Compare the translation of de La Vallée Poussin, *Muséon* (1910), pp. 315–16.

56. The "aggregation" is explained by *Mchan:* triple aggregation, such as a mirror, face, and appearance. The theory derives from dependent origination, no. 6, "contact" (*sparśa*), usually explained as contact of sense organ, sense object, and perception based on sense organ. Here the appearance (*snaṅ*) is in perception (*vijñāna*).

57. *Mchan:* are recognized for their false nature.

58. The sūtra passage which immediately follows in Candrakīrti's self-commentary, and which La Vallée Poussin did not identify, is in fact from the *Pitāputrasamāgama-sūtra,* and is extant in Sanskrit by quotation in the *Śikṣāsamuccaya* (cf. A. Wayman, "The Mirror as a Pan-Buddhist Met-

aphor-Simile," p. 259): "In the way that an image void of self-existence is seen in a very clean mirror, so Druma, understand these *dharmas.*"

59. This important passage, providing the Sanskrit name of the "realist," i.e., *vastusat-padārthavādin,* is among the Sanskrit fragments published by Mahāmahopādhyāya Haraprasād Shāstrī of Āryadeva's *Catuḥśataka* and Candrakīrti's commentary, in *Memoirs of the Asiatic Society of Bengal,* vol. III, no. 8 (1914). Nagao notes the passage therein at p. 492.13-15.

60. La Vallée Poussin, ed., p. 329.10-17, under XVII, 30.

61. Nagao notes, on k. 347, but V. Bhattacharya, partially reconstructing, in *The Catuḥśataka of Āryadeva,* p. 226, includes it on k. 348 (= chap. XIV, 23).

62. *Mchan* observes that when the realist asks this, the "entity" he has in mind is in fact the "extreme of entity" (*dṅos po'i mthar*) and the "truly produced" (*bden grub*).

63. "effects arising with the nature": This agrees with the Abhidharma theory of dependent origination as "cause," and the natures that arise as "effects."

64. Nagao notes, on k. 276, corroborated by V. Bhattacharya, pp. 134–35. Also, the verse citation is displaced from its position in Candrakīrti's commentary as in the Tanjur edition. This may reflect a different recension of the text, which Tsoṅ-kha-pa utilizes.

65. The expression "third possibility" (*phuṅ gsum*) is in Atīśa self-commentary on *Bodhipathapradīpa,* the *pañjikā,* PTT, vol. 103, p. 39-5-3: " 'The two' has no third possibility at all here" (/ gñis ka źes pa'i phuṅ po gsum pa ni 'ga' yaṅ 'di na med do /).

66. *Mchan's* way of stating the four alternatives: / yod pa daṅ min med pa yaṅ min de gñis ka yaṅ min de gñis ka ma yin pa yaṅ min źes /.

67. La Vallée Poussin, ed., p. 273.4-9, on XV, 11.

68. Nagao notes: the *Buddhapālita* on XV, 11.

69. La Vallée Poussin, ed., p. 495.12 to p. 496.9.

70. La Vallée Poussin, ed., p. 495.3-5.

71. In ancient Buddhism this sect was described by the doctrines of Ajita Keśakambalī, in *Dīgha-nikāya,* II, 22–24. Both the *Lam rim chen mo* (Tashilunpo edition) and the *Mchan 'grel* edition give here and later on the spelling *'jig rten rgyaṅ pan pa,* but the lexicons have *'phan pa.*

72. La Vallée Poussin, ed., p. 368.4-12. In J. W. de Jong, *Cinq chapitres de la Prasannapadā,* the passage is in sect. 13, "Pourquoi les Mādhyamika ne sont pas des nihilistes," pp. 25–26.

73. This Sanskrit expression, for both occurrences in this passage, is translated into Tibetan with neglect of the *bhāva.* The compound might intend: "void of a present thing's self-existence."

74. *Mchan* points out that they admit the present world because it is directly perceived. These then are the "naïve realists."

75. This type of seeing was traditionally credited in Buddhism to a faculty called the "divine eye" (*divya-cakṣus*), but ordinarily humans do not have this faculty.

76. La Vallée Poussin, ed., p. 368.13-15.

77. Ridiculous on the face of it!

78. La Vallée Poussin, ed., p. 368.16 to p. 369.4.

79. For the two sides, cf. note 51, above.

80. Nagao notes, k. 360A; in V. Bhattacharya, it is 359a–c.

81. Presumably Tsoṅ-kha-pa specifically mentions the chapter (i.e., XX) because the preceding chap. XIX is in fact devoted to the topic of "time" (cf. in translation, de Jong, *Cinq chapitres,* pp. 37–43), although the topic does spill over to chap. XX.

82. The word "examination" here and later should usually be understood with the sense of "search," since the context shows that the examination need not be successful, because there may be ability or inability in the examination.

83. By "form, etc." is meant form as the object of sight, sound as the object of hearing, and so forth. Or form, feelings, and so forth, as *skandhas.*

84. The implication is that these persons shrug off the negation by a principle, saying, "Oh well, your negation is just an inability."

85. This is part of a longer passage in the commentary on k. 311, which Tsoṅ-kha-pa cites a few folios later.

86. According to *Mchan*'s *snaṅ ba tsam,* for Tsoṅ-kha-pa's *yod du chug.* The Tibetan word *chug* seems to be an ancient word for "mere" or "merely," possibly as a form of *chog,* "to suffice." Modern dictionaries allow it only to be the imperative of *gźugs.*

87. Nagao notes that most of this passage has original Sanskrit extant, per M. H. Shāstrī's edition of fragments, p. 501.15-17.

88. *Mchan:* one does not see them in *ārya-samāpatti,* because in that state of voidness, duality appearance (*gñis snaṅ*) abates.

89. Ja says: "great translators and partisans" (*lo chen daṅ cha pa*).

90. *Mchan:* the "Mind-only" (Cittamātra) followers, the deniers (*'gog pa po*) of worldly convention (*'jig rten gyi kun rdzob*).

91. *Mchan,* 142b–4, 5 in the edition in my possession, explains this as a like capacity or incapacity to refute each other.

92. This last sentence, while in Tsoṅ-kha-pa's quotation, is in fact missing at that place in the edition published by V. Bhattacharya, p. 183.

93. While this passage, being the continuation of the previous citation, should be found in V. Bhattacharya's edition at p. 183, in fact it is not there. According to Nagao (note 79), it is in the Tibetan text of *Catuḥ-śataka-ṭīka,* which he consulted.

94. La Vallée Poussin, ed., p. 69.1-5.

95. This shows that Tsoṅ-kha-pa heard in his day the same remark one can hear nowadays, to wit, that *saṃvṛti-satya* is not *really* a truth (*satya*); only *paramārtha-satya* is indeed a truth.

96. This refers to the Buddhist terminology of the *āryas* as the disciples of the Buddha, and the non-*āryas* as the ordinary persons ("separate persons," *pṛthagjana*).

97. From the *Samādhirāja-sūtra,* IX, 23, as was previously cited.

98. Apparently, since the eye is an authority for reality, why bother with using the ears!

99. Ja identifies him as the logician type of realist. This is because the Buddhist logician, especially following Dharmakīrti, takes direct perception (*pratyakṣa*) to have as object the "particular" or "own-character" (*svalakṣaṇa*), which is *paramārtha-sat.*

100. When *vijñāna* is taken as a personality aggregate (*skandha*) it is also said to be illusory (*māyopama*) (cf. *Prasannapadā,* p. 41.11).

101. Nagao notes the place in Tibetan text and identifies as on chap. XIII, k. 301. However, this passage is not in that place of V. Bhattacharya, *The Catuḥśataka,* pp. 167 ff.

102. For "a swinging bell" the text *g'yer po* is to be read *g'yer kha. Mchan* glosses *g'yer po* with *kun tu g'yo ba'i,* "swinging."

103. Ja: the *spyi* (S. *sāmānya,* "universal"), to wit, "This is called. . . ."

104. Ja: the second *spyi* (*sāmānya*), to wit, "This is a kind of. . . ."

105. Cf. Masaaki Hattori, *Dignāga, On Perception,* pp. 25–26.

106. La Vallée Poussin, ed., p. 75.9.

107. Ja: "direct perception" (*pratyakṣa, mṅon sum*)=*yul mṅon gyur rtogs pa,* "what directly comprehends the object"; "inference" (*anumāna, rjes dpag*) = *yul lkog gyur tsam rtogs pa,* "what comprehends the object which is just out-of-sight"; "testimony" (*āgama, luṅ*) = *yul śin tu lkog gyur rtogs pa,* "what comprehends the object which is very much out-of-sight"; "analogy" (*upamāna, ñer 'jal*) = *mṅon lkog gi 'dra ba rtogs pa,* "what comprehends directly something similar to what is out-of-sight."

108. La Vallée Poussin, ed., p. 75.10-11.

109. Compare Stcherbatsky's conclusions, *The Conception of Buddhist Nirvāṇa,* p. 164, note.

110. La Vallée Poussin, *Muséon* (1910), p. 301, gives Sanskrit for VI, 25, as cited in *Bodhicaryāvatārapañjikā,* p. 353.13.

111. *Mchan:* The rest is such things as reflected images and echoes, as well as erroneous perceptions due to impaired senses.

112. That is, in the case of the conventional cognition it has (*a*) nonerror: senses unimpaired by personal causes; (*b*) error: senses impaired by personal causes. In the case of the conventional object it has (*a*) nonerror: when perceived by unimpaired senses; (*b*) error: when perceived by external causes for error, yielding hallucinations, etc.

113. Commentary that immediately follows VI, 25.

114. See Nagao's note no. 92 for variant spellings of this word, and that this poison causes one to see everything with a golden color.

115. Commentary that follows the previous citation, note 113, above.

116. *Mchan:* These three are the common bases for reflected images and accordingly generate error in eye-cognition.

117. *Mchan:* This generates error in ear-cognition.

118. *Mchan:* This special encounter causes a mirage, generating an error that there is water.

119. Candrakīrti by this remark verifies the information of notes 116–18, above.

120. If Bhāvaviveka's point is cogent, this is indeed a blow against the Yogācārin, who has a distinctive theory of three natures (*svabhāva*): the imaginary (*parikalpita*), the dependency (*paratantra*), and the perfect (*pariniṣpanna*).

121. Cf. Lamotte, *Saṃdhinirmocana,* chap. VII, sect. 3: dgoṅs nas chos thams cad ṅo bo ñid med pa'o. There are three kinds there stated: "non-self-existence" of character (*lakṣaṇa*), of origination

(*utpatti*), and of the absolute (*paramārtha*). As to Kamalaśīla's text, *Mchan* does not identify; it should be either the *Madhyamakāloka* or the *Madhyamakālaṃkāra-pañjikā* of works preserved in the Tibetan Tanjur.

122. Followers of the *Saṃdhinirmocana-sūtra* claimed it to have "final meaning" (*nītārtha*).

123. Cf. La Vallée Poussin, *Muséon* (1911), p. 250. And in the Tibetan text, the identification with this sūtra occurs in PTT, vol. 98, p. 136-1-1.

124. This interpretation of Tsoṅ-kha-pa's sentence is corroborated by Louis de La Vallée Poussin, *Vijñaptimātratāsiddhi,* II, p. 559, where the Parikalpitasvabhāva is identified as the *lakṣaṇa-niḥsvabhāva* (the non-self-existence of character), meaning "absolutely unreal." Here the Paratantras-vabhāva is the *utpattiniḥsvabhāva,* and the Pariniṣpannasvabhāva is the *paramārthaniḥsvabhāva.*

125. *Vijñaptimātratāsiddhi,* II, p. 559, agrees explicitly in the case of the Paratantra, observing that it is *sa-svabhāva.* But no similar statement is made at this point in the case of the Pariniṣpanna.

126. For their inaccessibility to sense perception, cf. La Vallée Poussin, *Vijñaptimātratāsiddhi,* I, p. 34. *Mchan* explains the simile: They are not material in the sense of a single moon.

127. The *Tarkajvālā* is Bhāvaviveka's own commentary on his *Madhyamakahṛdaya.*

128. This is the case of *niravayava* (without parts).

129. Perhaps Bhāvaviveka means: Why would not the same denial hold if they *are* material (*dravya*)?

130. For the eight substances, cf. *Abhidharmakośa,* II, 22, La Vallée Poussin, trans., p. 145. They are the speechless eight substances in the "realm of desire" (*kāma-dhātu*), to wit, four great elements (*mahābhūta*), and the four derived elements, the visible (*rūpa*), odor, taste, and tangible.

131. *Mchan* might understand a switch away from the Yogācārin as the adversary (*pūrvapakṣa*).

132. *Madhyamakāvatāra* of Candrakīrti, PPT, vol. 98, pp. 166-2-3 f. This is part of the concluding remarks of the work.

133. *Mchan* says Vaibhāṣikas, Sautrāntikas, etc., thus taking in all four Buddhist *siddhāntas* under the term *svayūthyā* (*raṅ gi sde pa*).

134. At first, this seems contradictory with the *Avatāra-Comm.* cited above. However, there the Mādhyamika accepts as *saṃvṛti* what some deviant Mādhyamikas take as *paramārtha* while explaining the Vaibhāṣikas and Sautrāntikas. The citation then does not apply to what these two schools themselves take as *paramārtha,* since the Mādhyamika is classified as a separate *siddhānta* from the Vaibhāṣikas and Sautrāntikas.

135. So far I have not located the citation.

136. Ja says that this disclaims Bhāvaviveka's taking of the "object-support condition" (*ālambanapratyaya*) as a substance (*dravya*).

137. This is part of a previous citation of *Catuḥ-śataka-ṭīkā,* XIII, 1 (cf. above, with note 99).

138. The Tibetan expression was previously discussed (note 86, above).

139. *Mchan:* "the ultimate manner-of-being of *dharmas*" (*chos kyi yin lugs mthar thug gi*). This is the *svabhāva,* also to be translated "real nature."

140. Tsoṅ-kha-pa appears to have included the various assertions in the category "affected by nescience" of the foregoing citation.

141. Ja: one is the convention of mind (*buddhi*) that understands all *dharmas* as illusory; the other is the conventional mind that takes only appearances as true. Cf. *Bodhicaryāvatāra,* IX, 2: "*buddhi* is called 'conventional.' "

142. *Mchan:* This is the "Mind-only school" that has not understood voidness.

143. Cf. *Bodhicaryāvatāra,* IX, 107: "If thus there is no conventional thing, then how are there two truths? But if it were by virtue of another convention, how would a sentient being get to Nirvāṇa?" Again, *ibid.,* IX, 3: "In this case, the world is seen as twofold—the yogin and the ordinary man. Among these, the world of ordinary men is repelled (*bādhyate*) by the world of yogins."

144. The line is *Avatāra,* VI, 28a (Sanskrit from *Bodhicaryāvatārapañjikā,* p. 353.3): *mohasvabhāvāvaraṇād dhi saṃvṛtiḥ. Mchan* glosses *raṅ bźin* (*svabhāva*): "the manner-of-being of dharmas" (*chos kyi yin lugs kyi*), and glosses *kun rdzob* (*saṃvṛti*): "all" (*kun*) means "all *svabhāva,*" and "obscuring" (*rdzob*) means "instilling obscuration."

145. In the passage cited from *Avatāra-Comm.* on VI, 28.

146. *Mchan:* That is, the passage does not refer to the basis of falsity consisting of form, etc.

147. Ja illustrates this, as when the theory that sound is permanent is not opposed by an inference which understands sound to be impermanent.

148. Ja: as when there is no opposition by conventional authority to the accomplishment in reality of sound (*sgra bden grub*).

149. *Mchan:* whether ordinary person (*pṛthagjana*) or disciple of the Buddha (*ārya*).

150. For "not acknowledged," *Mchan* gives: "entities out of sight" (*don lkog tu gyur pa*).

151. For "autonomy of a cognition," cf. the extended discussion of the same matter in Tsoṅ-kha-pa's commentary on the *Madhyamakāvatāra,* PTT, vol. 154, p. 42-3-3, including, "even though comprehended by the autonomy of a mundane intellect" (*/ 'jig rten pa'i blo raṅ dga' bas kyaṅ rtogs mod kyaṅ /*).

152. *Mchan: pradhāna* (T. *gtso bo*) here refers to the Sāṃkhya system, i.e., *prakṛti,* the state when the three *guṇas* are in harmony.

153. The four wayward objects are taking suffering as happiness, the impure as pure, impermanent as permanent, and nonself as self.

154. *Bodhicaryāvatārapañjikā,* 353.7-8, mentions two kinds of *saṃvṛti,* genuine (*tathya*) and deviant or misleading (*mithyā*) and defines them in the manner that Tsoṅ-kha-pa does now.

155. The eight are the four pairs itemized in note 153, above.

156. For this "ranging in sign-sources," cf. the Introduction, "Asaṅga on the Ancillaries . . . ," ancillary no. 7, "Restraint of Sense Organs."

157. *Bodhicaryāvatārapañjikā,* p. 352.6-7 says, " 'nescience,' 'delusion,' and 'waywardness' are equivalent terms" (*avidyā moho viparyāsa iti paryāya*).

158. *Mchan* says they are *śrāvakas* and *pratyekabuddhas.* According to the *Śrīmālā-sūtra* ("The Lion's Roar of Queen Śrīmālā"), the two would be *arhats* and *pratyekabuddhas,* where *pratyekabuddha* refers to the second of the two kinds of *pratyekabuddhas;* cf. Alex and Hideko Wayman, trans., p. 82. This interpretation is certified by Tsoṅ-kha-pa's qualification of the Bodhisattvas as those on the eighth and higher stages, and these are of course the *Śrīmālāsūtra*'s "Bodhisattvas who have attained power."

159. Hence, "eye, etc." means the five outer senses and the *manas* (mind) as a sixth sense.

160. These remarks just precede, in Candrakīrti's commentary, his verse VI, 36, whose first words are indicated by "In the phase of reality."

161. A portion of the commentary following VI, 36.

162. *Mchan:* ears (*rna ba*) are the basis for hearing; heart (*sñiṅ*) is the basis for remembering.

163. *Mchan:* "It is incumbent to hear the addition of the qualification 'by reason of self-existence' and to remember its meaning; and if one hears and remembers that way, then 'where is the possibility of disputing (us)' by asserting that 'arising in dependence' and 'not arising' are in contradiction!"

164. This verse is extant in Sanskrit and is much cited, e.g., in the *Prasannapadā,* which gives the scripture title *Anavatapta-hradāpasaṃkramaṇa-sūtra.*

165. *Mchan:* "heedful" means "set in the path of liberation." Cf. *Dhammapada* (21–23): "Heedfulness is the path to the deathless; heedlessness is the path to death. . . . The constantly meditative, the ever earnestly striving ones, realize the bond-free, supreme Nibbāna."

166. Presumably because *nirvāṇa* is counted as an *asaṃskṛta-dharma,* and the self-existence of *nirvāṇa* cannot be opposed. Various Western writers on the Mādhyamika have not recognized it this way; and there is no point in singling out for mention one of these writers whose viewpoint is probably not original with him anyway.

167. Kunst, ed., p. 27.

168. *Mchan:* In the example, the part "like somebody preventing a sound by the sound, 'Don't say it!' " is valid; but the part "likewise with non-self-existent words one can prevent non-self-existent entities" is not valid.

169. Nagao (note 132) mentions that this is found at the end of Buddhapālita's commentary on chap. XIII (verse 8 being the last one of this chapter).

170. Cf. the stock phrase in Buddhism, "lovely in the beginning, lovely in the middle, lovely in the end," especially applied to Buddhist practice.

171. La Vallée Poussin, ed., p. 247.4: ye tu tasyām api śūnyatāyāṃ bhāvābhiniveśinas.

172. *Prajñā-pāramitā-ratnaguṇa-saṃcaya-gāthā,* Sanskrit and Tibetan text edited by E. Obermiller: imi skandha śūnya parikalpayi bodhisattvo carato nimitta anupādapade asakto.

173. *Prasannapadā* cites it at p. 359.2:6 ātmānātmakṛte dṛṣṭī vavārāsmān mahānumiḥ.

174. *Mchan* cites the *Dar-ṭik* (Rgyal-tshab-rje's commentary on the *Ratnāvalī*) to the effect: "Because those views that self and nonself are accomplished by self-existence, are wayward views—the great Muni warded them off."

175. Tsoṅ-kha-pa here summarizes from the opening sentences of the larger version of the Heart Sūtra (*Prajñāpāramitā-hṛdaya-sūtra*).

176. Obermiller, ed.: prakṛtīasanta parijānayamāna dharmān eṣā sa prajñavara-pāramitāya caryā.

177. *Advitiyaṃ śiva-dvāraṃ*. Nagao (notes 139–40) presents the available Sanskrit from Shāstrī fragments, which includes the verse and much of the following citation of Candrakīrti's commentary. Cf. V. Bhattacharya, *The Catuḥśataka,* pp. 151–52.

178. Nagao (note 141) points out that this work is not available in Sanskrit or Tibetan, but is in Chinese as Taishō, no. 1660, a gāthā set attributed to Nāgārjuna (Taishō, XXXII, p. 532a). Possi-

bly this work was translated into Tibetan from Chinese in the early period (say eighth to ninth centuries) and, while not preserved in the canon, still remains through a verse or so handed down in the *Lam rim* literature. Translation of the verse was much aided by *Mchan.*

179. The three doors are standard in Buddhist literature as the "voidness" (*śūnyatā*), "signless" (*ānimitta*), and "wishless" (*apraṇihita*) doors or gates. The fact that the view observing the void of self-existence (*svabhāva*) is called the sole gate, and, as above, designated the substratum for the three gates to liberation seems to support the position taken in my article "Secret of the Heart Sūtra" (forthcoming in Conze honorary volume) that the view of the five personality aggregates as void of self-existence is the basis for the next realization of the sūtra which can be explained as the three gates to liberation, and that these gateways then lead to the "Truth of Cessation" (*nirodhasatya*), which some traditions identified with *nirvāṇa.*

180. For the two kinds of reflection (*rtog pa*), cf. the terminology "deviant reflection" (*mithyāvikalpa*) and "right reflection" (*samyag-vikalpa*) in the *kṣānti* section of Āryaśūra's *Pāramitāsamāsa,* called to my attention by the translation of this work as a doctoral dissertation by Carol Meadows at Columbia University.

181. The *lto ldir ba* kind of pot is one with a large globular or bulbous formation. Here the large bulbous pot, being a *kind of a pot,* can explain the pot by illustrating it, as when one would say, " 'a pot,' e.g., a large bulbous one."

182. For "basis" *Mchan* says, "any concomitant object-support and aspect" (*lhan skyes kyi dmigs pa daṅ rnam pa gaṅ gi*). Tsoṅ-kha-pa soon clarifies the *kind* of basis by giving a verse with the expression "nescience basis."

183. Kārikā VI, 141 is quoted in the *Subhāṣitasaṃgraha:* paśyann ahiṃ chidragataṃ svagehe / gajo 'tra nāstīti nirastaśaṃkaḥ / jahāti sarpād api nāma bhītim / aho ni nāmārjavatā parasya //.

184. It appears that Tsoṅ-kha-pa has composed this verse himself as a companion to *Avatāra,* VI, 140.

185. In the *Daśabhūmika-sūtra* (Rahder edition, p. 65): *eṣā sarvadharmāṇāṃ dharmatā,* referring to the *dharmadhātu,* or voidness of all *dharmas.*

186. The passage occurs in PTT, vol. 98, pp. 151-2-3 ff., immediately following the citation of *Madhyamaka-kārikā,* XV, 1–2, which two verses Tsoṅ-kha-pa has himself cited at the head of the present section.

187. This remark occurs in the *Daśabhūmika-sūtra,* Sixth *bhūmi* (Rahder, ed., p. 65), and was also said in early Buddhism, *Aṅguttaranikāya,* i.285.

188. La Vallée Poussin, ed., 263.5 to 264.4, on XV, 2.

189. In the light of the previous citations, this can be expanded: "This (*svabhāva*) while neither existing in objects as realists believe, nor failing to exist as the goal of Bodhisattvas—is not so by reason of own-nature."

190. Occurs in PTT, vol. 98, p. 151-4-1,2, on VI, 182.

191. Occurs just prior to the preceding citation, p. 151-3-4 to 151-4-1, on VI, 182. *Mchan* explains the *kye ma* ("fooey") as here a term of contempt.

192. Nagao (n. 154) points out that the Peking edition has *chos,* while the Kumbum edition has *khyad chos.* Both my Tashilunpo edition and the *Mchan* edition agree with the reading *khyad chos.*.

193. For these two faces of *buddhi*—voidness, or absent factual bases, on the one side; and the conventional presence of factual bases, on the other side—cf. Lessing and Wayman, *Mkhas grub rje's Fundamentals of the Buddhist Tantras,* pp. 210–11.

194. Ja: They are the Jo-naṅ-pa, who take the *Kālacakra* and *Uttaratantra* (i.e., the *Ratnagotravibhāga*) as sources.

195. More literally, have taken the wrong alternative at the road-fork, Tib. *gol sa. Mchan* gives synonyms, *lam gyi gol sa, lam gyi nor sa, lam gyi log sa.*

196. The comments are Ja's: "consciousness" (*sems*); "of consciousness" (*sems kyi*).

197. *Mchan* indicates two of the opposing arguments: *1*) the evidence of nonbirth from the four alternatives, opposing the birth of an entity by own-nature; *2*) the evidence of avoiding singleness and multiplicity, opposing the real existence of the shoot. Thus the opposing argument means the examination by principle.

198. The portion within brackets is not included in the present Sanskrit text (Johnston and Kunst, pp. 48–49). It is part of the Tanjur text as reproduced in Tucci. *Pre-Dinnāga Buddhist Texts on Logic from Chinese Sources,* using both the Narthang and the Peking editions of the *Vigrahavyāvartanī.*

199. For "wandering," *'byams pa = 'khyams pa,* according to *Mchan,* but this meaning is not attested in Sarat Chandra Das.

200. Ja cites here the *Bodhicaryāvatāra,* IX, 1: "The Muni stated this entire list for the sake of insight (*prajñā*); for that reason, through longing for the cessation of suffering, one should generate insight." *Mchan* adds that the refutation and proof are not for defeating an opponent or for gaining fame.

201. Nagao (n. 160) says these verses are part of a gāthā section at the end of the *Prasannapadā* that is missing in Sanskrit. But cf. J. W. de Jong, "La Madhyamaka-śāstrastuti de Candrakīrti." *Oriens Extremus* (1962), pp. 47 ff., where the verses here cited are the first two of de Jong's Sanskrit edition.

202. *Mchan* first gives the usual list of twelve: sūtra, geya, vyākaraṇa, gāthā, udāna, nidāna, avadāna, itivṛttaka, jātaka, vaipulya, adbhutadharma, and upadeśa; and goes on to say that the commentary on the *Laṅkāvatāra-sūtra* shows how to reduce them to nine by taking nidāna, avadāna, itivṛttaka, and jātaka in one group, in which nidāna is the chief one and the other three ancillary, thus suggesting that the group is called nidāna.

203. For the 84,000 defilements mentioned here by *Mchan,* and their adversary called *Dharmaskandha,* cf. *Mkhas grub rje's,* p. 57.

204. The theory here, according to *Mchan,* is that of adversaries, to wit, in order to get rid of one of these particular defilements, one must crowd it out of consciousness by means of its polar adversary. But the adversary is itself a kind of defilement, from the standpoint of ultimate truth.

205. Previously in the dependent origination discussion of the Middling Person section of the *Lam rim chen mo,* Tsoṅ-kha-pa refers to the *Śālistambasūtra* as "explaining that the seed of 'perception' (*vijñāna*) is planted in the field of *karma* which has the manure of 'nescience' (*avidyā*); and that it is moistened with the water of craving, and then the shoot of 'name-and-form' in the womb proceeds to completion." For the Sanskrit passage, cf. La Vallée Poussin, *Théorie des douze causes,* p. 84, 3rd paragraph.

206. *Mchan*'s additions of the two "arhats" at this point agree with its previous comment; cf. note 158, above. This points to a certain amount of ambiguity in the "arhat" terminology.

207. For the location of the Middling Person section, cf. the Introduction, "The Lineage," outline of the *Lam rim chem mo:* "The Ascetic Handbook for the Middling Person." In fact, in the dependent origination discussion in that part, Tsoṅ-kha-pa mentions Dharmakīrti's theory (from *Pramāṇavārttika,* I, 215cd–216ab) that nescience (*avidyā*) is the positing of self in personality (*pudgala-ātmagrāha*), which is tantamount to the "reifying view" (*satkāyadṛṣṭi*).

208. Ja says that the nescience connected with hindrance of the knowable is called mtshaṇ ṅid can gyi ma rig pa ("characterizing nescience"), which is not helpful. Later Tsoṅ-kha-pa specifies the two kinds as the co-natal nescience (*sahaja-avidyā*), which is the defiled kind, especially involved with the "reifying view," and the nescience of imaginations (*parikalpa*), which is the hindrance of the knowable. The matter is treated in my article, "Nescience and Insight, according to Asaṅga's *Yogācārabhūmi,*" forthcoming in the Rahula honorary volume. Although Tsoṅ-kha-pa employs other sources here—mainly Mādhyamika—Asaṅga's treatment is consistent. Using Asaṅga's explanations, the "co-natal" nescience means having the mental concomitants of defilement, and this is the confusion of heedlessness and the defiled confusion; while the nescience of "imaginations" is the confusion of not comprehending and the undefiled confusion.

209. By saying "nescience" is general, the author shows that it can be defiled or undefiled, as per note 208, above, while the reifying view is always counted as defiled.

210. This is a remark parallel to what Tsoṅ-kha-pa said in his discussion of Buddhist dependent origination in the Middling Person section: "Nescience is as stated in the (*Abhidharma-*) *Kośa* (in III, 28): 'the contrary of clear vision like enmity and untruth.' Besides, one should not regard enmity and untruth as just the negation of friendliness and truth, or as just different from those two; rather, as the opposite side which actively opposes friendliness and truth. Accordingly, nescience should not be regarded in the sense of an opposite as just the negation of clear vision or as just different from it; rather as the contrary side which actively opposes clear vision (*vidyā*)."

211. The whole verse, M.K. XXVI, 1, runs: "The one obscured by nescience, for rebirth, instigates the motivations (*saṃskāra*) of three kinds. By these acts (of three kinds) it proceeds to a destiny." Since *vijñāna* is the seed, it would normally be taken as the understood subject in the verse. It is what is obscured by nescience, instigates the *saṃskāras,* and proceeds to a destiny.

212. The whole verse, M.K. XXVII, 1, runs: " 'In past time, I arose,' 'I did not arise'—whatever the views taking the world as eternal, they are based upon the extreme of the past." XXVII, 2, gives analogous views that are based upon the extreme of the future.

213. They did not make the distinction which Tsoṅ-kha-pa established earlier, of a contrast between genuine and false discursive thought, and which he insists upon repeatedly.

214. The "perspicacity" follows *Mchan's dmigs phyed pa,* while Tashilunpo, ed. has *dmigs byed pa.*

215. *Mchan*'s explanation of *re yod par 'dzin pa* is "a situation independent of conventional cognition."

216. Sanskrit for this is extant in Shāstrī fragments, p. 473.17-18. Here "own-nature" is *svarūpa.*

217. Nagao (note 179) cites the extant Sanskrit from the Shāstri fragments, p. 497.23-24, but does not locate it in a chapter of the *Catuḥ-śataka-ṭīkā*. It has similar language to a citation of this text above, commentary on k. 348 in chap. XIV, but does not occur there.

218. *Mchan* says: included within the Vaibhāṣika school. The thesis here advanced is similar to the first thesis of the Sammatīya according to Bareau, *Les sectes,* p. 123. Presumably the mention of the Sammatīya at this point goes with Candrakīrti's commentary on the *Avatāra,* VI, 126; cf. La Vallée Poussin, *Muséon* (1911), pp. 290–92) and his reply to the Sammatīya in VI, 127, and commentary.

219. In commentary on VI, 133; cf. La Vallée Poussin, *Muséon* (1911), pp. 301–2.

220. Here I follow the *Mchan* reading, *brten nas btags pa'i,* rather than Tashilunpo's *brten nas brtags pa'i.*

221. PTT, vol. 98, p. 141-2-3, commentary on VI, 120.

222. *Ibid.,* p. 141-2-7,8, on VI, 120.

223. *Mchan's ran rkya ba'i.* Cf. *A Tibetan Dictionary,* ed. and published by Jampa Chogyal (Delhi, 1969), p. 17, where *rkya* is defined *ran rkya thub dan tshig rkya thub.* Apparently, the word *rkya* is taken from the *kya* in the title of Buddha, "Śā-kya thub pa" (Śākyamuni), where of course it is a transcription of a Sanskrit syllable, and so *rkya* has a meaning analogous to *śākya,* "capability."

224. Nagao (note 185) cites Shāstrī's fragments for the extent Sanskrit, for which a few corrections had to be made to represent the text from which the Tibetan translation was made. Following is the text corresponding to the Tibetan: / yadi ca amī padārthā alātacakranirmitādivad visamvādakatvād avastukā na syus tadā niyatam upapattyā vicāryyamāṇā jātarūpādivat spaṣṭataram upalabhyamānasvarūpāḥ syuḥ / na caite vicārāgni-santāpitā viparyyāsa-nibandhanatvāt svarūpābhāvaṃ nāsādayanti /. Candrakīrti here employs irony.

225. The phrase "the magical manifestation" (S. *nirmita*) is missing from the Shāstrī fragment.

226. Notice Tsoṅ-kha-pa's sequence: *1*) the Prajñāpāramitā scripture; *2*) Nāgārjuna; *3*) Buddhapālita; *4*) Candrakīrti. He thus expresses the lineage of the Mādhyamika-Prāsaṅgika school.

227. *Mchan:* who has set out with striving on the path to Nirvāṇa, has seven lives ahead of him, and so on.

228. *Mchan:* who returns by reason of *karma* and defilement (kleśa).

229. *Mchan:* who has destroyed all the defilement of the three realms.

230. *Mchan:* who in his last life does not rely on another instructor (*ācārya*), but realizes enlightenment (*bodhi*) by himself.

231. *Mchan:* who has generated the mind to bring to fulfillment the two aims—that for himself and that for others. (This is usually stated as enlightenment for himself, and *nirvāṇa* or liberation for others).

232. Nagao (note 191) mentions that this occurs at the end of Buddhapālita's commentary on chap. XXII (on the Tathāgata). Nevertheless, the verse included in his commentary is XXIV, 8.

233. Nagao (note 192) mentions that this directly follows the preceding, quoted passage.

234. That is to say, the first of the Madhyamaka-kārikā, I, 1, denies four alternatives of causation concerning the arising of things, but does not deny that things arise. Since the world agrees that things arise, the *paramārtha* distinction does not apply.

235. In the absolute sense, arising per se is rejected.

236. Nagao (note 197) cites *Prasannapadā,* pp. 25–26: na paramārthata (ādhyātmikāny āyatanāni) svata utpannāni / vidyamānatvāt / caitanyavad iti. In the *Avatāra* passage the *pakṣa* is *bhāvāḥ* rather than *ādhyātmikāny āyatanāni.*

237. *Mchan,* in the *Madhyamakahṛdayakārikā,* section of *Don dam par yod pa 'gog pa.*

238. The *Tarkajvālā* and *Madhyamaka-āloka* passages that directly follow clarity the intention of the two Tibetan expressions. They are here the logical terms *ma yin* (*paryudāsa*), the qualified negation; and *med* (*prasajya*), the unqualified negation. Thus, *der yod pa ma yin* means, according to the context, "There is no existence there (accomplished by self-existence)"; and (*der*) *med* means "It does not exist (there) (at all)."

239. Cf. Lessing and Wayman, *Mkhas grub rje's,* p. 91. This is one of the "three Eastern works of the Svātantrika." The other two are Jñānagarbha's *Ṣatyadvaya* (with a self-commentary), and Santarakṣita's *Madhyamakālaṃkāra* (with a self-commentary).

240. This is Kamalaśīla's commentary on Śāntarakṣita's work (note 239, above).

241. This inference, called *dṅos po'i stobs kyis źugs,* is the first of three kinds of inference given in Tsoṅ-kha-pa's "Guided Tour through the Seven Books of Dharmakīrti." The other two kinds are the "acknowledged in the world" and the "based on religious faith."

242. Nagao (note 202): the beginning of commentary on chap. XV.

243. Cf. note 54, above.

244. *Mchan:* Buddhapālita and Candrakīrti. However, it seems that Tsoṅ-kha-pa now reverts to the remark that opens this subsection, "c. Explanation of Treating. . . ." Since the Madhyamika-Svātantrika is headed by Bhāvaviveka, and the *Avatāra-Comm.* is of course by Candrakīrti, it appears that Tsoṅ-kha-pa means by "these two *ācāryas*" Bhāvaviveka and Candrakīrti, to show the area of agreement and to clarify their disagreement.

245. The sentence explains the name "Svātantrika," to wit: he refutes the opposing side by proving his own side.

246. The sentence explains the name "Prāsaṅgika," to wit: he clarifies his own position by showing the absurdity (*prasaṅga*) of the opponent's position.

247. Nagao (note 206): commentary on VI, 9–10.

248. Cf. Th. Stcherbatsky, *Buddhist Logic,* vol. II, p. 49, comment on *Nyāyabindu,* II, 4, Vinītadeva's remarks on inference, "since it has the character of definitely ascertaining the object (*artha-viniścaya-svabhāvatvāt*)."

249. Cf. in this quotation, below, "arises (from the object) alone." Here "alone" (the object) is meant to exclude "all" (*sarvam*). Hence, the inference of one object is the negation of all objects in the qualified sense, i.e., negation of all except the inferred object alone.

250. Meaning of *prādeśika* from Edgerton's *BHS Dictionary.*

251. For the three marks, cf., for example, Stcherbatsky, *Buddhist Logic,* vol. I, p. 244: 1. its presence in the subject of the inference, 2. its presence in similar instances, 3. its absence in dissimilar instances.

252. Ja: the translator Ku and so on, who were his followers. Here, Ku must refer to Khu Mdo-sde-'bar, who collaborated with Jayānanda in the translation of Jayānanda's *Tarkamudgarakārikā-nāma.* Roerich, *The Blue Annals,* vol. I, p. 94: "Now the Khu-pas: they belonged to the Lineage of Khu mDo-sde-'bar. He taught the Mādhyamika system. mDo-sde-'bar was a contemporary of Pa-tshab Ñi-ma grags." Hence, the twelfth century. Also, *The Blue Annals,* vol. I, p. 343: "rMa-bya Byaṅ-brtson was a disciple of Khu lo-tsā-ba mDo-sde-'bar and Kha-che Jayānanda. He composed a commentary on the *Tarkamudgarakārikā* written by Jayānanda. . . ." *The Blue Annals* contains

mention of various Mādhyamika works by this rMa bya Byaṅ-brtson, who thus appears to have expanded upon the method of applying Buddhist logic to the Mādhyamika system.

253. Ja: the method of refutation by the Prāsaṅgika.

254. "Common denominator" translates *mgo sñoms;* perhaps also, "reduction to par."

255. *Mchan* says: *lo-tsa-ba,* "translator"; hence, the translator Khu, as in note 252, above.

256. *Mchan* says: *lo-tsa-ba 'di dag* (these translators), indicating that these arguments now presented by Tsoṅ-kha-pa belong to the lineage of Khu and disciples.

257. Both this *Catuḥ-śataka-kārikā* and the *Vigrahavyāvartinī* verses 29–30, above are cited in *Prasannapadā,* p. 16, in commentary on *Madhyamaka-kārikā,* I, 1.

258. This alludes to the opening of the Third Position, "Nowadays, what some others claim to be Prāsaṅgika is as follows."

259. Ja: the position known as "peacock (*rma bya ba*)," etc., former followers of Pa-tshab.

260. For "authority aroused by strength of a present fact," cf. note 241, above. This is the first kind of inference, the formal syllogism, and is distinguished from the second kind, acknowledged by the world, which this Fourth Position accepts.

261. Ja: rejecting the school of the pandit Jayānanda.

262. T. *phyogs re,* defined by Dge-bśes-chos-kyi-grags dictionary as *ñi tshe ba* (hence, *prādeśika*).

263. *Mchan:* refutation of the translator followers of Jayānanda.

264. Cf. first paragraph of the rejection of the Second Position: ". . . is it your claim . . . or is it your claim . . .?" The portion, "or is it your claim" is the second case, now being answered.

265. *Mchan:* rejection of a Tibetan school claiming to be Prāsaṅgika. The author employs the most ample space for rejecting this school, which claimed support from passages in the works of Nāgārjuna, Āryadeva, and Candrakīrti. Since these passages are necessarily authoritative for Tsoṅ-kha-pa as well, he will not reject the quotations themselves but will seek to establish that their purport is different from the way in which this Third Position has understood them. In this section the paragraphing follows Ja's headings.

266. The words "avowing and then disavowing" are for T. *bsñon 'diṅs pa,* following definition in Dge-bśes-chos-grags dictionary. Cf. note 33, above.

267. The *Avatāra-Comm.,* PTT, vol. 98, p. 146-1, identifies the school as the Āryasammatīya (*'phags pa maṅ pos bkur ba pa*). The Sammatīya is one of the four sects that issued from the Vātsīputrīya (for which see Bareau, *Les sectes,* pp. 114 ff.).

268. See Bareau, *Les sectes,* p. 126, thesis no. 26 of the Āryasammatīya: "Le connaissable (*jñeya*) est à la fois exprimable (abhilāpya) et inexprimable (anabhilāpya)." Bareau notes that for lack of commentary, the meaning of this thesis seems enigmatic. However, the present context constitutes a kind of commentary on the thesis. It appears that the thesis held, in regard to the substantial self, that it is "expressible," but that its sameness or difference—the relation—with the aggregates is "inexpressible." But then the relationship is of absolute nature, which is unacceptable. Cf. Ruegg, *La théorie . . . ,* chap. V, "La nature inexprimable et inconnaissable de l'absolu."

269. For *źe ba,* cf. the Dge-bśes-chos grags dictionary.

270. Presumably Tsoṅ-kha-pa refers to Nāgārjuna's *Madhyamaka-kārikā,* XV, 7, the verse summarizing the Buddha's discourse to Katyāyana: "In the counsel of Katyāyana, the Lord, having un-

derstood presence and absence, has denied 'It is' and 'It is not.' " In the Pali canon, this is found in "The Kaccāyana," *Saṃyutta-Nikāya,* ii, 15, where avoidance of the two extremes is set forth as dependent origination.

271. Candrakīrti, PTT, vol. 98, p. 133-4, does not identify the source of the passage, including: "I do not fight with the world. When someone in the world holds that it exists, I too claim that it exists. When someone in the world holds that it does not exist, I too claim that it does not exist." La Vallée Poussin, *Muséon* (1911), p. 237, points to a passage of similar sentiments, *Prasannapadā,* p. 370, where the note refers also to *Saṃyutta-nikāya,* iii, p. 138; cf. in translation, de Jong, *Cinq chapitres de la Prasannapadā,* p. 27.

272. *Mchan:* the factual base is the shoot (in the foregoing thesis).

273. The beginning of k. 30, *Vigrahavyāvartinī.*

274. Nagao (n. 227) properly refers to *Prasannapadā,* p. 75, which was cited much earlier. Here it is of course a paraphrase.

275. Tsoṅ-kha-pa's text of the commentary apparently diverges from the text reproduced by V. Bhattacharya, *The Catuḥśataka,* pp. 296–97 (on chap. XVI, 25).

276. This occurs in PTT, vol. 98, p. 150–1, in commentary on *Avatāra,* VI, 175.

277. Tsoṅ-kha-pa summarizes the passage, found in PTT, vol. 98, p. 149-4,4 which itself appears to be in part a paraphrase of a passage found in the first part of the larger *Prajñāpāramitā* scriptures, just prior to the first Śakya chapter of this literature. Thus, in the *Aṣṭasāhasrikā prajñāpāramitā,* it is partially found toward the end of the first chapter, Sarvākārajñatācaryā (Coursing in the Knowledge of All the [Best] aspects), thus in the text, Vaidya edition, p. 15.10–12: āha / kiṃ punar āyuṣman subhūte anutpannena dharmeṇa anutpannā prāptiḥ prāpyate, utāho utpannena dharmeṇa anutpanna eva dharmo 'nutpannaḥ ? / And so forth.

278. See the previously cited *Prajñāpāramitā* passage with notes 227–31, above, which directly follows the foregoing passage as it is found in the *Avatāra-Comm.* on *Avatāra,* VI, 173.

279. Sanskrit is available for this verse, since it is cited in *Madhyamaka-vṛtti* (*Prasannapadā*), p. 413.

280. This statement directly follows from the formula of dependent origination, where no. 7, "feelings" (*vedanā*), arise on the condition of no. 6, "contact" (*sparśa*), where "contact" means contact between sense object, sense organ, and perception based on that sense organ.

281. That is to say, if the cause is cut off, it is not there to produce the effect, while if it is not cut off, the effect does not have opportunity to arise (because Buddhism, in contrast with Sāṃkhya, does not believe in the preexistence of the effect in the cause).

282. Cited in *Bodhicaryāvatārapañjikā,* p. 427, for IV, 34a–b; cf. note 44, above.

283. Candrakīrti, of course, reverts to *Madhyamaka-kārikā* XXIV, 18 (cf. above, with note 43). The point is that the followers of Nāgārjuna accept the designation of voidness when there is depending, and so of course accept Buddhist dependent origination, while the realists among the Buddhists accept only the dependent origination and not that designation. La Vallée Poussin in his translation, *Muséon* (1911), p. 320, took the understood subject "we" (F. *nous*) to govern both acceptances. I would have translated it that way also, had not *Mchan* indicated otherwise.

284. As given in Nāgārjuna's *Madhyamaka-kārikā,* I, 1.

285. The position known as "peacock."

286. This is the "indeed" meaning of *hi,* in this context almost equal to "but."

287. Because the Buddhist accepts only four elements (fire, air, water, earth) as the factors of becoming; and does not allow "space" (*ākāśa*) in the group.

288. Not acceptable, for example, to the Buddhist teacher Asaṅga (cf. *Analysis of Śrāvakabhūmi Manuscript,* Paramārtha-gāthā), who holds that things require a cause to arise, but no cause to pass away: they pass away through their own-nature of destruction, as was already mentioned, note 54, above.

289. Stcherbatsky, *The Conception of Buddhist Nirvāṇa,* pp. 109–10, translates this passage in rather free fashion, but agrees in sense with my rendering, which is literal but filled in from *Mchan.* Bhāvaviveka argues that inference for others is possible only if the two parties agree on the factual base (*dharmin*) and feature (*dharma*), and disregard further distinctions.

290. Stcherbatsky's translation (*The Conception,* pp. 110–11) of this passage (text, 29.7 to 30.11) is so remarkably free as to defy any attempt to relate it to actual Sanskrit, the Tibetan translation, or the expansion in *Mchan,* which I utilize, even though his version is applicable in a general way.

291. Nagao points out quite properly that Tsoṅ-kha-pa's sentence is based on *Prasannapadā,* text, p. 21. Hence, the syllogism (inference for oneself):

1. the sense base of form (*rūpāyatana*) does not arise from itself (*na svata utpannam*);
2. because it is present (*vidyamānatvāt*);
3. like a pot in front (*puro 'vasthitaghaṭavat*).

292. For "simplifying the discussion," T. *tshig tshegs bskyuṅ.*

293. For "meanwhile rest the matter," T. *re źig bźag.*

294. Ja goes to great length to show that the alternative to take (which Tsoṅ-kha-pa did not care to argue here) is that it is not necessary (*śin tu mi dgos te*) and cites in justification Mkhas-grub-rje's *Stoṅ-thun bskal bzaṅ mig 'byed.* Furthermore, Ja's comment on Tsoṅ-kha-pa's sentence is remarkably long, and indicates that this is a troublesome point.

295. The final phrase is different in Tibetan because of the syntax change; in Tibetan: "gaṅ gi tshe źes pa nas / dmigs pa ga la yod ces pa'i bar ro."

296. Of course, all this is directly opposed to the position of the Buddhist logicians that *indriya-pratyakṣa,* which is devoid of discursive thought and free from error, has as object the momentary particular (*svalakṣaṇa*) that is real (*paramārtha-sat*). But the logicians also accept other varieties of *pratyakṣa*—mental (*mānasa-p.*), introspective (svasaṃvedana-p.), and yogi's (yogi-p.).

297. This concludes the extended commentary on that *Prasannapadā* passage.

298. Text, p. 30.12–14; Stcherbatsky's translation, *The Conception,* p. 111.

299. Previously Tsoṅ-kha-pa cited Bhāvaviveka's statement on this matter.

300. These features may well be such ones as loudness, pleasing qualities, etc., i.e., sound is sound quite apart from whether people like it or not, and so on.

301. Ja has an extremely long comment just preceding this paragraph, and again resorts to Mkhas-grub-rje's *Stoṅ-thun* for authoritative remarks.

302. *Mchan:* by adhering to the extreme of permanence.

303. Ja points out that the Chinese teacher Hva-śaṅ and numerous Tibetan followers are intended.

304. Cf. the passage with note 59, above.

305. *Mchan* at this point shows clearly that the individual appearance realm (*snaṅ yul*) is the respective object of each sense awareness; while the clinging realm (*źen yul*) is the object of discursive thought.

306. Ja: which would be in conflict with the previous requirement of a universal (*spyi*) claimed by Bhāvaviveka.

307. This is the second kind of inference; cf. note 241, above. This does not mean the Mādhyamika would have to adopt what was called above the "Peacock Position," the Fourth Position, which Tsoṅ-kha-pa rejects.

308. For these terms *gźan rig* and *raṅ rig,* we may refer to Lcaṅ-skya Rol-pa'i-rdo-rje, *Grub pa'i mtha'i rnam par bźag pa gsal bar bśad pa thub bstan lhun po'i mdzes rgya śes bya ba las sde tshan,* p. 118, where he classifies the four *pratyakṣas* of the Buddhist logicians under these headings, taking the extroversion (*gźan rig*)—which is "unmistaken" because being a *pratyakṣa*—to cover the three *pratyakṣas:* of the outer sense organs, of the mind, and of the yogin; and taking the introversion (*raṅ rig*)—which is "unmistaken" for the same reason—to be the *pratyakṣa* of introspection. He defines what he means by "introspection" (*ibid.,* p. 119): "Introspection is the gazing inward that has the abatement of appearance of both the subject and object and is strong in the vacancy of apprehension." Since he does not define the "extroversion," he apparently intends it to be construed as the opposite, i.e., as arousing the appearance of subject and object, much as does the "imagination of unreality" (*abhūtaparikalpa*) of the *Madhyānta-vibhāga,* while in the latter tradition the subject-object relation is indeed mistaken.

309. Text, p. 31.1–5. In Stcherbatsky's translation of the chapter, *The Conception,* p. 112, he specifies Bhāvaviveka's opponent as a "Hīnayānist" (guessing?), while *Mchan* identifies him as the Dṅos smra ba, the realist, who may be the Buddhist as well as the non-Buddhist realist, but the remarks in the syllogism, e.g., "Because the Buddha has so declared," makes this opponent a Buddhist realist.

310. Text, p. 31.9–13.

311. This sentence does not appear in the Sanskrit text edited by La Vallée Poussin.

312. See Stcherbatsky, *The Conception,* pp. 115–16, for three syllogisms, of which the present one is the third. He says, p. 116, note 6, that the Tibetan schoolmen have much discussed these three syllogisms.

313. Ja: a rash statement (*bab chol smra*).

314. The rendition "isolation" is found in Sarat Chandra Das dictionary under the main verb *dgar ba* as "to separate, place apart." The idea here seems to be to emphasize the autonomy (which is castigated in this literature) as well as the limitation due to confinement.

315. The Tibetan *sbyor ba* (S. *prayoga*) is expanded by *Mchan: ṅag sbyor,* or *rtags sbyor.* The first kind, also written *sbyor ba'i ṅag,* is a term for "inference for others," so presumably the second kind, *rtags sbyor,* is used for "inference for oneself." Ja cites verses of Dharmakīrti defining inference as of two kinds—inference for oneself, which requires the three "marks," and inference for others, in which that meaning seen by oneself is revealed, i.e., by expression (*ṅag*).

316. Text, 34.4–5.

317. Text, 34.6–10. Compare Stcherbatsky, *The Conception,* pp. 117–18, whose syllogistic labels ("major premise," etc.) have been adopted here.

318. *Mchan:* The eye does not witness others, i.e., form, from its own side, because it does not see itself, like a jar (doesn't see itself).

319. This is called the *'phral gyi 'khrul gyi rgyu,* "cause of error," which is *'phral* (S. *akasmāt*), "without a why and a wherefore."

320. Paraphrased from the text as found in *Buddhapālitavṛtti,* Tibetan text, Max Walleser, ed., pp. 55–56, which cites the two verses from the *Catuḥśataka* that follow in quotation by Tsoṅ-kha-pa, as pointed out by Nagao (note 272).

321. Original Sanskrit extant for the verse, V. Bhattacharya, p. 188.

322. Original Sanskrit extant for the verse, V. Bhattacharya, p. 212.

323. The "hence" here according to *Mchan* seems based on the idea that only when the heat is of the fuel does fire occur; there is no intention of asserting that the fuel becomes the fire.

324. Text, pp. 34.13 to 35.4. Compare Stcherbatsky's translation, *The Conception,* pp. 118–19.

325. According to Ja, the precept (S. *jñāpaka;* T. *śes byed*), or truism, of the passage is the sentence, "As it is in common life. . . ."

326. Text, pp. 35.5 to 36.2. Compare Stcherbatsky's translation, *The Conception,* p. 119.

327. Ja here cites one verse from a work *Śāri'i sde'i luṅ:* "If the guides of the world, whether the Buddha or the Dharma, did not enter a concord with the world, who would be ignorant of the Buddha?" / gal te 'jig rten rnam 'dren rnams / 'jig rten mthun par mi 'jug na / saṅs rgyas chos ñid gaṅ yin daṅ / saṅs rgyas sus kyaṅ śes mi 'gyur /. The implication is that in such a case no one would be ignorant or knowing of the Buddha and Buddhism. The work he cites does not seem to be a separate work in the canon; the verse is likely one that occurred as a quotation in one of the śāstra works of the Tanjur.

328. Ja mentions that this is a *śrāvaka* scripture passage also cited by Bhāvaviveka. Cf. La Vallée Poussin, *Muséon* (1911), p. 303, for a comparison suggestion with *Saṃyutta,* i, p. 135. These are the verses of Sister Vajirā, including: "Why do you keep returning to the idea 'sentient being' (*satta*)? Māra, you are among false views. A mere heap of constructions, this! One does not apprehend a sentient being here. For just as when there is a collection of members, happens the word "chariot," so also when there are the personality aggregates, happens the assent 'sentient being.' "

329. Translation "individual relief" for *yan gar ba* is based on *Mchan*'s gloss, but the dictionaries only enter *gar ba* with the meanings "astringent," "strong."

330. Tsoṅ-kha-pa appears to allude by this remark to his previous refutation of identity or difference of the chariot from its members in terms of self-existence (*svabhāva*). The difference between the two examples (Devadatta's possession of cows, and Devadatta's possession of ears) seems to go with serving a different purpose and serving the same purpose. Compare also his Bodhisattva section earlier in the *Lam rim chen mo* when he cited Śāntideva's *Bodhicaryāvatāra* VIII, 137–138, including "These eyes, which are theirs, must no longer see my aim." Also, near the beginning of the Bodhisattva section mention is made that the animals seek only their own aim. Thus the mental orientations of the Bodhisattva path also amount to a loosening of the inveterate commonsense attachments to the personality aggregates with realistic imputations.

331. *caṅ med pa = ci yaṅ med pa.*

332. This language appears to refer to the refutation of the Yogācāra position, where a *paratantra-lakṣaṇa* (dependency character) is allowed some measure of reality in order to serve as a platform

("substratum") for designating a *parikalpita-lakṣaṇa* (imaginary character). Of course, Tsoṅ-kha-pa rejects the security of the *paratantra-lakṣaṇa*.

333. Here Tsoṅ-kha-pa uses language of Buddhist dependent origination, where "nescience" is no. 1 and "seed = perception" is no. 3, while "motivations" is no. 2, and the "shoot = name and form," is no. 4.

334. That this is a paraphrase is evident from the Tibetan text of Candrakīrti's commentary (PTT, vol. 98, p. 147-2-3), where for this part the remark is: "This fault is only yours!" (*ñes pa 'di ni khyed kho na la 'gyur te*).

335. This eye is in Tibetan *blo'i mig*. The word *blo* usually corresponds with Sanskrit *buddhi*. In an article about the Buddhist theory of these "eyes" ("The Buddhist Theory of Vision," *Añjali*, pp. 27–32), I included two passages from tantric works of Tsoṅ-kha-pa about this eye that is covered with the obscuration of nescience. In one passage it was shown that by removal of the nescience film, one generates the supernormal power of the "divine eye" (this eye sees forms in past and future, and has an ability to see beings going to different destinies). Another passage called this eye by another name, the "diamond eye" (*vajranetra*). But see the next note, 336.

336. Tsoṅ-kha-pa here insists that the yogin can use more than one faculty at the same time. He expands upon the point in his commentary on the *Madhyamakāvatāra*, PTT, vol. 154, p. 238-2: "When one applies eye ointment to the eye and the eye becomes bright, the eye (itself) is not nullified. In the same way, when one applies the eye ointment for seeing voidness and the eye of discrimination (*buddhi*) becomes bright, the eye of knowledge is not nullified." In that same article ("The Buddhist Theory of Vision") I showed that the knowledge eye is equivalent to the *dharma* eye. Since the eye that sees voidness is ordinarily called the "eye of insight" (*prajñā-cakṣus*) and sees the *dharmas* in the absolute sense (*paramārtha-tas*), while the "*dharma* eye" sees the *dharmas* in the conventional sense (*saṃvṛti-tas*), it would be a reasonable conclusion that this is what Tsoṅ-kha-pa means in the present context: When the yogin enters reality with the "eye of insight," this does not nullify the "eye of *dharma*" (or "knowledge eye"), which observes the convention of a chariot.

337. "Exemplary": T. *'tsham pa;* S. *pratirūpa*. *Mchan's* synonyms: "pleasant" (*bde*) for "not troublesome," and "easy" (*sla*) for "not difficult."

338. Original Sanskrit extant in Shāstrī fragments, p. 502.24–25. The last sentence, "Is this not wonderful," not included in the Sanskrit, per Nagao, note 295.

339. Original Sanskrit extant in Shāstrī fragments, p. 504.20–21.

340. The whirling firebrand might be implied in the fire-circle that constitutes the outer boundary of the *maṇḍala,* because *Mchan* refers to the illusory ring as a *khor yug*.

341. *Mchan* explains that, in this context, the expression *zla bcas* means "accompanied with partner or with rival" (*skabs 'di'i zla bcas ni zla bo daṅ bcas pa 'am ya bo daṅ bcas pa ste*). And *Mchan* adds: it is similar to the meaning of "having parts" (*cha bcas don 'dra*). This is not the same Tibetan expression, namely *cha śas can,* that translates *avayavin* (see previously the citation of *Avatāra,* 159a–c, in subsection "'Method of Demonstration by Way of Distinction of Names"). But here the reference is to the subjective side, with language analogous to the use of the term "composite" (*avayavin*) for the chariot.

342. There is Sanskrit for this, in *Prasannapadā,* p. 342, citing *Avatāra,* VI, 127, 128.

343. This momentary theory provided by *Mchan* of course stems from the *Prasannapadā;* cf. Jacques May, *Candrakīrti,* p. 283.

344. Cf. *Laṅkāvatāra-sūtra,* D. T. Suzuki, trans., p. 122, for mention of Buddha's former life as Māndhātṛ; more details in Malalasekera, *Dictionary of Pāli Proper Names,* under "Mandhātā."

345. *Mchod sbyin* = Yajñadatta, a name of Śarabhaṅga, a celebrated ascetic whose story is found in the Jātakas (see, for example, *Mahāvastu,* vol. III, trans. J. J. Jones, pp. 358 ff.).

346. This is a frequent type of sentence at the end of Jātakas.

347. *Mchan:* the view that self and the world are permanent.

348. These are among the sixty-two views of the celebrated *Brahmajāla,* which is the first scripture in the *Dīgha-Nikāya* of the Pāli canon. For the Tibetan *Brahmajāla-sūtra,* cf. Friedrich Weller, *Asia Major* (1933), pp. 195-332, 381–440. Besides, the sixty-two are stated briefly in Atīśa's *Dharmadhātu-darśana-gīti,* PTT, vol. 103, p. 193-2: four kinds that express eternalism (of self and world); four that some hold as eternal (because they call to mind their previous births even further back), four tracing their previous births to the extreme, four with inveterate holding (T. *mi spoṅ*), two that there is no cause—the "imagination of a former limit" (*sṅon mthar rtog*), sixteen saying, "I have the idea (saṃjñā) that . . .", eight holding (regarding one's self) that there is not, eight holding (regarding one's self) that there neither is nor is not, seven that express (regarding one's self) nihilism, and five claims about *nirvāṇa.* Tsoṅ-kha-pa's mention of the four wrong views probably refers to the first group of four (cf. *Dīgha-Nikāya,* part I, trans. T. W. Rhys Davids, pp. 27–29).

349. Mchan: gods, men, etc.; i.e., the bad destiny of animals, hungry ghosts (*preta*), and hell-beings; the good destiny of gods and men, as well as the demigods (*asura*).

350. Tsoṅ-kha-pa, in his Tibetan commentary on Candrakīrti's *Madhyamakāvatāra,* PTT, vol. 154, p. 52-5 to p. 53-2, mentions four theories to account for the effectiveness of *karma.* In brief, the four are: 1) that of certain "mind-only" (Cittamātra) followers who resort to the *ālayavijñāna* (store consciousness) to account for it. 2) that of a Vaibhāṣika school outside of Kashmir, as is explained by Avalokitavrata (a voluminous commentator on Bhāvaviveka's *Prajñāpradīpa*), crediting the *saṃskāras* ("motivations," the second member of dependent origination) with an indelible record of the debt to be paid. 3) that of the standard Vaibhāṣika school which claims that the *dharma* called "reach" (*prāpti*) has the capacity to get to the fruit. 4) that of a number of persons, both Vaibhāṣika and Sautrāntika, who hold that the stream of *vijñāna* ("perception," the third member of dependent origination) is suffused (from Chinese texts one would say "perfumed") with the habit-energy (*vāsanā*) of *karma* (the volitional act).

351. J. May, *Candrakīrti,* p. 285, notices the difficulty regarding the *tatra,* but seems to have overlooked that the two occurrences of *der* in the Tibetan translation show a double translation of the S. *tatra. Mchan,* as used to expand my translation of the verse suggests that the original Sanskrit verse intended both the *tatra* and the *amṛtaḥ* to be understood twice, as follows for k. 10c–d: "Accordingly, it (the prior self), *not having died,* would remain *there;* or, *not having died there,* would be reborn." Thus the contrast indicated by the "or" is between remaining there, or being reborn (which would presumably take the *saṃtāna* to a different place).

352. *Mchan* mentions a further absurdity from *Madhyamaka-kārika* XVII, 23a–b (*akṛtābhyāgamabhayaṃ syāt karmākṛtakaṃ yadi*): "Even if the act (*karma*) is not committed, there could be fear of encountering what was not committed (i.e., experiencing the fruit of a cause that never happened)."

353. Original Sanskrit missing for this verse; La Vallée Poussin's reconstruction, *Prasannapadā,* p. 580, is reasonable.

354. The example seems to mean that one can find the "footprints" left in the previous time of the stream of consciousness, compared to a pigeon, even if one cannot dip into the "milk" of the previous time. The grass lid appears to be moist because of milk seeping up through it.

355. Nagao (note 309) locates the Tibetan in commentary to k. 232.

356. *Mchan*'s "wet clay" glosses the citation's "mud" (*'dam*).

357. The passage alluded to is *Prasannapadā,* 343.5–6 (de Jong's translation of chap. XVIII, p. 4). My translation and understanding of the passage follows Ja's indications. The "substratum for conventional designation," because the substratum is unconstructed, apparently agrees with "like *nirvāṇa*"*:* while "there is not in the objective domain an apprehending as self," because the objective domain is unconstructed, apparently agrees with "like a flower in the sky" (said of that apprehending as self). The two formulations seem to have respectively a subjective and an objective reference.

358. The *Mchan* additions allude to the *blaṅ-dor* (accepting and rejecting), which, early in the *Lam rim chen mo,* Tsoṅ-kha-pa stresses as the life of the path, i.e., accepting the good and rejecting the bad.

359. Nagao (note 315) says the reference is to Buddhapālita's comment on XVIII, 1.

360. Here "characteristics of the aggregates" refers to the denotation (*nirukti*), as evidenced by the example of characteristic for the "aggregate of form," to wit, *rūpaṇā. Mchan* fills in the equivalent for the remaining aggregates: the nature of experiencing (i.e., "feeling," *vedanā*), the apprehension of sign-sources (i.e., "ideas," *saṃjñā*), instigation (i.e., "motivation," *saṃskāra*), and representing the various objects (i.e., "perception," *vijñāna*). Another way of saying it is Asaṅga's, in the *Śrutamayī bhūmi* (PTT, vol. 109, p. 286-4): "What is the possessor of objects (**viṣayin,* T. *yul can*)? Any aggregate of form. What is the level (**avasthā,* T. *gnas skabs*)? Any aggregate of feelings. What is the discursive speculation (**vikalpa,* T. *rtog pa*)? Any aggregate of ideas. What is the course of action (**caryā,* T. *spyod pa*)? Any aggregate of motivations. What is the indulgence (**upādāna,* T. *len pa*)? Any aggregate of perceptions."

361. Ja refers to the *Śrāvakabhūmi* for the four kinds of principles (*yukti*), and points out that the one meant here is the "demonstration-and-proof principle"; cf. Wayman, *Analysis,* p. 112: "By demonstration-and-proof principle, he thoroughly searches the three authorities (*pramāṇa*): lineage of the experts, inference, and direct perception, thinking, 'Is this the lineage of the experts, or is it not? Is it seen in direct perception or is it not? Is it reasoned with inference or not?' "

362. The other principles from the *Śrāvakabhūmi* are summarized in Tsoṅ-kha-pa's section "II. Varieties of Discerning," below.

363. Cited in *Prasannapadā,* p. 434. My translation follows La Vallée Poussin's in *Muséon;* de Jong's version (his pp. 74–75) is about the same.

364. Cited in *Prasannapadā,* p. 434. My translation follows La Vallée Poussin's in *Muséon,* with additions from *Mchan.*

365. *Mchan* explains the "mind and so on" as "mind and mentals" (*citta-caitta*).

366. This language alludes to the division of the five personality aggregates into *rūpa-skandha,* and the four "formless" *skandhas.* "Form" (*rūpa*) may be divided into "shape" (*saṃsthāna*) and "color" (*varṇa*).

367. Compare the two kinds of *buddhi* in note 141, above.

368. Ja: "translators and scholars in the time of the Tibetan kings."

369. Nagao (note 324) locates the Tibetan as commentary on k. 360c–d.

370. Sanskrit extant in Shāstrī fragments, p. 513.24–25, but with a textual problem, to wit, the Sanskrit equivalent to the Tibetan *so so nas* is corrupt.

371. *Mchan* now cites a verse from Tsoṅ-kha-pa's work, the *Tsha Kho Dbon por gdams pa.* This is presumably work no. 85 among his 135 minor works called *Thur bu,* having the one catalog number of 5275 in the Tohoku catalog of native Tibetan works. The verse may be rendered: "When, without alternating (between the extremes of nihilism and eternalism) but simultaneously one sees dependent origination without deception, the certainty cognition entirely destroys the grasping-pattern of the objective domain, and at that time one fulfills the examination of the view." (/ nam źig res 'jog med par cig car du / rten 'brel mi bslu mthoṅ ba tsam ñid nas / ṅes śes yul gyi 'dzin staṅs kun 'jig na / de tshe lta ba'i dpyad pa rdzogs pa lags /).

372. Cited several times in *Prasannapadā,* e.g., pp. 109–10.

373. Cited in *Prasannapadā,* p. 128.

374. The word "flimsiness" corresponds to S. *tuccha,* T. *gsog,* for which *Mchan* correctly says: *sñiṅ po med pa* (without pith), although Western Tibetan dictionaries do not register this meaning for *gsog.*

375. Cf. the similar material in note 271, above. The present passage is cited only as "Āgama" in *Prasannapadā,* p. 370.

376. Nagao (note 337) points to Jayānanda's commentary on *Madhyamaka-Avatāra.*

377. Cited in *Prasannapadā* at end of chap. IV.

378. Cited in *Prasannapadā,* p. 13.7–8.

379. The entire verse is cited in *Subhāṣita-saṃgraha.*

380. The four conditions (*pratyaya*) are *1*) the causal condition (*hetupratyaya*), *2*) the support-object condition (*ālambana-p.*), *3*) the immediately following condition (*samanantara-p.*), *4*) the controlling condition (*adhipati-p.*).

381. The entire verse is cited in *Subhāṣita-saṃgraha,* also *Prasannapadā,* 36.6-9.

382. Cited in *Subhāṣita-saṃgraha.*

383. As to "reliant on others," the reading *gźan la rag ma las* seems to lack the required negation of the context. *Mchan,* following Tsoṅkha-pa's explanation, qualifies "others" by *rtog pa bźag pa tsam* "only posited by discursive thought."

384. Previously quoted; cf. note 164, above.

385. Cited in *Prasannapadā,* p. 505, as "said by the Bhagavat." *Mchan* adds: *"luṅ de las"* (from that scripture), suggesting that it comes also from the *Anavataptanāgarāja-paripṛcchā.*

386. Cited in *Prasannapadā*, p. 388.1.

387. A play on words, since the Tibetan is a verbal form of *prapañca,* which in the Mādhyamika frequently means "verbal elaboration."

388. I.e., body, speech, and mind.

389. *Mahāvyutpatti,* CXXV; gain and loss, fame and infamy, praise and blame, pleasure and pain.

390. The association of discursive thought (*vikalpa*) with elaboration (*prapañca*) is given by Asaṅga in *Paryāya-saṃgrahaṇī,* PTT, vol. 111, p. 238-5. After mentioning that "clinging" (**saṅga,* T. *chags pa*) here means "lust" (*rāga*), "hatred" (*dveṣa*), and "delusion" (*moha*), he gives a list of four defilements (*kleśa*)—"discursive thought" (*vikalpa*), "elaboration" (*prapañca*), "clinging" (**saṅga*), and "ideas" (*saṃjñā*)—and goes on to say that the first two (discursive thought and elaboration) are the defilements on the side of the one gone forth to the religious life (*pravrajyā*), while the latter two (clinging and ideas) are the defilements on the side of the householder. Besides, there are two kinds of "elaboration," that of place and that of verbalization. So Atiśa in his self-commentary on "Light on the Path to Enlightenment" (PTT, vol. 103, p. 39-4) cites a verse (with a flavor of the Tantras): "Whoever engages with no place or verbalization belonging to all elaborations, he is declared by the diamond of mind (*cittavajra*) as wise (i.e., endowed with insight, *prajñā*)." The "verbalization" type of elaboration is well illustrated in Asaṅga's *Paramārtha-gāthā* with his own commentary (Wayman, *Analysis,* p. 178): "He shows the state of nothing anywhere to be elaborated (*sarvathāpy aprapañcanīyatvaṃ . . . paridīpayati*) with (such sentences as) "He becomes different, or not different, or beyond death does not exist," and so on (*anyo vā saḥ ananyo vā bhavati vā / paraṃ maraṇān na bhavati vety evamādi*). Hence, the kind of remark one finds in Buddhaguhya's "Driving away the hindering demons of the yogin's discursive thought" (PTT, vol. 103, p. 258-2-5): "Free from elaboration he avoids the extremes of existence and nonexistence, of eternalism and nihilism" (*spros bral yod med rtag chad mtha' spaṅs pa*). However, the present context suggests the "place" type of elaboration, as when the *Prasannapadā* refers to the (net of) elaboration, i.e., adding to or detracting from the entity which has been perceptually reached, and following this elaboration with discursive thought. Asaṅga uses language consistent with the present context in the *Cintāmayī bhūmi* (PTT, vol. 110, p. 15-3, 4) referring to the Arhat's mind as "transcending all elaboration, like the sky." The sky is neither adhered to by the clean nor adhered to by the unclean. "Likewise, the Arhat, like the sky, is not adhered to by any of the agreeable or the disagreeable *dharmas* of the world, to wit, gain and loss, and so on, to pleasure and pain."

391. The Tibetan text, here followed, differs by having a few less words than the Sanskrit, *Prasannapadā,* 350.16 to 351.4.

392. The Tibetan text, here followed, differs by having a few less words than the Sanskrit, *Prasannapadā,* 351.8-11.

393. This is terminology of the Abhisamayālaṃkāra exegesis of the *Prajñāpāramitā,* cf. E. Obermiller, "The Doctrine of Prajñā-pāramitā as Exposed in the Abhisamayālaṃkāra of Maitreya," *Acta Orientalia,* vol XI (reprint 1932), indexes.

394. Tsoṅ-kha-pa states in the Bodhisattva section of the *Lam rim chen mo* (f. 206b of the Tashilunpo edition), "In particular, in the phase of the Eighth Stage there is the end of all defilement (*kleśa*), so it is the time of being stationed in the absolute (*paramārtha*) when ceases all elaboration (*prapañca*); and at that time, the Buddhas could not have attained Buddhahood with only this full comprehension of voidness in that (Stage), because this nondiscursive thought is attained also by the Śrāvakas and Pratyekabuddhas." But at that place there is no citation of the *Catuḥśataka* commentary. Cf. note 158, above.

395. *lta źog,* "hopeless, miserable," according to definition in the dGe-bśes-chos-grags dictionary.

396. The implication is that the bulk of Tsoṅ-kha-pa's large section "The Method of Instruction in Discerning" is meant for the ordinary person, i.e., involves mundane intelligence. Then, having this intellectual preparation, in order to fulfill the discerning it is necessary to undertake the varieties of discerning, and then one may arrive at a discerning superior to mundane intelligence.

397. See previously, "Calming the Mind," note 6.

398. Cf. Wayman, *Analysis,* p. 110.

399. For this word "traversing" (S. *saṃtīrayan*), cf. previously, "Calming the Mind," note 8.

400. Cf. Pradhan, ed. *Abhidharmasamuccaya,* text, p. 75.16: / vipaśyanā kathamā / yā dharmān vicinoti pravicinoti parivitarkayati parimīmāṃsām āpadyate ca /.

401. This is part quotation and part paraphrase of the passage at Bihar MS. 11A.6-1a,b.

402. *Mchan* clarifies the three doors as the well-known three levels of insight: that consisting of hearing, that considering of pondering, and that consisting of cultivation.

403. Tsoṅ-kha-pa's following treatment of the six is based on the *Śrāvakabhūmi;* cf. Wayman, *Analysis,* pp. 111–13.

404. Cf. Genjun H. Sasaki, "The Three Aspects of Truth in Buddhist Epistemology," *Journal of the Oriental Institute Baroda* (March–June 1965), for the theory of an underlying factor for conventional and absolute truth, and where this factor is called *bhāva*—apparently equivalent to the *nidāna* of Asaṅga's text.

405. *Mchan* refers to the story previously given about the footprint left by the bluish pigeon; cf. note 354, above.

406. *Mchan* mentions that this "abiding true-nature" is, for example, that the *dharmas* are void of self-existence. It seems it could also apply to the *dharmatā* mentioned in certain sūtra passages about Buddhist dependent origination, as the "staying of *dhamma,* or *dharma*" (*dhammaṭṭhitatā*); cf. Walpola Rahula, "Wrong Notions of Dhammatā (Dharmatā)," *Buddhist Studies in Honour of I. B. Horner,* esp. pp. 187–88. Cf. the foregoing verses of Tsoṅ-kha-pa, ending "so that the teachings of the Jina may long endure," applied to the *Dharma* as the teaching.

407. For the third one, cf. Wayman, *Analysis,* p. 113.

408. Cf. Wayman, *Analysis,* p. 113.

409. Cf. Wayman, *Analysis,* pp. 109–10.

410. A work by Ratnākaraśānti.

411. Following Tashilunpo edition's *de ltar na śes kyaṅ*; but *Mchan* edition has *de ltar ma śes kyaṅ*.

412. The word *tsom,* "shocker," after *Mchan*'s explanation that its meaning is like *had de,* "to be surprised, shocked." There seems also to be a suggestion of "baiting," or harassment, to those who meditate along traditional lines, spend years studying the Buddhist books, etc.

413. *Third Bhāvanākrama,* G. Tucci, ed., p. 13.14 to p. 15.5.

414. The Tibetan word for "part" (*źe*), glossed by *Mchan* as *cha;* there seems no equivalent for this in the Sanskrit text, note 413, above.

415. From "That being the case, . . . to, his own views" is not in the Sanskrit text, as Tucci points out, p. 15 (note 120).

416. *Mchan* gives the six as Ārya-Nāgārjuna, Āryadeva, Asaṅga, Vasubandhu, Dignāga, and Dharmakīrti. Sometimes the six ornaments are increased by the "two best" (*mchog gñis*), who are Guṇaprabha and Śākyaprabha; cf. *Rgyan-Drug Mchog-Gnyis* (Gangtok: Namgyal Institute of Tibetology, 1962).

417. *Third Bhāvanākrama,* G. Tucci, editor, pp. 17–18.

418. Cf. note 336, above, for the ability to use simultaneously the "eye of knowledge" and insight as in the present context, where possibly one should render the *vispharitajñānacakṣuḥ* as "keeping the knowledge eye open."

419. *Avatāra,* VI, 120c-d, previously cited.

420. *Pramāṇasiddhi* chapter.

421. *Pratyakṣa* chapter.

422. "Acknowledged" for T. *grags* (S. *prasiddha*); note that Prajñākaragupta's *vṛtti* commentary takes the verse's *asaṃvṛtti* as meaning *prasiddhi,* and explains the term *āgopāla* as a stock example for "one highly confused."

423. For the two faces of *buddhi,* cf. note 193, above.

424. By "best *dharmas*" is here meant the fourth of the four "roots of virtue conducive to penetration" (the *nirvedha-bhāgīya*); cf. Wayman, "Buddhism," in *Historia Religionum* vol. II, pp. 437–38, for three versions of explanations of these four stages. By method of general meaning, Tsoṅ-kha-pa presumably refers to the version found in Vasubandhu's *Abhidharmakośa,* where the four degrees can be practiced only by beings in the realm of desire. Hence, the meaning of nonself stems from the experience of the higher stages, called *samāpatti,* and beings in the realm of desire do not understand nonself simply by being free from discursive thought (as happens when we are in dreamless sleep).

425. *Mchan:* like the *pratyakṣa* [of the Buddhist logicians].

426. *Mchan:* both that previous contemplation with no discursive thought and that nondiscursive thought of dreamless sleep.

427. Cited in Śāntideva's *Śikṣāsamuccaya* (Bendall edition, p. 189).

428. "Hearing," "pondering," and "cultivation" are, of course, the three degrees of "insight" (*prajñā*).

429. For these paths, cf. "Calming the Mind," note 153.

430. *Svārthānumānam* chapter. The verse is III, 49a-b, in the Sanskrit-Tibetan edition of the *Pramāṇavārttika-kārikā,* edited by Yūsho Miyasaka, *Acta Indologica II* (1971/72).

431. For the placement of the lesser person, cf. outline of the *Lam rim chen mo* in the introductory chapter "A. The lineage . . ." The meaning of 'assailant' and 'upholder' for the lesser person appears, by consultation of that section, to amount to the bad to be rejected and the good to be accepted, as already alluded to in "Discerning the Real," n. 358, above.

432. *Kāśyapa parivarta,* Staël-Holstein, ed., no. 69, but Sanskrit is not extant for this particular paragraph.

433. This citation of the *Samādhirāja* occurred near the outset of the "Discerning the Real" section.

434. *Third Bhāvanākrama,* G. Tucci, ed., p. 20.

435. In the first chapter, "Knowledge of All the (Best) Aspects"; Haribhadra's *Abhisamayālaṃkārāloka,* U. Wogihara, ed., p. 53.

436. While the text of the *Ratnaguṇasaṃcaya-gāthā,* Obermiller, ed., and also Yuyama's Recension A, has for this place, *vibhāvamānaḥ,* from the Tibetan one would expect **vibhedamānaḥ.*

437. *Third Bhāvanākrama,* G. Tucci, ed., p. 17.

438. *Ibid.,* p. 18.

439. *Ibid.*, pp. 19–20.

440. For "verbal elaboration," see note 390, above.

441. Sanskrit is extant for this citation, Stäel-Holstein, ed., no. 52.

442. *First Bhāvanākrama*, G. Tucci, ed., p. 212.

443. *Third Bhāvanākrama*, G. Tucci, ed., pp. 9–10.

444. While the lesser person is here mentioned, the treatment of the watches is actually to be found in the "General precepts for the three orders of persons," starting in the Tashilunpo edition at folio 40a-3 and ending at folio 41b-2. As a brief idea of what is meant, cf. Introduction, "Asaṅga on the Ancillaries of Calming and the Supernormal Faculties," especially "9. Practice of staying awake."

445. The rendition "very true" follows *Mchan*'s *śin tu mad par;* Tashilunpo edition has erroneously, *śin tu med par*.

446. Apparently the meditator's own meditations bring up problems which he brings to the attention of his spiritual guide. It is not necessary to try to anticipate all such problems.

447. This rather brief work by Atīśa is followed in the Tanjur by a rather extended commentary on the same, the *Madhyamakopadeśa-nāma-vṛtti* by Prajñāmokṣa.

448. This means what are in Tibetan tradition five works which Asaṅga obtained from Maitreya who dwells in the Tuṣita heaven. They are: 1) *Mahāyāna-Sūtrālaṃkāra*, 2) *Mahāyāna-Uttaratantra*, 3) *Dharmadharmatāvibhāga*, 4) *Madhyāntavibhāga*, 5) *Abhisamayālaṃkāra*. Of these works, the *Sūtrālaṃkāra* is certainly associated with Asaṅga's school. The *Uttaratantra* is now more usually referred to as the *Ratnagotravibhāga*, by Johnston's edition of the Sanskrit with this title.

449. Bihar MS., 12A.3-6a ff. (words italicized are corrections of manuscript corruptions): / tatra *kiyatā* śamathaś ca vipaśyanā cobhe *miśrī*bhūte samayugam vartate / yena yuganaddhavāhīmārga ity ucyate / āha / yo lābhī bhavati / navākārāyāṃ cittasthitau navamasyākārasya yad uta samāhitatāyāḥ sa ca taṃ pariniṣpannaṃ samādhiṃ niśritya adhiprajñāṃ dharmavipaśyanāyāḥ prayujyate / tasya tasmin samaye dharmān vipaśyataḥ svarasavāhana eva mārgo bhavaty anābhogavāhanaḥ anabhisaṃskāreṇa vipaśyanā pariśuddhā paryavadātā śamathānuyogatā-kalyatā-parigṛhītā pravartate / yathaiva śamatha*mārgas* tenocyate śamathaś cāsya vipaśyanā cobhe *miśrī*bhūte samayugan vartate / śamathavipaśyanāyuganaddhavāhī ca mārgo bhavatīti.

450. *Third Bhāvanākrama*, G. Tucci, ed., p. 9.

451. Ja explains the phase: "When one has achieved the third mental orientation—proceeding without interruptions, and the fourth mental orientation—proceeding without effort; and while examining, still one has not attained the cathartic."

452. By *Mchan*'s suggestion, the four are the "members" (Tashilunpo edition, f. 34b-5 to f. 35a-6), "confession of sins," "sympathetic joy," "exhortation (for the Buddha) to turn the wheel of the law," and "transference (of merit)."

453. From the extensive exposition of this topic in the Bodhisattva section, I have made a selection in a paper, "The Bodhisattva Practice according to the *Lam-Rim-Chen-Mo*," *The Tibet Society Newsletter*, vol. 1, no. 2 (July–Decemter 1967), pp. 85–100.

454. In Tsoṅ-kha-pa's sectional divisions, this "second" assumes as "first" "The method of instruction in the general Mahāyāna"—a division stated in the Bodhisattva section of the *Lam rim chen mo* and in the Tashilunpo edition at f. 214b-5. That is, having preceded with materials about "generat-

ing the mind of enlightenment," the author now goes into the detailed instruction, especially the six perfections (*pāramitā*) in the general Mahāyāna, which of course also includes the "Calming the Mind" and "Discerning the Real." Having then come to the "second"—the tantric path—the author gives only the briefest of indications, but later gives the extended materials on the subject in a separate book, the *Sṅags rim chen mo*.

455. Nagao (note 434) locates the line in T. G. Sāstri's edition, p. 101.9: *duḥśīlasya munindreṇa mantrasiddhir na coditā*.

456. For the ten practices, *Mchan* says, *yi ge 'bri, mchod, sbyin pa, la sogs pa*. Hence, *Mahāvyutpatti*, no. 902 (*daśa-dharmacaryāḥ*), listed, nos. 903–912: writing (i.e., copying scripture), offering, giving, listening, reciting (usually in unison), memorizing, teaching, silent recitation, pondering, and contemplating.

457. I.e., of the Dpal Gsaṅ-phu monastery; cf. Roerich, *The Blue Annals*, vol. I, p. 328.

458. Cf. Roerich, *The Blue Annals*, vol. I, p. 322.

459. This monastery was founded in the year 1056 by 'Brom Rgyal-ba'i 'byuṅ-gnas (1005–1064), who inaugurated the Bka'-gdams-pa school upon the basis of the master Atīśa's precepts and instructions.

Glossaries

The following two glossaries, I. English–Tibetan–Sanskrit; II. Tibetan–English, are of modest length (they could have been expanded fivefold), so as to stress those renditions that represent Tibetan terms of especially frequent use in the text or that are characteristic of the present translator. In the case of the first glossary, since Tsoṅ-kha-pa relies on the great texts translated from Sanskrit into Tibetan, whenever possible the normal Sanskrit equivalent for the Tibetan term will be given. For the translator's general procedures, cf. the introductory section "Apropos the translation."

I. ENGLISH–TIBETAN–SANSKRIT

English	*Tibetan*	*Sanskrit*
ability	bzod	kṣamā
absence	dṅos med	abhāva
absolute sense	don dam pa	paramārtha
absurdity	gnod pa	bādha
acknowledged	grags pa	pratīta, prasiddha
adversary, opponent	gñen po	pratipakṣa
aggregate	phuṅ po	skandha
agreement (show of)	mthun snaṅ	
alternative, limit	mtha'	koṭi
aspect	rnam pa	ākāra
assailant	gnod byed	bādhaka
authority	tshad ma	pramāṇa
authorized	gźal ba	pramita*
automatically	raṅ gi ṅaṅ gis	svarasena
autonomy	raṅ dga' ba, raṅ ga ba	
awareness	śes bźin	saṃprajanya
beginner	las daṅ po pa	ādikarmika
being (manner of)	yin lugs	
calming	źi gnas	śamatha

* Tentative reconstruction of Sanskrit word.

English	*Tibetan*	*Sanskrit*
category	phyogs	pakṣa
cathartic	śin tu sbyaṅs pa	praśrabdhi
cause	rgyu	hetu
clear vision	rig pa	vidyā
clinging	(mṅon par) źen pa	abhiniveśa
cognition	śes pa	jñāna
cognition, attitude, discrimination, intellect, intelligence	blo	buddhi, dhī, mati
condition	rkyen	pratyaya
consciousness, thoughts	sems	citta
consciousness (stream of)	sems rgyud	cittasaṃtāna
consideration	yoṅs su rtog pa	parivitarka
contradiction	'gal ba	virodha
convention	kun rdzob	saṃvṛti
cultivation, contemplation	bsgom pa	bhāvanā
deception	bslu ba	visaṃvāda
defilement	ñon moṅs	kleśa
delusion	gti mug	moha
dependent origination	rten ciṅ 'brel bar 'byuṅ ba	pratītyasamutpāda
disadvantage	ñes dmigs	ādīnava
discerning	lhag mthoṅ	vipaśyanā
discursive thought	rtog pa	vikalpa
distinction	khyad par	viśeṣa
distraction	rnam par g'yeṅ ba	vikṣepa
efficiency	don byed nus pa	arthakriyākaritva
effort	rtsol ba	ābhoga
elaboration	spros pa	prapañca
entity	don, dṅos po	artha, bhāva
equanimity	btaṅ sñoms	upekṣā
equipment	tshogs	saṃbhāra
equipoise	sñoms par 'jug pa	samāpatti
eternalism	rtag pa	śāśvata
evidence	rtags	liṅga
examination, scrutiny	dpyod	vicāra
example, illustration	dpe	dṛṣṭānta
exchange	yoṅs su 'gyur ba	parivṛtti
extreme	mtha'	anta
factual base	chos can	dharmin
fading	byiṅ ba	laya
fault, demerit	ñes pa, skyon	doṣa
feature	chos	dharma

English	*Tibetan*	*Sanskrit*
fixation	gnas pa	sthiti
flux	zag pa	āsrava
given thing	dṅos po	vastu
grasping pattern	'dzin staṅs	muṣṭibandha
habit-energy, propensity	bag chags	vāsanā
hindrance	sgrib pa	nīvaraṇa
idea	'du śes	saṃjñā
illusion	sgyu ma	māyā
image (reflected)	gzugs brñan	pratibimba
imagery	rnam pa	ākāra
indulgence	len pa	upādāna
inference	rjes dpag	anumāna
insight	śes rab	prajñā
instigation	mṅon par 'du byed	abhisaṃskāra
investigation	rnam par 'byed pa	vicaya
investigation (supernal)	rab tu rnam par 'byed	pravicaya
knowable	śes bya	jñeya
knowledge	ye śes, rig pa	jñāna, vidyā
layout	stod lugs	saṃsthāpana*
main part	dṅos gźi	maula, maulī
marks (three)	tshul gsum	trairūpya
meaning	don	artha
means	thabs	upāya
meditation	bsam gtan	dhyāna
meditative object, support of consciousness	dmigs pa	ālambana
mental orientation	yid la byed pa	manaskāra
merit	yon tan	guṇa
mind	yid	manas
mindfulness	dran pa	smṛti
motivation	'du byed	saṃskāra
nature	chos	dharma
nature (true)	chos ñid	dharmatā
negation (qualified)	ma yin	paryudāsa
negation (simple)	med	prasajya-pratiṣedha
nihilism	chod pa	uccheda
nihilist	med pa pa	nāstika
noumenon	ji lta ba	yathāvad-bhāvikatā
own-character, particular	raṅ gi mtshan ñid	svalakṣaṇa
own-nature, own-form	raṅ gi ṅo bo	svarūpa

* Tentative reconstruction of Sanskrit word.

English	*Tibetan*	*Sanskrit*
pair-yoked	zuṅ du 'brel pa	yuganaddha
path	lam	mārga
perception	rnam (par) śes (pa)	vijnāna
perception (direct)	mṅon sum	pratyakṣa
perfection	pha rol tu phyin pa	pāramitā
pervasion	khyab	vyāpti
phenomenon	ji sñed pa	yāvad-bhāvikatā
plane	sa	bhūmi
pleasure, ecstasy	bde ba	sukha
possibility (third)	phuṅ sum	rāśi-traya
principle	rigs pa	upapatti
problem	khegs	
profound comprehension	yoṅs su dpyod pa	parimīmāṃsā
proposition	sbyor ba	prayoga
rapture, delight	dga' ba	prīti
realist	dṅos po yod par smra ba	vastusatpadārthavādin
reason	rgyu mtshan, gtan tshigs	hetu
refutable	dgag bya	niṣedhya
scattering	rgod pa	auddhatya
self-existence	raṅ bźin	svabhāva
selflessness	bdag ṁed pa	nairātmya
serviceability	las su ruṅ ba	karmaṇyatā
side, position	phyogs	pakṣa
sign(-source)	mtshan ma	nimitta
situation	gnas tshul, gnas lugs	saṃniveśa
special *dharma*	khyad chos	
stoppage-cultivation	'jog sgom	
substratum	gźi	āśraya, ādhāra
syllogism	sbyor ba'i ṅag, sgrub byed	sādhana
theory system	grub mtha'	siddhānta
thesis, proposition	dam bca', bsgrub bya	pratijñā, sādhya
thesis, claim, belief	'dod pa, bźed pa	abhilāṣa
threshold	ñer bsdogs	sāmantaka
universal, general characteristic	spyi'i mtshan ñid	sāmānya-lakṣaṇa
view	lta ba	dṛṣṭi
view (reifying)	'jig tshogs lta ba	satkāyadṛṣṭi
vividness, distinctness, brightness	gsal ba	prakaṭa
voidness	stoṅ pa ñid	śūnyatā
waywardness	phyin ci log	viparyāsa

II. TIBETAN–ENGLISH
(in Tibetan alphabetical order)

Tibetan	*English*
kun rdzob	convention
rkyen	condition
skyon	fault
khegs	problem
khyad chos	special *dharma*
khyad par	distinction
khyab	pervasion
grags pa	acknowledged
grub mtha'	theory-system
dgag bya	refutable
dga' ba	rapture, delight
'gal ba	contradiction
rgod pa	scattering
rgyu	cause
rgyu mtshan	reason
sgyu ma	illusion
sgrib pa	hindrance
sgrub byed	proving
bsgom pa	cultivation, contemplation
bsgrub bya	thesis, to be proved
dṅos po	entity, given thing
dṅos po yod par smra ba	realist
dṅos med	absence
dṅos gźi	main part
mṅon par 'du byed	instigation
mṅon sum	perception (direct)
chod pa	nihilism
chos	feature, nature
chos can	factual base
chos ñid	nature (true)
ji sñed pa	phenomenon
ji lta ba	noumenon
'jig tshogs lta ba	reifying view
'jog sgom	stoppage cultivation
rjes dpag	inference
ñer bsdogs	threshold

Tibetan	*English*
ñes pa	fault, demerit
ñes dmigs	disadvantage
ñon moṅs	defilement
gñen po	adversary, opponent
sñoms par 'jug pa	equipoise
gtan tshigs	reason
gti mug	delusion
btaṅ sñoms	equanimity
rtag pa	eternalism
rtags	evidence
rten ciṅ 'brel bar 'byuṅ ba	dependent origination
rtog pa	discursive thought
lta ba	view
stoṅ pa ñid	voidness
stod lugs	layout
thabs	means
the tshom	doubt
mtha'	alternative, limit, extreme
mthun snaṅ	agreement (show of)
dad pa	faith
dam bca'	thesis, proposition
de ñid	reality
don	entity, meaning
don dam pa	absolute sense
don byed nus pa	efficiency
dran pa	mindfulness
bdag med pa	selflessness
bde ba	pleasure, ecstasy
bden pa	truth
'du byed	motivation
'du śes	idea
'dun pa	longing
'dod pa	claim, belief
gnas pa	fixation
gnas tshul, gnas lugs	situation
gnod pa	absurdity
gnod byed	assailant
rnam rtog	inquiry, adumbration
rnam pa	aspect, imagery

Tibetan	*English*
rnam par 'byed pa	investigation
rnam par g'yeṅ ba	distraction
rnam (par) śes (pa)	perception
dpe	example, illustration
dpyad sgom	examining-cultivation
dpyod	examination, scrutiny
spyi'i mtshan ñid	universal, general characteristic
spros pa	elaboration
pha rol tu phyin pa	perfection
phuṅ po	aggregate
phuṅ sum	possibility (third)
phyin ci log	waywardness
phyogs	side, position, category
bag chags	habit-energy, propensity
byiṅ ba	fading
blo	intellect, discrimination, cognition
sbyor ba	proposition
sbyor ba'i ṅag	syllogism
ma yin	negation (qualified)
ma rig	nescience
med	negation (simple)
med pa pa	nihilist
dmigs pa	meditative object, support of consciousness
rtsol ba	effort
brtson 'grus	striving
tshad ma	authority
tshul gsum	marks (three)
tshogs	equipment
mtshan ma	sign-source, image
'dzin staṅs	grasping pattern
źi gnas	calming (the mind)
źen pa	clinging, attachment
gźal ba	authorized

Tibetan	*English*
gźi	substratum
bźed pa	thesis, claim, belief
zag pa	flux
zuṅ du 'brel pa	pair-yoked
gzugs	form
gzugs brñan	image (reflected)
bzod	ability
yid	mind
yid la byed pa	mental orientation
yin lugs	being (manner of)
ye śes	knowledge
yoṅs su 'gyur pa	exchange
yoṅs su rtog pa	consideration
yoṅs su dpyod pa	comprehension (profound)
yon tan	merit
raṅ gi ṅaṅ gis	automatically
raṅ gi ṅo bo	own-nature, own-form
raṅ gi mtshan ñid	own-character, particular
raṅ dga' ba, raṅ ga ba	autonomy
raṅ bźin	self-existence
rab tu rnam par 'byed	investigation (supernal)
rig pa	clear vision, knowledge
lam	path
las daṅ po pa	beginner
las su ruṅ ba	serviceability
len pa	indulgence
śin tu sbyaṅs pa	cathartic
śes pa	cognition
śes bya	knowable
śes bźin	awareness
śes rab	insight
sa	plane
sems	consciousness, thoughts
sems rgyud	consciousness (stream of)

Tibetan	*English*
gsal ba	vividness, distinctness, brightness
bsam gtan	meditation
bslu ba	deception
lhag mthoṅ	discerning (reality)

Bibliography

REFERENCE WORKS

Brtsams pa'i brda dag miṅ tshig gsal ba, by Dge-bśes- chos-kyi-grags-pa native Tibetan dictionary with Chinese translation. Peking, 1954.

Buddhist Hybrid Sanskrit Grammar and Dictionary, vol. II: *Dictionary,* by Franklin Edgerton. New Haven, 1953.

Dictionary of Pāli Proper Names, by G. P. Malalasekera. London, 1960. 2 vols.

Dictionnaire Tibétain-Sanscrit par Tse-Ring-Ouang-Gyal, published by J. Bacot. Paris, 1930.

Index to the Bodhicaryāvatāra Pañjikā, Chapter IX, compiled by Takashi Hirano. Tokyo, 1966.

Index to the Mahāyāna-Sūtrālamkāra, by Gadjin M. Nagao (Part I, 1958; Part II, 1961), both Tokyo.

Mahāvyutpatti, edited by Ryōzaburō Sakaki. 2nd edn.; Tokyo, 1962. 2 vols.

Sanskrit-English Dictionary, by M. Monier-Williams. New edn.; Oxford, 1960.

Tibetan Dictionary, edited and published by Jampa Chogyal. Delhi, 1969.

Tibetan-English Dictionary, by Sarat Chandra Das. Reprint; Alipore, West Bengal, 1960.

TEXTS OR TEXT PORTIONS AND TRANSLATIONS BY TRADITIONAL AUTHOR OR BY TITLE

Abhisamayālaṃkāra. (*A*) T. Stcherbatsky and E. Obermiller, *Abhisamayālaṃkāra,* Sanskrit and Tibetan texts. Vol. 23. Bibliotheca Buddhica, 1929. (*B*) E. Conze, *Abhisamayālaṅkāra.* Rome, 1954.

Akṣayamatinirdeśa-sūtra, Tibetan translation. Vol. Pha. Narthang Kanjur, Mdo.

Aṅguttara-nikāya. (*A*) *The Aṅguttara Nikāya.* Vol. I, edited by Bhikkhu J. Kashyap. Varanasi, 1960. (*B*) E. M. Hare, translator, *The Book of the Gradual Sayings.* Vol. III (The Books of the Fives and Sixes).

Arthaviniścaya. (*A*) N. H. Samtani, *The Arthaviniścaya-sūtra and Its Commentary*

(*Nibandhana*). Patna, 1971. (*B*) *Artha-viniścaya-ṭīkā* (author unknown). Tibetan Tanjur. PTT, vol. 145.

Āryadeva. *Catuḥśataka.* (*A*) *Āryadeva's Catuḥśataka and Candrakīrti's Commentary. Sanskrit Fragments,* edited by Haraprasad Shāstrī, *Memoirs of the Asiatic Society of Bengal,* vol. III, No. 8 (1914). (*B*) Vidhushekhara Bhattacharya, *The Catuḥśataka of Aryadeva.* Calcutta, 1931.

Āryaśūra. *Jātakamālā,* edited by Hendrick Kern. Harvard Oriental Series. Cambridge, 1943.

—— *Pāramitāsamāsa,* edited by A. Ferrari. In *Annali Lateranensi,* vol. X (1946).

Asaṅga. *Abhidharmasamuccaya,* edited by Pralhad Pradhan. Santiniketan, 1950.

—— *Mahāyānasaṃgraha.* Étienne Lamotte, *La Somme du Grand Véhicule d'Asaṅga.* Vol. II. Louvain, 1939.

—— *Saṃgrahaṇī.* (*A*) *Viniścayasaṃgrahaṇī.* PTT, vols. 110–111. (*B*) *Paryāyasaṃgrahaṇī.* PTT, vol. 111.

—— *Sūtrālaṃkāra* or *Mahāyāna-Sūtrālaṃkāra.* (*A*) Sylvain Lévi, editor, Asaṅga: *Mahāyāna-Sūtrālaṃkāra.* Paris, 1097. (*B*) Sthiramati, *Sūtrālaṃkāra-vṛtti-bhāṣya,* Tibetan translation. PTT, vols. 108–109. (*C*) Asvabhāva, *Mahāyāna-Sūtrālaṃkāra-vṛtti.* PTT, vol. 108.

—— *Yogācārabhūmi.* (*A*) V. Bhattacharya, editor, *The Yogācārabhūmi of Asaṅga,* Part I. Calcutta, 1957. (*B*) *Samāhitabhūmi,* Tibetan translation. PTT, vol. 109. (*C*) *Śrutamayī bhūmi,* Tibetan translation. PTT, vol. 109. (*D*) *Cintāmayī bhūmi,* Tibetan translation. PTT, vol. 110. (*D*) A. Wayman, *Analysis of the Śrāvakabhūmi Manuscript.* Berkeley, 1961. (*F*) Karunesha Shukla, *Śrāvakabhūmi of Acārya Asaṅga.* Patna, 1973. (*G*) Unrai Wogihara, editor, *Bodhisattvabhūmi.* Vol. I. Tokyo, 1936.

Aṣṭasāhasrikā Prajñāpāramitā. (*A*) Edited by P. L. Vaidya. Darbhanga, 1960. (*B*) Haribhadra, *Abhisamayālaṃkārāloka.* Edited by U. Wogihara. Tokyo, 1934–1935.

Aśvaghoṣa. *Buddhacarita.* E. H. Johnston, *The Buddhacarita,* Part I. Sanskrit text. Calcutta, 1935; Part II, translation of Cantos i to xiv. Calcutta, 1936.

Atīsa. *Bodhipathapradīpa* and *Bodhimārga-pradīpa-pañjikā-nāma.* (*A*) Tibetan translation. PTT, vol 103, pp. 20 to 46. (*B*) Sarat Chandra Das, "Bodhipathapradīpa," *Journal of the Buddhist Text Society of India,* vol. I (1893). Alaka Chattopadhyaya, *Atīśa and Tibet.* Calcutta, 1967. Contains an annotated translation of *Bodhipathapradīpa.*

—— *Dharmadhātu-darśanagīti.* PTT, vol. 103.

Brahmajāla-sūtra. Friedrich Weller, "Über das Brahmajālasūtra," *Asia Major,* vol. IX (1933), pp. 195–332, 381–440.

Buddhaguhya. "Driving Away the Hindering Demons of the Yogin's Discursive Thought" (*Yogikalpa-vighna-nibarhaṇa-nāma*). PTT, vol. 103.

Candrakīrti. *Madhyamakāvatāra.* (*A*) *Madhyamakāvatāra-kārikā-nāma.* Two Tibetan translations. PTT, vol. 98. (*B*) *Madhyamakāvatāra-bhāṣya-nāma.* Tibetan translation. PTT, vol. 98. (*C*) Tsoṅ-kha-pa's commentary, the *Dgoṅs pa rab gsal.* PTT, vol. 154. (*D*) Louis de La Vallée Poussin. Translated from Tibetan, in *Le Muséon* (1907, 1910, 1911).

—— J. W. de Jong, "La Madhyamaka-śāstrastuti de Candrakīrti," *Oriens Extremus,* 9:1 (February 1962).

Bibliography

Daśabhūmika-sūtra. Edited by J. Rahder. Paris, 1926.

Dharmakīrti. *Pramāṇavārttika.* (*A*) Yūsho Miyasaka, editor, *Pramāṇavārttika-kārikā* (Sanskrit and Tibetan). *Acta Indologica,* II (1971/72). (*B*) S. Mookerjee and H. Nagasaki, *The Pramāṇavārttikam of Dharmakīrti, First Chapter, kārikās I-LI.* Nalanda, 1964. (*C*) Prajñākaragupta's *bhāṣya.* Patna, 1953.

—— Ernst Steinkellner, *Dharmakīrti's Hetubinduḥ.* Part II. Wien, 1967.

—— Tsoṅ-kha-pa's "Guided Tour through the Seven Books of Dharmakīrti" (*sde bdun la 'jug pa'i sgo don gñer yid kyi mun sel śes bya ba*). Sarnath, 1969.

Dīgha-nikāya. (*A*) *The Dīghanikāya,* I. Edited by Bhikkhu J. Kashyap. Varanasi, 1958. (*B*) T. W. Rhys Davids, *Dialogues of the Buddha,* Part I. London, 1956.

Dignāga. *Pramāṇasamuccaya.* Masaaki Hattori, *Dignāga, On Perception.* Cambridge, Mass., 1968.

Dpal-brtsegs. *Chos kyi rnam graṅs kyi brjed byaṅ.* PTT, vol. 147.

'Gos lo-tsā-ba. *Deb ther sṅon po.* George N. Roerich, *The Blue Annals.* Calcutta, 1949, 1953. 2 parts.

Guhyasamājatantra. A. Wayman, *Yoga of the Guhyasamājatantra; the Arcane Lore of Forty Verses.* Delhi, 1977.

Hsüan-tsang. Louis de La Vallée Poussin, translator, *Vijñaptimātratāsiddhi; La Siddhi de Hiuan-tsang.* Vol. I: Paris, 1928; Vol. II: Paris, 1929; Index: Paris, 1948.

Jñānakīrti. *Pāramitāyāna-bhāvanā-kramopadeśa.* PTT, vol. 103.

Kamalaśīla. (*A*) *First Bhāvanākrama,* edited in Sanskrit by G. Tucci, *Minor Buddhist Texts.* Part II. Rome, 1958. (*B*) *Third Bhāvanākrama.* E. Obermiller, "A Sanskrit Ms. from Tibet—Kamalaśīla's Bhāvanā-krama," *The Journal of the Greater India Society* (January 1935). G. Tucci, *Minor Buddhist Texts.* Part III. *Third Bhāvanākrama.* Rome, 1971.

Kāśyapaparivarta. Edited by Staël-Holstein. Shanghai, 1926.

Laṅkāvatāra-sūtra. (*A*) B. Nanjio, editor. Kyoto, 1956. (*B*) D. T. Suzuki, translator.

Lcaṅ-skya Rol-pa'i-rdo-rje. *Grub pa'i mtha'i rnam par bźag pa gsal bar bśad pa thub bstan. lhun po'i mdzes rgya źes bya ba las sde tshan.* Mussoorie, 1962.

Mahāvastu. J. J. Jones, translator, *The Mahāvastu.* Vol. III. London, 1956.

Mātṛceṭa. D. R. S. Bailey, "The Varṇārhavarṇa Stotra of Mātṛceṭa (II)," *Bulletin of the School of Oriental and African Studies,* XIII (1951).

Mkhas-grub-rje. F. D. Lessing and A. Wayman, translators, *Mkhas grub rje's Fundamentals of the Buddhist Tantras.* The Hague, 1968.

Nāgārjuna. *Mūlamadhyamakakārikā.* (*A*) Louis de La Vallée Poussin, editor, *Mūlamadhyamakakārikās de Nāgārjuna avec la Prasannapadā Commentaire de Candrakīrti.* St. Petersburg, 1903–1913; Japanese photographic reprint. (*B*) Translation of various chapters; S. Schayer, *Ausgewählte Kapitel aus der Prasannapadā.* Krakow, 1931. S. Schayer, "Feuer und Brennstoff," RO 7 (1931). Th. Stcherbatsky, *The Conception of Buddhist Nirvāṇa.* Leningrad, 1927; reprinted Shanghai, 1940. J. W. de Jong, *Cinq chapitres de la Prasannapadā.* Paris, 1949. Jacques May, *Candrakīrti: Prasannapadā Madhyamakavṛtti.* Paris, 1959. (*C*) Buddhapālita's *Mūlamadhyamakavṛtti.* Tibetan version edited in part by Max Walleser. St. Petersburg, 1913–1914.

—— *Ratnāvalī.* G. Tucci, "The Ratnavali of Nagarjuna," *Journal of the Royal Asiatic Society.* 1934: 307–325; 1936: 237–252, 423–435.

—— *Vigrahavyāvartinī.* (*A*) G. Tucci, translated from Chinese and Tibetan versions, in *Pre-Diṅnāga Buddhist Texts on Logic from Chinese Sources.* Baroda, 1929. (*B*) E. H. Johnston and Arnold Kunst, editors of Sanskrit text, MCB 9 (1948–1951).

—— Louis de La Vallée Poussin, "Les quatre odes de Nāgārjuna," *Le Muséon* (1913).

—— Étienne Lamotte, *Le Traité de la Grande Vertu de Sagesse de Nāgārjuna.* Vol. III (Louvain, 1970); vol. IV (Louvain, 1976).

Prajñāpāramitā, various sūtras. Edward Conze, *The Large Sutra on Perfect Wisdom, with the Divisions of the Abhisamayālaṅkāra.* Berkeley, 1975.

Prajñāpāramitā-Ratnaguṇasaṃcaya-gāthā. (*A*) E. Obermiller, editor, Sanskrit and Tibetan texts. The Hague, 1960. (*B*) Akira Yuyama, *Prajñāpāramitā-ratnaguṇasaṃcaya-gāthā* (Sanskrit Recension A). (Cambridge, England, 1976.)

Ratnagotravibhāga. Jikido Takasaki, *A Study on the Ratnagotravibhāga.* Rome, 1966.

Ratnakīrti. *Dharmaviniścaya-nāma-prakaraṇa* (Tibetan). PTT, vol. 114.

Samādhirāja-sūtra. Edited by P. L. Vaidya. Darbhanga, 1961.

Saṃdhinirmocana-sūtra. (*A*) Étienne Lamotte, editor of Tibetan version and French translation. Louvain, Paris, 1935. (*B*) Yüan-ts'ê, Chinese commentary on the *Saṃdhinirmocana-sūtra* as translated into Tibetan. PTT, vol. 106. (*C*) Jñānagarbha's *Ārya-saṃdhinirmocana-sūtre ārya-maitreya-kevala-parivarta-bhāṣya.* PTT. vol. 109.

Śāntideva. *Bodhisattvacaryāvatāra.* (*A*) Vidhushekhara Bhattacharya, editor of Sanskrit and Tibetan texts. Calcutta, 1960. (*B*) Louis de La Vallée Poussin, Prajñākaramati's *Bodhicaryāvatārapañjikā.* Ghent, 1902.

—— *Śikṣāsamuccaya.* P. L. Vaidya, editor. Darbhanga, 1961.

Saptaśatikā prajñāpāramitā mañjuśrīparivartāparaparyāyā, text as fixed by J. Masuda, in P. L. Vaidya, *Mahāyānasūtrasaṃgraha,* Buddhist Sanskrit Texts, no. 17. Darbhanga, 1961.

Sgam-po-pa. *Thar pa rin po che'i rgyan.* Herbert V. Guenther, translator, *Jewel Ornaament of Liberation.* London, 1959.

Śrī-Lakṣmī. *Pañcakrama-ṭīkā-kramārtha-prakāśikā-nāma* (Tibetan) PTT, vol. 63.

Śrīmālādevīsiṃhanāda-sūtra. A. Wayman and H. Wayman, translators, *The Lion's Roar of Queen Śrīmālā.* New York, 1974.

Subhāṣitasaṃgraha (anthology by unknown author). Cecil Bendall, editor, in *Le Muséon* (1903, 1904).

Tsoṅ-kha-pa. Biography (*Rnam thar*). (*A*) Mkhas-grub-rje's *Rje-btsun bla-ma Tsoṅ-kha-pa chen-po'i rnam par thar pa yoṅs su brjod pa'i gtam du bya ba dad pa'i 'jog ṅos źes bya ba* (Lhasa edition). (*B*) Akyā Blo-bzaṅ-bstan-pa'i-rgyal-mtshan Dpal-bzaṅ-po's *Rje thams cad mkhyen pa Tsoṅ-kha-pa chen po'i rnam thar gyi bsdus don cuṅ* zad brjod pa (Peking edition). (*C*). A portion of Dge 'dun grub's biography, in Alexandra David-Neel, *Textes tibétains inédit, traduit et présentés.* Paris, 1952. (*D*) Rudolf Kaschewsky, *Das Leben des Lamaistischen Heiligen Tsongkhapa Blo Bzaṅ-Grags-pa* (1357–1419). Wiesbaden, 1971.

—— *Lam rim chen mo.* (*A*). Edition of Tashilunpo monastery, with covering title: *Mñam med tsoṅ kha pa chen pos mdzad pa'i byaṅ chub lam rim che ba,* 491 folios. (*B*) Chinese translation by Fa-tsun. Peking, 1936. (*C*) Partial Russian translation by G. Z. Zubikov, *Bodhi Mör.* Vostochnye Institut, Vladivostok, *Isviestiia,* 1914. (*D*) Translation of *Vipaśyanā* ("Discerning the Real") section by Gadjin Nagao, *A Study of Tibetan Buddhism* [in Japanese]. Tokyo, 1954. (*E*) Edition of the *Lam rim chen mo* accompanied by four annotation commentaries with covering title: *Mñam med rje btsun tsoṅ kha pa chen pos mdzad pa'i byaṅ chub lam rim chen mo'i dka' ba'i gnad rnams mchan bu bźi'i sgo nas legs par bśad pa theg chen lam gyi gsal sgron źes bya ba,* presumably published in Mongolia. (*F*) Edition with four annotation commentaries: *Lam rim mchan bźi sbrags ma, Tsoṅ-kha-pa.* New Delhi, 1972. 2 vols.

Vasubandhu. *Abhidharmakośa.* (*A*) With his own *Bhāṣya* and *Sphuṭārtha* commentary of Yaśomitra. Edited by Dwarikadas Shastri, in four parts. Varanasi, 1970–1973. (*B*) Louis de La Vallée Poussin, translator, *L'Abhidharmakośa de Vasubandhu,* in six parts. Paris, 1923–1931.

——— *Madhyāntavibhāga* commentary, with subcommentary by Sthiramati. (*A*) Susumu Yamaguchi, *Sthiramati: Madhyāntavibhāgaṭīkā.* Tokyo, 1966. (*B*) Gadjin M. Nagao, *Madhyāntavibhāga-bhāsya.* Tokyo, 1964. (*C*) R. C. Pandeya, *Madhyānta-vibhāga-Śāstra.* Delhi, 1971.

MISCELLANEOUS BOOKS AND JOURNAL ARTICLES

Bareau, André. *Les sectes bouddhiques du Petit Véhicule.* Saigon, 1955.

Bhattacharya, Tarasankar. *The Nature of Vyāpti according to the Navya-Nyāya.* Calcutta, 1970.

Boyd, James W. *Satan and Māra: Christian and Buddhist Symbols of Evil.* Leiden, 1975.

Buddhadāsa, Bhikkhu. *Ānāpānasati. Mindfulness of Breathing.* Bangkok, 1971.

Chakraborty, Nirod Baran. *The Advaita Concept of Falsity—A Critical Study.* Calcutta, 1967.

De Jong, J. W. Review, Karunesha Shukla, ed. *Śrāvakabhūmi of Ācārya Asaṅga,* in *Indo-Iranian Journal,* vol. 18 (1976), pp. 307–10.

Demiéville, Paul. *Le Concile de Lhasa.* Paris, 1952.

Grousset, René. *Histoire de l'Extrême-Orient.* Paris, 1929.

Ingalls, Daniel Henry Holmes. *Materials for the Study of Navya-Nyāya Logic.* Cambridge, Mass., 1951.

La Vallée Poussin, Louis de. *Théorie des douze causes.* Gand, 1913.

May, Jacques. "CHŌJŌ," in *Hōbōgirin,* Quatrième Fascicule. Paris, Tokyo, 1967. pp. 353–360.

Mayeda, Sengaku. "On the Cosmological View of Śaṃkara," *The Adyar Library Bulletin,* Centenary issue, vol. 39 (1975).

Murti, T. R. V. *The Central Philosophy of Buddhism.* London, 1955.

Bibliography

Nakamura, Hajime. "A Brief Survey of Japanese Studies on the Philosophical Schools of the Mahāyāna," *Acta Asiatica* I. Tokyo, 1960.

Obermiller, E. "The Doctrine of Prajñā-pāramitā as Exposed in the *Abhisamayālaṃkāra* of Maitreya," *Acta Orientalia,* vol. 11, reprint 1932.

—— *Analysis of the Abhisamayālaṃkāra.* London, 1933.

Rahula, Walpola. "Wrong Notions of Dhammatā (Dharmatā)," *Buddhist Studies in Honour of I. B. Horner.* Dordrecht, 1974.

Rgyan-drug Mchog-gñis. Published by Namgyal Institute of Tibetology. Gangtok, 1962.

Ruegg, David Seyfort. *La théorie du Tāthāgatagarbha et du Gotra.* Paris, 1969.

Sasaki, Genjun H. "The Three Aspects of Truth in Buddhist Epistemology," *Journal of the Oriental Institute,* Baroda (March–June 1965).

Stcherbatsky, Th. *Buddhist Logic.* New York, 1962. 2 vols.

Tucci, Giuseppe. *Tibetan Painted Scrolls.* Rome, 1949. 2 vols. and portfolio of plates.

Wayman, Alex. "Introduction to Tsoṅ kha pa's Lam rim chen mo," *Phi Theta Annual,* vol. 3. Berkeley, 1952.

—— "The Bodhisattva Practice according to the Lam-Rim-Chen-Mo," *The Tibet Society Newsletter,* vol. 1, no. 2 (July–December 1967).

—— "The Buddhist Theory of Vision," *Añjali* (Wijesekera Felicitation volume). University of Ceylon, 1970.

—— "Observations on Translation from the Classical Tibetan Language into European Languages," *Indo-Iranian Journal,* vol. XIV, no. 3/4 (1972).

—— *The Buddhist Tantras; Light on Indo-Tibetan Esotericism.* New York, 1973.

—— "The Mirror as a Pan-Buddhist Metaphor-Simile," *History of Religions,* vol. 13, no. 4 (May 1974).

—— "Aspects of Meditation in the Theravāda and Mahīśāsaka Buddhist Sects," *Studia Missionalia,* vol. 25 (1976).

—— "Regarding the Translation of the Buddhist Terms *saññā/saṃjñā, viññāṇa/vijñāna,*" *Malalasekera Commemoration Volume.* Colombo, 1976.

—— "Who Understands the Four Alternatives of the Buddhist Texts?" *Philosophy East and West,* vol. 27, no. 1 (January 1977).

—— "Dependent Origination—The Indo-Tibetan Tradition," forthcoming, *Journal of Chinese Philosophy.*

—— "Secret of the Heart Sūtra," *Prajñāpāramitā and Related Systems.* (Berkeley Buddhist Studies Series, 1977).

Index

Index

Index

Liberation: progress toward it by realizing non-self, 183-84; from what: suffering and defilement, 175; phenomenal life, 189
Light: idea, contemplation of it, 129, 132-33; light of knowledge, of insight, cognizing reality, 174, 176, 407
Lokātītastava, 195, 307
Lokāyata, 211, 375

Madhyamaka-hṛdaya, 54, 119, 132, 134, 402, 414
Madhyamaka-kārikā (= *Mūla-prajñā*), 8, 62-63, 67, 182, 184, 192-94, 198, 201-2, 209-10, 247, 249, 253, 266, 283, 327, 349-53, 355-56, 369-72, 374, 376, 381, 383, 386
Madhyamakālaṃkāra, 181-82
Madhyamakālaṃkāra-pañjikā, 281
Madhyamakāloka, 179, 182, 281
Madhyamakāvatāra and auto-commentary, 8, 17, 21, 25, 63, 67, 72, 184-85, 190-91, 201, 217, 221-22, 226, 228, 232, 234-35, 240, 242-44, 251, 254-55, 257, 265, 272, 276, 278-79, 289, 295, 297-98, 301, 303-5, 308, 336, 339-46, 349, 351-53, 355-59, 367-76, 383-84, 394-95, 402, 414, 467 *n.* 218
Madhyamakāvatāra-ṭīkā, 284-85
Madhyamakopadeśa-nāma, 414
Mādhyamika: and kinds in early Tibetan history, 5, 181; topic in the monastic curriculum, 17; fourth among the four Buddhist theory-systems (*siddhānta*), 30; two main kinds, Prāsaṅgika and Svātantrika, 182; challenged by realist, 187; agreements and disagreements between it and Yogācāra, 23, 25, 156; Set of Mādhyamika Principles (=chief works of Nāgārjuna according to Tibetan tradition, 179, 260, 263, 394, 408; Śāntideva's two works represent path, 7; misrepresentations of Mādhyamika that it denies all views, 59, 65-66, or ubiquitously denies *svabhāva,* 66-67; the author's conclusion on authentic Mādhyamika view, teachers, and texts in summary verses, 385-86
Madhyāntavibhāga, 101-3, 129, 136, 138-39, 170, 260, 418, 472 *n.* 308
Madhyāntavibhāga-ṭīkā, 124, 130, 140
Mahāmati (interlocutor in *Laṅkāvatāra-sūtra*), 69, 408
Mahāvyutpatti, 5
Mahāyānaprasādaprabhāvana-sūtra, 83, 92, 176
Mahāyānasaṃgraha, 28, 51, 170
Mahāyāna-Sūtralaṃkāra and commentary, 7, 17, 28-29, 85, 98, 102, 117-18, 141-42, 148, 165, 170, 436-37
Maitreya, 9-10, 17, 22, 82, 85, 87, 102, 136, 138, 148, 156, 159, 172, 387; name of a chapter (in *Saṃdhinirmocana-sūtra*), 47, 55, 437; Maitreya-dharma (= five books traditionally credited to Maitreya), 414
Mañjughoṣa, 9, 17, 21-23, 427-28
Mañjuśrī, 9, 11, 45-46, 394
Mañjuśrī-Buddhakṣetraguṇavyūha-sūtra, 11
Māra, 164, 198, 453 *n.* 164, 457 *n.* 50
Mchan 'grel (a tantric annotation by Tsoṅ-kha-pa), 24
Mdun legs ma, 72
Meaning: as object-support, 47; special knowledge of it, 39; right contemplation of it, 83; the three incongruities, 348-49; provisional and final, 23, 177-80, 228-29, 260, 306, 319, 357, 385, 397, 399, 411, 418
Means (*upāya*): the first five perfections, 12; skill in it, 380; part of the Bodhisattva path, 392; goes with comprehending phenomenon, 456 *n.* 36
Meditative object (*ālambana*): object-support, 47, 50, 52; meditative object is virtuous, 82-83, 91, is expressionless, a mere given thing, 86; non-virtuous ones, pebble, etc., improper, 108; definition of meditative object, 114; exposition of the basic ones, 105-9; other possible topics for calming, 102, 113; discerning topics, 90; shifting to various meditative objects disallowed, 115; advanced meditations for discerning, classified, 388-89; eighteen kinds of voidness, 115; *see also* Image (reflected)
Mental orientation (*manaskāra*): the four, 146-47, in common between calming and discerning, 389, which are also involved in pair-yoking, 419; the seven, beginning with "realizing the characteristics," 165-69; a mental orientation called "furnished with a conviction favorable to calming," 148; a mental orientation called "equivalent to a conviction consistent with discerning," 415; when non-mental-orientation is allowed, 408

Index

Index

Translations from the Oriental Classics

Major Plays of Chikamatsu, tr. Donald Keene 1961

Four Major Plays of Chikamatsu, tr. Donald Keene. Paperback text edition. 1961

Records of the Grand Historian of China, translated from the Shih chi of Ssu-ma Ch'ien, tr. Burton Watson, 2 vols. 1961

Instructions for Practical Living and Other Neo-Confucian Writings by Wang Yang-ming, tr. Wing-tsit Chan 1963

Chuang Tzu: Basic Writings, tr. Burton Watson, paperback ed. only 1964

The Mahābhārata, tr. Chakravarthi V. Narasimhan. Also in paperback ed. 1965

The Manyōshū, Nippon Gakujutsu Shinkōkai edition 1965

Su Tung-p'o: Selections from a Sung Dynasty Poet, tr. Burton Watson. Also in paperback ed. 1965

Bhartrihari: Poems, tr. Barbara Stoler Miller. Also in paperback ed. 1967

Basic Writings of Mo Tzu, Hsün Tzu, and Han Fei Tzu, tr. Burton Watson. Also in separate paperback eds. 1967

The Awakening of Faith, Attributed to Aśvaghosha, tr. Yoshito S. Hakeda. Also in paperback ed. 1967

Reflections on Things at Hand: The Neo-Confucian Anthology, comp. Chu Hsi and Lü Tsu-ch'ien, tr. Wing-tsit Chan 1967

The Platform Sutra of the Sixth Patriarch, tr. Philip B. Yampolsky 1967

Essays in Idleness: The Tsurezuregusa of Kenkō, tr. Donald Keene. Also in paperback ed. 1967

The Pillow Book of Sei Shōnagon, tr. Ivan Morris, 2 vols. 1967

Two Plays of Ancient India: The Little Clay Cart and the Minister's Seal, tr. J. A. B. van Buitenen 1968

The Complete Works of Chuang Tzu, tr. Burton Watson 1968

The Romance of the Western Chamber (*Hsi Hsiang chi*), tr. S. I. Hsiung. Also in paperback ed. 1968

The Manyōshū, Nippon Gakujutsu Shinkōkai edition. Paperback text edition. 1969

Records of the Historian: Chapters from the Shih chi of Ssu-ma Ch'ien. Paperback text edition, tr. Burton Watson 1969

Cold Mountain: 100 Poems by the Tang Poet Han-shan, tr. Burton Watson. Also in paperback ed. 1970

Twenty Plays of the Nō Theatre, ed. Donald Keene. Also in paperback ed. 1970

Chūshingura: The Treasury of Loyal Retainers, tr. Donald Keene. Also in paperback ed. 1971

The Zen Master Hakuin: Selected Writings, tr. Philip B. Yampolsky 1971

Chinese Rhyme-Prose: Poems in the Fu Form from the Han and Six Dynasties Periods, tr. Burton Watson. Also in paperback ed. 1971

Kūkai: Major Works, tr. Yoshito S. Hakeda 1972

The Old Man Who Does as He Pleases: Selections from the Poetry and Prose of Lu Yu, tr. Burton Watson 1973

The Lion's Roar of Queen Śrīmālā, tr. Alex and Hideko Wayman 1974

Courtier and Commoner in Ancient China: Selections from the History of The Former Han by Pan Ku, tr. Burton Watson. Also in paperback ed. 1974

Japanese Literature in Chinese. Vol. I: Poetry and Prose in Chinese by Japanese Writers of the Early Period, tr. Burton Watson 1975

Japanese Literature in Chinese. Vol. II: Poetry and Prose in Chinese by Japanese Writers of the Later Period, tr. Burton Watson 1976

Scripture of the Lotus Blossom of the Fine Dharma, tr. Leon Hurvitz. Also in paperback ed. 1976

Love Song of the Dark Lord: Jayadeva's Gītagovinda, tr. Barbara Stoler Miller. Also in paperback ed. Cloth ed. includes critical text of the Sanskrit. 1977

Ryōkan: Zen Monk-Poet of Japan, tr. Burton Watson 1977

Calming the Mind and Discerning the Real: From the Lam rim chen mo of Tsoṅ-kha-pa, tr. Alex Wayman 1978

Studies in Oriental Culture

1. *The Ōnin War: History of Its Origins and Background, with a Selective Translation of the Chronicle of Ōnin,* by H. Paul Varley 1967
2. *Chinese Government in Ming Times: Seven Studies,* ed. Charles O. Hucker 1969
3. *The Actors' Analects (Yakusha Rongo),* ed. and tr. by Charles J. Dunn and Bunzō Torigoe 1969
4. *Self and Society in Ming Thought,* by Wm. Theodore de Bary and the Conference on Ming Thought. Also in paperback ed. 1970
5. *A History of Islamic Philosophy,* by Majid Fakhry 1970
6. *Phantasies of a Love Thief: The Caurapañcāśikā Attributed to Bilhaṇa,* by Barbara Stoler Miller 1971
7. *Iqbal: Poet-Philosopher of Pakistan,* ed. Hafeez Malik 1971
8. *The Golden Tradition: An Anthology of Urdu Poetry,* by Ahmed Ali. Also in paperback ed. 1973
9. *Conquerors and Confucians: Aspects of Political Change in Late Yüan China,* by John W. Dardess 1973
10. *The Unfolding of Neo-Confucianism,* by Wm. Theodore de Bary and the Conference on Seventeenth-Century Chinese Thought. Also in paperback ed. 1975
11. *To Acquire Wisdom: The Way of Wang Yang-ming,* by Julia Ching 1976
12. *Gods, Priests, and Warriors: The Bhṛgus of the Mahābhārata,* by Robert P. Goldman 1977
13. *Mei Yao-ch'en and the Development of Early Sung Poetry,* by Jonathan Chaves 1976
14. *The Legend of Semimaru, Blind Musician of Japan,* by Susan Matisoff 1977

Companions to Asian Studies

Approaches to the Oriental Classics, ed. Wm. Theodore de Bary 1959

Early Chinese Literature, by Burton Watson. Also in paperback ed. 1962

Approaches to Asian Civilizations, ed. Wm. Theodore de Bary and Ainslie T. Embree 1964

The Classic Chinese Novel: A Critical Introduction, by C. T. Hsia. Also in paperback ed. 1968

Chinese Lyricism: Shih Poetry from the Second to the Twelfth Century, tr. Burton Watson. Also in paperback ed. 1971

A Syllabus of Indian Civilization, by Leonard A. Gordon and Barbara Stoler Miller 1971

Twentieth-Century Chinese Stories, ed. C. T. Hsia and Joseph S. M. Lau. Also in paperback ed. 1971
A Syllabus of Chinese Civilization, by J. Mason Gentzler, 2d ed. 1972
A Syllabus of Japanese Civilization, by H. Paul Varley, 2d ed. 1972
An Introduction to Chinese Civilization, ed. John Meskill, with the assistance of J. Mason Gentzler 1973
An Introduction to Japanese Civilization, ed. Arthur E. Tiedemann 1974
A Guide to Oriental Classics, ed. Wm. Theodore de Bary and Ainslie T. Embree, 2d ed. Also in paperback ed. 1975

Introduction to Oriental Civilizations

Wm. Theodore de Bary, *Editor*

Sources of Japanese Tradition	1958	Paperback ed., 2 vols.	1964
Sources of Indian Tradition	1958	Paperback ed., 2 vols.	1964
Sources of Chinese Tradition	1960	Paperback ed., 2 vols.	1964